Time Out London

BARS
PUBS & CLUBS

timeout.com

CONTENTS

Time Out Guides Ltd
Universal House
251 Tottenham Court Road
London W1T 7AB
Tel + 44(0)20 7813 3000
Fax + 44(0)20 7813 6001
guides@timeout.com
www.timeout.com

Editorial
Editor Simon Cropper
Deputy Editors Simon Coppock, Sally Davies, Phil Harriss
Consultant Editor Andrew Humphreys
Researchers Jill Emeny, Cathy Limb, Rob Norman
Proofreader John Pym
Indexer Jonathan Cox

Editorial/Managing Director Peter Fiennes
Series Editor Sarah Guy
Deputy Series Editor Cath Phillips
Business Manager Gareth Garner
Editorial Co-ordinator Holly Pick
Accountant Kemi Olufawa

Design
Art Director Scott Moore
Art Editor Tracey Ridgewell
Senior Designer Oliver Knight
Designer Chrissy Mouncey
Digital Imaging Dan Conway
Advertising Designer Charlotte Blythe

Picture Desk
Picture Editor Jael Marschner
Deputy Picture Editor Tracey Kerrigan
Picture Researchers Helen McFarland, Monica Roche

Advertising
Sales Director Mark Phillips
Sales Manager Alison Gray
Advertisement Sales Ben Holt, Matthew Salandy, Jason Trotman
Advertising Assistant Lucy Butler
Copy Controller Amy Nelson

Marketing
Marketing Director Mandy Martinez
Marketing & Publicity Manager, US Rosella Albanese
Marketing Designer Simeon Greenaway

Production
Production Director Mark Lamond
Production Controller Samantha Furniss

Time Out Group
Chairman Tony Elliott
Managing Director Mike Hardwick
Group Financial Director Richard Waterlow
Group Commercial Director Lesley Gill
Group Marketing Director John Luck
Group General Manager Nichola Coulthard
Group Circulation Director Jim Heinemann
Group Art Director John Oakey
Online Managing Director David Pepper
Group Production Director Steve Proctor
Group IT Director Simon Chappell

Contributors
James Aufenast, Simone Baird, Simon Coppock, Chris Cottingham, Peterjon Cresswell, Rob Crossan, Christi Daugherty, Garrett Dearey, Guy Dimond, Jim Driver, Kevin Ebbutt, Richard Ehrlich, Jill Emeny, Dan Fielder, Will Fulfurd-Jones, Jan Fuscoe, Victoria Gill, Andrew Humphreys, Ruth Jarvis, Jack Jewers, Fran Kellett, Jill Knight, Kelley Knox, Tom Lamont, Sam Le Quesne, Jerry Lloyd-Williams, Sharon Lougher, Rhodri Marsden, Norman Miller, Emma Norton, Elise Rana, David Swift, Dave Swindells, Anne Tillyer, Pete Watts, Natalie Whittle.

The editor would like to thank Yuko Aso, Ismay Atkins, Guy Dimond, Becky Lucas, Lesley McCave, Simon Portman-Lewis.

Cover Photography Inc Bar & Restaurant, 7 College Approach, SE10 9HY.
Openers Photography Kingsley Barker.
Photography Alys Tomlinson, except pages 10, 11 Lukas Birk; pages 15, 16 Richard Haughton/Buzzin Fly Records and featured artists/illustration Dan Conway; pages 20, 27, 57, 65, 79, 105, 191, 196, 205, 212, 213, 221, 229, 234, 241, 245 Tricia de Courcy Ling; pages 53, 77, 133, 153, 173, 175, 187, 211, 223 Lukas Birk/illustration Dan Conway; page 60 Ming Tang Evans; pages 249, 250, 257, 259 Muir Vidler. The following images were provided by the featured establishments: pages 96, 97.

Illustrations Ian Keltie & Dan Conway.

Maps JS Graphics (john@jsgraphics.co.uk)
Street maps based on material supplied by Alan Collinson and Julie Snook through Copyright Exchange.

Repro Icon Reproduction, Crowne House, 56-58 Southwark Street, London SE1 1UN.
Cover printed by AGI Thamesdown, 1-2 Birch, Kembrey Park, Swindon, Wiltshire SN2 8UU.
Printed and bound by Cooper Clegg, Shannon Way, Tewkesbury Industrial Centre, Tewkesbury, Gloucestershire GL20 8HB.

ISBN 0 903446 19 7

Distributed by Seymour Ltd (020 7396 8000)

ABOUT THE GUIDE

This guide is arranged by area, because we reckon that's how most people drink. Area boundaries are often nebulous, so we include brief introductions to each section explaining our take on London geography. If you're after something other than just the closest or most convenient decent pub or ace bar, turn to **Where to go for...** on page 260, a rundown of drinking establishments by theme. Some of the best venues are highlighted in our **Critics' picks** boxes, scattered throughout the guide and indexed on page 261.

Opening times
We only list the opening times of the bar or pub at the time of going to press. We do not list those of any attached restaurant, brasserie or shop (though these may be the same).

Food served
We list the times when food is served in the bar or pub or, where relevant, in any attached restaurant or brasserie. 'Food served' can mean anything from cheese rolls to a three-course meal. When the opening times and food serving times are run together (Open/food served), it means food is served until shortly before closing time.

Admission
In some cases, particularly in central London, pubs and bars charge admission after a certain hour. Where there is a regular pattern to this, we list the details. Note that more and more venues are becoming members-only after a fixed time (usually when pubs close), although the rules are often blurred. We've chosen not to include in this guide places that are strictly members-only.

Credit cards
The following abbreviations are used: **AmEx** American Express; **DC** Diners Club; **MC** MasterCard; **V** Visa.

Babies and children admitted
Under-14s are only allowed into gardens, separate family rooms and restaurant areas of pubs and wine bars, unless the premises has a special 'children's certificate'. If the establishment has a certificate, children can go in as long as they're with an adult. Those aged 14-17 can go into a bar, but only for soft drinks. It's an offence for a licensee to serve alcohol in a bar to anyone under 18. Unless drinkers can prove they're at least 18, the licensee can refuse to serve them and may ask them to leave the premises.

Disabled: toilet
If a pub claims to have a toilet for the disabled, we have said so; this also implies that it's possible for a disabled person to gain access to the venue. However, we cannot guarantee this, so phone in advance to check.

Function room
Means the pub or bar has a separate room that can be hired for meetings or parties; some charge for this, some do not.

Late licence
We have listed any pub or bar that is open until midnight or later as having a late licence. Our **Late drinks** feature (*see pp100-101*) brings together all those places where it's possible to get a drink *after* midnight.

Music
Unless otherwise stated, this means live musicians and no entry fee. For a round-up of good DJ bars, *see p263*.

No-smoking room/area
Very few pubs or bars have a no-smoking room or area; we list those that do. Note that a designated no-smoking area is rarely much protection from the usual pub smoke.

TV
We tell you whether or not the pub has a TV, and also whether it's a subscriber to cable or satellite.

Reviews featured in this guide are based on the experiences and opinions of Time Out's reviewers. All pubs and bars listed are visited – anonymously – and Time Out pays the bill. No payment or incentive of any kind has secured or influenced a review.

ADVERTISERS

We would like to thank the companies that have advertised in this guide. However, we would like to stress that advertisers have no control over editorial content. No bar or pub has been included because its owner has advertised in the guide. An advertiser may receive a bad review or no review at all.

Liquid LONDON

The 12 months prior to the publication of this latest edition of our (renamed) guide to London's bars and pubs had the potential to turn the capital's drinking on its head. The issue of banning smoking in enclosed spaces including pubs, bars and clubs hung in the air like the mass exhalation of so many Gitanes, while the long-heralded 24-hour licensing bill finally came to pass. As it happens, neither issue has had any noticeable effect. Yet.

A government White Paper on health published at the end of 2004 calls for an end to smoking in pubs and bars that serve food, while allowing those that don't serve food the option of permitting smoking. For all the hot air expelled, and the various corresponding polls that showed a majority in favour of exiling smokers to the street, the government has, for the time being, backed away from bringing in any such legislation until 2008. Pub group JD Wetherspoon intends to ban smoking in all 650 of its pubs by the end of May 2006 and in ten per cent of them by May 2005, but to date only two pubs, the Polar Bear on Lisle Street in the West End and the Phoenix (*see p136*) on Throgmorton Street in the City, have taken matters into their own hands and instituted their own ban on lighting up.

As for round-the-clock opening: in theory yes, but in practice probably not, or not far and wide – and not until November 2005, anyway: *see right* **24 nil**.

Instead, changes that have occurred have been more stealthy. If there's one trend that stands out in our survey of 1,000-odd of the capital's drinking establishments, it's the continued increase in choice and quality. Big-brand lagers may still outsell all other beers by hundreds of barrels to one, but the evidence is there in the handpumps that London's boozy palate is becoming far more sophisticated. Take Hoegaarden, first introduced to British drinkers in

1994. We took our time pondering its cloudy appearance and distinctive sour-sweet taste, but 11 years on, the beer's distinctive ceramic dispenser is now a standard bar-counter fixture, to be found even in the high-street chains.

Never slow to overload a bandwagon, pub companies are pushing all manner of similar 'boutique beers' to the point where it's now unusual to find a boozer that doesn't serve one or more of the likes of Leffe, Erdinger, Paulaner, Wiekse Witte or Kronenbourg Blanc. Also, are we imagining it or is there also a resurgent interest in real ales? Not so long ago a single handpump delivering badly kept London Pride was frequently the only alternative to lager, lager, lager. These days, two or three pumps devoted to real ales seems to be the norm, with a far greater showing for the offerings of smaller brewery product: *see p85* **Raise a glass: Real ale**.

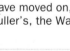

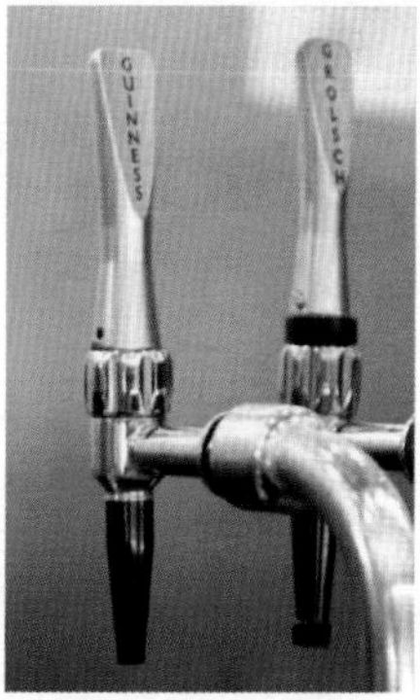

As an illustration of just how far things have moved on, less than a decade ago, Fuller's, the Wandsworth brewer, could contemplate launching its chain of upmarket bars, Fine Line, and have them stock only London Pride (strangely excluding the company's several other varieties of fine beer). Currently, pub-owning conglomerate Mitchells & Butlers (a Sony Corporation of the pubs and bars game, whose portfolio includes All Bar One and O'Neill's) is revamping some of its properties. We recently visited one such place, the White Hart (*see p106*) in Waterloo, and noted not just London Pride on draught but also Shepherd Neame Spitfire, Belgium's Hoegaarden and Leffe, Küppers Kölsch from Cologne and Früli, a wheat beer infused with strawberries. To say nothing of Chimay, Duvel and Frambozenbier, among many others, in bottles. And this from a company previously best known for pushing lowest-common-denominator brands served by staff with all the motivation of fast-food franchise employees.

And then there's the food. Love it or loathe it, the gastropub phenomenon

24 NIL

The new licensing act introduced on 7 February 2005 allows pubs, bars and clubs to apply for the necessary permission to remain open for extended hours – up to 24 hours daily. The law will not actually come into force until November. Even then, it is unlikely that venues will open around the clock; local authorities will decide how late a particular place can stay open. The new law also gives greater powers to the police to fight disorder around pubs and bars, and gives local residents more say over disturbance. As a result, according to a BBC report at the time of writing, only six pubs in Westminster (an area that includes Soho and Leicester Square) have applied for extended licences.

Each local council will decide what is appropriate for its own borough. A spokesman for Westminster Council told *Time Out* magazine that it would probably only consider extending hours until 11.30pm on weekdays and midnight on weekends. Similarly, Hackney Council will designate a triangle around Hoxton Square, Old Street and Shoreditch High Street as a 'Special Policy Area', where it will restrict granting licences to new venues and current premises will find it hard to extend their hours.

Additionally, in the run-up to November, the government is applying pressure to the drinks industry to curb happy hours, cheap-drinks deals and the practice of adapting pubs for 'vertical drinking' (stripping out the furniture to pack in more customers), all of which it believes promote binge drinking.

The effect of the new laws, then, is likely to be negligible. Chances are, if you want a drink after 11pm in the West End, that you're still going to have to search for it and fork out several quid at the door for the privilege.

means that pubs can no longer get away with food options that stop short at salt and vinegar or ready salted. It is now de rigueur that all but the most reprobate of backstreet boozers have a daily changing blackboard-listed menu that's decipherable only with the aid of a complete set of European language dictionaries. 'Two pints of Stella and a chicken liver parfait, please.' Sounds ridiculous? We overheard it.

This shift towards quality drinks and a greater focus on serving food suggests that the drinks industry is already well on its way to adopting the more continental (i.e. responsible and grown-up) approach that the government hopes to instill in Britain's drinkers by its relaxation of the licensing laws. Ironically, the proposed smoking ban may have the reverse effect: the British Beer & Pub Association estimates that over 16,000 pubs and bars will stop serving food in order to accommodate smokers. Which sounds like a step backwards to us.

As it happens, we've got a better idea. If the government is prepared to include curtailment of choice in any new legislation, then why not ban mass-market lagers? Let's see how many up-for-it weekend boozers are willing to indulge in bouts of binge drinking on £4 pints of white beer and £6.50 Martinis. *Andrew Humphreys*

HELLO!

Notable arrivals in the last year.

CENTRAL

Albannach
66 Trafalgar Square, WC2N 5DS (7930 0066/www.albannach.co.uk).
Handsome whisky encyclopedia – with glowing stag. *See p95.*

Cocoon
65 Regent Street, W1B 4EA (7494 7609/www.cocoon-restaurants.com).
Butterfly theme and a beguiling oriental flavour. *See p40.*

Crazy Bear
26-28 Whitfield Street, W1T 7DS (7631 0088/www.crazybeargroup.co.uk).
Bear-faced chic: style wonderland, cocktail heaven. *See p40.*

Bar Constante @ Floridita
100 Wardour Street, W1F 0TN (7314 4000/www.floridita london.com).
Havana good time yet? *See p80.*

43
43 South Molton Street, W1K 5RS (7647 4343/www.43southmolton.com).
'Claridge's on acid': classy drinking den with a sense of humour. *See p65.*

Island Restaurant & Bar
Lancaster Terrace, W2 2TY (7551 6070/www.island restaurant.co.uk).
Stylish minimalism, friendly service, great cocktails. *See p18.*

Shochu Lounge
37 Charlotte Street, W1T 1RR (7580 9666).
New bar, age-old drink: introducing shochu. *See p45.*

CITY

T
56 Shoreditch High Street, E1 6JJ (7729 2973/www.tbarlondon.com).
Lots of space, lots of cocktails. *See p130.*

Zetter
86-88 Clerkenwell Road, EC1M 5RJ (7324 4455/www.thezetter.com).
A hotel bar for the noughties. *See p119.*

EAST

Marie Lloyd Bar
289 Mare Street, E8 1EJ (8510 4500/www.hackney empire.co.uk).
A welcome injection of style on Mare Street. *See p151.*

NORTH

Anam
3 Chapel Market, N1 9EZ (7278 1001).
An Emerald Isle cocktail bar? A gem indeed. *See p172.*

SOUTH

Polar Bar
13 Blackheath Road, SE10 8PE (8691 1555).
Chilled vibe and drinks, hot music and food. *See p211.*

WEST

Defectors Weld
170 Uxbridge Road, W12 8AA (8749 0008).
Welcome, classy new gastrobar. *See p242.*

During the year-long lifetime of this guide, bars and pubs will inevitably change name, change hands or close. We strongly recommend giving the venue a ring before you set out – especially if your visit involves a long trip.

RAISING THE BAR

Where did it all go right? Britain has a pub culture built on ale, but in London, at least, we've overcome that handicap to end up as the 'cocktail capital of the world' – according to Salim Khoury (*see p77*), who, as head barman of the Savoy's American Bar, should know what he's talking about. Other bar professionals seem to agree – see the **Drinking aloud** boxes scattered throughout this guide. Which is all a bit rum given that little more than a decade ago, our city had barely a handful of decent bars to its name.

Bars used to be the things attached to hotels. They employed fake timber panelling, etched-glass panels and coppery knick-knacks in an attempt to resemble pubs, and sold beer from handpumps at a considerable mark-up. Only a few bucked the trend, including, notably, the aforementioned American Bar (*see p64*), which had its own glamorous heritage to trade on. Proper bars required a smart jacket, money to burn and swaggering self-confidence. All those attributes came to the fore in the boom years of the 1980s, when the trend for wine bars kept everyone happy until the berthing of the Atlantic Bar & Grill (*see p56*), a huge oceanic liner of a bar/restaurant in a former basement ballroom off Piccadilly Circus.

The Atlantic showed everyone just how glam glam could be. With the help of cocktail guru Dick Bradsell (the 'UK's leading barman'™), Dick's Bar at the Atlantic showed how good glam could taste, too. That was 1994. In 1997 the Met Bar (*see p66*) and the first of the Match bars opened (*see p43*), and the rest is, as they say, recent history.

From Alphabet (*see p78*) to 43 (*see p65*) to Pearl (*see p47*) Zeta (*see p68*), the capital is, in fact, spoiled for style bars. But what makes a great bar? As someone who has spent the past five years visiting and reviewing bars, not just in London but worldwide, I'd put concept at the top of the list. All the best bars

43. *See p65.*

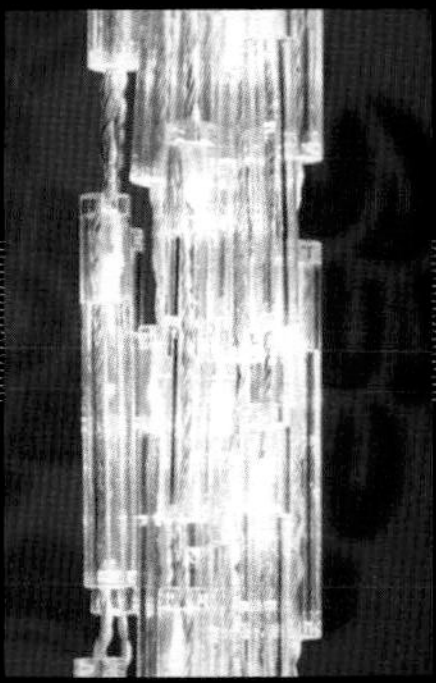

know exactly what they are about and, importantly, who their target customers are. Atlantic was all about delivering a bit of Manhattan glitz to London's West End, and crucial to the enterprise was the revival in the UK of the Martini – the ultimate embodiment of sophistication in a glass. The Met was an LA-style wrap party where the A-listers could let their hair down, protected from public and press by an exclusive door policy. Match offered quality drinks in a comfortable lounge environment and credited people with a bit of taste. None of this sounds particularly radical now, but that's because together these bars have spawned literally hundreds of imitators.

The best of their successors have come up with concepts of their own. Hoxton Square Bar & Grill (*see p127*), Shoreditch Electricity Showrooms (now closed, sadly) and Cantaloupe (*see p124*) promoted the stripped-down concept of bare concrete, baggy sofas and T-shirted staff matched with great drinks and food. Home (*see p127*), in the same neighbourhood, along with W1's Social (*see p45*), pioneered the DJ bar – with the result that today no bar worth its sound system plays anything that wouldn't make the NME's annual top 50 list. Zeta started the trend for hotel bars to exist as stand-alone style venues with their own entrances and profiles distinct from any corporate identity. Lab (*see p84*) brought mixological experimentation and club styling to Soho.

All these bars kicked off in the mid to late 1990s. Since that time it has

Pearl Bar & Restaurant. *See p47.*

become harder for any new venture to distinguish itself. All credit, then, to Loungelover (*see p128*) for introducing a welcome shot of high campery into the London drinking scene (in a former butcher's storage shed in Shoreditch, of all places), and to Chelsea's Apartment 195 (*see p29*) for adding a dash of femininity in the form of bar manager Charlotte Voisey and her all-girl staff – no mere gimmick, given that Ms Voisey won *Class* magazine's 'Best Bartender' award in 2004. Rockwell (*see p98*), winner of Time Out's best bar award in 2002, distinguishes itself through a devotion to bourbon, using it as a base spirit for some exceptional mixed drinks; Zuma (*see p55*) specialises in saké, while new arrival Shochu Lounge (*see p45*) does the same with little-known Japanese spirit shochu.

Given the incredible growth in quality and diversity over the past decade, it's hardly surprising that the momentum is on the wane. The past 12 months on the London bar scene have been remarkable only in their uneventfulness. What we're seeing instead is a replication of successful templates (with the inevitable dilution of quality that implies) plus, more positively, a spread of the bar phenomenon beyond the usual confines of the Circle line.

The class of the mid '90s, which includes figures like Jonathan Downey (Match Bar Group), Douglas Ankrah (Lab) and the Gorgeous Group (Rockwell, Steam), have done the groundwork; but at present there's no evidence of anyone picking up the baton. The bar industry has found its maturity – now it needs to look to its youth. *Andrew Humphreys*

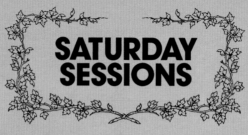

GROOVERS & SHAKERS

Ben Watt

Making it in London's clubbing scene? No easy achievement, especially when you consider that everything's been done before and then again in the name of irony. For all the thousands of pretenders, there are barely a handful of people who are actually pushing things forward. Gone are the days when there was a place for everybody, when the superstar DJ was employed by the superclub owner; now, the DJ is probably the promoter who has a side interest in a pirate radio station. If you can't wear several hats with ease, chances are that now is not for you. Of course, you don't have to be a local to make a big splash (you can even come from Birmingham, it seems), but you do have to be ultra-original. Step up, then, the people who will shape 2005.
Simone Baird

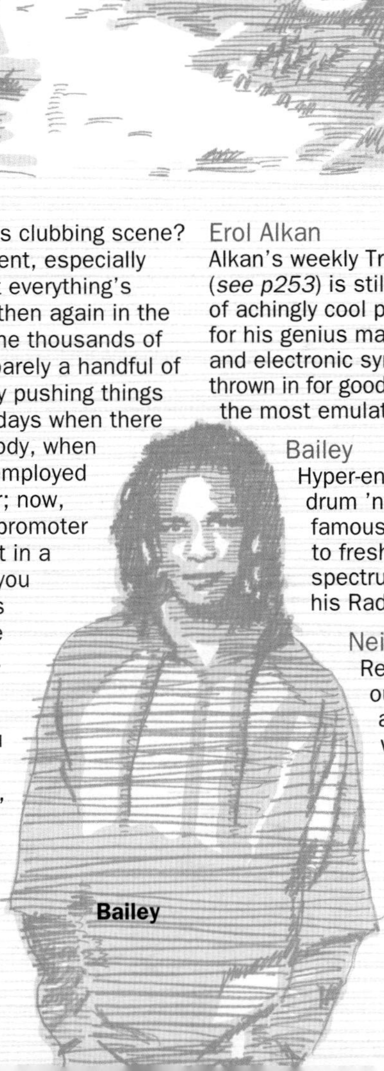

Bailey

Erol Alkan

Alkan's weekly Trash party at the End (*see p253*) is still generating queues of achingly cool people, all hankering for his genius mash-up of indie guitars and electronic synths, with pop classics thrown in for good measure. He's arguably the most emulated spinner out there.

Bailey

Hyper-enthusiastic about the drum 'n' bass scene, and famous for introducing junglists to fresh tracks right across the spectrum through his sets and his Radio 1Xtra show.

Neil Boorman

Responsible for packing out 333 (*see p259*) each and every Saturday. As well as DJing (although usually at his own gigs, he jests), he's the man behind the ace new freebie 'lifestyle magazine for cool people who live in London', also known as *Good For Nothing*,

Johnno Burgess

and he writes a weekly club column in the *Guardian*. We'd call him the Hoxton Prince, if that weren't such a ridiculous thing to call someone.

Johnno Burgess

Moved from Birmingham via Manchester in 1999, and added a big dose of cool to London clubland. Bugged Out at the End (*see p253*) brings together all manner of leftfield greats; as music programmer at the Legion, he actively hunts out fresh blood. Check out his infamous Erection Section nights; power ballads never sounded so good.

JoJo de Freq

Mere moments after getting off the boat from Canada, JoJo started one of the most essential club nights in town, Nag Nag Nag at the Ghetto (*see p253*). Her DJ star is rising fast as her reputation for playing lots of shit-hot records full of synths is cemented. Sadly, this means that she's often away doing international gigs, but catch her when you can: she really is something special.

Gaz Mayall

His Rockin' Blues party has been filling dancefloors since 1980 – and, boy, don't they go wild for his mix of ska, blues, reggae and rock 'n' roll. His dad is blues

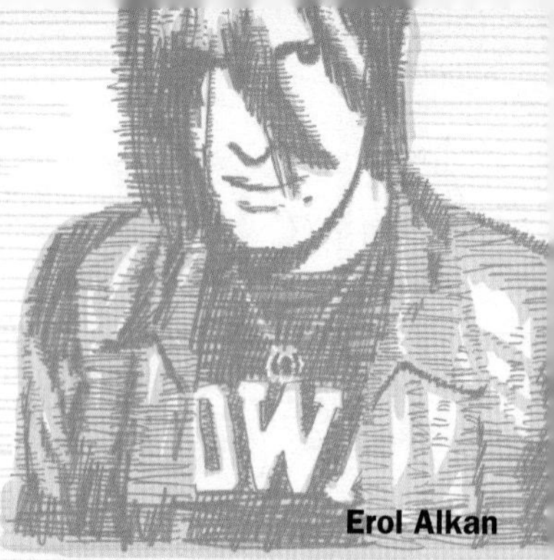

Erol Alkan

star John Mayall, and Gaz regularly tours with his own band, the Trojans. Keep your eyes open for his on-the-sly appearances at pubs around London; people always end up dancing on tables.

Ben Watt

There's many a string to this bloke's bow: his club Buzzin' Fly is deep house nirvana, his label of the same name launched last year and is going stellar rapidly – and you might just know him from Everything But The Girl days.

Tubbs West

Long a familiar face around the clubbing scene, he's now a superstar music programmer and largely responsible for turning a derelict King's Cross depot into 2004's clubbing success story, thanks to the mind blowing Cross Central festival in August. He's doing it again in spring and summer, which is great news for music fans, and his pet project the Key (*see p255*) continues to set the disco lit floor alight.

JoJo de Freq

CENTRAL

glass from a selection at www.urbanbar.com

CENTRAL

BAYSWATER & PADDINGTON

Hardly the most salubrious of London districts, Bayswater and Paddington nonetheless have a modest but solid share of worthwhile watering holes, from historic pubs such as **Victoria** and **Mitre**, to chic newcomers like **Island Restaurant & Bar** and **Salt Whisky Bar**.

Central

Archery Tavern

4 Bathurst Street, W2 2SD (7402 4916). Lancaster Gate tube. **Open** 11am-11pm Mon-Sat; noon-10.30pm Sun. **Food served** noon-3pm, 6-9.30pm Mon-Fri; noon-9.30pm Sat; noon-9pm Sun. **Credit** JCB, MC, V.

This laid-back, old-fashioned little boozer was built in 1840 to cash in on a steady flow of customers from the Royal Toxophilite (Archery) Society, whose practice grounds were within a stone's throw of the front door. Both have long since departed, but the Tavern remains, providing a country pub atmosphere among the raft of tourist traps hereabouts. Inside, almost every square inch of wall space is taken up with archery-related paraphernalia; there's even a faded copy of sheet music for *Robin Hood* by the front door, well scuffed by generations of passing regulars. Two open fireplaces add to the cosy atmosphere, and there's a quieter, if slightly more utilitarian, back room. The ales on tap come from Dorset's Badger Brewery and include K&B Sussex, Badger and Tanglefoot; there's HB lager, too.

Babies and children admitted. Games (board games, darts, fruit machine). Quiz (9pm Sun; £1). Tables outdoors (4, pavement). TV (satellite).

Cherry Jam

58 Porchester Road, W2 6ET (7727 9950/www.cherryjam.net). Royal Oak tube. **Open/food served** 6pm-2am Mon-Sat; 4pm-midnight Sun (times vary, call to check). **Happy hour** 6-8pm Mon-Sat; 4-7pm Sun. **Admission** £5 after 8pm Mon-Thur; £6 after 10pm, £7 after 11pm Fri, Sat. **Credit** MC, V.

Almost painfully hip when it first opened its inconspicuous doors three years ago, Cherry Jam isn't quite packing them in like it used to. However, the bar remains something of a beacon in an otherwise lifeless part of town. It's co-owned by Ben Watt (of Everything But The Girl fame), and the famously eclectic music policy means that you're as likely to find improvisational jazz or spoken word on the bill as such sub-genres as 'metropolitan' and 'outernational'. Wooden booths and recessed seating add a touch of privacy to the subtly lit, invariably crowded bar area, while there is above-average selection of wines, cocktails and bottled beers. There's also a good, if ethnically confused, bar menu, including dim sum, sushi, or burger and fries.

Disabled: toilet. Music (DJs 10pm Fri-Sun). Poetry (6pm-12.30am last Thur of mth). Specialities (cocktails).

Harlem

78 Westbourne Grove, W2 5RT (7985 0900/www.harlemsoulfood.com). Bayswater or Notting Hill Gate tube. **Open** 10.30am-2am Mon-Sat; 10.30am-midnight Sun. **Food served** 10.30am-midnight daily. **Credit** AmEx, DC, MC, V.

Reviews were so split when this trendy bar-restaurant opened in early 2004 that some wondered how long it would last. Personally, we would banish the naysayers into a corner to eat their words along with a fat, juicy burger and a side of corn cakes, because we love the place – and not only because it's one of the few boozers in town to serve Brooklyn beer. The venue is split between a ground-floor restaurant and a much cosier (verging on cramped) basement bar. Service is perhaps a little cool, but the all-American soul food is damn fine; there's a decent cocktail list too, in addition to the reasonable selection of bottled beers. The emphasis is on a party atmosphere, and the almost-nightly DJ spots attract big names; indeed, Harlem has become quite the place for celeb-spotting lately, which we hope is an indication of its staying power.

Babies and children welcome. Dress: smart casual. Function room. Music (DJ 9pm Mon-Sat). Restaurant.

Island Restaurant & Bar

Lancaster Terrace, W2 2TY (7551 6070/www.islandrestaurant.co.uk). Lancaster Gate tube. **Open** bar 10am-11pm Mon-Sat; 10am-10.30pm Sun. **Food served** noon-11pm daily. **Credit** AmEx, DC, JCB, MC, V.

Partly named after the huge traffic island on which it stands, this new adjunct to the Royal Lancaster Hotel pitches itself as a 'super-chic dining space overlooking Hyde Park'. A tad optimistic, as the view is really more of the busy road outside, but in all other respects Island pretty much hits the mark. The decor is stylishly minimalist: soaring white walls and vast windows, with the kitchen area on display. And if the bar seems like something of an afterthought – an overspill from the upstairs dining area, really – it's not cramped and the table service is friendly and attentive. The wine list is merely adequate; we far preferred the imaginative (and surprisingly inexpensive) cocktail menu. One sip of the Honey Berry Sour (Krupnik honey vodka, crème de fraise and lemon juice) and we were sold.

Babies and children welcome; children's menu; high chairs. Disabled: toilet. Restaurant (no-smoking).

Leinster

57 Ossington Street, W2 4LY (7243 9541). Bayswater or Queensway tube. **Open** noon-11pm Mon-Sat; noon-10.30pm Sun. **Food served** noon-2.30pm daily. **Credit** AmEx, MC, V.

How eyebrows were raised when this rather strait-laced boozer reinvented itself as a gay pub around the start of 2004. The interior had a much-needed makeover when the new management moved in, and the result was, for a time, rather upbeat: wisely preserving the essential elegance of the original building, but adding a certain muted flam-

positive eating + positive living

Island. *See p18.*

boyancy. Yet although the Leinster continues to wear its rainbow colours on its sleeve (or at least, on the shiny new pub sign outside), the place has already begun to look a little tawdry: somewhat battered, perhaps, after a successful first year. The staff are always likeable, though, and the eclectic customers make this the perfect spot for some choice people-watching. On tap is a fairly standard range of beers, and the selection of bottles includes Hoegaarden.
Games (fruit machine). Music (DJs and cabaret monthly). No-smoking area. Tables outdoors (14, patio). TV (satellite). **Map 10 B6**.

Leinster Arms

17 Leinster Terrace, W2 3EU (7402 4670). Lancaster Gate or Queensway tube. **Open** noon-11pm Mon-Sat; noon-10.30pm Sun. **Food served** noon-9pm daily. **Credit** AmEx, MC, V.
An unfussy sort of pub, the Leinster Arms is by no means unpleasant, but neither is it a place we've warmed to. We've always found the main bar area strangely unwelcoming, rather cramped and under-lit, and the side room is just a little too small to accommodate the pool table that dominates it (a polite notice asks punters to make use of the short cues for difficult shots, rather than backing up into the ladies toilets). However, the staff are friendly enough, and the crowd gets too rowdy (for reasons we've yet to fathom, this place is quite a favourite with pilots, hence the small displays devoted to aeronautical memorabilia). The adequate range of beers includes Bass, London Pride and Grolsch; cider devotees will be pleasantly surprised to see Addlestones on tap, quite a rarity in these parts.
Games (quiz machine, pool). Tables outdoors (3, pavement). TV.

Mad Bishop & Bear

Upper Concourse, Paddington Station, Praed Street, W2 1HB (7402 2441/www.fullers.co.uk). Paddington tube/rail. **Open** 7.30am-11pm Mon-Sat; 8.30am-10.30pm Sun. **Food served** 7.30am-9pm Mon-Sat; 8.30am-9pm Sun. **Credit** AmEx, MC, V.

A strange breed, the station pub: full of lone drinkers and people who, by definition, are just passing through. It's hard to escape the sense of melancholy, even in an above-average example like this. The lack of a front wall adds to the feeling that you've never quite left the station concourse but, such reservations aside, the Mad Bishop is a pleasant enough place in which to while away a spare hour. The unobjectionable decor keeps things nice and traditional: earthy red walls and Regency-style prints. It's the range of beers on tap that really sets this boozer apart. In addition to the usual selection of lagers, these include Chiswick, ESB and Jack Frost (it's a Fuller's pub), plus Tribute (an excellent Cornish ale), specials and seasonal variations. It's almost enough to make you miss your train.
Games (4 fruit machines). No-smoking area. Specialities (real ales). Tables outdoors (8, terrace). TV (satellite).

Mitre

24 Craven Terrace, W2 3QH (7262 5240). Lancaster Gate tube/Paddington tube/rail. **Open** 11am-11pm Mon-Sat; noon-10.30pm Sun. **Food served** noon-3pm, 6-10pm Mon-Fri; noon-4pm, 6-10pm Sat; noon-4pm, 6-9pm Sun. **Credit** AmEx, MC, V.
There's very little not to like about this grand old Victorian pub. On sunny days, light pours in through the beautiful, oversized, metal-framed windows; in the main bar, high ceilings give an impression of more space than there often is. Far cosier are the two side rooms, the larger of which has an open fireplace, while downstairs is a separate cellar bar (the aptly named Vault) which hosts an open-mic night every Sunday. The atmosphere is congenial and, despite being under the constant gaze of various dour gentlefolk, whose portraits line the walls, staff are friendly. The array of beers on tap includes Old Speckled Hen, London Pride and Cruzcampo lager, and the wine list is above average. The only off-note on our visit was the uninspiring (if muted) piped music.
Babies and children admitted (separate room). Downstairs bar available for hire. No-smoking area. Music (open mic 8pm Sun; free). Tables outdoors (8, pavement). Specialities (real ale).

Royal Exchange

26 Sale Place, W2 1PU (7723 3781). Paddington tube/rail. **Open** 11am-11pm Mon-Sat; noon-10.30pm Sun. **Food served** noon-10pm daily. **Credit** AmEx, MC, V.
There's been an inn on this site since the days when the Royal Mail coach would exchange letters with local post office wagons, a short distance away from the front door – hence the name. But although time has frayed the edges of this charming little boozer (which has been in its present form since the 1970s), it stands, battered but unbowed, as that rarest of breeds in a land of faceless theme bars: an Irish pub worthy of the name. Authentic-tasting Guinness and Murphy's sit beside Adnams and Brakspear on tap; Irish bar staff dispense dry Irish wit; and there's usually a lively debate going on in one corner or another. The bar food is excellent, too: all hearty, traditional stuff. The landlord happens to be a successful racehorse owner, hence the various equestrian knick-knacks cluttering the walls.
Tables outdoors (2, pavement). TV (digital, satellite).

Salt Whisky Bar

82 Seymour Street, W2 2JB (7402 1155/www.saltbar.com). Marble Arch tube. **Open** 5pm-1am Mon-Sat; 5pm-midnight Sun. **Food served** 6-10.30pm daily. **Credit** AmEx, MC, V.
This cosy, lounge-style bar (a curious adjunct to Salt, the modern Italian restaurant upstairs) is a favourite haunt of staff from Broadcasting House – and as such, it maintains a certain highbrow media chic. The vibe is more Radio 4 than Radio 1, so it was a shame the club-style piped music was turned up so loud on our visit: like techno on the *Today* programme, it just didn't fit. That aside, the bar is a place of sanctity for acolytes of the whisky bottle; the 200-strong selection is nothing short of spectacular. Prices vary from around £5 for an average dram of Scotch to an eye-watering £12,000 for a bottle of 1937 Glenfiddich. Our money-to-sense ratio held firm, but we couldn't resist a shot of Pappa Van Winkle's 20-year-old Bourbon: a little steep at £15, but still a discovery this side of the Mason-Dixon.
Babies and children welcome. Function room. Music (DJs 8pm Thur-Sun; free). Specialities (whisky). Tables outdoors (7, heated terrace). TV (satellite, widescreen).

Steam

1 Eastbourne Terrace, W2 1BA (7850 0555). Paddington tube/rail. **Open** noon-1am Mon-Wed; noon-2am Thur-Sat. **Food served** 11am-11pm Mon-Sat. **Admission** £5 after 11pm Mon-Thur; £7 after 11pm Fri, Sat. **Credit** AmEx, DC, JCB, MC, V.
As self-consciously posey as the Fashion TV that played constantly behind the bar on our last visit, Steam pitches itself at the young and hip crowd – missing the point that there are hipper places in which to spend an evening than the Hilton at Paddington station. In truth, Steam is usually more of a hangout for businessmen and local office workers than the bright young things it seeks to attract, despite the blaring, clubby music that never seems to let up, whatever the time of day. On the plus side, the spacious layout means that finding a table is rarely a problem, and there's a wide selection of bottled beers, plus a limited range of lagers on tap. The cocktail list is also a step in the right direction, but with names such as 'Organic Orgy' and 'Coconut Groove', it hardly screams sophistication.
Disabled: toilet (in hotel). Music (DJs 10pm Fri, Sat.). Restaurant. Specialities (cocktails). TV (big screen, satellite).

Victoria

10A Strathern Place, W2 2NH (7724 1191). Lancaster Gate/Paddington tube/rail. **Open** 11am-11pm Mon-Sat; noon-10.30pm Sun. **Food served** noon-3pm, 6-9.30pm Mon-Sat; noon-9pm Sun. **Credit** AmEx, MC, V.
Tiny and perfectly pretty, the Victoria is quite simply a lovely pub. Assorted items of Victoriana cover every available space of the faded pink walls. An ornate clock above the bar bears the date 1864, and there's even a charmingly unimpressive mini-museum in the corner, beside the larger of the two fireplaces. The crowd is surprisingly bohemian, probably due to the presence of the additional theatre bar upstairs, and the whole atmosphere is very relaxed and cosy. The place never takes itself too seriously, thank goodness, and the effect is all the more appealing because of it. Being a Fuller's pub, it has a fine selection of ales on tap, and the bar food isn't at all bad, either. A pub that's thoroughly worth the detour.
Function rooms (2). Quiz (9pm Tue; £1). Tables outdoors (7, pavement). Games (fruit machine). TV.

Also in the area...

All Bar One 7-9 Paddington Street, W1M 3LA (7487 0071).
Gyngleboy (Davy's) 27 Spring Street, W2 IJA (7723 3351).

Slug and Lettuce 47 Hereford Road, W2 5AH (7229 1503).
Tyburn (JD Wetherspoon) 18-20 Edgware Road, W2 2EN (7723 4731).

BELGRAVIA

The pubs of stately Belgravia cater to diplomats, army officers and staff from embassies whose flags colour the otherwise stern streets; punters who judiciously order from the carefully chosen drinks provided by the likes of the **Grenadier** and the **Star Tavern**. Even local day-jobbers prefer a discerning after-work pint in the **Horse & Groom**, while the world-class **Blue Bar** has international standards to keep.

Blue Bar

The Berkeley, Wilton Place, SW1X 7RL (7235 6000/ www.the-berkeley.co.uk). Hyde Park Corner tube. **Open** 4pm-1am Mon-Sat. **Food served** 4-11pm Mon-Sat. **Credit** AmEx, DC, JCB, MC, V.

Prices match the setting at this stylish and discreet bar beside the lobby of the Berkeley Hotel, but service is courteous and details memorable. Onion-flavoured crostini, a bowl of warmed, glazed mixed nuts, another of marinated black olives, a thin blue drinks menu, a napkin and a leather coaster were swift to arrive. Sit at the scented bar, or in the sunken side area overlooking the moneyed calm of an off-Knightsbridge close, or simply enveloped by the original Lutyens panelling, while you muse over a Berkeley cocktail classic (£10) – say, a Lotus of green Chartreuse and fresh mint, or a Berkeley champagne cocktail (£12) of cognac and angostura bitters, champagne and Grand Marnier. Dom Pérignons (costing three-figure sums), vintage Cristals, 50ml malts at £59 a shot, Cohiba cigars and Beluga caviar, or just a thimble of Achille Musetti espresso – all arrive with optimum grace. Impeccable.

Disabled: toilet. Function room. Restaurants. Specialities (cocktails).

Ebury

11 Pimlico Road, SW1W 8NA (7730 6784/www.the ebury.co.uk). Sloane Square or Victoria tube/rail/11, 211 bus. **Open** noon-11pm Mon-Sat; noon-10.30pm Sun. **Credit** AmEx, MC, V.

Of the same gastropub family as the Wells in Hampstead, Belgravia's Ebury has more of a restauranty vibe. Most of its neat, spacious ground-floor interior is dedicated to dining, and the bar counter heaves with oysters, crabs and langoustines. Such is the quality of drinks on offer, though, that popping in just for a drink isn't a bad idea at all. Cocktails are initially categorised as Classics (£6.50), Almost Classics (£6.50) and Twisted Classics (£6.50) – try the latter's Cappuccino Martini (Stoli, espresso and foamed milk) or Blueberry Mojito of Havana Anejo Blanco, fresh lime and blueberries – then branch out into Champagne (£8.50), Signature (£6.50) and London Selection (£6.50) varieties. An Ebury Martini of Stoli Vanilla, melon purée and Amaretto di Saronno, topped with champagne, would also be a wise choice; the London Selection is a Best Of by the bartenders of the Detroit, the Mac Bar et al. Equally expertly devised, the wine list starts with a Jacques Veritier Côtes de Gascogne at £3.50 a glass.

Babies and children welcome. Disabled: toilet. Function room. Restaurant. Specialities (cocktails).

Grenadier

18 Wilton Row, SW1X 7NR (7235 3074). Hyde Park Corner tube. **Open** noon-11pm Mon-Sat; noon-10.30pm Sun. **Food served** noon-2.30pm, 6-9pm Mon-Sat; noon-2.30pm, 6-9pm Sun. **Credit** AmEx, DC, JCB, MC, V.

Such is the military heritage of this tiny, eccentric anomaly – wedged up a staircase between two private cobbled mews – that you almost feel like saluting as you enter. There's even a sentry box outside. Wellington's guards had their mess here, and the ghost of a card-cheating officer is said to haunt this low-ceilinged, two-room tavern every September. By the crossed sabres and bearskin of the small, pewter-countered front bar, warmed in winter by a blazing fire, regulars quaff pints of Young's, London Pride or John Smith's while transatlantic tourists gee and phew over framed press clippings from their compatriots; decades ago the *Wall Street Journal*, the US edition of *Gourmet* and others described a scene similar to today's. In the back is an intimate restaurant, its seating marked with 'Inkerman 1846' and 'Tunis 1680', its tables regularly booked. As you were!

Babies and children welcome (daytime only). No piped music or jukebox. Restaurant (no smoking).

Horse & Groom

7 Groom Place, SW1X 7BA (7235 6980). Hyde Park Corner tube. **Open** 11am-11pm Mon-Fri. **Food served** noon-8.30pm Mon-Fri. **Credit** AmEx, MC, V.

In the maze of private mews dotted with cars sporting personalised number plates, in a dog-leg by the Vicolo Deli, this amiable little bar accommodates beer lovers and bods more suited to Balham or Borough. Friendly types talk football or the finer points of the guest ale, while squeezed on to two rows of simple banquettes in a lived-in wooden interior fronted by frosted glass spotted with 'As Featured In' stickers. On a bar manned by a genial staff of two (one pony-tailed), a towering Holsten beer pump joins more modest dispensers for Oranjeboom, Shepherd Neame Spitfire and, crowned by a recent award, Shepherd Neame Master Brew. Above this orderly calm, up a narrow staircase, is another bar room that's occasionally hired out for private functions. Then again, the Horse & Groom is private enough as it is, thank you.

Bar available for private hire Sat, late licence. Function room. Games (darts). Restaurant. Specialities (cocktails). Tables outdoors (10, pavement). TV.

Library

Lanesborough Hotel, Hyde Park Corner, W1J 7JZ (7259 5599/www.lanesborough.com). Hyde Park Corner tube. **Open** 11am-1am Mon-Sat; noon-10.30pm Sun. **Food served** 11am-midnight Mon-Sat; noon-10.30pm Sun. **Credit** AmEx, DC, MC, V.

Ask for a drinks menu in the Library – a decorous place, though there's no dress code – and the experienced barman brings a book. A standard range of cocktails (such as a Délice du Library Bar of champagne, amaretto, peach purée and fresh juices at £11.50, or any example from the Library Collection of high-end spirits in simple cocktail mixes for £11.50) is augmented by the likes of Dom Pérignon in three sizes, bottles of Krug at four-figure sums and lobster club sandwiches at £22. A real fire, towers of fresh flowers and a solitary red chaise longue surrounded by yellow half-moon chairs provide the setting in the back room. If your tastes are simple, try a bottle of Ruddles County (£4.50) or a glass of Mud House sauvignon blanc (£7.50). All orders come with a pot pourri of roast potato flakes, and attentiveness that outscores even a librarian's.

RAISE A GLASS: COCKTAILS

London's most exclusive cocktail, according to the Piano Bar of the Sheraton Park Tower, Knightsbridge, costs between £1,000 and £4,000. Its ingredients are 25ml of Rémy Martin Louis XIII ('a fine cognac carefully tended by three generations of cellar masters'), Heidsieck champagne, two drops of Angostura bitters, a sugar cube – and a diamond. Four gees gets you a one-carat upgrade. The PR blurb forgot to mention if this diamond-and-cognac mix was shaken, stirred or served straight up.

Exclusivity in the current cocktail craze isn't confined to gemstones. London has gone fruit loopy. Charlotte Voisey, general manager of **Apartment 195** (*see p29*), is excited about 'a new range of Colombian fruits' which includes the lulo, 'a green fruit with a spiky exterior, in taste similar to a gooseberry', and the mora, 'an Andean blackberry'.

Meanwhile, the cocktail vodka of choice is 42 Below, made with water drawn from 1,000 feet beneath an extinct volcano, 42 degrees below the equator in New Zealand. Its upmarket rival, Grey Goose, uses water naturally purified by champagne limestone from the Genté springs of Cognac, France.

Volcanic water? New Zealand vodka? (Isn't vodka meant to be Russian?) Spiky Colombian gooseberries? Four-grand diamonds? Waiter, there's a gimmick in my drink...

Behind this endless search for novelty festers a lack of genuine creativity in today's cocktail bars. 'It's been a really dull year,' complains Match Bars supremo Jonathan Downey. 'The last year has been about Nathan Barley bars.' And Downey knows a thing or two. Bringing mixology maestro Dale DeGroff over from New York to consult on ventures such as the **Match** bars (*see p43 and p116*) and **Milk & Honey** (*see p84*), Downey sparked a cocktail revolution this side of the Atlantic. DeGroff was the instigator of New York's cocktail boom of the late 1980s, the singed orange peel in his Cosmopolitan at the seminal Rainbow Rooms now the stuff of legend. DeGroff offered the perfect example of doing the simple things right. In no time, every bar worth its shaker was reinventing cocktail classics using prime ingredients, choosing the glass with care and presenting the drink with equal aplomb.

Harry Craddock would have approved. Another American, head barman at the Savoy from 1921, he introduced mixology to London. Europe was grey with post-war austerity, America was in the grips of prohibition. Craddock's **American Bar** (*see p93*) catered

to well-bred Brits and expat Americans. Craddock became London's first celebrity barman, part valet, part confidant, author of the influential *Savoy Cocktail Book*. The Savoy's success saw American Bars set up in Rome and Venice, then across Europe, attracting high-class travellers. London's cocktail bars were mainly confined to hotels, where staff could be properly trained. But somehow, as society became more egalitarian and women started going to pubs, cocktails became a gimmicky fad, all disco colours and paper brollies.

Alongside DeGroff, Dick Bradsell created a similar storm at the **Atlantic Bar & Grill** (*see p56*) in the early 1990s. Bars became lucrative add-on for hotels as well, and bar design began to matter. Soon came **Lab** (*see p84*), the **Met Bar** (*see p66*) and so on. Mixologists earned celebrity-chef reputations, using only premium spirits. The demand for Plymouth gin rescued it from extinction, Absolut started its own fruit range, Moët Hennessey launched Belvedere vodka, Dutch Ketel One became hip. Bottled pineapple for piña colada was out; back bars sprouted fruit. Now even Wetherspoons do cocktails.

In 20 years, the gimmick has come full circle, just dumbed up instead of dumbed down. It's not all bad – **Shochu Lounge** (*see p45*) makes imaginative use of a distilled rice spirit from medieval Japan, and the standard of cocktail mixing at high-end bars means more choice in London than anywhere else on the planet. Competition demands difference – and there are only so many ways you can mix a Martini. Isn't everyone satisfied? *Peterjon Cresswell*

Disabled: toilet. Function rooms. Music (pianist from 6.30pm daily). Restaurant. Specialities (cocktails, vintage cognac and whisky).

Nag's Head

53 Kinnerton Street, SW1X 8ED (7235 1135). Hyde Park Corner or Knightsbridge tube. **Open** 11am-11pm Mon-Sat; noon-10.30pm Sun. **Food served** noon-9pm daily. **No credit cards.**

The idiosyncratic layout of this charming, cheerful and often crowded little boozer reflects the building's former use as stables (and stable-hands' bar) nearly two centuries ago. From the Wendy House of a main bar (pygmy stools around its pygmy counter), a narrow corridor and staircase lead down to a standing-room-only area with its own counter service. Bitter, Broadside and Old Ale from Adnams, and Bitburger on draught, are complemented by bottles rare enough to drag discerning hopheads to this quiet strip on the Knightsbridge-Belgravia border. Yet idiosyncracy isn't confined to design or drinks. Covering the walls are line drawings of James Mason and Kenny Everett, of the pub's pretty window-boxed frontage set beside the gate of Anne's Close, and, by a different hand, of Grace-era cricket poses. Boasting a fire in winter, and an outdoor bench in summer, the Nag's is an outstanding pub for all seasons and all sorts of reasons.

No mobile phones. Tables outdoors (1, pavement).

Star Tavern

6 Belgrave Mews West, SW1X 8HT (7235 3019). Hyde Park Corner or Knightsbridge tube. **Open** 11am-11pm Mon-Sat; noon-10.30pm Sun. **Food served** noon-2.30pm, 6-9pm daily. **Credit** AmEx, MC, V.

Behind the heavily fortified German Embassy, through an arch and down a private cobbled lane past the Austrian Embassy, the Star – its golden 12-pointer shining amid the quaint, exclusive Belgravia façades – has attracted many types since its incarnation as a servants' inn. Gangsters, film stars and notoriety of every stripe would frequent the tiny bar area, expansive lounge and conspiratorial first-floor room. Today, Fuller's ales and two welcoming fires draw a mix of locals in their best work clothes; those happy to make a beeline for ESB, Chiswick or bottles of Golden Pride, and thirsty clerks with Germanic accents. The Star still has class in spades: Latin inscriptions on the maroon and olive-green lounge seating, stars carved into coloured window panes, and service that's more usually reserved for the nobs who frequent a different class of Belgravia bar. The Star is still of the people, and proud of it.

Babies and children admitted. Function room. No piped music or jukebox.

BLOOMSBURY & ST GILES

Eclectic is the easy but apt description of the drinking scene here. Grand, traditional public houses of stern mahogany draw tourists from the British Museum, some thrilled to rub shoulders with the ghosts of literary pre-war regulars. Hip DJ bar **AKA** and **Point 101** are more of an overspill from the West End, whose easy pickings attract a clutch of junkie hustlers (keep a sharp eye on your bags). **Oporto** is the leading player of the bar-starred border area where Bloomsbury, St Giles, Holborn and the West End collide at the High Holborn/Shaftesbury Avenue intersection.

AKA

18 West Central Street, WC1A 1JJ (7836 0110/www.akalondon.com). Holborn or Tottenham Court Road tube. **Open** 6pm-3am Tue-Thur; 6pm-4am Fri; 7pm-5am Sat; 10pm-4am Sun. **Food served** 6-11pm Tue-Fri; 7-11.30pm Sat. **Admission** £3 after 11pm Tue; £5 after 10pm Thur; £5 after 9pm, £7 after 10pm Fri; £10 after 9pm Sat; varies Sun. **Credit** AmEx, DC, JCB, MC, V.

Partner operation to adjoining nightclub the End, AKA stages DJ nights of equal renown in its expansive, two-floor industrial space – a former Victorian sorting office. A clubbing vibe exudes from the main downstairs bar, comprised of a long shiny zinc counter, curved-back seats and candlelit tables. Cocktails (£6.50-£8.50) are categorised by premium base spirits such as Ketel One vodka, Germana cachaça, Appleton white rum and Tanqueray gin, but pride of place goes to the champagne varieties: a Lost in Translation (Devaux champagne, sake, passionfruit puree and marmalade) or an 18 West (Zubrowka Bison vodka, passion fruit, pear and lemon juice topped with Devaux champagne). Bottled beers include Russian Baltika, Australian Crown and Belgian Grimbergen – although the ambitious food menu has been dropped in favour of pizzas shuttled round from Pizza Express in Coptic Street.

Bar available for hire. Disabled: toilet. Quiz (8pm 1st Tue of mth; free, book teams in advance). Music (DJs 10pm nightly). Specialities (cocktails). TV (projector screen). **Map 1 L6.**

Angel

61 St Giles High Street, WC2H 8LE (7240 2876). Tottenham Court Road tube. **Open** 11.30am-11pm Mon-Fri; noon-11pm Sat; 1-10.30pm Sun. **Food served** noon-9pm Mon-Sat; noon-6pm Sun. **Credit** MC, V.

This cosy Sam Smith's pub could easily be found in a snug Yorkshire village – instead, it's slap behind Centre Point, among shady streets worked by junkie hustlers. Once inside, though, the Angel is conviviality itself. The roaring fire, coal scuttle and tongs in the saloon bar, the thuds from the dartboard in a public bar decorated with old theatre posters, the modest tiled indoor courtyard, the comfort food of giant Yorkshire puddings filled with mince and mash (£5.50) – even Yorkshire pudding and gravy is considered a lite bite – and hearty pints of Old Brewery Bitter or Extra Stout from the Sam Smith's stable, all exude homely bonhomie. Ironically, in its previous Elizabethan incarnation, this was the Bowl, where last-request bowls of sustenance were offered to condemned men before the quick march to the nearby gallows.

Babies and children admitted (garden/weekend afternoons only). Games (chess, darts, cribbage, fruit machine). No piped music or jukebox. Tables outdoors (8, garden). **Map 7 K6.**

Daily Bar & Grill

36-38 New Oxford Street, WC1A 1EP (7631 0862). Tottenham Court Road tube. **Open** noon-11pm Mon-Thur; noon-midnight Fri, Sat. **Food served** noon-10pm Mon-Sat. **Credit** AmEx, DC, MC, V.

Little has changed here apart from the name: the Nudge nudged out in favour of the Daily, neither title particularly inspired. The place itself, though, isn't bad at all, comprising an upstairs of smart brown furniture, a neat bar and open kitchen, and a downstairs lounge space for after-dark intimacy. For the price (around £7) and quality, Stefano's daytime food (chalked up daily specials and main menu detailed on primitive clipboards) alone almost merits. Choose from upmarket pastas, Cumberland sausages

or burgers and hot sandwiches. Draught options of Leffe, Guinness and Hoegaarden, bottled Budvar, Cruzcampo and Peroni, wine at £11-£16 a bottle (white Marques de Caceres Rioja at £15), five of each colour in two sizes of glass from £3, standard cocktails at £6, pitchers at £12… The Daily is doing everything right, yet lacks loyal trade. Maybe New Oxford Street is just a bus lane after all.
Babies and children welcome (before 5pm). Disabled: toilet. Function room. Tables outdoors (2, pavement).

Grape Street Wine Bar

222-224A Shaftesbury Avenue, WC2H 8EB (7240 0686). Holborn or Tottenham Court Road tube. Bar **Open** noon-11pm Mon-Fri. **Food served** noon-3.30pm, 5-10pm Mon-Fri. **Credit** AmEx, MC, V.

Wedged into the corner where Shaftesbury Avenue meets Grape Street, this warm, friendly bar has 1980s throwback written all over it: salmon pink walls, wood-look shelving and a collection of corks in a range of framed boxes. Odd, that, since much of it was rebuilt in 1997. Clive Allen, formerly of the Cork & Bottle (*see p56*), took on the site eight years ago, but although cosy and atmospheric, the makeover doesn't have the stylish look of his other place. A calmer after-office crowd collects in groups at the well-spaced tables: couples in their late 30s and older men reading the paper over a few glasses of claret. The wine list is very good indeed, strong in aromatic styles like the excellent 2003 Mantineia from Domaine Tselepos in Greece (£18.95) and showing an acceptable total of 14 wines by the glass. Prices are keen, although who would order 2003 sauvignon de touraine (£11.95) – described on the list as 'the poor man's sancerre'?
Babies and children admitted. Function room. Tables outdoors (2, pavement). **Map 7 K6**.

Central

King's Bar

Russell Hotel, Russell Square, WC1B 5BE (7837 6470). Russell Square tube. **Open** 7am-midnight Mon-Sat; 8am-11pm Sun. **Food served** 7am-9pm Mon-Sat; 8am-9pm Sun. **Credit** AmEx, DC, MC, V.

The extensive overhaul of the century-old Russell Hotel has seen some sleek touches introduced to its ground-floor King's Bar. A new red-and-black logo has been slapped on the menus and back bar, incongruously so, given the genteel ambience exuded by the dark-wood-and-stucco interior dotted with pot plants and upholstered armchairs. That said, the new hi-tech toilets are redolent of a designer bar in competitive Soho, and yet this is still an average hotel bar in a quiet part of town. So how do you justify cocktails at £9 when they're two pounds cheaper in venues of far higher mixology renown? The cheapest wines – Hardy's and valpolicella classico – are just under £5 a glass – not cheap. And how can you charge £18 for a steak sandwich, however oniony the rings or zesty the Dijon mustard? The King's Bar isn't *that* regal.
Babies and children admitted. Disabled: toilet. Dress: no shorts. Function room (call hotel for details). No piped music or jukebox. Restaurant. **Map 1 L4**.

Lord John Russell

91 Marchmont Street, WC1N 1AL (7388 0500). Russell Square tube. **Open** 11.30am-11pm Mon-Sat; noon-10.30pm Sun. **Food served** noon-3pm Mon-Fri. **Credit** JCB, MC, V.

Well stocked, well run and well laid out, this admirable pub attracts a mix of discerning beer hounds, students and locals who reside in this no man's land northeast of the British Museum. The range of ales satisfy all, the grand pumps lining a sturdy bar counter that fronts a scrubbed-wood interior filled with old prints of London and simple furniture. Marston's Pedigree, John Smith's, Courage Director's, St Austell Tribute, Bombardier, Budvar, San Miguel, Früli, Kronenbourg Blanc and Guinness of either temperature – a draught XI to put most pubs to shame – are complemented by bottled Belgian brews such as Grimbergen. The food is along the scampi-and-chips line, with four daily specials (cajun chicken, savoury mince), at under £5, chalked up over the TV. Worth the trek from the British Museum – not that many tourists yet agree.
Babies and children welcome (daytime only). Games (board games, chess, draughts, quiz machine). Specialities (real ale). Tables outdoors (7, pavement). TV.

Museum Tavern

49 Great Russell Street, WC1B 3BA (7242 8987). Holborn or Tottenham Court Road tube. **Open** 11am-11pm Mon-Sat; noon-10.30pm Sun. **Food served** 11am-9pm Mon-Sat; noon-9pm Sun. **Credit** AmEx, DC, JCB, MC, V.

This is a rare example of a pub able to satisfy tourist and local alike. The visitor will delight in the Tavern's location directly opposite the British Museum, its historic longevity (as the Dog & Duck in the early 1700s it was surrounded by marshland, 150 years before William Finch Hill's ornate reconstruction) and its pub grub of the pie or roast variety. Some may even derive a thrill from sitting where famed regulars Orwell and Marx may have sat. Today's regulars, though, couldn't give a hoot about history, but remain perfectly happy to nurse a pint of Bombardier, Theakston's Old Peculiar, Courage Director's, Young's, Bateman's XXXB or Fuller's London Pride. The range of malts (Glenmorangie, Lagavulin and others) appeals to all-comers, but few locals would consider shelling out for the pub's logoed T-shirt.
Children admitted (over-14s only before 5pm). Games (boardgames). No-smoking area. Specialities (real ale). Tables outdoors (5-8, pavement). **Map 1 L5**.

mybar

11-13 Bayley Street, WC1B 3HD (7667 6000/www.myhotels.com). Goodge Street or Tottenham Court Road tube. **Open/food served** 11am-11pm daily (last food orders 10.30pm). **Credit** AmEx, DC, MC, V.

The flagship bar of this mid-range, New Age lifestyle hotel chain has had to differentiate itself from the glut of upmarket hotel bars an easy taxi journey away. Feng shui or no feng shui, punters want original cocktails at affordable prices. And lo! Ten signature drinks – sorry, mysignaturedrinks, £7.50 plus 12.5% service charge – feature such gems as the Wink! (South gin, bitters, Triple Sec and sugars shaken into an absinthe-washed glass); for the same price, mymartinis include the Bloomsbury of 42 Below vodka and rosehip stirred with 'bubbles', namely Graham Peck Brut NV champagne. Towards lunchtime, temptingly drizzled plates of brightly coloured vegetables and cheeses of varying hues form mydeli (£8.95, or £11.95 with a glass of wine). Mains, though, are good – stuffed Gressingham duck breast filled with baby spinach on couscous with black-olive sauce (£11.95), for example – and a bar vibe is engendered in the intimate mysnug at the back, with five tables and a plasma screen of trippy images. Could it be mydestination, perchance?
Babies and children admitted (until 6pm). Disabled: toilet. Function rooms. Tables outdoors (7, pavement). **Map 1 K5**.

Nags Head. *See p24.*

Oporto

168 High Holborn, corner of Endell Street, WC1V 7AA (7240 1548/www.baroporto.com). Holborn or Tottenham Court Road tube. **Open** noon-11.30pm **Food served** noon-11.30pm Mon-Sat. **Credit** MC, V.

Packed most evenings, petite two-floor corner bar Oporto manages to catch the drift from several crowds. A reasonably hip post-work bunch who wouldn't be seen dead in Freud's mingle with the younger element of the theatre crowd – Shaftsbury Avenue and Theatre are a step away – and Euro Londoners. A neat, continental design helps, as do draughts like San Miguel, London Pride, Staropramen and Früli, bottles such as Paulaner, Duvel and Budvar, wines from £11 a bottle and a reasonably priced chic lunch selection of light pastas, salads and curries. Illy coffee, too. In operation from springtime to the end of the warm weather, a row of tables outside adds an extra dimension – albeit a resolutely urban one. The wood-panelled downstairs bar is rather smart, though, with armchairs, a pool table and little fear of knocking over someone else's drink.

Function room. Games (pool). Music (DJ, Thur; varying programme of live entertainment). Tables outdoors (4, pavement). TV (satellite). **Map 1 L6.**

Plough

27 Museum Street, WC1A 1LH (7636 7964). Tottenham Court Road tube. **Open** 11am-11pm Mon-Sat; noon-10.30pm Sun. **Food served** noon-4pm Mon-Sat; noon-4.30pm Sun. **Credit** MC, V.

The middle-aged men in casual sweaters tell you that this traditional wooden corner boozer trades in real ale – and sure enough, there's Adnams and Adnams Broadside, Young's and Bass. But the twofer lunches (lasagne, chicken cacciatore) at under a tenner between Monday and Thursday see all kinds of employees parked on the neat banquettes or perched in the upstairs restaurant. Racks holding a good and well-priced wine selection and televised sport see steady business in the downstairs back room right through the day. Tourists, too, pop in after seeing the sign in four languages on their way from the British Museum (five minutes away). On summer afternoons, thirsty dispatch riders congregate on the busy right-angle of pavement outside, festooned with clusters of hanging baskets.

Babies and children admitted (upstairs bar). Comedy (7.30pm 2nd Fri of mth; £6). Function room. Games (fruit machine, quiz machine). Quiz (7.30pm 1st Wed of mth; £2). Tables outdoors (8, pavement). TVs (satellite). **Map 1 L5.**

Point 101

101 New Oxford Street, WC1A 1DB (7379 3112). Tottenham Court Road tube. **Open/food served** 4pm-2am Mon-Sat; 4pm-midnight Sun. **Credit** AmEx, MC, V.

The recent refit and classy overhaul of this unusual venue might just suit it down to the ground. The ground-floor reception area of the notorious, 35-storey Centre Point still harks back to 1960s municipal architecture, no matter how much purple the new management has splashed over it. But an adventurous nightly roster of DJs, new evenings-only opening hours and a carefully considered menu of food and drinks are welcome developments. The after-dark approach allows the bright staff to forgo what were slack lunchtimes. An array of well-made £6.50 cocktails now complements a varied wine list that runs from Catarratto chardonnay at £3.50 a glass to Paul Deloux Petit Chablis at £18 a bottle. Food includes Chinese-style crab claws and salad (£5.25). There are plans to extend the beer range beyond the current draught Staropramen and bottled Beck's and Budvar.

Function room. Music (DJs 10pm daily; free). Tables outdoors (4, pavement). **Map 7 K6.**

Queen's Larder

1 Queen Square, WC1N 3AR (7837 5627). Holborn or Russell Square tube. **Open** 11am-11pm Mon-Fri; noon-11pm Sat; noon-10.30pm Sun. **Food served** noon-6pm daily. **Credit** MC, V.

Almost every trace of this cosy corner pub's quirky past has been whitewashed from the history books by a refurbishment. Named after Queen Charlotte, whose consorting duties ran to hiding mad King George's medicaments here, the Queen's Larder lived happily with its legend, displaying framed pictures of royals around the tiny main bar. All is now white paint and recent Royal Opera House promotional posters. Even the historical plaques have gone. Greene King IPA, Adnams and London Pride remain on tap, although the more obscure ales, which once attracted customers from nearby Russell Square, have also disappeared. Just be thankful that the dumb waiter continues to groan under the weight of pies and potatoes at lunchtime, and that in warm weather terrace tables still give out on to the pretty pedestrian passage.

Function room. Games (board games, fruit machine). No-smoking area (restaurant). Restaurant. Tables outdoors (7, pavement). **Map 1 L5.**

Truckles of Pied Bull Yard

Off Bury Place, WC1A 2JR (7404 5338/www.davy.co.uk). Holborn or Tottenham Court Road tube. **Open/food served** 11am-10pm Mon-Fri; 11am-3pm Sat. **Credit** AmEx, DC, MC, V.

The Harvester-style makeover – yellow walls, pine floors, a couple of leather sofas – effaced this wine bar's old spit 'n' sawdust character. But in the process, Truckles has become a broader church, sucking in literary types from neighbouring London Review Bookshop as well as old boys in pinstriped shirts and patterned ties. There's a work crowd on weekday evenings; some even go to the occasional wine tastings organised by Davy's, the wine merchant that supplies the wine and owns the bar – it's one of 20 under its stewardship. 29 wines by the glass is a fine figure, but it's a patchy list, full of Davy's own-label tipples. Try the 2003 Domaine des Billards Saint-Amour (£5.05 a glass) instead, or Delaforce's 1985 port (£3.95 for a 50ml glass). There are just three beers, by the bottle, but they're all good – Becks, Budvar and Bishop's Finger – and five Cuban cigars, including an excellent Cohiba at £8.95.

Bar/restaurant available for hire. No-smoking area (restaurant). Restaurant. Tables outdoors (20, courtyard). **Map 1 L5.**

Also in the area...

All Bar One 108 New Oxford Street, WC1A 1HB (7307 7980).

CHELSEA

Follow rule number one of Chelsea drinking – get off the King's Road – and you'll find an engaging mix of top-notch gastropubs and great locals tucked away in the backstreets down towards the river or pushing against nearby South Ken and Fulham (take your A-Z as well as this guide). The leavening of older social housing in the area also provides welcome balance to the mix – it's not all about wall-to-wall Sloanes. A liberal dash of bohemia is an added bonus, spurred by an arty set linked to the Royal Court Theatre, Chelsea Arts Club and the art school.

Apartment 195

195 King's Road, SW3 5ED (7351 5195/www. apartment195.co.uk). Sloane Square tube/11, 22 bus. **Open** 4-11pm Mon-Sat; 4-10.30pm Sun. **Food served** 4-10.30pm daily. **Credit** AmEx, MC, V.

Apartment 195 arrived in a blaze of glory a couple of years ago, notching up Bar of the Year awards and getting male reviewers as much in a tizzy over its saucily clad all-women mixologists, marshalled by Charlotte Voisey (*see p211*) as its extensive cocktail list (which specialises in Mojitos, Martinis and Caipirinhas). But as these things do, the first flush of excitement has faded. The venue is still a lovely space, a wood-panelled gentlemen's club – brown and mauve palette, battered leather seats – sexed up with bright pop art and uptempo sounds; and women still rule the bar with flashes of flesh. Beers are limited to just two bottled lagers, presumably because beer just isn't a turn-on. Wine drinkers do better, and there's a decent bar menu tailored to deep pockets.

Function room. Specialities (cocktails). TV.

Builder's Arms

13 Britten Street, SW3 3TY (7349 9040). Sloane Square or South Kensington tube. **Open** 11am-11pm Mon-Sat; noon-10.30pm Sun. **Food served** noon-2.30pm, 7-9.30pm Mon-Sat; noon-4pm, 7-9pm Sun. **Credit** JCB, MC, V.

Tucked away amid residential streets just north of the King's Road, the Builder's ticks all the boxes dictated by its Chelsea demographics: casually filled bookshelves and leather sofas for conservative backdrop, tempered by surreal Dali-inspired oil paintings by way of bohemian colour. This all seems a bit wasted, though, on the twentysomething Sloanes that pack in on a weekend night, necking serviceable wine and unexciting bottled beer (though you can get a pint of London Pride or Adnams if you want to go against the grain). The food in the narrow back room dining area is more of a draw, pulling in well-heeled punters for the likes of red snapper with fennel, celery and thyme soup. But, for the most part, an evening here consists of cramming into the awkward, too-narrow spaces either side of the bar and looking out for Camilla or Toby.

Babies and children admitted. Disabled: toilet. Restaurant. Tables outdoors (2, pavement). TV.

Chelsea Potter

119 King's Road, SW3 4PL (7352 9479). Sloane Square tube. **Open** 11am-11pm Mon-Sat; noon-10.30pm Sun. **Food served** 11am-9pm daily. **Credit** AmEx, DC, MC, V.

Enjoying pole position as the first pub on the King's Road as you make west from Sloane Square, the Potter was a favourite of 1960s swinging Chelsea before becoming a gathering spot for gaudier 1970s punks looking to earn picture-for-a-pint dosh from tourists. That all seems a distant memory on weekend nights, when raucous folk in their twenties try to out-shout loud and lousy music while knocking back lager and house white. On the plus side, there's good beer to be had (Greene King IPA, London Pride, plus guests), and art nouveau touches – flowery mirrors, decorated iron columns – liven up an otherwise unremarkable interior. Large windows provide ringside viewing of the King's Road flow, making the pub popular with Top Shop misses and, on match days, less discerning Chelsea fans in search of a pint or three.

Babies and children admitted (until 6pm). Games (fruit machines). Tables outdoors (5, pavement). TV (big screen, digital, satellite).

Chelsea Ram

32 Burnaby Street, SW10 0PL (7351 4008). Fulham Broadway tube/Sloane Square tube then 11, 19, 22 bus. **Open** 11am-11pm Mon-Sat; noon-10.30pm Sun. **Food served** noon-3pm, 6.30-10pm Mon-Sat; noon-3.30pm, 6.30-10pm Sun. **Credit** MC, V.

Clued-up locals are drawn to the Ram like moths to a flame. This brightly lit corner beacon shines out in the rag-tag semi-lined backstreets at the gritty end of the King's Road. Pale wooden tables blend with light sepia walls in a main space warmed in winter by an open fire. Red stripy carpets and sparsely filled bookshelves create slightly more formal areas around the other two sides of the bar, where diners congregate to enjoy a fine menu ranging from the biggest fish cakes in Chelsea to wood pigeon salad with quails' eggs. While most of the customers seem as well scrubbed as the tables, a few dissolute-looking sorts temper the blend. The wines are an interesting mix too: nice to see Lebanese reds and organic whites. The taps dispense Young's ales alongside the standard lagers. Refined if you want it to be, down-to-earth if you don't.

Babies and children admitted. Function room. Tables outdoors (6, pavement). TV (big screen).

Cooper's Arms

87 Flood Street, SW3 5TB (7376 3120). Sloane Square or South Kensington tube. **Open** 11am-11pm Mon-Sat; noon-10.30pm Sun. **Food served** 12.30-3pm, 6.30-9.30pm Mon-Sat; 12.30-3pm Sun. **Credit** AmEx, MC, V.

This solid corner local lights up its residential backstreet. Nice touches abound: a moose head pokes out of the wine racks above the bar, while vintage Jak cartoons offer pleasant distraction in an alcove dominated by more taxidermy. The stuffed pig's head, though, is the only old boar amid the gaggle of raffish locals, luckier ones bagging a spot by the fireplace, others passing time by an old grandfather clock alongside pretty vintage travel posters. Dishes like Thai green monkfish curry dot a bar menu as warming as the sunny yellow walls; a short, well-chosen wine list augments Young's ales and Hoegaarden on tap. Papers are scattered on a massive central wooden table; grab one if you don't fancy eavesdropping on the local gents chatting up the barmaids.

Babies and children admitted (until 6pm). Function room. No piped music or jukebox. TV.

Cross Keys

1 Lawrence Street, SW3 5NB (7349 9111/www. thexkeys.co.uk). Sloane Square or South Kensington tube. **Open** noon-11pm Mon-Sat; noon-10.30pm Sun. **Food served** bar noon-3pm, 6-8pm Mon-Fri. **Credit** AmEx, MC, V.

Just back from the traffic roaring down the river road, the Cross Keys is a quirky, colourful oasis in the middle of staid Chelsea mansion blocks. Reds and golds adorn walls and chandeliers, while wacky stone and wood sculptures and reliefs peer down on a stone-floored bar warmed by two

Guanabara. *See p35.*

fires in winter. An exotic stained-glass triptych of monkeys and parrots adds to the air of warped bohemia; it's no surprise that the words 'Chelsea Arts Club' are etched on one of the large mirrors over the fireplaces. The beer's not bad, with Courage Directors and Wadworth 6X among the choice at the tiny red curved bar; wine seems to be reserved for diners in the more restrained stone back-room restaurant. Out front, there's a happy mix of young bohos and codgers, with a quiet soundtrack ranging from 1970s rock to Nick Drakey bongo-fuelled folk. Eclectic and charming.
Babies and children admitted (high chairs). Function rooms. No cigars or pipes (restaurant). Restaurant.

Fox & Hounds

29 Passmore Street, SW1W 8HR (7730 6367). Sloane Square tube. **Open** 11am-11pm Mon-Sat; noon-10.30pm Sun. **Food served** noon-2.30pm, 6.30-9.30pm Mon-Fri; noon-2.30pm Sun. **Credit** AmEx, DC, MC, V.
Hidden away on a backstreet near the Royal Court, this vintage bar is ideal for a pre- or post-theatre drink. It's a lovely, low-ceilinged old boozer. The stone-flagged front bar offers a few tiny alcoves; the carpeted space at the back attracts older, more dress-circle drinkers. Bright red walls, the result of a recent makeover, still look a little too fresh to match the dark wood panelling and stained glass elsewhere, but time will fix that. This is an unhurried place, where locals over 40 chat quietly about middle-aged matters, the ladies sipping house white while the blokes sup something from the Young's range of draught beers or maybe a bottle of Ramrod. An 'On This Day' blackboard adds to the old-time mood: it's updated daily by a landlady who clearly has a fondness for past glories – why else the stirring Kipling poems in the gents'?

Lots Road Pub & Dining Room

114 Lots Road, SW10 0RJ (7352 6645). Fulham Broadway tube then 11 bus/Sloane Square tube then 11, 19, 22 bus. **Open** 11am-11pm Mon-Sat; noon-10.30pm Sun. **Food served** 11am-3pm, 5.30-10pm Mon-Fri; 11am-10.30pm Sat; noon-10pm Sun. **Credit** MC, V.
Filling a big, sweeping corner site by Chelsea harbour and the old power station, this place exudes confidence in its magnetic power, despite an out-of-the-way location. By the door, leather seating and a few discreet alcoves create a slightly more upmarket sideshow for the bustling brasserie space that is the main attraction. Boisterous locals cram round little dark-wood candlelit tables, while staff at a big curving zinc-topped bar dispense rounds to drinkers mingling happily with diners. The wine list is matched by an exemplary gastro bar menu offering the likes of tiger prawns with chorizo and broad beans. A decent range of beers includes Wadworth 6X on tap; alternatively, try one of the delicious milkshakes, which provide sustenance while leaving you with a clear head before viewing or bidding at the nearby auction rooms.
Babies and children admitted. Disabled: toilet. No smoking (restaurant).

Orange Brewery

37-39 Pimlico Road, SW1W 8NE (7730 5984). Sloane Square tube. **Open** 11am-11pm Mon-Sat; noon-10.30pm Sun. **Food served** 11am-9pm Mon-Sat; noon-9pm Sun. **Credit** AmEx, DC, MC, V.
The engagingly unassuming Orange Brewery (now, sadly, a brewery no longer) sits on a tiny triangle of greenery in the shadow of St Barnabas Church at the meeting point between Chelsea and Victoria (the Edwardian decor – murky orange-brown walls, old wooden chairs, scuffed tables – is more reminiscent of Victoria). Music plays softly in the background, and there's a lovely dark-wood snug off the main space. The wine list squeezes some quality bottles on to a selection starting at under a tenner, but most punters are here for the beer (Abbot, Greene King IPA, a couple of Adnams ales among the eight cask offerings on our visit) served in friendly style. Food tends to be hearty and meaty. All in all, this is the sort of local that Royal furniture maker David Linley might pop into from his shop just along the road.
Babies and children welcome (restaurant). Function room. Games (fruit machines, quiz machine). Restaurant. Specialities (real ale). Tables outdoors (7, pavement).

Phene Arms

9 Phene Street, SW3 5NY (7352 3294). Sloane Square or South Kensington tube. **Open** 11am-11pm Mon-Sat; noon-10.30pm Sun. **Food served** noon-3pm, 6-10.30pm Mon-Sat; noon-4pm, 6-10.30pm Sun. **Credit** MC, V.
People who care about these things know that this was George Best's local, and it exhibits some of the flashy panache that the football legend had in his heyday. An ornate frieze tops one mirrored wall, while delicate rural scenes snake faintly across the façade of the tiny central bar. A backroom of brown leather sofas and abstract pictures adds to the arty air, even if the punters – a few rugby shirts here, nice couples there – don't quite match the decor. Food seems similarly mixed up: foie gras on one hand, Swedish meatballs on the other. The drinks list features some unexciting wines and so-so beers. To sum up: the Phene is OK for those living a short dribble away, perhaps, but isn't a venue we'd buy a season ticket to.
Babies and children admitted. Function room. Tables outdoors (27 garden, roof terrace). Restaurant. TV (satellite).

Pig's Ear

35 Old Church Street, SW3 5BS (7352 2908/www.thepigsear.co.uk). Sloane Square tube. **Open** 5-11pm Mon; noon-11pm Tue-Sat; noon-10.30pm Sun. **Food served** (bar) 7-10pm Mon; noon-3pm, 7-10pm Tue-Fri; noon-4pm, 7-10pm Sat, Sun. **Credit** AmEx, MC, V.
This popular gastropub is a colourful newcomer to a corner site a stone's throw from the King's Road. A glossy red ceiling glimmers in the light given out by antique lamps and chandeliers, and candlelight flickers from the dark wooden tables. Customers, most in their 20s and 30s, dine on robust, classy dishes like truffle, spinach and nutmeg risotto or pan-fried pig's tail. Staff at the high marble-topped bar dispense wine from a fine, 30-strong European list (starting at £13), as well as excellent Pig's Ear ale from Gloucestershire's Uley Brewery. Venture through a cosy side-bar past a blazing fire, and upstairs you'll find a lovely wood-panelled dining room also packing them in and serving up an expanded take on the bar menu. There's no smoking upstairs, and children enjoy the bustle along with their parents downstairs. Is this Chelsea continental? It's certainly a winner.
Babies and children admitted. Games (backgammon, cards, chess, Scrabble). No-smoking (restaurant). Restaurant.

Sporting Page

6 Camera Place, SW10 0BH (7349 0455/www.frontpagepubs.com). Fulham Broadway or Sloane Square tube/bus 11, 14, 19, 22, 328, 211. **Open**

11am-11pm Mon-Sat; noon-10.30pm Sun. **Food served** noon-3pm, 6-10pm Mon-Fri; noon-6pm Sat, Sun. **Credit** AmEx, DC, MC, V.

The long glass frontage means you can't miss this bar, with its bright lights spilling out on to a nondescript residential street. As the name suggests, there's a sporting theme, exemplified on a small scale by old prints, but much more grandly by tiled wall-panels depicting such sporting legends as tennis queen Suzanne Lenglen and jockey Lester Piggott; the little TV tuned silently into greyhound racing on our visit added a strange modern-day complement. This being Chelsea, the food is several notches above average sports bar fare – there's roast poussin, and salmon chowder soup – but you can have a steak and Guinness pie, too, accompanied by a pint of Bombardier (if you so choose) instead of something from the global wine list. The black-and-white stone flags and bright lights can make the interior seem a bit antiseptic, especially midweek – but with outside tables beneath a wide awning, the bar has more of a sporting chance on a summer's day.

Babies and children admitted. No piped music or jukebox. Tables outdoors (12, pavement). TV (big screen, digital, satellite).

Surprise in Chelsea

6 Christchurch Terrace, off Tite Street, SW3 4AJ (7349 1821). Sloane Square tube. **Open/food served** noon-11pm Mon-Sat; noon-10.30pm Sun. **Credit** MC, V.

Hidden away amid the luxury pads, and a stone's throw from the river, this unadorned old boozer is aptly named. Both toffs and toughs congregate around its tiny horseshoe bar beneath sketches of old Chelsea life, husky-voiced old geezers crooning standards in one corner, flat-capped stripy-shirted Sloanes looking for working-class grit in another. There's bar billiards, and when it comes to thirst, a blackboard promises 'lovely bubbly' for £15; less rarefied tastes can sup on London Pride and Adnams ales. A tiny maroon-walled hideaway in one corner contains a few battered red leather chairs, though for the most part the place is decked out in bare wood and peeling walls. And as we left, a quartet of codgers struggled engagingly to work out 'Doh, a Deer'. Surprise indeed.

Babies and children welcome. Games (bar billiards, board games, quiz machine). Quiz (Tue, fortnightly; £2). Tables outdoors (4, pavement). TVs (satellite).

Also in the area...

All Bar One 152 Gloucester Road, SW7 4TB (7244 5861).

Pitcher and Piano 871-873 Fulham Road, SW6 5HP (7736 3910).

COVENT GARDEN

Either staunchly traditional (the **Lamb & Flag**, the **Roundhouse**, the **Cross Keys**) or defiantly multinational (**Africa Bar**, **Lowlander**, **Maple Leaf**), many of the bars of Covent Garden show inklings of character, even if the streets around them are dreadfully bland. Notable places include **Detroit**, **Freud**, the **Porterhouse** and the **Retox Bar** – but they have more in common with the West End than the focal Piazza area where across-the-board inanity abounds. In this quagmire, the pleasing new arrival of the jazzy **Octave Jazz Bar** may be showing too much promise.

Africa Bar

Africa Centre, 38 King Street, WC2E 8JT (7836 1976). Covent Garden or Leicester Square tube. **Open** 12.30-3pm, 5.30-11pm Mon-Fri; 5.30-11pm Sat. **Food served** 12.30-2.30pm, 6-11pm Mon-Fri; 6-11pm Sat. **Credit** MC, V.

The Africa Centre – of Soul II Soul fame – has barely changed since its 1980s heyday. Within an institutional building flying the map of Africa, not two minutes from the bland commerce of Covent Garden Piazza, the main hall still stages essential music. Nor have the venue's other facilities been tampered with. Down a tatty, mural-patterned staircase, a sign points you to the Calabash restaurant, right, and the Africa Bar, left. This small corner, with shabby red furniture and a modest bar counter, would be no different in any other cultural institute were it not for the peeling posters of savannah sunsets and flapping elephants' ears, the bottles of Zimbabwean Zambezi, Kenyan Tusker and South African Castle in the fridge, the diverse rhythmic soundtrack and the immediate charm of the staff. The Guinness, though, seems (more's the pity) not to be of the strong Nigerian type.

Babies and children admitted (restaurant). Restaurant. Specialities (African drinks). TV (satellite). **Map 2 L7**.

Bacchanalia

1A Bedford Street, WC2E 9HH (7836 3033). Charing Cross or Covent Garden or Leicester Square tube. **Open** noon-11pm Mon-Sat. **Food served** noon-3pm, 5-10pm Mon-Sat. **Credit** AmEx, MC, V.

The younger sister of the more bohemian Phoenix Artist Club (*see p86*), the Bacchanalia is also undergoing transformation, with a change of management following the recent death of the previous manager – not that there was much wrong with the Bac before. A superior wine selection, a higher grade of grub, perhaps a few decorative touches to the spacious, neat, wooden interior, Sunday opening, even a little live jazz: all are being introduced before summer's tourist tide washes in (the bar is two minutes' walk from Covent Garden Piazza). Brinkhoff's No.1 Dortmunder Union on draught (a hefty £3.25 a pint), bottles of Asahi, Baltika, Lokowicz, Okocim and Leffe (from Japan, Russia, the Czech Republic, Poland and Belgium respectively, each at £3 a pop), draught Bombardier bitter from Bedford... Worse options typified the neighbourhood; the Bac's revamp can only improve it.

Babies and children admitted. No-smoking area. **Map 2 L7**.

Box

32-44 Monmouth Street, Seven Dials, WC2H 9BA (7240 5828/www.boxbar.com). Covent Garden or Leicester Square tube. **Open** 11am-11pm Mon-Sat; noon-10.30pm Sun. **Food served** 11am-5pm daily. **Credit** MC, V.

A lively-easy-going gay bar at Seven Dials, whose bright interior and come-one-come-all party vibe attracts almost as many straights. The formula is similar to that of many a high-street London drinkery: stack the back bar with primary-coloured pyramids of alcopops, fill the fridges with Beck's, Breezers and Buds, man the counter with pseudo-hip staff, fill the place with easy-on-the-ear pre-clubbing music – then add a few decorative touches such as a daft water-bubble arrangement behind the alcopops, and the kind of black-and-white photos preferred at certain barber shops. Light the blue touchpaper and retire. Box makes a reasonable fuss (with reasonable success) about food during the day, and its pavement tables are a

boon of a summer's afternoon. This is not the best venue in the busy bar-starred border between Soho and Covent Garden – but it's by no means the worst.
Babies and children admitted (daytime only). Tables outdoors (3, pavement). **Map 2 L6**.

Brasserie Max

Covent Garden Hotel, 10 Monmouth Street, WC2H 9LF (7806 1000/www.coventgardenhotel.co.uk). Covent Garden tube. **Open/food served** 7am-11pm Mon-Fri; 8am-11pm; Sat; 8am-10.30pm Sun. **Credit** AmEx, MC, V.

The rather classy bar after the lobby of the Covent Garden Hotel offers relaxed breakfasts and casual evening cocktails to the business community (note the subtle but omnipresent house logo of suited man reclining on stripy sofa). These striped banquettes provide alcove intimacy, while a reasonably lively buzz is fostered around the whistle-clean bar counter. Cocktails aren't cheap (who cares when you're ex-ing it?) but are well made, using premium spirits and fresh fruit; a Tamarillo Martini (£10.50) features the rare red South American fruit of the same name, Belvedere vodka, Cointreau and gomme syrup. Twenty wines, categorised into light, medium and full bodied, come by the glass or bottle, starting at £4.50 for an Argentine Libertad malbec bonarda or vin de pays de l'Aude Croix Blanche. Light snacks and bottled beers are also to be had.
Babies and children admitted. Dress: smart casual. Entertainment (film club from 6pm Sat, dinner plus film £30). Function rooms. **Map 1 L6**.

Bünker

41 Earlham Street, WC2H 9LX (7240 0606/www.bunkerbar.com). Covent Garden tube. **Open** noon-11pm Mon-Sat; noon-10.30pm Sun. **Food served** noon-10pm Mon-Sat; noon-4pm Sun. **Credit** MC, V.

The former Freedom Brewing Company is still thriving as a beer-making concern, its copper vats bubbling away behind a glass screen that reflects rows of merry drinkers enjoying the tasty results at what are now Biergarten tables. In fact, the grafted-on pseudo-German theme – who the hell put that umlaut on the name? – detracts from this fine operation. Three house draughts (Pilsner, Bok and organic) come in pint or two-pint forms, with a try-before-you-buy option. International bottled beers (Budvar, San Miguel, Nastro Azzurro) and standard cocktails (£6.50) are probably better enjoyed in the cooler loungey area rather than the beer hall. The food is pukka bar fare (own-made burgers of beef, coriander and mustard, plus trimmings, £8.50), the service swift and the toilets pristine – with signs that hilariously read 'Himm' and 'Herr'.
Music (DJs, 7pm Fri, Sat; free). Specialities (micro-brewed beer). TV (big screen). **Map 2 L6**.

Café des Amis

11-14 Hanover Place, WC2E 9JP (7379 3444). Covent Garden tube. **Open** 11.30am-1am Mon-Sat. **Food served** 11.30am-midnight Mon-Sat. **Credit** AmEx, DC, MC, V.

Dodge the metal flower pots outside its sister restaurant, through the adjacent entrance and down into this bustling basement bar. Metal spotlights guide you into a small, minimalist room that's more business class airport lounge than sexy style bar: Habitatesque fittings and blokes in Thomas Pink shirts. A large wine rack is in full view behind the large central bar, showing off an impressive array of bottles that's divided (how French) into 'Vins Français' and 'Les Etrangers' on the wine list. There's the odd gem, such as Rolly Gassmann's 2000 Riesling (£30), and an impressively large selection of 23 wines by the glass (though you should steer clear of Michel Laroche's merlot-grenache and a soupy De Loach pinot noir). The Côtes de Gascogne vin de pays again comes up trumps, with Carrele's 2003 colombard chardonnay a particularly refreshing example (£3.70 a glass, £14.50 a bottle).
Babies and children admitted (restaurant). Function room. Restaurant. Specialities (wine). Tables outdoors (10, courtyard). **Map 2 L6**.

Christopher's

18 Wellington Street, WC2E 7DD (7240 4222/www.christophersgrill.com). Covent Garden tube. **Open/food served** noon-11pm Mon-Sat. **Credit** AmEx, DC, MC, V.

Though not quite outré or adventurous enough to be a destination bar in its own right, neat, chic Christopher's more than fits the bill for a pre-theatre cocktail or an aperitif prior to climbing the grand staircase to the dining room upstairs. Your first drink can be added to your restaurant bill, it's suggested, but you can't go far wrong with what's offered downstairs. Christopher's Classic and Special cocktails (£6.50), well mixed with high-end spirits, can be accompanied by a charcuterie plate of salamis, prosciutto and red pepper (£6.50) or small plates of zucchini tempura fries (£3). Wines are well chosen and well priced: six of each colour from £3.50 a glass, and £14 a bottle. Dalliance is encouraged by arty touches to a plain white room blessed with natural light, brown furnishings and friendly staff.
Babies and children welcome (children's menu; high chairs). Function room. Restaurant. Specialities (cocktails). TV (plasma). **Map 2 L7**.

Coach & Horses

42 Wellington Street, WC2E 7BD (7240 0553). Covent Garden tube. **Open** 11am-11pm Mon-Sat; noon-10.30pm Sun. **Food served** noon-2.30pm daily. **Credit** MC, V.

A genuine, expat Irish pub, from the Guinness of Dublin provenance to the hurling pictures in the corner. The array of beers also helps attract many a discerning drinker here, delighted to get a decent pint a stone's throw from Covent Garden Piazza. Marston's Pedigree, John Smith's, Courage Best, Beamish and Beck's all get a look in, and can be chased by any of five dozen malts and whiskies from either side of the Irish Sea. Hulking great lumps of pork and beef sizzle away on the hot-counter, ready for use in sandwiches. Sporting talk buzzes around the tiny main bar, regulars putting in their penn'orth before returning their noses to the *Irish Times*. It's the kind of place that could make a fortune from tourism, but doesn't feel it has to.
Specialities (whisky). TV. **Map 2 L6**.

Cross Keys

31 Endell Street, WC2H 9EB (7836 5185). Covent Garden tube. **Open** 11am-11pm Mon-Sat; noon-10.30pm Sun. **Food served** noon-3pm Mon-Sat, noon-2.30pm Sun. **Credit** AmEx, MC, V.

This coalmine-dark and neatly upholstered pub is resolutely old school. Venerable blokes swap army stories over pints of Young's or Shepherd Neame Spitfire, while others of similar age and experience tuck into Keys fry-ups or chicken tikka masala. Old brass kettles and diving equipment hang from the ceiling; more character is provided by landlord Brian, whose collection of pop oddities decorates the bar counter: press cuttings about his successful £500 bid for Elvis Presley's napkin make up its centrepiece; said napkin is mounted, along with numerous Beatles memorabilia – not least a poster for the band's

Central

Royal Command Performance of 1963, the day that changed British pop forever. Should Brian ever sell up, his paraphernalia might be worth more than the pub itself.
Function room. Games (fruit machine). Tables outdoors (3, pavement). TV. **Map 2 L6.**

Detroit

35 Earlham Street, WC2H 9LD (7240 2662/www.detroit-bar.com). Covent Garden or Leicester Square tube. **Open** 5pm-midnight Mon-Sat. **Food served** 5-10.30pm Mon-Sat. **Happy hour** 5-7pm Mon-Sat (£7 cocktail & food deal). **Credit** AmEx, DC, MC, V.
One of London's most revered style bars, the cool and cosy Detroit celebrates its tenth anniversary in 2005. The retro sci-fi decor (Tardis doors leading to a warren of alcoves, curved forms meeting the eye as it adjusts to the changing floor and ceiling heights) has not dated – and nor has the expert cocktail-making. The three dozen Martinis, short and long drinks (all £6.80) are created with aplomb and flair; try the house Detroit (Wyborowa vodka, mint and sugar syrup) for a fine example. Beers include Estonian A Le Coq, Asahi and Duvel, in 33cl bottled forms. The superior snacks, such as Parma ham and honey crostini, are in the £5 range. During Seven-Heaven, from 5pm to 8pm, a choice of six cocktails plus a platter costs £7.
Function room. Restaurant. Specialities (cocktails). **Map 2 L6.**

Freud

198 Shaftesbury Avenue, WC2H 8JL (7240 9933). Covent Garden or Tottenham Court Road tube. **Open** 11am-11pm Mon-Sat; noon-10.30pm Sun. **Food served** noon-4.30pm daily. **Credit** MC, V.
This basement done out in cool slate was an early example of bar minimalism in London – and surprisingly, not much has changed since it opened in 1986. A metal staircase leads you from a utensils shop of the same name to a smallish bar space mercifully ventilated by huge ceiling fans. Art of the Lucien Freud school adorns the walls, but your attention is quickly drawn to a busy tall bar counter in the centre, headed by a huge board of drinks choices. The range of cocktails (£5-£6) and short drinks (£4.20) is pretty much standard everywhere now, as are bottled beers such as Erdinger, Warsteiner and Pilsner Urquell. In the time it's been open, its clientele has barely blipped from hip.
Babies and children admitted. Music (jazz 3-5pm Sun). No-smoking tables (until 4.30pm). Specialities (cocktails). TV. **Map 1 L6.**

Guanabara

New London Theatre, Parker Street (corner of Drury Lane), WC2B 5PW (7242 8600/www.guanabara.co.uk). Holborn tube. **Open** 5.30pm-2.30am Mon-Sat; 5.30pm-midnight Sun. **Food served** 5.30-11pm daily. **Credit** AmEx, MC, V.
Occupying two floors of a wing of the New London Theatre, the Guanabara warms to its theme immediately, a huge screen of live Brazilian TV covering one wall. Ahead is a Rio beach mural – Guanabara is the bay of Rio – and within, a fiery nightspot of classic lore. A dozen long wooden tables, waited on by car-ad-worthy *brasileiras*, radiate from a central dancefloor and stage. The music programme of samba bands, resident and guest DJs is as modern and inventive as the Caipirinha and Caipiroska house cocktails (£5), also offered at the upstairs bars. There are 20 varieties of cachaça (£5), three kinds of Daiquiris (£5.50), and the beers (Bravara, Brahma, Palma Luca) cross the border into Argentina (Quilmes) and Peru (Cusquena). An equally exotic range of mains (£10-£13) and starters (£5) includes Brazilian classics such as feijoada (pork and black-bean stew) and salt-cod fishcakes.
Disabled: toilet. Games (football tables). Music (DJ 5.30pm nightly; occasional bands). Specialities (cocktails). TV (big screen, satellite). **Map 1 L6.**

Lamb & Flag

33 Rose Street, WC2E 9EB (7497 9504). Covent Garden tube. **Open** 11am-11pm Mon-Sat; noon-10.30pm Sun. **Food served** noon-3pm Mon-Fri, Sun; noon-4.30pm Sat. **Credit** MC, V.
Historians disagree about this place. Conflicting accounts mounted beneath the original wooden frames and low ceilings of this indubitably ancient inn recall the 'Bucket of Blood' and bare-knuckle fighting days – but the Survey of London doesn't mention it at all. Still, millions of customers have imbibed here, a few earning a name plaque. Today's are treated to Young's and a changing line-up that might include Bombardier, Courage Best, Ridley's IPA and Rumpus, Löwenbräu and Hoegaarden on tap. There are ploughman's lunches and doorstep sandwiches downstairs, full pub grub on red checked tablecloths in the Dryden room upstairs. It's said that the poet John Dryden was beaten up outside, on still-eerie Rose Street, in 1679. What's certain is that you'll find little but standing room in either of the two downstairs bar areas any time after five.
Babies and children admitted (mornings only). Music (jazz 7.30-10.30pm Sun). No piped music or jukebox. Restaurant. Specialities (real ales). TV. **Map 2 L7.**

Langley

5 Langley Street, WC2H 9JA (7836 5005/www.thelangley.co.uk). Covent Garden tube. **Open/food served** 4.30pm-1am Mon-Sat; 4-10.30pm Sun. **Credit** AmEx, MC, V.
This popular party bar has few pretensions about it, doing a good job to provide reasonable – and reasonably cheap – cocktails for nine-to-fivers on the pull. Two large bar areas, one of bare brick and thumping music, the other with waitress service and swirly decor, operate the same drinks menu. Cocktails Now (a Toblerone of Frangelico and vanilla vodka, a Cool Melon of Smirnoff and melon schnapps) and Then (Mint Julep with Maker's Mark, Singapore Sling with Gordon's) are each a snippy £5.35, while the standard champagne cocktails run to £6.95. Bar food consists of 'plates' (Thai fishcakes with dipping sauce, Chinese barbecue ribs) at around £5, seven of them laid out to form the Langley Bar Platter (£15.95). Sandwiches include the seriously retro fish-fingers with Heinz ketchup in thick-cut white bloomer, burgers, steak baguettes and so on.
Disabled: toilet. Music (DJs 8pm Wed-Sat; £3 after 10pm Thur; £5 after 10pm Fri, Sat). Restaurant. **Map 2 L6.**

Lowlander

36 Drury Lane, WC2B 5RR (7379 7446/www.lowlander.com). Covent Garden or Holborn tube. **Open** noon-11pm Mon-Sat; noon-10pm Sun. **Food served** noon-10pm Mon-Sat; noon-9.30pm. **Credit** AmEx, MC, V.
For once, the words in the window – 'London's premier Dutch and Belgian beer café' – are right: this is a superior gastrobar featuring the best of Benelux. Fourteen draught beers (De Koninck, Forest fruit beer, Brugs Tarwerbier, Westmalle Dubbel) are poured from neatly logoed pumps into half-pint or two-pint logoed glasses, and the 40 bottles are split into Trappist & Abbey, Pilsner, Wheat and other categories. Both the all-day deli selections (Dutch and Belgian cheeses, eight hot snacks from Holland) and the

Shochu Lounge. *See p45.*

mains (mussels, waterzooi) get the starched white napkin treatment from efficient waiting staff in brasserie uniform. A main bar area, of close rows of light-wood communal tables, is decorated with retro beer ads and the Lowlander logo of a skimmed beer head; it's overlooked by a mezzanine often hired out for private bashes. As good as it gets, on either side of the Hook or the North Sea.
Babies and children admitted. Function room. No-smoking area. Specialities (Belgian beer). Tables outside (5, pavement). **Map 1 L6**.

Maple Leaf

41 Maiden Lane, WC2E 7LJ (7240 2843). Covent Garden tube. **Open** 11am-11pm Mon-Sat; noon-10.30pm Sun. **Food served** noon-9pm daily. **Credit** (over £5) AmEx, DC, MC, V.
As the blurb says, the Maple Leaf is 'a little piece of Canada in the heart of London'. With Molson and Sleeman Silver Creek on draught, Moosehead by the bottle, a stuffed bear, framed ice hockey paraphernalia and mounted Mounties set within the log-walled bar, Canadian it most certainly is. Actually, it's a pretty big piece of Canada: a large all-in-one bar area and logged lounge, with one bar counter by the door and snug corners dotted within. There's also room for some Premiership football, along with American football (NFL) and basketball (NBA), on six screens (no NHL owing to logistical problems; Canucks will have to watch their hockey elsewhere). Food is the kind of pub grub you'd get anywhere. What really makes the place unmistakably Canadian, though, is the hockey scoreline engraved on the wall: Canada 5, USA 2, Olympics 2002.
Babies and children admitted (before 5pm). Games (fruit machine, quiz machine). No-smoking area (before 5pm). TV (satellite). **Map 2 L7**.

Octave Jazz Bar

27-29 Endell Street, WC2H 9BA (7836 4616/www.octave8.com). Covent Garden tube. **Open/food served** noon-11pm Mon-Wed; noon-1am Thur-Sat. **Credit** AmEx, MC, V.
A suitably blueish light imbues this new jazz bar, a large, sleek operation offering six dozen cocktails, saucy American cuisine and musicians three nights a week (combos play in two sets, at 9pm and 10.30pm, in the corner of this expansive lounge). During the day and at the start of the week, the Octave is simply a pleasant spot for lunch or sipping cocktails (mixed with high-end spirits, all cost £7). Champagne cocktails such as the Smooth Jazz (Southern Comfort, champagne and apricot liqueur) or Kir Lethal (raisin-steeped vodka and champagne) go for £8.50; beers (1664, San Miguel) come in half-pint measures (£2); and the menu includes pan-fried catfish on roast corn mash (£14.95) and a New York Strip of 10oz sirloin beef on bourbon sauce (£18.50). Nodding in approval are the jazz greats artistically depicted over the walls: far worse things have been done in their name.
Disabled: toilet. Music (live jazz 9pm Thur-Sat; free). Restaurant. Specialities (cocktails). **Map 1 L6**.

Opera Tavern

23 Catherine Street, WC2B 5JS (7379 9832). Covent Garden tube. **Open** noon-11pm Mon-Sat. **Food served** noon-3pm, 5-8pm Mon-Sat. **Credit** AmEx, MC, V.
Named after the Irish playwright Sheridan Knowles in 1846, ornately rebuilt in dark wood and frosted glass (and renamed) in 1879, standing opposite the Theatre Royal and no distance from the Royal Opera House, this two-floor public house turns a tidy penny with its tradition and location. Current interval times are chalked up to entice the-

atre-goers into a pre-ordered swifty, while tourists might revel in the native delights of steak and ale pie, British bangers and chocolate fudge cake, which can be devoured in the upstairs Baddeley bar and restaurant. Downstairs, locals tuck in to draught Fuller's London Pride and, from Greene King, Abbot and IPA (although the Double Diamond promised by the back-bar advertising has long gone). Old globe light fittings complete the classic setting.
Babies and children welcome (restaurant). Games (fruit machine, quiz machine). Restaurant (no-smoking). Tables outdoors (2, pavement). TV. **Map 2 L6**.

Porterhouse

21-22 Maiden Lane, WC2E 7NA (7836 9931/www.porterhousebrewco.com). Covent Garden tube/Charing Cross tube/rail. **Open** 11am-11pm Mon-Wed; 11am-11.30pm Thur-Sat; noon-10.30pm Sun. **Food served** noon-9pm Mon-Sat; noon-7pm Sun. **Credit** AmEx, MC, V.
The London branch of Liam LaHart and Oliver Hughes's justifiably successful Bray-based brewing operation, the Porterhouse is one of the capital's key destinations for beer lovers. In fact, make that one of Europe's key destinations: with nine house beers on draught (Wrasslers 4X stout from West Cork, Oyster stout brewed with fresh oysters, house Weiss, Pilsner, reds and coppers) and an encyclopaedic gazetteer (Ethiopia, Indonesia, Lebanon, Palestine, Tahiti) of the bottled variety, you'd be hard pushed to find better. The setting (over several levels, with copper, wood and glass-fronted cupboards filled with curiously international beers) is comfortable and stylish. The slightly 'nerr-nerr' tone in the thick drinks brochure ('beware of BUL – brewed under licence'), £10 souvenir baseball caps and £25 rugby shirts is forgiven as soon as you sip your first Temple Bräu. *Sláinte*!
Disabled: lift; toilet. Dress: smart casual. Function room. Music (bands 8pm Wed-Sat; Irish band 4-8pm Sun; free). Tables outdoors (3, pavement). TV (big screen, satellite). **Map 2 L7**.

Punch & Judy

40 The Market, WC2E 8RF (7379 0923). Covent Garden tube. **Open** 11am-11pm Mon-Sat; 11am-10.30pm Sun. **Food served** noon-7pm Fri, Sat; noon-5pm Sun. **Credit** AmEx, MC, V.
The 'World Famous' Punch & Judy proves that even lame Londoners like to be seen dead in a place otherwise mobbed by ill-travelled provincials on the pull. Chalet numbers can be exchanged in the alcoves of this dark basement bar, the recesses of what was once a fruit-market warehouse are now flooded with the aural pap of the hits du jour, and the long bar counter is propped up by single men with a roving eye. 'Hen and stag parties welcome' – and they are certainly welcome to the standard nitrokegs and the chips-with-everything fodder. An upstairs bar overlooking the modern market hall, open at lunchtime-only in winter, fills from noon to night in summer, when tables creep out ever closer to the epicentre of the unicycle-plagued Piazza.
Babies and children admitted. Games (fruit machines, quiz machines, video juke box). No-smoking area (restaurant). Restaurant. Tables outdoors (6, courtyard). TVs (plasma). **Map 2 L7**.

Retox Bar

The Piazza, 11-12 Russell Street, WC2B 5HZ (7240 5330/www.retoxbar.com). Covent Garden tube. **Open/food served** 5pm-1am Mon-Wed; 5pm-3am Thur, Fri; 6pm-3am Sat. **Admission** £5 after 9.30pm Thu-Fri. £6 after 9.30pm Sat. **Credit** AmEx, MC, V.
Hidden beneath the awning of Tutton's Brasserie, this gimmicky little basement bar specialises in 'replenishing toxic substances' – that is, strong shots 'perfect for group bonding or individual delirium'. A fully illustrated drinks menu aims to instruct in this four-step, ten-point programme, culminating in '9: Swallow' and '10: Take off'. By the time you're bonded or delirious, you'll be aboard a shiny metal starship, all slatted and swirly, six squillion light years from Covent Garden. Helping you achieve this goal are five-shot numbers such as the Saga (with Sagatiba and cachaça) or a trio of KOs, rationed at one per night per person. Who could resist oblivion at the hands of a Devil's Advocaat (£14.50) of Blavod vodka, black sambucca, advocaat, J&B rare and blue curaçao? Filling bar snacks (deep-fried gnocchi, spicy potato wedges, all £3) provide back-up.
Function room. Music (DJs 9pm Mon-Sat). Restaurant. Specialities (cocktails). **Map 2 L6**.

Roadhouse

35 The Piazza, WC2E 8BE (7240 6001/www.roadhouse.co.uk). Covent Garden tube. **Open** 5.30pm-3am Mon-Sat; 5.30pm-1am 2nd Sun of month; 1pm-12.30am last Sun of mth. **Food served** 5.30pm-1.30am Mon-Sat. **Admission** £3 after 10.30pm Mon-Wed; £5 after 10pm Thur; £5 after 9pm, £10 after 10pm Fri; £7 after 8pm, £10 after 10pm Sat; £5 after 7pm Sun. **Credit** AmEx, DC, MC, V.
This late-opening house of grunge is thriving, owing to the unholy trinity of Americana, rock and biker chic. Over the door, manned by bouncers delighted to send away punters aghast at paying a £5 fee, the term 'lubrication' entices drinkers – mostly Antipodeans and continental types – to part with their wonga. Inside, a centrepiece octagonal bar counter topped by a Harley chopper is surrounded by

diner-style booths, pinball tables and old Coke and automobile signage. A somewhat smarmy drinks menu boasts 'These Are Ours' (£5.50 house cocktails such as the Roadhouse Root Beer: amaretto, Galliano, Kahlúa and Coke) and 'Of Course We Do' for Martinis and Long Islands. The beer of choice is Miller. Such acts as Grouper, Lobotomy and the Tide yell on a small stage which is occupied by punters on BYOA Mondays: Bring Yer Own Axe.
Music (bands 2nd Sun of mth). Specialities (cocktails).

Round House

1 Garrick Street, WC2E 9BF (7836 9838). Covent Garden or Leicester Square tube. **Open** 11am-11pm Mon-Sat; noon-10.30pm Sun. **Food served** 11am-9pm daily. **Credit** AmEx, JCB, MC, V.
A classy, traditional T&J Bernard pub, the Roundhouse occupies a busy, pedestrian-friendly intersection of Theatreland. It started life as the Petters Hotel soon after Garrick Street opened as an access road to Covent Garden market in the 1860s. Luvvies and traders rubbed shoulders here, and today's clientele, set against a backdrop of stucco and old prints, is still mixed. With the dumbing down of West End theatre and disappearance of the market, the beer lovers stand out. They're treated to Shepherd Neame Spitfire, Theakston Old Peculiar, Young's, John Smith's and guest ales ('Adnams and London Pride coming next month!'); beer mats deck the long bar counter. The pies (beef and Guinness, chicken and stilton) are freshly baked, the wines are well chosen and well priced (from £2.80 a glass and £8 a bottle) – and even the coffee comes in a dinky cafetière with biscuits.
Games (fruit machine). No-smoking area. TVs. **Map 2 L7**.

Also in the area...

All Bar One 19 Henrietta Street, WC2E 9ET (7557 7941).
Bar 38 1-3 Long Acre, WC2E 9AD (7836 7794).
Crusting Pipe (Davy's) 27 The Market, WC2E 8RD (7836 1415).
Mullins of Covent Garden (Davy's) Unit 27a, The Market, WC2E 8RD (7836 8345).
O'Neill's 40 Great Queen Street, WC2B 5AA (7242 5560); 14 New Row, WC2N 4LF (7557 9831).
Walkabout 11 Henrietta Street & 33 Maiden Lane, WC2E 8PS (7379 5555).

EARL'S COURT

The Antipodean community having long since scattered around London, Earl's Court is not the 'kangaroo valley' it once was – though there's still enough cheap accommodation to maintain a steady flow of international travellers and keep unremarkable pubs and cafés in a steady trade. For charm or character, discerning drinkers should head off the main thoroughfare to local favourite the **King's Head**, or up the road and upmarket to the historically hip hangout the **Troubadour**.

Blackbird

209 Earl's Court Road, SW5 9AN (7835 1855). Earl's Court tube. **Open** 11am-11pm Mon-Sat; noon-10.30pm Sun. **Food served** noon-4pm, 5-8.45pm daily. **Credit** MC, V.
Every day feels like Sunday afternoon in the Blackbird: newpapers spread out for a leisurely read, pints being supped and savoured, life sliding by unhurried in near-silence. During lunchtimes and evenings, however, the pace picks up a little with the arrival of hungry local workers, plus an ever-changing roster of convention-attenders and gig-goers from nearby Earl's Court. Thrown in for good measure is the odd tourist blown off course from Kensington, and lured by the traditional feel of the Blackbird's sober stylings. Food is of the underwhelming pub grub variety (though it's passable when accompanied by one of the well-kept Fuller's ales). If you're in search of something refined, this boozer is unlikely to hit the mark; but for a peaceful pie and a pint, the Blackbird is more than adequate.
Games (fruit machines). TV.

King's Head

17 Hogarth Place, SW5 0QT (7244 5931). Earl's Court tube. **Open** noon-11pm Mon-Sat; noon-10.30pm Sun. **Food served** noon-3pm, 5-9.30pm Mon-Fri; noon-9.30pm Sat, Sun. **Credit** AmEx, MC, V.
Nothing provides better proof that Earl's Court is no longer the scuzzy backpacker ghetto immortalised in cult Oz movie *The Adventures of Barry McKenzie* than this, the film's star location. Antipodeans may occupy both sides of the bar, but they're not spraying each other with beer in a Midnight Oil singalong – they've refined their tastes, as the popularity of the new-look KH demonstrates. Mismatched furniture gives a comfortably battered retro feel – one that suits the multinational crowd who've been here long enough to prefer the relaxed off-street location and the low-key cool atmosphere to the blare of the main drag. The Aberdeen Angus burger with fat-cut wedges is still a highlight of the consistently good menu, and the variety of rotating guest beers hasn't gone unappreciated either: Russian Baltika was a recent favourite, though perhaps for its bargain-basement price as much as for its exoticism. Some travelling habits die hard.
Bar available for hire. Disabled: toilet. Games (retro video games). Music (DJs 7pm Fri, Sat; girls' pamper night 8pm monthly, Tue; free). Specialities (Belgian beer). TVs (digital, plasma).

Troubadour

265 Old Brompton Road, SW5 9JA (7370 1434/www.troubadour.co.uk). Earl's Court tube. **Open/food served** 9am-midnight daily. **Food served** 7.30-11pm daily. **Credit** MC, V.
The brightly painted tin coffee pots lining the window are a subtle reminder that the Troubadour has been around since places like this were known as coffee shops – the 1960s, in other words, when this was the folkies' hangout of choice and Dylan drank here. A generation later and there's no longer an easy category for the place: it's at once an excellent delicatessen that sets high standards in produce, a café serving notable breakfasts and even more notable burgers – and, come evening, a wine bar (supplementing the drinks list with cocktails and boutique beers) and live music venue, showcase for singer-songwriters and weekly comedy. There's a refined continental air to the intellectual types who conspire around the candlelit tables, but relaxed bohemianism still reigns. You can usually find one of the Troubadour's two laid-back moggies snoozing on the prime seats.
Club available for hire. Function room. Games (board games). Music (live bands 8pm Thur-Sat; £5-£15; singer-songwriter evenings 8pm Tue, Wed £5/£2.50

Musicians' Union). No-smoking area (in restaurant). Poetry (8-10pm alternate Mon; £5.50). Tables outdoors (20, garden, pavement). TV (big screen).

Warwick Arms

160 Warwick Road, W14 8PS (7603 3560). Earl's Court or High Street Kensington tube. **Open** noon-midnight Mon-Sat; 10am-10.30pm Sun. **Food served** noon-3pm, 5.30-11.30pm Mon-Fri; 5.30-11.30pm Sat; 5.30-10pm Sun. **Credit** MC, V.

With the volume of traffic thundering down the Warwick Road, you might need a side order of ear plugs before you might actually enjoy an alfresco drink at the picnic tables parked optimistically outside the Warwick; and yet the warm glow within makes this pub a comfortable stop. The Fuller's brews – London Pride, ESB – tend not to be poured with particular care, but this isn't really a place for ale purists; rather, it's a reliably quiet destination in which to put the world to rights over a pint. This most useful function is performed by local men, in the main (amid the pots, pans and assorted kitchen clutter hanging from the rafters), but the atmosphere is politely convivial enough to make all comers and sexes welcome. Somewhat incongruously, given the overall traditional feel, the food here is North Indian – as your nose will instantly tell you the moment you walk through the door.

Tables outdoors (6, pavement). TV.

Also in the area...

O'Neill's 326 Earls Court Road, SW5 9BQ (7244 5921).

FITZROVIA

Christened after and once defined by the seminal **Fitzroy Tavern**, this area north of Soho is now characterised by the Noho media haunts that the now standard-issue FT overlooks. Most of these are restaurants, although a high-quality resto-bar culture, already in place with **Oscar**, is starting to bloom – and the upmarket **Crazy Bear** and **Shochu Lounge** are as much about sassy, unusual cocktails (and decor of similar ilk) as doing lunch. The buzz has not yet abated around the hip,

CRITICS' PICKS

For beers and ales
Bünker (*see p33*), **Clachan** (*see p81*), **Mash** (*see p43*), **Orange Brewery** (*see p31*), **Pillars of Hercules** (*see p86*), **Porterhouse** (*see p37*).

For cocktails
Cactus Blue (*see p92*), **Goring Hotel** (*see p102*), **Lab** (*see p84*), **Match Bar** (*see p43*), **Thirst** (*see p89*), **22 Below** (*see p89*).

For the strong stuff
Albannach (whisky; *see p96*), **Baltic** (vodka; *see p104*), **Boisdale** (whisky; *see p99*), **Na Zdrowie** (vodka; *see p47*), **Salt Whisky Bar** (whisky; *see p21*), **Shochu Lounge** (shochu; *see p45*), **Zuma** (shochu; *see p55*).

For wine
Cork & Bottle (*see p56*), **Crown & Two Chairmen** (*see p83*), **Gordon's** (*see p97*), **Kettner's** (*see p84*), **Pearl Bar & Restaurant** (*see p47*), **Hush** (*see p66*).

For sheer style
Cocoon (*see p56*), **43** (*see p65*), **Hakkasan** (*see p41*), **Lobby Bar** (*see p94*), **Long Bar** (*see p43*), **190 Queensgate** (*see p93*).

For some open sky
Angel (*see p24*), **Anglesea Arms** (*see p92*), **Prince of Wales** (*see p51*), **Windsor Castle** (*see p52*).

For fine views
Shepherd's Tavern (*see p67*), **Studio Lounge** (*see p77*), **Tenth Bar** (*see p52*).

For a blast from the past
Albert (*see p99*), **Fitzroy Tavern** (*see p41*), **French House** (*see p84*), **Lamb** (*see p47*), **Old Coffee House** (*see p84*), **Princess Louise** (*see p48*), **Troubadour** (*see p38*).

For fun and games
George IV (pool; *see p94*), **Hope** (board games; *see p41*), **Horse & Groom** (bar billiards, darts; *see p22*), **ICA Bar** (board games; *see p98*), **Oporto** (pool; *see p28*), **Surprise in Chelsea** (bar billiards; *see p32*).

For real fires
Churchill Arms (*see p51*), **Cross Keys** (*see p29*), **CVO Firevault** (*see p40*), **Nag's Head** (*see p24*), **Star Tavern** (*see p24*), **Paxton's Head** (*see p55*).

For surroundings with a theme
Coach & Horses (Irish; *see p33*), **Costa Dorada** (Spanish; *see p40*), **Courthouse Hotel** (prison; *see p81*), **Lowlander** (Belgian; *see p35*), **O'Conor Don** (Irish; *see p63*), **Royal Exchange** (Irish; *see p21*), **Toucan** (Irish; *see p89*).

For good food
Newman Arms (*see p44*), **Page** (*see p75*), **Pig's Ear** (*see p31*), **Pillars of Hercules** (*see p86*), **Seven Stars** (*see p95*), **Spice Lounge** (*see p89*), **Villandry** (*see p46*).

For the sound of music
Ain't Nothin' But? The Blues Bar (*see p78*), **Endurance** (*see p83*), **Octave Jazz Bar** (*see p36*), **Roxy** (*see p44*), **Social** (*see p45*), **William Wallace** (*see p63*).

streetwear-friendly area just north of Oxford Circus on Market Place – although the bars themselves now seem tired – and everywhere else is either a happy-hour post-work basement drinking trough or traditional pub.

Bradley's Spanish Bar

42-44 Hanway Street, W1T 1UT (7636 0359). Tottenham Court Road tube. **Open** noon-11pm Mon-Sat; 3-10.30pm Sun. **Credit** MC, V.

Brazenly boho, yet still Iberian, Bradley's Spanish Bar carries on packing 'em into its two-floor retro casket of velour every night of the week. There's a constant turnover of Spanish and Portuguese alternative types, who run the bar that was once overseen by the much-loved Luis. Although the crowd is the same – youngish cosmopolitans who spill on to narrow Hanway Street in taxi-blocking bonhomie – the old music has gone. No more White Horses or Wandrin' Star: instead, Nirvana, Pearl Jam and the Vines blast out of the old-style jukeboxes on both tiny floors (basement and ground). Pints from the decent, if pricey, range of keg beers (Bitburger, Budvar, San Miguel, John Smith's, Amstel) are still accidentally spilled over the wobbly, thinly covered bar stools and banquettes. There's not much by way of food these days, though.

Map 7 K6.

Cock Tavern

27 Great Portland Street, W1W 8QE (7631 5002). Oxford Circus tube. **Open** 11.30am-11pm Mon-Sat; noon-10.30pm Sun. **Food served** noon-3pm, 5.30-8.30pm Mon-Thur; noon-3pm Fri; noon-6pm Sat, Sun. **Credit** MC, V.

Quite an unusual pub this one, strutting amid the landmark style bars that now radiate from Market Place. The century-old Cock Tavern has got nothing to prove: its interior is a work of art, and will no doubt outlast by years the up-to-the-minute decor sported by neighbouring young contenders. Ornately carved in dark wood, the one main bar counter is embellished with thin movable panes of glass; the front and back areas are divided by a grand arch. Certainly, the Cock would have been a glitzy boozer in its day; but nowadays the pub is merely a historical anomaly – although one that carries the full range of Sam Smith's beers on draught (Ayingerbräu lager and Pils, Prinz, Old Brewery Bitter) and in bottles (Taddy Porter, Oatmeal Stout).

Games (fruit machines). No piped music or jukebox. Tables outdoors (3, pavement). **Map 1 J5**.

Costa Dorada

47-55 Hanway Street, W1T 1UX (7636 7139). Tottenham Court Road tube. **Open** 5pm-3am Mon-Sat. **Food served** 7pm-2am Mon-Sat. **Credit** AmEx, DC, JCB, MC, V.

Once upon a time, late-night drinking venues, such as this has always been, were a rarity. Now, though, there are plenty of other options in the vicinity of nearby Soho Square – where can't you get a late drink these days? Laudably, Costa Dorada has responded to the competition by playing to its strengths, upping the quality of what it has to offer. Other Spanish bars may give you a past-midnight bottle of Estrella Damm and a microwaved plate of albóndigas (meatballs), but this cavernous venue not only has space in spades, its kitchen turns out quality hot snacks to be enjoyed in comfort at one of the long wooden tables: the food includes such appetising bites as oven-baked Mediterranean vegetables (£4.75) and deep-fried paprika-flavoured whitebait (£3.75). Flamenco shows run twice nightly from Thursday to Saturday.

Babies and children welcome. Music (DJ/live flamenco 9-10pm Thur-Sat). **Map 1 K5**.

Crazy Bear

26-28 Whitfield Street, W1T 7DS (7631 0088/www.crazybeargroup.co.uk). Goodge Street or Tottenham Court Road tube. **Open** noon-11pm Mon-Fri; 6-11pm Sat. **Food served** noon-3pm, 6-10.45pm Mon-Fri; 6-10.45pm Sat. **Credit** AmEx, JCB, MC, V.

An offshoot of the renowned Oxfordshire pub, boutique hotel and Thai restaurant of the same name, Fitzrovia's Crazy Bear features a restaurant upstairs and a bar down an ornate staircase. The hospitable hostess leads you to a spot – on a swivelling cowhide bar stool, a red padded alcove, or low leather armchair – in an art deco, mirrored wonderland. Drinks include impeccable long (£7.50), 'short and muddled' (£7.50), champagne (£8.50) and Martini (£7.50) cocktails, created with such ingredients as fresh tomatoes, lemongrass syrups and raspberry purées, chilli-infused vodkas and Buffalo Trace bourbons; flavoured vodkas include Fox's Glacier Mint and Jelly Baby. Six quality wines of each colour are available by the glass, and there's a more extensive choice by the bottle; Paulaner wheat beer and Timothy Taylor Landlord are two prime beers on draught. Top-quality pan-Asian food, steamed, satayed or deep-fried, comes in canapé and snack form. Perfect: we couldn't fault the place.

Restaurant. Specialities (cocktails). TV (plasma, satellite). **Map 1 K5**.

Crown & Sceptre

26-27 Foley Street, W1W 6DS (7307 9971). Oxford Circus tube. **Open** noon-11pm Mon-Sat; noon-10.30pm Sun. **Food served** noon-9.30pm daily. **Credit** AmEx, MC, V.

A classic example of how to transform a landmark public house into a modern lounge bar without losing any character, the Crown & Sceptre is a valuable addition to local drinking options. The sturdy pentagonal bar counter has been retained, as have the high ceilings, the ornate interior and the regular customers. The main addition has been a chill-out/dining area where a range of gastro options is served (tagliatelle with char-grilled tuna steak, £9, plus various light meal and 'between bread' choices). Funky lighting, a striking back-bar painting of a pair of stylish ladies, and a superb soundtrack of down-tempo, funky sounds (DJ nights on Wednesdays) complete the modern makeover. A continental beer selection (Küppers Kölsch, Früli and Leffe on draught; bottled Duvel, Bellevue Kriek, Chimay Red and Karmeliet Tripel) complements British draught Deuchars IPA and bottled Spitfire and Black Sheep. Wines include cheapie bin-ends such as Oliver Savary Chablis at £3.25/£13. Commendable.

Disabled: toilet. Music (DJ 7.30pm Wed). Tables outdoors (4, pavement). **Map 1 J5**.

CVO Firevault

36 Great Titchfield Street, W1W 8BQ (7636 2091/www.cvofirevault.co.uk). Oxford Circus tube. **Open** noon-11pm Mon-Sat. **Food served** noon-3pm, 6-10.30pm Mon-Sat. **Credit** AmEx, MC, V.

A postmodern version of the BHS cafeteria, CVO Firevault has a client base beyond those just shopping for heaters in this stylish store (though you might need a snifter after laying out three grand on a van Outersterp blue-flame fire

bowl). Those in the know make their way downstairs, past fortunes going up in flames, for a quality selection of wines and cocktails in cool, if wonderfully heated, surroundings. The 20 CVO cocktails (£7.50) include a Passion Fruit Martini made with real passion fruit (the puréed version and 42 Below vodka are almost ubiquitous throughout the selection); Deutz is used in the champagne varieties (£8.50). Wine comes by the bottle (Domaine de la Bastide, the cheapest at £15.50), half-bottle (Rincón de Baroja crianza rioja, £15.50) or glass (£4.50). Imaginative alcohol-free refreshments are also available, and the Modern European kitchen attracts a steady traffic of lifestyle commentators making entrances to do lunch.
Babies and children admitted. Function room. Restaurant. Specialities (cocktails). **Map 1 J5**.

Eagle Bar Diner

3-5 Rathbone Place, W1T 1HJ (7637 1418/www.eaglebardiner.com). Tottenham Court Road tube. **Open/food served** noon-11pm Mon-Wed; noon-midnight Thur, Fri; 11am-1am Sat; 11am-6pm Sun. **Credit** MC, V.
This American-style brunch-to-bedtime operation reigns supreme as *the* dine-and-drink spot between Soho and Noho. The Eagle soars above the local competition for its range of cocktails, beers and all-day breakfasts. Choosing cocktails means perusing a creative list including Eagle Martinis (£6.45; try the Peanut Butter Martini, containing Finlandia vodka with a hint of Elvis's ruin), Old Fashioneds (£6.95-£12.95) based on bourbons from Buffalo Trace to Old Portrero, and Eagle Seasons (£6.50), like a Central Park of amaretto with Campari shaken with orange juice. Shakes with booze (a Liberty of Stoli Vanilla with vanilla ice-cream and strawberries, £6.50) add a humorous touch. Dixie, Liberty, Brooklyn and Anchor feature among the bottled beers. Food, to be devoured at the diner-style booths, has gone global: burgers of kangaroo and red wine, emu and black-mountain pepper, ostrich and cranberry. Good ol' Arkansas barbecue grills are still keeping the regulars in shape, all the same.
Babies and children welcome (until 9pm if dining). Disabled: toilet; ramp. Music (DJs 8pm Wed-Sat). Specialities (cocktails). **Map 7 K6**.

Fitzroy Tavern

16 Charlotte Street, W1T 2LY (7580 3714). Goodge Street tube. **Open** 11am-11pm Mon-Sat; noon-10.30pm Sun. **Food served** noon-2.30pm, 6.30-9.30pm Mon-Thur, Sat, Sun; noon-2.30pm Fri. **Credit** AmEx, MC, V.
Neither Soho nor Bloomsbury, Fitzrovia was first named for the notorious bohemian shenanigans going on at this Tavern in its heyday, as described by gossip columnist William Hickey in the *Daily Express* in 1940. Hickey hardly had his work cut out, for the Fitzroy was rife with artistic intrigue. Under the stewardship of the Allchilds, this ornate Victorian pub attracted Dylan Thomas, George Orwell, Nina Hammett and dissolute shag-around painter Augustus John, who would pat any passing children in case they were his. In 1955, the police closed the place. Now serving the full range of Sam Smith's beers, lunchtime baguettes and burgers, today's Tavern pays homage to its history, with wartime cuttings on the walls, portraits of the Allchilds and an alcove dedicated to John. Downstairs, decorated with pictures of Spanish Civil War-era Orwell, a stage is set up for weekly stand-up comedians.
Babies and children welcome (lunchtime only). Comedy (8pm Wed; £7). Function room. Games (fruit machine, quiz machine). No piped music or jukebox. Tables outdoors (9, pavement). **Map 1 K5**.

Hakkasan

8 Hanway Place, W1T 1HD (7907 1888). Tottenham Court Road tube. **Open** noon-12.30am Mon-Wed; noon-1.30am Thur-Sat; noon-midnight Sun. **Food served** noon-2.45pm, 6-11pm Mon-Wed, Sun; noon-2.45pm, 6-midnight Thur, Fri; noon-4pm, 6pm-midnight Sat; noon-4pm Sun. **Credit** AmEx, MC, V.
The long cocktail counter, named Ling Ling, at this Time Out award-winning postmodern Chinese restaurant always played second fiddle to the exclusive food (and clientele) on view through the slatted wooden partition that separated the narrow bar area from the main attraction; but now the bar has expanded to fill a decent side space with button stools and candlelit tables. Bar-hoppers still call it the Hakkasan, as lit up in cobalt blue on the corner of Hanway Street and Hanway Place, and the cocktails are still unbeatable. Pay £9.61 (including service charge) and you'll get a Hakkatini (Grey Goose l'Orange, Campari, Grand Marnier) or Saketini (Saké, Hendrick's gin, Rain vodka) of such sublimity you'll wonder why you bothered sipping cocktails elsewhere. Long and short drinks match the price and quality of the customised Martinis: a cornucopia of Ketel One and Rain vodkas, sakés, fresh fruits and ginseng spirits. Saké comes cold or hot, the beer is Yebisu.
Babies and children welcome. Disabled: toilet. Music (DJ 9pm daily). Restaurant. Specialities (cocktails). **Map 1 K5**.

Hope

15 Tottenham Street, W1T 2AJ (7637 0896). Goodge Street tube. **Open** 11am-11pm Mon-Sat; noon-6pm Sun. **Food served** noon-4pm Mon-Fri; noon-3pm Sat, Sun. **Credit** MC, V.
This lunchtime landmark on the corner of Whitfield Street and Tottenham Street entices an amiable mixture of office workers, builders, discerning ale drinkers and international students to its cosy, two-floor operation. The attraction? Quality draught beers and a stunning variety of sausages (£5.95). Here you can tuck into trios of creole smoky, pork, stilton and celery, or venison and wild mushroom combinations, complemented by the chips, mash, peas or beans of your choice, all while supping on a pint of Adnams, Shepherd Neame Spitfire or Fuller's London Pride, either in the busy downstairs bar or in the more comfortable surroundings of the upstairs dining room, decked with Victorian prints. Board games and a large TV come into play once most of the punters have drifted back to work, sleep or study.
Babies and children admitted (until 7pm). Function room. Games (board games, fruit machine). Tables outdoors (6, pavement). TV (big screen, satellite). **Map 1 J5**.

Horse & Groom

128 Great Portland Street, W1W 6PS (7580 4726). Great Portland Street or Oxford Circus tube. **Open** noon-11.30pm Mon-Sat; 11am-3pm, 7-11pm Sun. **Food served** noon-2.30pm, 5.30-8.30pm Mon-Fri; noon-5pm Sat. **Credit** MC, V.
This warming and friendly pub, all frosted glass and cosy banquettes, divides itself between a pint-glugging front bar and versatile back bar; at the rear, darts, bar billiards and table football are all on offer. Alternatively, there's the chance of a winter afternoon's snuggle over a pub lunch (there are plenty of vegetarian dishes among the pies and curries) next to a roaring fire. Obscure vintage team line-ups and jockey portraits around the walls hint

at a sporting past, but the Horse & Groom's main function these days is to serve Sam Smith's full range of ales and lagers to its regulars. On quieter days, a stranger's face can turn heads, but otherwise this is a real home from home: more like the reading room of an ivy-clad seat of learning than a raucous boozer.
Function room. Games (darts, fruit machine). Tables outdoors (4, pavement). **Map 1 J5**.

Jerusalem

33-34 Rathbone Place, W1T 1JN (7255 1120/www.the breakfastgroup.co.uk). Tottenham Court Road tube. **Open** noon-11pm Mon; noon-midnight Tue, Wed; noon-1am Thur, Fri; 7pm-1am Sat. **Food served** noon-3pm, 6-10.30pm Mon-Fri; 7-10.30pm Sat. **Credit** AmEx, MC, V.
Shaun Clarkson's eclectic wood-and-brick interior design might be showing its eight years, but the Jerusalem continues to be packed throughout the week. The prime attractions are superior food and beers, and 'twofer' offers on main courses at lunchtimes (plus two-course dinners at £10 of an early evening). Beers include draught Hoegaarden, Leffe, San Miguel and standard and extra-cold Grolsch, plus bottles of Bellevue Kriek, Sol and Pilsner Urquell. Wines start at £2.90 a glass, either a white Viura or a red Tempranillo from the Pleno stable. Generous main dishes – like char-grilled rib-eye steak, or braised lamb shank with creamy mash – sneak over the £10 mark, but there's an attractive Thai platter at £9.80. Fat medieval candles and red velvet drapes create a vaguely Gothic atmosphere during the mid-afternoon lull.
Music (DJs Thur-Sat; £5 after 9pm Fri, after 10pm Sat). Restaurant. **Map 1 K5**.

Long Bar

Sanderson Hotel, 50 Berners Street, W1P 3AB (7300 1400). Oxford Circus or Tottenham Court Road tube. **Open** noon-12.30am Mon-Sat; noon-10.30pm Sun. **Food served** noon-11pm Mon-Sat; noon-10pm Sun. **Credit** AmEx, DC, MC, V.
The sleek flagship lounge bar beside the lobby of Philippe Starck's über-stylish Sanderson Hotel is still a landmark rendezvous spot for urban shakers – even though the decor, drinks menu and Japanese garden have hardly changed since the place opened in 1999. The long bar in question is a thin rectangle of a silver, white and glass counter dotted with Dalí-esque eyeball-embellished stools. An attentive waiter slides you a silver drinks menu. The dozen Martinis include a Picasso (Wyborowa apple, crème de cassis and blueberries) and a Citroen (Ketel One citron slowly stirred with limoncello, elderflower water and lemon zest). There are also champagne cocktails such as Bubbles & Bling (Hennessey, caramel and cinnamon charged with Laurent Perrier) and Hi Balls like Sweet Thing (crushed strawberries and Cariel vanilla vodka). All cocktails cost about £10; wines start at £6.50 a glass. The finger food matches the setting for style and price.
Babies and children welcome (terrace); high chairs. Disabled: toilet. Music (DJs 7pm-12.30am Wed-Fri; free). Specialities (cocktails). Tables outdoors (20, terrace). **Map 1 J5**.

Market Place

11 Market Place, W1W 8AH (7079 2020/www.marketplace-london.com). Oxford Circus tube. **Open/food served** 11am-midnight Mon-Wed; 11am-1am Thur-Sat; 1-11pm Sun. **Admission** £7 after 11pm Fri; £3 8-11pm, £7 after 11pm Sat. **Credit** AmEx, MC, V.
The West End two-floor flagship of the otherwise City-based Cantaloupe Group has a distinctly ethnic feel. A mixed international bunch, strong on the Latin American and European, is drawn by Iberian-influenced food (£4 empanadillas, £3 tapas, £12.50 platters of jamón ibérico, piri-piri pork and salchichón) and bottled beers (Sagres, Dos Equis, Voll Damm, large Cruzcampos). The cocktails (£6) emphasise the exotic, with Mount Gay rum in the Bajan rum and Caipirissima, and Bacardi eight-year-old cropping up in the Moscow Mules, Mojitos and Daiquiris. Cava, Navaran Brut, makes a pleasing appearance, albeit at a displeasing £19 a bottle. Overall the ambience is as *caloroso* as the menus suggest. Upstairs accommodates diners and pint-sippers (draught Amstel, Budvar and Erdinger); downstairs, DJs in a brightly lit booth conjure up Trojan, jazz-funk and Afro beat sounds.
Disabled: toilet. Music (DJs 8pm daily). Specialities (cocktails). Tables outdoors (8, terrace). **Map 1 J6**.

Mash

19-21 Great Portland Street, W1W 8QB (7637 5555/www.mashbarandrestaurant.co.uk). Oxford Circus tube. **Open** 11am-2am Mon-Sat. **Food served** 8am-11pm Mon-Fri; 4-11pm Sat. **Credit** AmEx, DC, MC, V.
Once a cool brew pub, Mash is now a catch-all, breakfast-to-bedtime provider of meals and drinks. After the breakfast area empties, the expansive bar behind it serves lunch (spicy pork belly or duck pizzas, £10.50-£11.50; charcuterie platters, £11.50) – as crucial to trade as the £6.30-£7 classic cocktails. Creativity still pervades the place; the dozen Mash Original Cocktails include a Tiki (Myer's dark rum, apricot brandy, passion fruit and orange juice), and an Amalfi Sunset (amaretto, cherry brandy and lemon). And, of course, Mash's vats, gleaming from behind glass at the back of the main bar, still produce micro-brewed beer: Vienna-style lager, Festival Golden, Mash blonde and Belgian wheat, all in the £3-per-pint bracket. The decor, curvaceous and orange, remains essentially retro, the highlight being, in the sunken lounge, the tongue-in-cheek, off-kilter mural of 1970s families at play.
Babies and children welcome; high chairs. Disabled: toilet. Entertainment: DJs 10pm Thur-Sat. Function room. Tables outdoors (4-8, pavement). **Map 1 J6**.

Match Bar

37-38 Margaret Street, W1G 0JF (7499 3443/www.matchbar.com). Oxford Circus tube. **Open** 11am-midnight Mon-Sat. **Food served** 11am-11pm Mon-Sat. **Credit** AmEx, MC, V.
The West End Match makes up in atmosphere what it might lack in decorative cool. That's not to say Match W1 is shabby – just that its narrow shape, from the front lounge area to the bar counter buried inside, doesn't lend itself to inventive murals or retro motifs. The lounge comes into its own for the venue's trademark sharing bowls: big stir-fries and casseroles savoured communally (£12 for two, £20 for four). Other mains include superior classics: the £7.50 fish and chips is haddock, deep-fried in Proof lager batter, the Cuban burger (£7.50) is of Inverurie beef and chorizo sausage, and so on. The drinks, of course, are sublime. Recent Match Originals (£6-£6.50) include Sam Jeavons' Fa'afafene (42 Below passion fruit vodka, shaken with lime and apple juices, honey and syrups) and Kevin Armstrong's Tequila Treacle (Cuervo Tradicional stirred with agave syrup, apple juice and angostura bitters).
Babies and children admitted (until 5pm). Disabled: toilet. Music (DJs 8pm Thur-Sat; free). Tables outdoors (2, pavement). **Map 1 J6**.

Newman Arms

23 Rathbone Street, W1T 1NG (7636 1127/www.newmanarms.co.uk). Goodge Street or Tottenham Court Road tube. **Open** noon-11pm Mon-Fri. **Food served** noon-3pm, 6-9pm Mon-Thur; noon-3pm Fri. **Credit** MC, V.

This cosy corner pub and Famous Pie Room on the first floor are a world away from the media dealings of Charlotte Street round the corner. The friendly, family-run Newman belongs to another era, perhaps when George Orwell (who mentions it in *1984*) and Dylan Thomas were regulars, or 1960 when Michael Powell filmed *Peeping Tom* in the adjoining alleyway – or even before any bohemian fizz was put into Fitzrovia. Today, regulars banter over pints of London Pride or Bass. The nautical knick-knacks on the walls accentuate the ship's cabin feel – the pub's certainly small enough. Book for the pie room, such is its fame; favourites such as chicken, gammon and leek, and beef and Guinness, plus daily specials such as mutton with plums and ginger, or pork with mushrooms and cider, arrive puffed up perfectly like car air-bags. They are put down on the checked tablecloths with impeccably cooked potatoes and veg. Timeless.

Restaurant. Specialities (pies). **Map 1 J5.**

Nordic

25 Newman Street, W1T 1PN (7631 3174/www.nordicbar.com). Tottenham Court Road tube. **Open** noon-11pm Mon-Fri; 6-11pm Sat. **Food served** noon-3pm. **Credit** AmEx, DC, JCB, MC, V.

This Scandinavian theme bar has changed little in four years. The ice-cool selection of beers, spirits, shots, cocktails and food has been embellished by arrivals such as Gotland rum Alaissima Noll, and canned Mac Arctic beer from the world's northernmost brewery. Draught Carlsberg, Faxe and Red Erik, bottled Lapin Kulta, Spendrups Crocodile and a range of Absoluts, Pölstars and Finlandias are still the mainstays of the drinks menu, interspersed with Alborg akvavit, Kirsberry liqueur and humorously themed strong cocktails (£6.50). Muddled raspberries or fresh ginger, flavoured Absoluts and lingonberry juices create striking concoctions such as Sex in the Snow, Norwegian Blue and the Scandapolitan. To eat, Nordic cheeses and seafood salads are complemented by a pick 'n' mix smörgåsbord (£2.75 an item). A triptych mural of Max von Sydow necking akvavit and a gallery of famous Scandinavians (Victor Borge! Allan Simonsen!) greet arrivals at each of the two hideaway entrances, on Newman Street and Newman Passage.

Babies and children welcome. TVs. **Map 1 J5.**

Oscar

Charlotte Street Hotel, 15 Charlotte Street, W1T 1RJ (7806 2000/www.charlottestreethotel.com). Goodge Street or Tottenham Court Road tube. **Open/food served** 11am-11pm Mon-Sat; 5-8pm Sun. **Credit** AmEx, MC, V.

The lobby bar of the media-swamped Charlotte Street Hotel is a suitably chic spot for deal-clinching cocktails. A long chrome bar counter, lined with brown stools, faces a casual chatting area of comfortable low purple, red and orange seats, at right-angles to french windows overlooking Charlotte and Windmill Streets. To the other side is a busy dining area and open kitchen. Attentive, blue-shirted staff serve £9.50 cocktails with aplomb, earning their 12.5% service charge. Combinations of Grey Goose l'Orange, Plymouth gin, Havana Club rum and Absolut Kurrant are mixed with fresh raspberries, angostura bitters and Mozart chocolate liqueurs to create cocktails in categories such as Sweet Indulgence and Long Cooling. The signature drink remains Charlotte's Secret (Grey Goose Citron, lychee juice, Passoa liqueur, and Crème de Mûre, crowned with Beaumont des Crayeres champagne). This high-quality selection is completed by 20 wines of each colour by the glass and bottle, and quality Vietnamese, Indian and Japanese platters (£9.50).

Babies and children admitted. Film Club (8pm Sun; £30 incl meal, book in advance). Function rooms. No-smoking area (restaurant, lunch only). Tables outdoors (6, pavement). **Map 1 K5.**

Potion

28 Maple Street, W1T 6HP (7580 6474). Warren Street tube. **Open** 11am-11pm Mon-Sat. **Food served** noon-9pm Mon-Fri; 6-9pm Sat. **Credit** AmEx, MC, V.

This simple but stylish two-floor bar-diner on the corner of Maple and Fitzroy Streets fills a gap in north Fitzrovia. It won't win any awards for originality, but what it does, it does well: Potion is a handy port in a storm when local workaday pubs are filled with sozzled workers on payday. Draught Cobra, Grolsch, Heineken and John Smith's, and bottled Asahi, Crown, Tiger and Michelob are complemented by 15 cocktails, including a Mai Tai (with Appleton Estate rum, Bacardi and Cointreau) and a Manhattan (with Maker's Mark), generously priced at £5.40 or £3.50 during happy hours (between 4pm and 9pm). Wines start at £3 a glass, for Jacob's Creek semillon chardonnay or shiraz cabernet. The Thai food, best enjoyed in the dinky space upstairs, features authentic curries of various meats and colours, and stir-fried specialities.

Babies and children admitted. Function rooms. Specialities (cocktails). Tables outdoors (6, pavement). TVs. **Map 1 4J.**

Roxy

3 Rathbone Place, W1T 1HJ (7255 1098/www.theroxy.co.uk). Tottenham Court Road tube. **Open/food served** 5pm-3am Mon-Fri; 9.30pm-3.30am Sat. **Credit** AmEX, MC, V.

'Yet another post-work happy-hour trough,' you may groan – but the Roxy rocks. Why? Because this spacious basement bar understands the meshing of classic underground/indie music with the dishevelled malcontents of this world, whatever their age. Young blokes who discreetly comb their fingers through their tousled hair as they approach the bar counter; mixed groups of wastrels, garrulous after dipping their communal beaks into £7.95 happy-hour pitchers of Iced Tea or Sex on the Beach – these are not the frustrated office workers who frequent other West End binge buckets. And the soundtrack! Velvet Underground's 'Rock & Roll' 1969 live version, a blast of Mary Chain, a touch of Teardrops. What's more, there's Beck's on tap, Condessa de Leganza wine of either colour at £3.60 a glass, £6 cocktails, ciabatta toasties and disco lights to boot.

Games (board games). Music (DJs 6pm nightly). **Map 1 K6.**

Ship

134 New Cavendish Street, W1W 6YB (7636 6301). Oxford Circus tube. **Open** 11am-11pm Mon-Fri. **Food served** 11.30am-5pm Mon-Fri. **Credit** MC, V.

This nautical oddity is a pub of the old school: of quiet natter or soulful contemplation over a pint of Caffrey's, Bass or Worthington. Its regimental accent attracts men of late middle age who did their time in the services. A cosy all-in-one bar lounge is decorated with shiny copper

Social

knick-knacks (beer taps, things that presumably help a ship keep going, neon signs for little-known lagers) and regimental crests. The Irish and Polish staff keep the banter lively, occasionally running round next door to the Sky 2 caff to fetch plates of set breakfasts, jacket potatoes and burgers. The somewhat disconcerting 'No Soliciting' sign over the gents' seems a little harsh, for although sailors do pass by, they're here to talk tides and tillers. Grolsch and Dry Blackthorn are the non-bitter draught varieties.
Babies and children admitted. Function room. Games (fruit machine). Tables outdoors (2, pavement). TV. **Map 1 J5**.

Shochu Lounge

37 Charlotte Street, W1T 1RR (7580 9666). Goodge Street or Tottenham Court Road tube.
Open 5pm-midnight Mon, Sat, Sun; noon-midnight Tue-Fri. **Food served** noon-2.30pm, 5.30-11.30pm Mon-Sat; 5.30-10.30pm Sun. **Credit** AmEx, DC, MC, V.
A sumptuous basement beneath the equally stylish Japanese restaurant Roka, Shochu Lounge is a wonderfully original newcomer. Shochu, a vodka-like spirit made of buckwheat, barley, sweet potato or rice, has been around in Japan since the 14th century, but has only come to the attention of Londoners in the 21st. Here Tony Conigliaro has mixed it with fresh fruits and spices to create cocktails (£6-£7.50) chilled (Tanuki Peach: shochu, peach purée and sugar) or hot (shochu, cinnamon and pear), in Martini, short, long, flute or goblet form. Rows of preserving jars are part of the striking semi-rustic, semi-boutique decor, accentuating centuries-old tradition and modern taste. A table heaving with old kitchen utensils almost seems part of the island bar counter, except it's lined with customers. The red-shaded, raised back area is a bar lounge with a design that spans seven centuries. Saké and Sapporo beer are also available, and the bar snacks and mains (brought down from the restaurant) are superb.
Disabled: toilet. Music (DJ 8pm Sun). Restaurant. Specialities (Shochu). **Map 1 J5**.

Social

5 Little Portland Street, W1W 7JD (7636 4992/www.thesocial.com). Oxford Circus tube. **Open/food served** noon-midnight Mon-Fri; 1pm-midnight Sat. **Credit** AmEx, MC, V.
The formula for this bar has become so successful that it has spawned imitators as far away as Bondi Beach. The Social is divided into two areas: one at street level for daytime play, the other downstairs for after dark. Through a fairly hidden doorway, a lunchtime crowd fills five rounded booth tables, parallel to a long bar counter. Changing photo displays provide decoration – in this case, William English's vintage shots of Vivienne Westwood – and the Heavenly Jukebox is set to Aretha Franklin on Atlantic. To eat, there are square pies (wild mushroom and asparagus, steak and Guinness, £6.20), snacks and ruggedly proletarian sandwiches (sausage,

fish-finger). Both caff and basement share the same drinks menu: unusual and somewhat sickly cocktails (£5.40) such as a Black Forest Gâteaux (Marnier cherry liqueur, cream and chocolate sprinkles) or Social (Frangelico hazelnut liqueur and Teichenné butterscotch). Draught (San Miguel, Grolsch, Guinness) and bottled beers (Tsing Tao, A le Coq, Red Stripe, Kasteel) are equally eclectic. Downstairs, DJs six nights a week attract a relaxed, hip crowd.
Babies and children admitted (until 5pm). Music (DJs 7pm Mon-Sat; occasional bands Mon). **Map 1 J5**.

Villandry

170 Great Portland Street, W1W 5QB (7631 3131/ www.villandry.com). Great Portland Street tube. **Open** 8am-11pm Mon-Fri; 9am-9pm Sat. **Food served** 8am-3.30pm, 5-9pm Mon-Fri; 9am-4pm Sat. **Credit** AmEx, DC, MC, V.
A high-class delicatessen and bar-restaurant in one, Villandry has standards to maintain. Adjoining a bright store abundant with Italian preserves and French cheeses is a classy, monochrome dining area headed by a low lit stone bar counter. Here, cocktails (£7-£8) of classic and champagne varieties are dispensed, along with carefully chosen wines, and the finest produce for the plates (£7-£8.50) of cheese, meze and charcuterie. Ketel One vodka is used in the Bloody Mary, Plymouth gin in the Raffles' Singapore Sling, and Wyborowa vodka in the Rising Sun. Albert Beerens is the champagne of choice, as featured in the Parisian Spring Punch of calvados, Noilly Prat, freshly pressed apple juice, lemon juice and champers. A Marsanne Languedoc (£3.25) and Michel Laroche grenache (£3.50) kick off the extensive wine list. The list of grappas, schnapps, digestives and dessert wines would put hotel bars of far greater swank to shame.
Babies and children welcome (restaurant); children's menu, high chairs. Function room. No smoking (restaurant). Tables outdoors (13, pavement).

Wax

4 Winsley Street, W1N 7AR (7436 4650/www.wax-bar.co.uk). Oxford Circus tube. **Open/food served** noon-3am Mon-Sat. **Happy Hour** 5-7pm Mon-Sat. **Credit** AmEx, MC, V.
A place where you can get mullered at £3 per after-work cocktail might give off something of a scary atmosphere after the post-discount watershed of 7pm – but not a bit of it. Such is the layout of this spacious basement venue (where Bar Madrid once strutted its stuff) – two long bar counters, a loungey chat area at the back and a prop-up chat-up area at the front – that a spirited party atmosphere is the norm, and customers are courteous. Cocktails, chronologically split between 'Yesterday' and 'Today', cost only a fiver later in the evening anyway, so the party keeps going until close of play at 3am. Finger food (Thai spiced chicken skewers, honey-roasted sausages) and sarnies (lamb koftas, spicy chicken fajitas) are similarly priced. Bottled beers include Michelob and Red Stripe.
Babies and children welcome (before 5pm). Bar available for hire. Music (DJs 9pm Thur-Sat; £7 after 10pm Fri, £10 after 10pm Sat). **Map 1 J6**.

Also in the area...

Jamies 74 Charlotte Street, W1T 4QH (7636 7556).
Lees Bag (Davy's) 4 Great Portland Street, W1N 3HD (7636 5287).
O'Neill's 4 Conway Street, W1T 6BB (7323 5965).

Central

HOLBORN

To fans of proper pubs, Holborn is one of the best districts in central London. It's also one of the worst if you end up on Kingsway, which is nothing but one chain boozer after another. The richest pickings are to be found around Lamb's Conduit Street and east to Gray's Inn Road and the **Calthorpe Arms**. With such exceptions as the **Perseverance** and the revamped **Yorkshire Grey**, venues tend to be blokey and old school: 'A pint of your finest please, landlord, and a Hamlet cigar.' If that doesn't really sound like your glass of beer, well – there's always Kingsway.

Calthorpe Arms

252 Gray's Inn Road, WC1X 8JR (7278 4732). Russell Square tube. **Open** 11am-11pm Mon-Sat; noon-10.30pm Sun. **Food served** noon-2.30pm, 6-9.30 Mon, Tue, Thur, Fri; noon-2.30pm, 7-9.30pm Wed; noon-2.30pm Sat, Sun. **Credit** MC, V.
Proudly bearing the Calthorpe crest on the sign outside, with the motto 'Gradu diverso una via' (the same way by different steps), this splendid corner pub serves a diverse clientele. Set in no man's land between Holborn and King's Cross, its pavement tables marking the boundary of the old Calthorpe estate, this boozer brings together discerning drinkers and sympathetic locals on first-name terms. Cosy, round, brown banquettes bookend the largish bar space, a patterned carpet from your grandma's day accentuating the comfort. Two Young's beer on draught, Bitter and Special, are complemented by bottled Old Nick, Champion, Waggle Dance, Double Chocolate Stout, Oregon Amber, Oatmeal Stout, Ramrod and other ales to protect you from the winter chill. Well-priced Coto Rioja/Blanco and Crystal Brook of both colours come by the glass and bottle; scampi, lasagne and ploughman's lunches provide sustenance.
Babies and children welcome. Function room. Games (fruit machine). No piped music or jukebox. Tables outdoors (6, pavement). TV (satellite). **Map 3 M4**.

Duke

7 Roger Street, WC1N 2PB (7242 7230/www.dukepub.co.uk). Chancery Lane, Holborn or Russell Square tube. **Open** noon-11pm Mon-Sat; noon-10.30pm Sun. **Food served** noon-10pm Mon-Sat; noon-9.30pm Sun. **Credit** MC, V.
For our money, this has to be the most gorgeous little retro pub in town. The tables are topped with primary red Formica, the floor is tiled with the original black, red and yellow squared lino, and the walls are half 1950s wood panelling, and half mustard yellow. The whole thing looks like it might have been knocked together by the set designer from *Ready, Steady, Go!*. There's no Wurlitzer jukebox, but there is a blazing-red upright piano. The selection of beers is decent enough (Greene King IPA and Adnams Broadside on a recent visit) and the food is excellent: fish cakes, leek and mushroom risotto, and sirloin steak, for instance. Dishes all cost around £8 to £10 and are served in a green-hued rear dining room so very petite that cat-swinging would definitely not be an option. The Duke can be a little tricky to find, sitting at the bottom of pretty little Doughty Mews, off Guildford Street, but perseverance will be rewarded.
Babies and children welcome. Restaurant (no-smoking). Tables outdoors (3, pavement). **Map 3 M4**.

King's Arms

11A Northington Street, WC1N 2JF (7405 9107). Chancery Lane or Russell Square tube. **Open** 11am-11pm Mon-Fri. **Food served** noon-9.45pm Mon-Fri. **Credit** AmEx, DC, MC, V.

The colour TV at the King's jars: a black-and-white model would be more apt. As it is, you still half expect the bar to offer nothing but Watney's Pale Ale and sherry. A one-room corner pub with a black-painted wooden floor, red velvet drapes and well-weathered furniture, the place hasn't changed since the days when the Charrington brewery ruled the roost. It's well on the way to becoming a capital treasure. You'll always find a choice of three well kept real ales – Timothy Taylor Landlord, Adnams bitter and Greene King IPA when we last visited. Upstairs are a couple of function rooms, the smaller doubling as a no-smoking area, and the tiniest gents' outside a motor caravan. Regulars are a motley bunch ranging from solicitors to workers in boiler suits. Things get busy at lunchtime, when a Thai menu is served; evenings are generally quiet.

Function room. Games (darts, pool). No-smoking area. Tables outdoors (2, pavement). TVs (big screen, plasma, satellite). **Map 3 M4**.

Lamb

94 Lamb's Conduit Street, WC1N 3LZ (7405 0713/ www.youngs.co.uk). Holborn or Russell Square tube. **Open** 11am-11pm Mon-Sat; noon-4pm, 7-10.30pm Sun. **Food served** noon-2.30pm, **Credit** AmEx, MC, V.

A runner-up in the Best Pub category of the 2004 Time Out Eating & Drinking Awards, this outstanding Grade II listed structure was built around 1730 over William Lamb's river dam (conduit). Thanks to a sympathetic restoration in the 1960s, the ornate Victorian interior has been left largely intact. The mahogany island bar is edged with rotating etched-glass snob screens, complemented by matching mirrors and windows and racing-green upholstery. Walls are heavy with pictures of Victorian thespians, and the round-topped tables have funny little brass balustrades that at some point in the evening you're sure to catch with the bottom of your glass. The partitioned non-smoking section (more of a cubicle) is a nice idea but completely ineffective. The complete range of Young's beers is on tap, including seasonal ales. Drinkers are a mix of local office types, along with students and academics from the nearby halls of London University.

Function room. No piped music or jukebox. No-smoking area. Specialities (real ale). Tables outdoors (3, patio; 3, pavement). **Map 3 M4**.

Na Zdrowie The Polish Bar

11 Little Turnstile, WC1V 7DX (7831 9679). Holborn tube. **Open** 12.30-11pm Mon-Fri; 6-11pm Sat. **Food served** 12.30-10pm Mon-Fri; 6-10pm Sat. **Credit** MC, V.

With its tiled floor, plastic-topped stools and silvery plastic chairs, all crammed into a spartan, tiny wedge of a room, Na Zdrowie could be the local for factory workers in Lodz. What's more, this little slice of Slavic chic serves more than 60 vodkas, all fascinatingly described: from Dlaczego ('green mint vodka: just ask for Polish crème de menthe') at 25% proof, to such heavy-duty rocket fuels as Starka ('aged in old wine barrels so it's a bit like whisky') at 60%. There's also a fine range of Polish bottled beers, although when we visited most of the after-work crowd opted for draft Amstel or Stella. The food is far better than you might expect, and comprises good Baltic dishes like herring with sour cream, potato fritters with mushroom sauce and sour cream, and carefully handmade pierogi dumplings with fillings of potato and cheese or meat and cabbage.

Specialities (vodka). Tables outdoors (3, pavement). **Map 4 M5**.

Old Nick

20-22 Sandland Street, WC1R 4PZ (7430 9503). Holborn tube. **Open** 11.30am-11pm Mon-Fri. **Food served** noon-3pm Mon-Fri. **Credit** MC, V.

The interior of the Nick looks as 'old' as a half-timbered Barratt Home, but full marks for trying. This was formerly a much-loved Young's pub, the Three Cups, until a 2003 sale and refit saw it knocked through into the café next door. The result is a big, comfortable, dark-wood and ketchup-red boozer with a nest of nooks around a central serving area. Only the lamps and bar-back are original. But the place is welcoming enough; on a wintry Monday evening when most nearby hostelries were sad, empty affairs, the Old Nick was packed and buzzing. It helps that the counter has a great line-up of beers courtesy of the owners, Dorset's Hall & Woodhouse brewery: Badger Best, Tanglefoot, K&B Sussex bitter. The food is a cut above most pub grub, too: big sarnies and bistro-style dishes for between £5 and £8.

Bar available for hire (weekends). Disabled: toilet. TV (digital, plasma). **Map 3 M5**.

Pearl Bar & Restaurant

252 High Holborn, WC1V 7EN (7829 7000/www.pearl restaurant.com). Holborn tube. **Open** 11am-11pm Mon-Fri; 6-11pm Sat. **Food served** (restaurant only) noon-3pm, 6-10pm Mon-Fri; 6-10pm Sat. **Credit** AmEx, DC, JCB, MC, V.

Just what Holborn needs: a real destination bar. Even within the swish five-star Chancery Court business hotel, Pearl shines. Past the courtyard entrance and a revolving door, a narrow bar drips and sways with strings of pearls: from huge, tubular brown lights, over the windows and dividing the six groups of armless chairs and banquettes of uniform fawn. Everything curves where it should, and at night the strings twinkle as piano keys tinkle. Fat olives and sugared nuts are swiftly delivered. The thick menu lists 44 cocktails (£9-£10.50), including a Pink Pearl of Rémy Martin VSOP and spiced berry cordials, topped with pink champagne; Zubrowkas and flavoured Absoluts inform the Martinis. Wine, though, is where Pearl really sings. Aided by a back-bar Cruvinet nitrogen machine that keeps bottles fresh, a clear cold room in the adjoining restaurant and equally switched-on staff, Pearl can provide 450 types by the bottle, and 54 choice varieties by the glass. A custom-made carrier allows the delivery of three 125ml glasses at once, sold (£25) as a differing but complementary trio of high-end chardonnays, for example. Swinging after dark, but as yet dead by day.

Babies and children welcome (before 7pm): high chairs. Disabled: toilet. Music (pianist 6pm nightly). Restaurant (no smoking). Specialities (cocktails, wine). **Map 4 M5**.

Perseverance

63 Lamb's Conduit Street, WC1N 3NB (7405 8278). Holborn or Russell Square tube. **Open** 4-11pm Mon-Sat; 4-10.30pm Sun. **Food served** 5.30-10pm Mon-Fri; 4-10pm Sat. Sun. **Credit** AmEx, DC, MC, V.

Not quite as dazed or confused as its Soho sibling, the Endurance (*see p83*), the Percy is nonetheless by far the hippest outpost in WC1. Its foppish attire of flock wallpa-

Princess Louise

per, baroque mirrors and mounted animal heads continues to wear well, and the line-up of beers has improved from the single real ale of old: on a recent visit we found Courage Directors, Deuchars IPA and Old Speckled Hen. Wines are similarly well represented: a busy blackboard has space to list only the highlights, so oenophiles are instructed to ask for the 'full menu'. The food served in the small, boxy dining room upstairs is a not overly ambitious roster of European standards, but the quality is consistently excellent. The crowd here is convivial and shops some way off the high street. The only disappointment is the lack of a killer jukebox to match the one at the Endurance.
Babies and children admitted (lunch only). Function room. Restaurant. Tables outdoors (6, pavement).
Map 3 M4.

Princess Louise

208 High Holborn, WC1V 7EP (7405 8816). Holborn tube. **Open** 11am-11pm Mon-Fri; noon-11pm Sat; noon-10.30pm Sun. **Food served** noon-2.30pm, 6-8.30pm Mon-Fri; noon-8.30pm Sat, Sun. **Credit** AmEx, MC, V.
If the moulded ceiling, tall engraved mirrors and intricately carved woodwork at this wonderful gin palace don't do it for you, you deserve to be banished to an All Bar One (in fact, there's a branch just round the corner on Kingsway). The pub was built in 1872 and named after Queen Victoria's fourth daughter. Most of the spectacular work we see today is the result of an 1891 refurbishment, conducted by WH Lascalles & Co. The centrepiece is the magnificent horseshoe wooden bar, long enough to race dogs on, and complete with its original clock, mirrors and spidery globe lamps. Even the loos are magnificent. All the place lacks are the partitions that separated the various drinking areas until Watney's saw fit to rip them out in the 1960s. The Princess is now under the benevolent control of the Samuel Smith brewery; just a shame about the drinks, then (Sam Smith's own-brand beers, lagers and spirits).
Games (fruit machines). No piped music or jukebox.
Map 1 L5.

Rugby Tavern

19 Great James Street, WC1N 3ES (7405 1384). Holborn tube. **Open** 11am-11pm Mon-Fri. **Food served** noon-2.30pm, 5.30-9.30pm Mon-Fri.
Credit AmEx, MC, V.
We can't remember seeing a neater, cleaner, more polished and well-lacquered pub. Nor one in which the lights (BHS fittings, we're sure) were brighter – all the better to show off the pristine state of the plush, patterned carpet. No wonder the sign at the door reads 'Smart, tidy dress only'. The place has the air of a great aunt's front parlour, albeit one that has a whopping island bar stuck in the middle. On a recent visit, the staff reluctantly broke off their game of backgammon to serve us something from the full range of Shepherd Neame beers. Company on this night consisted of a large gathering of beefy blokes. The pub's name derives from adjacent Rugby Street, but the

hostelry rises to what's expected of it, with pictures of Dr Arnold's public school, old scorecards and photographs of long-forgotten try-scorers.
Games (darts). Tables outdoors (10, pavement). TV. **Map 1 L5**.

Vats Wine Bar

51 Lamb's Conduit Street, WC1N 3NB (7242 8963). Holborn or Russell Square tube. **Open** noon-11pm Mon-Fri. **Food served** noon-2.30pm, 6-9.30pm Mon-Fri. **Credit** AmEx, DC, MC, V.
Scene of many a rowdy *Spectator* party, this well-established watering hole is as popular with local solicitors as with media types. The current owners have built up a regular clientele of suited 40s-plus men and women who like a drink or ten. Thanks to the roaring coal fire, panelled walls, wood benches and large sash windows, there's a Dickensian feel to the place (and staff can become as severe as Mr Gradgrind at lunchtime, when boozers are confined to the bar or two small benches by said fire). Avoid the obvious temptations of 1997 Château Bastor-Lamontagne from Sauternes (£22.50) and try something new – Bual Madeira (£4.95 a glass), perhaps, or Moscatel Superior from Lustau (£5.50 a glass). There's no beer – the licence would have to be altered to serve it. But 27 wines by the glass isn't bad, and Domaine de Grangeneuve's 2000 Vielles Vignes from the Rhône (£5.25 a glass) is the best tipple outside of the sweet wines.
Babies and children admitted. Disabled: toilet. Function room. Tables outdoors (4, pavement). **Map 3 M4**.

Yorkshire Grey

29-33 Gray's Inn Road, WC1X 8PN (7405 2519/www.theyorkshiregrey.co.uk). Chancery Lane or Holborn tube. **Open** noon-11pm Mon-Sat. **Food served** noon-3pm, 5-9pm Mon-Sat. **Credit** DC, MC, V.
Not long ago, the Yorkshire Grey was beloved of beer enthusiasts for its range of own-brewed real ales, all with names relating to the legal profession. Then things went downhill; the real ales were ditched and successive managements came and went faster than a pint at last orders. The pub was shunned by all and became near derelict. So, a big welcome back to the newly revamped 'YG Pub & Kitchen'. Shame that it's such a half-hearted return, though, with a by-the-numbers interior (bare floorboards, mix-and-match furniture), just one real ale (Shepherd Neame Spitfire) among the four handpumps, and a menu that on the night we visited was limited to just chips – and then the chef burned his hand and stopped at 7.30pm. Things can only get better: the drinks selection will expand, and food platters are promised. Hey, just be thankful the place didn't get turned into an O'Neill's.
Function room. Tables outdoors (6, pavement). **Map 3 M5**.

Also in the area...

All Bar One 58 Kingsway, WC2B 6DX (7269 5171).
Bierodrome 67 Kingsway, WC2B 6TD (7242 7469).
Bung Hole (Davy's) Hand Court, 57 High Holborn, WC1V 6DX (7831 8365).
Knights Templar (JD Wetherspoon) 95 Chancery Lane, WC2A 1DT (7831 2660).
Penderel's Oak (JD Wetherspoon) 283-288 High Holborn, WC1V 7PF (7242 5669).
Pitcher and Piano 42 Kingsway, WC2B 6EX (7404 8510).
Shakespeare's Head (JD Wetherspoon) Africa House, 64-68 Kingsway, WC2B 6BG (7404 8846).

HOLLAND PARK

This is not an inspiring area for drinking. There are some handsome Victorian pubs, but attempts to update them have erased much of their character. Although posey and a touch stilted, the **Castle** is good for continental beers, while the **Prince of Wales** can work up a good head of steam at the weekends. For a quiet pint, head for the **Ladbroke Arms**, a traditional pub that wouldn't be out of place in the wilds of Hampshire.

Academy

57 Princedale Road, W11 4NP (7221 0248). Holland Park tube. **Open** noon-11pm Mon-Sat; noon-10.30pm Sun. **Food served** noon-3.30pm, 6-10.30pm Mon-Sat; noon-10pm Sun. **Credit** MC, V.
Its name might be better suited to a nightclub, but otherwise this place hits all the right sophisticated notes: gallery-white paint, venetian blinds and elegant flower arrangements, with wooden floors underfoot. A fake fire takes the edge off the slightly draughty room in winter, and in summer the bar's light colours make it a pleasantly bright spot in which to pore over the weekend papers with a pint. Friendly staff behind the horseshoe bar dispense the likes of Leffe, Staropramen and Grolsch to a mixture of young, cliquey hipsters and their slightly more mellowed forerunners; in general the atmosphere is quieter than at the Prince of Wales just across the road.
Babies and children admitted (until 7pm). Function room. Tables outdoors (8, pavement). **Map 10 Az7**.

Castle

100 Holland Park Avenue, W11 4UA (7313 9301). Holland Park tube. **Open** noon-11pm Mon-Sat; noon-10.30pm Sun. **Food served** noon-3pm, 5.30-9pm Mon-Fri; noon-9pm Sat, Sun. **Credit** MC, V.
Is the Castle a pub that wants to be a bar, or the opposite? It's hard to decide, since one wing of the place is a fusion of old and modern, with ornate Victorian bar, squishy sofas and deep cherry-red banquettes – while the other has loungey white sofas and trashy David LaChapelle-esque photography. It doesn't all quite hang together, and during the weekends the DJs make matters worse (we think) by thrusting an incongruous house soundtrack into the proceedings. There are some nice details, though, such as the pretty mini chandeliers, in an art deco style, hanging above the bar. The clientele is of trusty Holland Park stock, mostly under 30 and well dressed. To the Castle's credit, the 'international' beer list ventures past Hoegaarden and Leffe to include Früli, Duvel, Brooklyn, Schneider wheat beer and the ever-popular cherry beer Kriek.
Disabled: toilet. Games (board games). Quiz (8pm Tue; £1). Music (DJs 7.30pm Thur, Fri; free). Specialities (beers of the world). **Map 10 Az7**.

Julie's Wine Bar

135 Portland Road, W11 4LW (7727 7985/www.juliesrestaurant.com). Holland Park tube. **Open** 9am-11.30pm Mon-Sat; 10am-10.30pm Sun. **Food served** 9-11am, 12.30-2.45pm, 7.30-10.30pm Mon-Sat; 12.30-3pm, 7.30-10.30pm Sun. **Credit** AmEx, MC, V.
With its pseudo-Marrakesh dark wood partitions, this is something of a late 1970s precursor to Momo (*see p61*). It may have kept out of the cocktail action in nearby Notting Hill, but it's still the place for west Londoners in the know – the scene of Prince Charles's first engagement party and

familiar territory for familiar faces even today. In the last year the bar has gained a coffee machine, so cappuccinos are go; and the bar food is ambitious (try Jerusalem artichoke puree with fried ginger and armagnac sauce, £17.50). An exceptionally well-chosen wine list includes 1998 Girardin Volnay Premier Cru (£50 a bottle) if you're feeling flush; more reasonable options include a Morton Estate sauvignon blanc (£22), the lovely organic Novas from Chile (£18 a bottle), or the Mitchell cabernet sauvignon from the Clare Valley in Australia (£5 a glass). Or there's the unusual 14-year-old Oban malt, kept in a wooden model of the Albert Memorial behind the bar.
Babies and children admitted (crèche 1-4pm Sun, £10 including food). Function room. Restaurant. Specialities (organic food, wines). Tables outdoors (10, pavement).

Ladbroke Arms

54 Ladbroke Road, W11 3NW (7727 6648). Holland Park tube. **Open** 11am-11pm Mon-Sat; noon-10.30pm Sun. **Food served** noon-2.30pm, 7-9.45pm Mon-Sat; noon-3pm, 7-9.30pm Sun. **Credit** MC, V.
Standing serenely between lofty white mansionettes, this quiet-minded establishment comes neatly draped in fronds of ivy. It has the feel of a gentrified country pub, with older couples taking early suppers in the plush mezzanine dining area and discussing horse-racing at the bar – but the Ladbroke is by no means shunned by younger drinkers. The bar space is pleasant, with wooden tables, bench seating and beautiful stained-glass detailing that dates from the Victorian original. Only a handful of beers are on tap, but San Miguel and Budvar are welcome among them. Bar snacks aren't cheap (£2.50 for a bowl of chips), so it's probably better value to pick a starter from the gastropubby menu: perhaps Spanish octopus with white bean stew (£6). Not a place for a wild night out, but inoffensive enough.
Children admitted (dining only). No piped music or jukebox. Tables outdoors (12, terrace).

Prince of Wales

14 Princedale Road, W11 4NJ (7313 9321). Holland Park tube. **Open** noon-11pm Mon-Sat; noon-10.30pm Sun. **Food served** noon-3pm, 6-10pm Mon-Fri; 11am-10pm Sat; noon-9pm Sun. **Credit** AmEx, MC, V.
The Prince is probably Holland Park's liveliest pub, despite cramped drinking conditions and an island bar taking up almost two-thirds of the room. The traditional pictorial sign hanging from the exterior reminds you that this was once an old-school boozer. The memory is distant, though, since the interior now sports a boutique-chic look, with delicate gold and blue flock wallpaper, parquet flooring and a pink satin Chinese-style lantern. Scattered around in various low-lit corners are clusters of seats, but you're likely to have more fun propping up the bar and spying across the room. At weekends, the pub attracts young and up-for-it Holland Park life, knocking back Grolsch and Hoegaarden; in summer the reasonably sized beer garden comes into play.
Babies and children welcome (before 6pm). Disabled: toilet. Games (board games). Music (musicians 8pm every 2nd Thur; free). Tables outdoors (15, garden). TV.

KENSINGTON

For one of London's most moneyed locales, Kensington is strangely lacking in quality drinking venues. Unless you like your booze with a view (the **Tenth Bar**'s main draw), try veering a little off the Manolo-trodden path of the High Street to reach the eccentric delights of the **Scarsdale**, the **Churchill Arms** or the **Windsor Castle**.

Abingdon

54 Abingdon Road, W8 6AP (7937 3339). Earl's Court or High Street Kensington tube. **Open** 12.30-11pm Mon-Sat; 12.30-10.30pm Sun. **Food served** 12.30-2.30pm, 6.30-11pm Mon-Sat; 12.30-3pm, 7-10.30pm Sun. **Credit** AmEx, DC, MC, V.
The peeling dark blue paint and slightly chipped plaster of this popular boozer's exterior clash with the neighbouring cutesy Georgian housing and manicured trees. Its age (it opened, as the Abingdon Arms, in 1861) notwithstanding, it moves with the times, pulling a well-heeled local crowd with its unusual hybrid of cosy gastropub and urban style bar, achieved with some clever design. Large, curving windows provide light and space at one end, where there are sofas and low-slung tables; at the other, low lighting and a dramatically curved, overhanging bar provide a setting suitable for cocktails (21 listed, all at £5.50). The star on the exemplary wine list is the 2002 Cullen chardonnay (£38 a bottle) from Australia – although the 2003 Rias Baixas (£22.50), a lovely, grapefruit-scented albariño from Spain, runs it close. 16 wines by the glass isn't bad: try the silky 2003 Château Val Joanis Côtes du Luberon (£5). Staropramen is the only unusual beer on tap; service is efficient rather than friendly.
Babies and children welcome; high chairs. Restaurant. Tables outdoors (4, pavement).

Bar Cuba

11-13 Kensington High Street, W8 5NP (7938 4137/www.barcuba.info). High Street Kensington tube. **Open** 5pm-2am Mon-Thur; noon-2am Fri, Sat; 5pm-12.30am Sun. **Food served** 5pm-1am Mon-Sat; 5-11pm Sun. **Credit** AmEx, DC, MC, V.
Buzzy Bar Cuba sports a cheerfully Latin American decor scheme – faded citrus tones, fruity mural above the bar, quirky black signatures across one terracotta wall – well suited to consumption of cheap (around the £4 mark), largely rum-based cocktails. There's authentic Cuban food in the raised dining section at the back (there's also a wide selection of tapas plates for around £4), and an impressive range of cigars, of which the most expensive is a £22 Cohiba the size of a baguette sandwich. Popular with local office workers and the area's international crowd, Cuba has an upbeat vibe, even if the Latin American concept is looking a little tired these days. The owners stage live music thrice weekly, and also hold 'hot hot hot' salsa lessons in the basement and even have a 'half-price fajita night'.
Babies and children welcome. Dance classes (7.30-9.30pm Mon-Sat; 6.30-8.30pm Sun). Music (DJs 9.30pm nightly, singer 8.30pm Wed, live jazz 8.30pm Sun; free Wed, Sun, £3-£10 other nights). Specialities (cocktails).

Churchill Arms

119 Kensington Church Street, W8 7LN (7727 4242). Notting Hill Gate tube. **Open** 11am-11pm Mon-Sat; noon-10.30pm Sun. **Food served** noon-9.30pm Mon-Sat; noon-8pm Sun. **Credit** AmEx, MC, V.
A corker of a pub, the Churchill is so thickly adorned with eccentric paraphernalia that it gives you the feeling of having just stepped into a tinker's yard. A curious collection of pots, pans and kettles – well almost anything, really

(there are also ye olde signposts, a pram and miniature violin case) – adorns the ceiling; out back, in the converted garage, is a Thai dining room. Here, foliage hangs in profusion, like an upside-down, overgrown garden; a glass-encased butterfly collection mounted on the walls adds to the tropical feel. Two open fireplaces, a frenetic, buzzy vibe, Fuller's ales on draught (Chiswick, London Pride, ESB and a seasonal brew), plus a hip yet diverse crowd render this boozer one of the stars of the Kensington pub trail.
Babies and children admitted. Games (fruit machine). No-smoking area. Restaurant. TV (satellite). **Map 10 B8**.

Elephant & Castle

40 Holland Street, W8 4LT (7368 0901). High Street Kensington tube. **Open** 11am-11pm Mon-Sat; noon-10.30pm Sun. **Food served** noon-3pm, 6-8pm Mon-Thur; noon-3pm Fri-Sun. **Credit** MC, V.
Enter this corner boozer and you wonder where its charm lies. It's a boxy, dark, airless space, and unless you consider cheese, tomato and chutney sandwiches a delicacy, you'll probably decide to overlook the food menu altogether and just stick to pints of London Pride. The photographs of Victorian printworks seem incongruous, and the signed England flags covering the windows failed to impress us – but the Elephant comes into its own during the summer months. It's situated on one of the most charming streets in west London (all chi-chi boutiques and leafy trees), and in warm weather the locale's pretty people come out to play in such droves that they spill on to the road and have been known to block traffic. The regularly changing guest ales (Badger Tanglefoot and Timothy Taylor Landlord were recently on draught) add to the attraction.
Games (fruit machines). No piped music or jukebox. Tables outdoors (4, pavement). TV.

Scarsdale Tavern

23A Edwardes Square, W8 6HE (7937 1811). Earl's Court or High Street Kensington tube. **Open** noon-11pm Mon-Sat; noon-10.30pm Sun. **Food served** noon-10pm Mon-Sat; noon-9pm Sun. **Credit** AmEx, MC, V.
Approach the Scarsdale and you'd be forgiven for thinking you were somewhere far removed from the retail mecca of High Street Ken. Set on a charming square with an overgrown, botanical wilderness at its centre, the Scarsdale was constructed by a hapless builder who, anticipating an impending Napoleonic invasion, transported a 'French Arcadia' to what he believed would soon be a Gallic outpost. The foliage outside and friendliness within (staff greet regulars by name) set a pleasantly countrified vibe; the original wooden floorboards, string of glass lanterns above the bar, church seating and fabulous British food all add to the rustic feel, as does the oft-changing roster of guest ales (Black Sheep Special from Masham, North Yorkshire, say). Customers are a mix of tourists in search of 'authentic' Englishness and home-grown beer drinkers who fit the role to a T: welcome to Barbour country.
Babies and children admitted (in restaurant). Games (fruit machine). Tables outdoors (8, garden). TV (digital).

Settle Down

Barkers Arcade, Kensington High Street, W8 5SE (7376 0008). High Street Kensington tube. **Open** noon-11pm Mon-Fri. **Food served** noon-3pm, 6-10pm Mon-Fri. **Credit** AmEx, MC, V.
The blackboard out front says 'Best Basement Bar in Kensington' (are there any others?), 'great food', and 'friendly people'. While we can't vouch for the food, the people are friendly enough, even if they do appear to have staggered in on a jolly from Swindon. The Settle Down is somewhere between a wine bar and a pub, and is set deep within Barkers Arcade. There are two rooms, one of which is tatty enough to be a student union – complete with ceiling that looks as if it survived the asbestos era, curling faux-wood floorboards and a bizarre Bacardi Breezer pyramid atop the bar. The other room's a better bet: decorated in a drawing-room style, this boasts a marble fireplace, battered leather chesterfields and tartan walls and upholstery, all of which make for a decent bolt-hole in which to enjoy the strong selection of New World wines.
Babies and children admitted (until 6pm). Function room. TV.

Tenth Bar

Royal Garden Hotel, 20-24 Kensington High Street, W8 4PT (7361 1910/www.royalgardenhotel.co.uk). High Street Kensington tube. **Open/food served** noon-5pm, 6pm-midnight Mon-Fri; 6pm-midnight Sat. **Credit** AmEx, DC, MC, V.
The lofty location on the tenth floor of the fabulous Royal Garden Hotel gives the Tenth Bar an clear selling point: views. These extend across Hyde Park, as far Canary Wharf and the London Eye in the distance. Furnishings are nothing special – brown leather seating and curved corner bar give the place a 1980s Manhattan feel – but most of the time your eyes will be turned outwards anyway. Customers are largely drawn from the upper echelons of the local office fraternity. We were surprised to see such a limited wine list (just three each of red and white), but at these heights, champagne seems obligatory – and there are about 20 types to choose from; come on a Wednesday between 5.30pm and 8.30pm when prices are halved – that's £44 for a bottle of Vintage Veuve Cliquot with great Thames views.
Disabled: lift; toilet. Function room. Restaurant.

Whits

21 Abingdon Road, W8 6AH (7938 1122/www.whits.co.uk). High Street Kensington tube. **Open** noon-11pm Tue-Sat. **Food served** 5.30-8pm Tue-Sat. **Credit** AmEx, MC, V.
There's been a change of management at the former Goolies (ouch), and the dining side of the operation has been upped by the hiring of a former La Gavroche chef as consultant; tables that were formerly for drinking in the bar area at the front, too, now have tablecloths. But eating is not compulsory: perch at the bar on spindly metal chairs and sip champagne, preferably a half bottle of the excellent Billecart-Salmon rosé (£35), or, perhaps, sample a cocktail. Their excellent collection of liqueurs includes Gabriel Boudier crème de pêche, Lejay-Lagoute Chocolat (mixed with cappuccino to make a Wicked Chococino, £5) or Guyot cassis for a superior Kir Royale (£8.50). The wine list is strong, too, from entry level – the more than drinkable Culpeo cabernet merlot (£3.50) – to Antinori's superb and underrated 1998 Tignanello. Fine dessert wines include the Quady winery's delicious 2003 Black Muscat (£6 a glass).
Children admitted (restaurant). Restaurant.

Windsor Castle

114 Campden Hill Road, W8 7AR (7243 9551/www.windsor-castle-pub.co.uk). High Street Kensington or Notting Hill Gate tube. **Open** noon-11pm Mon-Sat; noon-10.30pm Sun. **Food served** noon-10pm daily. **Credit** AmEx, MC, V.

When this pub was built in 1835, its three separate areas – Campden, Private and Sherry Rooms (watch your head as you negotiate the tiny doorways between them) – were intended for the lower orders, the upper classes and women respectively. Today, the Windsor Castle remains an unspoilt, dark-wooded boozer with a warm, inviting feel that's helped in winter by a real fire. It's tucked away from the main Kensington tourist trail, so customers tend to be wealthy and refined locals. Beer drinkers are treated to a splendid range that includes Früli, Leffe Blonde, Deuchars IPA, Back Row (from Wiltshire's Hopback Brewery), and Adnams Broadside; there's Addlestones cider too. The kitchen serves predominantly meaty, British food a notch above pub grub, and the beer garden (with its spectacular plane tree) is the best for miles around – though on a fine day you'll be hard pressed to find a table.
Games. No piped music or jukebox. No-smoking area (noon-4pm Mon-Fri). Tables outdoors (20, garden, 4, pavement). **Map 10 A8**.

KING'S CROSS & EUSTON

Most people going for a night out in King's Cross tend to bypass the pubs and go straight to the top of eerie York Way for the cavernous clubs. However, regeneration is now in full swing and Camden's relentless clean-up operation is bearing fruit. The success of **06 St Chad's Place** is still the best indication of the gradual influx of trendy urbanites to the area, but it can only be a matter of time before the stressed-out proprietors of overcrowded nearby Islington realise there are richer pickings to be made down here.

06 St Chad's Place

6 St Chad's Place, WC1X 9HH (7278 3355/www.6stchadsplace.com). King's Cross tube/rail. **Open** 8am-11pm Mon-Fri. **Food served** 8-10am, noon-2.30pm, 6-9.30pm Mon-Fri. **Credit** MC, V.
The walk down a dark, cobbled alley seems an appropriate approach to this converted Victorian warehouse. It's one of King's Cross's few cool style café-bars, and would be good enough to hold its own anywhere in the city. The handful of comfy sofas are vastly outnumbered by rows of wooden tables, indicating that food is the priority here; breakfast is available from 8am and there's a Mediterranean-leaning gastro lunch menu that changes every week. Evening sees a daily changing selection of posh finger food and there's a suitably sophisticated wine and cocktail list to complement it. Still, for drinking there's a small, choice selection of draught beers that includes Paulaner and Peroni, and the final touch is a flawless sound system. The self-consciously trendy design succeeds very well – until you get to the toilets: whoever decided to make the women share their mirror space with the men has a very poor sense of humour.
Babies and children welcome (before 6pm). Bar available to hire. Disabled: toilet. Music (DJ 7pm Fri; free). Tables outdoors (10, pavement). TV (plasma, satellite, widescreen).

Head of Steam

1 Eversholt Street, NW1 1DN (7383 3359). Euston tube/rail. **Open** 11am-11pm Mon-Sat; noon-10.30pm Sun. **Food served** noon-2.30pm, 5-8pm Mon-Fri; noon-3pm Sat. **Credit** MC, V.

DRINKING ALOUD
ROXY BEAUJOLAIS

Who are you? I guess I'm a publican (at the Seven Stars, *see p95*) – for 20 years I've been selling real ale and cooking – but I call myself an ale wife, and I've got a bunch of merry, outrageous wenches working for me. I'm doing a Seven Stars cookbook – in between the cooking, and the pouring of beer, and the drinking, and the befuddlement...
Drinking in London: what's good about it? Quite honestly, my drinking is done in my own place – the only other place I go to is Norman's Coach & Horses in Soho (*see p81*); I managed a pub next door to him for ten years.
What's the secret of a good pub? I don't sell alcopops, and I don't really allow children. For me, it's a place for adults, it's about secrets, conversation, conviviality and outrageousness – all those things that should make something magical. There's a Max Beerbohm story called *The Golden Drugget*, in which he talks about 'the siren call of the public house'. One should come home from the inn contented (my first cookbook was called just that, *Home from the Inn Contented*), and people should rub their belly and think fondly of the establishment they've just left.
The new licensing law: good or bad? The *Daily Mail*'s going to say it will be like the 18th century, and there'll be gin lanes all over city centres – outrageous drinking, 24-hour drinking, women lying on streets with their legs apart, suckling children, people with pock marks. But people only have a certain amount of time and a certain amount of money to spend on drinking. Who's going to open at 3am? Perhaps big venues with music. But most people want to go to sleep!
Anything to declare? I refuse to refer to 'the drinks trade' – it's just running a good joint. As I say to my girls, we don't come here to be ignored, we come here to be adored!

Very smokey and very blokey: the ratio of men to women was 16:1 on our visit (though the women aren't made to feel uncomfortable). Draught lagers include Grolsch, Stella and Top Totty (now there's one you won't find in an All Bar One) from Staffordshire's Eccleshall brewery, as well as a regularly changing choice of nine cask ales such as Holts Bitter and Hopback Summer Lightning. The characterful interior successfully distracts you from the soulless 1960s office block it inhabits, with all things train-related lining the walls. These were obviously painstakingly arranged by a genuine enthusiast: who else would include a display box of cutlery and door handles from steam journeys of yesteryear? A snug carriage-shaped booth with train seating completes the railway experience. The telly shows sport, and for unenthusiastic ale-swillers who do venture in there's a surprisingly adequate choice of wines. Sunday lunches were about to be introduced as we went to press.
Babies and children welcome. Games (fruit machine, quiz machine). No piped music or jukebox. No-smoking area. Specialities (real ales). TVs (satellite).

King Charles I

55-57 Northdown Street, N1 9BL (7837 7758). King's Cross tube/rail. **Open** 11am-11pm Mon-Fri; 5-11pm Sat; 5-10.30pm Sun. **Credit** AmEx, MC, V.
This hostelry (formerly the Craic House) changed management in February 2005, but its regulars have kept coming, and make up the bulk of the crowd (though they're not unfriendly to newcomers). You may have to wait for a while to get served, but it's hard to see how they could up the speed of the service: they couldn't fit any more staff behind the tiny bar even if they wanted to. There are no meals on offer, but you can bring your own – or even order at one of the caffs over the road and have them deliver it directly to you. As well as such mainstays as Foster's, Beck's, Kronenbourg and San Miguel, seasoned drinkers can choose from two real ales on rotation – though when we visited, only Courage Best was available. An open fire adds to the general cosiness, and a jukebox covers all corners from cool to country, played at a level conducive to chatter.
Tables outdoors (5, pavement).

Ruby Lounge

33 Caledonian Road, N1 9BU (7837 9558/www.ruby.uk.com). King's Cross tube/rail. **Open** 4-11pm Mon-Wed, Sun; noon-midnight Thur; 2pm-2am Fri, Sat. **Food served** 4-8pm daily. **Credit** MC, V.
This modern-retro cocktail bar does its best to engineer a mood of intimacy, with red walls, red ceiling, red lights and who knows what red else. It succeeds, up to a point, and wall-to-wall curved seating further encourages drinkers to settle in for a prolonged session. A fabulous shell chandelier is the centrepiece over the circular bar (staff are on show from every angle, thus shy and retiring types need not apply), and there's a token selection of draught beers that includes the now obligatory wheat beer option, Hoegaarden, to supplement the cocktails; all apart from the champagne concoctions are a reasonable £5. There's a panini grill if you fancy a snack of decent size, though on busy nights this option stops early. It's the late opening hours at weekends, when DJs provide the beats with a mix of hip hop and 1980s tunes that really seal Ruby's success: there aren't many places like it, with free entry, in this corner of town.
Music (DJs 9pm Thur-Sat; free). Specialities (cocktails). Tables outdoors (3, pavement).

Smithy's

15-17 Leeke Street, WC1X 9HZ (7278 5949). King's Cross tube/rail. **Open** noon-11pm Mon-Fri. **Food served** noon-2.30pm, 6-10pm Mon-Fri. **Credit** AmEx, MC, V.
Hidden from the flashing arcades, burger shops and hotels of Euston Road, this rambling warehouse is more like Clerkenwell than King's Cross: at the end of a dark, narrow street, a small green door opens onto a vista of exposed air ducts, grey iron supports and skylights. Smithy's was formerly a blacksmith's shop, but the alarmingly undulating cobbled floor – beware if you're carrying a tray of drinks – now rings to the sound of high heels, not horseshoes; and though once popular with scruffy indie kids and a better class of tramp, it now draws high-fliers from nearby design firms. There's a fine array of beers: Nastro Azzurro and Budvar on tap, plus London Pride, Greene King IPA and the little-seen Kronenbourg 1664 Blanc. Most punters, though, stick to the above-average wines: 15 by the glass (and better whites than reds). Try the 2003 La Vigne Blanche sancerre (£6 a glass) from fine Loire producer Henri Bourgeois or 2001 Reserve chardonnay from top South African wine-maker Glen Carlou (£26.30 a bottle).
Bar available for hire (weekends).

Also in the area...

Davy's of Regent's Place Euston Tower Podium, Regent's Place, NW1 3DP (7387 6622).
O'Neill's 73-77 Euston Road, NW1 2QS (7255 9861).

KNIGHTSBRIDGE

Finding somewhere decent for a drink in this part of London is hard work. Two of its better bars, **Swag & Tails** and **Townhouse**, are all but invisible to passing trade; otherwise the tale here is one of swanky cocktail bars – like **Zuma** or newcomer **Pengelley's** – and slightly down-at-heel boozers, with shamefully little in between.

Australian

29 Milner Street, SW3 2QD (7589 6027). Sloane Square tube. **Open** noon-11pm Mon-Sat; noon-10.30pm Sun. **Food served** noon-3pm, 6-8pm Mon-Fri; noon-6pm Sat, Sun. **Credit** AmEx, DC, MC, V.
In summer the Australian gets so overgrown with ivy that you'll be hard-pressed to see the sign. Inside, the bar staff are famed for their friendliness, the clientele is heavy on Y-chromosomes, and the decor is cricket-themed. Don't be fooled by the name, as this is not particularly a hangout for Antipodeans: it got its Oz moniker after the Australian cricket team adopted the place in 1878. Nowadays, the Australian connection is not much more than Castlemaine XXXX on tap (no stuffed 'roos or 'Darwin 3,500km' signs here); otherwise, there's Adnams bitter, Tetley and Bass for the real-ale drinkers, plus an adequate wine list. The menu is meat-based, and brunch is served for most of the day.
Babies and children admitted (until 6pm). Games (darts). Quiz (7pm Thur; £1). Tables outdoors (5, pavement). TV (satellite).

Beauchamp

43-44 Beauchamp Place, SW3 1NX (7581 8886). Knightsbridge tube. **Open** 11am-11pm Mon-Sat; noon-10.30pm Sun. **Food served** noon-7pm daily. **Credit** AmEx, MC, V.

This is one of those pub-bar hybrids that isn't particularly good at being either. It's all pale wooden floors and light-coloured walls, with flat-screen TVs here and there, and it's far too bright. Turning up the music is not the way to make a place that doesn't look like a bar feel like a bar. Staff are friendly enough, but on our visit were achingly slow: a pint and a glass of wine took five minutes to pour – we'd forgotten what we'd ordered by then. Abbot Ale and Greene King IPA are on tap, there's a reasonable wine list, but nothing really stands out. Still, the crowd of regulars doesn't seem to mind any of these weaknesses: drawn by the affordable menu and comfortable leather chairs, no doubt. Nothing else seemed worth making the trip for.
Babies and children welcome. Bar available for hire. Restaurant. Tables outdoors (6, pavement).

Mandarin Bar
Mandarin Oriental Hyde Park, 66 Knightsbridge, SW1X 7LA (7235 2000/www.mandarinoriental.com). Knightsbridge tube. **Open** 11am-2am Mon-Sat; 11am-10.30pm Sun. **Food served** 11am-11.30pm daily. **Admission** £5 after 11pm daily. **Credit** AmEx, DC, MC, V.
You walk past a lot of marble in the Mandarin Oriental Hotel's lobby to reach this surprisingly enjoyable modern bar, where the staff are endlessly patient and the bar nuts are plentiful and top-notch. Jetlagged businessmen come here to get smashed on single-malt Scotch: watch them waving thick cigars and engaging in passionate conversations about hedge funds. Such is their excitement, the eavesdropping could pass for entertainment. Skip the whisky and go straight for the fruity cocktails – Mai Tais and the like – for around £11; take in the (not bad) jazz combo; and start a conversation with whoever's nearby. It's the sort of place where people talk to strangers about their investment portfolios, which is rather sweet in a way.
Disabled: toilet (in hotel). Function room. Music (jazz trio 9pm Mon-Sat, 8pm Sun). Restaurants. Specialities (cocktails).

Paxton's Head
153 Knightsbridge, SW1X 7PA (7589 6627). Knightsbridge tube. **Open** 11am-11pm Mon-Sat; noon-10.30pm Sun. **Food served** noon-3.30pm, 5.30-10.30pm Mon-Fri; noon-10.30pm Sat; noon-9pm Sun. **Credit** MC, V.
This rambling, traditional old pub is just the kind of place you want to be in on a cold winter's night. A fire blazes in the hearth and the Sloaney crowd is cheerfully buzzy, but minds its manners amid the dark wood and frosted glass. The range of beers on tap isn't bad, with options like tasty Bavarian wheat beer Paulaner and German Amstel, alongside Adnams bitter and Bombardier. The menu is another attraction, divided into 'East' and 'West': spring rolls (£3.75) and Thai dishes in the former, fish and chips (£7.50) in the latter. What's more, the bar staff are absurdly friendly. Our only complaint concerns the music, which was turned up far too loud.
Babies and children welcome (restaurant). Function room. Games (fruit machines). Music (DJs 9pm Fri; free). Restaurant (no-smoking). TV (big screen, satellite).

Pengelley's
164 Sloane Street, SW1X 9QB (7750 5000/www.pengelleys.com). Knightsbridge tube. **Open** noon-1am daily. **Food served** noon-11pm daily. **Credit** AmEx, JCB, MC, V.
An adjunct to the glamorous new Asian restaurant of the same name, this cocktail bar is a suitably slick operation. Abundances of time and money have clearly been spent on the look of this place, touting a kind of 1960s futurism; waitresses are clad in tailored, ankle-length dresses, and the lighting is intricately designed, from the tiny halogens spots that make the booze glow amber behind the bar, to the oversized Japanesey lamps that appear to float in the middle of the ceiling. The cocktail menu is compact but excellent; our Islay Old Fashioned was perfectly mixed, smoky and dark, as it should be; the Mai Tai was rather sour – not a bad cocktail, just not what we'd call a Mai Tai. The bar food comprises a delicious selection of dim sum, although we have to say that eating a bowl of soup from a below-knee-high table proved a bit of a challenge.
Disabled: lift, toilet. Restaurant. Specialities (cocktails).

Swag & Tails
10-11 Fairholt Street, SW7 1EG (7584 6926/www.swagandtails.com). Knightsbridge tube. **Open** 11am-11pm Mon-Fri. **Food served** noon-3pm, 6-10pm Mon-Fri. **Credit** AmEx, MC, V.
They couldn't hide Swag & Tails better if they tried: the staff ought to stand on Knightsbridge handing out maps to the place. Or perhaps not: on reflection, this wine-bar-cum-pub, with a good wine list and a decent choice of beer on tap (Hoegaarden, Marston's Pedigree and John Smith's) is probably the better for being something of a secret. Inside, there are potted plants on tables and a fairly standard pub menu priced for Knightsbridge affluence (£10-£15 for main courses like beer-battered haddock with fat chips). All in all, a nice enough neighbourhood drinking spot – but we'd only frequent it if we could afford to live around here.
Babies and children admitted (restaurant only). Bar available for hire. Restaurant. Tables outdoors (11, conservatory). TV.

Townhouse
31 Beauchamp Place, SW3 1NU (7589 5080/www.lab-townhouse.com). Knightsbridge tube. **Open** 4pm-midnight Mon-Fri; noon-midnight Sat; 4-11.30pm Sun. **Food served** 4-11.30pm Mon-Fri; noon-11.30pm Sat; 5-11pm Sun. **Credit** AmEx, MC, V.
From the street the Townhouse is little more than a discreet sign and a doorway – and even that is hidden behind a meaty bouncer. Get past him and you'll find a sleek, narrow bar, with a tiny seating area at the back kitted out with leather sofas (which on our visit were filled with young lovestruck couples). Aside from the rather preening crowd, the place is pleasantly chic, the bar staff (all women, all young, all beautiful) are friendly and the cocktail list is as big as a phonebook. Said list features moreish fruity concoctions (for £10) like Very Berry, which apparently had some vodka under all that sweet blueberry juice, and Cool Hand Luke, a tart mixture of lime juice, brown sugar, rum and crushed ice: delicious. We'll come again, but not without our sunglasses and Chanel.
Function room. Music (DJs 8.30pm-midnight Wed-Sat). Over-21s only. Specialities (cocktails). TVs (plasma, satellite).

Zuma
5 Raphael Street, SW7 1DL (7584 1010/www.zumarestaurant.com). Knightsbridge tube. **Open** 5.30-10.45pm Mon-Sat; 5.30-10pm Sun. **Food served** 6-10.45pm Mon-Sat; 6-10pm Sun. **Credit** AmEx, DC, MC, V.

In an anonymous back street lurks this temple to conspicuous consumption: Zuma is one of London's most upmarket sushi restaurants. No surprise, then, that it attracts such a well-dressed crowd; if you want to feel comfortable, clad yourself to match. The bar, green-hued and candlelit with granite-look walls of almost Stonehenge proportions, occupies a big square space at the front; there's limited seating but lots of leaning room. Come nine o'clock in the evening, when the restaurant's packed, the bar gets even more heaving. In keeping with the Far Eastern thrust of its adjoining dining room, there's a glorious range of ample saké and shochu options (of the former, we loved the Ozeki Daiginjo); otherwise there are cocktails like the Vanilla Espresso, which contains Polstar vodka, vanilla and espresso (£8.50).
Babies and children welcome; high chairs (restaurant). Disabled: toilet. Function rooms. Restaurant (no-smoking). Specialities (cocktails). Tables outdoors (5, pavement).

LEICESTER SQUARE & PICCADILLY CIRCUS

If Piccadilly is showing slight signs of inventive new bar culture – **Cocoon** joining **Jewel** and the admittedly poorly ageing **Atlantic** – then Leicester Square remains the same neon-lit tourist-swamped dodo it always has been. The closure of the much-loved Dive Bar leaves a huge gap, although its staff have moved on revive the potentially sassy **Blue Posts** of Rupert Street. Much else is a hangover from the gay and/or tacky drinking culture of surrounding Soho. Full marks to the **Salisbury**, then, which manages to balance tradition with good taste, tourism with a decent range of ales and a smile for the locals.

Central

Atlantic Bar & Grill

20 Glasshouse Street, W1B 5DJ (7734 4888/www.atlanticbarandgrill.com). Piccadilly Circus tube. **Open** noon-3am Mon-Sat. **Food served** noon-3pm Mon-Sat. **Credit** AmEx, DC, MC, V.
Rucksacked bods in souvenir tour T-shirts shouting 'Yeah?' into rock-ringtoned mobiles – is this the Atlantic of classy lore? The stylish ocean-liner decor of the old Regent Palace Hotel ballroom may have changed little since Dick Bradsell, godfather of mixology, turned it into the celeb hangout of the mid 1990s – but the clientele certainly has. The light vetting at the VIP ropes at street level once ensured an agreed decorum among the non-celebs simply after a quality cocktail in sexy surrondings, but these days it's token – or non-existent. Of the cocktails, though, praise is still appropriate. Classic or contemporary, £7.50-£8.50, they're both traditional and inventive, where high-end spirits slide easily with fresh fruit combinations: a Bossanova of Stoli Orange, fresh passion fruit, raspberry purée and fresh apple juices, for example, or a Chin-Chin of Chivas 12-year shaken with vanilla sugar and fresh apple juices and layered with Taittinger champagne. With such class in the glasses, isn't it time for a full makeover of Dick's delectable drinkerie a decade on?
Babies and children welcome (daytime only). Disabled: toilet. Function room. Music (DJ 10pm Tue-Sat; free). Restaurant. **Map 2 J7**.

Blue Posts

28 Rupert Street, W1D 6DJ (7437 1415). Leicester Square or Piccadilly Circus tube. **Open** 11am-11pm Mon-Sat; noon-10.30pm Sun. **Food served** noon-9pm daily. **Credit** MC, V.
A dinky little bar this, much loved by its regulars ('Hello, Carlos! The usual?'), and now augmented by the genial bar staff from the late lamented Dive Bar the other end of Gerrard Street. The small, wood and bare-brick interior is quickly filled – and don't expect Carlos to give up his seat – so standing room only is the norm; but with Hoegaarden, Leffe Blonde, London Pride and Timothy Taylor Landlord on draught, and decent Illy coffee in the machine, no one can have any grounds for complaint. If you can find a table, there's standard pub grub until mid-evening, and a couple of good malts (Talisker, Glenlivet) for late-night relaxation. The only mild – no, make it major – annoyance is the preponderance of those nodding Japanese lucky cats behind the bar. As Trini Lopez once sang, 'If I had a hammer…'
Babies and children admitted (until 6pm). Function room. No-smoking area. Tables outdoors (2, pavement). **Map 7 K7**.

Cocoon

65 Regent Street, W1B 4EA (7494 7609/www.cocoon-restaurants.com). Piccadilly Circus tube. **Open/food served** noon-3pm, 5.30-1am Mon-Fri; 5.30-1am Sat; 5.30-11pm Sun. **Credit** AmEx, MC, V.
Stéphane Dupoux's groundbreaking design at this exclusive Asian-style bar/restaurant is laid out in step with the six-stage life cycle of the butterfly, but do the cocktails make it worth the effort of getting to the pretty, winged expanse of lounge bar at the end? Of course they do. Priced between £7 and £9 (Luxury Cocktails excepted), these Classic, Contemporary or Oriental Twist varieties are flights of a fanciful imagination, high-end and handsome. A Jerry Collins features 42 Below Feijoa vodka shaken with fresh kiwi fruit and apple juice, then mixed with ginger beer; an Espresso Martini has Wyborowa Almond shaken with espresso, cognac and vanilla. As for the Oriental mixes, an Asayake comprises crushed red grapes shaken with plum wine, fresh cloudy apple juice and Bombay Sapphire, decorated with rose petals; shochu, seasonal berries and jasmine are used with abandon elsewhere. The Luxury items are absurdly decadent (frozen Johnnie Walker Gold? Smirnoff Penka and beetroot sangrita?), though most are only in the £12 range. There are fine choices of saké and shochu, and dim sum bar food, too.
Babies and children welcome. Disabled: toilet. Function room. No-smoking (restaurant). Restaurant. **Map 2 J7**.

Cork & Bottle

44-46 Cranbourn Street, WC2H 7AN (7734 7807). Leicester Square tube. **Open/food served** 11am-11.30pm Mon-Sat; noon-10.30pm Sun. **Credit** AmEx, DC, JCB, MC, V.
This old-fashioned wine bar is a world away from its neighbours – sex shop and purveyor of kebabs. Beyond a discreet glass door, a narrow spiral staircase winds down into two small rooms, heavily decorated with art nouveau posters for Moët & Chandon and Mumm. It's a gorgeous space: small tables sit on a battered red tiled floor and an alcove dives under the street, into a blue-painted space for six. Owner Don Hewitson loves his wine, and has compiled a list that has top choices from the Rhône, California and New Zealand. Te Mata's 2002 sauvignon blanc from New Zealand is a must-try at £29.50 a bottle, and wines by the glass – such as the 2003 Domaine L'Aulnay (£4.95), from

St Nicholas de Bourgueil – have improved since Hewitson installed a Verre de Vin preservation system. Drink with Hemingway's favourite, a burger that combines beef, pork and lamb, with chips (£10.95).
Babies and children welcome. No-smoking area (daytime). Restaurant. Specialities (wine). **Map 7 K7**.

De Hems

11 Macclesfield Street, W1D 5BW (7437 2494). Leicester Square tube. **Open/food served** noon-midnight Mon-Sat; noon-10.30pm Sun. **Credit** AmEx, DC, JCB, MC, V.
Nearly every bar these days boasts at least two Lowland beers on tap and probably half a fridge of bottled options – some (like the Lowlander, *see p35*, or L'Auberge, *see p103*) even specialise in it. What they don't have is century-old Dutch pub De Hems' history. Once a refuge for homesick Dutch sailors, the Macclesfield was taken over by a Dutchman by the name of De Hems and was a rallying point for the Dutch Resistance during the World War II. Today, this spruced-up, dark wood bar boasts towering beer pumps of Amstel and Oranjeboom, Früli and Grolsch, and three types of Leffe; rare Orval and Rochefort hide among the bottles of Chimay and Vedett. The Dutch range of bar food features an uitsmijter of poached eggs, cheese and ham, frikandellen sausages, bitterballen and sambalaletjes. Dutch TV plays in the background, while an Ajax-themed staircase leads to an upstairs bar mainly used for private functions.
Disabled: toilet. Function room. Games (fruit machine). Music (DJ 8pm Sat; free). Tables outdoors (2, pavement). TVs (big screen, plasma, satellite). **Map 7 K6**.

International

116 St Martin's Lane, WC2N 4BF (7655 9810/www.theinternational.co.uk). Leicester Square tube/Charing Cross tube/rail. **Open/food served** noon-2am Mon-Sat; noon-10.30pm Sun. **Credit** AmEx, DC, MC, V.
Set between the National Portrait Gallery, the English National Opera and Trafalgar Square, the International could only be a class act. In a stylish interior of cool maroon and brown furnishings and glitzy silver and mirrors, a premium selection of drinks and foodstuffs awaits. An Asian influence pervades both, whether in the sharing platters (£13.95-£14.95) of Thai snacks and seafood, or in the cocktails (£6.95-£7.95) categorised by champagne or spirit base. A Katana comprises chilled saké shaken with jasmine tea, fresh ginger and Orange Curaçao; an Absolutely Asian Mandarin is vodka mixed with fresh watermelon, topped with champagne. A satisfying wine selection starts off with a humble Italian Casada of each colour at £3.50, £6.25 and £13 according to glass size or bottle, and the smart, friendly bar staff do justice to the shaking and the surroundings.
Babies and children admitted (restaurant). Disabled: toilet. Function room. Restaurant. **Map 2 L7**.

Jewel

4-6 Glasshouse Street, W1B 5DQ (7439 4990/www.jewelbarlondon.co.uk). Piccadilly Circus tube. **Open/food served** 4pm-1am Mon-Sat; 6-12.30am Sun. **Credit** AmEx, MC, V.
The glitzy Jewel is a convoluted story. It burst dramatically on to a bland Piccadilly bar scene in the autumn of 2002, and was doing a tidy business – attracting a pretty clientele with themed cocktails, starburst chandeliers, flickering candlelight and much crystal – when the management took over the Spot club/bar in Covent Garden's

Julie's Wine Bar. *See p49.*

Maiden Lane. Imposing the same interior combination of twinkling Jewel bar in one half and Moorish-styled Bar Blanca in the other, they then sold their original Piccadilly site (you can see it from the front window here). Thus there are, for the interregnum, two Jewels of similar make-up within two tube stops of each other. In this one, the mood is low-lit and cool. Cocktails at £7 (categorised Ruby, Garnet, Pearl and so on, well mixed with flavoured Absoluts and vintage Havana Clubs) are sipped by well-heeled romantic couples and upmarket, cosmopolitan tourists. The food (lamb koftas, chicken satays, £7) is equally neat, the service keen to impress.
Disabled: toilet. Function rooms. Music (DJs 8pm Wed-Sat; bands 9pm Mon-Thur, Sun). **Map 2 J7**.

Ku Bar

75 Charing Cross Road, WC2H 0NE (7437 4303/ www.ku-bar.co.uk). Leicester Square tube. **Open** 1-11pm Mon-Sat; 1-10.30pm Sun. **Happy hour** all day Mon-Fri, Sun; 1-9pm Sat (cocktails). **No credit cards**.
Where boys like to party before going on to GAY round the corner. Ku, set along a redbrick arcade of tacky tourist shops and 24-hour grocer's opposite the second-hand book trade of the Charing Cross Road, has always had its tongue firmly in its... cheek when it comes to entertainment. Kitsch pop icons get pride of place in the downstairs bar, with posters of Take That and framed memorabilia of Boyzone and Celine Dion overshadowing the disco ball and glitter mural. The bar's awash with gaudily coloured alcopops, neat pyramids of After Shock, Archer's, WKD, and £1 shooters such as Cocksucking Cowboy of butterscotch schnapps and Bailey's. Beers comprise Stella, Sol and Grolsch by the bottle. Upstairs is a little more intimate, and staff are of that cheeky, naughty ilk: just looking for a slap – or, possibly, a tickle.
Babies and children welcome (before 9pm). Bar available for hire. Jukebox. Specialities (cocktails). Tables outdoors (12, pavement). TV (satellite). **Map 7 K6**.

Salisbury

90 St Martin's Lane, WC2N 4AP (7836 5863). Leicester Square tube. **Open** 11am-11pm Mon-Fri; noon-11pm Sat; noon-10.30pm Sun. **Food served** noon-9pm daily. **Credit** AmEx, DC, MC, V.
The venerable Salisbury is not just a glittering temple to Victorian interior pub design, it's a first-rate, well cared-for boozer with a fine range of ales and a quality kitchen. The history, though, is unavoidable. As the Coach and Horses, it staged fights by famed bare-knuckle fighter Ben Caunt, the Torkard Giant, who lost two children here in a pub fire. Renamed Ben Caunt's Head, then the Salisbury after the Prime Minister who leased it, it was transformed into a grand public house of carved mahogany, etched glass, beautifully curved banquettes and art nouveau lamps. Kept pristine by Jas and his staff, it offers six ales on tap (St Austell Tribute, Marston's Resolution, Courage Director's and Bombardier among them), draught Beck's and bottled Budvar for lager drinkers, plus superior pub food such as Chablis chicken, and Brie and Broccoli Bake famous face mingle amid the gleaming ostentation.
Games (chess). No-smoking area. Specialities (real ales). Tables outdoors (8, pavement). **Map 2 L7**.

Sports Café

80 Haymarket, SW1Y 4TE (7839 8300/www.thesports café.com). Piccadilly Circus tube. **Open** noon-3am Mon-Wed, Fri; noon-2am Thur; 11am-3am Sat; noon-12.30am Sun. **Food served** noon-midnight daily. **Admission** £5 after 11pm Mon, Tue, Fri, Sat; £3 after 11pm Wed, Thur. **Credit** AmEx, DC, JCB, MC, V.
London's most showy sports bar, slap-bang on Haymarket is of a type you see everywhere – in fact, it has a mini chain stretching from Birmingham to Glasgow. This particular two-storey barn is filled with sporting memorabilia, from the baseball door handles to the hanging racing car, the American Football helmets over the bar counter and almost every inch of wall space – which is a lot of wall space – mounted with a signed shirt, bat, club or glove. It has '125 TV monitors, nine plasma screens and four superscreens' – but not one quality beer. Although the menu plays on the play theme – End Zone, Seconds Out and Golden Goal among the cocktails (£4.65) and shooters – it falls into the sports bar trap of appealing to the lowest common denominator. To be fair, the new lounge zones are a boon, kids are well catered for, weekday lunches (spaghetti bolognese, burgers) are under a fiver, and the pool lounge is a winner.
Children admitted (until 6pm, dining only). Disabled: toilet. Music (DJs 10pm Mon, Tue, Fri, Sat). Restaurant. TVs (plasma, satellite, widescreen). **Map 2 K7**.

Waxy O'Connors

14-16 Rupert Street, W1D 6DD (7287 0255/www.waxy oconnors.co.uk). Leicester Square or Piccadilly Circus tube. **Open** noon-11pm Mon-Sat; noon-10.30pm Sun. **Food served** noon-10pm daily. **Credit** AmEx, DC, JCB, MC, V.
Six floors, four bars, a confession box, a wall of alchemists' drawers, a bloody big beech tree, any amount of Oirish toot – road signs, plaques, quotations – and a heaving mass of humanity keen to see the rugby or get laid and ideally both – such is the vast, over-the-top Waxy O'Connor's, whose premises seem to stretch over and under half of Soho. To keep punters merry and mingling there are Caffrey's, Murphy's, Guinness, Beamish and Magners cider on tap, plus Bushmills and Jamesons of various vintages. The bar food and main meals in the on-site Dargle restaurant are quality Irish fare, whether it's a chargrilled steak sandwich (£5.95) with your pint or a plate bearing a rack of Irish lamb (£12.95) or half-a-dozen Rossmore oysters (£7.25).
Function rooms. Music (Musicians 8.30pm Mon, Tue, Sun; free). Restaurant. TV's (big screen, satellite). **Map 7 K7**.

Also in the area...

All Bar One 84 Cambridge Circus, WC2H 8AA (7379 8311); 48 Leicester Square, WC2H 7LT (7747 9921).
Champagne Charlies (Davy's) 17 The Arches, off Villiers Street, WC2N 4NN (7930 7737).
Hog's Head 5 Lisle Street, WC2H 7BG (7437 3335).
Montagu Pyke (JD Wetherspoon) 105-107 Charing Cross Road, WC2H 0BP (7287 6039).
Moon Under Water (JD Wetherspoon) 28 Leicester Square, WC2H 7LE (7839 2837).
O'Neill's 166-170 Shaftesbury Avenue, WC2H 8JB (7379 3735).
Pitcher & Piano 40-42 William IV Street, WC2N 4DE (7240 6180).
Slug & Lettuce 14 Upper St Martin's Lane, WC2N 9DL (7379 4880).
Tappit Hen (Davy's) 5 William IV Street, WC2N 4DW (7836 9839).

MARYLEBONE

Normally known for its foodie run of speciality delicatessen and wine shops, this area – defined for the purposes of this guide by Regent Street, Edgware Road, Oxford Street and Euston Road – also boasts some attractive pubs and bars. The former, like the **Barley Mow**, are mostly homely institutions that have stood for decades, daily homes to a following of devout regulars; the latter, such as **Low Life**, cash in on Marylebone's influx of the smart and rich; they're doing a pretty good job of it, too.

Barley Mow

8 Dorset Street, W1U 6QW (7935 7318). Baker Street tube. **Open** 11am-11pm Mon-Sat; noon-6pm Sun. **Food served** noon-3pm daily. **Credit** AmEx, DC, MC, V.

The square bar inside the Barley Mow yields an interesting surprise. Two sides by the entrance cater for the everyday punter, but the other two? The pub has retained the class-divide partitioning of days gone by. Latchable booths house benches for small groups, and a tabled area at the back has a whole stretch of bar to itself (useful for a party group). We love it, especially the booth full of such raucous drink that the whole cabinet rattled to their jokes and hysterics. The Mow also has a wide choice of ales: Adnams Bitter, Bombardier, Tetley's, Greene King IPA, Shepherd Neame Spitfire, Marston's Pedigree. Outside, the building is quite pretty, and a sign that can be read from roads away reveals it was established in 1791. The world may have changed, but this pub clings with a cheeky smile to the gentry-peasant divide of yesteryear.

Babies and children welcome (lunch only). Games (fruit machine, quiz machine). Tables outdoors (3, pavement). TV (satellite).

Beehive

7 Homer Street, W1H 4NU (7262 6581). Edgware Road or Marylebone tube. **Open** noon-11pm Mon-Sat; noon-10.30pm Sun. **Food served** noon-3pm Mon-Fri. **Credit** AmEx, MC, V.

In last year's guide, we asked: 'Could this be the friendliest pub in London?' In previous editions, too, we've praised the welcome provided by regulars. This time, as strangers to what is evidently a tight-knit crowd, we received much attention, though not entirely friendly at first. 'This is football,' said one barfly, pointing at the screen. 'English football.' A quick confession of our affiliation to a London club smoothed progress to the bar somewhat – but many newcomers would have turned tail and legged it at once. Not a pub for the timid, then, but the Beehive is charming enough in its way. Standard-issue beers (plus London Pride) are on draught, the telly is treated like a fellow customer, and everyone gets a goodbye from the regulars. Friendly, but prepare to be scrutinised.

Tables outdoors (4, pavement). TV (satellite).

Carpenters Arms

12 Seymour Place, W1H 7NE (7723 1050). Marble Arch tube. **Open** 11am-11pm Mon-Sat; noon-10.30pm Sun. **Food served** noon-9pm daily. **Credit** AmEx, MC, V.

'Pint of Pigswill, please' was the first phrase we heard upon entering the Carp'. A few such cheerily named real ales (the one in question, from Wiltshire's Stonehenge brewery) help raise this pleasant corner pub a notch above the competition. On the whole, though, there's nothing extraordinary about the place. It's a home for local workers and young 'uns necking a quickie before a night on the tiles. If you're in the area, though, this is a decent bet, with plenty of seats around the horseshoe bar (many on a raised platform, once a stage, by a large bank of windows), and a tabled area tucked away at the back. Sport on the telly is a mainstay, and informs much of the atmosphere: not a bad thing when Arsenal are winning, as most of the singing punters seem to support them.

Babies and children admitted (until 7.30pm). Function room. Games (darts, fruit machines). Tables outdoors (3, pavement). TV (satellite).

Chapel

48 Chapel Street, NW1 5DP (7402 9220). Edgware Road tube. **Open** noon-11pm Mon-Sat; noon-10.30pm Sun. **Food served** noon-2.30pm, 7-10pm daily. **Credit** AmEx, DC, MC, V.

A chap at the bar was complaining about the poor service here as we approached. Perhaps this is something the Chapel should work on, as we've heard whispers of staff causing affront before. Nevertheless, we found them friendly, if abrupt, while we enjoyed a bottle at the bar from the broad wine list. This place won a Time Out food award a few years back, yet has stumbled a bit since. The venue is still (just) trendy enough to attract a decent-sized crowd, and it benefits from the location near Edgware Road station. Seating is all very low and squidgy: perfect, we'd imagine, for a relaxing Sunday with the papers. The food is still very good, too – all large white plates and gastro-pub flourishes – and seemed to be pleasing the local suits as they loosened their ties after a day at the grind.

Babies and children admitted. Function room. Tables outdoors (12, garden; 4, pavement). TV (big screen).

Dover Castle

43 Weymouth Mews, W1G 7EQ (7580 4412). Oxford Circus or Regent's Park tube. **Open** 11.30am-11pm Mon-Fri; 12.30-11pm Sat. **Food served** noon-3pm, 6-9pm Mon-Thur; noon-3pm Fri. **Credit** MC, V.

There's nothing revolutionary here, but you will find the odd quirk at this Sam Smith's pub. Beer's cheap for a start, including the tasty Ayingerbräu lager. Furnishings are cosy and old fashioned (plenty of sepia prints on the walls). The pub also has the advantage of being just a short walk from Oxford Street (up Portland Place), yet its tucked-away location in a corner of a residential hideaway means that traffic outside is rare. However, expect to draw some attention if you aren't a regular; a gaggle of veterans at the bar spoiled our visit somewhat, launching a discussion about us while we ordered. Perhaps this was an aberration, as the Dover Castle draws an eclectic mix: casual thirtysomethings chatting in groups and posh locals on their way back from a shopping trip, on our visit. We didn't feel welcome, though, and left after one drink.

Babies and children admitted (lunchtime only; separate room). Games (quiz machine). No piped music or jukebox. Tables outdoors (6, pavement).

Duke of Wellington

94A Crawford Street, W1H 2HQ (7224 9435). Baker Street or Marylebone tube. **Open** 11am-11pm Mon-Sat; noon-10.30pm Sun. **Food served** noon-3pm, 6-9pm Mon-Fri; 12.30-4pm Sun. **Credit** AmEx, MC, V.

Don't be confused by the bizarre road numbering – this broad-fronted red pub, halfway down Crawford Street, is hard to miss if you hunt for it. Old junk (sorry, antiques)

Cocoon. *See p56.*

in the window sets the tone: the Duke is a cheeky, cluttered pub that tries to be a little different. Its heart is in the right place, but its interior is a bit of a mess: exhibits A and B, the soiled red carpet and worn chairs that could do with a good scrub. Some would call the gentle grubbiness cosy, others plain grubby; we think the former. The Duke himself plays a role in the decor: his bust sits in the window, and a signpost inside points to the locations of all the battles he won. Like old Wellington himself, this pub is battle-hardened and all the better for it; there's London Pride and Adnams on tap, too.
Tables outdoors (4, pavement). TV.

Dusk

79 Marylebone High Street, W1U 5JZ (7486 5746). Baker Street tube. **Open** 10am-11pm Mon-Sat; 10am-10.30pm Sun. **Food served** 10am-10.30pm Mon-Sat; 10am-10pm Sun. **Credit** MC, V.
A big, corner building; an open, well-windowed space; three decent wheat beers on tap – all are positives for Dusk. Why, then, did we come away feeling so flat? Possibly because of the staggering lack of imagination. Dusk has all the prerequisites of a popular London bar: better-than-IKEA furniture; single-syllable name that vaguely alludes to a coolness within; black-clad, black-hearted staff; car showroom spotlights. But it's missing that all-important ingredient: character. Although the bar is generally agreed to be an improvement on the Rising Sun pub it replaced, we wish the owners had pushed a bit further with their prime space – at least one quirk or idiosyncrasy would have been nice. A broad wine selection: yes. Decent food menu: yes. But a reason to come here, rather than to London's many, many similar venues: sorry, no. At least Low Life down the road (*see below*) takes a few risks.
Disabled: toilet. Specialities (imported beers). Tables outdoors (6, pavement).

Golden Eagle

59 Marylebone Lane, W1U 2NY (7935 3228). Bond Street tube. **Open** 11am-11pm Mon-Sat; noon-7pm Sun. **Food served** noon-2.30pm Mon-Fri. **No credit cards**.
An attractive corner pub, the Golden Eagle has a pleasingly Dickensian exterior (trained ivy and smoky windows) – yet the inside doesn't quite measure up. It's pleasant enough, sure, but the blue carpet and matching booths hardly had us swooning with delight. Real ale buffs should be pleased with the rotating selection (Tribute from St Austell was a recent choice), and music lovers are catered for, too: instead of the usual pop play-list, the Eagle has its own pianist. Mr Fingers plays blues and oldie classics every Tuesday, Thursday and Friday. These nights are justifiably popular, and can be fantastic fun. Bar staff are friendly, and regulars are quite passionate about the pub: one couldn't wait to expound on how much he loved the place for being 'real'. After a few tunes, we were beginning to see his point.
Games (fruit machines). Music (pianist 8.30pm Tue, Thur, Fri; free). TV.

Low Life

34A Paddington Street, W1U 4HG (7935 1272). Baker Street tube. **Open** 5-11pm Mon-Sat; 3-10.30pm Sun. **Food served** 5-10.30pm Mon-Sat; 4-10pm Sun. **Credit** AmEx, MC, V.
This fuzzy, bill-postered underground bar is popular, and it has an appealing 'we don't fit, we don't care' attitude. Menus have a comic-book theme, a DJ spins inexpertly at a booth in the corner, beer comes in bottles only (Red Stripe, what else?) and the cocktails are served sloppily in chunky glasses. This might sound like criticism, but it isn't. Low Life tries hard not to try hard, but the laid-back atmosphere works a treat. The bar will certainly be a little too studenty for some (though not for the crowd on our visit, nearly half of whom hadn't seen the inside of a hall of residence for a decade), but there are cave-like booths along one side to give groups some privacy. Sceptics should hold their nose and dive in – this could prove a nice surprise.
Bar available for hire. Games (retro games). Music (open decks 5-11pm Mon; DJs 7.30pm Wed-Sun). Specialities (cocktails). Tables outdoors (4, pavement).

Marylebone Bar & Kitchen

74-76 York Street, W1H 1QN (7262 1513). Marylebone tube/rail. **Open** 11am-11pm Mon-Sat; noon-10.30pm Sun. **Food served** noon-10pm daily. **Credit** MC, V.
Someone here likes red: there's a red sign, red lamps, red walls, red lacquered ceiling, even a red cocktail – it's like Valentine's Day all year round. This might sound like a nightmare scenario for some, but the decor makes for a cosy, intimate space; through the dimmed lights you're barely aware of the next table. Not that groups are excluded: they're well catered for on the long tables in the middle, and can also be accommodated in the cheeky hideaway of sofas and lamps in the far corner. White beers like Affligem are served from the bar, and we can vouch for the long and short cocktails from the extensive list; we chose an interesting Espresso Martini (just the right bitter-sweet balance) and a fruity number called Sex in the Marylebone. If all this romance gets too much, try the table football.
Games (table football). Tables outdoors (4, pavement). TV.

Mason's Arms

51 Upper Berkeley Street, W1H 7QW (7723 2131). Marble Arch tube. **Open** noon-11pm Mon-Sat; noon-10.30pm Sun. **Food served** noon-2.30pm, 6-9pm Mon-Thur, Sun; noon-3pm, 6-9pm Fri, Sat. **Credit** MC, V.
This Hall & Woodhouse boozer is easily missed on the Portman-to-Edgware path, but we think it would be a travesty to overlook such a welcoming pub. It's a compact space, although there's overflow seating upstairs. The barman was helpful and the young, local crowd at the wooden central bar wasted no time in inviting us over for a drink. Badger Best and Tanglefoot are the real ale options, though there are various draught lagers including Stella. The interior has a hearty glow: attributable in part to two open fireplaces, but also to the mellow, feel-good sounds. A notice on the exterior proclaims that the Mason's cellars were once home to a motley crew awaiting execution. Their shackles are still on display and, if you believe what you read, their souls have never left. Someone should tell them to stop hanging out in the basement: it's far more fun upstairs.
Babies and children admitted (separate area). Games (fruit machine). Tables outdoors (5, pavement). TV (digital).

Momo at Selfridges

2nd Floor, Selfridges, 400 Oxford Street, W1C 1JT (7318 3620/www.momoresto.com). Bond Street tube. **Open** 10am-8pm Mon-Wed, Fri, Sat; 10am-9pm Thur; 11.30am-6pm Sun. **Food served** 10am-7pm Mon-Wed, Fri, Sat; 10am-8pm Thur; 11.30am-5pm Sun. **Credit** AmEx, DC, JCB, MC, V.

A destination venue par excellence, Momo Selfridges is the latest concept from the celebrated team who brought Sketch and Momo Heddon Street to town. The fashionable French staff compete with the beauty of the Moorish decor – teak screens, and earthy, carved cedarwood tables with mother-of-pearl mosaics – that provides an inspired visual contrast to the ultra-contemporary Marni backdrop. The 'Tea Room' holds an elaborately carved marble-topped bar, and all the seating – from the low chairs to the high stools – is covered in cross-stitched horsehair. The real pièce de résistance, though, is the glass 'tent' that doubles as a smoking room: a cube of tranquillity whose North African chill-out sounds and exotic furnishings temporarily transport you to somewhere a long, long distance from a West End department store. The art deco lighting flatters the narghile-smoking, cocktail-sipping cosmopolitans who recline in this atmospheric space.
Babies and children welcome; children's menu. Disabled: toilet. No smoking. Restaurant. Specialities (cocktails).

O'Conor Don

88 Marylebone Lane, W1U 2PY (7935 9311/www.oconordon.com). Bond Street tube. Bar **Open** noon-11pm Mon-Wed, Fri; noon-1am Thur. **Food served** noon-3pm, 5.15-10pm Mon-Fri. **Credit** AmEx, MC, V.
Named after the head of the most ancient royal Irish house, the O'Conor Don is one of the most attractive Irish theme pubs we've seen. Alpha males predominate, mainly doctors and legal eagles; table service, on the other hand, is all-blonde, all-beautiful, all mini-skirted – which begs that chicken and egg question. The wine list is extensive (there are over 40 bottles to choose from, although, when we visited, most punters plumped for Guinness) and the food menu is a global collection of dishes augmented by more traditional cooking, including Irish mussels meunière, open soda bread sandwiches, and Guinness rarebit. The decor is divine; among the nationalistic tributes you'll see a magnificent, marble-topped mahogany bar and a selection of vintage clocks gracing the walls.
Function room. Music (DJ, 10pm Thur). Restaurant available for hire; all areas available for hire Sat, Sun. TV (digital, plasma).

Queen's Head & Artichoke

30-32 Albany Street, NW1 4EA (7916 6206/www.theartichoke.net). Great Portland Street or Regent's Park tube. **Open** 11am-11pm Mon-Sat; noon-10.30pm Sun. **Food served** 12.30-3pm, 6.30-10.15pm Mon-Fri; 6.30-10.15pm Sat; 12.30-10.15pm Sun. **Credit** AmEx, MC, V.
The appeal of this beautifully maintained, corner gastropub is obvious as soon as you enter. There are fresh lilies in on the bar (and, less immediately obvious, in the toilets); other greenery includes potted plants, cacti, and huge evergreens outside. A long tapas menu (dishes start from just £2) is available in the bar, while the upstairs restaurant offers heartier meals: crab, leek and ginger tart followed by a Scottish rib-eye, for instance. Customers are young, funky and look as though they might do something important within the legal, design and media industries; they packed this place full on the night we visited. Wicker stools, oak tables and chairs and battered leather sofas provide the furniture. The drinks list includes over 50 wines (as well as mulled wine and prosecco by the glass), plus lagers (Grolsch, Löwenbraü) and real ales (Ushers, Pedigree) on draught. The background music's good, too.
Babies and children admitted. Function room. Restaurant. Tables outdoors (6, garden; 6, pavement).

William Wallace

33 Aybrook Street, W1U 4AP (7487 4937). Baker Street or Bond Street tube. **Open** noon-11pm Mon-Sat; noon-10.30pm Sun. **Food served** noon-3pm, 6-10pm Mon-Fri; 5-10pm Sat. **Happy hour** 5-7pm Mon-Fri. **Credit** AmEx, DC, MC, V.
Save for an incongruous collection of sporting pictures and photos of Mel Gibson circa *Braveheart*, there's not much by way of decoration at the Scottish-themed Wallace, but the high proportion of pretty people provides some compensation. The L-shaped room has a welcoming saloon feel, with high ceilings and old-fashioned hanging lights; the walls, floor and bar are constructed in attractively contrasting shades of tawny wood. It's the atmosphere, though, that really grabs you. Staff and customers are friendly, and there's a great choice of tunes on the jukebox. Deuchars IPA is the only real ale, but there's also the usual line-up of lagers, plus Guinness and Strongbow. There's also a good-value Thai menu and a nightly happy hour.
Function room. Games (fruit machine). Tables outdoors (4, pavement). TVs (big screen, satellite).

Windsor Castle

29 Crawford Place, W1H 4LJ (7723 4371). Edgware Road tube. **Open** 11am-11pm Mon-Sat; noon-10.30pm Sun. **Food served** noon-3pm, 6-10pm Mon-Fri. **Credit** MC, V.
An eccentric bone china collection lines the windows, and a glass-encased sentry guards the door outside. Inside, you'll find open fireplaces, a buzzy atmosphere and a pleasingly upbeat crowd spanning the generations. Among the curiosities lining the walls is a homage to the 'Handlebar Club' – a Pythonesque society formed in the 19th century for gentlemen with luxuriant moustaches (the club continues to this day – members meet here on the first Friday of each month). The eclectic decorations also include a lovely grandfather clock, Victorian arcade-style fortune-telling machines, a 'House of Stuart' table and 'reserved' brass date and name plates fixed to the bar for last century's patrons. The beers on tap are relatively mundane, running from Stella, Caffreys, Guinness and Carling to (the one exception) Adnams Best. There's also decent Thai food.
Babies and children welcome. Function room. No-smoking area. Restaurant. Tables outdoors (5, pavement).

Also in the area...

All Bar One 289-293 Regent Street, W1B 2HJ (7467 9901).
Davy's at Basement 92 92 Wigmore Street, W1U 3RE (7224 0170).
Dock Blida (Davy's) 50-54 Blandford Street, W1H 3HD (7486 3590).
Marylebone Tup 93 Marylebone High Street, W1M 3DE (7935 4373).

MAYFAIR

Mayfair is one of London's most monied areas, but with a hard swallow and a careful-hazy squint at the menu, you can drink at some rather swanky bars without too much bank-breaking heartache. The **Mô Tea Room** and the **Zeta Bar**, in particular, are very welcoming to all; and if you do decide to splash some cash, there are few better places than the fab **43** and **Hush**.

American Bar

Connaught Hotel, 16 Carlos Place, W1K 2AL (7499 7070/www.savoygroup.com). Bond Street or Green Park tube. **Open** 5.30-11pm Mon-Sat. **Credit** AmEx, DC, MC, V.

The Connaught Bar at the front of the hotel (turn right upon entering) is more popular, but the American Bar (walk past reception and turn left) is the spot you want. While other hotel bolt-holes wear their sophistication as a badge of honour, this old-fashioned, atmospheric and peaceful bar is simply a lovely, classic room in which to have a lovely, classic drink. Sure, it's upmarket, but if you treat the place with the respect it deserves – look smart, choose a classic cocktail (there's no menu), keep your voice down – then respect will be yours in return. The new barman mentioned a few adjustments he'd like to make to the wood-panelled, sofa-lined room, but the changes, if they occur, sound more like tweaks than major alterations. Of course, the most troubling change would be if it were suddenly to become popular; please, then, keep it to yourself.

Dress: smart casual.

Audley

41-43 Mount Street, W1K 2RX (7499 1843). Bond Street or Green Park tube. **Open** 11am-11pm Mon-Sat; noon-10.30pm Sun. **Food served** 11am-9.30pm Mon-Sat; noon-9pm Sun. **Credit** AmEx, DC, MC, V.

The grandest pub in Mayfair is also its largest. The Audley looks imposing from the outside; but for once, the exterior is matched by the interior, a handsome, unspoilt and only slightly self-conscious evocation of a classic British taproom. The light that glows from the three chandeliers is cheapened by the blinking fruit machine – but, well, that's progress for you. Things get a little more troublesome when you order: while the list of wines served by the glass and ales served by the pint (five, including Young's and London Pride) is impressive, the latter could be better kept, and more or less every dish on the food menu costs 50 per cent more than it should.

Babies and children admitted (until 6pm). Function rooms. Games (fruit machines). Tables outdoors (5, pavement). TV.

Cecconi's

5A Burlington Gardens, W1S 3EW (7434 1500/ www.cecconis.co.uk). Green Park or Piccadilly Circus tube. **Open** 11am-11pm Mon-Sat; 7-10.30pm Sun. **Food served** 8-11am, noon-3pm, 6.30-11pm Mon-Fri; 10am-4pm, 6.30-11pm Sat; 10am-4pm, 6.30-10.30pm Sun. **Credit** AmEx, DC, JCB, MC, V.

Its tables lined uniformly against windows around the bar, Cecconi's is very much a restaurant first, cocktail bar second – though said tables provide great opportunities for people-watching, both inside and outside. Cocktails are pricey (some nudging a tenner), but are crafted with enough care to make the expense seem bearable. Of particular interest was a cheeky little Martini made with strawberries and balsamic vinegar: very tasty, and not the sharpish shock you might expect. The prevailing aroma of high-end food was appealing, though unwelcome if you haven't the pocket-power to afford it in the dining room across the bar – and be prepared to play second fiddle to the high-rollers knocking back cocktails before sitting down to their meal. To all appearances a classy operation, then – but it only takes the sneer of a waiter to make Cecconi's seem quite the opposite.

Babies and children welcome; high chairs. Disabled: toilet. Restaurant. Specialities (cocktails). **Map 1 J7**.

Claridge's Bar

Claridge's Hotel, 49 Brook Street, W1K 4HR (7629 8860). Bond Street tube. **Open** noon-1am Mon-Sat; 4pm-midnight Sun. **Food served** noon-11pm daily. **Credit** AmEx, DC, MC, V.

Described by the Baedeker guidebook in 1860 as 'the first hotel in London', Claridge's still offers the last word in Mayfair elegance; on our way in, we found two employees conducting a terrifyingly formal conversation about the location of luggage belonging to 'Prince Valentine'. Sadly, the sophistication of the hotel, the impeccably stylish design of its bar and the delicious cocktails served within it (try the bourbon-rich Kentucky Highroller in winter, or the airier Davies Street in summer) are not matched by the ghastly people who drink in it. On one table, a cluster of PRs, draining bottle after bottle of chardonnay. On another, the obligatory beer-suckers, blithely forking out £4.50 for a Peroni. Everywhere, braying men sucking on bargepole cigars. Above the din of conversation could be heard the unmistakeable tones of Jamie Cullum, appropriate in so many ways. Cheekily, your bill will include a tip, but your credit card chit will have a gap left for a gratuity. Oh, and check your bank statements afterwards. We were charged twice.

Disabled: toilet. Function room. Restaurant.

Coach & Horses

5 Bruton Street, W1J 6PT (7629 4123). Bond Street, Green Park or Oxford Circus tube. **Open** 11am-11pm Mon-Fri; 11am-8pm Sat. **Food served** 11am-9.30pm Mon-Fri; 11.30am-6pm Sat. **Credit** AmEx, DC, MC, V.

It almost gets away with it from a distance. But upon entering this pokey little corner pub, it quickly becomes clear that the Tudor is mock. It's a bit of a mess, this place, unsure of what it wants to be and how to go about being it. On the one hand is the olde-worlde exterior and the fine range of ales, which included the rarely seen Black Sheep on our visit. On the other, regrettably, are some rather awful red banquettes, ordinary food, too-bright lights, and both fruit and quiz machines in a room that's not really big enough to hold either. Still, approach without high expectations and you might be pleasantly surprised.

Babies and children admitted (restaurant). Games (fruit machines, quiz machines). No-smoking (restaurant). Restaurant (available for hire). TV.

Dorchester Bar

The Dorchester, 53 Park Lane, W1K 1QA (7629 8888/ www.dorchesterhotel.com). Hyde Park Corner tube. **Open** 11am-11pm Mon-Sat; noon-10.30pm Sun. **Food served** noon-11pm Mon-Sat; noon-10.30pm Sun. **Credit** AmEx, DC, JCB, MC, V.

A grand illusion of a long-vanished London (it's housed in one of the swankiest hotels in the world), or a simpering tilt at glamour that lacks the style to match it? The bar at the Dorchester is a little bit of both, but we like it regardless. The problems are plain and painfully clear: the airport muzak that bleeds dry the ears between jazz-inflected sets from the house pianist; the tacky blue neon that stripes the stairs; the relentless ostentation of the room itself, all gold and glass and glory-be (good grief, just look at the grand piano). And yet it stays on just the right side of the line that separates 'sophisticated' from 'Liberace', thanks largely to deferential wait staff and some impeccably mixed cocktails. Good for a treat, then.

Disabled: toilet. Music (pianist 7-11pm Tue-Wed, 7-10.30pm Sun; jazz band 7-11pm Thur-Sat). Restaurant. Specialities (cocktails).

Claridge's Bar. See p64.

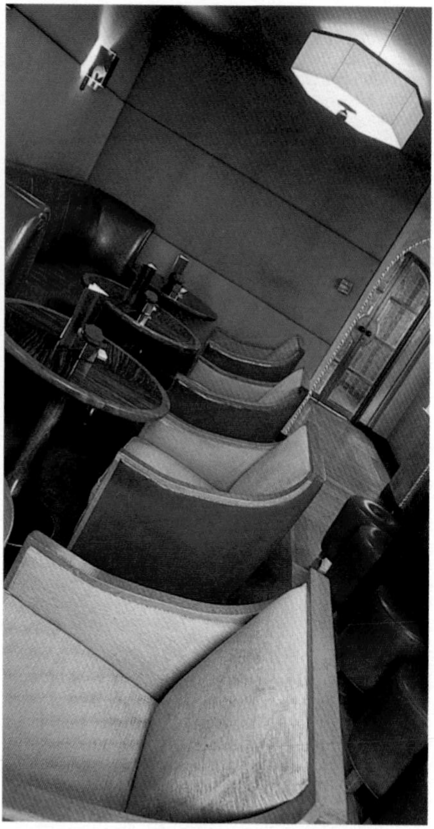

43

43 South Molton Street, W1K 5RS (7647 4343/ www.43southmolton.com). Bond Street tube.
Open/food served 11.30pm-1am Mon-Sat.
Credit AmEx, MC, V.

Understatement of the year: you need to get here early. Jasper Tay, formerly of the impossibly successful phone-ahead-or-members-only Milk & Honey, has pulled out all the stops to create a four-bar establishment run along similar lines in pedestrianised South Molton Street. Its faceless frontage and name is part of the gag, as is the retro retail decor – a nod by interior designer Russell Sage to the bland commerce evident in this Bond Street tributary – in the intimate bar/diner at street level, the only space easily accessible to the general public; larders full of Scotti porridge oats boxes, Listerine, Brasso and old Beano annuals form the decorative punchline. More eccentrica looms in the clubby basement ('Claridge's on acid!' says Jasper), while the private dining and drinking rooms upstairs, accessible next door, are boho clad and comfortable. The provisional drinks menu sparkles with invention – a house Bloody Mary (£8) features horseradish-infused vodka, a Dam French 75 (£9) includes Damson gin, a Silver Coin (£8) margarita with Cointreau. The house beer is bottled Asahi, the bar menu (sliced duck, fennel and avocado, £6.50) in suitably good taste.

Babies and children welcome. Function room. Music (DJs 7pm daily). Restaurant. Tables outdoors (5, pavement).

Ye Grapes

16 Shepherd Market, W1J 7QQ (no phone). Green Park or Hyde Park Corner tube. **Open** 11am-11pm Mon-Sat; noon-10.30pm Sun. **Credit** (over £15 only) MC, V.

Location, location, location? This venerable old boozer certainly has a plum one at the heart of Shepherd Market, a curiously louche corner of London that's home to a mix of cheap restaurants and pricey prostitutes. Ye Grapes is helped by the fact that the three pubs nearest it are, for various reasons, best avoided; and so this high-ceilinged, dimly lit, eccentrically cluttered room does brisk business; too brisk, indeed, for our liking. Service managed to be both distracted ('over here!'), inept (our pint arrived with an inch of head) and rude (the look we got when we asked for a top-up would have slain weaker men) in the space of 90 seconds – impressive in a way. Finding a seat afterwards proved beyond our capabilities; even standing room was a precious commodity. We drained and left. Ye Grapes? Ye Gods.

Babies and children admitted (until 2.30pm). Function room. Games (fruit machine).

Guinea Grill

30 Bruton Place, W1J 6NL (7499 1210/www.youngs.co.uk). Bond Street or Green Park tube. **Open** 11am-11pm Mon-Fri; 6.30-11pm Sat. **Food served** noon-2.30pm Mon-Fri. **Credit** AmEx, DC, JCB, MC, V.

The doors creak open, and in you walk. You don't have walk in very far, for the room is small and busy and the bar is almost within touching distance; but you do walk in very fast, for you can feel yourself being watched. Everybody, it immediately becomes apparent, knows everybody else at this historic, subdued backstreet Young's pub, and nobody knows you. So you scout the taps as discreetly as you can, choose your pint; and when it arrives, you stand still at the bar and sip it gently, perhaps sparking a smoke to go with it. And within seconds, the men in the suits and the overcoats and the unloosened ties return to their beers and their gossip, comfortable at last that you somehow belong.

Function room. No piped music or jukebox.

Hush

8 Lancashire Court, Brook Street, W1S 1EY (7659 1500/www.hush.co.uk). Bond Street tube. **Open** 11am-12.30am Mon-Sat. **Food served** noon-11pm daily. **Credit** AmEx, DC, MC, V.

Now the secret's out, and the management happy to let the general public traipse up to the main bar above the restaurant tucked in a cobbled courtyard by the Handel Museum, improvements are on the cards at the previously exclusive Hush. New covers and carpets will grace the spacious bar area, although the signature pictures of celebrities with index fingers on lips stay put. The ambitious drinks menu, grouped by base spirits, will be halved from five dozen cockails to 30; let's hope that the inventive fresh fruit Bellinis (£8) are equally sacrosanct. The pre-revamp selection of ten Martinis (£7.50) includes a sizzling Forest Fruit Gâteau of muddled blackberries and raspberries, Cartron crème de mûre and Wyborowa vodka, while the Twinkle features Belvedere vodka with a dash of elderflower and a Taittinger Rosé float. The staff are still in three-bags-full mode from serving thirsty celebrities, and the wine list would do justice to the signature bar of a five-star hotel.

Babies and children welcome. Disabled: toilet. Function rooms. Restaurant. Specialities (cocktails). Tables outdoors (15, pavement).

Met Bar

Metropolitan Hotel, 18-19 Old Park Lane, W1K 1LB (7447 1000/www.metropolitan.co.uk). Hyde Park Corner tube. **Open/food served** 11am-6pm daily (members only from 6pm). **Credit** AmEx, DC, MC, V.

Launched in 1997, the Met is probably best known as a haven for the sort of paparazzo-prey soap stars so extensively anthropologised in the gossip mags. It's a small, dark and not unattractive room – gloomy enough for the cast of *EastEnders* to get hammered in relative privacy before they stumble out to greet their crowd of loyal snappers. In fairness to the place, its barman was extremely friendly on our visit (unlike the bouncers on a previous, abortive, attempt) and the raspberry Martini he crafted was superb. Lava-like lighting makes for a pretty enough atmosphere, and there are pricey bar snacks available from the highly rated Nobu restaurant upstairs. But, really: do you want to go to this much trouble getting past mean door staff, just to share dance space with *Holby City* regulars? If you do, fine; if not, try Zeta Bar (*see p68*) down the road.

Disabled: toilet. Music (DJs 10pm Mon-Sat). Restaurant.

Mô Tea Room

23 Heddon Street, W1B 4BH (7434 4040/ www.momoresto.com). Piccadilly Circus tube. **Open** noon-11pm Mon-Wed; noon-midnight Thur-Sat. **Food served** noon-10.15pm Mon-Wed; noon-11.15pm Thur-Sat. **Credit** AmEx, DC, MC, V.

The sweet smell of sheesha pipes and mint dominates proceedings at Mô, and they take their Moroccan stylings seriously. Decor is pretty flawless in this respect, all clutter and colour, though a mite claustrophobic; tables, couches and stools (most of them mismatched) run along either side of the thin room, and low hanging lamps and drapes make for cosiness or discomfort, depending on your taste and height. Cocktails are good – especially the Peach Julep (though, for £8, would it be picky of us to expect a more exotic glass than a straight-edged classic?). Momo, the famed Moroccan restaurant next door, is virtually inaccessible if you haven't booked, and its spill-over makes this affiliate bar busy, too. Still, arrive early enough, and you'll find the Tea Room to be a lovely little nook in which to spend an evening.

Babies and children admitted. Bookings not accepted. Tables outdoors (3, terrace). **Map 1 J7**.

Polo Bar

Westbury Hotel, New Bond Street, W1S 2YF (7629 7755/www.westburymayfair.com). Bond Street or Oxford Circus tube. **Open/food served** 11am-11pm daily. **Credit** AmEx, DC, JCB, MC, V.

This is a pretty little red bar, apparently named after a polo ground on Long Island. The sport is a theme of sorts: dramatic portraits capture the drama of the equine battle, though, surprisingly, when we visited there were none of the open-necked yar-yars you might expect; instead, a knot of rather glum businessmen sat at the bar. This is very obviously part of a hotel – more than once we noticed the unmistakable look of the drinker desperate to finish his business meeting and get off home. Still, the cocktails are pretty and tasty, many – like the Manhattan, Sidecar and Boxcar – have an American bent, in homage to the Westbury's sister hotel in New York. One note: the Westbury hotel is on the corner of New Bond Street and Conduit Street: it would be easy to spend ages looking for the place and cursing its affected, number-free address.

Function rooms. Music (pianist 6-10pm Mon-Fri). Restaurant. TV (satellite).

Punch Bowl

41 Farm Street, W1J 5RP (7493 6841). Green Park tube. **Open** 11am-11pm Mon-Fri; 11am-6pm Sat. **Food served** noon-4pm, 6-9pm Mon-Fri; noon-5pm Sat. **Credit** MC, V.

It's difficult to identify what makes the Punch Bowl stand out. Indoors, this is very much your London pub archetype: hints of history tempered by 'advancements' brought on by chain affiliation (in this case to Scottish & Newcastle). You'll find familiar real ales (Courage Best, Old Speckled Hen, Bombardier), telly, chef behind his heat lamps – all present and correct. But there's a cheery atmosphere – the place is popular with locals and not unfriendly to strangers – and the reasonably priced pub grub looked decent enough, especially the pies. That said, there isn't really enough space to separate eaters-and-drinkers from the hardcore pint-seekers, so food smells dominate. The best seats are either side of the door: tables in booths with plenty of space for a group of five or six.

Babies and children admitted (until 7pm). Function room. No-smoking area. Tables outdoors (3, pavement). TVs (satellite).

Red Lion

1 Waverton Street, W1J 5QN (7499 1307). Green Park tube. **Open** 11.30am-11pm Mon-Fri; 6-11pm Sat; noon-3pm, 6-10.30pm Sun. **Food served** noon-2.30pm, 6-9.30pm Mon-Fri, Sun; 6-9.30pm Sat. **Credit** AmEx, MC, V.

The fire doesn't quite roar, and the bar is tended not by a robust, ebullient old codger but by a handful of youngsters. Otherwise, though, this delightful pub is the closest Mayfair gets to a village local. The isolated location helps: it's tucked away off unassuming Waverton Street, a small thoroughfare famous only as the home of London's smallest petrol station. As such, the people who drink in the Red Lion have made the effort to find it – a useful filter that keeps the atmosphere relaxed and sometimes almost clubbable. The five beers included Young's and Spitfire on our visit; there are also 14 wines by the glass and a board proudly detailing the sausage of the day. For our money, it's the best pub in Mayfair. Take a date.

Babies and children admitted (lunch only). Function room. Music (pianist 7pm Sat; free). Restaurant. Tables outdoors (2, pavement).

Running Horse

50 Davies Street, W1K 5JE (7493 1275). Bond Street tube. **Open** noon-11pm Mon-Sat. **Food served** noon-3pm, 6-9pm Mon-Thur; noon-3pm Fri; noon-4pm Sat. **Credit** AmEx, MC, V.

Bought a while back by gastro-revamper Tom Etridge (the man responsible for the transformation of hotspot the Farm in Fulham, among other pubs), the Running Horse has been groomed a little over the past year. For all that, it has yet to live up to its pedigree. Dark wood panelling and ultra-chic light fittings make this a very attractive boozer, and a few luxury leather sofas raise the comfort level – but does it stand out? Has it been properly Etridge-d? We'd say no, but don't rule out changes in the near future. Expect big improvements for food-lovers, and maybe an expansion in the ale selection (currently it only features Courage Best and London Pride). Trendy, friendly, and wholly likeable – but until now, without that winner's edge.

Babies and children admitted (daytime only). Tables outdoors (4, pavement).

Shepherd's Tavern

50 Hertford Street, W1J 7SS (7499 3017). Green Park or Hyde Park Corner tube. **Open** 11am-11pm Mon-Sat; noon-10.30pm Sun. **Food served** 11am-10.30pm Mon-Sat; noon-9.30pm Sun. **Credit** AmEx, MC, V.

The riotous football spectatorship on both our visits underlined that this is a pub, if not a game, of two halves. The Shepherd's, you see, is boldly bicephalous. Downstairs is a dark, tightly spaced (though not unattractive) room where vociferous local workers and suited smarts come to watch a spot of footie on the big screen while sampling interesting brews like Adnams Broadside or Young's Special. Upstairs, it's all change: a well-lit dining room of sorts (though drinkers looking for a quieter atmosphere are welcome), with gorgeous wood-panelled walls and a great view of the area's surrounding tweeness. A sign on the staircase says 'Come up and be pampered' – so we did, and were delighted with delicious pie and mash for £6 (there are usually three or four own-made specimens on the menu). A very nice pub: the kind of place you might choose for Mayfair on a Monopoly board pub crawl.

Babies and children admitted (under-10s dining area only). Games (fruit machines). Restaurant (available for hire). TV (satellite).

Trader Vic's

Hilton Hotel, 22 Park Lane, W1K 4BE (7208 4113/ www.tradervics.com). Hyde Park Corner tube. **Open/food served** noon-1am Mon-Thur; noon-3am Fri; 5pm-3am Sat; 5-11.30pm Sun. **Credit** AmEx, DC, MC, V.

First, greatest and silliest of the international theme bars. It's been seven decades since Victor Bergeron established the first one in Oakland, California, and yet this Americo-Polynesian establishment never fails to both baffle (why?) and delight (who cares?). There's nothing authentic about it at all; indeed, as we all travel more and the world grows smaller, the already over-the-top theme seems even more preposterous – and, if you look very closely in the dim light, a little shabbier. But still, it's a hard heart that remains uninspired by this cheerily unsophisticated spot, especially after a couple of the good-value atomic cocktails. The Mai Tai, invented by Bergeron himself, is always a wise choice; other good bets include the rum-rich Samoan Fog Cutter, served in an absurd ceramic vase, and Doctor Funk of Tahiti – purely because it's such fun asking for one.

Babies and children welcome; high chairs. Disabled: toilet (in hotel). Function room. Music (musicians 10.30pm daily). No smoking (restaurant only). Restaurant. Specialities (cocktails).

Windmill

6-8 Mill Street, W1S 2AZ (7491 8050). Oxford Circus tube. **Open** 11am-11pm Mon-Fri; noon-4pm Sat. **Food served** noon-3pm, 6-9.30pm Mon-Fri; noon-4pm Sat. **Credit** AmEx, DC, MC, V.

The Windmill's hard-hitting aesthetic incorporates red walls, intensely patterned carpet, golden cherubs at head height, and – on our visit – 20 or so tuxedoed, elderly gentlemen (cause for celebration unknown). All this might provoke a measure of surprise if you happen to sidle through the door for a sly one after a day's shopping in Oxford Street or Mayfair. But the Windmill has more going for it. Location, primarily: it's nice and close to those aforementioned consumer shrines, but without the price hikes you might expect in such an area (two pints from the ale selection barely clipped a fiver). Our eyes were drawn to the pies on the menu, but we didn't order; staff at this Young's pub looked over-worked dealing with yet another private party in a lowered area at the back.

Function room. No piped music or jukebox. No-smoking area (lower bar). Restaurant.

Windows

Hilton Hotel, Park Lane, W1K 1BE (7493 8000/ www.hilton.co.uk). Green Park or Hyde Park Corner tube. **Open/food served** noon-2am Mon-Thur; noon-2.30pm Fri; 5.30pm-2.30am Sat; noon-10.30pm Sun. **Credit** AmEx, DC, MC, V.

One knows one has reached a certain worldly comfort level in one's adult life when one realises that Hilton hotels aren't actually that posh. Even so, the fall from grace of this 28th-floor bar (great views, of course, over Hyde Park Corner, Green Park and the grounds of Buckingham Palace), has been swift and demeaning. The lofty surrounds once inspired a casual exclusivity; no longer. Staff, once formal, are now merely terse. The drinks list contains a selection of Budvar cocktails (whisky, Drambuie and lager, anyone?); even the piano, that archetypal signifier of provincial class, has gone, replaced by a central-European busker of indeterminate accent mispronouncing his way through songs by Bob Marley and U2 with the help of an acoustic guitar and the hindrance of a drum machine. The final

straw? Asking, quite clearly, for a glass of the house white and being brought – and billed for – a rather more expensive glass of chablis.
Babies and children welcome: 50% discount for under-10s; high chairs (restaurant only). Disabled: toilet. Music (musicians 7pm-1.30am Mon-Sat). No-smoking tables (restaurant).

Zeta Bar

35 Hertford Street, W1J 7SD (7208 4067/ www.zeta-bar.com). Green Park or Hyde Park Corner tube. **Open** 5pm-1am Mon, Tue; 5pm-3am Wed-Sat; 9pm-1.30am. **Food served** 6pm-12.30am Mon-Sat. **Admission** £10 after 11pm Mon-Sat. **Credit** AmEx, DC, MC, V.
Entry will either provoke a cry of delight or a sneer of derision. With no bouncers on a weekday night, the Zeta Bar was easy to miss – the dark, industrial exterior is pretty much anonymous. But pull open the heavy, factory-like door to be bathed in golden light and… it's like the moment Dorothy steps from black-and-white to Technicolor in *The Wizard of Oz*. Luscious brown and beige couches (as deep as small beds) are a highlight; so too are the wooden divisions that make the bar maze-like in its slow revealing of space. The cocktails aren't cheap. Toto, a so-so orangey champagne cocktail, rang in at £7 (about average), but a £13 'Hemingway Daiquiri' worked out at approximately a quid a delicious swallow. Silhouettes of passers-by sweep across the frosted windows, quite unaware of the delights on the other side.
Bar area available for hire. Dress: smart casual. Music (DJs 9pm daily). TV (satellite).

Also in the area...

All Bar One 5-6 Picton Place, W1M 3PR (7487 0161).
Balls Brothers Mulligan's of Mayfair, 14 Cork Street, W1S 3NS (7409 1370); 34 Brook Street, W1Y 1YA (7499 4567).
Chopper Lump (Davy's) 10C Hanover Square, W1R 9HD (7499 7569).
Hog's Head 11 Dering Street, W1S 1AR (7629 0531).
Pitcher & Piano 1 Pollen Street, W1R 0PH (7629 9581).
Slug & Lettuce 19-20 Hanover Street, W1R 9HG (7499 0077).

NOTTING HILL, LADBROKE GROVE & WESTBOURNE GROVE

Most of the better venues are nowhere near what's generally considered the heart of Notting Hill – Notting Hill Gate and its tube station. The action lies much further north, in an east-west spread concentrated between Westbourne Park Road and Westbourne Grove. This is an area that in the last couple of years has nurtured a spate of new quality bars including, notably, the **Lonsdale**, **Tom & Dick's** and **Trailer Happiness**. Similarly, Notting Hill has more than its fair share of fine gastropubs, including the **Cow**, **Golborne Grove**, **Grand Union**, **Prince Bonaparte** and the **Westbourne**. No wonder the denizens of W11 often come across as smug.

Beach Blanket Babylon

45 Ledbury Road, W11 2AA (7229 2907). Notting Hill Gate tube. **Open** noon-11pm Mon-Sat; noon-10.30pm Sun. **Food served** noon-3.30pm, 7pm-midnight Mon-Sat; noon-4pm, 7-10.30pm Sun. **Credit** MC, V.
This place is fabulously camp, from the palatial front doors to the faux-Roman temple fireplace in the corner. Things get even more outlandish as one passes from the modest-sized, crimson back bar into the dining area – via a plank-and-chain footbridge and a spiral staircase. It resembles the city of the Elves from *The Lord of the Rings*, all heavenly white walls and low stone arches. The food is actually rather fine, although we wish snackier alternatives were available downstairs. The wine and cocktail lists are excellent, too, but otherwise it's bottle city as far as drinks are concerned (there's Grolsch on tap). We'll forgive this one failure of imagination, though: it's the only such in this weird and wonderful place.
Babies and children admitted (daytime). Function rooms. Music (DJ 6pm Sun; free). Restaurant. Tables outdoors (10, garden). **Map 10 A6**.

Bed

310 Portobello Road, W10 5TA (8969 4500). Ladbroke Grove tube. **Open/food served** 5-11pm Mon-Thur; noon-11pm Fri, Sat; noon-10.30pm Sun. **Credit** MC, V.
Inspired by its location in the heartland of London's North African community, Bed first opened a few years back as a Moroccan flavoured drinking den. It had lounging platforms, kilims, tea lights and a definite whiff of the kasbah about it. Now, we're not sure if it's a change of direction or simple neglect, but the place seems to be in the process of reverting to the scruffy old boozer it was before the makeover. The ethnic trappings are largely gone, leaving behind bare, drab, nicotine-filmed surfaces that are battered and scuffed. The general appearance suggests that no one any longer cares. That's borne out by the drinks, with just three types of lager, plus Guinness, available at the bar. Looks to us like it's way past bedtime.
Music (DJs 7.30pm Thur-Sun). Specialities (cocktails). **Map 10 Az5**.

Cow

89 Westbourne Park Road, W2 5QH (7221 0021). Royal Oak or Westbourne Park tube. **Open** noon-11pm Mon-Sat; noon-10.30pm Sun. **Food served** noon-3.30pm, 6-10.30pm Mon-Sat; noon-3.30pm, 6-10pm Sun. **Credit** MC, V.
The Cow is to your average high street pub what Fortnum & Mason is to Somerfield's. They're both licensed premises offering alcoholic beverages and food, but that's as far as the similarities go. Operated by Tom Conran, the Cow is a modestly sized shrine to the gentrified good life. Its wines and spirits are selected with a connoisseur's eye and the two real ales (London Pride and Harvey's Bitter) are supplemented by a good selection of bottled Belgian brews. The largely seafood menu, served in the back and also in the upstairs dining room, keeps things simple, but includes some superb fare. The only drawback is the bumptious crowd that hangs out here. Money may buy a platter of rock oysters on ice to scoff at the bar with your Guinness, but it sure doesn't buy good manners.
Babies and children admitted. Function room. Restaurant. Tables outdoors (4, pavement). TV. **Map 10 A5**.

Eclipse

186 Kensington Park Road, W11 2ES (7792 2063/ www.eclipse-ventures.com). Labroke Grove or Notting Hill Gate tube. **Open/food served** 5pm-midnight Mon-Fri; noon-midnight Sat; noon-10.30pm Sun. **Credit** AmEx, MC, V.

There's very little to dislike in this intimate little cocktail lounge. Okay, it gets a little cramped on a busy night; but, frankly, we're just glad it seems to be doing so well. With its orangey tones and exposed brick, the decor fosters a warm and sultry atmosphere (a theme upheld by the excellent, Mediterranean-style bar food). The seating is upholstered stools and long leather banquettes, while in winter months an open fire blazes away at one end of the room. The cocktails are stand-outs – we tried the watermelon Martini and the cherry and coconut sour, both of which were delicious. The prices are surprisingly reasonable for a place of this kind, especially given its location – a mere cocktail olive's throw from Portobello Market.

Babies and children welcome. Specialities (cocktails). Tables outdoors (2, pavement). **Map 10 Az5**.

Elbow Room

103 Westbourne Grove, W2 4UW (7221 5211/ www.elbow-room.co.uk). Bayswater or Notting Hill Gate tube. **Open/food served** noon-11pm Mon-Sat; 1-10.30pm Sun. **Credit** MC, V.

Since first appearing in the mid 1990s, Elbow Room has spread its unique formula far beyond the confines of Westbourne Grove (there are branches in Islington, Shoreditch and even out of town); but this place is their original combination of beer and baize. It's all about a game here, and the game in question is pool. Six full-sized American tables dominate the room, symbolically separated from the main bar with an almost reverential awning of velvet curtains. Get your name chalked up quick, and you'll be summoned over the PA system when a table's free; while you wait, sit in one of the low-lit booths with your drinks. Unlikely as it may sound, the combination of pool hall and bar-nightclub is hugely successful, as proved by the dedicated following of punters that keeps this place short of its namesake on a busy night. The bar food is of the superior nachos and burgers variety, while the modest range of draught beers includes Korenwolf.

Games (7 pool tables). Music (DJs weekly; free). Specialities (cocktails). TV. **Map 10 Az5**.

Electric Brasserie

191 Portobello Road, W11 2ED (7908 9696/www.the-electric.co.uk). Ladbroke Grove tube. **Open** 8am-midnight Mon-Sat; 8am-11pm Sun. **Food served** 8am-11pm Mon-Fri; 8am-5pm, 6-11pm Sat; 8am-5pm, 6-10pm Sun. **Credit** AmEx, DC, MC, V.

The wildly successful, too-cool-for-art-school vibe of the adjoining Electric Cinema transfers comfortably to this sophisticated café-bar. This is a brasserie in the true sense of the word, a place where you feel as comfortable dropping in for tea and pâtisserie as for something stronger: in other words, not the sort of venue you'd choose for some pub-style lager-glugging. The food lives up admirably to the brasserie tag, too, with dishes such as roast hake Viennoise and duck cottage pie sitting alongside British versions of steak frites and the like. There are also fine-looking breakfast and brunch menus on offer, and at the back in the more formal, à la carte restaurant, the steaks are raised even higher. The Electric Brasserie may be a obvious choice if you're letting your palate decide – but your wallet may have other ideas.

Babies and children welcome; high chairs. Disabled: toilet. Restaurant. Tables outdoors (7, courtyard). **Map 10 Az5**.

Elgin

96 Ladbroke Grove, W11 1PY (7229 5663). Ladbroke Grove tube. **Open** 11am-11pm Mon-Sat; noon-10.30pm Sun. **Food served** noon-10pm daily. **Credit** AmEx, MC, V.

Another runner-up in 2004's Time Out Eating & Drinking Awards, the Elgin is W11's most handsome pub. Built in 1853 by Dr Samuel Walker, a property-speculating clergyman who blew a sizeable inheritance in four years, it was then the only structure in Ladbroke Grove aside from a convent. For the treasure-trove of spectacular stained-glass screens, lavish decorative wall tiles and delicious carved mahogany, we owe thanks to William Dickinson, who acquired the pub in 1892 and decorated it in opulent style. In the 1970s the pub became famous as a centre for the *Time Out*-wielding 'alternative' society. The 101ers (precursors to The Clash) performed here every Thursday; Alexei Sayle and Keith Allen launched their careers in the back room. More recent additions to admire at this three-bar, high-ceilinged boozer include three rotating real ales, boutique brews such as Wieckse Witte and a decent supply of Belgian bottled beers. There's also good value food (£4-£8), outdoor bench seating for warmer weather, twofer drinks deals, two pool tables, big screen sports and an on-site ATM. Maybe you can please all the people all of the time?

Babies and children welcome (before 6pm). Games (fruit machine, pool tables, quiz machine). Music (Elvis 8pm 1st Fri of mth; karaoke 9pm 2nd Sat of mth; both free). Tables outdoors (12, pavement). TVs (big screen, satellite). **Map 10 Az5**.

Golborne Grove

36 Golborne Road, W10 5PR (8960 6260/ www.groverestaurants.co.uk). Westbourne Park tube. **Open** 11am-11pm Mon-Thur; 11am-11.30pm Fri, Sat; noon-10.30pm Sun. **Food served** 4-7pm daily. **Credit** DC, MC, V.

Since changing ownership some two years back (this used to be a terrific gastropub by the name of Golborne House), the place has lost its finesse and gone a bit All Bar One. It's still the same big, L-shaped, open-plan pub with large windows delivering a view of Ernö Goldfinger's Trellick Tower over the road, but any individuality has been leached out of the operation. Instead, expect a default-setting stripped-down interior, lots of lager on tap but only one real ale (London Pride), two-pint jugs of sangria or vodka and Red Bull, a menu of giggly cocktails (Woo Woos and Slippery Nipples) and happy hours from 4pm to 7pm. The uniformed staff are pleasant enough and the food is reportedly still noteworthy, but otherwise it's all a bit depressing. They play Sting on the sound system, too.

Babies and children admitted. Function room. Restaurant. Tables outdoors (4-10, pavement). TV (big screen, satellite). **Map 10 Az4**.

Grand Union

45 Woodfield Road, W9 2BA (7286 1886). Westbourne Park tube. **Open** noon-11pm Mon-Sat; noon-10.30pm Sun. **Food served** noon-10pm Mon-Sat; noon-9pm Sun. **Credit** AmEx, DC, MC, V.

The interior to this appealing little boozer displays an endearing degree of shabbiness. Indeed, despite the warning signals given off by the prerequisite bare boards and

scant illumination of the interior, the place displays little of the wearisome artiness that one has come to expect from the gastro-centric watering holes in this neck of the woods. Perhaps it's a hangover from the not-too-distant past when this was a rather shabby old hangout for rail and bus workers from the depots down the road. On tap are Amstel, Hoegaarden, Adnams Bitter and Broadside, and the wine list is thoughtfully put together; the bar food isn't half bad. In summer, step outside to the large and extremely pretty summer terrace that overlooks the Grand Union Canal.
Babies and children admitted (until 6pm). Function room. Music (DJ 7pm Sun; free). Restaurant (available for hire). Tables outdoors (20, canalside). TV.
Map 10 A6.

Lonsdale

44-48 Lonsdale Road, W11 2DE (7228 1517/ www.thelonsdale.co.uk). Ladbroke Grove or Notting Hill Gate Park tube. **Open** 6pm-midnight daily. **Food served** 6.30-11.30pm Mon-Sat; 6.30-11pm Sun. **Credit** AmEx, MC, V.
This sassy little joint was Time Out's bar of the year in 2003, and yet it's easy to see how things could have gone badly wrong, given the plethora of pretentious bars in this almost insufferably trendy neck of the woods. Yet the Lonsdale pulls off a genuinely exciting formula with just enough balls-out chutzpah to make it the perfect example of how to do tongue-in-cheek: cheerfully, and with style. The decor is an explosion of post-space-age chic, a kind of 1970s vision of how we would be living in the 21st century: glinting bronze hemispheres protrude from metallic walls and an enormous skylight spirals above the bar, as if preparing to suck everybody out through the roof. The long cocktail list is suitably imaginative: our Thyme Daiquiri was earthy and unusual, while the New York Sour was tart and perfectly mixed (although at £8 a pop, we'd expect it to be).
Disabled: toilet. Function room. Music (DJs 9pm Fri, Sat). Specialities (cocktails). **Map 10 A6**.

Mall Tavern

71-73 Palace Gardens Terrace, W8 4RU (7727 3805). Notting Hill Gate tube. **Open** noon-11pm Mon-Sat; noon-10.30pm Sun. **Food served** noon-3pm, 6-10.30pm Mon-Thur; noon-3pm, 6-11pm Fri; noon-4pm, 6-11pm Sat; noon-4pm, 7-10.30pm Sun. **Credit** AmEx, MC, V.
This is the kind of pub where the haughty blonde behind the bar hands back your change on a silver plate; house matches come in one of those boxes shaped like a mini After Eights box; and wines occupy three times as much space in the chiller cabinet as the bottled continental beers. There are no real ales, just three draught lagers: Stella and Hoegaarden and Leffe at a fairly staggering £5.50 a pint. Foodwise, a burger can't just be a burger, naturally: it's a beef, chorizo and walnut burger. None of which is to say we don't like the Mall, which is not without its charms. It's a very elegant corner pub, duck-egg green of wall and bare of floorboard; there are newspapers neatly spread on the bar counter and a very full rack of current style and fashion mags. And it's perfectly right for the location, where Notting Hill shades into High Street Ken: check out the gorgeous, Tuscan-style open staircase on the Mall Chambers building opposite.
Babies and children admitted. Function room. Restaurant. Tables outdoors (6, patio).
Map 10 B7.

Market Bar

240A Portobello Road, W11 1LL (7229 6472). Ladbroke Grove or Notting Hill Gate tube. **Open** 11am-11pm Mon-Sat; noon-10.30pm Sun. **Food served** noon-3pm Mon-Fri, Sun. **Credit** MC, V.
Up near the Westway, where the fruit and veg stalls give way to sub-Camden trinketry and hand-me-down fashion, the Market stands as the quintessential '90s-style yoof pub: rough wooden floorboards and terracotta paintwork, a sofa and coffee table to complement other sundry items of mismatched wooden furniture, giant candelabras sporting storks' nests of wax, local artwork on the walls, a chilled soundtrack and a DJ booth for weekend use, and a blackboard wine list, but no decent beer apart from fancy lagers (Leffe, San Miguel). If you like that sort of thing, it's fine. Plenty do, and the pub draws a colourful mix of muso types and ravenous locals waiting for a sought-after table at the highly regarded Market Thai restaurant upstairs (food is also served at tables downstairs). On a recent visit the place also boasted the most gorgeous barmaid on Portobello, but given that it took her 10 minutes to ring up the bill she may no longer be around when you visit.
Babies and children admitted (restaurant). Music (DJs 7pm Sat; jazz 4-7pm Sun). No smoking (restaurant). Restaurant. TV. **Map 10 Az6**.

Number Ten

10 Golborne Road, W10 5PE (8969 8922). Westbourne Park tube. **Open** 11am-midnight daily. **Food served** 11am-10.30pm daily. **Credit** AmEx, DC, JCB, MC, V.
An enormous amount of effort and money has clearly been put into this cheerily left-field gastrobar, which until recently was just a dilapidated old boozer overshadowed by the landmark Trellick Tower. It's paid off, though, from the suitably avant-garde live music ('skew wiff stuff from deviant DJs', said the promotional material on the night we visited) to the gleaming main bar that vaguely reminded us of a 1950s departure lounge; all wood and Formica trim. We didn't venture to the separate restaurant or the members-only floors (we've heard good things about both), but found very little to complain about downstairs. The cocktail menu, while small, is good, and we've certainly paid more for less in this neighbourhood: our perfectly mixed Gibson set us back precisely six pounds. Draught lagers include Cobra and Red Stripe, with Negra Modelo and Especial the best among a modest range of bottled beers.
Babies and children welcome. Music (bands 7pm Wed, Thur; free). Restaurant. Tables outdoors (5, pavement).

Portobello Gold

95-97 Portobello Road, W11 2QB (7460 4900/ www.portobellogold.com). Notting Hill Gate tube. **Open** 10am-midnight Mon-Sat; 10am-10.30pm Sun. **Food served** 11am-11pm Mon-Sat; 1-9pm Sun. **Happy hour** 5.30-7pm daily. **Credit** AmEx, DC, MC, V.
Following a brief closure, courtesy of a fire in October 2004, the Gold reopened early in 2005. Happily, little has changed. The bar area has been reconstructed much as it was, merely looking a bit newer and sporting a different paint scheme. And thank goodness for that. In other ways, too, the place remains as idiosyncratic as ever, doubling as an international restaurant of renown (the multi-levelled dining area is at the rear, specialising in seafood with an Asian twist, such as Thai moules and Japanese-style rock oysters), a gallery, small hotel and an internet café. The draught line-up at the bar includes the punchy quintet of Spitfire, Brakespear Bitter, Leffe, Hoegaarden and Grolsch,

while bottled beers run to Budvar, Chimay, Duval, Früli, Pilsner Urquell and Thatcher's cider, among others. The wine list offers nine reds and whites by the glass, champagnes include Bollinger NV, Dom Perignon and Louis Roederer Cristal, and there's an appealing list of post-prandial digestifs. Fire cannot whither her: the Gold remains the best pub on Portobello by a long chalk.
Babies and children admitted. Function room. Internet access. Restaurant. Specialities (world beers, wines). Tables outdoors (3, pavement). TV (satellite). **Map 10 A6**.

Prince Bonaparte

80 Chepstow Road, W2 5BE (7313 9491). Notting Hill Gate or Royal Oak tube/7, 28, 31, 70 bus. **Open** noon-11pm Mon-Sat; noon-10.30pm Sun. **Food served** noon-10pm Mon-Thur; noon-9pm Fri-Sun. **Credit** AmEx, MC, V.
A big, open-plan corner pub with a spacious front bar area and a dining room at the back the size of a mess hall, the Boney is a hugely comfortable venue. It also boasts some serious class: clock the draught beer choices of Timothy Taylor Landlord, Leffe, Hoegaarden, Küppers Kölsch from Cologne and Belgium's De Koninck – an impressive line up. Then there's a widely travelled wine list, lettered out on one blackboard and a long, long food menu of some ambition scrawled on a second. The dining area also does duty as a surprisingly serious gallery space. Considering its plum location in the serious wealth belt just north of Westbourne Grove, the crowd seems gratifyingly normal and down to earth – although we don't reckon there are too many cashiers or labourers among them.
Disabled: toilet. Games (backgammon, cards, chess). Specialities (Belgian beer). **Map 10 A5**.

Sun in Splendour

7 Portobello Road, W11 3DA (7313 9331). Notting Hill Gate tube. **Open** noon-11pm Mon-Fri; 11am-11pm Sat; noon-10.30pm Sun. **Food served** noon-4pm, 6-10pm Mon-Fri; noon-8pm Sat, Sun. **Credit** MC, V.
This charmingly boho little boozer has the laid-back, faintly bewildered air of a landlocked surfer joint. The likes of Neil Finn and Jack Johnson play on the stereo, while the clientele is a suitably chilled mixture of locals, arty types, and local arty types; low-slung bar staff pull pints of Früli, Leffe and Hoegaarden; mismatched wooden furniture adds a certain scavenger chic to the proceedings; and almost-tasteful erotica hangs on elegantly papered walls. However, what might, at first glance, appear to be a haphazard case of creative disarray is actually a successful little operation. We've had some fine lunches here, and the wine list is surprisingly varied.
Games (quiz machine). Music (DJ 8pm Wed; free). Tables outdoors (8, garden). **Map 10 A7**.

Tiroler Hut

27 Westbourne Grove, W2 4UA (7727 3981/ www.tirolerhut.co.uk). Bayswater or Queensway tube. **Open** 6.30pm-1am Tue-Sat; 6.30pm-midnight Sun. **Food served** 6.30pm-midnight Tue-Sat; 6.30-11.30pm Sun. **Credit** AmEx, DC, MC, V.
You could be forgiven for thinking that everyone associated with this magnificent little basement bar was a couple of slices short of a bratwurst, but fear not – they just seem to have an exceptionally well developed sense of fun. Don't get us wrong: this is no tedious theme bar where jollity is forced upon you, and we had a fabulously good time here. It's just that the whole thing is a bit, well, bonkers – a magnificent spectacle of kitsch, from the accordion and cowbell show that started up midway through the evening, to the ebullient waiting staff – who, if the photos plastered across the walls are anything to go by, are not adverse to preserving the most raucous nights for posterity. The food is Austrian and plentiful; the beer is of appropriately Germanic origin: Dortmunder Union on draught, and Erdinger wheat beer and Austria's Gösser in bottles.
Babies and children admitted. Music (cowbell show 9pm Wed-Sat). Restaurant.

Tom & Dick's

30 Alexander Street, W2 5NU (7229 7711/ www.tomanddicks.com). Royal Oak tube. **Open** 6.30pm-midnight Mon-Sat; 11am-3pm, 6.30-10.30pm Sun. **Food served** 6.30pm-midnight Tue-Sat; 11am-3pm, 6.30-10.30pm Sun. **Credit** MC, V.
A luscious yet homely little drinking haunt where auction-house furniture, hand-painted antique silk wallpaper and assorted curios create an atmosphere that's two parts camp to one of calculated cool. Wafted with incense and lit by tea candles and brass lanterns, it's like the front room boudoir of a batty old friend who once danced cabaret in Bombay. It has a fruity cocktail menu (big on apples, berries and citrus, each glass at around £7) and excellent snacks (tempura veggies, seared scallops, chicken and mushroom dumplings, £5-£8). Add changing displays of art and mini flatscreens the size of cigar boxes (showing *DangerMouse*!), not to mention a gorgeous set of upstairs rooms used for dining and occasional Sunday afternoon art-house movies (with high-spec surround sound) but otherwise for hire – and you have the sweetest, kookiest little bar since Audrey Hepburn's last house party.
No-smoking area. Rooms available for hire. **Map 10 B5**.

Trailer Happiness

177 Portobello Road, W11 2DY (7727 2700/ www.trailerhappiness.com). Ladbroke Grove or Notting Hill tube. **Open** 5-10pm 1st Mon of mth; 5-11pm Tue-Fri; 6-11pm Sat; 6-10.30pm Sun. **Food served** 6-10.30pm Tue-Sat. **Credit** AmEx, MC, V.
For once, we'll let the bar's own PR do the talking: 'Trailer H is a retro-sexual haven of cosmopolitan kitsch and faded trailer park glamour – cork tiles and shag pile, love songs and vol-au-vents, Lynch prints and Tiki drinks.' It's not far off, although the reality is a basement bar of limited proportions with a sliver of an entrance on the corner of Portobello and Elgin Crescent. The decor is fairly negligible (brown, brown and brown, with some of those soft-focus, doe-eyed dusky lady portraits that were flogged by Woolworths throughout the 1970s): all the attention falls on the spotlit bar, stocked with 37 largely Caribbean rums and centre for the preparation of some absolutely killer cocktails. The menu has an 'homage' section ('drinks we like making') of international bar creations, 'house favourites' – and, best of all, Tiki specials (£7-£15), which are some of the fruitiest, frothiest, most luridly coloured, knock-out concoctions going. And, yes, they do a Zombie, but it's so evil it's limited to two per person per night.
Music (DJs 8pm Thur-Sun; free). Specialities (cocktails). **Map 10 Az6**.

Visible

299 Portobello Road, W10 5TD (8969 0333). Ladbroke Grove tube. **Open/food served** 4-11pm Mon-Thur; 10am-11pm Fri, Sat; 10am-10.30pm Sun. **Credit** AmEx, MC, V.

Central

We wonder if the name of this genial little cocktail bar is meant to be ironic, given its almost apologetically low-key exterior. More deserving of apology on our last visit was the ear-splittingly loud piped music, easily audible from a few doors away. It felt a little silly, screaming to be heard – on a Tuesday afternoon. In other respects, the vibe here is distinctly un-clubby, with twinkly nightlights casting a glow across low-slung wooden tables, and a preponderance of bottom-pleasing, plush sofas along the bare brick walls. Staff are cheery and the cocktail menu is nothing short of excellent. The Middle Eastern-style bar snacks we tried weren't bad, either. We've heard the live jazz on Thursday nights is pretty good – though should we venture back at any other time, we might just invest in some earplugs first.
Babies and children welcome (before 7pm). Music (musicians 8pm Thur, 6pm Sun; free). Specialities (cocktails). Tables outdoors (4, pavement). TVs (plasma). **Map 10 Az5**.

Westbourne

101 Westbourne Park Villas, W2 5ED (7221 1332). Royal Oak or Westbourne Park tube. **Open** 5-11pm Mon; 11am-11pm Tue-Fri; noon-11pm Sat; noon-10.30pm Sun. **Food served** 7-10pm Mon; 12.30-3pm, 7-10pm Tue-Thur; 12.30-3pm, 7-9.30pm Fri; 12.30-3.30pm, 7-9.30pm Sat, Sun. **Credit** AmEx, MC, V.
The Westbourne is so trendy, so beyond trendy, that even supermodels falter at its door. It's also hugely popular and consistently packed; if you want to eat (and the food is sufficiently good that the place features in the 2004 edition of the Michelin Guide) we suggest coming early in the week: that you way you might have a table by Friday. The drinks selection is excellent, with draught Hoegaarden, Leffe, Dortmunder Union and Old Speckled Hen, lots of potent bottled Belgian brews, and an equally fine range of wines. We do like the ragtag decor of assorted posters and prints, although most evenings anyone less than six feet tall is unlikely to see anything other than the backs of the heads of the Georgies, Jesses and Camerons at the bar. There's a great front terrace that is a poseurs' magnet come warmer weather (perfect for head-turner arrivals in your new Porsche Boxster). On our last visit, we auctioned off our seats before leaving and made a tasty profit on the evening.
Babies and children admitted. Games (board games, chess). Tables outdoors (14, terrace). **Map 10 B5**.

Also in the area...

All Bar One 126-128 Notting Hill, W11 3QG (7313 9362).

PIMLICO

The pubs scattered across Pimlico must have heard many a dark secret, as customers include members of MI6 from the opposite embankment and employees from the royal estate near the tube stop. But the pubs are as quiet as the well-swept,

Argyll Arms. *See p78.*

residential streets around them, and dutifully serve decent pints of ale and quality lunches. The **Morpeth Arms** and **Gallery** are typical of the genre.

Chimes

26 Churton Street, SW1V 2LP (7821 7456). Pimlico tube or Victoria tube/rail. **Open/food served** noon-2.30pm, 5.30-10.15pm Mon-Sat; noon-3pm, 5.30-10pm Sun. **Credit** AmEx, DC, MC, V.

This rustic, traditional English restaurant accommodates – nay, welcomes – non-dining drinkers. The main attractions here are not only the cosy wooden right-angles of seating around a homely bar or the light-filled back lounge decked out in house plants, but the drinks themselves. Wines and ciders, some of unusual and affordable variety, are the order of the day (though there's also bottled Beck's and Kronenbourg). The ciders come in draught (half-pint glass or two-pint jug) and keg versions, starting with a house medium dry (£1.40-£5.60 draught), moving on to a Weston's Old Scrumpy from the orchards of Worcestershire, Kent-produced Biddenden and slightly sparkling kegs of Stowford Press. Wines of each colour, from the house Jacques Veritier (£2.55 a glass, £10.20 a bottle), include half-bottles of Château Favrey pouilly fumé (£9.95) and bottles of Sicilian Mandra Rossa syrah (£13.95). Add some fine pies and pâtés, and a pleasantly sozzled lunch can be yours.

Function room. Restaurant. Specialities (cider). Tables outdoors (3, pavement).

Gallery

1 Lupus Street, SW1V 3AS (7821 7573). Pimlico tube. **Open** 9.45am-11pm Mon-Sat; 9.45am-10.30pm Sun. **Food served** 9.45am-2.30pm, 5.30-9.30pm Mon-Sat; 9.45am-2.30pm, 5.30-9pm Sun. **Credit** AmEx, DC, MC, V.

A home from home among grand townhouses and private courtyards, the mildly upmarket Gallery ('no soiled clothing') treats a mainly white-collar clientele to decent draught ales, more than reasonable wines and good grub from breakfast to late evening. The gallery in question, only open at peak times, is a relaxing lounge of light wood and house plants, bathed in natural light, while the spacious downstairs lounge comprises relaxing sofas and banquettes, and a long bar counter. There you'll find Spitfire, London Pride and Greene King IPA on tap, and a blackboard of six wines of each colour by the bottle and by two sizes of glass. Red or white Marques de Turia is an acceptable first offer, although a quid or so more will get you a better El Coto crianza rioja. Fresh cod in Hoegaarden batter or home-made beef, ale and leek pie (both £7.95) star on the food menu.

Disabled: toilet. Function room. Games (fruit machines). No-smoking area. Tables outdoors (4, pavement). TV.

Jugged Hare

172 Vauxhall Bridge Road, SW1V 1DX (7828 1543). Victoria tube. **Open** noon-11pm Mon-Sat; noon-10.30pm Sun. **Food served** noon-9pm Mon-Sat; noon-8pm Sun. **Credit** AmEx, DC, MC, V.

café de Paris
since 1924
5 BARS
1 RESTAURANT
TIMELESS GLAMOUR
3 Coventry Street, Piccadilly,
London, W1. 020 7395 5806
www.cafedeparis.com

G·A·Y·L·O·R·D
RESTAURANT
Why not bring your family, friends and business colleagues to experience Gaylord - the pioneer of Indian Tandoori and Muglai dishes around the world.
Gaylord takes pride in delivering the very best in Indian exotic food in splendid surroundings which promises to leave a lasting impression.
We also specialise in catering for wedding receptions.
79 - 81 Mortimer Street, London W1W 7SJ.
Tel: 0207 580 3615 / 636 0808. Fax: 0207 636 0860.

Bröderna OLSSON'S
GARLIC & SHOTS®
EVERYTHING WITH GARLIC
BEWARE
OF
GARLIC
Garlic Restaurant, the one and only
14 Frith Street, Soho, London W1. 020-7734 9505
FOLKUNGAG. 84, STOCKHOLM. 0046 8 6408446

In what must have been a bank, this huge T&J Bernard 'ale and pie house' does the full range of Fuller's ales and traditional beery pies in high-ceilinged, upholstered grand surroundings. The large painting of medieval London, with cheery market traders clinking tankards, sets the tone. Draught ESB, Chiswick, London Pride and a seasonal ale are complemented by rarer beers by the bottle, like 1845 and London Porter, originally a mix of malts popular with the workers at Billingsgate and Smithfield. It's used in the stews and pies sold (in the £8 range) at lunchtime and early evening. Eight wines come in each colour, five by the glass, including an Australian Five Mile Point cabernet merlot. An attractive gallery affords the best spots to sample what's on offer; a convivial back lounge is a no-smoking zone. An enormous painting in the main bar area shows a chaotic inn – also called the Jugged Hare – circa what looks like a time coterminous with the publication of *The Pickwick Papers*.
Gallery area available for hire (seats 40). Games (fruit machine). No-smoking area. TV (digital).

Millbank Lounge

30 John Islip Street, SW1P 4DD (7932 4700). Pimlico or Westminster tube. **Open** 11am-11pm Mon-Sat; noon-10.30pm Sun. **Food served** 11am-10pm Mon-Sat; noon-9.30pm Sun. **Credit** AmEx, DC, MC, V.
Tucked in behind the Embankment, the Pimlico branch in the stylish, urban, business City Inn hotel chain is the classiest thing around these parts. Beyond the open-plan lobby bustle, a flight of stairs leads you to this light-filled lounge, lined with four rows of furniture, a middle pair of red settees flanked by beige ones and dining tables. Inventive cocktails are divided into Classically Chic (£7.50, perhaps a Millbank Martini of Absolut Blue, calvados, vermouth and orange bitters), Modernist (£6.75, perhaps a Paradise Martini of Absolut Vanilla, strawberry liqueur and fresh strawberries), Latino Chic (£7.50, perhaps a Millbank Mojito made with Havana Club 7, fresh blackberries and lime juice) and Sparkles (£8.50, perhaps a Millbank Classic of Rémy Martin Grand Cru with a brown sugar cube soaked in apple schnapps and bitters, doused in pressed apple juice). Wines, six of each colour by the bottle and just two by the glass (Concha y Toro chardonnay or merlot), are complemented by draught Deuchars IPA or Bitburger.
Function room. Music (DJs 7pm Fri; free). Restaurant.

Morpeth Arms

58 Millbank, SW1P 4RW (7834 6442). Pimlico tube. **Open** 11am-11pm Mon-Sat; noon-10.30pm Sun. **Food served** noon-9pm Mon-Fri; 12.30-4pm Sat, Sun. **Credit** AmEx, DC, MC, V.
What could be more traditional than a good pint and a doorstep cheese-and-pickle sandwich after a hard morning's spying? Its modest front terrace facing the Thames and MI6 building opposite, the cosy Morpeth Arms makes the best of its location and its history: its walls remember its former life as Millbank Prison, Paul Dangerfield having transformed it into a public house of little nooks in 1845. The Morpeth is a Young's pub, with the usual Young's range of ales by the pump and bottle. Along with the aforementioned sandwiches (£3-£3.85, stilton and apple chutney another option), mains include catch-of-the-day fish in Young's beer batter (£6.95) and steak and Young's ale pie (£7.50). Off-duty spooks might also enjoy the traditional Sunday roasts. Five wines of each colour, two by the glass, include a reasonable Coto Bianco Rioja and superior Coto Crianza.
Function room. Games (fruit machine, quiz machine). No piped music or jukebox. Quiz (8.30pm every other Mon; £1). Tables outside (14, riverside terrace). TV.

Page

11 Warwick Way, SW1V 4LT (7834 3313). Pimlico tube/Victoria tube/rail. **Open** 11am-11pm Mon-Sat; noon-10.30pm Sun. **Food served** noon-3pm, 6-10pm Mon-Fri; noon-4pm, 6-10pm Sat; noon-4pm, 6-9.30pm Sun. **Credit** AmEx, MC, V.
Upmarket *Sporting Page* bars – pubs that think they're newspapers: first with the sports coverage, relaxing at lunchtimes – have their heartland in Hampstead, Putney and Richmond. This one is the Pimlico branch, brimming with Bollinger and Rothko-type art. It takes its tucker seriously too, winning ethnic pub food awards for its superior Thai kitchen, turning out either quality 'Express' (dim sum, tempura, soups) or 'Main' courses. Infused with Thai sweet basil, fresh chillies, coconut milk and cashews, with varieties such as slow-cooked pork with caramel dark soya sauce or roasted duck slices cooked in a red curry, and in the £7-£8 range, they really do put most pub lunches to shame. Not surprisingly, there's an upstairs restaurant. Beers are equally well chosen: draught London Pride, Hogs Back Brewery Traditional English Ale, and Beck's, Tiger and Nastro Azzurro by the bottle. Bollinger comes by the glass (£8), half-bottle (£21) and bottle (£38), and the large wine selection begins with a Baron Philippe de Rothschild sauvignon blanc or cabernet sauvignon at £3 a glass.
Babies and children admitted (before 6pm). Restaurant (available for hire). Tables outdoors (4, pavement). TV (big screen, satellite).

White Swan

14 Vauxhall Bridge Road, SW1V 2SA (7821 8568). Pimlico tube. **Open** 11am-11pm Mon-Sat; noon-10.30pm Sun. **Food served** noon-9pm daily. **Credit** AmEx, DC, JCB, MC, V.
A prominent, tourist-friendly, blokey boozer halfway between Victoria Station and the river, this traditional hostelry in the T&J Bernard stable excels in its range of ales. Pumps of Adnams Broadside, Marston's Pedigree, Morland Old Speckled Hen, Young's Best, Courage Directors and London Pride line the imposing bar counter, behind which stand fridges full of Brug's Beertje, Baltika, Budvar and Grimbergen. Freshly baked pies stand out among the standard pub lunches, best enjoyed in the raised, no-smoking front area of this long, capacious pub. Wooden banquettes lead to a back area piled with flyers advertising entertainment for tourists, and all is covered in metal knick-knacks, horseshoes and the like. Also mounted is an esoteric motto, relating the tale of the Swan who left her pond to dip her bill in Porter: it confuses local and tourist alike.
Games (fruit machine, quiz machine). No-smoking area. Tables outdoors (2, pavement).

ST JAMES'S

The streets basking in the reflected glory of the Ritz and St James's Palace north of the park of the same name contain pubs with historic overtones and bars of classy – and pricey – character. Three **Lions**, one Golden and two Reds, set the tone in terms of pub profile (polished and traditional), while keynote bars such as **Aura**, **Calma** and the astronomically priced **Rivoli at**

Central

the Ritz keep the well-heeled in classic and occasionally inventive cocktails.

Aura

48-49 St James's Street, SW1A 1JT (7499 6655/ www.the-aura.com). Green Park tube. **Open** 11.30am-3am Tue-Sat; 9.30pm-1.30am Sun. **Food served** 7-9.30pm Tue-Sat. **Credit** AmEx, DC, MC, V.

Aura has a new cocktail menu, but that aside, little has changed at this high-end bling of a bar, its tone set by the glittery topless mural that strikes you as you enter. So, if the mirrored surfaces, high ceilings, plum-coloured banquettes and Claridge's ballroom chandeliers are still in place – most of the staff, too – what of the cocktails? Well, at £7-£9 they promise much – and deliver. A Rum Monkey punched above its weight thanks to a dash of Myer's to complement the Appleton's VX, mint and watermelon; a little Chambord gave a kick to the Stoli, raspberries, blackberries and cranberry juice in the Berry Yogurty. Old favourites remain, especially the fruit Martinis (lychee, mango, passion fruit and three berries), and house classics like the Apple Seedless Martini of Pölstar Apple, grapes, Stoli and Chambord. It's diners (reserved in both senses of the word) and members only at weekends.

Music (DJs midnight Tue-Sun; £20; members only Fri). **Map 2 J7**.

Calma

23 St James's Street, SW1A 1HA (7747 9380/www. shumi-london.com). Green Park tube. **Open** noon-1am Mon-Fri; 6.30pm-1am Sat. **Food served** noon-3pm, 6.30-10pm Mon-Sat. **Credit** AmEx, MC, V.

A name change and a few Soviet propaganda posters, but this cool lounge bar is still very much part of the upstairs restaurant, Shumi, whose name it also used to share. It has the restaurant's automatic, convex doors, and the same fine Tuscan meats star in its lunchtime and evening snack selection. Here, though, cocktails rule: fresh fruit Bellinis (£8.50) in six flavours, dozens of classic Martinis (£8.50), plus contemporary concoctions and sours in the £7-£8 range. It's Grey Goose, Junipero and Myer's all the way, plus Taittinger champagne in the London Special flute (£8.50) to top the orange zest, bitters and sugar. Even the beers (Little Creatures Pale Ale £4, Peroni Gran Reserva £4.50) have been carefully chosen, complemented by a comprehensive selection of vintage rums, malts and grappas. The wine list is strong on Tuscan reds, and the olive-green chaises longues and swishy venetian blinds provide suitably dignified decor.

Babies and children welcome (restaurant). Function room. Music (band 7.30pm Wed; free). Restaurant. Specialities (cocktails). Tables outdoors (13, pavement). **Map 2 J8**.

Golden Lion

25 King Street, SW1Y 6QY (7925 0007). Green Park or Piccadilly Circus tube. **Open** 11am-11pm Mon-Fri; noon-6pm Sat. **Food served** noon-9pm Mon-Fri; noon-5pm Sat. **Credit** AmEx, MC, V.

This sturdy boozer might appear somewhat faux historic, given all the heraldic tat stacked round the interior – but the protruding circular exterior and upstairs bar are both hangovers from the time it served drinks to Oscar Wilde at the adjoining St James's Theatre (despite a campaign by Laurence Olivier and Vivien Leigh, who both performed there, the theatre was knocked down in 1957): a plaque even records the Lion's service as the Golden Theatre Bar from 1762, although today the crowds – mainly blokey, mainly lunchtime – are here for the draught ales, meaty mains and notable selection of malts. Morland Old Speckled Hen, London Pride and Harvey's Sussex are the draught options, Marston's Pedigree Spitfire and Abbot come by the bottle. Wines (Valdivieso sauvignon blanc, Marktree chardonnay) begin at £3.30 a glass. The almost regal snugness of the downstairs lounge is occasionally fractured by the bleeping of the fruit machine – try to get a table upstairs.

Restaurant. Specialities (real ale). Tables outdoors (3, pavement). TV. **Map 2 J8**.

Red Lion

23 Crown Passage, off Pall Mall, SW1Y 6PP (7930 4141). Green Park or St James's Park tube. **Open/food served** 11am-11pm Mon-Sat. **Credit** MC, V.

'London's oldest village inn' belongs to a time long before sandwich chains: indeed, this low-ceilinged, wooden pub is anachronistically conspicuous down a busy, pedestrianised alleyway between King Street and Pall Mall. Once you get inside, though, time slows down amid a decor of glazed windows, horse brasses and plates. The beers, too, lend themselves to unhurried quaffing: draught Adnams, Bass and John Smith's sipped by sturdy types around the four-square bar counter in the corner. Some might also accompany their pint with a malt from the three dozen on offer, the history of Glenfiddich depicted in the vintage cases lining the back bar. The staff are of the cheery, timeless type, whose forebears may have served nearby resident Nell Gwynne as she waited for the next bout in her liaison with King Charles II – who, legend has it, used to nip over from St James's Palace.

Babies and children admitted (daytime). Function room. TV. **Map 2 J8**.

Red Lion

2 Duke of York Street, SW1Y 6JP (7321 0782). Piccadilly Circus tube. **Open** noon-11pm Mon-Sat. **Food served** noon-4pm Mon-Sat. **Credit** V.

Everything is just so in this lovely example of detailed Victorian pub interior design. The woodwork and manifold glass, delicately carved and chiselled, are kept pristine and polished, allowing the island bar to stand out in the intimate, two-space interior. The ales – Wadworth 6X, London Pride, Adnams, Tetley's and Bass Premium – are equally cared for, and the lunchtime choice of pub dishes is created with a discerning, well-turned-out public in mind: no stringy steaks or sloppy pies here. What they can't do – heaven forbid – is alter the dimensions, which means that lunchtimes and post-work of a late weekday prove to be the tightest of squeezes. In summer the pavement doubles up as a front terrace; in winter, come back when things are quieter. It'll be worth it.

No piped music or jukebox. **Map 2 J7**.

Rivoli at the Ritz

Ritz Hotel, 150 Piccadilly, W1J 9BR (7493 8181). Green Park tube. **Open** noon-11pm Mon-Sat; noon-10.30pm Sun. **Food served** noon-10pm daily. **Credit** AmEx, MC, V.

Old school from its dress code (jackets only) to its bar snacks (olives, mixed nuts, roasted crisps), the brown lacquered Rivoli bar in the lobby of the Ritz (take a hard right by the piano player) offers reassuringly crafted cocktails at assuredly absurd prices. The 20 champagne cocktails (all priced at £16 – including a Kir Royale!) and 15 after-dinner varieties (£14) cover all bases – Manhattan, Brandy

Alexander, Bellini and French 75 – with a few house concoctions thrown in. Along with a Ritz Fizz (Amaretto, Blue Curaçao, lemon juice and champagne) and a Ritz Whiskers (Blanton's whisky, vanilla vodka, Amaretto, apple juice), a Cesar Ritz of Armagnac, peach liqueur, grenadine and champagne and Raw Deal Martini of vodka, Pomme Verte, fresh carrot juice and fresh apple juice add character. Small bottles of beer (including the rarer Boddington's and Nyevskoe) begin at £6, and even an espresso will cost you a fiver. But it's not cheap to keep barstaff in white linen jackets and the tables stacked with fresh flowers, after all.
Disabled: toilet. Dress: jacket (no jeans or trainers). No piped music or jukebox. **Map 2 J8**.

Studio Lounge

5th floor, Waterstone's, 203-206 Piccadilly, W1J 9HA (7851 2400). Piccadilly Circus tube. **Open** 10am-10pm Mon-Sat; noon-5pm Sun. **Food served** noon-4pm, 6-9pm Mon-Sat; noon-5pm Sun. **Credit** (over £10) AmEx, MC, V.

Every bookstore should have one! Instead of providing just sticky buns and frothy coffees – although these are also available – the panoramic café of Waterstone's Piccadilly does a nice line in cocktails with a view. The surroundings are pretty grand anyway (this was once the prestigious Simpsons department store), but the fifth-floor venue offers the kind of eye candy you can normally only get at the bar of a five-star hotel or high-rise financial building. It's run by Searcy's, responsible for landmark venues such as Portrait in the National Portrait Gallery and the Amphitheatre restaurant at the Royal Opera House, so quality is assured. Champagne cocktails, Martinis (£6.50-£8.50) and drinks short and long cover the classics with style and decent measures of quality spirits. The mixing breaks few boundaries, but your Manhattan or French 75 would stand up to most of the competition around town. The beer choice includes bottled Asahi and Paulaner wheat, wines come in six of each colour, from £3.30 a glass and £13.50-£27 by the bottle. Bar snacks maintain standards – at a price.
Babies and children admitted (until 5pm). Disabled: toilet. Function rooms. Restaurant. **Map 2 J7**.

Also in the area…

Davy's at St James Crown Passage, Pall Mall, SW1Y 6QY (7839 8831).
Tapster (Davy's) 3 Brewers Green, Buckingham Gate, SW1H 0RH (7222 0561).

SOHO

Perhaps it's the sky-high rates; maybe it's the fact that every location is taken; but Soho has been suffering from a dearth of new drinking venues. The classic haunts on and off spinal Old Compton Street – **Lab**, the **French House**, **Café Bohème** – have changed little, nor have the ones dotted between Regent Street and Wardour Street. The gay scene, roughly concentrated around the Old Compton-Wardour T-junction, hasn't really evolved, either. There's still plenty to do, and plenty to do late at night, but you feel as if Soho needs a couple more keynote venues to liven things up.

DRINKING ALOUD
SALIM KHOURY

Who are you? I'm head barman and bar manager of the Savoy (*see p93*). I came to England and to the Savoy on the same day – 4th June 1969. And I'm still here…
Drinking in London: what's good about it? You know, my whole life is in cocktails – so when I go out, I'm afraid I don't drink cocktails, I have a gin and tonic. Best drink in the world.
What could be improved? The gin and tonic! It's the pride of England, but in how many bars can you get a decent one? Very few. If you ask for ice, the barman looks at you as though you've come from outer space. A slice of lime instead of lemon? Long tumbler? He thinks you're interfering with his job. But that's just one example. Beers – we don't want flat beers… Why not always serve the best?
What's caught your eye in the last year? Cocktails are more popular than ever – and London is now the cocktail capital of the world. You can have whatever you want, all the ingredients are available. 20 years ago we didn't have mango juice, we didn't have cranberry juice, passion fruit juice, we had only one or two kinds of vodkas – now there are hundreds of vodkas, hundreds of juices.
What's in your crystal ball? The traditional head barman as we know him now is, perhaps, losing his independence: food and beverage managers like to run the bar like everything else. But I still run my bar the way I want to!
New licensing law: good or bad? The British people have been waiting for this for a hundred years. There's nothing wrong with it. People come to London from all over the world – why shouldn't they have a drink after 11?

Admiral Duncan

54 Old Compton Street, W1D 4UD (7437 5300). Leicester Square or Piccadilly Circus tube. **Open** noon-11pm Mon-Sat; noon-10.30pm Sun. **Credit** MC, V.

The chubby gent swinging over the pink and purple frontage of this landmark gay bar looks somewhat smug, but then he has every reason to be. Since it unfurled the rainbow flag a decade or more ago, this once unremarkable boozer halfway down Old Compton Street has blossomed, surviving the homophobic bombing of April 1999 in which three people died, coping with the aftermath with grit and dignity. Today it's a party venue for a slightly more mature, more mixed crowd than frequents the likes of Compton of Soho (*see p81*) and G.A.Y. nearby – although shooters (three for £5) are still necked by the bucketload. By day the Duncan is as sedate as a library, the only sounds being the quiet sipping of Kronenbourg or John Smith's and the spinning of the fruit machine.

Games (fruit machines, quiz machine). **Map 7 K6.**

Ain't Nothin' But? The Blues Bar

20 Kingly Street, W1B 5PZ (7287 0514/www.aintnothinbut.co.uk). Oxford Circus or Piccadilly Circus tube. **Open** 6pm-1am Mon-Wed; 6pm-2am Thur; noon-3am Fri, Sat; 7.30pm-midnight Sun. **Credit** MC, V.

This rather splendid music enthusiasts' bar and modest live venue is celebrating '10 Rockin' Years', and well it might. Its name is a slight reworking of a title by Georgia White, whose Decca 78 is mounted alongside the 12-bar sheet music, photos and concert bills of hangdog bluesmen opposite the bar; a wall of fame covers a tiny staircase and cellar. In the back area of benches and bar tables, a small stage hosts the likes of Hucklebuck, The Bluematics and others. Saturday afternoon is open-mic time: a whole mess of wailing about slavery and cotton, while shoppers struggle down Kingly Street with bulging bags from nearby Liberty. Draught Adnams Bitter and Broadside, Everards, Murphy's and Red Stripe keep things nicely rocking, as do Southern Comfort, JD and Jim Beam – and everyone has a rare ole time.

Music (jazz/musicians nightly; open mic 2pm Sat). **Map 2 J6.**

Akbar

77 Dean Street, W1D 3SH (7437 2525/www.redfort.co.uk/akbar). Leicester Square, Piccadilly Circus or Tottenham Court Road tube. **Open** 5pm-1am Mon-Sat. **Food served** 5-11pm Mon-Thur; 5-11.30pm Fri, Sat. **Happy hour** 5-6pm Mon-Sat. **Credit** AmEx, MC, V.

Occupying an exotic, mood-enhancing basement, Akbar has changed little since it was established as part of the makeover of the Red Fort Indian restaurant above in 2001. Its cocktails – with names such as Zaafroon, Jahangir and Great Mughal (named, presumably, for Akbar, who was himself one) – still feature the zesty delights used in the high-class cuisine upstairs: ginger, lemongrass and chilli among others. Most cost a reasonable £6.50-£7 a throw, with a 60-minute 'twofer' happy hour from 5pm. Bar snacks (nizami samosas, seekh kebabs, £6) are similarly spicy, and the bottled house lager is southern India's Kingfisher. Low red lights and two alcoves at either end of the narrow cellar space encourage intimacy, as does the midweek lounge music. More uptempo DJ sets from Thursday to Saturday see bar stools cleared away and the smart, young professional clientele hit the dancefloor.

Bar available for hire. Music (DJs 8pm Thur-Sat). Restaurant. TV (digital, plasma). **Map 7 K6.**

Alphabet

61-63 Beak Street, W1F 9SS (7439 2190/www.alphabetbar.com). Oxford Circus or Piccadilly Circus tube. **Open** noon-11pm Mon-Fri; 5-11pm Sat. **Food served** noon-5pm, 5-9pm Mon-Fri; 5-9pm Sat. **Credit** AmEx, JCB, MC, V.

One of London's most notable examples of cool bar design – the A-Z street-plan floor of the basement at Alphabet – has been removed in a recent spring clean, leaving this ever-popular west Soho landmark somewhat bereft. Upstairs too, where you'll find the main bar and chatty diners from lunchtime to mid-evening, the walls are bare; Chito's dripping CDs downstairs are prettty much all the in-house art left. The menu, though, is pretty much unaltered: half a dozen bottles of each colour of wine, three each by the glass starting from £4.50 (for Spanish El Muro Bodegas Lozano white and Chilean Casa de Piedra cabernet sauvignon); bottles of Asahi, Cruzcampo, Hoegaarden, Negro Modelo and San Miguel at £3.30 each. The lunch menu changes daily, ensuring return custom, and the DJ decks downstairs still kick ass of an evening.

Babies and children admitted (until 5pm). Music (DJs 7.30pm Thur-Sat). Specialities (cocktails). **Map 2 J6.**

Amber

6 Poland Street, W1F 8PS (7734 3094/www.amberbar.com). Oxford Circus tube. **Open** noon-1am Mon-Sat. **Food served** noon-midnight Mon-Sat. **Credit** AmEx, MC, V.

The younger, more prim and proper sister of the rather wilder Alphabet, Amber combines a Latin-tinged cocktail lounge with a superior tapas bar. Upstairs at street level, diners partitioned off into separate booths tuck into dishes divided into fish (filo prawns with orange mayo, £4.90), meat (half-rack of baby back-ribs in barbecue sauces, £5.50) and vegetarian varieties, while in the more loungey downstairs room, a sleek, neat, youngish crowd chatters over (generally) £6.30 cocktails of the Creamy, Bubbly and Martini type. Although Chivas, Ketel One and Wyborowa are used, the house specialities are made with tequila: Buena Vista, South of the Border, Dirty Sanchez and the tangy Agave Julep (Aguavero tequila, mint, ginger, lime and sugar). Bottled beers include Mexican Pacifico and Negro Modelo, and the mainly Latin wine list starts at £4.50 a glass.

Function room. Music (DJs 8pm Thur-Sat). Restaurant. Tables outdoors (2, pavement). **Map 2 J6.**

Argyll Arms

18 Argyll Street, W1F 7TP (7734 6117). Oxford Circus tube. **Open** 11am-11pm Mon-Sat; noon-10.30pm Sun. **Food served** 11am-10pm Mon-Sat; noon-9pm Sun. **Credit** AmEx, MC, V.

When Robert Sawyer redesigned this grand pub as an ornately partitioned ground-floor public area and first-floor mahogany-lined Palladium Bar, he had in mind the social classes of the late 1890s, not the global, consumerist London of a century later. The delicately carved snugs that once differentiated servant from clerk now accommodate shoppers and tourists from Australia to Alaska and a steady tide of W1 workers, movers and chancers. The Argyll is slap next to Oxford Circus tube exit; no more central or crowded rendezvous pub could be imagined, unless a modern-day Sawyer builds one beneath the neon of Piccadilly Circus. The world and his wife are catered for with Bombardier, Greene King IPA and London Pride on tap, standard lagers and pub grub. The wines are those common to pubs of the Nicholson's stable: Hardy's Nottage Hill (£8) and up.

Dog & Duck. *See p83.*

Babies and children admitted (restaurant). Games (fruit machines). No-smoking (upstairs bar). Restaurant (available for hire). Tables outdoors (5, pavement). **Map 1 J6**.

Bar Chocolate

27 D'Arblay Street, W1F 8EN (7287 2823). Oxford Circus or Tottenham Court Road tube. **Open/food served** 10am-11pm Mon-Sat; noon-10.30pm Sun. **Credit** MC, V.

This one-time boho bar – come to mention it, this much-revered erstwhile Bar Tactical – is now as mainstream as any downtown drinkerie, laminated menus and all. Many of the customers are barely out of their teens, an impression accentuated by the school furniture arrayed across the checkered lino floor. Several are here for the food: tortillas, ciabattas and salads in the £6 range, accompanied by wine (from £3.10 a glass of Coteaux d'Ardèche to £25 a bottle of chablis). The £6 cocktails include a Bar Chocolate of Myers rum, Crème de Cacao and Bailey's; Budvar, Beck's and Baltika are among the bottled beers. All is as it should be, except that the cool crowd left thataway a long time ago.

Babies and children admitted (until 6pm). Tables outdoors (3, pavement). **Map 1 J6**.

Barcode

3-4 Archer Street, W1D 7AP (7734 3342/ www.bar-code.co.uk). Leicester Square or Piccadilly Circus tube. **Open** 4pm-1am Mon-Sat; 4-10.30pm Sun. **Happy hour** 4-7pm daily. **Admission** £3 after 11pm Fri, Sat. **Credit** AmEx, MC, V.

An off-Rupert Street meat market that takes its fun seriously. Well-packed honchos with bristly moustaches muscle their way around this two-level up-for-it gay bar; you might as well be at a body-building club, except that everyone's buzzing on shooters (Quick Fuck, Landslide, Dave, Goldfinger and Adios Mutherfucker among the 30 offered), Archer's or Breezers, and looking for action. You're more likely to find it in the dimly lit industrial space downstairs, not least on Thursday's Homosocial ('street-style snogging'), or Monday's ultra-cheap Happy Hour evening. Tuesdays bring comedy, Saturdays pre-clubbing liveners. Beers include draught Kronenbourg Blanc and John Smith's, and bottled Budvar and Beck's ('not the footballer'). Check out the flyers stuck on the wall for further titters; hirsute machos with ridiculous names are all the rage.

Comedy (8pm, Tue, £7/£5 members). Music (DJs 9pm-1am Mon, Wed-Sat). Specialities (shots). **Map 7 K6**.

Bar Constante @ Floridita

100 Wardour Street, W1F 0TN (7314 4000/www. floriditalondon.com). Tottenham Court Road tube. **Open/food served** 5.30-2am Mon-Wed; 5.30pm-3am Thur-Sat. **Credit** AmEx, Dc, MC, V.

Floridita allows the opportunity to fraternise in the old-fashioned way – as well it should, given the pedigree. Beneath his now tapas-oriented Mezo (formerly Mezzo) restaurant, Terence Conran has teamed up with Cuba's renowned (if tourist-pitched) Floridita bar to open this London branch. Glitzy couples gaze absent-mindedly at the film-set scene of hot waitresses swaying past with clanking trays of exotic drinks, to the experienced rhythm of the house band. It's all a little forced, really: pearls before undiscerning swine. The quality of the cocktails, though, cannot be gainsaid. Fairly priced (£7-£8), categorised Cuban or international, old or new, they are flawless. Pride of place goes to the Daiquiri, invented at the venue's Havana counterpart and here offered in five classic and reinvented varieties, with Havana Club Anejo Blanco as the base. Churchill (with fresh lime and Earl Grey tea syrup) or Pomegranate may be inventive, but you can't beat the old timers. It's all in the maraschino.

Disabled: toilet. Function room. Music (DJ/live band 8pm nightly; £10 Thur-Sat after 10pm). Restaurant. Specialities (cocktails). **Map 2 K6**.

Bar Soho

23-25 Old Compton Street, W1D 5JQ (7439 0439). Leicester Square or Piccadilly Circus tube. **Open/food served** 4pm-1am Mon-Thur; 4pm-3am Fri, Sat; 4pm-12.30am Sun. **Admission** £3 after 11pm Mon-Thur; £5 after 9.30pm; £8 (for men) after 11pm Fri-Sat. **Credit** AmEx, DC, MC, V.

Thanks to its position slap in the centre of Old Compton Street, Soho's high street, Bar Soho is as busy as any venue in West One. From mid-afternoon until past midnight, seven days a week, this cosy, conspiratorial bar echoes with incessant chatter. Light from the fat medieval candles flickers over the naughty sculptures on the long, sturdy counter. Behind them, fridges of Beck's, Buds and Breezers are on hand. There's a constant traffic of mainly straight punters, who perch on the heavy furniture spread over the stone floor. Long mirrors reflect the moving tableau of action. After dark, a glitterball and the DJ decks come to the fore, and folk poodle out to obey the five-lettered instruction mounted across the back, and DANCE.

Function room. Music (DJs 9.30pm nightly). Tables outdoors (4, pavement). **Map 7 K6**.

Barsolona

15-17 Old Compton Street, W1D 5JH (7287 9932). Leicester Square or Tottenham Court Road tube. **Open** 6pm-3am Mon-Sat; 6-11pm Sun. **Credit** AmEx, MC, V.

Way back when Barcelona was newly hip, this basement tapas bar, ideally located at Soho's epicentre, manned by hip Latins and mobbed by party-minded punters with their snouts in troughs of sangría, was all the rage. There's still no shortage of lively Latin bar staff – or sangría at £14.30 a jug – but the thrill, most certainly, has gone. Not that Barsolona does anything wrong (apart from the dreadful name): standard cocktails cost less than £6; champagne cocktails and Martinis go for £6.50; vinos blancos and tintos start at £3.50 a glass; standard tapas are £5 each. The setting's fine, too: a fairy-lit, tiled cellar cornered with intimate alcoves. Yet not even two hours of reduced drink prices (weekdays only) can raise the tempo here. Perhaps by now everybody has visited the real city of Barcelona and don't need a hand-me-down version.

Music (DJs 11pm Mon-Sat; £3-£4 Fri, Sat). Specialities (cocktails). TV (satellite). **Map 7 K6**.

Café Bohème

13 Old Compton Street, W1D 5JQ (7734 0623/ www.cafeboheme.co.uk). Leicester Square tube. **Open** 8am-3am Mon-Sat; 8am-10.30pm Sun. **Food served** 8am-2.30am Mon-Sat; 8am-10pm Sun. **Credit** AmEx, DC, MC, V.

This stylish French brasserie serves breakfast and late-hour cocktails with equal aplomb. Whether it's quality coffee, freshly squeezed orange juice, fluffy brioches and the day's newspapers from either side of the Channel, or just drinks finely mixed with high-end spirits, the starched-shirt service is crisp from one end of the day to the other. Of an evening, a reasonably hip crowd gathers for chic, original cocktails such as Toblerone (Stoli vanilla and Frangelico), Absinthe Minded (over caramelised sugar),

Xan (fresh ginger, Xante pear liqueur, Absolut Citron) and Death by Chocolate (Bailey's, Absolut, Crème de Cacao and chocolate ice-cream), an excellent selection of wines from £3.30 a glass, and 'petits plats' (£5) including tiger prawns and quality charcuterie. The bouncer on the door reminds you that you're in W1 and not the 4th *arrondissement.*
Babies and children admitted (before 7pm). Music (jazz 4-6pm Thur, Sun). Restaurant. Tables outdoors (9, pavement). **Map 7 K6**.

Candy Bar

4 Carlisle Street, W1D 3BJ (7494 4041/www.thecandybar.co.uk). Tottenham Court Road tube. **Open/snacks served** 5-11.30pm Mon-Thur; 5pm-2am Fri, Sat; 5-11pm Sun. **Happy hour** 5-7pm daily. **Credit** AmEx, DC, MC, V.

Formerly a members' club, London's leading lezzer bar (ten years young in 2006) has stuck firmly to its entry criteria: lesbian or bisexual women, and men only if gay and accompanied. Its narrow confines are split into two distinct areas: the discreet ground-floor lounge bar with leather seating, neutral colours and glass, where halves of Red Stripe and toasted ciabattas can be consumed at leisure; downstairs is a bear pit. It's this raucous, sweat-soaked basement, where women in party mood can romp with wild abandon, that has earned the Candy Bar its notoriety. The fashionable, pretty and party-oriented clientele can also indulge in the less hectic pursuits of midweek pool and karaoke; weekend DJ nights incur a modest entrance fee.
Entertainment (strip night 8.30-11.30pm Tue, Thur, £3; 8.30pm-2am Sat, £6. Karaoke (9pm Wed; free). Music (DJs 9pm nightly; £5). **Map 7 K6**.

Clachan

34 Kingly Street, W1B 5QH (7494 0834). Oxford Circus tube. **Open** 11am-11pm Mon-Sat; noon-10.30pm Sun. **Food served** noon-10pm daily. **Credit** (over £10) AmEx, MC, V.

Gaelic for 'Meeting Place', the Clachan, once the Bricklayer's Arms, then part of neighbouring Liberty, is one of the more classy operations in the Nicholson's stable. 'Regional hand-pulled ales' are promised, and sure enough, Adnams, Timothy Taylor Landlord, London Pride and guest beers such as Ushers Winter Storm and Haggis Bash, are served to a mainly blokey clientele in the invariably crowded front bar. Hidden behind the ornate, finely carved back bar is a modest lounge area featuring a cosy raised alcove. Upstairs the surroundings are more sedate and include an open fire; this room is mainly used for private evening bashes or for dining (sausages a speciality: mushroom and tarragon or pork and leek, for instance). A dozen varieties of wine begin at less than £8 a bottle – though this is for Hardy's Nottage Hill. Otherwise, the Clachan is heartily recommended.
Function room. Games (fruit machine). Specialities (real ale, whisky). **Map 2 J6**.

Coach & Horses

29 Greek Street, W1V 5LL (7437 5920). Leicester Square or Piccadilly Circus tube. **Open** 11am-11pm Mon-Sat; noon-10.30pm Sun. **Happy hour** 11am-4pm Mon-Fri, Sun. **Credit** MC, V.

Watching the West End's self-proclaimed rudest landlord terrorise staff and customers, we had a brilliant idea: 'I'm A Celebrity, Last Orders Please', in which ten Z-listers labour under the baleful eye of said landlord Norman Balon to convince sceptical customers that £3.10 is not too much to pay for a pint of London Pride. We could be witness to the horror of Tara Palmer-Tompkinson as she heads into the ever-grim Coach loos; the hissy fits of Antony Worrall Thompson as he grapples with the culinary phenomenon that is the Coach's £1 all-day sandwiches; and the gradual disintegration of the fixedly smiling Hamiltons as they wither under a barrage of insults from the spivs, hacks, queens, trannies, would-bes and has-beens that make up the (ir)regulars at this corner pub. Only drawback: it would be hard to persuade Norm to hold off sacking the whole bunch before the end of the first show.
No piped music or jukebox. TV. **Map 7 K6**.

Comptons of Soho

51-53 Old Compton Street, W1D 6HJ (7479 7961/www.comptons-of-soho.co.uk). Leicester Square or Piccadilly Circus tube. **Open** noon-11pm Mon-Sat; noon-10.30pm Sun. **Happy hour** 7-11pm Mon. **Credit** AmEx, MC, V.

Comptons, one of Soho's landmark gay bars, doesn't do subtlety. By day, drinkers drool over passers-by from the vast front windows; these folk in turn may occasionally look in as if choosing a puppy in a pet store. Inside, a large circular bar counter is surrounded by blokes pretending to look busy – flicking through magazines, whistling to themselves, staring at the ceiling. It may as well be a dentist's waiting room, or a practice venue for trainees at spy school. But as it's a bar, alcohol is sold: Carling and London Pride on draught, Asahi, Beck's and Breezers by the bucketload. Now and then blokes poke their heads round the half-wall of a padded open back lounge. Upstairs, after dark… well, find out for yourselves.
Games (fruit machines, pool table). Music (DJs 8-11pm Mon, Fri, Sat; free). TV (big screen, satellite). **Map 7 K6**.

Couch

97-99 Dean Street, W1D 3TE (7287 0150). Tottenham Court Road tube. **Open** 11am-11pm Mon-Fri; noon-11am Sat; noon-10.30pm Sun. **Food served** 11am-9pm Mon-Thur; 11am-6pm Fri; noon-9pm Sat, Sun. **Credit** AmEx, MC, V.

Why complain about Couch? It does fine cocktails (Strasberi Slings with Pimms and Stoli raspberry, £5.80; Honey Mules with 42 Below vodka, Manuka honey and ginger beer, £6.90), its wines are well chosen (Grillo, Duca di Castelmonte from Sicily, £6 a large glass; a Bodega Ondarre Rioja Reserva, £6.50) and its food is more than a cut above: cinnamon-roasted duck breast in a rich cherry sauce at £10.95, for example. It's a comfortable spot, with lounge seating in three corners and simple wooden tables in between. Draught beers are OK, if limited: San Miguel, Guinness and Kronenbourg. So where's the snag? Well, Couch is gastrobar-by-rote, a soulless operation for smug couples, foursomes and solitary *Standard* readers. It's everything Clapham is and Soho shouldn't be – and, deep in Dean Street (albeit opposite Tesco), this grates.
Music (DJs 8-11pm Sat; free). **Map 7 K6**.

Courthouse Hotel

19-21 Great Marlborough Street, W1F 7HH (7297 5555). Oxford Circus tube. **Open/food served** 11am-11pm daily. **Credit** AmEx, DC, MC, V.

The Courthouse Hotel, in its early 'soft launch' period as we went to press, promised interesting things. In a former incarnation as the Great Marlborough Street Magistrates' Court it was the setting for several historic brushes with the law, including Oscar Wilde's 'Queensberry' case, the trial involving John Lennon's 'obscene' (some said merely

the Green

The Green is as much pub as bar, with toothsome Timothy Taylor Landlord on draught and an unpretentious pubby feel. There's a good selection of spirits, decent wines, and worthwhile bottled beers such as Duval. In the evenings the food is an array of good quality Spanish tapas: boquerones, chorizo, roasted pepper salad, cubes of manchego in olive oil. At lunchtime the menu's more extensive, and might include Cornish crab salad followed by roast pheasant with chestnuts and cranberries. The staff are welcoming and professional, setting the tone for the kind of simple bar that's a pleasure to linger in. Guy Dimond. Time Out.

29 Clerkenwell Green, EC1R 0DU
020 7490 8010
Hours: Open Mon-Sat 12noon-12midnight;
Sun 12noon-11.30pm
Nearest tube ⊖ Farringdon tube/rail

TOM & DICK'S
BAR & DINNING

WWW.TOMANDDICKS.COM TEL: 020 7229 7711
30 ALEXANDER STREET, LONDON W2
NEAREST TUBE - ROYAL OAK

MONDAY TO SATURDAY: 6.30PM - 12.30AM
SUNDAY: 6.30PM - 10.30PM
SUNDAY BRUNCH: 11.00AM - 4.00PM

TWO FLOORS OF LAVISH ART DECO AND OUTSTANDING FURNITURE
THE RIGHT ATMOSPHEAR FOR ALL OCCASIONS.

DINNER SERVED - TUESDAY TO SATURDAY (BOOKINGS ESSENTIAL)

BOOK CLUB : SUNDAY MOVIES : ART EXHIBITIONS : COCKTAIL BAR : MODERN BISTRO : ECLECTIC MUSIC

bad) lithographs, and various drugs-related Rolling Stones run-ins. The bar plays on these associations. Opening off a low-lit, slate- and leather-furnished main room are three prison cells converted into private booths, complete with urinal ice buckets (we're not joking). The modish and appealing cocktail list includes such penal-themed concoctions as Behind Bars (pear cognac with white crème de cacao and cream, sprinkled with with nutmeg 'bars') and Red Silk (raspberries, raspberry vodka, Campari and lemonade). When we visited, service and atmosphere were a little strained; however, given the exenuating circumstances – bar manager Angelika Hammerer had yet to take up residence – we reserve judgment.
Babies and children welcome. Disabled: toilet. Function rooms. Restaurants. **Map 1 J6**.

Crobar

17 Manette Street, W1D 4AS (7439 0831/ www.crobar.co.uk). Tottenham Court Road tube. **Open** 5pm-3am Mon-Sat. **Happy hour** 5-9pm Mon-Sat. **Credit** MC, V.
Guarding the Borderline, this rather quaint hairies' bar beside one of London's major rock venues is, if anything, just a little too tidy. No initiation ceremonies here, no sirree. Even if you felt like walking round the bar wearing the toilet seat, you'd find it's been superglued down. Round-shouldered young musos clutching record-sleeve-shaped carrier bags shamble in from Hanway Street, almost rubbing shoulders with the peacock-proud and hairy-chested types posing with their JDs (on special offer) at the narrow bar counter. In a comic-muralled back area, guitar followers of both sexes congregate around £16 cocktail jugs. If you're after a serious pre-gig sesh – the Astoria is also around the corner – hit the £3 shooters such as Brain Haemorrhage (Archer's and Bailey's) or Viva Knievel (sambuca and Blue Aftershock) before inventing an equally ridiculous name plus one for a guest-list blag.
Jukebox. Specialities (bourbon). **Map 7 K6**

Crown & Two Chairmen

31 Dean Street, W1D 3SB (7437 8192). Tottenham Court Road tube. **Open** noon-11pm Mon-Sat. **Food served** noon-7pm Mon-Fri. **Credit** AmEx, MC, V.
The name, legend has it, comes from Queen Anne's chairmen, who would deposit her across the road to have her portrait painted, then nip in here for a crafty pint. Today they would have a field day, what with Adnams, Greene King IPA and London Pride on draught, Amstel if they were feeling European and fiver-a-bottle plonk (£1.65 a glass!) if they were short of the readies. If they were hungry, bingo! Mains – smothered chicken in barbecue sauce, rump steak – come in standard, large and king-size varieties, from around £5 to £10, and can be devoured on comfy banquettes in the more intimate back area. Front of house means sport on three TVs and pop quiz machines, and there are comedy shows of a Saturday evening.
Comedy (8pm Mon; free; 8pm Sat; £8/£9). Function room. Games (fruit machines, golf machine). TVs (satellite). **Map 7 K6**.

Dog & Duck

18 Bateman Street, W1D 3AJ (7494 0697). Tottenham Court Road tube. **Open** noon-11pm Mon-Sat; noon-10.30pm Sun. **Food served** noon-9pm daily. **Credit** AmEx, MC, V.
This venerable corner pub, the size of a largish newsstand, crams a lot into its pretty, tiled and mirrored interior. Good beers, for a start: pumps of Timothy Taylor Landlord, London Pride, and Greene King IPA line the wooden bar counter occupying half of the front bar. Bottles of Beck's, Budvar and Pilsner Urquell cater to non-ale drinkers, and there's Addlestone's cloudy cider on draught. If there's no room out front, and there won't be, grab a seat in the intimate, comfortably upholstered back area, with its vintage stamp machine on the wall. Between front and back, there's a staircase leading up to the George Orwell wine bar, and overspill tables for diners tucking into brie, wensleydale or cheddar ploughman's, or various mains (stuffing pie!) with chips and peas.
Function room. **Map 7 K6**.

Edge

11 Soho Square, W1D 3QE (7439 1313/www.edge.uk.com). Tottenham Court Road tube. **Open/food served** noon-1am Mon-Sat; noon-10.30pm Sun. **Credit** MC, V.
The only bar to make full use of Soho Square's prime pavement space, the Edge leads a double life. By day, it's a laid-back bar-diner, its downstairs clientele perched on half-a-dozen tables in a modest lounge corner, consuming £5 daily specials (chicken korma, pastas), soups and salads, pints of Stella or Boddingtons or £3.30 glasses of Reynier Blanc Sec or Rouge. The after-dark life upstairs is hinted at with tacky pop videos on a large screen in the lounge area, offers of combinations of vodka and Red Bull for £10, and flyers in gaudy colours showing phallic bananas. Once the sun sets and punters drift away from those convivial pavement pints, a nominal sum is demanded for entry to the piano bar and dance club upstairs, and a mainly gay crowd lets rip.
Babies and children welcome (until 6pm). Function rooms. Music (pianist 9pm-midnight Tue-Thur; DJs from 9pm Thur-Sun). Tables outdoors (6, pavement). TV (plasma screen, satellite). **Map 7 K6**.

Endurance

90 Berwick Street, W1F 0QB (7437 2944). Tottenham Court Road or Oxford Circus tube. **Open** noon-11pm Mon-Sat; 12.30-10.30pm Sun. **Food served** 12.30-4pm Mon-Sat; 1-4.30pm Sun. **Credit** MC, V.
Combining the best elements of pub and bar, hidden amid Berwick Street market (look out for the wild boar logo), the sassy Endurance fills its swanky black banquettes from noon till night. It is most cherished by the vinyl fraternity; Sister Ray and at least four other record stores do good business nearby. The jukebox is as cared for as the selection of bourbons (Wild Turkey 8, and the like) and beers. Deuchar's IPA, London Pride, John Smith's and Hoegaarden all feature on tap, but it's the quality of food (until 4pm) that raises the Endurance above the level of a drop-in centre for Soho music obsessives: gilthead sea bream, fennel and confit tomatoes (£10.95), venison-and-bitter pie (£9.95), if you please. Tidy black-and-red wallpaper and the odd stuffed animal head complete the picture.
Babies and children welcome (before 5pm). Games (darts). Tables outdoors (8, garden). **Map 2 J6**.

Freedom

66 Wardour Street, W1F 0TA (7734 0071). Leicester Square or Piccadilly Circus tube. **Open** 5pm-3am Mon-Sat; 5-10.30pm Sun. **Food served** 5pm-2am Mon-Fri; 2pm-2am Sat; 2-9.30pm Sun. **Admission** £5-7 after 10.30pm Fri, Sat. **Credit** AmEx, MC, V.
Freedom has become a workaday gay/straight party bar, the likes of which are ten-a-penny in the West End – but it wasn't so long ago that this venue, on the busy Brewer,

Wardour and Old Compton Street cruising crossroads, revelled in naughty exclusivity. Now open to a wider public, Freedom hints at its colourful past with leopard-skin furniture, Lanson champagne at £8 a glass, and a reasonably 'let's get sloppy, who cares?' late-opening basement DJ bar. Above, a cheerfully mixed crowd dives into standard cocktails (£6.50-£9), six wines by the glass, Kronenbourg Blanc and Budvar on draught, and Hahn, Negro Modelo and Michelob by the bottle, in a funky lounge presided over by a bright disco ball. There are worse places.
Disabled: toilet. Function room. Music (DJs 10.30pm Fri, Sat). **Map 7 K6.**

French House

49 Dean Street, W1D 5BG (7437 2799). Leicester Square or Piccadilly Circus tube. **Open** noon-11pm Mon-Sat; noon-10.30pm Sun. **Food served** noon-3pm Mon-Sat. **Credit** AmEx, DC, MC, V.
It's more arty and minimal these days, with John Claridge's black-and-white shots of Tommy Cooper and other luminaries on the walls – but the French House was built on legends larger than these. The French connection came between the wars when Victor Berlemont took charge, inviting over the cabaret stars of the day, Maurice Chevalier and friends. General De Gaulle and his Free French had their office upstairs (that's his schnozz in the photo over the bar), and under Victor's son Gaston, the wild post-war era involved Brendan Behan, Dylan Thomas, Francis Bacon and other world-champion drinkers. A boho vibe lingers, the narrow bar area and back tables a-buzz with lively banter, though more are sipping house Argentier (£2.60) wines of each colour, Kronenbourg or bottles of Theakston than the Ricard of old.
No piped music or jukebox (restaurant). Restaurant. Specialities (champagne, wine). **Map 7 K6.**

Intrepid Fox

99 Wardour Street, W1F 0UF (7494 0827). Leicester Square or Piccadilly Circus tube. **Open** noon-11pm Mon-Sat; 3-10.30pm Sun. **No credit cards.**
Here is a perfectly good bar, a classic old interior, in fact – and Goths have filled it with lit-up spiders, skeletons and pseudo-ghoulish tat, just so the disaffected youngsters of the world can come and commune over pints of Stella or Strongbow (does nobody drink snakebite-and-black these days?) before going back to whatever sad place they escaped from. House rules: No Ties Allowed! Wow! No football or rugby colours either (as if Julian from Clapham would ever set foot inside the place). Clear away the spiders and give the bar some proper edge, Fox. Leave ghost trains to Fred Pontin, and you'll get a broader spiky – or post-spiky – clientele keen to hear a little thrash of an evening (though not so keen they'll stand in a theme bar to do so).
Comedy (7.30pm Wed; £3). Function room. Games (fruit machine, pool table). Music (DJs 7-11pm Fri, Sat; free). **Map 7 K6.**

Kettner's

29 Romilly Street, W1D 5HP (7734 6112/ www.kettners.com). Leicester Square or Piccadilly Circus tube. **Open/food served** 11am-1am Mon-Sat; 11am-10.30pm Sun. **Credit** AmEx, DC, MC, V.
This stylish champagne bar in the heart of seedy Soho was founded in 1867 by Auguste Kettner, former chef to Napoleon III – though why here, exactly, no one can say. Today's drinks menu would do Auguste proud: 26 'marques' in all. The cheapest of the ten half-bottles is Mercier at £21, and lesser-known brands such as H Blin, Billecart-Salmon and Nicolas Feuillatte compete with Taittinger, Lanson and Louis Roederer. House champers by the glass is Brice NV/Jacquart NV at £7.25; similarly priced champagne cocktails include the Kettner Breeze of champagne and cranberry juice. The bar, decked out with tasteful brown furnishings and framed paintings, is divided into different areas, the back one for reclining, the front for enjoying the piano tinkle from the nearby restaurant.
Babies and children welcome; high chairs (restaurant only). Function room. Restaurant. **Map 7 K6.**

Lab

12 Old Compton Street, W1D 4TQ (7437 7820/ www.lab-bar.com). Leicester Square or Tottenham Court Road tube. **Open** 4pm-midnight Mon-Sat; 4-10.30pm Sun. **Snacks served** 6-11pm Mon-Sat, 6-10.30pm Sun. **Credit** AmEx, MC, V.
A recent revarnish has brightened up this landmark cocktail bar, which has trained and nurtured some of the best mixers in the business. Naturally enough, its glossy drinks menu, where alchemy meets urban cool, is a treat. Set amid striking images of Soho, the cocktail categorisation of Streets Ahead (for instance, Big Apple with Jameson's and apple schnapps), Respect (Dick Bradsell Bramble with Plymouth gin and Crème de Mure) and Hall of Fame (15 classics) is, well, streets ahead of nearly all the competition, and reasonably priced at that (around £7). And therein lies the problem. This two-level bar is at best petite, at worst poky, especially upstairs, so the chances of finding any space amid the moderately retro decor on a Friday night are slim indeed. That apart, Lab is a thoroughly commendable operation.
Music (DJs 9pm Mon-Sat). **Map 7 K6.**

Milk & Honey

61 Poland Street, W1F 7NU (7292 9949/0700 655 469/www.mlkhny.com). Oxford Circus tube. **Open/food served** *Non-members* 6-11pm Mon-Fri; 7-11pm Sat. *Members* 6pm-3am Mon-Fri; 7pm-3am Sat. **Credit** AmEx, DC, MC, V.
Milk & Honey, winner of the Best Bar gong in Time Out's 2004 Eating & Drinking awards, oozes exclusivity, with the unmarked door and ring-for-entry arrangement of a Prohibition-era speakeasy. The interior is fantastic: a jazz age affair of dimly lit booths, a low ceiling covered in diner-style aluminium and a business-like corner bar area, lit like a Hopper painting. Staff are the very model of professionalism, and the cocktails they prepare are sublime (not too bad at £7-£8.50). Discounting the caviar and oysters, bar snacks barely add up to half a dozen choices, but they are fantastic, particularly the spicy fishcakes (£6). And the best thing of all? Despite the air of exclusivity, anyone can visit. Just phone in advance and make a reservation for a two-hour slot. It's a simple caveat, but it keeps the tourists at bay. M&H also operates as a members' bar; come 11pm, when you are asked to leave, members can linger smugly until 3am.
Function room (members only). **Map 1 J6.**

Opium

1A Dean Street, W1D 3RB (7287 9608/www. opium-bar-restaurant.com). Tottenham Court Road tube. **Open** 5pm-3am Mon-Fri; 7.30pm-3am Sat. **Food served** 6-9.30pm Mon-Fri; 7.30-9.30pm Sat. **Admission** £10 after 10pm, £15 after midnight Thur-Sat. **Credit** AmEx, JCB, MC, V.
This sumptuous French-Vietnamese bar-restaurant has gone from strength to strength since opening in late 2003. It's divertingly attractive, and the luxurious sunken interior and alluring, low-lit, delicately carved alcoves reveal

RAISE A GLASS: REAL ALE

It was recently calculated that 412 British brewers were producing some 2,342 different real ales. Sad, then, that four out of five pints of all beer sold in London are brewed by just four companies. These conglomerates spend millions promoting a handful of premium lagers and nitro-keg bitters – and practically nothing on real ale. Owing to the extra profitability of lager, there's nothing the big brewers would like more than to see real ale disappear altogether. In fact, they've spent most of their efforts and promotional budgets over the last 50 years trying to achieve just that.

But what exactly is this dangerous and subversive drink? The Chambers Concise Dictionary defines real ale as 'beer which continues to ferment and mature in the cask after brewing'. All lagers and bitters start out in much the same way – only the quality of the ingredients varies – but the 'unreal' stuff is pasteurised, filtered and effectively killed before leaving the brewery. Such keg and nitro-keg beers then have to be 'reactivated' by forcing CO_2 into them at the pump. Pasteurisation kills flavour and artificial carbonation leaves beer gassy and flabby.

Real ale is a natural product. Retaining its own yeast, it should be flavoursome but not fizzy, and never served warm. It does require a little extra work in the cellar – which can be comprehensively taught in a couple of hours – but the results are worth it. Cask-conditioned and bottle-conditioned (look out for sediment in the bottom of the bottle) ales are the premier cru of the beer world. Think the difference between farmhouse Stilton and Kraft cheese slices, between crusty organic baguettes and white sliced supermarket loaves. Thanks largely to the efforts of CAMRA (the Campaign For Real Ale; *see also p173*), London's real ale presence is at an all-time high. Practically every pub sells at least one and, frankly, places that don't bother aren't worth our custom. Is there anything more ludicrous than a boozer boasting of its gourmet kitchen and extensive, well-chosen wine list, when the range of beers doesn't rise above the level of canned ravioli and Piat d'Or?

The problem is that few London pubs sell well-kept real ale. As a general rule, it pays to avoid managed pubs owned by big pub-owning companies, where minimum-wage staff don't know their ASB from their Elgood's. After strenuous and extensive research – well, someone has to do it – we've concluded that, generally speaking, the most reliable place

to sample a brewery's real ale is in a pub owned and run by that brewery. Young's beers taste better in Young's pubs, Fuller's beers in Fuller's pubs, and so on. For some reason, the nearer the brewery, the sweeter the beer. You'll be hard-pressed to find a better pint of 'ordinary' than that served at Wandsworth's **Alma** (*see p222*) or more toothsome Pride than at Chiswick's **Mawson Arms** (*see p231*). Regional brewers from further afield with celebrated London presence are topped by Harvey's of Lewes at the **Royal Oak** (*see p200*), and Salisbury's Hop Back at Time Out's 2004 Pub of the Year, the **Sultan** (*see p226*).

Then there are free houses. A free house is an independently owned pub that's not bound to any particular pub group or brewery and can stock whatever beers it wants (though in practice, most settle for the easy option of getting whatever real ale their lager provider sells cheapest). London free houses that put effort into their ale purchases and subsequent care are headed by the **Wenlock Arms** (*see p130*), the **Dog & Bell** (*see p206*) in Deptford and the **White Horse** (*see p234*) at Parson's Green. So – what's yours? *Jim Driver*

Chinese and Moorish touches. Hired out for fashion and photo shoots by day – with certain tables reserved for private parties by night – Opium hasn't lost its focus in serving the (reasonably) smart set. Imaginative, original cocktails of fine quality and oriental influence (Ca Phe Frappé of Stoli Vanilla, Tia Maria and Toussaint coffee liqueur; Opium Martini of Stoli Rasberi stirred with Momokawa raspberry saké and shaken with pineapple juice) are all under a tenner; house cocktails are £5.50. The Opium Twists, giving oriental zest to classic cocktails, are especially inspired. Bar food (marinated tiger prawns, £6.50, barbecued duck pastry parcels, £5.50) is of the highest quality, and the early-evening 'Unbelievable Upgrade' lets you splurge on a budget. DJs start at 10.30pm.
Music (DJs 10.30pm Fri, Sat). **Map 7 K6.**

Phoenix Artist Club

1 Phoenix Street, Charing Cross Road, WC2H 0DT (7836 1077/www.thephoenixartistclub.co.uk). Leicester Square or Tottenham Court Road tube. **Open** noon-8pm Mon-Fri; 5-8pm Sat. *Members* noon-3.30am Mon-Fri; 5-3.30am Sat. **Food served** noon-10.30pm Mon-Fri; 5-10.30pm Sat. **Membership** from £50/yr. **Credit** AmEx, MC, V.

Rumours of the demise of the Phoenix – or at least its restructuring – have been greatly exaggerated. The new management, which also oversees Bacchanalia (*see p32*), may yet make a few changes, but for the time being it's 'as you were'. Which means a delectably louche, late-opening bar combining basement arty boho beer-hall steeped in theatrical lore, with an outstanding range of bottled beers (Baltika, Bitburger, Lobkowicz, Okocim) and a damn good spread of draughts (Brinkhoff's Number One, Dortmunder Union, Red Stripe). Wine starts from £3.10 a small glass, £4.15 a large one and £10.90 a bottle, and food includes Greek meze (£4.95), big combo meat-and-veg platters (£9.95 for two) and char-grilled burgers (£7.75). Take note: the late opening is only for those already ensconced before 8pm, or bar members.
Map 7 K6.

Pillars of Hercules

7 Greek Street, W1D 4DF (7437 1179). Tottenham Court Road tube. **Open** 11am-11pm Mon-Sat; noon-10.30pm Sun. **Food served** noon-8pm daily. **Credit** AmEx, DC, MC, V.

The mock Tudor façade and old sign stretching over the adjoining passage of Manette Street could be mistaken for hiding a centuries-old former coaching inn, but what Hercules lacks in historical authenticity it more than makes up for in pub tradition. At the narrow, low-ceilinged bar counter you'll find draught ales of fine quality: Young's Ordinary, Young's Special, Caledonian Six Nations, Brains SA and Hyde Jekyll's Gold. All wines cost around a tenner a bottle, the stellar pies (beef and Young's Special Ale, bean and chilli) are a fiver. Framed old pictures of London around the raised back area and period-piece lights flickering over the counter accentuate the historical hue. Customers are a mix of hoary locals, young tourists in bright colours and men just gagging for a decent pint.
Games (fruit machine). Music (DJs 6.30-10pm Wed). TV. **Map 7 K6.**

22 Below. *See p89.*

Player

8 Broadwick Street, W1F 8HN (7494 9125/www.thplyr.com). Oxford Circus or Tottenham Court Road tube. **Open** 5.30pm-midnight Mon-Wed; 5.30pm-1am Thur, Fri; 7pm-1am Sat. **Food served** 6-11pm Mon-Fri; 7-11pm Sat. **Credit** AmEx, MC, V.

The Soho member of the Match family is something of an anomaly. It was opened in 1998 by local star Dick Bradsell, a mixer so legendary he had a bar named after him at the seminal Atlantic, the only other non-hotel cocktail lounge of note at the time. For three years, this basement bar was top of the pile. Its closure saw Dale DeGroff take over, standardising the menu and installing those stripy lampshades of Match lore. Today, judging from the clientele (some barely a notch above All Bar One status), Player seems close to being all played out – but the cocktails (£6.50 apiece, champagne varieties £7.50) are still mixed with pride and pedigree by a fresh new bar staff under manager Irina Miroff. An extra £3.50 lets you upgrade the vodka in your cocktail from standard to Grey Goose l'Orange. Food is imaginative (sushi dishes such as Salmon Rushdie, Torvill & Dean and I Hate Sushi).

Bar available for hire. Disabled: toilet. Music (DJs 8pm Thur-Sat; £3-£5 after 9pm). Specialities (cocktails). **Map 7 K6**.

Pop

14 Soho Street, W1D 3DN (7734 4004/www.thebreakfastgroup.co.uk). Tottenham Court Road tube. **Open/snacks served** 5pm-3am Mon-Thur; 5pm-4am Fri; 8pm-5am Sat; 7pm-midnight Sun. **Happy hour** 5-8pm Mon-Fri. **Admission** £3-£5 after 9pm Mon-Thur; £7-£8 guest list, £12 door after 9pm Fri; £15 guest list only Sat. **Credit** AmEx, MC, V.

Has Pop finally eaten itself? This late-night retro-styled bar should have everything going for it. Located a busy step from Soho Square and Oxford Street, it offers quality cocktails (Ketel One in the Cosmopolitan, Zubrowka Bison in the Vodka Martini, Plymouth in the gin variety) at around £7, decent bottled beers including Estonian A Le Coq and Red Stripe, and platters (£10) from either side of the Atlantic – British with fish and chips, scampi and chipolatas; American with buffalo wings and mini burgers. With its pseudo sci-fi seating, flower murals and over use of Fanta orange, Pop couldn't be more retro. It's spacious, too – maybe too spacious. With live music twice a week, half-price early-evening food and a cheap Grolsch promotion, Pop still has problems even half-filling the space. What can be done?

Function room. Music (DJs 9pm daily). Specialities (cocktails). **Map 7 K6**.

Revolution

2 St Anne's Court, W1F 0AZ (7434 0330/www.revolution-bars.co.uk). Tottenham Court Road tube. **Open** 11.30am-11pm Mon-Sat; 1-10.30pm Sun. **Food served** 11.30am-9pm Mon-Wed; 11.30am-10pm Thur-Sat; 1-9pm Sun. **Credit** AmEx, MC, V.

For some reason (cheap shots?) this gimmicky cod-Russian bar tucked away in a Soho sidestreet is immensely popular. Perhaps it's the pricing, attractively and communally

set: £25 for 15 shots, £45 for 30 shots, £14 for pitchers of Pölstar, Wyborowa, Finlandia and Absolut Kurrant, with cocktails in the £6 range (not least a Revolution Breezer with Ketel One Citron). Perhaps it's the intimate areas running along the side, cosy and comfy. Perhaps it's the DJ. It's probably not the long and impersonal bar itself, nor the almost complete absence of anything Russian in the food or vodka selection – despite the misuse of Cyrillic in the logoed name. It's certainly not the artwork, woeful mural and all, though the overall decor is neat. So why do so many pre-clubbers come here?
Disabled: toilet. Music (DJs 7pm daily; free). Specialities (vodka). **Map 7 K6.**

Romilly Room

Teatro Club, 93-107 Shaftesbury Avenue, W1D 5DY (7494 3040/www.teatrosoho.co.uk). Piccadilly Circus or Leicester Square tube. **Open** 5.30pm-3am Mon-Fri; 5.30pm-3am Sat. **Food served** 5.30pm-2am Mon-Sat. **Credit** AmEx, DC, MC, V.
It's that classic contradiction. There you were before, wishing you had the right connections to get into the Teatro members' bar – and now they open up part of it to the public as the Romilly Room, let in pretty much anybody, and you toy with your SoHo Bloody Mary (celery-infused Wyborowa vodka and Teatro's own spicy Mary mix, £7.50) and look bored. What was all the fuss about? Well, the Romilly Room is stylish all right, its first-floor windows looking out over Greek Street, the low tables of its cool, extensive interior waited on by busy staff. The drinks menu, much like Teatro's, is upmarket and well conceived. Twenty contemporary cocktails (£7.50-£9) brim with Grey Goose l'Orange, 42 Below Passionfruit, Absolut Raspberi and so on. The champagne variety, such as the J'Amora of Krupnik honey vodka, black raspberry and honey liqueur, topped with Jean Moutardier Brut Nu, are equally nifty. Lack of exclusivity may be a terrible thing, but there's certainly nothing wrong with the cocktails.
Disabled: toilet. Music (DJs 10.30pm Tue-Sat; £10 after 9pm, £15 after 11pm). Restaurant. Specialities (cocktails). TV (big screen, digital). **Map 2 K6.**

Rupert Street

50 Rupert Street, W1D 6DR (7292 7141). Leicester Square or Piccadilly Circus tube. **Open** noon-11pm Mon-Sat; noon-10.30pm Sun. **Food served** noon-5pm Mon-Thur; noon-6pm Fri-Sun. **Credit** AmEx, MC, V.
This bright, light, landmark gay bar on a busy corner attracts custom mainly from after-work professionals aged over 25; punters are nevertheless party-minded, and most certainly up for it from Thursday to Sunday. The boy band element drifts through during the day, before drifting off to the perhaps fresher pastures of Village Soho (*see p91*). Once darkness falls, the volume is pumped up and serious quantities of standard lager (and alcopops) are consumed. The venue doesn't have the universal appeal of, say, the Admiral Duncan (*see p78*) – there's too much eye contact going on for that – but it's all very jovial, and the bar staff seem in on the joke. Food is served at lunchtimes; in summer, tables spread out on to the pavement.
Disabled: toilet. Tables outdoors (5, pavement). TV (big screen, satellite). **Map 7 K6.**

Shampers

4 Kingly Street, W1B 5PE (7437 1692). Oxford Circus or Piccadilly Circus tube. **Open** 11am-11pm Mon-Sat (*Aug* closed Sat). **Food served** noon-11pm Mon-Sat. **Credit** AmEx, DC, JCB, MC, V.
Incongruously old-fashioned, on a road that contains celebrity style bar Red and ad agency Bartle Bogle Hegarty, Shampers attracts the older, rugby-loving man and girls in pairs. It's an odd mix of the youthful and fuddy-duddy that only works later on at night, when the room fills up. If you want a drink, prepare to be squeezed around three tables at the back, next to a noisy glass-washing machine and a draughty back door. Otherwise, there are plenty of tables to eat at, served by friendly French waitresses beneath bottles of wine and precarious-looking lighting. The look is trad-flimsy, but a wine list more than compensates, thanks to choices such as the eccentric Josmeyer's 1997 pinot gris vieilles vignes (£27) and a half-bottle of Heidsieck Dry Monopole, a bargain at £14.50. The 31-strong by-the-glass selection includes Lustau manzanilla sherry (£2.95) – worth trying if you're feeling adventurous.
Babies and children welcome. Function room. Restaurant and bar available for hire. Specialities (wine). Tables outdoors (3, courtyard). **Map 2 J6.**

Ship

116 Wardour Street, W1F 0TT (7437 8446). Piccadilly Circus or Leicester Square tube. **Open** noon-11pm Mon-Sat. **Food served** noon-3pm. **Credit** MC, V.
Woven into rock's rich tapestry by dint of its location by the old Marquee, the intimate corner Ship still attracts the leather-trouser, leopardskin-top brigade. Former regulars Jimi Hendrix and Keith Moon have long gone, but you're bound to bump into some fat bass player from a 1970s band on the retro circuit, or better yet, a roadie with gossip on same. The 'No Dancing No Entry' sticker illustrated by a Pan's People figurine in loons tells all. Even tackier is the unwise nod towards a pirate theme – plastic parrots, cardboard ships and skull and crossbones logo (the cute models of Sid and Joey R behind the bar would have been enough). London Pride, Caffrey's and standard lagers account for the drinks; the vibe is of chatty intimacy (grab the table under the stairs if entertaining *à deux*).
Games (fruit machine). **Map 2 K6.**

Soho

12-13 Greek Street, W1D 4DL (7025 7844/www.thesohobar.co.uk). Leicester Square or Tottenham Court Road tube. **Open/food served** 4pm-1am Mon-Wed; 4pm-3am Thur-Fri; 5pm-3am Sat. **Happy hour** 5-7pm daily. **Credit** AmEx, DC, MC, V.
This run-of-the-mill basement after-work trough is a pub/bar mongrel comprising a rabbit warren of alcoves, each the ideal conduit to flog the dead horse of that post-Christmas-party office affair. Happy hours of £3 champagne cocktails, half-price wine (decent Rioja for a tenner) and £3 bar food bring in the punters. Once they're halfway down their second bottle of £10 reduced champers, their bellies full of chicken satay skewers and Thai fish cakes, they may look at the extra three quid on a Martini (normally £5.50), look at their now prospective partner, look at their watch and say to themselves, 'Sod it!' Bingo! Another customer hooked and shelling out tenners until 3am.
Dress: smart casual. **Map 7 K6.**

Spice Lounge

124-126 Wardour Street, W1F 0TY (7434 0808/www.sohospice.co.uk). Leicester Square or Tottenham Court Road tube. **Open** 5pm-midnight Mon, Tue; 5pm-3am Wed-Sat. **Credit** AmEx, MC, V.
The Spice Lounge is the simple but stylish basement bar of the newly refurbished Soho Spice, with dancefloor, Latin DJs and hot snacks ('flavours across the Tiger Belt' – mainly

affordable Indian, actually). Drinks carry the odd exotic ingredient and reasonable price tag. Cardamom pods, lemongrass and elderflower water feature in the modest list of cocktails (£5.75), including a Soho Caipiroska of Smirnoff vodka, crushed limes, mango and passion fruit, stirred with brown sugar. Fine enough – and at these prices, they don't throw around Grey Goose. Ten wines of each colour, four by the glass, start at a standard Vin du Pays du Gers at £3, and include an unoaked chardonnay from the Beelgara vineyards of Australia at £4; affordable, if hardly outstanding. Fruit lassis (£2.25-£2.95) complement the non-alcoholic cocktails; the beers are only Cobra or Stella. The star is the kitchen open until 3am; the bar snack version of pot-roasted quails, tandoor grilled lamb best ends and shashlik duck breast is, at £10, £2 cheaper than its restaurant counterpart – and equally delicious.
Music (DJs 5pm Fri, Sat). Restaurant. **Map 1 J6.**

Spice of Life

37-39 Romilly Street, W1D 5AN (7437 7013). Leicester Square or Tottenham Court Road tube. **Open** 11am-11pm Mon-Sat; noon-10.30pm Sun. **Food served** noon-9pm daily. **Credit** AmEx, DC, MC, V.
This landmark meeting place tucked in behind Cambridge Circus is enjoying a second lease of life thanks to the eclectic events programme featured in its basement bar. 'Live music nightly' could be midweek jazz (attracting seventysomethings who can tell a tale or two), open-mic Mondays, Sunday karaokes or second-banana bands on the circuit at weekends; but in any case it brings a more committed type of punter to this otherwise large, busy, neutral space. The spice of life indeed. The flavouring is provided by top-notch bitters (McMullen Country Best, McMullen AK) as well as six types of reasonably priced, well-chosen wines of each colour by the bottle, and daily specials of pasta or rice at under £6.
Over-14s only. Disabled: toilet. Downstairs bar available for hire. Music (open mic 6.30pm Mon; blues 7pm Tue; jazz 8pm Wed, Thur; £3-£5; acoustic guitar & bands 7.30pm Fri, Sat; karaoke 7.30pm Sun). Tables outdoors (5, pavement). **Map 7 K6.**

Sun & Thirteen Cantons

21 Great Pulteney Street, W1F 9NG (7734 0934). Oxford Circus or Piccadilly Circus tube. **Open** noon-11pm Mon-Fri; 6-11pm Sat. **Food served** noon-3pm Mon-Fri. **Credit** AmEx, DC, MC, V.
Named after a 17th-century pub that stood on this site and the cantons of Switzerland, this stylish pub-cum-brasserie attracts discerning media types to its tidy two-room operation. The front bar area offers London Pride, Staropramen, South African chenin blanc and Australian cabernet merlot at £2.70 a glass respectively. In the elegant back dining room of green-and-white tiling and marble-topped tables, you're more likely to order a superior £20 Domaine Durand sancerre – or Château Hostens Picant bordeaux – to go with the Thai food of green curry or pad thai noodles (£5.25). The row of sexy scooters parked outside enhances the palpable continental atmosphere.
Function room (seats 50). Music (DJs 7pm occasional Thur, Fri; free). **Map 2 J6.**

Thirst

53 Greek Street, W1D 3DR (7437 1977/www.thirstbar.com). Tottenham Court Road tube. **Open/food served** 5pm-3am Mon-Sat. **Happy hour** 5-9pm Thur; 5-7pm Fri, Sat. **Admission** £3 after 11pm Mon-Thur; £5 after 10pm Fri, Sat. **Credit** AmEx, MC, V.
Standing on the busy corner of Greek and Bateman Streets, Thirst (the downstairs bar at least) is one of Soho's funkiest and most commendable drinking dens. Prices are staggered according to time zones. Those caning menu cocktails from opening time at 5pm get them at half-price for two hours: Stupid Hour. Then follows Happy Hour, the middle zone; and by the time you reach the end zone, which starts at 9pm, you'll be joining the sweaty mob jigging in the sunken area by the DJ ('No Requests!' – no matter how many Thirstinis of Bombay Sapphire, cassis and apple schnapps you've sunk). There's even a cloakroom, admirable for a bar the size of an in-flight toilet. The upstairs space, configured into little booths, is less lively but still hopping.
Music (DJs 8pm-3am Mon-Sat). Specialities (cocktails). **Map 7 K6.**

Toucan

19 Carlisle Street, W1D 3BY (7437 4123/www.thetoucan.co.uk). Tottenham Court Road tube. **Open** 11am-11pm Mon-Fri; 1-11pm Sat. **food served** 11am-3pm Mon-Sat. **Credit** MC, V.
This well-established two-cabin Irish boozer functions as both bar and museum, for the Toucan must contain more Guinness publicity memorabilia than anywhere outside St James's Gate, Dublin: even the bar stools resemble pints of stout. Toucans abound: pecking, flying, imploring you to drink more of the black stuff, from ad campaigns launched generations before the current budget-busting celluloid variety. House cocktail concoctions include Black Velvet (Guinness and champagne), Poor Man's Black Velvet (Guinness and cider), Black Maria (Guinness and Tia Maria), and so on. Naturally, there's also Magners cider and every whiskey known to man. In summer, custom spills on to the pavement overlooking Soho Square: it has to, since neither the ground floor nor the claustrophobic basement could comfortably accommodate more than 50 people. Kronenbourg, Fosters and Beck's by the bottle are possibilities for those who don't fancy the black.
Specialities (Irish whiskey). TV (digital). **Map 7 K6.**

22 Below

22 Great Marlborough Street, W1F 7HU (7437 4106/www.22below.co.uk). Oxford Circus tube.
Open 5pm-midnight Mon-Fri; 7.30pm-midnight Sat. **Food served** 5-10.30pm Mon-Fri; 7.30-10.30pm Sat. **Credit** AmEx, DC, MC, V.
A suitable candidate for best new venture of 2004, this fresh, frisky cocktail basement is hidden beside the street-level Café Libre opposite the Carnaby Street estuary. The neat interior combines photo gallery, aka The Dark Room (where Rosa Lykiardopoulos' provoking prints are strung up by clothes pegs), mini-cinema (short-film showcases, Kurosawa), public iPod (with cherry-picked tunes nightly) and comedy stage (Old Rope on Mondays). Most of all, it gives good cocktail. Previously hired by some of the most prestigious bars of South-East Asia, South Africa and Soho, the bar manager has devised a menu of wit and verve. Named after mates, muses and musical memories, it's a crazy scrapbook (with a pulp fiction cover) of mixology, inventive and inspired, in which fresh-fruit Martinis take centre stage. Priced in the same range (£6-£7) as the Asian bar snacks, the cocktails are as inviting here as the intelligently foxy vibe throughout.
Comedy (8pm Mon; £3-£5). Music (DJs 8pm Fri; jazz 1st Thur of mth). Specialities (cocktails). TV (plasma, widescreen). **Map 2 J6.**

Ayoush

The North African Members' Bar & Restaurant,
58 James St, London, W1U 1HG
T: 020 7935 9839 www.ayoush.com F: 020 7935 1708

The smell of incense, exotic herbs, the aroma of Me'assel tobacco and mint tea are all part of the sweet melange of Ayoush, which mesmerises all its members, foreigner and locals alike.

Every Tuesday, Ayoush hosts a Bedouin Night. If you have never experienced the magic of Bedouin Night at Ayoush, visit www.ayoush.com to share the experience where we have our staff members and custome (if they wish) dressed up in traditional Egyptian attire.

Your mind will be blown away by our North African set-up as well as the charm of the belly dancer and Arabic music.

Every Wednesday, Ayoush hosts Ladies Night and this is the chance for all ladies to let their hair down an enjoy our special half-price cocktails while they can boogie down with our House DJ's latest mixed hits.

Every Sunday, Ayoush hosts a family day where you can bring along all family members especially childre The mood will drive your imagination far from the London scene into Cairo bazaars and Moroccan Souq The Egyptian house www.egyptianhouse.co.uk will be sponsoring the papyrus and the cartouche that th children can draw and colour.

Located at James Street, Ayoush restaurant and the private dining club have become landmarks in this part of town.

Two Floors

3 Kingly Street, W1B 5PD (7439 1007). Oxford Circus or Piccadilly Circus tube. **Open** noon-11pm Mon-Sat. **Food served** noon-5pm Mon-Sat. **Credit** AmEx, DC, MC, V.

This unassuming yet splendid venue does so many things right. It's loungey but not achingly so; the institutional furniture, primitive bar stools, low-slung sofa at ground level and basement slouch pit allow for relaxation without being posey. The cocktails are rather good, too. Vanilla and cinnamon are flavours of choice, in Cairpirinha or Caipiroska, but there are also eight sours and champagne cocktails at a bargain £6.50. Quality spirits are used throughout. Bottles of Kirin, Brooklyn, St Peter's Organic, Cruzcampo, Hoegaarden and Modelo cost £3 each – is this a centralised economy? – and wines, from humble Herve Varenne sauvignon blanc or grenache (£3 a glass, £11 a bottle) upwards, are just as snippy. Ciabattas (£4), served until 4.30pm, are stuffed with chorizo, parma ham, chèvre or mozzarella; service is sharp but personable. Two Floors: three cheers.

Babies and children admitted (daytime only). Downstairs bar available for hire (except Fri). Tables outdoors (2, courtyard). **Map 2 J6.**

Village Soho

81 Wardour Street, W1D 6QD (7434 2124). Leicester Square or Piccadilly Circus tube. **Open/food served** 4pm-1am Mon-Sat; 4pm-midnight Sun. **Happy hour** 4-8pm daily. **Admission** £3 after 10pm Fri, Sat. **Credit** AmEx, MC, V.

You can enter from either end here, through the chaotic, crowded Brewer Street side or the bright pink, more clubby Wardour Street entrance. In business since 1991, the Village is one of Soho's many gay landmarks, a byword for go-go glam and good times. Hang out at the Brewer Street side – a shambolically camp ambience slapped together with candlestick and fireplace – and you'll find a crush of non-threatening homosexuality around the old wooden bar counter. Blend with the more mixed gang at the top end of the L-shape on Wardour Street, and expect an unpretentious time of poppy tack and alcopop heaven. Singapore Slings, Sea Breezes, Slow Comfortable Screws (£6 a glass, £12.50 a jug) and the like are mixed with Smirnoff, Bacardi and Gordon's. Shooters, of the Quicky and Blow Job ilk are downed by the bucketload. Basement karaoke takes place on Thursdays.

Entertainment (pole dancers 11.15pm-1am Fri, Sat). Function rooms. Music (DJs 8pm Thur-Sat). Specialities (cocktails). Tables outdoors (4, patio). **Map 7 K6.**

Yard

57 Rupert Street, W1D 7PL (7437 2652/www.yardbar.co.uk). Piccadilly Circus tube. **Open** 4-11pm Mon-Sat; 4-10.30pm Sun. **Credit** AmEx, MC, V.

A more mature crowd hangs out in the heated courtyard of this popular gay bar, the sought-after five square metres of shaded bar tables also attracting straight custom in the dog days of summer. Inside, it's a scout hut of simple decor and composition: bar counter, fruit machine, pumping music, take it or leave it. In the smoky loft, accessed through the courtyard, there's a more subdued second bar space with chesterfield seating and colonial-style ceiling fans twirling indolently from a beamed barn roof. Pre-clubbing is the key throughout, with DJ Gary H spinning tunes until standard pub closing time at the weekend, and advance tickets for Heaven available at the bar. All in all, a right-on place of respectable rendezvous: even the Russian bouncer on the door cracks the occasional smile.

Comedy (7.30pm every other Wed; £3/£4). Function room. Music (DJs 8pm Fri, Sat). Tables outdoors (4, covered/heated & open courtyard). TV (plasma). **Map 7 K6.**

Zebrano

14-16 Ganton Street, W1V 1LB (7287 5267/www.zebrano-bar.com). Oxford Circus tube. **Open** 5-11pm Mon-Wed; 5pm-midnight Thur-Sat. **Food served** 5-10.30pm Mon-Wed; 5-11.30pm Thur-Sat. **Credit** AmEx, MC, V.

Changes are afoot at the sassy, sexy Zebrano, a sashay away from Carnaby Street. The main basement bar has been shorn of its cacti and screen dividers to create a more expansive lounge space, now with counters at either end; this makeover will continue through the spring of 2005. What's more, a complete overhaul is under way in the formerly nondescript street-level café, due to form a two-storey unit of chic sustenance from noon till night. The menu is being revamped, too – although the selection of zingy cocktails (£7-£8) such as the Zebrano Bellini (lychee liqueur, lychee purée topped with champagne) and Devil's Dandruff (Stoli Raspberi, butterscotch schnapps, Kahlúa, Frangelico and Half & Half) should remain. The modest food choice of grilled, vegetarian and Asian platters (£10-£12.50), chicken wings and raclette cheeseburgers may be increased; meanwhile, the foxy factor – guys and gals getting it on in low-lit red intimacy – can barely be improved upon.

Bar available for hire. Café. Music (DJs 7pm-midnight Thur-Sat). Specialities (cocktails). Tables outdoors (6, pavement). **Map 2 J6.**

Also in the area...

All Bar One 36-38 Dean Street, W1D 4PS (7479 7921).
Jamies 58-59 Poland Street, W1D 3DF (7287 7500).
Moon & Sixpence (JD Wetherspoon) 183-185 Wardour Street, W1V 3FB (7734 0037).
O'Neill's 34-37 Wardour Street, W1D 6PU (7479 7941); 7 Shepherd Street, W1J 7HR (7408 9281); 38 Great Marlborough Street, W1F 7JF (7437 0039).
Pitcher & Piano 69-70 Dean Street, W1D 3SE (7434 3585).
Slug & Lettuce 80-82 Wardour Street, W1V 3LF (7437 1400).

SOUTH KENSINGTON

Sloanes, rootless cosmopolitans and crims mingle in the upscale watering holes of South Ken. Black cabs trawl the Fulham and Brompton Roads, on and off which are found some of London's most pristine pubs and cocktail bars. Typical of the genre would be the **Collection**, clever, expensive and all a little soulless unless you're part of a moneyed clique. The more amenable **Anglesea Arms** and **190 Queensgate** would stand out anywhere. Here, they're gold dust.

Admiral Codrington

17 Mossop Street, SW3 2LY (7581 0005). South Kensington tube. **Open** 11.30am-11pm Mon-Sat; noon-10.30pm Sun. **Food served** noon-2.30pm, 7-11pm Mon-Sat; noon-4pm, 7-10.30pm Sun. **Credit** AmEx, MC, V.

In its heyday 20 years ago, it was the haunt of Di, Fergie and Andy; today, its modest bar area heaving with Hoorays, the Admiral Cod has not lost its cachet. It's pleasant enough, even today, but perhaps its attraction was its anonymous location, hidden down a South Ken backstreet. Even now, the modest terrace lined with umbrella heaters is tucked away, and you could park yourself at most points of the bar without realising there's an upmarket restaurant attached to it. The food (in two servings) is classy here, too – superior steaks and game when season demands – and such is the pressure of space on the square bar counter, that there's only room for two bitter pumps, Black Sheep and Bombardier, plus taps for San Miguel, Hoegaarden and Guinness. A warming fire and military prints augment the sense of decorum.
Babies and children admitted. Games (backgammon, bridge, Perudo). Restaurant (available for hire). Tables outdoors (6, garden).

Anglesea Arms

15 Selwood Terrace, SW7 3QG (7373 7960/www.capitolpubcompany.co.uk). Gloucester Road or South Kensington tube. **Open** 11am-11pm Mon-Sat; noon-10.30pm Sun. **Food served** noon-3pm, 6.30-10pm Mon-Fri; noon-5pm, 6-10pm Sat; noon-5pm, 6-9.30pm Sun. **Credit** AmEx, MC, V.
One of the best pubs in the area, the well run Anglesea does so many things right. Its choice of ales – Adnams, Adnams Broadside, Young's, Hogs Back Brewery T.E.A., London Pride and Barnsley Red Heart – is superb. Its lagers, San Miguel on draught, plus Leffe, Budvar and Beck's by the bottle, are acceptable. The wine list is extensive, with ten of each colour by the glass and bottle, from a humble Terrain Vin de Pays d'Oc sauvignon blanc and cabernet sauvignon (£3.10 per glass) through to a £9.50-per-glass 2002 Vaillons chablis premier cru and an £8-per-glass 1998 rioja. The food, also served in the sunken back dining area, front terrace beer garden and cosy main bar, more than meets these high standards. Decor? Some frosted glass, a few old prints and romantic paintings (the main one semi-erotic). The day's papers, cheery, polite regulars, staff of like demeanour… And it's even got a colourful legend attached: Bruce Reynolds is said to have planned the Great Train Robbery here.
Babies and children admitted (restaurant; before 6pm in bar). Dogs welcome. No piped music or jukebox. Tables outdoors (12, terrace). TVs (satellite).

Cactus Blue

86 Fulham Road, SW3 6HR (7823 7858). South Kensington tube. **Open/food served** 5.30pm-midnight Mon-Fri; noon-midnight Sat; noon-11pm Sun. **Happy hour** 5.30-7.30pm daily. **Credit** AmEx, DC, MC, V.
A landmark cocktail bar with a loose North American theme, Cactus Blue feels as big as Texas. The spacious street-level bar area, with its imposing square counter and back dining area, is only one of four floors, a little basket winching up drinks to the one immediately above. As the others are often hired out, the action takes place in the main bar, decked out in Navajo chic murals, patterned banquettes and alike. The food and drinks are Tex-Mex. Tequila cocktails (£6.50) are the speciality, such as the house Margarita with El Jimador Silver, Triple Sec and lime juice, or a Dirty Cosmopolitan (£6.95) with Sauza Hornito, Triple Sec, fresh limes and cranberry juice. Sol and Dos Equis feature among the bottled beers, and the bulky bar snacks include a Queso Fondito (£6), a sharing plate of fondue with corn chips, guacamole and pico salsa. Wines include a couple of beauties from Pepperwood Grove, California, a Viognier (£5.75 a glass) and a Zinfandel rosé (£5.45 a glass). Springy bar stools and the hide-coloured bar counter complete the cowboy fantasy.
Babies and children admitted (daytime, restaurant only). Function room. Restaurant. Tables outdoors (4, pavement).

Collection

264 Brompton Road, SW3 2AS (7225 1212/www.the-collection.co.uk). South Kensington tube. **Open/food served** 5-11pm daily. **Credit** AmEx, MC, V.
Cross the illuminated bridge, guarded by sculptured metal rams, and you enter someone's bar fantasy. It's a mess, really: part industrial (the metallic bar counter), part ethno (the mask logo, material TV screens and bead curtains), part medieval (the fat orange candles), with a mezzanine for diners and snug half-moon banquettes for lovers. Nothing wrong with the drinks, though. Five house specials (£8.50) include an Aussie Tart of passion fruit muddled with Seriously vodka and vanilla schnapps, and a Lost in Space of Seriously, Bombay Sapphire and Chambord. Martinis (£7.50) are made with Belvedere, Zubrowka and Miller's gin, and Chivas 12-year-old features in the Manhattan. A cherry-picked wine list includes a Concha y Toro chardonnay and a cabernet sauvignon from Maipa Valley, Chile at £4.50 a glass; the bar snacks (£3-£4) of olives, nuts and so on are marinated and roasted. There's even a flunky in the toilets. Hey, that decor wasn't so bad, after all.
Disabled: toilet. DJs (8pm nightly; free). Restaurant. Specialities (cocktails). TV (big screen, satellite).

Cross Bar

99 Fulham Road, SW3 6RH (7225 2244). South Kensington tube. **Open** 9am-11pm Mon-Sat; 10am-6pm Sun. **Food served** 9am-10pm Mon-Sat; 10am-6pm Sun. **Credit** AmEx, DC, JCB, MC, V.
A stone's throw from Bibendum, this is a redesigned reincarnation of what used to be the Crescent. Zinc still frames the narrow façade, as well as topping the bar in a tiny street-level space which, despite a mirrored wall, suggests cat-swinging be attempted immediately; some very groovy 1960s lighting adds a cool touch, complemented by other Pop Art flourishes. The much bigger space downstairs, however, goes for blandness as a tradeoff for extra room. Sure, there's nice new leather on the seats, pale wood tables and bright repros of old drinks posters on the wall, but it's comfort without character. If you like your wine, though, this place offers over 100, with 25 by the glass, and there's decent enough food in a modern British meets Med style. The early opening makes it an option for a working brekky but it's more likely to be a stop-off after the museums, perhaps, or for a post-work run-through of the wine list.
Babies and children welcome. Restaurant. Specialities (fine wine). Tables outdoors (2, pavement).

Drayton Arms

153 Old Brompton Road, SW5 0LJ (7835 2301). Earl's Court or Gloucester Road tube. **Open** noon-11pm Mon-Sat; noon-10.30pm Sun. **Food served** noon-2.30pm, 6-10pm Mon-Fri; noon-9pm Sat; noon-8pm Sun. **Credit** MC, V.
It's the range of beers that impresses here, in this pub-bar hybrid on a busy South Ken intersection. Küppers Kölsch, London Pride, Bombardier, Hoegaarden, Früli, Staropramen, Grolsch and Guinness all feature on draught, plus rare Belgian Trappist varieties (Westmalle

Dubbel, Karmeliet Trippel, Liefmans Framboize), with Asahi, Brooklyn and Baltika by the bottle. The wine and food are almost as formidable. A Chilean Palena sauvignon blanc (£3.50 a glass) hides among the standard array of Silverland chardonnays and malbecs (£2.55 a glass); lamb rump steak (£8.90), set on roasted root vegetables, was garnished with baby potatoes and mint gravy; bean cassoulet (£5.90) was the stand-out of the vegetarian options. Squashy sofas, scuffed wooden furniture, house plants and a red-lit back dining area lend the place bar credibility, while the blokey clientele and manly Irish staff lend it pub personality.
Disabled: toilet. Music (DJs 8pm Sat; Bands 8pm Sun). Tables outdoors (6, pavement). TVs.

Iniga

2a Pond Place, SW3 6QJ (7589 6589/www.iniga.com). South Kensington tube. **Open** noon-11.30pm daily. **Food served** noon-3pm, 6-11.30pm daily. **Credit** AmEx, DC, MC, V.
Formerly of Aura (*see p76*), Marcello Santese knows his cocktails. Mixer desperately sought chef, and the resultant restaurant, Iniga, is romantic modern Italian with a fair dollop of bling, and a corner of cushions, beds and a bright red bar counter. Here's where Marcello struts his stuff. Fresh fruit ingredients, Ketel Ones, Matusalems and Belvederes are splashed with abandon, in a Tall Cocktail selection (£9) themed by base spirit. A Squeeze Me! includes Matusalem Classico, fresh mandarin and apricot liqueur; a Vain Ketel Citron, Cariel vanilla and fresh strawberries. The list is long – but the wines cover Italy from Piedmont to Sardinia. Behind the bar, two machines keep whites and reds at exact temperatures, allowing you to order a Barolo or a Montepulciano by the glass. Rare, pricy troves hail from Puglia, Campania and Sicily. Mention must be made of the exquisite free bar snacks, tiny wheat crackers piled with peppers and carrots, or breadsticks wrapped in Parma ham. The music (ah, those Italians!) envelops dating thirtysomethings, which is fine, unless you're after something a little less Bazza. Mixer desperately seeks mixer?
Bar available for hire. Music (jazz 7pm Wed-Sun; free). Restaurant. Specialities (cocktails).

190 Queensgate

190 Queensgate, SW7 5EU (7584 6601). Gloucester Road or South Kensington tube. **Open** 4pm-1am Mon-Sat; 4-11pm Sun. **Food served** (bistro) 7am-midnight Mon-Fri; 7.30am-midnight Sat; 7.30am-11.30pm Sun. **Credit** AmEx, DC, MC, V.
The perfect pub, cocktail lounge and destination bar, this annexe of the Gore Hotel would grace any area. Set in no man's land between the Albert Hall and the Bulgarian Embassy, it's bloody miraculous. Pubwise, it has upholstered seating, carved dark wood a-plenty and a sturdy bar without the transactional bullshit of the metal change tray. Barwise, it has table service, bar food of the charcuterie plate and smoked haddock fish cake variety, and an ambient soundtrack. It also has cocktails. Twisted classics (£8.95) include a Kensington Sidecar of Martell VSOP, Grand Marnier and chocolate schnapps; Martini 'Ishes' (£7.50) feature a 190 of Smirnoff Penkar, elderflower cordial and orange Curaçao; Rain vodka swishes with Angostura bitters and blackberries in a Prom Night (£7.95). Wines include a Pinot Grigio della Venezia (£5.75 a glass) or a tasty red from Curatolo, Sicily (£4.50 a glass), bottled beers Cruzcampo and Sleeman's Silvercreek. The hotel element allows for automatic doors, sweet-smelling toilets and an intimate side lounge. Oh yes, and beds upstairs.
Restaurant. Specialities (cocktails).

Oratory

234 Brompton Road, SW3 2BB (7584 3493/www.brinkleys.com). South Kensington tube. **Open** noon-11pm daily. **Credit** AmEx, MC, V.
The newest branch of the West London Brinkley's chain is a rather funky little brasserie spread out on to a busy pavement near the Michelin Building. A lunchtime crowd of chatty shoppers and mums happy to park the pram give way to a more buzzy one (men also!) after dark. Although bright enough – baubled chandeliers, tangled vine patterns over light blue walls, pinkish banquettes down the sides – the space can feel a little cramped, not least if you find yourself parked up on the wrought iron seats at the tiny bar. Wine is the order of the day, four of each by the glass (Marques de Riscal rioja at £5, Louis Jadot chablis at £6), five each by the half-bottle (Villa Antinori sangiovese at £9.50, Guy Saget pouilly fumé at £6.50) and some 20 each by the full bottle, from a humble caliterra (£7.50) to a 2001 Vergisson pouilly fumé (£27.50) and 1995 Château Pontet-Canet pauillac (£30). Main dishes include platters of mezze (£6), with plenty of salads; there are also four daily specials.
Babies and children welcome (restaurant). No-smoking. Restaurant. Tables outdoors (9, pavement).

STRAND & ALDWYCH

The Strand itself is a disappointment, its decent drinking establishments limited to high-end hotel bars (**Lobby Bar**, **American Bar**) – but explore the eastern end around Aldwych (particularly near LSE and the law courts) and you'll unearth some quirky gems. Pride of place goes to Roxy Beaujolais' **Seven Stars**, a pub extraordinaire, although it might be a squeeze at lunchtime. **Edgar Wallace**, **Nell Gwynne** and **George IV** both offer a decent range of drinks and a little pub heritage. Since the closure of the Columbia Bar, the long established, pricy **Bank** is the only real bar in the area.

American Bar

Savoy Hotel, Strand, WC2R 0EU (7836 4343/www.the-savoy.co.uk). Embankment tube/Charing Cross tube/rail. **Open** 2pm-1am Mon-Sat. **Food served** 2-11pm Mon-Sat. **Credit** AmEx, DC, JCB, MC, V.
The American Bar is trapped in time, but what a time it was. Harry Craddock, he of the seminal Savoy Cocktail Book, brought the concept of cool mixed drinks from prohibition-era America to London (today's maestro is Salim Khoury, *see p77*). As the black-and-white portraits of celebrity drinkers – Lee Marvin, Richard Burton – silently testify, the American Bar was the talk of the town, and spawned similar establishments in Venice and beyond. In deference, you dress smartly, and wait to be seated before a dish of fat olives and salted nuts is brought to your table. Today's menu nods to the modern, with concoctions such as savoy.com (absinthe, Cointreau and lime juice, £11.50) and Martinis (£11.50) with Ketel One, Grey Goose or Plymouth. You're paying for the linen-jacket-and-dickie-bow service, the art deco decor and all those memories, but find a table overlooking the Thames embankment, and you'll regret ever spending money at any standard c.1996 designer bar.

Disabled: toilet. Music (pianist/vocalist 7pm-midnight Mon-Thur; 7pm-1am Fri, Sat). Restaurant. Specialities (cocktails). **Map 2 L7**.

Bank Aldwych

1 Kingsway, WC2B 6XF (7379 9797/www.bankrestaurants.com). Holborn or Temple tube. **Open** 11.30am-11pm Mon-Sat; 11.30am-10pm Sun. **Food served** 5.30-11pm Mon-Sat; 5.30-9.30pm Sun. **Credit** AmEx, DC, MC, V.

The Aldwych branch of the Bank chain was indeed a bank, before opening as a swish, designer bar-restaurant in 1996. The boardwalk mural and red banquettes around the spacious front bar now seem somewhat dated, although the action around the imposing, round bar counter is still lively – and pricily upmarket. Cocktail prices dip either side of the tenner mark, but you're getting quality. The Bank Signature (£8.75) features Absolut Citron, Cointreau, Framboise liqueur, juices and champagne; Martinis (£7.50 or thereabouts) are mixed with Absolut, Grey Goose, Plymouth and Tanqueray. The fresh fruit Bellinis (£8.50) aren't shabby, either. A dozen wines come by the glass and bottle, including a St-Claire petit chablis at £6.40 a glass, a Conde de Valdemar rioja reserva at £6.75, and the house chardonnay or merlot at £3.60. Bottled Estrella, De Koninck and Bitburger comprise the beers. Your nose will feast on smells from the open kitchen nearby (the restaurant lies beyond), your wallet will choke on the prices: £12.95 for an open chicken sandwich!

Babies and children welcome; children's brunch menu; high chairs; nappy-changing facilities (restaurant). Disabled: toilet. Function room. Music (jazz 11.30am-3pm Sat, Sun). **Map 4 M6**.

Coal Hole

91 Strand, WC2R 0DW (7379 9883). Embankment tube/Charing Cross tube/rail. **Open** 11am-11pm Mon-Sat; noon-10.30pm Sun. **Food served** noon-10pm daily. **Credit** MC, V.

A bizarre venue, this. Originally a cellar bar for dypsomaniac coal-heavers, its low-life reputation lived on when it was patronised by bacchanalian actor Edmund Kean and his louche Wolf Club fraternity. After Kean died on stage and the coal-heavers left for the Ship & Shovell (*see p98*), the bar was demolished and rebuilt as part of the grand Savoy Hotel complex. It's still grand today, with baronial-style wooden beams, fancy stained glasswork and Greco-Roman marble nymph friezes. A stunning art nouveau fireplace sits below a gallery area, named the Wolf Club. It's a Nicholson's pub, and does a tidy range of ales (London Pride, Adnams, Timothy Taylor Landlord, Greene King IPA) and meaty pub dishes in three sizes. Busy at lunchtimes and post-work, it's otherwise dotted with a handful of confused tourists. Send for Kean and his shovellers!

Games (fruit machines). Tables outdoors (2, pavement). **Map 2 L7**.

Edgar Wallace

40 Essex Street, WC2R 3JE (7353 3120). Temple tube. **Open** 11am-11pm Mon-Fri. **Food served** noon-8pm Mon-Fri. **Tapas** 4-9pm Mon-Fri. **Credit** AmEx, MC, V.

In a sidestreet between Fleet Street and the Royal Courts of Justice, this was where one-time *Daily Mail* journalist and prolific writer Edgar Wallace, his contemporaries and colleagues, would fraternise. Then called the Essex Arms, it was renamed after him on the centenary of his birth in 1975; his widow and later his daughter held meetings of the Edgar Wallace Society upstairs – this is now open lunchtimes only. His life story can be read in detail by the staircase, but most come here for the superb range of ales (Timothy Taylor Landlord, Greene King IPA, Deuchar's IPA, Abbot Ale, King & Barnes Sussex Draught) and daily specials of steaks and pies. Wines range from a standard merlot (£3 a glass) to a Campo Viejo rioja (£4 a glass), and a pinot grigio (£3 a glass) to a sancerre (£4 a glass), and a modest makeover has seen slight contemporary overtones in the decor.

Function room. Games (golf machine, quiz machine). Restaurant. TVs. **Map 4 M6**.

George IV

28 Portugal Street, WC2A 2HE (7404 0526/www.massivepub.com). Holborn or Temple tube. **Open** 11am-11pm Mon-Fri. **Food served** 11am-3pm, 5-9pm Mon-Fri. **Credit** MC, V.

Once a landmark boozer ('Hoare & Co's Celebrated Three Guinea Stout' runs the proclamation among amid wrought iron above), this high-ceilinged monolith has had a bar refit and attracted many an LSE student from across the road. To satisfy pubgoer and barhopper, there are Greene King IPA, Courage Best and Bombardier on draught, Baltika, Beck's and Budvar by the bottle, and San Miguel on tap. The dozen wines include a standard Puerta Cerrada of either colour at £3, a Pinot Grigio Pavia at £3.70 a glass and an Australian Promenade Old Vine Shiraz at £18 a bottle. Pubgoer may be pleased with the sturdy dark-wood furniture; barhopper is more thrilled by the steady pulse of the electronic musical backdrop. Upstairs, surrounded by portraits of judges, is pool and a window over the busy, almost traffic-free Portsmouth and Portugal Streets intersection.

Function room. Games (pool table). **Map 4 M6**.

Lobby Bar

1 Aldwych, WC2B 4RH (7300 1070/www.onealdwych.com). Covent Garden or Charing Cross tube/rail. **Open** 9am-midnight Mon-Sat; 9am-10.30pm Sun. **Food served** 9am-midnight Mon-Sat. **Credit** AmEx, DC, JCB, MC, V.

A star among hotel bars. Brilliantly conceived, with its high-back chairs, bizarre rowing sculpture and moving tableau of London buses from the vast windows, well run by impeccable staff, and always having ace cocktails up its sleeve, the lounge Lobby Bar of lifestyle hotel One Aldwych walks tall. Warmed, spiced nuts arrive as you peruse the comprehensive compendium of cocktails. Martinis (£8.95) come in Apple Strudel (apple schnapps, crème de cacao), Hazelnut (Potocki vodka, Frangelico) and Thai (ginger-infused Wyborowa, fresh coriander, lemongrass) flavours, to name but three of 22 imaginative varieties, not to mention the 22 high-end gins and vodkas available for the simple vermouth version. Passing over pear & rosemary Bellinis and Number Ones of Wyborowa and De Venoge champagne (both £9.90), seasonal cocktails such as the Aldwych Alexander (£8.80) allow for a mixologist's riot of nutmeg-infused cognac shaken with fresh vanilla custard and caramel liqueurs. Sushi – fish (£12.95) and veggie (£10.95) versions – can stand in if your budget doesn't run to Oscietra caviar (£35).

Babies and children welcome; nappy-changing facilities (in hotel). Disabled: toilet. Restaurants. Specialities (cocktails). **Map 4 M6**.

Lyceum Tavern

354 Strand, WC2R 0HS (7836 7155). Covent Garden. **Open** 11.30am-11pm Mon-Sat; noon-10.30pm Sun. **Food served** noon-3pm, 5.30-8.30pm Mon-Sat; noon-3pm, 5.30-8pm Sun. **Credit** MC, V.

Once attached to the nearby theatre of the same name, this Sam Smith's pub is an odd fish. Finely crafted in wood panelling and intimate booths, its decorative touches echo its illustrious past; old publicity posters for Edwardian leading ladies and Harry Houdini add to the illusion. An upstairs lounge and food bar boasts tapestries and quieter conversation. The full range of Sam Smith's ales and lagers – Old Brewery, Ayingerbräu, Prinz, Extra Stout – provides the alcohol accompaniment. All is reasonably well. Then you notice the cheap house doubles, the thud of the dartboard and the blaring TV. Arrive at lunchtime, and downstairs feels like a raucous works canteen, were a raucous works canteen to serve lager. Disappointed tourists who didn't notice the Coal Hole on the other side of the road hurry down their 'small beer, please'. All in all, it's a bit Jekyll and Hyde (the play of which premiered next door in 1888).
Babies and children admitted (before 9pm). Games (darts, quiz machines). No-smoking tables (when food is served). **Map 2 L7.**

Nell Gwynne

1-2 Bull Inn Court, WC2R 0NP (7240 5579). Covent Garden tube/Charing Cross tube/rail. **Open** 11am-11pm Mon-Sat. **Food served** noon-3pm Mon-Fri. **No credit cards.**

Lovely little pub, this, 'the friendliest freehouse in the West End'. And sure enough, there are cheery grins from the staff and breast-shaped lampshades over the bar counter. Squeezed in to a tiny, lived-in interior as cosy as Christmas are old framed prints, a little frosted glass and a fireplace. Old Speckled Hen and Courage Best star among the beers, the food is filling and invariably sandwich shaped, and most punters are at least on nodding, if not first-name, terms. Why Nell Gwynne? Well, when this was the Old Bull Inn – possibly the Black Bull Inn, historians differ – at the time of King Charles II, his aforementioned mistress performed on the stages of nearby theatres. It would be nice to think that they liaised here – perhaps nipping out for a crafty one in the alleyway, now decoratively tiled.
Babies and children admitted. Games (darts, fruit machines). Tables outdoors (pavement). TVs (satellite). **Map 2 L7.**

Ye Old White Horse

2 St Clement's Lane, WC2A 2HA (7242 5518). Holborn or Temple tube. **Open** 11am-10.30pm Mon-Fri. **Food served** noon-2pm Mon-Fri. **Credit** MC, V.

The gruff Cockney voices give it away before you even see the 'No Students' sign on the door. This is a geezers' pub, within two steps of the LSE. Jagger wasn't long out of there when they last changed the decor in here, a few mounted caricatures, pinkish globe lights on the bar, a bar gas fire from bedsitland. Still, the beer's fine – Timothy Taylor Landlord, Woodford's Wherry, Deuchar's IPA, Brakspear's, John Smith's and Guinness – and there's a lunchtime spread invariably requiring Colman's, HP or Heinz. Invariably, too, it'll be quiet, with voices whispering around the dim, maroon stucco interior, glances noticed in the mirrors, the occasional lighter flickering in the frosted glass. It would be the ideal film set for the post-heist scene of a cheap gangster movie. Just don't mention this too loudly.
Specialities (real ales). TV. **Map 4 M6.**

Seven Stars

53-54 Carey Street, WC2A 2JB (7242 8521). Chancery Lane, Holborn or Temple tube. **Open** 11am-11pm Mon-Fri; noon-11pm Sat. **Food served** noon-3pm, **Credit** AmEx, MC, V.

Imagination runs riot in this fabulous little place. It was built as a pub in 1602, hence the wooden front and wonky beamed interior. The blackboard of gastronomic fare (rabbit stew and mash, chargrilled sea bream, both £8.50), and green-and-white checked tableclothed dining areas at either end of the narrow bar, give it a rustic, French appeal. The eccentricity (and beers), though, are Anglo: feathers and skull in the window, the Boulting Brothers film posters of British legal yore, the pumps of Adnams, Butcombe Blond and Pride. Gastropub queen Roxy Beaujolais (*see p53*), boho Aussie Sohoite, passionate authoress on innkeeping food, is the force behind the Seven Stars. Considering well-sourced meat and fish as a continental achievement, and having the urban savvy to find same, she provides exquisite lunches for lawyers from the nearby Royal Courts of Justice, plus decent (and decently-priced, from £2.95 a glass) wines, Aspall's Suffolk Cyder and Bitburger. Upstairs, Spence and Kate Hepburn, from opposing sides of the bar in *Adam's Rib*, complete the picture.
Specialities (real ale). **Map 4 M6**

Also in the area...

Savoy Tup 2 Savoy Street, WC2R 0BA (7836 9738).
Walkabout Temple Station, WC2R 2PH (7395 3690).

TRAFALGAR SQUARE & CHARING CROSS

With the probable exception of the shiny new **Albannach**, and possible exception of **Rockwell**, few bars around tourist-swamped Trafalgar Square would really stand out anywhere else in the capital – but then few capitals would have this range of bars slap in the city centre. **Gordon's** (especially) and the **Harp** are steeped in tradition, the **ICA Bar** is arty, and more style bars will surely appear before too long. The norm, though, is the post-work glughouse, whose punters need only stagger over the road for Charing Cross and the sticks.

Albannach

66 Trafalgar Square, WC2N 5DS (7930 0066/www.albannach.co.uk). Charing Cross tube/rail. **Open/food served** noon-1am Mon-Sat; noon-midnight Sun. **Credit** AmEx, MC, V.

Unrivalled location overlooking Nelson's column, striking design, postmodern Scottish theme and fare, Caledonian-inspired cocktails from Tony Conigliaro... But can this lavish new venue succeed? A certain steady trade is guaranteed from the gazillion guzzling Scots passing through town thanks to a polemically ancient Scottish name (meaning 'he of Alba' – as opposed to Sassenach). There's even an illuminated stag in the basement bar. Behind the venture is entrepreneur Niall Barnes, with limited experience at this game, but limitless passion and guile. He has created a fabulous walk-in bar-diner, tinged with tartan, above which is a classy restaurant, and below is a stylish evening-only cocktail lounge. The cocktails, in the reasonable £7.50 bracket, include a Rob Roy of Balvenie Double Wood, angostura and Martini Rosso, and a Liquorice Whisky Sour of Bailie Nicol Jarvie with fresh lemon and liquorice. The whisky menu is encyclopaedic,

culminating in the £12,000 bottle of 1937 Glenfiddich. Oak-smoked salmon and smoked venison (both £9.50) feature in the ground-floor bites. Nothing has been left to chance. Now all it needs is some Sassenachs to patronise it.
Disabled: toilet. Function rooms. Restaurant. Specialities (malt whisky). **Map 2 K7**.

Clarence

53 Whitehall, SW1A 2HP (7930 4808). Embankment tube/Charing Cross tube/rail. **Open** 9am-11pm Mon-Sat; 10am-10.30pm Sun. **Food served** 9am-9pm Mon-Sat; 10am-9pm Sun. **Credit** AmEx, DC, MC, V.
'Famous since 1862' (the date stamped on the staff uniform, lest you forget), this is one of several tourist-friendly boozers lining the lucrative route between Trafalgar Square and Westminster. And it does a fair job, providing colonials and continentals with English ales (Bombardier, London Pride, Young's bitter and Special), standard main dishes (around £7) and a cheery smile when they order from the bar. The beamed interior is cosy enough, with a no-smoking dining area at the front, while the wood-panelled Parliament Room upstairs boasts a warming fire and a little peace from the constant multi-lingual mobile yack. And sure, if you were weekending in Bruges or Heidelberg, you might yack while scribbling postcards over a hearty, beery lunch in vaguely historic surroundings. Here the local trade is limited to employees breaking from or leaving work, with little reason to linger.
Babies and children admitted. Function room. Games (fruit machine). Tables outdoors (3, pavement). TV. **Map 2 L8**.

Gordon's

47 Villiers Street, WC2N 6NE (7930 1408/www.gordonswinebar.com). Embankment tube/Charing Cross tube/rail. **Open** 11am-11pm Mon-Sat; noon-10pm Sun. **Food served** noon-10pm Mon-Sat; noon-9pm Sun. **Credit** AmEx, MC, V.
Unchanged since *Brief Encounter*, this crumbling, candlelit wine bar was invented for affairs. Wallpapered with press cuttings covering Britannia's proud rule from the time when the *Mail* and *Express* were broadsheets, Gordon's is still of its time. Madeira is served from the wood in dock glasses, Graham's LBV comes by the schooner, beaker or bottle, and doorsteps of cheddar form the backbone of the €6.95 ploughman's.You almost feel like paying in old money – God knows how the seen-it-all staff working the tiny bar counter in front of hulking sherry barrels are going to cope with the euro. Wine is the drink of choice, by the glass, half-bottle or bottle, from every corner of the globe from a tenner a bottle. If you're finding this cramped two-space basement too crowded – and finding a table is near impossible more often than not – there are tables outside along Watergate Walk overlooking Embankment Gardens.
Babies and children welcome. No piped music or jukebox. Tables outdoors (10, terrace). **Map 2 L7**.

Albannach. See p95.

Harp

47 Chandos Place, WC2N 4HS (7836 0291). Charing Cross tube/rail. **Open** 11am-11pm Mon-Sat; noon-10.30pm Sun. **Food served** noon-10pm daily. **Credit** MC, V.

Resistant to modern bar mores, the cosy Harp prides itself on pub tradition. 'Award-winning sausages' (was there a ceremony?), rare ales and racing-form banter by the narrow bar counter: it could be 2005 – or 1965, the era enshrined by the film stars on the walls. Rare beermats over the bar also testify to well-sourced tradition; at present you'll find Cain's Raisin, George Gale Revenge, Black Sheep and Harvey's Sussex by the pump. Draught Caffrey's fits nicely with the Irish harps glowing in the panels of coloured glass protecting the pub from an outside world of All Bar Ones and revamps. They even guard a secret ingredient to their ceremonial sausages (note warm pan on the bar counter), something to do with sea salt and pepper – and indeed, the Creole Jazz and Best Scottish Beef varieties zing like billy-o. Unreconstituted kitsch decor completes the picture.

Specialities (real ale). TVs. **Map 2 L7**.

ICA Bar

The Mall, SW1Y 5AH (7930 3647/www.ica.org.uk). Charing Cross tube/rail. **Open** noon-11pm Mon; noon-1am Tue-Sat; noon-10.30pm Sun. **Food served** noon-2.30pm, 5-10.30pm Mon; noon-2.30pm, 5-11pm Tue-Fri; noon-4pm, 5-11pm Sat; noon-4pm, 5-10pm Sun. **Admission** £1.50 Mon-Fri; £2.50 Sat, Sun; free all week to ICA members. **Credit** AmEx, MC, V.

Formerly a live venue and now a weekend spot for DJs, this corner of the ICA has always been sought after. These days, even for a quiet lunchtime pint, they slap a £1.50 temporary membership to get in – something to do with the proximity to Buckingham Palace (did you ever wonder why the Mall wasn't lined with boozers?). Once inside though, this little space is spiffy. Wieckse Witte, Budvar, Guinness and Affligem comprise the draught options, Früli and Hahn come by the bottle. Standard house Chevanceau of either colour flows at £3.50 a glass, and there are cocktail varieties, too (Champagne £6.50, Martini £5.50, Classic £5.25). A slightly retro backdrop lets you pose while you while away the hours over games of Cluedo, Jenga and Monopoly kindly provided by the management. At night it can be hopping, proving that a palace location can be dishy – even desirable.

Babies and children admitted; nappy-changing facilities. Disabled: toilet. Function rooms. Internet access. Restaurant. **Map 2 K8**.

Lord Moon of the Mall

16-18 Whitehall, SW1A 2DY (7839 7701). Charing Cross tube/rail. **Open** 10am-11pm Mon-Sat; 10am-10.30pm Sun. **Food served** 10am-10pm Mon-Sat; 10am-9.30pm Sun. **Credit** AmEx, DC, MC, V.

What makes this Wetherspoon rise above any others? Well, for a start, it's set in a great echoing banking hall (erstwhile headquarters of Cocks, Biddulph & Co), with huge high ceilings, reading corners and a long library (of admittedly unreadable subjects) to choose from. The choice of beers is equally obscure, but worth investigation: Marston's Burton, Spitfire, Nethergate, Butcombe and Brewery Drop complement the London Pride, Abbot and Greene King on tap. Bottled lagers, now that JD's have gone global, are equally eclectic: Windhoek, Negro Modelo, Baltika, Castle and Zywiec are only a sample. It's also two steps from Trafalgar Square, and the cheapest sit-down meal option around. Given the setting, you get swank and thrift in one fell swoop. In fact, so proud are JDW that founder Tim Martin has had his portrait commissioned in grand Regency style in the main room.
Babies and children welcome. Disabled: toilet. Games (fruit machine, quiz machine). No piped music or jukebox. No-smoking area. Specialities (real ale). **Map 2 K8**.

Old Shades

37 Whitehall, SW1A 2BX (7321 2801). Embankment tube/Charing Cross tube/rail. **Open** noon-11pm Mon-Sat; noon-10.30pm Sun. **Food served** noon-8pm daily. **Credit** AmEx, MC, V.
How old is the Old Shades? Does it matter? The tourist blurb kindly provided by the pub's umbrella group Nicholson's blabs on about Whitehall's Tudor origins and King Charles I's execution, but really it's just a lived-in boozer, standing half-used and underrated in a row of semi-historic tourist traps. In fact, the scuffed furniture and warming radiators are an authentic relief from all the polished horsebrasses and logoed staff uniforms. There's room, too, in the three-space interior (note the cupola over the middle bar counter) – no bum bag or cagooled elbow digging into you. Beerwise, Adnams, Timothy Taylor Landlord, London Pride and Hoegaarden do the business, with a guest appearance by Robin's Revenge. Lanson is sold at a bargain £5 a glass (or £20 a bottle), so you can sink cheap champers in the expansive back dining area. Standard food served almost throughout the day.
Games (fruit machine, quiz machine). No-smoking area. TV (big screen). **Map 2 L8**.

Queen Mary

Waterloo Pier, Victoria Embankment, WC2R 2PP (7240 9404/www.queenmary.co.uk). Embankment or Temple tube. **Open** *Summer* noon-11pm Mon-Thur; noon-2am Fri, Sat; noon-10.30pm Sun. *Winter* noon-11pm Mon-Thur; noon-2am Fri, Sat; noon-6pm Sun. **Food served** *Summer* noon-8pm daily. *Winter* noon-8pm Mon-Sat; noon-6pm Sun. **Admission** £5 after 8pm Fri, Sat. **Credit** AmEx, MC, V.
Decent riverboat locations near the West End being all too rare, the big, blue Queen Mary is a welcome feature on the horizon – but once you get inside, it's pretty ordinary, really. It consists of a slightly claustrophic main bar, known as the Ward Room; the Hornblower's nightclub (£5 till 2am) opposite; and, in summer, the top-flight, open-air Sundeck Bar. There are a few seats on deck outside the main bar, too. All gently rock with the Thames, a pleasing sensation. The pleasure is all pretty lowbrow, though, as its laminated menus and brash posters boast of cheap early-week pints, standard lagers and dinners (cod, chips and mushy peas, £5.75). Blossom Hill (are you Blue Nun in disguise?) of both colours starts at £1.99 a glass, house champagne at £15. Now, there's nothing wrong with Beck's at £1.50 a pint of a Tuesday – but amid tatty furniture and tacky decor, you'd do just as well taking a couple of cans to the Embankment.
Function rooms. Games (quiz machine). Music (DJs 9pm Fri, Sat). Tables outdoors (15, deck). **Map 4 N7**.

Rockwell

The Trafalgar Hilton Hotel, 2 Spring Gardens, SW1A 2TS (7870 2959/www.thetrafalgar.hilton.com). Embankment tube/Charing Cross tube/rail. **Open** 8am-1am Mon-Sat; 8am-10.30pm Sun. **Food served** noon-10.30pm Mon-Sat; 10.30am-10pm Sun. **Credit** AmEx, DC, MC, V.
And what of the recent revamp at Rockwell – this chic, well-located (mainly) whisky lounge, winner of Time Out bar awards three years ago? Well, it's stripped down and not so sleek, for a start, even hosting a harp player some lunchtimes. And it's broadened out from bourbon, too – although cocktails (£9.50) such as Remember The Maine (Woodford Reserve stirred with absinthe and sweet vermouth) and Bourbon Preserve (Van Winkle 10-year, breakfast marmalade and Peychaud bitters) remain – as does the improbable selection of same by the bottle or tasting tray. But now the drinks menu is led by £9 Cosmopolitans and Chilli Jam Martinis (premium vodka with strawberry jam preserve and a hint of chilli), presumably in a bid to attract ladies on the lash, previously dissuaded by blokey bourbon. Fine wines and tapas, too – but does it work? Hmm… And in the meantime, across the square stands the equally upmarket, shiny new Albannach.
Disabled: toilet. Music (DJs 8pm Tue-Sat; £5 after 11pm). Tables outdoors (5, roof garden). **Map 2 K7**.

Sherlock Holmes

10 Northumberland Street, WC2N 5DB (7930 2644). Embankment tube/Charing Cross tube/rail. **Open** 11am-11pm Mon-Sat; noon-10.30pm Sun. **Food served** noon-10pm daily. **Credit** MC, V.
Elementary, my dear Watson. Take a singular old hotel (the Northumberland) that featured in *The Hound of the Baskervilles*. Turn it into a theme bar, before bars became theme bars – namely in 1957. Fill the place with encased knick-knacks associated with Conan Doyle's creation (some from the author's own family – but perhaps not the head of a bloodhound) and… by jove! I think we've got it! Fifty years of easy, thriving tourist trade, TV crews and tour groups. To be fair, it's not all tacky beer mugs, although these do exist. There are decent ales – Greene King, Abbot, London Pride, Old Speckled Hen and the strange case of Sherlock Holmes's own Fine brew, said to be Adnams – plus steaks, soups and more knick-knacks in the upstairs restaurant. Outdoor seating provides respite from the tourist rigmarole within – although you'll be missing out on the TV re-runs of Basil Rathbone.
Babies and children admitted (until 6pm). Games (fruit machine). Restaurant (no smoking; available for hire). Tables outdoors (4, pavement). **Map 2 L7**.

Ship & Shovell

1-3 Craven Passage, WC2N 5PH (7839 1311). Charing Cross tube/rail. **Open** 11am-11pm Mon-Fri; noon-11pm Sat. **Food served** noon-3pm Mon-Fri; noon-4pm Sat. **Credit** AmEx, MC, V.
Pub historians differ about the name of this establishment, with its two facing premises. Some claim its name derives from the coal-heavers driven from the nearby Coal Hole (*see p94*); others, from the much maligned Sir Clowdisley (perhaps Cloudisley) Shovell who lost his fleet off the Isles

of Scilly in 1707. The maritime prints in both would favour the latter option, but in any case each venue is a simple, upstanding boozer boasting fine ales (King & Barnes Sussex, Badger, Tanglefoot) from the Hall & Woodhouse brewery, independent since Sir Clowdisley's century. Lunchtimes (pub grub) and post-work slots bring busy trade from nine-to-fivers, and after nine a flurry of clubbers drifts in, taking advantage of the Ship's (or the Shovell's) location beside the arches of Heaven.
Babies and children admitted (Sat only). Function room. Games (fruit machines). No piped music or jukebox. TV (satellite). **Map 2 L7**.

VICTORIA

The selection of pubs in Victoria tends towards the solidly traditional (the **Albert**, the **Cask & Glass**) or the somewhat trendy (**Bbar**, **Zander**), with nothing particularly outstanding in between. The station itself has a standard (if lofty) Wetherspoon inside it, and a cubby hole near the platform for swifties; failing those, you're going to have to dive into the Thistle Hotel for the collegiate-style, wooden-panelled **Harvard Bar**, or the newly-revamped **Chez Gérard** on the opposite side of the lobby.

Albert

52 Victoria Street, SW1H 0NP (7222 5577). St James's Park tube/Victoria tube/rail. **Open** 11am-11pm Mon-Sat; noon-10.30pm Sun. **Food served** 11am-10pm Mon-Sat; noon-9.30pm Sun. **Credit** AmEx, DC, MC, V.
This gleaming palace of Victoriana, steeped in Parliamentary tradition, is a credit to the tourist trade. What with well-kept ales (Young's, London Pride, Bombardier, Courage Director's), eight reasonably decent wines of each colour (Ropiteau Frères chablis, £3.90 a glass, Campo Viejo Gran Riserva £16.35 a bottle), sausages of various types (pork, apple and cider, Cajun Dixie) and puddings of the treacle sponge sort, the customer is well catered for. Meanwhile, motivated staff work under the watchful eyes of Winston Churchill and the happily wed couple from the time of the pub's ornate makeover. Ornate is a sizeable understatement: the Albert, named after the husband in question shortly after his death, was recast in hand-cut glass, carved dark wood and old gas light fittings. Its main claim to fame, though, is its upstairs carvery. Accessed by a staircase lined with portraits of Prime Ministers past and present, it houses a division bell once used to usher dining members back to the House.
Babies and children admitted. Games (fruit machines). No-smoking area. Restaurant. TV.

Bbar

43 Buckingham Palace Road, SW1W 0PP (7958 7000/www.bbarlondon.com). Victoria tube/rail. **Open** 11.30am-11pm Mon-Fri (available for hire at weekends). **Food served** noon-10.30pm Mon-Fri. **Credit** AmEx, DC, MC, V.
Once a little tacky, the South African-themed Bbar is now doing a tidy trade in classy lunches, fine wines and upmarket cocktails, opening an intimate basement bar for the post-work overflow. The evening bar menu alone puts it a class above: tiger prawns with a pear and kiwi salsa, tempura of rock oysters with crispy rocket and tangy tomato sauce (both £8.95); it's South African Boerewors sausages at lunchtimes. The cocktails are well priced (£6-£7), extensive and inventive: consider the Guatemalan Blazer of Zacapa 23-year-old tequila with fresh raspberries, blackberries, cinnamon and orange, all set ablaze, or a Warsaw Pact of Krupnik and Poire Williams eau de vie. Martinis are made with 42 Below, Grey Goose and Finlandia. Among the bottled beers are southern African Windhoek, Savanna and Castle (draught is Budvar and Pilsner Urquell), while the huge wine list is categorised by flavour. You can sip your Boland Chenin Blanc (£4.30 a glass) amid leopard-spotted lampshades and savanna scenes. *Gesondheid*!
Babies and children admitted. Disabled: toilet. Function room. No-smoking area (lunchtime). Restaurant. Specialities (cocktails). Tables outdoors (4, pavement).

Boisdale

13 Eccleston Street, SW1W 9LX (7730 6922/ www.boisdale.co.uk). Victoria tube/rail. **Open/food served** noon-1am Mon-Fri; 7pm-1am Sat. **Admission** £10 (£3.95 if already on premises) after 10pm Mon-Sat. **Credit** AmEx, DC, MC, V.
Before the arrival of the Albannach on Trafalgar Square, this was the thane of Scottish bars, and is still a top-notch place. You can't argue with 147 malt whiskies – and nor should you want to. It's a superbly run operation, with an outstanding range of wines to match the whiskies, and an excellent kitchen, too. Though it's open to all (table reservation recommended), it moves mountains for its members, who are whisked off to Cuba to be treated by boss Ranald Macdonald and associates to the establishment's other key whims, cigars and music. Jazz greats line the walls, the seriously top-notch Boisdale Blue Rhythm Band have a residency, and cases of their CDs, plus rows of Cuban cigars, line the narrow, tartan-carpeted hallway. And there's the rub. Because if jazz and cigars aren't your thing, and you feel uncomfortable around well-heeled, middle-aged businessmen, then the Boisdale isn't for you. But for fine wine and rare whisky, you may not find better outside Scotland.
Babies and children admitted (restaurant). Function room. Music (jazz 10pm-midnight Mon-Sat). Restaurant.

Cardinal

23 Francis Street, SW1P 1DN (7834 7260). Victoria tube/rail. **Open** 11.30am-11pm Mon-Sat; noon-10.30pm Sun. **Food served** noon-3pm, 5.30-9pm Mon-Fri; noon-3pm Sat. **Credit** AmEx, MC, V.
Tarted up at the front, and conspicuous among the red brick buildings immediately behind Westminster Cathedral, the somewhat staid Cardinal cannot hide a life of dull, beery, blokey banter no matter what it now puts on its newly laminated menus. Chargrilled specials (£6.95) are most certainly welcome, though, like flamed Cumberland sausage (£6.95) or flamed leg of lamb steak in rosemary jus (£8.95); there's even Mediterranean risotto (£6.25) and Thai spiced crab cakes (£6.50). These are best enjoyed in the back dining area, separated from the rest of the rather gloomy bar by a wooden divider. It's still a Sam Smith's pub, so there's Old Brewery Bitter, Ayingerbräu and Prinz on tap, plus bottles of JS standards such as Waggle Dance and Oatmeal Stout. A row of cardinals still stare impassively from the walls. Flamegrilled? Thai spiced? There'll be a new broom at the Vatican next.
Babies and children welcome. Function room. Games (darts, fruit machine). No piped music or jukebox. No-smoking area (lunchtime).

RAISE A GLASS: LATE DRINKS

The long-promised change to the licensing laws allowing all-night drinking has finally come to fruition – but, as we explain in **24 nil** (*see p7*) that doesn't mean London is about to become a 24-hour kind of place. Round-the-clock drinking will largely remain the stuff of dreams (or *Daily Mail* nightmares), but there are still plenty of witching-hour watering holes across the city. At the time of going to press, all the venues below were open until at least midnight on at least one night in the week; many stay open later, more often. Door policies vary: some charge admission, while others prefer to keep things free and easy. For clubs and DJ bars, *see p248*.

CENTRAL

Bayswater & Paddington
Cherry Jam (*p18*) 2am Mon-Sat; midnight Sun.
Harlem (*p18*) 2am Mon-Sat; midnight Sun.
Salt Whisky Bar (*p21*) 1am Mon-Sat; midnight Sun.
Steam (*p21*) 1am Mon-Wed; 2am Thur-Sat.

Belgravia
Blue Bar (*p22*) 1am Mon-Sat.
Library (*p 22*) 1am Mon-Sat.

Bloomsbury & St Giles
AKA (*p24*) 3am Tue-Thur; 4am Fri, Sun; 5am Sat.
Point 101 (*p28*) 2am Mon-Sat; midnight Sun.

Covent Garden
Café des Amis (*p33*) 1am Mon-Sat.
Detroit (*p35*) midnight Mon-Sat.
Guanabara (*p35*) 2.30am Mon-Sat; midnight Sun.
Langley (*p35*) 1am Mon-Sat.
Octave Jazz Bar (*p36*) 1am Thur-Sat.
Retox Bar (*p37*) 1am Mon-Wed; 3am Thur-Sat.
Roadhouse (*p37*) 3am Mon-Sat; 1am 2nd Sun of mth; 12.30am last Sun of mth.

Earl's Court
Troubadour (*p38*) midnight daily.
Warwick Arms (*p39*) midnight Mon-Sat.

Fitzrovia
Costa Dorada (*p40*) 3am Mon-Sat.
Eagle Bar Diner (*p41*) midnight Thur, Fri; 1am Sat.
Hakkasan (*p41*) 12.30am Mon-Wed; 1.30am Thur-Sat; midnight Sun.
Jerusalem (*p43*) midnight Tue, Wed; 1am Thur-Sat.
Long Bar (*p43*) 12.30am Mon-Sat.
Market Place (*p43*) midnight Mon-Wed; 1am Thur-Sat.
Mash (*p43*) 2am Mon-Sat.
Match Bar (*p43*) midnight Mon-Sat.
Roxy (*p44*) 3am Mon-Fri; 3.30am Sat.
Shochu Lounge (*p45*) midnight daily.
Social (*p45*) midnight Mon-Sat.
Wax (*p46*) 3am Mon-Sat.

Kensington
Bar Cuba (*p51*) 2am Mon-Sat; 12.30am Sun.
Tenth Bar (*p52*) midnight Mon-Sat.

King's Cross & Euston
Ruby Lounge (*p54*) midnight Thur; 2am Fri, Sat.

Knightsbridge
Mandarin Bar (*p55*) 2am Mon-Sat.
Pengelley's (*p55*) 1am daily.
Townhouse (*p55*) midnight Mon-Sat.

Leicester Square & Piccadilly Circus
Atlantic Bar & Grill (*p56*) 3am Mon-Sat.
Cocoon (*p56*) 1am Mon-Sat.
De Hems (*p57*) midnight Mon-Sat.
International (*p57*) 2am Mon-Sat.
Jewel (*p57*) 1am Mon-Sat; 12.30am Sun.
Sports Café (*p58*) 3am Mon-Sat; 12.30am Sun.

Marylebone
O'Conor Don (*p63*) 1am Thur.

Mayfair
Claridge's (*p64*) 1am Mon-Sat; midnight Sun.
43 (*p65*) 1am Mon-Sat.
Hush (*p66*) 12.30am Mon-Sat.
Mô Tea Room (*p66*) midnight Thur-Sat.
Trader Vic's (*p67*) 1am Mon-Thur; 3am Fri, Sat.
Windows (*p67*) 2am Mon-Thur; 2.30am Fri, Sat.
Zeta Bar (*p69*) 1am Mon, Tue; 3am Wed-Sat; 1,30am Sun.

Notting Hill, Ladbroke Grove & Westbourne Grove
Eclipse (*p69*) midnight Mon-Sat.
Electric Brasserie (*p69*) midnight Mon-Sat.
Lonsdale (*p70*) midnight daily.
Number Ten (*p70*) midnight daily.
Portobello Gold (*p70*) midnight Mon-Sat.
Tiroler Hut (*p71*) 1am Tue-Sat; midnight Sun.
Tom & Dick's (*p71*) midnight Mon-Sat.

St James's
Aura (*p76*) 3am Tue-Sat; 1.30am Sun.
Calma (*p76*) 1am Mon-Sat.

Soho
Ain't Nothin' But? The Blues Bar (*p78*) 1am Mon-Wed; 2am Thur; 3am Fri, Sat; midnight Sun.
Akbar (*p78*) 1am Mon-Sat.
Amber (*p78*) 1am Mon-Sat.
Barcode (*p80*) 1am Mon-Sat.
Bar Constante @ Floridita (*p80*) 2am Mon-Wed; 3am Thur-Sat.
Bar Soho (*p80*) 1am Mon-Thur; 3am Fri, Sat; 12.30am Sun.
Barsolona (*p80*) 3am Mon-Sat.
Café Bohème (*p80*) 3am Mon-Sat.
Candy Bar (*p81*) 2am Fri, Sat.
Crobar (*p83*) 3am Mon-Sat.
Edge (*p83*) 1am Mon-Sat.
Freedom (*p83*) 3am Mon-Sat.
Kettner's (*p84*) 1am Mon-Sat.
Lab (*p84*) midnight Mon-Sat.
Opium (*p84*) 3am Mon-Sat.
Player (*p87*) midnight Mon-Wed; 1am Thur-Sat.
Pop (*p87*) 3am Mon-Thur; 4am Fri; 5am Sat; midnight Sun.
Romilly Room (*p88*) 3am Mon-Sat.
Soho (*p88*) 1am Mon-Wed; 3am Thur-Sat.
Spice Lounge (*p88*) midnight Mon, Tue; 3am Wed-Sat.
Thirst (*p89*) 3am Mon-Sat.
22 Below (*p89*) midnight Mon-Sat.
Village Soho (*p91*) 1am Mon-Sat; midnight Sun.
Zebrano (*p91*) midnight Thur-Sat.

South Kensington
Cactus Blue (*p92*) midnight Mon-Sat.
190 Queesgate (*p93*) 1am Mon-Sat.

Strand & Aldwych
American Bar (*p93*) 1am Tue-Sat.
Lobby Bar (*p94*) midnight Mon-Sat.

Trafalgar Square & Charing Cross
Albannach (*p95*) 1am Mon-Sat; midnight Sun.
ICA Bar (*p97*) 1am Tue-Sat.
Queen Mary (*p98*) 2am Fri, Sat.
Rockwell (*p98*) 1am Mon-Sat.

Victoria
Boisdale (*p99*) 1am Mon-Sat.
Zander Bar (*p102*) 1am Wed-Sat.

Waterloo
L'Auberge (*p103*) midnight Mon-Fri.
Cubana (*p104*) midnight Mon, Tue; 1am Wed-Sat.

CITY

Clerkenwell & Farringdon
Al's Bar Cafe (*p109*) midnight Mon; 2am Tue-Sat.
Cellar Gascon (*p111*) midnight Mon-Fri.
Charterhouse 38 (*p111*) midnight Wed, Sun; 1am Thur; 2am Fri, Sat.
Cock Tavern (*p112*) 2am Fri, Sat.
Dollar Grills & Martinis (*p109*) 1am Mon-Sat.
Easton (*p114*) 1am Fri, Sat.
Fluid (*p115*) midnight Mon-Wed; 2am Thur-Sat.
Green (*p115*) midnight Thur-Sat.
Match EC1 (*p116*) midnight Mon-Sat.
Medcalf (*p116*) 12.30am Fri.
Mulligans (*p116*) midnight Mon-Sat; 1am Sun.
Pakenham Arms (*p116*) 1am Mon-Sat.
Potemkin (*p117*) midnight Sat.
Smiths of Smithfield (*p118*) midnight Mon-Thur; 1am Fri, Sat.
Well (*p119*) midnight Mon-Sat.

Hoxton & Shoreditch
Anda de Bridge (*p122*) midnight Mon-Sat.
Bar Kick (*p124*) midnight Thur-Sat.
Barley Mow (*p124*) midnight Fri, Sat.
Bedroom Bar (*p124*) midnight Thur; 2am Fri, Sat.
Bluu (*p124*) midnight Fri, Sat.
Catch (*p125*) midnight Tue, Wed; 2am Thur-Sat; 1am Sun.
Charlie Wright's International Bar (*p125*) 1am Mon-Wed, Sun; 2am Thur; 3am Fri, Sat.
Cocomo (*p125*) midnight Mon-Sat.
dreamsbagsjaguarshoes (*p125*) midnight Mon; 1am Tue-Sat; 12.30am Sun.
Drunken Monkey (*p125*) midnight Mon-Sat.
Elbow Room (*p126*) midnight Mon, Tue, Sun; 1am Wed, Thur; 2am Fri, Sat.
Grand Central (*p127*) midnight Mon-Wed, Sun; 1am Thur; 2am Fri, Sat.
Great Eastern Dining Room (*p127*) midnight Mon-Thur; 1am Fri, Sat.
Home (*p127*) midnight Mon-Sat.
Hoxton Square Bar & Kitchen (*p127*) 1am Mon-Thur, Sun; 2am Fri, Sat.
Juno (*p127*) midnight daily.
Legion (*p127*) midnight Mon-Thur; 2am Fri-Sun.
Light Bar & Restaurant (*p128*) midnight Mon-Wed; 2am Thur-Sat.
Loungelover (*p128*) midnight Mon-Thur; 1am Fri, Sat.
Mother Bar (*p128*) 3am Mon-Wed; 4am Thur, Sun; 5am Fri, Sat.
Pool (*p129*) 1am Mon-Thur; 2am Fri, Sat; midnight Sun.
Reliance (*p129*) midnight Mon-Wed, Sun; 2am Thur-Sat.
Smersh (*p129*) midnight Mon-Sat.

Sosho (*p129*) midnight Tue; 1am Wed, Thur; 3am Fri, Sat.
T (*p130*) midnight Thur, Fri; 2am Sat.
Tabernacle (*p130*) 1am Mon-Thur; 2am Fri, Sat.
Troy (*p130*) 1am Tue-Thur; 2am Fri, Sat.
Zigfrid (*p130*) midnight Mon-Sat.

Liverpool Street & Moorgate
Public Life (*p132*) midnight Mon-Wed; 2am Thur; 3am Fri, Sat.

Mansion House, Monument & Bank
Pacific Oriental (*p136*) 1am Thur, Fri.

EAST

Bethnal Green
Napoleon Bar (*p140*) midnight Mon-Sat.
Pleasure Unit (*p141*) midnight Mon-Thur; 2am Fri, Sat.
Sebright Arms (*p143*) midnight Thur; 2am Fri, Sat.

Bow & Mile End
New Globe (*p144*) midnight Mon-Wed, Sat; noon-2am Thur, Fri.
Soma (*p145*) 12.30am Mon, Tue, Sun; 1.30am Wed-Sat.

Docklands
Gun (*p148*) midnight Mon-Sat.
Via Fossa (*p148*) midnight Thur-Sat.

Hackney
Central 1 Lounge Bar & Diner (*p150*) midnight Tue-Sun.
Jazz Bar Dalston (*p151*) 1am Mon-Thur, Sun; 3am Fri, Sat.
Marie Lloyd Bar (*p151*) 1am Mon-Sat; midnight Sun.
Royal Inn on the Park (*p151*) midnight Fri, Sat.
291 (*p151*) midnight Tue, Sun; 2am Wed-Sat.
Wellington (*p152*) midnight Mon-Sat.

Limehouse
Booty's Riverside Bar (*p153*) midnight Fri, Sat.

Whitechapel
Big Chill Bar (*p157*) midnight Mon-Sat.
Blind Beggar (*p157*) 1am Mon.
Lane (*p158*) midnight Mon-Wed; 1am Thur-Sat.
Urban Bar (LHT) (*p158*) midnight Mon-Wed, Sun; 1am Thur-Sat.
Vibe Bar (*p158*) 1am Fri, Sat.

NORTH

Camden Town & Chalk Farm
Bar Solo (*p161*) 1am daily.
Bartok (*p161*) 1am Mon-Thur; 2am Fri, Sat; midnight Sun.
Bullet (*p161*) midnight Mon-Wed, Sun; 1am Thur; 2am Fri, Sat.
Cuban (*p161*) 1am Mon-Sat; midnight Sun.
Monkey Chews (*p164*) midnight Fri, Sat.
Quinn's (*p164*) midnight Mon-Wed, Sun; 2am Thur-Sat.
Singapore Sling (*p164*) midnight Mon-Thur, Sun; 1am Fri, Sat.

Crouch End
Queen's Hotel (*p166*) midnight Thur, Sat.
Viva Viva (*p166*) midnight daily.

Finsbury Park & Stroud Green
Chapter One (*p166*) midnight Mon-Thur, Sun; 12.30am Fri, Sat.
Salisbury Hotel (*p166*) 1am Mon-Wed; 2am Thur-Sat; midnight Sun.
Triangle (*p166*) midnight Tue-Sun.

Highgate
Boogaloo (*p169*) midnight Thur; 1.30am Fri, Sat.

Holloway
Landseer (*p171*) midnight Mon-Sat.
Nambucca (*p171*) midnight daily.

Islington
Anam (*p172*) 2am Tue-Fri; 3am Sat.
Chapel (*p173*) midnight Thur; 2am Fri, Sat.
Elbow Room (*p174*) 2am Mon-Thur; 3am Fri, Sat; midnight Sun.
Embassy Bar (*p174*) midnight Mon-Thur, Sun; 2am Fri, Sat.
Keston Lodge (*p177*) 2am Fri, Sat.
King's Head (*p177*) 1am Mon-Thur, Sun; 2am Fri, Sat.
Matt & Matt Bar (*p177*) 1am Tue-Thur; 2am Fri, Sat.
Medicine Bar (*p177*) midnight Mon-Thur, Sun; 2am Fri, Sat.
Northgate (*p178*) midnight Mon-Sat.
Rosemary Branch (*p178*) midnight Fri, Sat.

Kilburn
Black Lion (*p180*) midnight Mon-Sat.

Maida Vale
Graze (*p181*) 1am Tue-Sun.

Muswell Hill & Alexandra Palace
Victoria Stakes (*p182*) midnight Fri, Sat.

West Hampstead
Gallery (*p188*) midnight Fri, Sat.
No.77 Wine Bar (*p188*) midnight Wed-Sat.

SOUTH

Balham
Bedford (*p190*) midnight Thur; 2am Fri, Sat.
Duke Of Devonshire (*p190*) midnight Mon-Thur, Sun; 2am Fri, Sat.
Exhibit (*p190*) midnight Fri, Sat.
Lounge (*p191*) midnight Tue-Sat.

Battersea
Artesian Well (*p190*) 1am Thur; 3am Fri, Sat.
Corum (*p193*) 1am Mon-Wed, Sun; 2am Thur; 3am Fri, Sat.
Dusk (*p193*) 12.30am Mon-Wed; 1.30am Thur-Sat.
S Bar (*p194*) midnight Fri, Sat.
Tea Room des Artistes (*p194*) 1am Fri, Sat.

Bermondsey & Rotherhithe
Spice Island (*p196*) midnight Fri, Sat.

Blackheath
Cave Austin (*p197*) 1am Wed-Sat.
Railway (*p197*) midnight Thur-Sat.
Zero Degrees (*p197*) midnight Mon-Sat.

Brixton & Streatham
Brixton Bar & Grill (*p200*) midnight Tue, Wed; 1am Thur; 2am Fri, Sat.
Brixtonian Havana Club (*p200*) midnight Mon-Wed, Sun; 2am Thur-Sat.
Dogstar (*p201*) 2am Mon-Thur, Sun; 4am Fri, Sat.
Far Side (*p201*) midnight Fri, Sat.
SW9 (*p201*) 1am Fri, Sat.
Tongue & Groove (*p201*) 3am Thur; 5am Fri, Sat.
White Horse (*p202*) 1am Mon-Thur, Sun; 3am Fri, Sat.
Windmill (*p202*) midnight daily.

Camberwell
Castle (*p202*) midnight Mon-Thur; 2am Fri, Sat.
Funky Munky (*p202*) midnight Mon-Wed, Sun; 2am Thur-Sat.
Old Dispensary (*p203*) midnight Mon-Sat.

Clapham
Arch 635 (*p204*) midnight Mon-Thur, Sun; 1am Fri; 2am Sat.
Bar Local (*p204*) midnight Mon-Sat.
Sand (*p205*) 2am Mon-Sat; 1am Sun.
SO.UK (*p206*) midnight Mon, Sun; 2am Tue-Sat.

Deptford
Live Bar (*p206*) 2am Wed-Sun.

Dulwich
East Dulwich Tavern (*p207*) midnight Thur-Sat.
Franklin's (*p207*) midnight Thur-Sat.
Liquorish (*p207*) midnight Mon-Sat.

Forest Hill
Bar Equal (*p207*) midnight Mon-Wed, Sun; 2am Thur-Sat.

Greenwich
Bar du Musée (*p210*) midnight Mon-Fri; 1am Sat.
Inc Bar & Restaurant (*p210*) midnight Mon-Thur, Sun; 2am Fri, Sat.
Polar Bar (*p211*) 1am Mon-Thur; 2am Fri, Sat.
Trafalgar Tavern (*p212*) midnight Fri, Sat.

Herne Hill
Half Moon (*p213*) 1.30am Fri, Sat.

New Cross
Goldsmiths Tavern (*p215*) 2am Mon-Sat; midnight Sun.

Peckham
Rye Hotel (*p216*) midnight Fri, Sat.

Stockwell
Bar Estrela (*p219*) midnight daily.
Swan (*p220*) 2am Thur, Sun; 3am Fri, Sat.

Tooting
smoke bar diner (*p220*) midnight Mon-Sat.
Spirit Bar Café (*p222*) midnight Mon-Sat.

Wimbledon & Earlsfield
Bar Sia (*p224*) midnight Mon-Thur; 2am Fri, Sat.
Common Room (*p225*) midnight Sat.
Eclipse (*p225*) midnight Tue-Fri.

WEST

Acton
Grand Junction Arms (*p228*) midnight Fri, Sat.

Ealing
Baroque (*p232*) 2am Fri, Sat.

Hammersmith, Ravenscourt Park & Stamford Brook
Brook Green Hotel (*p235*) midnight Thur, Fri, Sun; 1am Sat.

Kensal Green
Greyhound (*p236*) midnight Fri, Sat.
William IV (*p236*) midnight Thur-Sat.

Richmond, Isleworth & Twickenham
A Bar & Restaurant (*p239*) 12.30am Mon-Thur.
Coach & Horses (*p239*) midnight Tue, Fri, Sat.

Shepherd's Bush
Defectors Weld (*p242*) midnight Fri, Sat.
Seven Stars Bar & Dining Room (*p242*) midnight Thur-Sat.

Southall
Glassy Junction (*p242*) 1am Thur; 2am Fri, Sat.

Cask & Glass

39-41 Palace Street, SW1E 5HN (7834 7630). Victoria tube/rail. **Open** 11am-11pm Mon-Fri; noon-8pm Sat. **Food served** noon-2.30pm Mon-Sat. **Credit** AmEx, DC, MC, V.

Its quaint, cottage-like frontage festooned with Best Beer stickers, the flagship venue of Faversham brewery Shepherd Neame can do little wrong. Its intimate interior hasn't changed in years, nor has it needed to. As many tables as can be squeezed in – five at most – are nabbed not long after opening time. 'Standing room only' at least allows you to admire the rather splendid collection of civil aircraft running the length of the top shelf. That there is Shepherd Neame Spitfire, Best and Master Brew goes without saying, but you'll also find draught Oranjeboom and Holsten Export, plus perhaps the more recent arrival of Asahi by the bottle. A modest wine list commences with Paree sauvignon (£2.75 a glass) and Boonaburra shiraz (£3.25), and simple snacks and sandwiches are served of a lunchtime.

Tables outdoors (4, pavement). TV (satellite).

Chez Gérard

101 Buckingham Palace Road, SW1W 0SJ (7868 6249/www.chezgerard.co.uk). Victoria tube/rail. **Open/food served** 6-11pm daily. **Credit** AmEx, DC, JCB, MC, V.

Now part of the Chez Gérard group of Frenchified eateries, this lovely space by the lobby of the Thistle Hotel in Victoria Station has changed hands a couple of times of late. The latest changeover, stripy menus and all, sees the donning of beret and baguette. A café-resto by day – amuse-bouches of beignets de crevette (six tiger prawns in pastry, £5.95), pâté de foie de volaille (£5.50), assiettes de chèvre chaud (£8.75), steak hâché (£9.25) and cheeses – it becomes a bar by night. Wines come four of each colour by the glass, large glass, 50cl carafe and bottle, thus the price of a Paul Deloux chablis ranges from £6.60 to £26, a Marie-Louise Parisot pinot noir from £5.50 to £22.50. Cocktails, the forte of the previous incumbent here, are of the standard variety (unspecified tequila in Margaritas, unspecified rum in Piña Coladas, etc), and all at £7.50.

Babies and children welcome; high chairs. Music (jazz Sun).

Goring Hotel

Beeston Place, Grosvenor Gardens, SW1W 0JW (7396 9000/www.goringhotel.co.uk). Victoria tube/rail. **Open** 7am-11pm daily. **Food served** 11am-11pm daily. **Credit** AmEx, DC, MC, V.

How many other hotel bars change their drinks menu monthly? The Goring is indeed a rare trove, tucked away as it is down a sidestreet of a Victoria Station estuary – albeit fronted by flapping flags of many countries and a braided flunky straight out of the movies. The discreet greeting, the gentlemen's club decor in smallish bar area and spacious back room, the three-sided complimentary dish of olives, roasted potato chips and cheesy shortbread, all indicate a class act. And so it is. The cocktails (£9-£11.50) are delicately conceived and dangerously strong. Some feature under-rated R de Ruinart champagne, such as the Goring Royal Pimm's (also with Pimm's No.1 and crème de fraise), or in the first-rate Bellinis. There's whisky galore, too: Highland, Island and Lowland, from Auchentoshan to Tamdhu, of many a vintage.

Babies and children welcome (lounge). Disabled: toilet. No piped music or jukebox. No-smoking area. Restaurant. Specialities (cocktails). Tables outdoors (9, terrace).

Plumbers Arms

14 Lower Belgrave Street, SW1W 0LN (7730 4067). Victoria tube/rail. **Open** 11am-11pm Mon-Fri. **Food served** 11am-9.30pm Mon-Thur; 11am-2.30pm Fri. **Credit** AmEx, DC, MC, V.

A very popular boozer, thanks to its homely, intimate pub feel and decent beers on tap. Bombardier, Young's and London Pride are usually joined by a guest ale, often seasonal (in this case Usher's Winter Storm). The better lager – Budvar, Beck's – comes by the bottle. Laphroaig and Talisker number among a handful of classy malts, and the wine list is 18 strong. It's proud of its history, too, social or notorious. A plaque by the couple of beer tables outside describes the pub erected in honour of master builder Thomas Cubbitt, whose tradesmen, servants and footmen were allocated different drinking areas (it still feels somewhat partitioned). Meanwhile, inside, on one of the pillars, a newspaper report relates the exciting moment in November 1974 when Lady Lucan burst in to announce the murder by her husband of their nanny.

Function room. Games (board games, darts, quiz machine). Tables outdoors (3, pavement). TV (satellite).

Tiles

36 Buckingham Palace Road, SW1W 0RE (7834 7761/www.tilesrestaurant.co.uk). Victoria tube/rail. **Open** noon-11pm Mon-Fri. **Food served** noon-2.30pm, 5.30-10pm Mon-Fri. **Credit** AmEx, DC, JCB, MC, V.

Love is in the air on the ground floor of this charming bar, with tables for two, Communion candles, low lighting and large bowls of flowers setting a resolutely smoochy tone. Named for its blue and white diamond-patterned ceramic floor, Tiles also has room in the basement (pine floor here, plus modern lamps, the odd sofa and trendy pictures of wine bottles) for those who want to hang out with mates rather than just their mate. There are 22 wines by the glass to choose from, but few catch the eye. Antares' 2003 chardonnay (£3.75) confirms the view that one should avoid most entry-level Chilean whites; opt instead for the 2003 San Estaban carmenère from the same country (£4.75) – or, if you have the cash, sample Léoville-Barton's second bordeaux wine, 'La Réserve de' from the cracking 2000 vintage (£37 a bottle). Decent food includes an old Tiles favourite – fish cakes with caper mayonnaise.

Babies and children welcome. Function room. Tables outdoors (6, pavement).

Zander Bar

45 Buckingham Gate, SW1E 6BS (7379 9797/ www.bankrestaurants.com). St James's Park or Victoria tube/rail. **Open** 11am-11pm Mon, Tue; 11am-1am Wed-Fri; 5pm-1am Sat. **Food served** noon-2.45pm, 5.30-11pm Mon-Fri; 5.30-11pm Sat. **Credit** AmEx, DC, MC, V.

In the same stable as Bank Aldwych (*see p94*), Zander is in many ways a far better bar – albeit a far more isolated one. Stuck on a quiet road between St James's Park and Victoria Station, Zander has cool drinks in spades, plus a bloody long bar counter at which to enjoy them. A dozen original Zander cocktails include the Zander Cosmo (£6.85) of Absolut Kurrant shaken with Grand Marnier and fresh pomegranate; a Polish Breeze (£7) comprises Zubrowka with fresh apple, cinnamon and apple schapps; champagne cocktails are concocted with Piper Heidsieck; Martinis come in cinnamon, grape and watermelon flavours. The classics are made with premium and super premium base spirits, allowing use of Knob Creek nine-year-old, Grey Goose and Matusalem 15-year-old. The bottled beers are

Früli, Bitburger and De Koninck from Antwerp. Spanish (£9.50) and Greek (£5.95) plates allow for an easy snack, the home-made Zander burger (£5.75) less so.
Babies and children welcome (restaurant): children's menus, high chairs. Function rooms. Music (DJs 8.30pm Fri, Sat; free). Restaurant. Tables outdoors (60, terrace).

Also in the area...

Balls Brothers 50 Buckingham Palace Road, SW1N 0RN (7828 4111); 20 St James Street (Ryder Street entrance), SW1A 1ES (7321 0882).
Wetherspoon's Unit 5, Victoria Station, Victoria Island, SW1V 1JT (7931 0445).
Willow Walk (JD Wetherspoon) 25 Wilton Road, SW1V 1LW (7828 2953).

WATERLOO

Waterloo has scrubbed up its drinking scene in the past few years. If you're after places so close to the train station that your pint glass rattles, try spit-and-sawdust joints like the **Hole in the Wall**, or rather more sophisticated numbers like **L'Auberge** or **Archduke**. The Southwark end of the Cut now has three great options: the **Hope & Anchor** (a fine gastropub), the **Ring** (a homage to boxing) and **Baltic** (a cocktail paradise).

Anchor & Hope

36 The Cut, SE1 8LP (7928 9898). Southwark or Waterloo tube/rail. **Open** 5-11pm Mon; 11am-11pm Tue-Sat. **Food served** noon-2.30pm, 6-10.30pm Tue-Sat; 6-10.30pm Sun. **Credit** MC, V.
A thick red tapestry divides this alpha gastropub into two spaces for dining and drinking: the former with an open kitchen and the latter a chunky wooden bar. The A&C is a smartened version of a traditional pub, with dog-eared green velvet furniture, deep red walls and globe lights. The food has an excellent reputation, and the chef has a sense of humour: tripe and chips (£11), or pea, ham and pig's ear soup (£5), anyone? That said, our toast with duck rillettes was surprisingly greasy, and staff can get shirty when the place is overrun in the early evenings. The wine list is extensive, but kicks off with a thimble-sized glass of so-so house red (£1.80); beers include the rather poor Greek lager Crest, plus Red Stripe and Bombardier. An upright piano stands in one corner; maybe Kevin Spacey will come in from the Old Vic for a singalong one day.
Babies and children welcome. No-smoking (dining area). Restaurant available for hire.

Archduke

Concert Hall Approach, South Bank, SE1 8XU (7928 9370). Waterloo tube/rail. **Open** 8.30am-11pm Mon-Fri; 11am-11pm Sat. **Food served** 11am-11pm Mon-Sat. **Credit** AmEx, DC, MC, V.
Tourists and harassed parents on the South Bank are glad of the rest and relative privacy of this glass-fronted, split-level bar beneath dark Victorian railway arches. Large, fake plastic plants hang down from baskets, competing with heavy metal lamps as trains boom overhead. Archduke is like an art gallery tea room during the day, when fathers sport carry-pouches with young babies, and large groups in their 40s discuss the latest exhibition; at night, the bar gleams with coloured lights and rings to the sound of jazz. There's an upstairs restaurant, targeted at pre- and post-Royal Festival Hall crowd, with jazz-themed sketches hanging from the arch, as well as an outside conservatory. The wine list covers all the right bases. New Zealand sauvignon blanc? Check. Good value southern Italian red? Check. And the examples are good ones – respectively, the up-and-coming Waipara Estate's 2002 bottle (£23.75) and Madonne della Grazie's 2002 primitivo di Puglia 'A Mano' (£20.55).
Babies and children welcome. Conservatory (available for hire). Music (jazz 8.30-11pm Mon-Sat; free). No-smoking area. Restaurant. Tables outdoors (3 garden, 6 terrace).

L'Auberge

1 Sandell Street, SE1 8UH (7633 0610). Waterloo tube/rail. **Open/food served** noon-midnight Mon-Fri; noon-11pm Sat. **Credit** AmEx, DC, MC, V.
A cosy little Belgian set-up underneath Waterloo East sub-station, L'Auberge is one of the better drinking options within sprinting distance of Waterloo's platforms. The wooden bar room, with its scuffed floor, candlelight and low buzz of conversation, feels relaxed and well used. Continental beer fanciers have a gratifying menu to work from: Chimay Red, Duvel, potent Rochefort, raspberry and cherry varieties (£3.45-£3.95). Kwak (£3.95) is served according to tradition, in a wooden holder and test tube. Stella, Hoegaarden and Leffe on tap are also available in two-pint glasses (£5.75-£9.75) known, aptly (and in French), as *sérieux*. Eight wines of each colour are available by the glass. The mainly Gallic food is fairly average, though: it tries to please all tastes and comes up with some bizarre hybrids: moules Thailandaise, for example, with chips (£5.45). Stick to the beers and you can't go wrong.
Babies and children admitted. Restaurant.

Baltic

74 Blackfriars Road, SE1 8HA (7928 1111/www.balticrestaurant.co.uk). Southwark tube. **Open/snacks served** noon-11pm; Mon-Sat; noon-10.30pm Sun. **Credit** AmEx, MC, V.
On the ground floor of a frost-white townhouse, behind a heavy wooden door, Baltic really is a looker, with flocks of admirers to prove it. Its lofty, wood-beamed restaurant is its real raison d'être, but of an early evening the long, granite-hued bar to the front of the premises goes into cocktail-making overdrive for the Old Vic pre-theatre contingent. It's a classy but relaxed venue, enhanced by a fabulous cocktail menu that changes every four or so months, though always drawing on an impressive arsenal of Russian and Polish spirits. Baltic Martinis (£6.25) include the feisty Polish Passion, a blend of 42 Below Passion Fruit, champagne and fresh chilli. The fizzy Baltic Flutes (£6.75) are sublime; try the Cracow '75 with Chivas, white peach, vanilla and champagne. Beer includes Lapin Kulta, Okocim, Lech and Le Coq. Bar food is overpriced but tempting: Russian-style zakuski (various starters) with red pepper relish (£5.50); blinis with assorted caviars (£4.50-£24). There's a lofty, wood-beamed white restaurant to the rear.
Babies and children welcome; high chair. Disabled: toilet. Function room. Music (jazz 7-10pm Sun). Tables outdoors (5, courtyard).

Crown & Cushion

133-135 Westminster Bridge Road, SE1 7HR (7803 0573). Lambeth North tube or Waterloo tube/rail. **Open** 11am-11pm Mon-Sat; noon-10.30pm Sun. **Food served** noon-3pm, 6-11pm Mon-Sat; noon-3pm, 6-10.30pm Sun. **Credit** MC, V.

An unreconstructed, geezerish pub. Legend has it that the Crown & Cushion used to be a hangout for agents from the former MI5 office opposite. Yet while it's fun to imagine the spies playing darts and flicking through the jukebox, this is a pretty standard local. (The real arrows players conform to the beer gut stereotype, keeping score on a blackboard and throwing darts with St George cross flights.) Vintage beer promotion mirrors, Tupperware jugs and old London street signs line the walls, with a roasting electric fire in winter and a small beer garden available in summer. For 21st-century pursuits, there's also a wood-panelled room at the back with two internet points. Beer pumps feature the unremarkable choices of Greene King IPA, Worthington's, Carling and Grolsch; there's also bottled Budweiser. Pub grub is similarly straightforward.
Babies and children welcome. Disabled: toilet. Games (fruit machines, pool). Internet access (free). Restaurant. Tables outdoors (10, garden). TV (satellite, widescreen).

Cubana

48 Lower Marsh, SE1 7RG (7928 8778/ www.cubana.co.uk). Waterloo tube/rail. **Open** noon-midnight Mon, Tue; noon-1am Wed-Fri; 6pm-1am Sat. **Food served** noon-3pm, 5-11pm Mon-Fri; 6-11pm Sat. **Credit** AmEx, DC, JCB, MC, V.
On a dull night on Lower Marsh, Cubana's various sources of light – chilli-shaped fairy lights, huge cartoonish chandelier, rope lights – shine out with the promise of novelty. In truth, this place has nothing you won't have already seen on other Latino-themed premises, but it's still fun. One bar area is sunk below a huge street-level window and has just enough room to dance (there's salsa here at weekends) while the other contains a motley collection of tables. Drinks cover the classics (Caipirinhas and decently made Mojitos) and there are some moreish smoothie-style in-house numbers, such as the Revolution (with strawberries, pineapple, lime and white rum). Many of the cocktails are available by the jug, and there's also Sol, San Miguel and Budvar for beer drinkers. Outside are wrought-iron tables and chairs painted in rainbow colours; they look at some fairly nondescript buildings, but aren't bad for a summer booze-up.
Disabled: toilet. Function room. Music (live band 11pm-1am Wed-Sat). Restaurant. Specialities (cocktails). Tables outdoors (4, pavement).

Film Café

National Film Theatre, South Bank, SE1 8XT (7928 3535). Waterloo tube/rail. **Open** 11am-11pm Mon-Sat; noon-10.30pm Sun. **Food served** *Café only* 9am-9pm Mon-Sat; 10am-9pm Sun. **Credit** MC, V.
The NFT's in-house café hasn't blown the budget on decor (only two flat-screen displays suggest a movie theme), but this is a handy place for film-goers and tourists. Wedged underneath one end of Waterloo Bridge, it looks out on a busy stretch of the Thames through picture windows, with the best views at counter-top stools. The long wood-and-aluminium benches outside are packed during summer, but from here you can peel off to browse the outdoor second-hand book market opposite, or the various local cultural powerhouses. The blue-lit bar does Stella and Hoegaarden on tap, plus four wines by the glass (mostly of New World origin) and a modest tapas selection. Matinee-goers have the better option of a deli sandwich bar, which has fresh, if pricey, breads and fillings. At night the otherwise mundane canteen-style room becomes more atmospheric thanks to strings of fairy lights along the river.
Babies and children welcome. No-smoking tables. Tables outdoors.

Fire Station

150 Waterloo Road, SE1 8SB (7620 2226/www.wizardinns.co.uk). Waterloo tube/rail **Open** 11am-11pm Mon-Sat; noon-10.30pm Sun. **Food served** 11am-9pm Mon-Sat; noon-9.30pm Sun. **Credit** AmEx, MC, V.
This handsome red-brick 1910 fire station became a watering hole without drastic alterations, which means you don't have to think too hard to see it as a draughty, lofty room ideal for sleeping engines. Nevertheless, the original cream tiling (which covers all the wall space), bold red girders and stone floor work well with the present decor, which includes a seating area of wooden benches and tables, a zinc bar and tall pot plants. The bar is never less than busy, filled with the loud chatterings of thirtysomething boozers and a slightly clubby soundtrack. The restaurant at the back also does a tidy business, although some consider it a notch or two overpriced. The long wine list is chalked up above the bar, and includes a generous five different champagnes. The beer line-up includes London Pride, Shepherd Neame Spitfire, Marston's Pedigree and Young's bitter.
Babies and children welcome: children's menu (weekends); high chairs. Function room. Tables outdoors (4, pavement). TV (big screen, satellite).

Hole in the Wall

5 Mepham Street, SE1 8SQ (7928 6196). Waterloo tube/rail. **Open** 11am-11pm Mon-Sat; noon-10.30pm Sun. **Food served** noon-8pm Mon-Sat; noon-4pm Sun. **No credit cards**.
Yes, it's a hole in the wall, and a dent in the station, too – right underneath the rails of Waterloo. This place lives out the day's train timetable with intermittent wall-rattling that nobody pays much attention to. It's not the most glamorous place in the world (in a former life it was a cider house), and we strained hard to see signs of an apparent makeover; but it does have a certain scuffed charm, along with plenty of post-work/pre-commute drinkers. The bar in the large, arched wood-floored main room has a full hand of Adnams bitters, the usual lagers plus Spitfire and Hoegaarden. Sandwiches (£3.55) and snacks such as potato wedges (£2.65) are ferried out of the open kitchen. Assorted rough diamonds prop up the bar; other customers, seated on wooden benches and tatty velvet banquettes, are mainly young and blokey.
Babies and children admitted (until 6pm). Games (fruit machines, pinball, quiz machine). TV (big screen, satellite).

King's Arms

25 Roupell Street, SE1 8TB (7207 0784). Waterloo tube/rail. **Open** 11am-11pm Mon-Sat; noon-10.30pm Sun. **Food served** noon-3pm, 6-10.30pm Mon-Fri; 6-10.30pm Sat. **Credit** AmEx, DC, MC, V.
In the shadow of Waterloo East, Roupell is one of London's loveliest inner city streets: a narrow squeeze of two-up-two-down Victorian terraced houses that fetch upwards of half a million on the property market. Though it isn't cobbled, you feel it ought to be – yet it does get the pub it deserves in the King's Arms, a neat, corner boozer with a tiny two-bar interior in the classic tradition: stained glass, fireplace, old prints of the area. It pulls a fast one by opening out into a spacious, stone-paved conservatory at the rear, but this is so tastefully done that it doesn't seem out of place. Draught Adnams Bitter, London Pride and Young's Special are complemented by a fine selection of single malts, a well-priced wine list and Thai food.
Babies and children admitted (until 6pm Mon-Fri, all day weekends). Function room. TV.

Red Lion. See p67.

Laughing Gravy

154 Blackfriars Road, SE1 8EN (7721 7055). Southwark tube/Waterloo tube/rail. **Open** noon-11pm Mon-Fri; 7-11pm Sat. **Food served** noon-10pm Mon-Fri; 7-10pm Sat. **Credit** MC, V.

The name of Laurel and Hardy's dog, Laughing Gravy was also a hush-hush synonym for alcohol during Prohibition. While this place is far too civilised to be a speakeasy, the location – on a lonely stretch of Blackfriars Road – might suit such a venue. Inside is a cheerily decorated front bar with chunky wooden counter and bohemian curios (including perhaps London's only wooden Beefeater lamp stand). Beyond this is a pleasant, glass-roofed restaurant with decent food. The cherry-picked beer menu boasts everything from Barbar Honey Ale from Belgium to Brazilian Bravara (all around £3). Four wines of each colour are available by the glass, and the list also includes oddities like Gumpers' Block shiraz from Australia (£22.50). Bar snacks are of gastro pedigree; we had excellent own-made houmous with roasted chorizo and pitta slices (£2.95). A quiet and relaxed place, worth the detour.

Babies and children welcome: high chairs. Disabled: toilet. Games (board games). Restaurant (available for hire). Tables outdoors (2, pavement).

Ring

72 Blackfriars Road, SE1 8HA (7620 0811). Southwark tube. **Open** 11am-11pm Mon-Sat; noon-10.30pm Sun. **Food served** 11am-3pm, 6-10.30pm Mon-Sat; noon-4pm Sun. **Credit** MC, V.

Black eyes and bruises are a thing of the past at this boxing-themed pub, which used to have a training gym above it and has Blackfriars Ring (founded in 1910) opposite. These days it's a surprisingly sophisticated affair after a recent refurbishment, with a whiff of gentlemen's club in its dark wooden furnishings and elegant lamp lighting. Smartly framed memorabilia of old knuckle men covers all available wall space. It's all hugely entertaining: from curling, sepia photos of moustachioed featherweights to a poster heralding a match with Ted Broadribb, 'Great Britain's outstanding boxing mogul'. A TV screen (tucked discreetly in a corner, with the sound off) replays the sport's greatest moments, but doesn't interfere with the enjoyment of the non-pugilistic drinker. The bar doesn't pretend to offer much more than the standard lager-and-crisps fare (with the exception of a Hoegaarden pump), but no one's complaining. Not that they'd dare.

Babies and children admitted (lunch only). Tables outdoors (8, pavement). TV.

White Hart

29 Cornwall Road, SE1 8TJ (7401 7151). Waterloo tube/rail. **Open** noon-11pm Mon-Sat; noon-10.30pm Sun. **Food served** noon-10pm Mon-Sat; noon-9.30pm Sun. **Credit** AmEx, MC, V.

What was until recently the most decrepit and beyond-the-pale of backstreet boozers has now been reborn as a smart little venue that wouldn't look out of place in SW6. Owners the pub company Mitchell & Butler have done an amazing job, from the wispy parlour palms and brasserie-style seating on the pavement to the bottled Chimay, Duvel and Frambozenbier (wrapped in its own logoed paper) on the back bar shelves. With sofas, kitchen chairs and benches, beaded curtains and candles, the feel is part lounge bar, part gastropub (the food menu offers light bites, standard sandwiches, salads and mains such as smoked haddock fish cakes, gnocchi with wilted spinach and Aberdeen Angus burger, all at around £6-£8). Draught beers include ales Spitfire and London Pride, and boutique beers Hoegaarden, Leffe, Früli and Küppers Kölsch. Really not bad at all. The young, smiley female staff seem far too young to be working in a bar, and the clientele aren't much older – which makes for a buzzing and charged atmosphere.

Disabled: toilet. Games (retro machine). Specialities (Belgian beers). Tables outdoors (5, pavement).

Also in the area...

All Bar One 1 Chicheley Street, SE1 7PY (7921 9471); 34 Shad Thames, Spice Quay, Butlers Wharf, SE1 2YG (7940 9771); 28-30 London Bridge Street, SE1 9SG (7940 9981).
Balls Brothers The Hop Cellars, 24 Southwark Street, SE1 1TY (7403 6851); Hay's Galleria, Tooley Street, SE1 2HD (7407 4301).
Cooperage (Davy's) 48-50 Tooley Street, SE1 2SZ (7403 5775).
Heeltap & Bumper (Davy's) Chaucer House, White Hart Yard, Borough High Street, SE1 1NX (7407 2829).
Hog's Head 52-54 Stamford Street, SE1 9LX (7928 1154).
Pommeler's Rest (JD Wetherspoon) 196-198 Tower Bridge Road, SE1 2UN (7378 1399).
Slug & Lettuce 32 Borough High Street, SE1 1UX (7378 9999); North Block (1-63), 5 Chicheley Street, SE1 7PJ (7803 4790).

WESTMINSTER

You can't get away from parliamentary matters or parliamentarians in this corner of governmental London. Our version of Westminster runs from the Palace of Westminster, north up Whitehall and west to just shy of Westminster Cathedral (which we reckon is actually in Victoria). Most pubs around here draw in a mix of low-rent tourists and the less elevated end of the political spectrum: these we avoid. In those we include, sightings of bigwigs are nearly guaranteed.

Red Lion

48 Parliament Street, SW1A 2NH (7930 5826). Westminster tube. **Open** 11am-11pm Mon-Fri; 11am-9.30pm Sat; noon-7pm Sun. **Food served** noon-2.30pm daily. **Credit** MC, V.

No bar – or, at least, no public bar – sums up Westminster as well as this famous boozer yards from the Houses of Parliament. Upstairs is a grill room, and the cellar (not always open) holds a nice bar; but the handsome, skinny ground floor, complete with division bell, TV screening BBC Parliament and walls lined with memorabilia, is where the action is. The conversation here often hums with rumour and power-speak: the man ostentatiously wearing a 'Bush-Cheney 04' badge on our visit was not, as we first suspected, a guileless tourist but rather a quasi-important politico. Though this structure dates to 1900, the original building went up in 1733; it was where David Copperfield asked for a glass of 'genuine stunning ale', which he was then served with a kiss. You won't be quite so lucky these days, not least because the glass of Adnams we sampled was in pretty ropey condition. A pity, too, that Taylor Walker have kitted their staff out in tacky T-shirts and covered any spare wall space in posters advertising competitions and rugby games, but it's unlikely the power-brokers, deep in shop talk and gossip, would ever notice.

Babies and children welcome (restaurant). Bar and restaurant available for hire. No-smoking (restaurant). Tables outdoors (5, pavement). TV.

St Stephen's Tavern

10 Bridge Street, SW1A 2JR (7925 2286). Westminster tube. **Open** 11am-11pm Mon-Sat; 11am-10.30pm Sun. **Food served** noon-10pm daily. **Credit** MC, V.

With so many classic old pubs across the capital either closing or suffering a stripped-pine refit in recent years, here's a story to warm the cockles. This Victorian pub, owned by the Palace of Westminster, shut its doors in the mid-1980s, whereafter it served (among other things) as the site office during the construction of Portcullis House. Then, in 2003, it was restored by Hall & Woodhouse with many of its original fixtures and fittings, to fairly convincing effect. The two-room pub lacks the highly charged atmosphere of the Red Lion a few steps away; while politicos do drink in here, it's also popular with tourists. However, one major selling point is the fact that, unlike the other two largely chair-free pubs reviewed in this section, there's usually somewhere to sit and rest your decent pint of Badger.

Disabled: toilet. Function room. No piped music or jukebox.

Westminster Arms

9 Storey's Gate, SW1P 3AT (7222 8520). St James's Park or Westminster tube. **Open** 11am-11pm Mon-Fri; 11am-8pm Sat; noon-6pm Sun. **Food served** 11am-8pm Mon-Fri; noon-4pm Sat, Sun. **Credit** AmEx, MC, V.

On some nights, it can be difficult to move in here, the room a crush of MPs, lobbyists and other cogs in our beloved parliamentary machine. However, on evenings when the political demi-monde is back in its sundry constituencies, off on its summer holidays or away seeing its various mistresses, this feels like the saddest pub on earth. Aside from a few battered barstools near the door, there are no seats in here and precious little decoration, save for a vast TV screen and a handful of bashed-up portraits. Without a crowd in to fill the room, it's not much more than a barn – albeit a barn with seven taps pouring out real ales. On these lonely nights, you're better off downstairs in the more intimate Storey's Wine Bar.

Babies and children admitted. Function room. Games (fruit machine). No-smoking tables. Tables outdoors (4, pavement).

CITY

glass from a selection at Heals

CITY

CHANCERY LANE

Lawyers getting sloshed: that's the prevailing sight in Chancery Lane boozers. Doesn't matter how nice the pub, nor how plain – the conversation is all torts and courtroom politics. It's the worst eavesdropping in the city. Luckily, the architecture around here saves the day: two pubs – **Ye Olde Mitre** and the **Cittie of Yorke** – are gorgeous.

Cittie of Yorke

22 High Holborn, WC1V 6BN (7242 7670). Chancery Lane or Holborn tube. **Open** 11.30am-11pm Mon-Sat. **Food served** noon-3pm, 5-9pm Mon-Sat. **Credit** AmEx, MC, V.

You can probably guess from the name that this is no sleek, modern wine bar. Housed in an elegant Gothic building dating from 1430, the Cittie of Yorke is all about history, architecture and hard-backed wooden pews; there's also an abundance of wood panelling, wooden tables and wooden seating. The backroom bar was once the longest in the Empire, and the tall bottles above the bar held spirits, wines and sherries; at the centre is a triangular metal stove with an underground chimney. Much of ye olde furnishings in the front room are actually quite recent, but the gorgeous wooden cubicles in the back are Victorian. They were designed for lawyers from the nearby inns, and such characters still make up the bulk of the pub's clientele. The Cittie is now part of the no-nonsense Samuel Smith chain, which means Yorkshire prices for Old Brewery Bitter, Ayingerbrau and organic Pilsner.

Babies and children admitted (downstairs, before 5pm). Function rooms. Games (darts, fruit machine). **Map 3 M5**.

Ye Old Mitre

1 Ely Court, Ely Place (beside 8 Hatton Gardens), EC1N 6SJ (7405 4751). Chancery Lane tube/Farringdon tube/rail. **Open** 11am-11pm Mon-Fri. **Food served** 11am-9.30pm Mon-Fri. **Credit** AmEx, MC, V.

Settle yourself in one of the tiny rooms here – and mind your head: the low ceilings are deadly after a pint or two. Clearly people were shorter in 1546, when this pub was founded. The Mitre's name derives from its use as quarters for the retainers of the Bishops of Ely, on whose land it stands and whose church is still next door. The building was reconstructed in the 18th century using the original plans and materials. The decor is an eccentric hotchpotch of wood panelling, exposed stonework, low doorways and comfy chairs. Oliver Cromwell once owned the property, which he is said to have converted into a hospital and then a prison during the Civil War. Real ales include Adnams Best, Adnams Broadside, Tetley's and a monthly changing guest; cheese toasties head the rudimentary snack menu. Customers are a mix of legal types and tourists.

Function room. Games (cribbage, darts, dominoes). No piped music. Specialities (real ales). Tables outdoors (barrels, pavement).

Tooks Bar & Restaurant

17-18 Tooks Court, Cursitor Street, EC4A 1LB (7404 1818). Chancery Lane tube. **Open** noon-11pm Mon-Fri. **Food served** noon-3.30pm Mon-Wed; noon-3.30pm, 6.30-9.30pm Thur, Fri. **Credit** AmEx, MC, V.

This is a strange, oxymoronic place: a Belgian pub that looks like a breakfast restaurant in seaside France. Lights are bright, tables are polished pine; the whole feel is distinctly non-bar. It's like drinking in your gran's favourite teashop. Still, that doesn't stop Tooks attracting a regular crowd of legal eagles – although they all seem to go to bed early (on our visit the place was empty by 10pm). Beers are all in bottles and pleasantly Flemish; there's the rich Grimbergen Blonde, and the smooth De Koninck as well as a couple of fruity versions. Food is as big an attraction as the beer, if not bigger: Donald Russell beef, line-caught trout and tarte aux pommes were recently on the menu. Bar staff are friendly and authentically Belgian.

Babies and children admitted. Disabled: toilet. Function room. games. No-smoking area. Restaurant. **Map 4 N6**.

White Swan Pub & Dining Room

108 Fetter Lane, EC4A 1ES (7242 9696). Chancery Lane or Holborn tube. **Open** 11am-11pm Mon-Fri. **Food served** noon-3pm. **Credit** AmEx, MC, V.

Everything the Cittie of Yorke isn't, the White Swan is: scrubbed clean of nearly all trace of history (some old exposed brick is about the only visible link with the past), and heavy on cheesy art, brushed chrome and creamy walls. Behind the sleek bar, glass shelves groan under the weight of trendy booze, but the emphasis here is on lager – so it's San Miguel and Hoegaarden all round. On our Tuesday night visit, the place had no customers except for two large tables of extremely drunk, suited types. Staff were nicer than might be expected, given the noise levels. The Swan has gastropub ambitions, serving Modern European cuisine at fairly reasonable prices; the wine list isn't bad either, and glasses start at £3.60.

Function room (weekends only). Restaurant. Specialities (real ales). TV.

Also in the area...

Bottlescrue (Davy's) Bath House, 53-60 Holborn Viaduct, EC1A 2FD (7248 2157).

CLERKENWELL & FARRINGDON

Clerkenwell is almost north London, Farringdon is on the fringes of the City. The two meet at Clerkenwell Road, an office-dreary, traffic-clogged east-west artery, yet also the epicentre of the new

London drinking scene. The area remains second only to Hoxton and Shoreditch as a growth area for new venues (particularly around Smithfield and Exmouth markets), although like its near-neighbour to the east, new venues tend to be pale imitators of what's already there.

Abbaye

55 Charterhouse Street, EC1M 6HA (7253 1612). Chancery Lane tube/Farringdon tube/rail. **Open** noon-11pm daily. **Food served** noon-10.30pm. **Credit** AmEx, MC, V.

Abbaye is a mini chain of three Belgian bar-brasseries (the other two being in Bromley and on the Old Brompton Road). At the Smithfield venue, sashay past the seated diners (tucking into plates heaped with moules or steak and stoemp mash) to a bar area of bare brick, cast-iron columns, piano and potted palm. On the counter are taps dispensing Hoegaarden, Leffe, Stella Artois and Belle Vue Kriek cherry beer; behind, in plainly tempting view, are three chiller cabinets stuffed full of enticing bottles offering all manner of Belgian brews, including obscure Trappist ales and beers made with raspberry, banana, pineapple and even plum. Most are served, as befits Belgian tradition, in their own variously shaped logoed glasses that range from goblets to flutes to the complicated bulb-bottomed test-tube-and-wooden-holder arrangement designed for the conveyance of Kwak.

Babies and children admitted. Function room. Music (jazz Wed, Sat). No-smoking area. Restaurant. Tables outdoors (4, pavement). **Map 3 O5**.

Al's Café Bar

11-13 Exmouth Market, EC1R 4QD (7837 4821). Angel tube/Farringdon or King's Cross tube/rail. **Open** 8am-midnight Mon; 8am-2am Tue-Fri; 10am-2am Sat; 10am-11pm Sun. **Food served** 8am-10pm Mon-Fri; 10am-10pm Sat; 10am-9pm Sun. **Credit** AmEx, JCB, MC, V.

Al's is still the same four-square room with a concrete slab of a serving area, but the seating now is a mix of chunky pine furniture and baggy sofas, while the walls are a sultry claret, hung with fashionable kitsch. At heart it remains a bustling diner serving all-day breakfasts, burgers, and other great-value grub. The drinks include a choice selection of draught Euro beers (including Hoegaarden, Leffe, Pilsner Urquell, Paulaner and Warsteiner), with plenty more intriguing stuff in bottles, plus cocktails and fresh juices. There's an unappealing, bunker-like basement room to take up the overspill; far better (in summer) are the pavement tables on pedestrianised Exmouth Market.

Babies and children admitted. Function room. Games (board games). Music (DJ 10pm Thur-Sat). No-smoking (downstairs, lunch only). Tables outdoors (12, pavement). **Map 3 N4**.

Bishops Finger

9-10 West Smithfield, EC1A 9JR (7248 2341). Farringdon tube/rail. **Open** 11am-11pm Mon-Fri. **Food served** noon-3pm, 6-9pm Mon-Thur; noon-3pm Fri. **Credit** AmEx, MC, V.

The Finger is operated by Faversham brewery Shepherd Neame, Britain's oldest: it's been fermenting since 1698, which, as the legend on the pub clock points out, makes it 'very old indeed'. Hand pumps at the bar counter dispense the brewery's complete range of real ales including, naturally enough, Bishops Finger, as well as Master Brew and Spitfire (slogan: 'No Fokker comes close' – although maybe you need to be a childhood reader of *Battle* comic to fully appreciate the pun). To some, the Finger finds fame as 'Smithfield's well-known sausage pub', with 13 varieties including lamb, lime and chilli, or venison and red wine or tomato and mozzarella. The trad look (high ceiling, candles and fresh flowers on the many tearoom-style tables) belies a progressive attitude; witness the sticker on the window informing all that the pub is a 'WiFi zone'.

Babies and children admitted. Disabled: toilet. Function room. Tables outdoors (3, pavement). TV. **Map 3 O5**.

Cellar Gascon. *See p111.*

Bleeding Heart Restaurant, Tavern & Bistro

Bleeding Heart Yard, 19 Greville Street, EC1N 8SQ (7404 0333). Farringdon tube/rail. **Open** 11am-11pm Mon-Fri. **Food served** *Bar* 11am-10.30pm Mon-Fri. *Tavern* noon-3pm, 6-10.30pm Mon-Fri. **Credit** AmEx, DC, MC, V.

It's a tavern with a maître d' – and thus a tavern with class (or pretensions). The place is a restored version of a pub first opened in 1746, and oozes a rich history of bloody murders and royal weddings, celebrated in the publicity literature. It does good beers (Adnams Best, Broadside and, on a recent visit, Oyster Stout), but of greater note is the wine list, which runs to 450 varieties and reads like a who's who of viticulture. Open at 7am for breakfasts (continental at £5.95, full English at £6.95), at lunch it takes on the appearance of a boardroom; every table surrounded by suits and spreadsheets piled between plates of grilled bavette steak and seared bream (mains cost a tenner or so). Further into the yard, the Bleeding Heart Bistro keeps up the good work with outstanding French cuisine and yet more fine wines.

Babies and children admitted. Function room. No piped music or jukebox. Restaurant. Tables outdoors (10, terrace, May-Sep only). **Map 3 N5.**

Café Kick

43 Exmouth Market, EC1R 4QL (7837 8077/www.cafekick.co.uk). Angel tube/Farringdon tube/rail/19, 38 bus. **Open** noon-11pm Mon-Sat; 5-10.30pm Sun (spring-summer only). **Food served** noon-3pm, 6-10.30pm Mon-Fri; noon-10.30pm Sat. **Happy hour** 4-7pm Mon-Sat. **Credit** MC, V.

Not so much a celebration of football as of the international pageantry and bonhomie that characterises the game at its best, Kick is a multi-hued, worn and weathered shack, long, thin and dotted with memorabilia – pennants, programmes and centre spreads. The scout hut aesthetics are the setting for competitive high jinks, courtesy of three well-oiled René Pierre table-footie tables: reservations are taken, rules are posted and there are regular monthly tournaments. An area at the back with Formica-topped café tables offers sparse seating and menus listing a Champions' League of Euro beers: 14 by the bottle, including Kronenbourg (France), Peroni (Italy), Duvel (Belgium), San Miguel (Spain), Sagres (Portugal), Krombacher Pils (Germany) and Brahma (a ringer from Brazil). Cocktails come in the form of 'long kicks' and 'short kicks', food is tapas, platters and sandwiches, and the cigarettes sold behind the bar are, appropriately enough, Lucky Strikes. Premier league stuff.

Babies and children admitted (lunch only). Games (table football). Specialities (cocktails). Tables outdoors (2, pavement). TVs. **Map 3 N4.**

Cellar Gascon

59 West Smithfield, EC1A 9DS (7796 0600). Barbican tube/Farringdon tube/rail. **Open/food served** noon-midnight Mon-Fri. **Credit** AmEx, JCB, MC, V.

With almost missionary zeal, the proprietors of this stylish little wine bar (and, indeed, of the neighbouring restaurant that spawned it) are educating London drinkers in the vinous and culinary treasures of the eponymous region of France, Gascony. These are presented in the form of a giant wine list (there are around 120 bottles, all from the south-west) and a list of addictive *dégustations* (read: fancy bar snacks) that range from the familiar (slippery, rich foie gras) to the unusual (*andouille de Benejac*). If you must, you can stray from the wine list and try a regional aperitif – perhaps a glass of Floc de Gascoigne – but if it's a beer you're after, you really have come to the wrong place. Slick design rather than space is what characterises the interior here, so come early to be sure of a seat.

Bar available for hire. Tables outdoors (3, pavement). **Map 3 O5.**

Charterhouse 38

38 Charterhouse Street, EC1M 6JH (7608 0858/www.charterhousebar.co.uk). Farringdon tube/rail. **Open** noon-11pm Mon, Tue; noon-midnight Wed, Sun; noon-1am Thur; noon-2am Fri; 5pm-2am Sat. **Food served** noon-10pm Mon-Fri; 5-9pm Sat; noon-5pm Sun. **Happy hour** 5-7pm daily. **Credit** AmEx, MC, V.

C38's narrow, pie-slice premises work both for and against it. Visit by day and the tall, narrow interior is a delight, airy and well illuminated by long windows. By night, however, the slice rapidly becomes overfilled, especially towards the weekend when the ground floor acts as a busy conduit to the basement, where you'll hear champion sounds ranging from deep, soulful house and lounge to Pump the Funk's ghetto-fabulous hip hop. Refreshment comes in the form of bottled beers, a short list of classic cocktails (£5.75-£6.50) or a decent wine list that includes a good Chilean house red. The chef has gone beyond his remit for basic bar snacks like nachos and chicken skewers: the small menu also includes such gems as salad niçoise with sesame-crusted tuna.

Function room. Games (board games). Music (DJs 8pm Thur-Sun; free). Tables outdoors (2, pavement). TV (big screen). **Map 3 O5.**

Cicada

132-136 St John Street, EC1V 4JT (7608 1550/www.cicada.nu). Farringdon tube/rail. **Open** noon-11pm Mon-Sat. **Food served** noon-10.30pm Mon-Sat. **Credit** AmEx, DC, MC, V.

While most other local establishments cater to pre-clubbers, pool sharks and urban survivalists, punters here are a little more mature – in attitude, at least. This may have something to do with the calm and clean-lined space (stone-flagged floor, chunky chocolate furniture), half of which is sectioned off for diners (Chinese, Japanese and Thai food), with a solid bar counter occupying the centre ground. This counter is embellished with towering silvery taps dispensing boutique beers, but atop each table is an extensive menu of Martinis and drinks ('long & cool', 'short & fat', or 'top shelf classics' – all £6-£7.50). These mixed drinks are more exotic and lively than the crowd would suggest: a Shanghai Freeze of Zubrowka, mint, cranberry and lemon; a strawberry and basil Martini with Bombay Sapphire.

Babies and children admitted. Function room. No-smoking area. Restaurant. Tables outdoors (6, pavement). **Map 3 O4.**

Clerkenwell House

23-27 Hatton Wall, EC1N 8JJ (7404 1113). Chancery Lane tube/Farringdon tube/rail. **Open** noon-11pm Mon-Fri; 6-11pm Sat; 1-10.30pm Sun. **Food served** noon-3pm, 6-10pm Mon-Fri; 6-10pm Sat; 1-7pm Sun. **Credit** AmEx, MC, V.

Clerkenwell House is looking decidedly retro these days; trouble is, the period it references is the mid 1990s – a bit too recent for nostalgia. So the large ground-floor room has a slouch-perfect assortment of ageing leather sofas and assorted skip-ready furniture, which means, to be fair, punters feel at home, hoisting feet up on coffee tables, drawing on rollies and necking bottles of lowest-common-denominator lager. But it hardly makes for a destination venue. It's also

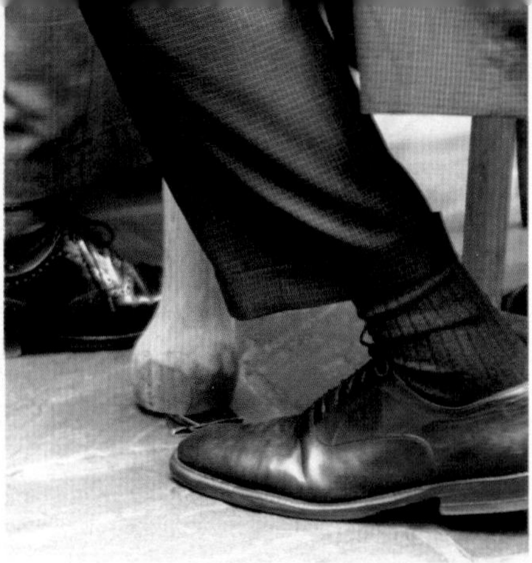

Gunmakers. *See p115.*

all a bit out of keeping with the ambitions of the large open kitchen, which turns out stuff like oven-baked trout and roast lamb shank (well priced at under a tenner). Down a tight spiral staircase is another large room with two pool tables and a DJ booth, but this looks even more neglected. A notice in the gents', however, promises a major refurb soon.
Bar available for hire (weekends). Games (pool). Music (DJs 7pm Thur, Fri). Restaurant. TVs. **Map 3 N5**.

Coach & Horses

26-28 Ray Street, EC1R 3DJ (7278 8990/www.the coachandhorses.com). Farringdon tube/rail/19, 38, 55, 63, 243 bus. **Open** 11am-11pm Mon-Fri; 6-11pm Sat; noon-3pm Sun. **Food served** noon-3pm, 7-10pm Mon; noon-3pm, 6-10pm Tue-Fri; 6-10pm Sat; noon-3pm Sun. **Credit** MC, V.

It takes some nerve to open a gastropub within a shallot's toss of the granddaddy of them all, the Eagle (*see p113*). But the gamble has paid off, and this was Time Out's favourite gastropub of 2004. It was once a neglected boozer next door to the offices of the *Guardian*; nowadays it looks well scrubbed, with a panelled bar, lovely moulded ceiling and some modern but unobtrusive lights. There's even a new patio garden with heaters. Draught beers include Adnams bitter, London Pride and Timothy Taylor Landlord, well kept but sold at West End prices (£3 a pint). The wine list is great (and well annotated), and the service is never less than charming. The superlative food comes from a daily-changing seasonal menu, supplemented by a snackier bar menu, which might include a pint of prawns and mayonnaise, oysters, or fish stew.
Babies and children welcome; high chairs. Specialities (wine). Tables outdoors (16, garden). **Map 3 N4**.

Cock Tavern

East Poultry Avenue, Central Markets, EC1A 9LH (7248 2918). Farringdon tube/rail. **Open** 6am-11pm Mon-Thur; 6am-2am Fri; 4-2am Sat. **Food served** 6-10.30am, noon-4pm Mon-Fri. **Credit** AmEx, MC, V.

There are several pubs around Smithfield that open early for breakfast, but there's only one that the butchers and bummarees use, and that's the Cock. Buried beneath the market building, this place is the real deal, the social centre for the meat marketeers once their hard day's morning is at an end. As much greasy spoon as pub, it's a great big bunker of fluorescent strip lights, Formica tops and lino

floors. It opens at 6am five mornings a week to serve up arteriosclerosis on a plate, accompanied by cheap pints. Recent changes have included a fancy lunchtime menu featuring the likes of marinated chicken with a julienne of mixed peppers, or honey roast ham with parsley sauce. The pub has also applied for a late weekend licence to provide the pre-clubbing crowd with an alternative and unusual party venue. It has already proved a big hit hosting after-show soirées for the Barbican.
Babies and children admitted. Bar available for hire. Games (fruit machine, quiz machine). Music (DJs 9pm Fri, Sat; free). TV (satellite, widescreen). **Map 3 O5**.

Crown Tavern

43 Clerkenwell Green, EC1R 0EG (7253 4973). Farringdon tube/rail. **Open** noon-11pm Mon-Sat; noon-9.30pm Sun. **Food served** noon-5pm, 6-9.30pm Mon-Thur; noon-5pm Fri-Sun. **Credit** AmEx, MC, V.
A couple of years back, local competition forced the old Crown to up its game. The lovingly polished mahogany and etched glass have been retained, but a careful hand has added a new varnished wooden floor, potted shrubs, padded leather seating and some ceiling fans. The result is a little trad, a little modern, a little continental and altogether classy. Blackboard menus detail choice beer, wine and food. Draught Adnams Bitter lines up alongside Staropramen, Hoegaarden and Früli strawberry beer, backed by an international array of bottled brews. There are over 20 choices of wine, with half a dozen of each colour by the glass, while food is above-average pub grub (gnocchi, Angus beef burger, steak and ale pie, £6.80-£8.90). Upstairs, in a space that vaguely echoes the building's former use as a Victorian music hall, is a high-ceilinged room with copper wallpaper and an American pool table that we've yet to find in working order.
Function room. Games (pool). Tables outdoors (10, pavement). **Map 3 N4**.

Dollar Grills & Martinis

2 Exmouth Market, EC1R 2EA (7278 0077). Farringdon tube/rail. **Open** 6pm-1am Mon-Sat. **Food served** 6pm-midnight Mon-Sat. **Credit** MC, V.
Anchoring Exmouth Market to Farringdon Road, the matt black façade of this former posties' boozer now wraps around a two-floor late-night bar and diner. The name, apparently, is all about trashy glamour, expressed in the ground-floor dining area's silver tables, glossy black tiles, mirror-mosaic pillars and huge blow-ups of Vegas neon. The menu is a New Yorkish mix of grills, including steak and quality burgers, and a crustacea bar. The drinks bar is downstairs in a low-ceilinged space done out in vampish black and red. Its leather-upholstered cube seating is as low as the lighting, making for a woozy well-past-tube-time feeling even when it's 6.15pm. There's also a lovely row of arched brick nooks lined in leather banquettes. There might be some bottled beers in a fridge somewhere, but the single-sheet menu lists only mixed drinks, leading with Martinis and running through contemporary classics and champagne cocktails to shorts, longs and shots.
Babies and children admitted. Bar available for hire. Music (8pm Fri, Sat; free). Restaurant. Specialities (cocktails). **Map 3 N4**.

Dovetail

9 Jerusalem Passage, EC1V 4JP (7490 7321/www.belgianbars.com). Farringdon tube/rail. **Open** noon-11pm Mon-Sat. **Food served** noon-3pm, 6-10pm Mon-Sat. **Credit** MC, V.
In a tiny alley between Clerkenwell Green and Clerkenwell Road, the Dovetail is a modestly proportioned homage to all things alcoholic and Belgian. In addition to 12 Lowland beers on draught, it offers 101 varieties by the bottle, including Trappist, Abbey, Gueze, Pilsner, wheat beers, golden ales, fruit beers, sour red beers, saison beers, pale ales, dark, triple, amber and blonde beers… One bottle, Rochefort 10, clocks in at a staggering (and you will be) 11.3% ABV. In a nod to Belgian ale's Trappist heritage, the place is monastically spartan – bare brick walls, stone-flagged floor, subdued lighting – with a few theatrical touches like the Gothic high-backed seating, and frivolity added by framed Tintin covers. Food takes the form of own-recipe sausages and burgers (ostrich, wild boar, mixed game, all marinated in booze), as well as kedgeree, Flemish fish stew and, of course, moules-frites.
Babies and children admitted. Disabled: toilet. No-smoking area. Specialities (Belgian beer). **Map 3 O4**.

Duke of York

156 Clerkenwell Road, EC1R 5DU (7837 8548). Farringdon tube/rail. **Open** 11am-11pm Mon-Sat; noon-10.30pm Sun. **Food served** noon-3pm, 6-10pm Mon-Fri; 5.30-10pm Sat. **Credit** MC, V.
Several cycle courier companies used to have their offices in the grey area of Clerkenwell Road, between City proper and the West End – so the big, red-fronted Duke became an off-duty bikers' social centre. On Thursdays and Fridays they still pack the place out, all Lycra shorts, dreads and tattoos, while every available post within 100 metres of the pub is festooned with chained-up bikes. At other times the large, high-ceilinged front room is almost as full and rowdy, but always entirely good-natured. A smaller back room holds a pool table, table football and an open fire. The crowd fuelled from a bar line-up of Bombardier, Directors, Stella and Guinness, with added nourishment courtesy of a cooked-to-order menu by the resident Thai chef, with dishes around £5. There are monthly art exhibitions and sport screened on two wall-mounted TVs.
Babies and children admitted (until 7pm). Games (fruit machine, pool, table football). Tables outdoors (2, pavement). TVs (2, digital). **Map 3 N4**.

Eagle

159 Farringdon Road, EC1R 3AL (7837 1353). Farringdon tube/rail/19, 38, 63, 341 bus. **Open** noon-11pm Mon-Sat; noon-5pm Sun. **Food served** 12.30-3pm, 6.30-10.30pm Mon-Fri; 12.30-3.30pm, 6.30-10.30pm Sat; 12.30-3.30pm Sun. **Credit** MC, V.
Every time we approach the Eagle we half expect to find it blockaded by a militant splinter group of CAMRA, raging at the viral spread of menus littered with lentils, beds of rocket and balsamic dressings and the attendant poncification of drinks offerings – New World wines and cocktails made with prosecco. The Eagle would be the object of wrath because it is widely regarded as the original gastropub. But, we'd point out, the Eagle's choice of drink is as splendid as its food, with a range of Charles Wells beers on draught, plus several continental white beers and a good selection of wines. Yes, the protesters would respond, but it's impossible to get a seat because all the tables in the pub's one modestly sized room are taken up by diners. And on that score, they'd be right. But for anyone prepared to stand at the polished wooden bar counter that runs the length of the back wall, the Eagle remains an excellent venue for the soaking up of decent booze and company.
Babies and children admitted. Tables outdoors (4, pavement). **Map 3 N4**.

Easton

22 Easton Street, WC1X 0DS (7278 7608/www.theeaston.co.uk). Farringdon tube/rail/19, 38 bus. **Open** noon-11pm Mon-Thur; 12.30pm-1am Fri; 5.30pm-1am Sat; noon-10.30pm Sun. **Food served** 12.30-3pm, 6.30-10.30pm Mon-Fri; 6.30-10.30pm Sat; 1-4pm, 6-10pm Sun. **Credit** MC, V.

There's a real neighbourhood feel to the Easton – a kind of sunny, 'I'm OK, you're OK' vibe – which is particularly impressive given its slightly tucked-away location north of Rosebery Avenue. Part of the reason for its popularity undoubtedly resides in the look of the place (big windows, wonderful retro wallpaper, beaten-up chairs and tables) and in the friendliness of the staff. It doesn't, sadly, rest with the drinks, which are limited to nitrokeg lager plus gastro stand-by Hoegaarden. The wine list is far better, with a short selection of inexpensive, good value bottles, and the food is excellent. The choice may not be vast (the day's dishes are on the blackboard), but what is done is done well. There's bench seating to accommodate outside boozing in the warmer months.

Babies and children admitted (daytime only). Music (DJs 9pm Fri). Tables outdoors (5, pavement). **Map 3 N4**.

Fluid

40 Charterhouse Street, EC1M 6JN (7253 3444/www.fluidbar.com). Barbican tube/Farringdon tube/rail. **Open** noon-midnight Mon-Wed; noon-2am Thur, Fri; 7pm-2am Sat. **Happy hour** 6-7pm Mon-Fri. **Food served** noon-10pm Mon-Fri. **Admission** £3 after 9pm, £5 after 10pm Fri, Sat. **Credit** AmEx, MC, V.

More than just a pit stop en route to Fabric, Fluid is a smart little venue in its own right. It's not so much a Japanese theme bar as a Japanese style bar relocated to London. Red-tinted windows reveal two floors of burnt orange ambient lighting, low-slung black leather seating and industrial metal vents and flues, with arcade games machines (including 1978 Space Invaders and tabletop Galaxians), a bright orange Sapporo beer machine and huge, manga-style Fluid logos. The food menu is all miso, tempura, sushi and sashimi, and the drink choices include draught Kirin backed by bottled Asahi Super Dry, Sapporo and ginseng beer. No saké, but there are plenty of oriental-themed cocktails (all at £6, or £3 between 6pm and 7pm Monday to Friday). Smooth jazz and downbeat house sounds give way to something more energetic at weekend DJ sessions.

Babies and children admitted (until 9pm). Function room. Games (retro arcade games). Music (DJs 7pm Tue-Sat). Tables outdoors (3, pavement). **Map 3 O5**.

Fox & Anchor

115 Charterhouse Street, EC1M 6AA (7253 5075). Barbican tube/Farringdon tube/rail. **Open** 7am-7pm Mon-Fri. **Food served** 7am-2pm Mon-Fri. **Credit** AmEx, MC, V.

What is possibly London's finest pub façade – a terracotta-tiled nouveau beauty, complete with twin gargoyles and glazed fox and anchor vignette – is sinking. The good news is that the owners, pub company Mitchell & Butler, have, after much shilly-shallying, decided to take the plunge and pay for repairs. These should stretch to a refit of the slightly shabby interior, which, although it looks authentically ancient, is in reality only a clever 1970s refit. What *are* old, though, are the wood-panelled booths at the rear of the pub, much sought after by early eaters who show up here at 7am for its celebrated full English breakfast. So prized are these private dining chambers that they're usually booked up weeks in advance. The Fox gets by on its breakfast and lunch trade, but at the time of writing was experimenting with an extension of evening hours until 9pm to cash in on the swift-one-before-home crowd.

Babies and children admitted (lunchtime). Function room. Tables outdoors (3, pavement). **Map 3 O5**.

Green

29 Clerkenwell Green, EC1R 0DU (7490 8010). Farringdon tube/rail. **Open** noon-11pm Mon-Wed; noon-midnight Thur, Fri; 4pm-midnight Sat; noon-10.30pm Sun. **Food served** noon-3pm, 6-11pm Mon-Fri; 6pm-midnight Sat; noon-4pm, 6-10.30pm Sun. **Credit** AmEx, MC, V.

Clerkenwell has gained a new corner bar where the prominent Novelli restaurant once stood (not actually on Clerkenwell Green, but round the corner facing Clerkenwell Road as it passes over the Circle Line tracks). The Green is as much pub as bar, with toothsome Timothy Taylor Landlord on draught (£2.70 a pint) and an unpretentious feel, though large groups can dominate a room that would feel small without its large windows. There's a good selection of spirits, decent wines, and worthwhile bottled beers such as Duvel. In the evenings the food is an array of decent Spanish tapas such as boquerones, chorizo, roast-pepper salad, and manchego in olive oil. At lunchtime the menu's more extensive, and might include Cornish crab salad followed by roast pheasant with chestnuts and cranberries.

Babies and children admitted. Disabled: toilet. Function room. Games (cards, dominoes). Music (DJ 6pm Sat, Sun; free). Tables outdoors (6, pavement). **Map 3 N4**.

Gunmakers

13 Eyre Street Hill, EC1R 5ET (7278 1022). Farringdon tube/rail. **Open** noon-11pm Mon-Fri. **Food served** noon-3pm, 5-9pm Mon-Fri. **Credit** AmEx, DC, MC, V.

Traffic on Clerkenwell Road passes largely ignorant that just 100 metres north, scarcely visible down Eyre Street Hill – flagged by the RAF roundel of the Ben Sherman offices – is the most perfect of little pubs. Just two rooms small, the Gunmakers boasts a tiny, duck-egg blue front bar with one red leatherette bench facing a serving area barely large enough to accommodate the smiles of the bar girls. Up two creaking steps is a similarly modest back-room, with a handful of tables that manages to magic cramped into intimate. Patrons are offered a draught line-up of Charles Wells Bombardier, Greene King IPA, Hoegaarden and Pilsner Urquell, and a lengthy wine list with four of each colour by the glass. No-nonsense pub food of superior quality is also served: expect the likes of rock oysters or braised oxtail with celeriac mash.

Babies and children welcome (before 6pm). Function room. Quiz (7pm Mon; £2). Tables outdoors (10, conservatory). **Map 3 N4**.

Hand & Shears

1 Middle Street, EC1A 7JA (7600 0257/www.handandshears.com). Barbican tube. **Open** 11am-11pm Mon-Fri. **Food served** noon-3pm Mon-Fri. **Credit** AmEx, MC, V.

According to a plaque mounted beside the rounded corner entrance to the Hand & Shears, the pub was constructed 1849 on the site of an alehouse built in 1123; the pub used to serve condemned prisoners their last drink before they were led to the scaffold at nearby Newgate. It has largely escaped the attentions of the refurb merchants, and has the unusual quality of actually feeling old rather than just looking it. In addition to wood-panelled walls and bare floorboards, the pub still retains its original partitions, dividing

what is already a small pub into three smaller snugs. It creaks and groans under the weight of its customers (who are largely lawyers). Expect Courage Best and Directors on draught, supplemented by monthly guest beers (Theakston's XB on our latest visit); the traditional, no-frills pub grub comes at good, old-fashioned prices (rump steak and chips at £6.50; sausage and mash at £4.50).
Games (darts). Function room. No piped music or jukebox. Restaurant. **Map 3 O5**.

Jerusalem Tavern

55 Britton Street, EC1M 5UQ (7490 4281/www.stpetersbrewery.co.uk). Farringdon tube/rail. **Open** 11am-11pm Mon-Fri. **Food served** noon-3pm Mon-Fri. **Credit** MC, V.
The Jerusalem is the solitary London representative of the St Peter's Brewery, based near Bungay in North Suffolk. Its beers are dispensed in marsh-green bottles that have the whiff of the apothecary. This is entirely appropriate given the druids'-balm-and-snake-oil nature of the brews: combinations such as lemon and ginger, cinnamon and apple or, in the case of King Cnut Ale, a re-creation of a typical beer of the first millennium using barley, nettles and juniper. The pub itself is a marvellously mad affair composed entirely of niches, nooks and crannies, with a tiny front room leading to a squeezed corridor between bar counter and tiny raised gallery, and, beyond that, a minuscule backroom adorned with stuffed fox and fowl. Floors are warped, flat surfaces scarce. This is possibly our city's most eccentric little hostelry and a thing to be cherished.
Babies and children admitted. Bar available for hire (Sat, Sun only). No piped music or jukebox. Specialities (real ales). **Map 3 O4**.

City

Match EC1

45-47 Clerkenwell Road, EC1M 5RS (7250 4002/www.matchbar.com). Farringdon tube/rail. **Open** 11am-midnight Mon-Fri; 5pm-midnight Sat. **Food served** noon-11pm Mon-Fri; 6-11pm Sat. **Credit** AmEx, DC, MC, V.
London's bar entrepreneurs have had around eight years now to scrutinise Match and roll out their own copycat establishments. And sure enough, there have been a gazillion imitators hereabouts, but on a slow Tuesday evening we found them all very light on custom while Match was packed. Why? It's the drinks, stupid. The cocktail list is put together by 'king of cocktails' Dale DeGroff and regularly updated. To DeGroff's originals on the current list are added some new 'Match originals' including the Fa'afafene (Sam Jeveons, 2004) of 42 Below passion fruit vodka with lime and apple juices, honey and a dash of grenadine; sweet and fruity but potent – after two you'll even be able to pronounce it. The place itself is modest of size with a sunken 'pit' area for serious upright drinking and ringside seating for cocktails or dining from a brief snacky menu (stuffed pitta, jerk chicken sandwich, Cuban burger; £6-£8).
Specialities (cocktails). Tables outdoors (4, pavement). **Map 3 O4**.

Medcalf

40 Exmouth Market, EC1R 4QE (7833 3533). Angel tube/Farringdon tube/rail. **Open** noon-11pm Mon-Thur, Sat; noon-12.30am Fri; noon-5pm Sun. **Food served** noon-3pm, 6-10pm Mon-Thur; noon-3pm Fri; noon-4pm, 6-10pm Sat; noon-4pm Sun. **Credit** MC, V.
A butcher's shop from 1912 until very recently, Medcalf now looks like a restaurant and tastes like a restaurant (Best Local Restaurant in Time Out's 2004 Eating & Drinking Awards, in fact), but it also functions beautifully as a bar. An assertive bar counter part-way down the room has Erdinger on draught for fans of wheat beer and offers a very decent selection of wines, largely from France, Italy and Spain. In fact, there's no dinner at all on Friday after 8pm, when the place transforms into the 'Clerkenwell funk pit' with 'choice cuts' (their pun, not ours) of jazz, soul and funk with a roster of special nights like the monthly Manchester Direct (flat caps optional). Otherwise, food is served throughout the day, beginning with breakfast and switching to a daily menu of largely organic British fare.
Babies and children welcome (before 7pm). Bar available for hire. Disabled: toilet. Music (DJs 7pm Fri; free). Tables outdoors (5, garden, 2, pavement). **Map 3 O4**.

Mulligans

8 Tysoe Street, EC1R 4RQ (7278 7630). Angel tube/19, 38 bus. **Open** 11am-midnight Mon-Sat; noon-1am Sun. **Food served** noon-3pm Mon-Fri, Sun. **Credit** MC, V.
The landlord and garrulous bar matron are English, but Mulligans retains the affinity to the Emerald Isle established when the pub was previously run by and named after the esteemed Gerry O'Hanlon. There are no Oirish knick-knacks; instead six handpumps delivering Young's ales, London Pride, Timothy Taylor and guest beers are backed by Guinness and a shelf of fine Irish whiskeys (Black Bush, Bushmills, Paddy and so on). The food menu includes Irish stew, boiled bacon and cabbage, and Irish cheeses served with imported Guinness mustard or stout relish with, of course, Irish coffee as digestif. There's a large, pull-down screen for sports; rugby's a big draw, but in the afternoon it keeps punters informed of goings-on at Aintree, Haydock Park and Newmarket.
Babies and children admitted (weekends). No-smoking area (12.30-2.30pm). Tables outdoors (2, pavement). TV (big screen, digital). **Map 3 N3**.

19:20

19-20 Great Sutton Street, EC1V 0DB (7253 1920). Farringdon tube/rail. **Open** noon-11pm Mon-Fri; 5pm-11pm Sat. **Food served** noon-3pm, 6-10pm Mon-Fri; 6-10pm Sat. **Credit** AmEx, MC, V.
The house menu offers its own (superfluous) four-step operational explanation of 19:20: '01 Bar; 02 American Pool; 03 Food; 04 Clerkenwell'. This requires some elucidation. 01 Bar: large, low-ceilinged, warmly-lit basement space, loud and leery in nature, amorphous in shape and lined with red-padded seating, with a poor selection of draught beers, four or five red and white wines by the glass, an array of £6 cocktails. 02 American Pool: four orange-baize tables on the ground floor, hired at £9 an hour or £6 before 5pm, invariably occupied by slacking office lads. 03 Food: gourmet burgers in five varieties with a choice of salads and sides (£6.50-£8), served up for just a fiver at lunch, plus a choice of two platters in fish or meat flavours. 04 Clerkenwell: borough of London notable for a profusion of less-fashionable-than-they-once-were bars.
Babies and children admitted (lunchtimes only). Games (4 pool tables). Music (DJs 7pm Fri-Sat; free). Tables outdoors (pavement). TV (satellite). **Map 3 O4**.

Pakenham Arms

1 Pakenham Street, WC1 0LA (7837 6933). Russell Square tube/King's Cross tube/rail. **Open** 9am-1am Mon-Sat; 9am-10.30pm Sun. **Food served** 9.30-11.30am, noon-2pm, 6-9pm Mon-Fri; 10am-6pm Sat, Sun. **Credit** MC, V.

Black Friar. *See p120.*

All things to all men, during the day this large, single-bar, old-school local serves postmen from the Mount Pleasant sorting office across the road. In the evening, darts players and sports fans – served by two TVs and several big pull-down screens – join real ale freaks and daytime stragglers. Real ale freaks because the Pakenham takes its beer very seriously indeed. A regular fixture in the North London CAMRA newsletter, it offers eight different ales on draught including representatives from Adnams, Fuller, Harveys of Sussex and Timothy Taylor. The pub opens for breakfast – the usual infarction-inducers – then it's simple lunches (Irish stew, Cumberland sausage and champ, haddock and chips, all at around £5) and similar in the evenings, when the pub remains open until 1am.
Disabled: toilet. Games (darts, fruit machines). Tables outdoors (3, pavement). TV (satellite). **Map 3 M4**.

Peasant

240 St John Street, EC1V 4PH (7336 7726/www.thepeasant.co.uk). Angel tube/Farringdon tube/rail/19, 38 bus. **Open/food served** (bar) noon-11pm daily. **Credit** AmEx, DC, JCB, MC, V.

A grand Victorian corner gin palace, spacious in layout and high of ceiling, with original dark wooden fittings and a fine mosaic floor. As with a great many pubs in the neighbourhood, it's been spruced up (beautifully, we might add) and the clientele of old sent off to some other joint. They've been replaced by self-conscious young hipsters in NHS specs, soothed by chilled tunes and refreshed by pints of Charles Wells Bombardier and something called Archers Golden (from Swindon), as well as Hoegaarden and bottles of prize continental brews like Leffe and Duvel in the chiller cabinet. They're further pandered to by a bar menu of enticing tapas, while proper food (prawn and monkfish spiedini, grilled kangaroo fillet, smoked paprika roast pork, all in the £10-£15 range) is served in the lovely upstairs dining room. The unlikely triumvirate of Chairman Mao, Che Guevara and Iggy Pop graces the wall behind the bar.
Babies and children welcome; high chairs. Games (board games). Restaurant. Specialities (organic cider). Tables outdoors (4, garden terrace; 5, pavement). **Map 3 O4**.

Potemkin

144 Clerkenwell Road, EC1R 5DP (7278 6661/www.potemkin.co.uk). Farringdon tube/rail. **Open** noon-11pm Mon-Fri; 6pm-midnight Sat. **Food served** noon-10.30pm Mon-Fri; 6-10.30pm Sat. **Credit** AmEx, DC, JCB, MC, V.

The mirrored basement restaurant is where Potemkin gets most business; upstairs is a small, well-rounded but harshly lit vodka bar. The menu runs to around 130 varieties, from standards like Smirnoff to Kauffman Private Vintage at

CRITICS' PICKS

For beers and ales
Abbaye (*see p109*), **Bar Kick** (*see p127*), **Bishops Finger** (*see p109*), **Dovetail** (*see p113*), **Jerusalem Tavern** (*see p116*), **Old Bell Tavern** (*see p120*), **Pakenham Arms** (*see p116*), **Wenlock Arms** (*see p130*).

For cocktails
Bonds Bar & Restaurant (*see p134*), **Cicada** (*see p111*), **Cocomo** (*see p125*), **Match EC1** (*see p116*), **1 Lombard Street** (*see p135*), **Sosho** (*see p129*), **Zetter** (*see right*).

For the strong stuff
Drunken Monkey (*see p125*), **Great Eastern Dining Room** (*see p127*), **Potemkin** (vodka; *see p117*), **Smersh** (vodka; *see p129*).

For wine
Balls Brothers (*see right*), **Bow Wine Vaults** (*see p134*), **Cellar Gascon** (*see p111*), **Corney & Barrow** (*see p131*), **La Grande Marque** (*see p120*), **Jamies at the Pavilion** (*see p132*).

For sheer style
Counting House (*see p134*), **Dollar Grills & Martinis** (*see p113*), **Loungelover** (*see p128*), **Zetter** (*see right*).

For fine views
Samuel Pepys (*see p121*), **Vertigo 42** (*see p132*).

For a blast from the past
Black Friar (*see p120*), **Cittie of Yorke** (*see p108*), **Hamilton Hall** (*see p131*), **Hand & Shears** (*see p115*), **Ye Olde Cheshire Cheese** (*see p121*), **Ye Olde Watling** (*see p135*), **Ye Old Mitre** (*see p108*), **Viaduct Tavern** (*see p122*), **Williamson's Tavern** (*see p137*).

For fun and games
Catch (pinball, pool; *see p125*), **Elbow Room** (pool; *see p126*), **Fluid** (vintage arcade games; *see p115*), **Pool** (pool; *see p128*).

For real fires
Dragon (*see p125*), **Duke of York** (*see p113*), **Golden Heart** (*see p131*).

For surroundings with a theme
Bar Kick (football; *see p124*), **Café Kick** (football; *see p111*), **Fluid** (Japan; *see p115*), **Smersh** (Soviet Russia; *see p129*).

For good food
Bishops Finger (*see p109*), **Coach & Horses** (*see p112*), **Dovetail** (*see p113*), **Eagle** (*see p113*), **Medcalf** (*see p116*), **Tooks Bar & Restaurant** (*see p108*).

£540 a bottle. The list includes many 'sweet sipping' and herbal types; almost all can be sampled by the shot (£2.80-£3.50). Kudos to the management for not insisting on the supremacy of Russian vodkas to the exclusion of others: there are Scandinavian and Polish vodkas, too (as well as Estonian beer and Georgian wine). Cocktails (£4.95 each) are a real let down, though. The choice is limited to nine; we've tried three and don't rate any. Neither can you order off-menu – although our waiter did consent to make us the house Beige Russian (vodka, Kahlúa, milk and Coke) without the Coke, giving us an ersatz watery White Russian. Grigori Aleksandrovich would not have approved.
Bar available for hire. Restaurant (no-smoking). Specialities (vodka). **Map 3 N4.**

Sekforde Arms
34 Sekforde Street, EC1R 0HA (7253 3251). Angel tube/Farringdon tube/rail. **Open** 11am-11pm Mon-Fri; 11am-6pm Sat; noon-4pm Sun. **Food served** noon-9.30pm Mon-Fri; noon-3pm Sat, Sun. **Credit** MC, V.
The Sekforde's a pub where a 'long drink' means a glass of lemonade, and the only 'drizzling' that goes on near the food is when somebody shakes vinegar on their chips. It's the most authentic pub in the neighbourhood, a backstreet corner house that's as unaffectedly traditional as they come, from the red swirly carpet, swagged curtains and frilly lightshades to the dust-coated trophies in the cabinet by the dartboard and the framed photo of Prince Charles pulling pints. These days, pint-pulling is done by a husband and wife team, plus bar help, who man the four handpumps that deliver pints of Wandsworth's finest (Young's ales). Food is refreshingly unpretentious (jacket potatoes, fish and the aforementioned chips) and reasonably priced. Unfashionable? Certainly – but whenever we've visited in recent years the place has been packed.
Babies and children admitted (restaurant only). Function room. Games (darts). Quiz (sports, 2-3 per week). Restaurant. Tables outdoors (10, pavement). TV. **Map 3 O4.**

Slaughtered Lamb
34-35 Great Sutton Street EC1V 0DX (7253 1516). Barbican tube or Farringdon tube/rail. **Open** noon-11pm daily. **Food served** noon-10.45pm daily. **Credit** AmEx, DC, MC, V.
Despite being a new-build (set up within former office premises in spring 2004), the Slaughtered Lamb relatively successfully conjures up the appearance and atmosphere of a local of long-standing and style. It's a big, single-room boozer, put together by numbers – bare-board floors, mix 'n' match furniture with a side order of leather sofa and kitsch pics on kitsch wallpaper – but well done and brightened by big picture windows. The bar impresses with offerings of Timothy Taylor Landlord, Bombardier, Affligem and Paulaner, although most punters stick with Red Stripe. The kitchen has stolen a leaf out of the Social cookbook with its offerings of fishfinger butties supplemented by Cornish pasties, sausage and mash, or chips with curry sauce. Downstairs there's a small black-painted brick basement, host to regular live music and open mic events.
Babies and children admitted. Disabled: toilet. Function room. Tables outdoors (3, pavement). TV.

Smiths of Smithfield
67-77 Charterhouse Street, EC1M 6HJ (7251 7950/ www.smithsofsmithfield.co.uk). Farringdon tube/rail. **Open** *Cocktail bar* 5.30-midnight Mon-Thur; 5.30pm-1am Fri, Sat. *Ground floor bar/café* 11.45am-midnight

Mon-Sat; 11.45am-10.30pm Sun. **Food served** *Cocktail bar* 5.30-midnight Mon-Thur; 5.30pm-1am Fri, Sat. *Ground floor bar/café* 7am-5pm Mon-Fri; 10am-5pm Sat; 9.30am-5pm Sun. **Credit** AmEx, DC, MC, V.
SOS (as the logoed T-shirts have it) is a massive complex of bar, cocktail bar, brasserie and restaurant, spread over four floors of a listed building facing Smithfield market. The serious drinking part of the operation is on the ground floor, a vast former warehouse with bare concrete, steel columns, huge ducts and industrial light fittings. It's defiantly blokeish, softened only slightly by picture windows and plain leather and oak furniture. Post-work it gets boozy with young professionals fuelling up on pints of the house Czech lager. On the next floor up is a red plastic-sheathed Martini and champagne bar of great appeal, where mixologists conjure up Applesinthes (absinthe shaken with passion fruit, lime and apple), Peach Flings (orange Stolichnaya shaken with peach and lime) and Bellinis made with St Evremond champagne and peach purée; prices are a reasonable £6-£7. The toilets are well worth a visit for their gritty urban views of Farringdon station sidings.
Babies and children admitted. Bar available for hire. Disabled: lift; toilet. Music (DJ 8pm Wed-Sat; free). Function room. Restaurants. Specialities (cocktails). **Map 3 O5**.

Three Kings of Clerkenwell

7 Clerkenwell Close, EC1R 0DY (7253 0483). Farringdon tube/rail. **Open** noon-11pm Mon-Fri; 7.30-11pm Sat. **Food served** noon-3pm Mon-Fri. **No credit cards**.
Also known as the Clerkenwell Green Social Club: home from home for a disparate bunch of amiable slackers. In the company of like-minded folk, pints are nursed (Young's, Pride, Speckled Hen), cigs are rolled and the pub cat is indulged. Walls are of mustard and red, a rhino head thrusts out over a fireplace, glitter balls glitter, tube lights twinkle and candles in bottles (encrusted with centuries of accumulated wax drippings) slowly and waxily drip. Upstairs, above the gents (supplied with London's smallest hand basin), are two tiny and seductively loungey rooms: one green, with a cabinet collection of snow globes; one red, with a Prestige jukebox loaded with killer tunes by the Clash, Toots and the Maytals, and the Marvelettes. If Withnail existed, this is where you'd find him.
Babies and children admitted (daytime only). Function rooms. Games (board games). No-smoking area (lunchtime only). TV (satellite). **Map 3 N4**.

Well

180 St John Street, EC1V 4JY (7251 9363). Farringdon tube/rail. **Open** 11am-midnight Mon-Fri; 10.30am-midnight Sat; 10.30am-10.30pm Sun. **Food served** noon-3pm, 6-10.30pm Mon-Fri; 10.30am-4pm, 6-10.30pm Sat; 10.30am-4pm, 6-10pm Sun. **Credit** AmEx, DC, MC, V.
Not quite pub, nor bar, nor restaurant, the Well finds success outside the pigeonholes. It's one modestly sized main room of chunky wooden tables on bare floorboards in a simple brick-walled setting. Most tables carry place settings, but a couple at the back are earmarked for drinkers. The bar line-up is a decent offering of draught Budvar, Hoegaarden, Leffe, Paulaner and San Miguel, with more choice by the bottle and a thoroughly excellent array of wines. The food menu is similarly superior – kept sharp, no doubt, thanks to the ever increasing competition on this northern stretch of St John Street. Downstairs is a closet-sized, designer-ish lounge area with tropical fish tanks and smart brown leather sofas. The Well comes into its own during the summer months, when the screen windows are slid open to allow alfresco dining and drinking.
Babies and children welcome; high chairs. Bar available for hire. Music (DJs 8pm Fri; free). Tables outdoors (6, pavement). **Map 3 O4**.

Zetter

86-88 Clerkenwell Road, EC1M 5RJ (7324 4455). Farringdon tube/rail. **Open/food served** 7am-11pm Mon-Fri; 7.30am-11pm; 7.30am-10.30pm Sun. **Credit** AmEx, DC, JCB, MC, V.
Within days of opening, the Zetter made it into *Condé Nast Traveller*'s list of the 50 coolest new hotels in Europe. And while its ground-floor bar is no more than a few tables squeezed into the pointed extremity of the crescent-shaped restaurant, boozing here is a fine experience. There's a handsome arc of a black marble bar counter and huge picture windows overlooking St John's Square; waitresses attend the tables, so you don't have to budge. Cocktails are pricey (£8-£8.50) but feature such rare ingredients as fennel, kumquats and blueberries. There's lots of fizzy stuff, made with prosecco, as well as some inviting Martinis. The bunch we sampled were all exceptional: best was the Zen Zero Zetter – ginger and lychees muddled with vodka and gin. Beer drinkers have to content themselves with bottled Beck's or Moretti and the attendant shame of lowering the tone of the establishment.
Babies and children welcome; children's portions; crayons; high chairs. Disabled: toilet. Function rooms. Restaurant. Specialities (cocktails). Tables outdoors (4, pavement). **Map 3 N4**.

Also in the area...

All Bar One 91-93A Charterhouse Street, EC1M 6HL (7553 9391).
Betjemans (Jamies) 43-44 Cloth Fair, EC1A 7JQ (7600 7778).
Hog's Head Unit E, Cowcross Place, Cowcross Street, EC1M 6DH (7251 3813).
Printworks (JD Wetherspoon) 113-117 Farringdon Road, EC1R 3AP (7713 2000).
Puncheon (Davy's) Unit 5, Cowcross Place, Cowcross Street, EC1M 6DQ (7250 3336).
Sir John Oldcastle (JD Wetherspoon) 29-35 Farringdon Road, EC1M 3JF (7242 1031).

FLEET STREET, BLACKFRIARS & ST PAUL'S

Once the centre of the newspaper industry, the area around Fleet Street is now more of a mongrel. Reuters hangs on, and Channel 4 is here, but there's not much media activity. Instead, the district buzzes with law firms and financial corporations; it's all worsted wool and testosterone. The drinking scene reflects this state of affairs, but this is also where you'll find some of London's most charming historic pubs.

Balls Brothers

6-8 Cheapside, EC2V 6AN (7248 2708/www.ballsbrothers.co.uk). St Paul's tube. **Open** 11am-10pm Mon-Fri. **Food served** 11.30am-9pm Mon-Fri. **Credit** AmEx, DC, MC, V.

With its elaborate Victorian tiling and dark wooden floors and panelling, you might expect this branch of the Balls Brothers wine bar chain to feel historic, traditional and a little stuffy. Yet the place has been artfully decorated to strike a modern note with one of relaxed, upmarket comfort. It's a mix deeply appreciated by the City-slicker regulars who pack in here for a bottle of wine and a meal; in fact, dining, rather than drinking the night away, seems the main pursuit. There's a general conviviality to the place at lunchtime, when business groups crowd in to the restaurant for the pâté starters and salmon fillets; in the bar, you can spend much less if you don't mind sticking to sandwiches or sausages and mash. The wine list relies heavily on French labels, with some very expensive champagnes.
Children admitted (garden only). Separate area for parties. Tables outdoors (16, courtyard).

Black Friar

174 Queen Victoria Street, EC4V 4EG (7236 5474). Blackfriars tube/rail. **Open** 11.30am-11pm Mon-Sat; noon-9pm Sun. **Food served** noon-9pm daily. **Credit** AmEx, MC, V.

It's not often one uses the word 'beautiful' to describe a pub, but no adjective better fits this extraordinary little gem – for all its surrounding noisy traffic and modern office buildings. The gorgeous stained glass window at the front is an indicator of what awaits inside, and the original 1905 decor of wooden floors and elaborately carved marble is unchanged. The main bar is attractive enough, but the side room is simply extraordinary, an Aladdin's cave of alabaster and gold, with fanciful mosaics depicting the friars who occupied this site in the Middle Ages. The outstanding selection of ales always includes several guests – Back Row and Tiger bitter on our last visit – beside Adnams bitter, London Pride and Timothy Taylor Landlord. The bar food is excellent, too: home-made pies are a speciality, and worth every accolade the crowd of loyal regulars and passing connoisseurs can throw at them.
Games (quiz machine). No smoking. Tables outdoors (10, pavement). TV. **Map 4 O6**.

Cockpit

7 St Andrew's Hill, EC4V 5BY (7248 7315). Blackfriars tube/rail. **Open** 11am-11pm Mon-Sat; noon-2.30pm, 7-10.30pm Sun. **Food served** 11am-2.30pm, 5-9pm Mon-Fri. **Credit** MC, V.

This somewhat pokey little boozer is full of cocks: rather lame papier-mâché cocks of the avian variety along its blood-red walls. Depending on your view, the place is either one of a dying breed that offers much-needed refuge from the larger, more commercial pub enterprises in this neck of the woods – or the sort of place that should really have faded away in the 1970s, along with the three-day week and Brotherhood of Man. We lean more to the latter opinion, although we'll admit the Cockpit has a certain rough-and-ready appeal. Shabby, scruffy and with barely enough room to swing a cock (this has to be one of the smallest pubs in the city), it's usually filled with a dour smattering of local geezers and after-work drinkers come the evening. On tap are Directors and Marston's Pedigree.
Games (fruit machine, shove ha'penny table). TV (satellite). **Map 4 O6**.

Evangelist

33 Blackfriars Lane, EC4V 6EP (7213 0740). Blackfriars tube/rail. **Open** noon-11pm Mon-Fri. **Food served** noon-9pm Mon-Wed; noon-8pm Thur, Fri. **Credit** AmEx, MC, V.

Occupying a sweeping, split-level space on the ground floor of a modern office building, the Evangelist is furnished with big wooden tables, giving it the feel of a posh, non-denominational church hall. Music is kept at a reasonable level, and the bar was crowded with twenty- and thirtysomethings. Couples mostly kept to the back spaces, where they could disappear into the shadows; business groups sat at the large tables where they could spread out and enjoy the cocktails, wine, and lagers that dominate the drinks list. Bombardier was the only ale to be had, but most customers opt for wine or San Miguel. Food from an above-average gastropub menu is cooked in an open-plan kitchen; the bar area is decorated with big religious mosaics, as a nod to the venue's name and its semi-religious theme. We were converted.
Babies and children admitted (lunchtime only). Disabled: toilet. Function room. Restaurant. TV (big screen). **Map 4 O6**.

La Grande Marque

47 Ludgate Hill, EC4M 7JU (7329 6709/www.lagrandemarque.com). St Paul's tube/Blackfriars tube/rail. **Open/food served** 11.30am-11pm Mon-Fri. **Credit** AmEx, DC, JCB, MC, V.

So subtle is this gorgeous and sophisticated champagne bar that it doesn't even have a proper sign: just an elaborate M engraved in the glass on the doorway. Through this can be seen the stunning, intricately carved Victorian ceiling. Inside, the charismatic French manager Olivier told us the story of the place over glasses of excellent pinot noir (£5.75). The beautiful premises, dating from 1891, were once headquarters to City Bank, and the marble-topped bar stands precisely where the bank counter used to be in the 19th century (try to spot the outline marked in the original mosaic floor). Walls are wood-panelled, seats are wooden – and unforgiving. There's no music, but conversation is plentiful. The wine list is first rate, if pricey, with champagne dominating the selection.
Function room. No piped music or jukebox. **Map 4 O6**.

Old Bank of England

194 Fleet Street, EC4A 2LT (7430 2255). Temple tube. **Open** 11am-11pm Mon-Fri. **Food served** noon-9pm Mon-Thur; noon-8pm Fri. **Credit** AmEx, MC, V.

There's grandeur in spades at this immense Fuller's boozer: high ceilings, vast arched windows, a huge Victorian clock above the bar, a mezzanine seating level overlooking the action below, and big torches burning outside. A recent renovation has polished up the edges, but the former home of the Bank of England remains an impressive spectacle. Bar staff are European and efficient, several of Fuller's beers are on draught (including a seasonal ale) and the pub food isn't bad at all for the money. The main negatives here are the music (bland pop played too loud) and the crowds (the place can get packed with lawyers and bankers) and tends to be very smoky. Otherwise, this is an enjoyable venue. The pub stands, according to lore, on the site of the Haunch of Venison – Sweeney Todd's local.
Babies and children admitted (lunchtime only). Function room. No-smoking area. Restaurant. Specialities (pies). **Map 4 N6**.

Old Bell Tavern

95 Fleet Street, EC4Y 1DH (7583 0216). Blackfriars tube/rail. **Open** 11.30am-11pm Mon-Fri. **Food served** noon-9pm Mon-Fri. **Credit** (over £10) AmEx, MC, V.

The picturesquely named Wynkyn de Worde is reputed to have operated the first print shop in London from a building on this site, thus beginning the association between

Fleet Street and print that continues to this day (even though all newspapers but one upped and left long ago). Thankfully, this fine old pub is still going strong, despite the loss of the steady stream of journalistic traffic that once passed through its door; nowadays, the crowd is more a mixture of City types and lawyers from the various Inns of Court. Stone floors and twin fireplaces contribute to the cosy atmosphere, and there's usually a respectable selection of guest ales on tap: Timothy Taylor Landlord and Badger Best were in the offing on our last visit, alongside such Fuller's favourites as London Pride.
Babies and children admitted. Games (fruit machine, quiz machine). TV (digital). **Map 4 N6**.

Ye Olde Cheshire Cheese

145 Fleet Street, EC4A 2BU (7353 6170/www.yeoldecheshirecheese.com). Blackfriars tube/rail. **Open** 11am-11pm Mon-Sat; noon-2.30pm Sun. **Food served** noon-9.30pm Mon-Fri; noon-8.30pm Sat; noon-2.30pm Sun. **Credit** AmEx, DC, MC, V.
This marvellous labyrinth of a pub has ten rooms of varying size and personality – from the comfortable wood-panelled room closest to the entrance (with a fire blazing in the hearth in winter), through church-like dining spaces furnished with pews, to the very last bar in the cellar (past perilously low beams), which is believed to pre-date the Great Fire. So thoroughly and accurately has the Samuel Smith brewery restored the place, its former regulars (including Dr Johnson, Dickens, Thackeray, Conan Doyle and Stanley Baldwin) would probably feel right at home were they to pop in for a pint today. There are four rooms for dining and six for drinking; the beer, being Sam Smith's, is cheap and palatable. A mix of legal eagles and clever tourists frequents the establishment; only a tiny sign on Fleet Street lets you know of the Cheese's existence, and the entrance is tucked down a narrow alley.
Babies and children admitted (restaurant). Function rooms. No piped music or jukebox. Restaurant (no-smoking area). TV. **Map 4 N6**.

Punch Tavern

99 Fleet Street, EC4Y 1DE (7353 6658). Blackfriars tube/rail. **Open/food served** 7am-11pm Mon-Fri. **Credit** AmEx, MC, V.
If you haven't been to the Punch Tavern for a while, you might not recognise the place. Aside from the Victorian entrance, with its frosted glass and floor mosaics, almost everything else has changed. Gone is the green and red decor reminiscent of a Victorian music hall; now it's all cushioned benches, candles in bowls, intimate lighting and pop music. The high ceilings and mirror-lined walls of the Grade II listed building thankfully survive, but the rest is modern-by-numbers – not that the City types and lawyers seem to mind. The food has been poshed up a bit, with steaks and salads topping the list; there's an above-average wine list, and the draught beers include Timothy Taylor Landlord alongside San Miguel.
Babies and children admitted. Function room. Games (board games). Quiz (6.30pm 1st Mon of mth; £10 per team). No-smoking area (lunch). **Map 4 N6**.

Red Herring

49 Gresham Street, EC2V 7EH (7606 0399). St Paul's tube. **Open** 11am-11pm Mon-Fri. **Food served** noon-3pm, 5-9pm Mon-Fri. **Credit** AmEx, MC, V.
Here's one red herring that won't lead you up the garden path. It is, in fact, a surprising find – a pleasant pub/bar with panoramic views of the craggy, historic architecture around St Paul's. You can stretch out on one of the comfortable sofas and armchairs and take in the view, or hide away to get a little privacy behind one of the many potted plants. Youngish City workers account for the largest group of drinkers, although there's a sprinkling of lawyers and the occasional tourist as well. It's easy to see the attraction of the Red Herring: a combination of Fuller's ales, a decent wine list and good, bistro-style food in the basement dining area. Small wonder the crowds keep coming in.
Disabled: toilet. Function room. Games (fruit machine). Restaurant. TV (big screen). **Map 6 P6**.

Rising Sun

61 Carter Lane, EC4V 5DY (7248 4544). St Paul's tube/Blackfriars tube/rail. **Open** 11am-11pm Mon-Fri. **Food served** noon-3pm, 5.30-10.30pm Mon-Fri. **Credit** AmEx, DC, MC, V.
On our visit, a wide screen taking up a significant portion of one wall was showing a Man U game; the crowd in the bar was all male and almost all suited. The Rising Sun is a rather ordinary local pub, with fruit machines here and there, raucous macho laughter, and Shepherd Neame Spitfire and Adnams bitter on the hand pumps. The pub has a historic connection: it stands on the site of the long-demolished Hart's Horn Tavern, where Guy Fawkes conspired to blow up Parliament. Another point in its favour are the surroundings; you'll find the pub on a corner, in a lovely medieval labyrinth of streets near St Paul's. There's a Thai menu, should hunger strike.
Babies and children admitted. Games (fruit machine). Restaurant. TV (big screen, satellite). **Map 4 O6**.

Samuel Pepys

Stew Lane, High Timber Street, EC4V 3PT (7634 9841). Mansion House or St Paul's tube. **Open** noon-11pm Mon-Fri. **Food served** noon-8pm Mon-Fri. **Credit** AmEx, MC, V.
The main attraction at this pleasantly modern brick-and-wood conversion near the Millennium Bridge is the sweeping view it offers across the Thames towards the South Bank. Inside, the pub has a combination of leather sofas, high bar tables and dining furniture spread across a first-floor loft conversion. The long serving area runs almost all the way down one side. Two real ales (London Pride and Adnams Best) are on draught, along with lagers such as Staropramen; bottled imports include Anchor Steam, Duvel, Orval and Chimay. The wine list is well thought out, with plenty of interesting options that are changed regularly; food is of the traditional British school – fish and chips, salmon fish cakes and the like – at City prices. Stew Lane doesn't refer to the pub's menu; it was from here that ferries left for the 'stews' or brothels of Tudor Southwark.
Disabled: lift; toilet. Function room. Restaurant (no-smoking). **Map 6 P7**.

Shaw's Booksellers

31-34 St Andrew's Hill, EC4V 5DE (7489 7999). St Paul's tube/Blackfriars tube/rail. **Open** noon-11pm Mon-Fri. **Food served** noon-9pm Mon-Fri. **Credit** AmEx, DC, MC, V.
Don't be fooled – there's never been a bookshop here, although the story behind the name is rather fun. Formerly a paper merchant's, the building lay empty in the mid 1990s, during which time it was used as a location for the film *The Wings of the Dove*. When Fuller's took over the place and turned it into a pub shortly afterwards, they kept its screen name. This is a friendly, likeable sort of spot, and one that manages to transcend its rather gastropub-by-

numbers design trappings: appealingly quirky touches, like a staircase that doesn't appear to go anywhere, sum this place up far better than the preponderance of planed wood and voguish artwork on display. Amiable staff dispense pints of Cumberland Ale and Honeydew.
Disabled: toilet. TV. **Map 4 O6**.

Tipperary

66 Fleet Street, EC4Y 1HT (7583 6470/www.tipperary pub.co.uk). Blackfriars tube/rail. **Open** 11am-11pm Mon-Fri; noon-6pm Sat, Sun. **Food served** 11am-10pm Mon-Fri; noon-5.30pm Sat, Sun. **Credit** MC, V.
The tall, narrow Tipperary was named to honour Fleet Street print-workers returning from the front after World War I, yet its renown as the Boar's Head stretches back centuries. Legend has it that the place was built in 1605 from the ruins of the Whitefriars monastery, and that its stone construction saw it through the Great Fire. When Dublin brewer SG Mooney took over the lease in 1700, it became London's first Irish pub – the first to sell Guinness, too. The Greene King brewery bought the building in the 1960s and restored it to its 18th-century state; the ground floor is tiled with shamrock mosaic, and upstairs has aged wood panelling. After 40 years, though, the place looks a little tired. You'll still find the black stuff on draught here, along with Greene King IPA and Abbot Ale, and Caffrey's.
Babies and children admitted. Function room. Games (fruit machine). TV. **Map 4 N6**.

Viaduct Tavern

126 Newgate Street, EC1A 7AA (7600 1863). St Paul's tube. **Open** 11am-11pm Mon-Fri. **Food served** noon-6pm Mon-Fri. **Credit** AmEx, MC, V.
Opened in 1869 (the same year as the Holborn viaduct), this fine old Victorian pub has long been a traditional refuge for lawyers, clients and assorted trial hangers-on from the Old Bailey across the road. The legal associations don't end there: the cellars are believed to be the last surviving cells of the infamous Newgate prison, renowned as a place of torture and ghoulish goings-on as far back as Shakespeare's day. (Tours can sometimes be arranged; call for details.) Terrible trivia aside, the Viaduct Tavern is rather an attractive place. The walls are lined with murals of the four viaduct statues: *Commerce, Agriculture, Science* and *Fine Art* (ask the friendly bar staff about the damage to *Fine Art* – it's a good story). On tap is a solid range of ales, including London Pride and Timothy Taylor Landlord, and the bar food is good, hearty stuff.
Games (quiz machine). TV. **Map 4 O6**.

El Vino

47 Fleet Street, EC4Y 1BJ (7353 6786/www.elvino. co.uk). Chancery Lane tube or Temple tube/Blackfriars tube/rail. **Open** 8.30am-9pm Mon; 8.30am-10pm Tue-Fri. **Food served** 8.30am-8pm Mon; 8.30am-9pm Tue-Fri. **Credit** AmEx, JCB, MC, V.
Both wine merchant and wine bar, El Vino has a long history. The firm started trading in 1879 and is now run by the fourth generation of the same family; these premises opened in 1923, and until 1982 (after a ruling by the Court of Appeal) women were forbidden to stand and be served at the bar. Lawyers account for much of the clientele, populating the slightly dingy, wooden interior which is bathed in rather harsh lighting. The wine list is long and largely European, claret being a forte. The New World isn't overlooked, though, and 2003 De Martino chardonnay, from Chile's Maipo valley, was recently the top-selling label. The food menu is an uninspired list of international standards, including pâté starters and egg-and-mayonnaise sandwiches. In common with many City venues, this place can get deserted early in the week and later of an evening.
Function room. Tables outdoors (2, pavement).

Also in the area...

All Bar One 44-46 Ludgate Hill, EC4M 7LA (7653 9901).
Balls Brothers 5-6 Carey Lane, EC2V 8AE (7600 2720).
Bar Under the Clock (Balls Brothers) 74 Queen Victoria Street, EC4N 4SJ (7489 9895).
City Pipe (Davy's) 33 Foster Lane, EC2V 6HD (7606 2110).
Corney & Barrow 3 Fleet Place, EC4M 7RD (7329 3141).
Davy's 10 Creed Lane, EC4M 8SH (7236 5317).
Heeltap & Bumper (Davy's) 2-4 Paul Street, EC2A 4JH (7247 3319).
Hog's Head 5-11 Fetter Lane, EC4A 1BR (7353 1387); 78 Ludgate Hill, EC4M 7LQ (7329 8517).
Jamies 34 Ludgate Hill, EC4M 7DE (7489 1938).
O'Neill's 2-3 New Bridge Street, EC4V 6AA (7583 0227).

HOXTON & SHOREDITCH

The über-cool elite claim to have smelt over-ripeness in the Shoreditch Triangle (formed by Old Street, Great Eastern Street and Shoreditch High Street) and now stay away. Or pretend to. Certainly, the fins, mullets and bangs are but a droopy memory, and some of the style and DJ bars are dated; but you still don't have to try too hard to home in on a good thing or two here. The real problem putting drinkers off is the overcrowding: there are hordes of people here at the weekend.

Anda de Bridge

42-44 Kingsland Road, E2 8DA (7739 3863/www.anda debridge.com). Old Street tube/rail/26, 48, 55, 67, 149, 242, 243 bus. **Open/food served** 11am-midnight Mon-Sat. **Main courses** £5-£10. **Credit** AmEx, DC, MC, V.
Set, unsurprisingly, under a bridge, this engaging slice of Kingsland Caribbean pulsates to classic reggae and dub, which drown out any train noise; wooden blinds help shut out the urban grime beyond the windows. Inside, you'll find warm but subdued lighting, a rough red stone floor, a main bar with low-slung seats, and a back room where a neon Red Bull sign shines cheerily above a red chesterfield. Steel ducts are draped with winking rainbow-hued lights; the punters are likewise a rainbow selection, drawn by excellent food and drink as much as the music. Fine rum cocktails (around £6) and draught Red Stripe help soak up the curry goat or 'fry fish and dumplin'. If you think the faded pics of Bob Marley are predictable, see the pretty back-room angel made from bottle tops and other cast-offs.
Babies and children admitted. Disabled: toilet. Music (DJs 8pm Fri, Sat; free). Restaurant. Specialities (cocktails). TV (digital, projector). **Map 5 R3**.

Artillery Arms

102 Bunhill Row, EC1Y 8ND (7253 4683). Old Street tube/rail. **Open** 11am-11pm Mon-Fri; noon-11pm Sat; noon-10.30pm Sun. **Food served** noon-3pm Mon-Fri. **Credit** AmEx, MC, V.

RAISE A GLASS: MUSICAL BOOZERS

Rock 'n' roll history can be found in the most unlikely venues: take the **Princess Louise** (*see p48*) in Holborn. The guidebooks will happily bang on about its ornate Victorian decor, carved woodwork, engraved mirrors and implausibly lavish loos – but how many will mention that this is the place where Pete Townshend devised the fake adverts that can be heard in between songs for the Who's *The Who Sell Out*? Or of its time as the Ballad and Blue Club, hosted by Ewan McColl, writer of great London anthem 'Dirty Old Town'? Or that Davey Graham and Bert Jansch both played here?

But then London changes so quickly, history often gets left behind. Take the monstrous three-floor **O'Neills** (35 Wardour Street, W1, 7479 7941) near Leicester Square. Way back in the 1960s, its basement housed the Flamingo Club, and upstairs was Whiskey A Go Go (later Wag). The Flamingo was a celebrated jazz dive (John McLaughlin was in the house band), while the Whiskey/Wag has been a home for R&B (the Stones played here), hip hop (Grand Master Flash and the Furious Five and Afrika Bambaataa), rare groove, house and Britpop. On the Soho side of Wardour Street is the **O-Bar** (83 Wardour Street, W1, 7437 3490), once the Roundhouse, home of the Blues Barrelhouse Club, an early venue for Blues Incorporated and where Muddy Waters and Big Bill Broonzy played.

Soho's current rock pubs are easier to spot. The **Intrepid Fox** (*see p84*) and **Crobar** (*see p83*) wear their mullets on their sleeve, while the **Ship** (*see p88*) oozes a sweaty vibe – although even here you'll never learn that Jimi Hendrix once passed out in a corner, or that the Clash wrote a song under the staircase in another.

The Kinks immortalised the pub in which they signed their first contract, the **Archway Tavern** (1 Archway Close, N19, 7272 2840), by posing there for the cover of their superb 1971 album *Muswell Hillbillies*. The Jam tried to do the same for the Red Cow, now **Latymer's** (157 Hammersmith Road, W6, 8741 2507) in Baron's Court by putting it on the cover of *In The City*; half of it is now a Thai restaurant.

Some places don't need to advertise: everybody knows that during Britpop, the **Good Mixer** (30 Inverness Street, NW1, 7916 6176) was the place to go to if you wanted to see the drummer from Menswear (the pub has recently shown signs of recovering from this terrible association). And even now, the **Hope & Anchor** (207 Upper Street, N1, 7354 1312) hosts dozens of hapless indie bands hoping to emulate the success of Joy Division, who made their London debut here. Incidentally, one of the band's last London shows was at the **Railway** (100 West End Lane, NW6, 7624 7611), where Ian Curtis had an epileptic fit on stage. The pub also hosted U2's London debut and was the venue for John Mayall's live album *John Mayall plays John Mayall*.

Finally, wash the sweat out of your hair with a wander along the river to Chiswick's **City Barge** (*see p231*). If it looks familiar, it's because this was where the Beatles sought refuge when chased by menacing bagpipers in *Help!*. Although Ringo ended up in the cellars with only a tiger for company, the other three were able to escape by jumping through the pub's window frontage. And you don't get more rock 'n' roll than that. *Peter Watts*

City

Some lunchtimes, thanks to a no-frills but reliable food policy and the consistent quality of the Fuller's beer range, the compact Artillery Arms is prone to the level of overcrowding that led in 1854 to the closure of the Bunhill Fields cemetery (the last resting place of William Blake) opposite. A dark wooden bar divides the downstairs space – all wood, frosted glass and old light fittings – where punters in suits quaff London Pride, ESB and Chiswick, and scoff toad-in-the-hole beneath military-themed prints. Upstairs, beyond the kitchens, is an attractive, cosy, L-shaped retreat with leaf tables and a glorious green-grey marble fireplace in which logs blaze come cold weather.
Function room. Games (board games, darts, fruit machine). TV (satellite). **Map 5 P4**.

Bar Kick

127 Shoreditch High Street, E1 6JE (7739 8700/www.cafekick.co.uk). Old Street tube/rail then 55 or 243 bus. **Open** noon-11pm Mon-Wed, Sun; noon-midnight Thur-Sat. **Food served** noon-3.30pm, 5-10pm Mon-Fri; noon-11pm Sat; noon-10.30pm Sun. **Credit** MC, V.

Welcome to bar heaven. Beneath flags from around the world, there's a truly continental feel to Bar Kick that goes beyond the authentic *fut* (table football) tables. The zinc bar and mismatched tables, chairs and battered sofas give the place a cosy retro vibe. There's a great range of bottled beers (almost as varied as the flags): Früli, Belgian Duvel, clean-tasting Italian Peroni and malty Portuguese Superbock, to name but a few. Then there's the food, made with top ingredients: serrano ham from Aragon, Campagna mozzarella cheese, Helsett Farm organic Cornish ice-cream. The crowd is mixed, too: from suits to Shoreditch locals to those from further afield looking for a bar that does everything right. This is it. Sister venue Café Kick (*see p111*) is in Exmouth Market.

Babies and children admitted (lunchtime only). Basement available for hire. Disabled: toilet. Entertainment (films 8pm Mon, Tue; table football tournaments 7pm last Thur of mth). Games (table football). Tables outdoors (4, pavement). **Map 5 R4**.

Barley Mow

127 Curtain Road, EC2A 3BX (7729 3910). Old Street tube/rail/55 bus. **Open** noon-11pm Mon-Thur; noon-midnight Fri; 4pm-midnight Sat; 3-10.30pm Sun. **Credit** MC, V.

As the name suggests, this lovely old boozer harks back to a time long before Hoxton's style graph began to rise. Trendy lighting and furniture shops may surround it now, but step inside and nothing much seems to have changed for decades – apart from the demise of one of the regulars, whose funeral service details were pinned up to edify the other habitués. Cause to down a Chiswick Bitter in his honour, perhaps – though you could also have one of the Belgian selection (including unusual options like Floris Chocolate) or maybe a Fentimans Curiosity Cola if you're driving. There are other unexpected flourishes, too: tango accordion music as sprightly background; Wi-Fi access in a lo-fi setting. Charmingly eccentric, and very English.

Babies and children admitted (until 6pm). Function room. Music (DJs 9pm Fri, Sat; 7pm Sun; free). Quiz (8pm Mon; £1). **Map 5 R4**.

Bedroom Bar

62 Rivington Street, EC2A 3AY (7613 5637). Old Street tube/rail. **Open** 7pm-midnight Thur; 7pm-2am Fri, Sat. **Food served** 7-10pm Thur-Sat. **Admission** £3 after 10.30pm Fri, Sat. **Credit** MC, V.

Next door to Rivington Street's Comedy Café is this compact (nay, tiny) bar with the eponymous bed for lounging on tucked in a corner. More seating is provided by way of banquettes and leather-topped stools made from dustbins; upside-down buckets double as fun lampshades, and tealights add a romantic air. The DJ plays lurve tunes and there are suitably named, reasonably priced cocktails such as Sex on the Bed or the Shoreditch Shag (butterscotch schnapps and Bailey's) on the drinks menu. As well as draught Guinness and Budweiser on tap, there's a host of bottled beers. Nibbles include home-made chips (£2.50) and veggie chimichanga (£4.95). Even on a Friday night this is a fine place for relaxation, as there's almost always plenty of room to sit, lie, or whatever.

Music (DJs 7pm Thur-Sat). **Map 5 R4**.

Bluu

1 Hoxton Square, N1 6NU (7613 2793/www.bluu.co.uk). Old Street tube/rail/55 bus. **Open** 11am-11.30pm Mon-Thur; 10am-midnight Fri, Sat; 11am-10.30pm Sun. **Food served** noon-9pm daily. **Credit** AmEx, MC, V.

Bluu is almost next door to the hipper-than-hip White Cube gallery, so perhaps it's less a mediocre chain bar (outlets in Nottingham and Manchester among others) than an installation about soul-sapping mediocre chain bars. This long, thin venue – all bare brickwork and neat seating – is spread over two levels, with the basement offering a little more encouragement by way of a few sofas and slightly more diverting lighting. Everything, though, is aimed at the lowest common denominator, resulting in so-so beer, so-so cocktails (grouped as 'Something Old', 'Something New' or 'Something Bluu') and so-so music. The most interesting 'bluu' here is the blue plaque revealing that the building was once the home of James Parkinson, discoverer of the iguanodon, early describer of appendicitis and expert on the 'shaking palsy' that now bears his name.

Babies and children admitted (until 7pm). Music (DJs 9pm Thur-Sun; free). Specialities (cocktails). **Map 5 R3**.

Bricklayer's Arms

63 Charlotte Road, EC2A 3PE (7739 5245/www.333mother.com). Old Street tube/rail/55 bus. **Open** 11am-11pm Mon-Fri; noon-11pm Sat; noon-10.30pm Sun. **Food served** noon-3pm, 6-11pm Mon-Fri; 2.30-11pm Sat; 1.30-9pm Sun. **Credit** MC, V.

The Bricklayer's Arms is an endearingly tatty surprise. It's such an authentic local, the notion occurs that you've wandered on to a set and the regional accents will turn RADA the minute you leave. An oasis of cheerful seediness, what it lacks in unusual booze – there's draught Grolsch, Fuller's London Pride and Old Speckled Hen, with bottles of Corona and Hoegaarden – the Bricklayer's Arms more than makes up for on atmosphere. An ancient mutt and its owner amiably commune together as you peruse the menu of the Thai restaurant upstairs. DJs also make appearances here, judging by the decks across from the *Star Wars* pinball machine. All in all, highly convincing and enjoyable.

Games (pinball). Restaurant. **Map 5 R4**.

Cantaloupe

35 Charlotte Road, EC2A 3PB (7613 4411/www.cantaloupegroup.co.uk). Liverpool Street or Old Street tube/rail/55 bus. **Open/food served** 11am-midnight daily. **Credit** AmEx, DC, JCB, MC, V.

The Cantaloupe has certainly got the knack of making people want to linger. The sturdy tables and seating in the main bar area offer a perfect location for sampling the

draught Amstel, Budvar and exceptional König Ludvig wheat beer. The global mix of enticing food in the bar menu is drawn from a number of countries – none of which, significantly, is England – and the ample wine list is drawn up to offer appropriate choices. Music is a complementary fusion of bossa and trip hop. The back room houses a restaurant section, and a raised, soft-seated retreat partially secluded by a curved red wall, as well as a bar for weekends and emergencies. Leather settees and armchairs join forces with low tables and potted greenery to make the connecting room an intimate alcove.
Babies and children admitted. Disabled: toilet. Music (DJ 8pm Fri-Sun). Restaurant. **Map 5 R4**.

Catch

22 Kingsland Road, E2 8DA (7729 6097/www.thecatchbar.com). Old Street tube/rail/55 bus. **Open** 5.30pm-midnight Tue, Wed; 5.30pm-2am Thur, Fri; 6pm-2am Sat; 5.30pm-1am Sun. **No credit cards.**
This provides a nice complement to the neighbouring dreambagsjaguarshoes (*see p125*) and Anda de Bridge (*see p122*). Rather than the industrial chic of the former or ethnic grooviness of the latter, Catch offers simple pleasures: a game of pool, retro fun on the pinball machine by the door, and the chance to catch a set from some young hopeful combo in the cavernous upstairs bar. It's a nice space, too: worn white clapboard on one side and half a dozen raised dark wooden booths along the other. When these fill up, squeeze on to the old leather seats in the tiny alcove at the front and watch the world go by. The drinks are a standard-issue line-up: Carling, Grolsch, Staropramen and Bitburger on tap, plus bottled lagers and breezers.
Function room (club upstairs). Games (pinball, pool). Music (DJs Tue-Sun; free). **Map 5 R3**.

Charlie Wright's International Bar

45 Pitfield Street, N1 6DA (7490 8345). Old Street tube/rail/55 bus. **Open** noon-1am Mon-Wed, Sun; noon-2am Thur; noon-3am Fri, Sat. **Food served** noon-3pm, 5-10pm daily. **Admission** £3 after 10pm Fri, Sat. **Credit** MC, V.
You can't scoff at the name in a place where Belgium meets Thailand under the cheerful eye of a Ghanaian weightlifter, can you? First impressions, mind, are of a venerable old boozer: the dark wood-panelled walls that divide the space have doubtless been buffed by countless beery nights and give off a nostalgic glow; there's also table football at the back. Down one side, however, a restaurant serves decent Thai food for around a fiver to office workers. Drinkers can choose from a fine range of Belgian brews, bitters and luscious African Guinness. Music adds to the mix of vintage and cosmopolitan, with classic black grooves (from 1960s soul to hip hop) sprinkled with the odd indie session. Entrance is often free of charge, though you might have to fork out a few quid if you haven't grabbed your seat early.
Babies and children admitted (until 7pm). Games (fruit machine, pool). Music (DJs 8pm Thur-Sun). Restaurant. TV (big screen, satellite). **Map 5 Q3**.

Cocomo

323 Old Street, EC1V 9LE (7613 0315). Old Street tube/rail/55 bus. **Open/food served** 11am-midnight Mon-Fri; 6pm-midnight Sat; 6-11pm Sun. **Credit** MC, V.
Vaguely Middle Eastern, definitely funky, Cocomo is one of the best of the Shoreditch bars. Sure, some of the style touches are a tad forced – from the Moroccan lights to the small mirrors that fail to make the tiny downstairs lounge feel a bit bigger – but the basic blueprint is sound: welcoming vibe, good drinks, great sounds. The diminutive size is fine in the week, when the place seems like your own cosy, hip hideout (especially if you can bag a spot downstairs, amid the tatty chic furnishings); but at weekends you can hardly move for people with the same idea. Rather than draught Red Stripe, treat yourself to one of the fine Martinis on the cocktail list. Cocomo has links with DJs like Rob Da Bank, so the music is on the cool side of chilled.
Music (DJs 8pm Thur-Sat; free). **Map 5 R4**.

Dragon

5 Leonard Street, EC2A 4AQ (7490 7110). Liverpool Street or Old Street tube/rail. **Open** noon-11pm Mon; noon-midnight Tue, Wed; noon-1am Thur; noon-2am Fri, Sat; noon-11pm Sun. **Credit** (over £10) MC, V.
There's little to alert you to this little corner hideaway, set apart from the rest of the Hoxton hip hangouts just off the City Road: no sign, no light, just the name marked in small letters on one step. Yet Dragon is a justly popular hangout. As if to emphasise the fact, the floor in the narrow street-level bar is impregnated with the scuzz of a thousand good nights. De rigueur soft leather seats are spread around the ground floor and the even more secluded little basement bar. To go with the open fire there are open decks, where you get everything from hip hop to 1960s psychedelia played by dudes who style themselves 'underground DJs' (though others might call them 'enthusiastic amateurs'). But everyone's friendly, there's Gulpener, Staropramen and Caffrey's on draught (with a decent choice of bottled beers), and one floor is kept just quiet enough to hear yourself think. Now that's thoughtful.
Babies and children admitted (daytime). Music (DJs, 8pm all week; open mic 7pm 1st Sun of mth; both free). Tables outdoors (5, pavement). **Map 5 Q4**.

dreambagsjaguarshoes

34-36 Kingsland Road, E2 8DA (7729 5830/www.dreambagsjaguarshoes.com). Old Street tube/rail. **Open** 5pm-midnight Mon; 5pm-1am Tue-Sat; 5pm-12.30am Sun. **Credit** MC, V.
Like many of Hoxton's more cutting-edge dives, this perennial favourite has smartened up a little as it has grown older. The worn shop signs of the two former fashion emporia that provide the name remain over the door, as does the basic concrete look, but the grey stuff is now covered with decent paintings, the artfully distressed seating looks a little more ordered, and on a weekend night you'll even find a pleasant chap on door inspection. What he's looking for isn't clear, mind, as no one here is particularly dressed up or cool: just a bunch of young Hoxton folk content to knock back the lager rather than any of the fancier Belgian bottles (such as Chimay). The rockabilly DJ on our visit created a relaxed, light-hearted mood.
Bar available for hire. Music (DJs 8pm Wed-Sun; free). **Map 5 R3**.

Drunken Monkey

222 Shoreditch High Street, E1 6PJ (7392 9606/www.thedrunkenmonkey.info). Liverpool Street tube/rail/35, 47, 242, 344 bus. **Open** noon-midnight Mon-Fri; 6pm-midnight Sat; noon-11pm Sun. **Food served** noon-11pm Mon-Fri; 6-11pm Sat; noon-10.30pm Sun. **Credit** AmEx, MC, V.
Detail counts with this Drunken Monkey, from the matt-black paintwork punctuated by tall mirrors and enhanced by raised golden motifs that lead you to the long bar and its line of large red Chinese lanterns, to the fetching deep-red crackled glaze on the wall opposite. Here, a small alcove

Juno

borders the dark intimacy of the Concubine Room. Up some stairs, past an oriental screen, is the music-free haven (DJs are a daily feature on the ground floor) of the Wu Dan dining room. Though food is obviously a speciality, its range of quality booze is splendid, from Breton cider through a wine list bursting with New and Old World treats to the distinctive 'House Liquors' (among them Cuban Matusalem Platino Rum) that form the basis for the Drunken Monkey's cheery cocktail selection.
Babies and children admitted. Function room. Music (DJs 9pm Tue-Sun. Restaurant. TV (big screen, digital). **Map 5 R4**.

Elbow Room

97-113 Curtain Road, EC2A 3BS (7613 1316). Old Street tube/rail/55 bus. **Open/food served** noon-midnight Mon, Tue, Sun; noon-1am Wed, Thur; noon-2am Fri, Sat. **Happy hour** 5-8pm Mon-Fri. **Credit** (over £10) MC, V.
This is one of the most popular links in the Elbow Room chain, offering bar, restaurant and plenty of bookable pool tables to a blend of City boys and Hoxtonites opting out of the style game. The array of purple-baize pool tables, copious booze deals and a menu of grilled meats draws the office blokes keen to brandish their cues and eye up any chicks with sticks; more serious players congregate at the rear tables, where things aren't quite as raucous. It's a big, cluttered space, wrapped around a bar that dishes out lagers and white wine as DJs pump out jazzy funk and other background mundanities. This place is big enough (you're almost certain to get a seat) and loud enough to make its customers forget the misery of office life.
Disabled: toilet. Games (7 pool tables). Music (DJs 8pm Wed-Sat; 4pm Sun; free). TV. **Map 5 R4**.

Fleapit

49 Columbia Road, E2 7RG (7033 9986/www.thefleapit.com). Old Street tube/rail. **Open** 11am-11pm Tue-Sat; 9am-2pm Sun. **Food served** 11.30am-10.30pm Tue-Sat. **Credit** AmEx, JCB, MC, V.
Fabulous furniture fills the inappropriately named Fleapit. There are teak-sided leather sofas, rattan S-shaped dining chairs, Dralon armchairs and vinyl button-back settees – all neatly arranged around a variety of Formica, glass-topped and G-plan tables. Food starts with breakfasts (cereal with yoghurt at £2.20, or croissants with jam at £1.55), then a range of lunch specials (like curry with butternut, tomato, onion and potato, £6.50). As well as teas, coffees and juices, there's an all-organic beer line-up (bottles only) that includes Eco Warrior pale ale and Shoreditch Stout from the local Pitfield Brewery, plus Samuel Smith's lager. The wine list is organic, too, and changes monthly. The mood is mellow during the week, but gets slightly more buzzy at weekends, when Columbia Road flower market draws another crowd. There's a decent-sized gallery at the rear where art exhibitions and film screenings are held.
Babies and children admitted. Disabled: toilet. Film club (8pm last Thur of mth; free). Function room. Internet access (free). Specialities (organic beer). Tables outdoors (3, pavement).

Fox Dining Room

28 Paul Street, EC2A 4LB (7729 5708). Old Street tube/rail. **Open** noon-11pm Mon-Fri. **Food served** (restaurant) 12.30-3pm, **Credit** MC, V.
One of those gastropubs with an old-school bar downstairs and an upmarket wood-panelled restaurant above, the Fox is a foodie beacon in an otherwise desolate tangle of Hoxton backstreets. City types (naturally) are to the fore rather than Shoreditch trendies, but it's a quality gaff where rough boards meet pale sepia walls, with decent wine (around a dozen each of red and white, from £11 a bottle) and jazz playing quietly in the background – a nice change from the pumping beats that prevail hereabouts. The peckish would do well to phone ahead for a table in the dining room, which serves modern British fare like mackerel with fennel or salt marsh lamb with swede (two courses for £15). The bar pumps include Bombardier and Hoegaarden.
Babies and children admitted (dining only). Restaurant available for hire. Tables outdoors (6, terrace). **Map 5 Q4**.

George & Dragon

2 Hackney Road, E2 7NS (7012 1100). Old Street tube/rail/55 bus. **Open** 4-11pm Mon-Thur; noon-11pm Fri, Sat; noon-10.30pm Sun. **Food served** noon-4pm Fri. **Credit** MC, V.
If you want to see how to do a gay-friendly makeover of a classic boozer, head for this fine little corner bar near the junction of Old Street and Kingsland Road. From the pub design box, take old, dark wood tables, nicotine-stained wallpaper and splashes of brick-red paintwork. Then add

skeins of red, heart-shaped lights, vintage cowboy and cowgirl signs, a few oil paintings of chaps in hunting gear enjoying bucolic pleasures, and top it all off with a fabulous modern light, a gorgeous centrepiece of glowing glass circles. A chatty, friendly gay crowd (both sexes) comes to show its appreciation and enjoy DJ nights (Saturday's Radio Egypt has a good rep), with plenty of louche classics. There's a touch of kitsch to the beer selection, too, with Double Diamond alongside Cruzcampo on tap.
Disabled: toilet. Music (DJs 8pm nightly). **Map 5 R3**.

Grand Central

91-93 Great Eastern Street, EC2A 3HZ (7613 4228/ www.grandcentral.org.uk). Old Street tube/rail/55 bus. **Open** 10am-midnight Mon-Wed; 10am-1am Thur; 10am-2am Fri; 7pm-2am Sat; 7pm-midnight Sun. **Food served** 10am-3pm, 5-10pm Mon-Fri; 7-10pm Sat. **Happy hour** 5-7pm Mon-Fri. **Credit** MC, V.
Its big corner site looks impressive enough, but there's nothing especially grand about this place. Tables are corralled around the side following the sweep of the windows, separated from the bar area behind dividers lined with beautiful multicoloured strips that produce rainbow hues beneath high ceiling lights. The lack of seating in the middle focuses attention on a similarly adorned bar that can knock up a decent cocktail – maybe a spiced raspberry Daiquiri or apple-tinged Mojito – but tends to spend more time dispensing lagers and white wine to a crowd of dressed-up party minxes and casual lads attracted by the eye candy. If you want some privacy, there's a comfy-seated alcove to the rear, but the music is louder here – and given how dire it can be, that's not good.
Babies and children admitted (until 5pm). Music (DJs 8pm Fri-Sun; free). No-smoking area (10am-3pm). Specialities (cocktails). Tables outdoors (6, pavement). **Map 5 Q4**.

Great Eastern Dining Room

54-56 Great Eastern Street, EC2A 3QR (7613 4545). Old Street tube/rail/55 bus. **Open** *Ground floor bar* noon-midnight Mon-Fri; 6pm-midnight Sat. *Below 54 bar* 7.30pm-1am Fri, Sat. **Food served** *Ground floor bar* noon-10.30pm Mon-Fri; 6-10.30pm Sat. *Below 54 bar* 7.30-10.30pm Fri, Sat. **Credit** AmEx, DC, MC, V.
A new white bar counter and the extra chrome of a couple of continental pumps has left the minimal feel of the decor in the bar area of this tri-pronged enterprise relatively untouched. The Great Eastern has a successful and imaginative Asian restaurant in the back room, the out-on-a-limb Below 54 club in the basement at weekends, and this light yet private quaffing section, where a gas fire flickers away in its own metal-chimneyed box in the corner, chrome lights hangs from the ceiling, and the silver-grey paintwork contrasts with the dark wood-grained panelling. Spirit gems, like Matusalem rum and Baker's B7 bourbon, lurk among the more readily available brands. The wine list is extensive and expensive.
Babies and children admitted (restaurant only). Bars available for hire. Music (DJs 8pm Fri, Sat; free). Restaurant. Specialities (cocktails). TV (big screen, projectors). **Map 5 R4**.

Home

100-106 Leonard Street, EC2A 4RH (7684 8618/ www.homebar.co.uk). Liverpool Street or Old Street tube/rail. **Open** 5pm-midnight Mon-Fri; 6pm-midnight Sat. **Food served** 6-10pm Mon-Sat. **Credit** AmEx, DC, JCB, MC, V.
Grolsch, Grolsch, Grolsch, say a trio of taps at the bar, which may explain the shocking sight of grown men drinking white wine. Home remains a popular destination for upmarket sorts frightened by Hoxton's more cutting-edge options but looking for a rough approximation of cocktail glamour. The low-ceiling bar has swapped places with the street-level restaurant, offering a blend of comfortable seats with a judicious mix of pale wood and light panels spread through several small rooms. The venue clearly makes people feel like they're having a good time, if the wiggling mass of young workers eyeing up each other is anything to go by. Perhaps it's a case of hormones over experience – why worry about over-priced bar snacks, uninspired cocktails or mediocre music when you might get lucky?
Disabled: ramp. Music (DJs 9pm-midnight Thur-Sat). Function room. Restaurant. Specialities (cocktails). TVs (big screen, digital, projector). **Map 5 R4**.

Hoxton Square Bar & Kitchen

2-4 Hoxton Square, N1 6NU (7613 0709). Old Street tube/rail. **Open** 11am-1am Mon-Thur, Sun; 11am-2am Fri, Sat. **Food served** noon-10pm daily. **Credit** AmEx, MC, V.
Once upon a time this was the rather lovely Lux Bar (named after a much-missed cinema), one of the Hoxton pathfinders with a blend of pared-back industrial style, in-your-face art, sharp music and interesting clientele. A bunker, yes, but one from which to plan a decent campaign. Now all is lost, and the barbarians have flooded through the huge glass doors, looking like extras from an All Bar One. One memento of the old days: you can at least still get something decent to imbibe – St Peter's and Samuel Smith's organic beers, De Koninck – if you can get through the throng of lager drinkers. DJs pump out mediocre backbeat in a dark rear bar, where a big empty space awaits punters drunk enough to dance to such crud. The dismal photo 'art' on display is Trendy as defined by committee.
Babies and children admitted (before 6pm). Cinema. Disabled: toilet. Music (DJs 9pm Thur-Sun; free-£3). Restaurant. Tables outdoors (4, patio). **Map 5 R3**.

Juno

134-135 Shoreditch High Street, E1 6JE (7729 2660/ www.junoshoreditch.co.uk). Liverpool Street tube or Old Street tube/rail. **Open** noon-midnight daily. **Food served** noon-10pm daily. **Credit** AmEx, MC, V.
Anyone who associates gloom with doom should try Juno on a winter's evening. There isn't a white light bulb to be seen, yet the place couldn't be more welcoming. Industrial bling being the decorative order of the day, metal ducts are proudly displayed. Settees and armchairs lead you to the bar area, where more low seating and tables await beneath a mural of a guy in boxing gloves. Backlit dark orange and blue, the bar offers an adequate wine list, cocktails that include the worryingly named 'Sicilian Kiss', and Pilsner Urquell and Tiger among the bottled beers. Food is unfussy and made in an open kitchen. Music played on our visit was a concise history of early dub; a downstairs bar has DJs some nights and comfy nooks always.
Babies and children admitted (before 6pm). Function room. Games (retro arcade machines). Music (DJs 8pm Wed, Thur; free). **Map 5 R4**.

Legion

348 Old Street, EC1V 9NQ (7729 4441). Old Street tube/rail. **Open** 5pm-midnight Mon-Thur; noon-2am Fri; 5pm-2am Sat; 1pm-2am Sun. Food served noon-10pm daily. **Credit** AmEx, DC, MC, V.

'Social club', proclaims the sign outside, but you're more likely to find assorted yoof in search of knees-ups and Breezers than old geezers (or anyone over 30) supping a quiet ale. The Legion is a long, cavernous space with big, rough planks bolted to the brickwork; one side is broken up by a bar containing a half-hearted selection of wines, alcopops and standard beers (both the real ales, Adnams and London Pride, were 'off' on our last visit). Music rather than booze is the main selling point, though, with events taking place pretty much every night. An excellent jukebox does, however, provide solace if you happen to get the karaoke evening – especially as it's free.
Disabled: toilet. Music (ring for event details; DJs 8pm Fri-Sun; free). TV (projector, satellite). **Map 5 R4**.

Light Bar & Restaurant

233 Shoreditch High Street, E1 6PJ (7247 8989/www.thelighte1.com). Liverpool Street tube/rail. **Open** noon-midnight Mon-Wed; noon-2am Thur, Fri; 6.30pm-2am Sat; noon-10.30pm Sun. **Food served** noon-10.30pm daily. **Admission** £2 Thur-Sat (upstairs bar).
Credit AmEx, DC, MC, V.
This former railway warehouse is a big player in every sense. It's a huge space, with bare brickwork, concrete floor and girders criss-crossing high above the hubbub – but even so, it feels like a sardine tin at weekends, as ties-loosened City types pile in with locals who can't be bothered to walk up to the Old Street action. Booze is a cut above average, with the likes of Paulaner and Duvel, but most seem happy necking standard-issue lagers and house wine to an accompaniment of MOR dance music. The burger and salad menu is similarly unadventurous, though if you want something better, there's a restaurant upstairs. A courtyard offers overspill in warmer weather.
Babies and children admitted (restaurant). Disabled: toilet. Dress: no suits in upstairs bar. Function room (Mon-Thur, Sun). Music (DJs Thur-Sat; free). Restaurant. Tables outdoors (9, courtyard). **Map 5 R5**.

City

Loungelover

1 Whitby Street, E1 6JU (7012 1234/www.loungelover.co.uk). Liverpool Street tube/rail then 8, 388 bus. **Open** 6pm-midnight Mon-Thur; 6pm-1am Fri; 7pm-1am Sat.
Food served 6.30-10.30pm Tue-Fri; 7-11pm Sat.
Credit AmEx, MC, V.
Bringing glorious camp to a barren Shoreditch backstreet earned Loungelover Best Design gong at Time Out's 2004 Eating & Drinking awards. It's an eye-popping riot of colour and gaudy styling – stuffed hippo's head, grandfather clock, revolving dummy, 1960s chairs, Victorian gas lamps, Japanese lanterns, coloured Perspex lights, glass fronted cases displaying the wine, big gold letters spelling out 'lover' over the bar, and some fabulous chandeliers – but success seems to have gone to their heads. Those who don't bag a seat in any of the nooks (booking needed at weekends) are corralled into a tiny space by the bar and given orders not to wander or distract the bar staff. The cocktails (divided into Current Obsession, Moment of Madness and Old Flame) are great, but at £11 you'd expect that, and a dash of courtesy.
Disabled: toilet. Music (musician/singer 10.30pm Fri, Sat; free). Specialities (cocktails). **Map 5 R4**.

Mother Bar

333 Old Street, EC1V 9LE (7739 5949/www.333mother.com). Old Street tube/rail/55 bus. **Open/snacks served** 8pm-3am Mon-Wed; 8pm-4am Thur, Sun; 8pm-5am Fri, Sat. **Credit** MC, V.
The mothership of Shoreditch's downbeat style retains every bit of its glamorous-seedy appeal. Stumble up the wanly lit stairs, and instead of cards advertising a 'Friendly Model' you'll find a large anteroom with a mish-mash of old seats scattered around a chessboard floor. Linger here if the chaise longue beckons, or carry on into the bohemian ballroom beyond, decorated with old chandeliers, polka-dot walls and a disco ball that spins merrily with the generally excellent DJs attending their decks beneath a giant painting. No one's here for the beer (Guinness, Red Stripe on tap, Staropramen by the bottle), just the warming darkness and friendly vibe. Late in the evening, you may have to queue to get in.
Music (DJs 10pm Mon-Thur, Sun; 8pm Fri, Sat; free). **Map 5 R4**.

New Foundry

84-86 Great Eastern Street, EC2A 3JL (7739 6900/www.foundry.tv). Old Street tube/rail/55 bus. **Open** 4-11pm Tue-Fri; 2-11pm Sat; 2-10.30pm Sun.
No credit cards.
Like a gloriously scuzzy sixth-form den in a boho school, this bank conversion is one of Hoxton's most engaging drinking spots. Peeling paintwork, headless dolls hanging above cracked lino, a rickety old piano, random stacks of old computers and floor-to-ceiling graffiti in the downstairs gallery space: the Foundry raises decrepitude to the level of art. The art, meanwhile, tends to decrepitude, though a large board engagingly challenges the 'I Could Do Better Than That' brigade to put up or shut up. All this seems to attract artists and buyers, the shabby and woollen-hatted relaxing with the urban stylistas. It's a friendly vibe, with standard lubricants augmented by such unusual bottled offerings as Pitfield's Shoreditch Stout and Eco Warrior. A 'Slow Sound System' provides a suitably cool score for artful draping on the mish-mash of battered seating.
Art gallery. Music (pianist 6pm Tue). Poetry readings (9pm Sun; free). Specialities (organic ale). Tables outdoors (5, pavement). **Map 5 Q4**.

Owl & the Pussycat

34 Redchurch Street, E2 7DP (7613 3628). Bethnal Green tube/Liverpool Street or Old Street tube/rail.
Open noon-11pm Mon-Fri; 5-11pm Sat; noon-10.30pm Sun. **Food served** noon-3pm, Mon-Fri; 2-6pm Sun.
Credit MC, V.
At 9pm on a Tuesday, this particular pea-green boat is vibrant and buzzing, thanks to the predominantly youthful crowd on board. It has a steady approach to the concept of draught 'Edward' (Edward Lear, beer) that includes Hoegaarden and London Pride. Food is geared towards the traditional carnivore, with sirloin steak, lamb shank and sausage and mash in the traps every day, as well as a carvery every Sunday. The lounge area at the back offers a bar billiards table, and there's a garden for use in perkier climatic conditions.
Babies and children admitted (restaurant). Games (bar billiards, fruit machine). Quiz (8.30pm Tue; £1). Restaurant (available for hire). Tables outdoors (8, garden). **Map 5 R4**.

Pool

104-108 Curtain Road, EC2A 3AH (7739 9608/www.thepool.uk.com). Old Street tube/rail/55 bus. **Open** noon-1am Mon-Thur; noon-2am Fri; 5.30pm-2am Sat; noon-midnight Sun. **Food served** noon-3pm, 5.30-10.30pm Mon-Fri; 5.30-10.30pm Sat; noon-midnight Sun. **Credit** MC, V.

Sosho

The ground floor here is a peaceful place in which to get some cue action, thanks to a wise decision to keep the music in its darker, spacious basement bar. And Pool trumps its rival in more than this: the drinks are better and cheaper, there's Thai food instead of burgers, and the music is funkier. You'll even discover a welcome nod to arty Hoxton here, with regular film nights downstairs. At street level, a pair of red-topped tables take up half the space, offering a spotlit arena for City boys to show off their deep screw while the laydeez knock back two-for-one cocktails and the evening builds to its shagfest finale. Sunday is a good day, when free tables and an absence of office workers let locals remember a time when Pool was leader of the rack.
Babies and children admitted (until 5pm). Games (pool; £5/hr before 6pm, £7/hr after; Sun free). Music (DJs 8pm Mon-Sat; 6pm Sun). **Map 5 R4**.

Reliance

336 Old Street, EC1V 9DR (7729 6888). Old Street tube/rail/55 bus. **Open** noon-midnight Mon-Wed, Sun; noon-2am Thur-Sat. **Food served** 12.30-3pm, 6-9pm Mon-Fri; 6.30-9pm Sat; 5-9pm Sun. **Credit** AmEx, DC, MC, V.

Until recently a standard-issue gastropub, the Reliance now has two women owners who have helped the place rediscover its roots. A couple of old sofas by the door provide a prime slouching spot from which to appraise new arrivals or, through the big windows, just watch Hoxton life pass by. Elsewhere, old Hoxton worn wooden seating is mixed with new Hoxton exposed brickwork and distressed floorboards. There's a strong continental flavour at the beer pumps, which feature Belgian and eastern European brews (Affligem, Hoegaarden, Früli, Litovel, Zubr). Quality bangers 'n' mash and the like are promised (in place of anything too fancy) once the new menu settles in, though whatever is served seems unlikely to put off the punters – chilled twentysomethings nodding along to a fine jukebox – who know a good gaff when they see one.
Babies and children admitted (upstairs only). Disabled: toilet. Function room. Games (board games, darts). Music (DJ 7pm Sun; free). Specialities (Belgian beer). **Map 5 R4**.

Smersh

5 Ravey Street, EC2A 4QW (7739 0092/www.smershbar.com). Liverpool Street or Old Street tube/rail. **Open** 5pm-midnight Mon-Sat. **Credit** (over £10) AmEx, DC, MC, V.

You have to like a place that names itself after a counter-espionage wing of the KGB, as described in early Bond novels. Add a slap of red paint in the tiny basement space, Cold War newspaper cuttings in the loos, and eastern European booze – Polish beers, excellent vodkas – and we like it even more. Bar staff are friendly, too, happy to suggest spirits to the uninitiated (they were spot on with the Soplica vodka), though most of the good folk who crowd in seem happy to raise their spirits on the more common pepper- or honey-flavoured variants. Full marks also go to the enthusiastic musical mix; regular nights range from Northern soul to a Norwegian female DJ spinning honky-tonk and country swing. A venue for vodka aficionados to add to SE1's Baltic (*see p103*) and Holborn's Na Zdrowie (*see p47*), Smersh will also be appreciated by decadent western music lovers, whatever their poison.
Bar available for hire (Sat). Music (DJs 7pm Mon-Sat). **Map 5 Q4**.

Sosho

2 Tabernacle Street, EC2A 4LU (7920 0701/www.sosho3am.com). Moorgate or Old Street tube/rail. **Open** noon-10pm Mon; noon-midnight Tue; noon-1am Wed, Thur; noon-3am Fri; 7pm-3am Sat. **Food served** noon-11pm Mon-Fri; 7-11pm Sat. **Credit** AmEx, DC, JCB, MC, V.

The zeal of the amiable and informative Argentine barman is appropriate, since, as part of the Match chain, Sosho is indeed on a mission: to enhance the reputation of the cocktail. Walk past the 14 eyes of the pop art *Magnificent Seven* prints on the wall, and you get to an award-winning space of industrial brickwork and leather settees, where the bar benevolently looms. A massive, kitsch, plastic chandelier overhangs a staircase leading to a cosy low-seating alcove, and ultimately to a discreetly lit lounge bar, where a range of DJs has boosted the establishment's reputation. Bottled beers from the Meantime micro-brewery, along with wines

and cocktails from the imagination of the celebrated Dale DeGroff, testify to Sosho's insistence on quality, and should ensure the joint continues to buzz.
Babies and children admitted (daytime only). Disabled: toilet. Function room. Music (DJs 9pm Wed-Sat; £3-£5 after 9pm). **Map 5 Q4**.

T

56 Shoreditch High Street, E1 6JJ (7729 2973/www. tbarlondon.com). Liverpool Street or Old Street tube/ rail. **Open** 9am-11pm Mon-Wed; 9am-midnight Thur, Fri; 7pm-2am Sat; 11am-10.30pm Sun. **Food served** 9am-10pm Mon-Fri; 11am-10pm Sun. **Credit** MC, V.
Part of the Tea Building (home to a design agency and a gallery), T is a behemoth of a drinking venue. What it lacks in atmosphere it makes up for in space, space and space. The Brave New World interior is part warehouse, part chi-chi bar with colour-coded areas: black and white retro furniture, black leather sofas, odd 1970s-style jungle murals, luxurious red-curtained areas and velvet couches. There's beer and wine, but the main line is cocktails (around £5.50): along with the classics, these include concoctions like Bethnal Green Tea (five spirits) or East End Sour (scotch, orgeat syrup, lemon juice and egg white). The short food menu lists sandwiches and bar snacks; on Sunday, there's breakfast, brunch and lunch. T might not be out of the ordinary, but we reckon it's the only venue in Shoreditch with room to shake a leg on a Friday night.
Disabled: toilet. Music (DJs 9pm Thur-Sat; free). Restaurant. Specialities (cocktails). **Map 5 R4**.

Tabernacle

55-61 Tabernacle Street, EC2A 4AA (7253 5555/ www.tabernaclebargrill.com). Old Street tube/rail. **Open/food served** *Ground floor bar* noon-1am Mon-Thur; noon-2am Fri; 6pm-2am Sat. *Lounge bar* 7pm-1am Thur; 7pm-2am Fri; 7pm-2am Sat. **Credit** AmEx, DC, JCB, MC, V.
'This is a place for grown-ups, not the kids,' says the barman, and he's probably right. The street-level bar in this Victorian warehouse conversion is a big, high room, with modern seats nicely spaced across the polished black floorboards; it contrasts with the 'late night lounge bar' downstairs, which is all red leather and bare brick. Drinks in both are focused on cocktails and wine, rather than beer, with the former split into 'Contemporary' and 'Classics with a Twist' (around £6). Food is a cut above your average bar snacks: dishes include peppered lavosh and Tabernacle crackling, along with Mediterranean mains like tagliatelle with broad beans and pancetta. There's also an adjacent restaurant. The place can be a bit soulless during the day, but if you fancy impressing a date with a classy post-work drink, try this welcome newcomer.
Babies and children admitted (restaurant). Disabled: lift; toilet. Function room. Music (DJs 6pm Thur-Sat; admission varies). Restaurant. Specialities (cocktails). **Map 5 R4**.

Troy

10 Hoxton Street, N1 6NG (7739 6695). Old Street tube/rail. **Open** noon-1am Tue-Thur; noon-2am Fri, Sat; noon-10.30pm Sun. **Food served** noon-9.30pm Tue-Sat; noon-6pm Sun. **Credit** MC, V.
Wander up the backstreet to Troy's glowing orange sign and peek through its orange curtains too early in the evening, and you may be alarmed to see an empty bar and a DJ warming up for an audience of empty seats. Sometime after 10pm, though, Troy comes alive, taking advantage of late opening to celebrate the midnight hour and beyond. They keep things simple. Grab a drink from the tiny bar by the door – basic booze options only – and wander through to the main space, where refectory-style furniture and warm painted walls give the feel of some sort of student club where all comers are welcome; very pleasant if you're relaxed and happy to nod along to a fine soundtrack of classic black grooves or chance your ears with whoever turns up for the regular open mic nights.
Music (open mic 9pm Tue; DJs 8.30pm Thur, Sat; live jazz 9.30pm Fri). Restaurant. **Map 5 R3**.

Wenlock Arms

26 Wenlock Road, N1 7TA (7608 3406/www.wenlock-arms.co.uk). Old Street tube/rail/55 bus. **Open** noon-11pm Mon-Sat; noon-10.30pm Sun. **Food served** noon-9pm daily. **No credit cards**.
Sixty-odd years ago, when the Luftwaffe demonstrated its true priorities by missing the the nearby munitions factory and taking out the local brewery, the Wenlock Arms was mercifully spared. So we can still gaze upon the high, dark-wood, mirror-backed bar, as scuffed as the regulars leering out of the black and white photomontage on the wall, where top shelves teem with dusty bottles and real ale awards. Punters can sample the delights of draught Kriek, Paulaner wheat beer or an Independence Party-defying Harviestoun Belgian White, brewed in Scotland. Food is basic, and half-a-loaf sausage sarnies go down a treat with lunchtime office workers, enjoying the coke-fuelled warmth emanating from the brick fireplace. The Wenlock: a paean to micro-brews and pan-European co-operation.
Babies and children admitted. Function room. Games (darts). Music (blues/jazz Fri, Sat; 3pm Sun). TV (satellite).

Zigfrid

11 Hoxton Square, N1 6NU (7613 1988/www.zigfrid.com). Old Street tube/rail. **Open** noon-midnight Mon-Sat; noon-11.30pm Sun. **Food** noon-3pm, 5-10pm Mon-Fri; noon-4pm, 6-10pm Sat; noon-9.30pm Sun. **Credit** MC, V.
Zigfrid's prime position, with huge windows overlooking the top end of Hoxton Square, means nowt when the designer, bar guru Paul Daly, seems to have done the job after a heavy session with that Llewelyn-Bowen chap. The decor typifies the instant artificial 'style' you might see on *Changing Rooms*: concrete walls softened by rich curtains, a scattering of artfully distressed leather chairs with too-fancy flourishes, plus a few old standard lamps. A dining area runs along one side of the long L-shaped bar, serving food that's as unexceptional as the drinks. The jukebox is a bit better, with an eclectic mix of older stuff: trip hop and classic disco playing on a lunchtime visit, though you could have Joy Division or the *Easy Rider* soundtrack too. But you couldn't imagine Fonda and Nicholson staying for more than a track or two before firing up the Harleys again.
Babies and children admitted. Disabled: toilet. Jukebox. Music (DJs 9pm Thur-Sat, 3pm Sun; free). Tables outdoors (25, terrace). TV (big screen, digital).

Also in the area...

Colonel Jaspers (Davy's) 190 City Road, EC1V 2QH (7608 0925).
Masque Haunt (JD Wetherspoon) 168-172 Old Street, EC1V 9PB (7251 4195).
Pulpit (Davy's) 63 Worship Street, EC2A 2DU (7377 1574).

LIVERPOOL STREET & MOORGATE

Liverpool Street has something of a Jekyll and Hyde personality. On Thursdays and Fridays, it's a heaving monster of City workers with annihilation on their minds. For the rest of the week (when the party animals are in recovery or in board meetings) the pubs and bars echo eerily. Overall, the vibe is smarter and dressier than in nearby Shoreditch or on Old Street; but as with many other City venues, most places here shut at the weekend – and there's little more disappointing than standing outside **Vertigo 42** rattling the glass doors.

Corney & Barrow

19 Broadgate Circle, EC2M 2QS (7628 1251/www.corney-barrow.co.uk). Liverpool Street tube/rail. **Open** 7.30am-11pm Mon-Fri. **Food served** 7.30am-10pm Mon-Fri. **Credit** AmEx, DC, MC, V.

Flagship of the swanky, City-based chain, this branch of C&B curls around the circumference of Broadgate Circle. It's a corridor-like, glass-fronted space, flooded with natural light during the day. By the windows are high tables around which young, self-assured City types sit on dark-blue stools. Outside there are heated canopies; in winter you get a bird's-eye view of the ice rink. The drinks list is updated every couple of months, and is very user-friendly. Wines are ordered by grape variety, with helpful, concise tasting notes (Chocapalha 2000 from Portugal is 'a temptress of a wine, with pepper dark chocolate and vanilla cream'), and the choice is wide yet unintimidating. To eat, there's breakfast, modern brasserie fare during the day (posh sandwiches, warm salads and mains like chicken breast stuffed with halloumi, chorizo hash and roasted red pepper jus) and an evening selection of bar bites.

Bar available for hire. Disabled: toilet; lift. Tables outdoors (30, balconies and terrace). TV (satellite). **Map 5 Q5**.

Dirty Dick's

202 Bishopsgate, EC2M 4NR (7283 5888). Liverpool Street tube/rail. **Open** 11am-10.30pm Mon-Fri. **Food served** noon-2.30pm Mon-Fri. **Credit** AmEx, MC, V.

'Dirty Dick' was a wealthy ironmonger by the name of Nathaniel Bentley, whose fiancée died on the eve of their wedding. Presaging Dickens's Miss Havisham, Dick locked up his house – complete with wedding breakfast – and retreated into a life of filth and squalor. When he died in 1809, a Georgian entrepreneur bought up all his possessions and displayed them in his house, recently converted into a tavern. The building was reconstructed in 1870 and all that now remains of the old house are the cellars. Young's are now in charge, and make sure that every level is used to the full, from the downstairs 'wine vaults' to the ground-floor bar and the first-floor Hobson's bar and dining room. The taps dispense Young's standards and seasonal varieties (Winter Warmer on our visit).

Bar for hire. Games (fruit machines). No-smoking area. Restaurant. TVs. **Map 6 R5**.

Fleetwood Bar

36 Wilson Street, EC2M 2TE (7247 2242). Liverpool Street or Moorgate tube/rail. **Open** 11am-11pm Mon-Fri. **Food served** 11.30am-9pm Mon-Fri. **Credit** AmEx, MC, V.

With its stainless-steel bar taps, warm beech furniture and smooth cream walls, Fleetwood Bar is strangely reminiscent of a cruise ship. Everything here is clean, inoffensive and slightly bland. From Monday to Wednesday, older suits exchange takeover tales and play FTSE; they make way for younger colleagues later in the week (and even a few creative types). This is a Fuller's bar, yet the most popular drinks seem to be lager, wine and mixers, along with a cocktail and shooters list that pleases the more hedonistic drinkers. There's also draught London Pride, Hoegaarden and Honey Dew Organic Golden Ale, should Slippery Nipples not be your thing. The menu of pub food includes a retro selection of fishfinger sandwiches and hot dogs.

Games (fruit machines, quiz machine). Tables outdoors (8, pavement). TVs (big screen). **Map 5 Q5**

George

Great Eastern Hotel, 40 Liverpool Street, EC2M 7QN (7618 7400). Liverpool Street tube/rail. **Open** 11am-11pm Mon-Sat; noon-10.30pm Sun. **Food served** noon-2.30pm, 6-9.30pm Mon-Fri; noon-5pm, 6-9.30pm Sat; noon-5pm, 6-9pm Sun. **Credit** AmEx, DC, MC, V.

This Conran venue is a smart, understated pub with a Tudor twist. Leaded windows shut out the City traffic, while dark wood panelling and a carved ceiling create an atmospheric, enclosed bar. There are plenty of modern touches, too: funky George Cross ashtrays on the tables, and staff kitted out in special shirts (which make them look a little like England rugby fans). The clientele is predominantly professional and includes guests from the adjoining Great Eastern Hotel. Greene King IPA, Rumpus from Essex's Ridleys brewery and Bombardier account for the ales; there's a standard draught lager selection; and the house sauvignon blanc and merlot aren't extortionately priced (£13.50 a bottle). An enticing food menu offers a range of traditional British fare, with mains like braised beef and spring onion mash at around £8.

Babies and children admitted: high chairs. Function room. **Map 6 R6**.

Golden Heart

110 Commercial Street, E1 6LZ (7247 2158). Liverpool Street tube/rail. **Open** 11am-11pm Mon-Sat; 11am-10.30pm Sun. **Credit** JCB, MC, V.

Trendies rub shoulders with traders at this happily shambolic, old-school Spitalfields boozer. The atmosphere is enhanced by a blazing coal fire in winter; the walls are lined with old photos of the market and its stallholders; and plenty of the latter come here to warm their toes during the day. The lager line-up holds no surprises (Stella, Kronenbourg and Carling), though there are a couple of ales – Adnams bitter and Broadside. Despite the pub's traditional feel, the art crowd has made its mark: the Heart hit the headlines a while ago when landlady Sandra Esquilant took 80th place in a list of the 100 most powerful figures in contemporary art, and Tracey Emin has been known to make an appearance. Oh, and looming over the ladies' loo is a bit of Brit Art stating: 'Stand still and rot'. Right-o.

Babies and children admitted. Function room. Jukebox. Specialities (real ales). Tables outdoors (4, pavement). TV (satellite).

Hamilton Hall

Unit 32, The Concourse, Liverpool Street Station, EC2M 7PY (7247 3579/www.jdwetherspoon.co.uk). Liverpool Street tube/rail. **Open/food served** 7.30am-11pm Mon-Fri; 10am-11pm Sat; 10am-10.30pm Sun. **Credit** MC, V.

This former ballroom of the Great Eastern Hotel – still standing next door – has been sympathetically restored by the JD Wetherspoon chain to something like the glory it would have enjoyed a century ago. There are chandeliers, a pale blue and lemon colour scheme, large mirrors and ornate gold mouldings, while the mezzanine sensibly offers a seated no-smoking area. At the pumps lager drinkers will find Stella, Carling, Kronenbourg and San Miguel; ale aficionados have Abbot, London Pride, Pedigree and a guest or two (Tournament from Gloucestershire's Goffs brewery on our visit) to choose from. Unfortunately, despite the grand decor, Hamilton Hall remains a railway pub, and a loud one, at that; and every Friday night brings a serious session before the last train leaves Liverpool Street.
Disabled: toilet. Games (fruit machines). No-smoking area. Tables outdoors (15, pavement). **Map 6 R6.**

Jamies at the Pavilion

Finsbury Circus Gardens, EC2M 7AB (7628 8224/ www.jamiesbars.co.uk). Liverpool Street or Moorgate tube/rail. **Open** 11am-11pm Mon-Fri. **Food served** 11am-3pm, 6-9pm Mon-Fri. **Credit** AmEx, JCB, MC, V.
A refuge from the City's finance factories, this branch of the Jamies chain is in a pavilion that's also the clubhouse for the City of London Bowling Club. Best enjoyed in summer, the venue is surrounded by an emerald bowling green and a circle of trees and shrubbery. The wine list changes three times a year, with advice on new labels being provided by Willie Lebus of Bibendum. The choice is sound and pretty evenly split between Old World and New. Sensibly ordered by grape variety, the selection includes several items under £20: 2002 Alamos Mendoza cabernet sauvignon from Argentina (£19.50); and 2002 Pierre Sparr pinot blanc from Alsace (£18.50), for instance. Most wines are available by the glass, making Jamies a good spot for experimentation. To eat there are shared snack plates, sandwiches and more substantial main courses.
Function room. Restaurant. Specialities (wine). **Map 6 Q5.**

Public Life

82A Commercial Street, E1 6LY (7375 1631). Aldgate East tube/Liverpool Street tube/rail. **Open** noon-midnight Mon-Wed; 9pm-2am Thur; 9pm-3am Fri, Sat. **Credit** MC, V.
Sitting in the shadows of Nicholas Hawksmoor's grand and spooky Christ Church is an unobtrusive glass box, the only above-ground sign that this tiny, subterranean 'events-led artists' bar' exists. Public Life used to be a public toilet, and it still has its original black and white tiles; where the cubicles used to be is now the serving area. These days it's not so much a bar as a place in which to experience loud DJ-driven music while gulping down mixers or bottled beers like Budweiser and Stella. There's very little in the way of seating, and ditto in the way of space (so you won't have a chance to exhibit your more extrovert dance moves), but at least there's nothing bog-standard about the place.
Bar available to hire. Music (DJs 9pm Thur-Sat; £2-£5 Fri, Sat). Tables outdoors (6, pavement).

St Paul's Tavern

56 Chiswell Street, EC1Y 4SA (7606 3828). Barbican tube/Moorgate tube/rail. **Open** 11am-11pm Mon-Fri. **Food served** noon-8pm Mon-Thur; noon-6pm Fri. **Credit** AmEx, MC, V.
Post-work banter melds with chart music at this large, unpretentious pub. It used to be the brewery-tap for the Whitbread Brewery, which stood next door from 1750 until recently; the building is still there, but it's been converted into offices. Meanwhile, the Tavern's stripped-wood floors, brick pillars and festive red and green colour scheme aren't going to win any design awards, but the atmosphere is cosy and relaxed. There's a more varied crowd here than in many of the City boozers; thirtysomething City types form the majority, but not all of them wear suits. However large the thirsty throng becomes, the bar staff run a quick, efficient ship, and there's a good choice of ales, including Abbot, Adnams bitter, Fuller's London Pride, and a regular guest ale (Caledonian's Six Nations on our visit). Food is cheap and cheerful, with steak and ale pies, burgers and fish 'n' chips all priced at around a fiver.
Games (golf machines). No-smoking tables (lunchtime only). Specialities (real ales). TV. **Map 5 Q5.**

Vertigo 42

Tower 42, 25 Old Broad Street, EC2N 1PB (7877 7842/www.vertigo42.co.uk). Bank tube/DLR/Liverpool Street tube/rail. **Open** noon-3pm, 5-11pm Mon-Fri. **Food served** noon-2.15pm, 5-9.30pm Mon-Fri. **Credit** AmEx, DC, JCB, MC, V.
Champers and charming staff aside, there's only one thing that really counts at Vertigo 42: the view. Situated on the 42nd floor of the tallest edifice in the City, the bar enjoys a truly stunning panorama , and the tourists, suits and romantics who come here all react in much the same way: 'Wow!' Everyone gets a view, as the seating lines the windows; perfect, as the space within has the feel of an upmarket airport lounge. As champagne bars go, Vertigo isn't cheap, but there's also a (slightly) less expensive wine list with a good choice of wines by the glass; a glass of full-bodied Château La Gasparde côtes de castillon will set you back £6.95. There's also a small food menu, featuring some very expensive caviar and some very tasty desserts.
Bar available for hire. No cigars or pipes. Specialities (champagne). **Map 6 Q6.**

Also in the area...

All Bar One 18-20 Appold Street, EC2A 2AS (7377 9671); 127 Finsbury Pavement, EC2A 1NS (7448 9921); 106-107 Houndsditch, EC3A 7BD (7283 0047).
Balls Brothers 158 Bishopsgate, EC2M 4LN (7426 0567); 11 Bloomfield Street, EC2M 1PS (7588 4643); Gow's Restaurant, 81 Old Broad Street, EC2M 1PR (7920 9645); 52 Lime Street, EC3M 7BS (7283 0841); Mark Lane, EC3R 7BB (7623 2923).
Bangers (Davy's) Eldon House, 2-12 Wilson Street, EC2H 2TE (7377 6326).
Bishops Parlour (Davy's) 91-93 Moorgate, EC2M 6SJ (7588 2581).
City Boot (Davy's) 7 Moorfields High Walk, EC2Y 9DP (7588 4766).
Corney & Barrow 5 Exchange Square, EC2A 2EH (7628 4367); 111 Old Broad Street, EC2N 1AP (7638 9308); 1 Ropemaker Street, EC2N 1AP (7382 0606).
Davy's 2 Exchange Square, EC2A 2EH (7256 5962).
El Vino 125 London Wall, EC2Y 5AP (7600 6377).
Hog's Head 25 St Mary Axe, EC3A 8LL (7929 0245).
Jamies 155 Bishopsgate, EC2A 2AA (7256 7279).
O'Neill's 31-36 Houndsditch, EC3A 7DB (7397 9841); 64 London Wall, EC2M 5TP (7786 9231).

Orangery (Jamies) Cutlers Gardens, 10 Devonshire Square, EC2M 4TE (7623 1377).
Pitcher & Piano 200 Bishopsgate, EC2M 4NR (7929 5914).
Slug & Lettuce 100 Fenchurch Street, EC3M 5JD (7488 1890).

MANSION HOUSE, MONUMENT & BANK

Slow change is afoot in the taverns and bars of this historic, financial quarter. Traditionally, hostelries here were about giving City workers a slap-up lunch and slurp of decent wine or ale, in revamped grandeur: old banking houses, coffee houses and city offices. Leadenhall Market arcade is a classic example. But just opposite, in **Prism**, you have an old banking house venue trying to break with tradition. If it catches on, what with more flexible working hours, it might also mean a weekend scene as well. For now, nearly all venues are open Monday to Friday only.

Bar Bourse

67 Queen Street, EC4R 1EE (7248 2200/2211). Mansion House tube. **Open** 11.30am-11pm Mon-Fri. **Food served** 11.30am-3pm Mon-Fri. **Credit** AmEx, JCB, MC, V.

The 'BB' (as logoed on the handles of its sleek double doors and wherever stylishly possible inside) is a chic basement bar/restaurant with a showy City crowd around the bar and secretive couples in affair intimacy along the surrounding tables. The wine list (20 of each colour) dominates the drinks menu, with five each by the glass (Cortenova delle Venezie pinot grigio at £4, Marques de Griñon rioja at £4.25, or Montgras merlot at £4.50) and two each by the half bottle (La Côte de Sury sancerre at £13.50, Château de Malleret haut médoc at £15). Along with the classic champagne (£8) and vodka (£6) varieties, cocktails include a Blurry Martini of Chambord, raspberries and strawberries topped with a Blavod vodka float (£6.50), while favourites like tiger prawn tempura (£10) make up bar food menus; heavier items, such as home-made venison and red onion sausages (£7.50), are also available. *Babies and children admitted. Bar/restaurant available for hire.* **Map 6 P7**.

Bar Under the Clock

74 Queen Victoria Street (entrance on Bow Lane), EC4N 4SJ (7489 9895/www.ballsbrothers.co.uk). Mansion House tube. **Open** 9am-11pm Mon-Fri. **Food served** 9am-3pm, 5.30-9pm Mon-Fri. **Credit** AmEx, DC, MC, V.

The sassiest branch of the 17-strong Balls Brothers' bar-and-restaurant chain across the City and West End, this modern basement is nearly as strong on beers and cocktails as it is on wines, Balls' stock in trade for 150 years or more. Bottles of Lapin Kulta, London Pride, Peroni, Chimay and other Trappist varieties vie for attention behind the long, well-stocked bar, along with £4.50 cocktails such as French 75, Creole Punch and Bailey's Comet. As for the wines, there are 16 reds and whites, four each by the glass, from the humble Central Valley Chilean sauvignon (£3.30) to a 1997 Viña Real Reserva rioja (£27.50 a bottle), and from a Clivus pinot grigio (£3.80) to a Domaine de la

DRINKING ALOUD
JONATHAN DOWNEY

Who are you? I'm the owner of the Match Bar Group [which includes the Match bars, *see p116* and *p43*; Sosho, *see p129*; Player, *see p87*; and Trailer Happiness, *see p71*].
Drinking in London: what's good about it? I like the passion and creativity of the best bartenders in the world. And I like the fact that almost every single non-chain bar east of Greek Street plays really good music.
What's caught your eye in the last year? Well, I think it's been a really dull year. I think it's been about Nathan Barley bars, if you know what I mean – so out there, so lad, so *wanky*. They're trying so hard to be cool, and they're so dire. They serve Foster's. They haven't got a clue.
What could London do with more of? More women owning and operating bars – I think women do things better. We need more than just the usual blokes who own bars! I'd also like to see more bars owned by gay men – not gay bars as such, but places like Loungelover (*see p128*). And property prices need to come down to lower the entry level for young, potentially interesting new bar entrepreneurs.
What's in your crystal ball? Recently there's been a resurgence of really good bands and music – look at the NME Awards and the Brits, there's some really good British music around. In the same way, I think there could be a generation of new bar owners opening really exciting bars in the next few years – a lot like the mid to late '90s, my generation.
New licensing law: good or bad? Irrelevant. To most drinkers in central London, it will make absolutely no difference whatsoever.
Anything to declare? Thank God for *Time Out* and the *Time Out Bars* guide!

City

Boissoneuse Chablis (£21 a bottle). Mains include a beef and Guinness pie at £8.95 and honey-roast chicken and spring onion mash at £7.75. A reasonably funky soundtrack matches the arty decor.
Bar area available for hire. **Map 6 P6**.

Bell

29 Bush Lane, EC4R 0AN (7929 7772). Cannon Street tube/rail. **Open** 11am-10pm Mon-Fri. **Food served** noon-2.30pm Mon-Fri. **Credit** AmEx, MC, V.
Our first attempt to visit the Bell was frustrated by the place closing early, but our post-work return revealed a saloon bar bustling with pre-commuters. Ignore the 'oyez, oyez, oyez' schtick outside – perhaps inevitable for a pub thought to be the oldest in the City – and you'll find an atmospheric little half-timbered boozer. There's so much wood it's a surprise to learn that this was one of the few buildings on Bush Lane to survive the Great Fire; the uncharitable might suggest the mustard-yellow textured wallpaper, horse brasses and coaching prints date back as far. Suited gents form the quorum, perched on tall stools or standing at the narrow shelves that run along the front and back walls, but a few couples help keep things relaxed. Ales include Courage Best, Battersea, Spitfire, Young's Bitter and Deuchars IPA, but visitors without beards can avail themselves of a dozen wines (£3 a glass) from a blackboard list. Sandwiches are made to order.
No piped music or jukebox. Specialities (real ales). **Map 6 P7**.

Bonds Bar & Restaurant

Threadneedle Hotel, 5 Threadneedle Street, EC4R 8AY (7657 8088). Monument tube/Bank tube/DLR. **Open** 11am-11pm Mon-Fri; noon-8pm Sat, Sun. **Food served** noon-2.30pm, 6-10pm Mon-Fri; noon-2.30pm, 6-8pm Sat, Sun. **Credit** AmEx, DC, MC, V.
Fabulously upmarket, Bonds Bar & Restaurant benefits from Spanish management, as discerning as it is caring. Cocktails come first, and when you're sitting at a brown swivel bar stool at the long glass bar counter lined with a leather rail, so they should. Along with the champagne (£10-£12.50) and classic (£7.50-£9) varieties, there are two score or more original concoctions (£8-£9), prepared with immaculate precision. Diamond Geezer (Château du Breuil VSOP, apple schnapps and fresh green apple juice), the Exchange (Grey Goose l'Orange, apple schnapps and fruit juices), and Wild Diamond (Bacardi, Midori and lychee purée) appeal to a moneyed clientele. Lager-guzzling office juniors can sink their Stellas elsewhere: beer is kept to a minimum, bottled Asahi and Cobra at £4.50 each. The Iberian influence shines with the well-sourced tapas (roast whole piquillos de Lodosa from Navarre, £4.50; lomo de Teruel, £6) and wines (a Castillo de Clavijo rioja at £6 a glass or a Quinta de Covela rosé at £8 a glass).
Babies and children admitted (restaurant only). Disabled: toilet. Function rooms. Restaurant. Specialities (cocktails). **Map 6 Q6**.

Bow Wine Vaults

10 Bow Churchyard, EC4M 9DQ (7248 1121/www.motcombs.co.uk). Mansion House or Monument tube/Bank tube/DLR. **Open** 11am-11pm Mon-Fri. **Food served** noon-3pm Mon-Fri. **Credit** AmEx, DC, MC, V.
After a major makeover at the end of 2003, this bar, bistro and restaurant is a thoroughly smart place to do lunch or drinkies. The latter are best enjoyed at the back bar subtly divided from the bistro within the neat, wooden interior – although you'll also find continental chairs and tables set outside on the pedestrianised passage by St Mary le Bow church. You can stick to the acceptable house white or red (£3.50 a glass or £13.50 a bottle), but a quid or three extra will get a Chilean Château Los Boldos chardonnay or a rioja. To push the boat out, opt for a £30 1996 gran reserva rioja from the Bodegas Montecillo, or a £35 Montée de Tonnerre premier cru chablis, from the William Fèvre estate. Along with succulent sandwiches (prime Scotch fillet steak with French mustard, £5.95), there are Bow platters of various antipasti at £11.95 for two, or £15.95 for three.
Restaurant available for hire. Specialities (wines). Tables outdoors (30, pavement). TV (satellite). **Map 6 P6**.

Counting House

50 Cornhill, EC3V 3PD (7283 7123). Monument tube/Bank tube/DLR. **Open** 11am-11pm Mon-Fri. **Food served** noon-9pm Mon-Fri. **Credit** AmEx, DC, MC, V.
This absurdly ornate Fuller's pub was built as Prescott's Bank in 1893 by HC Boyes, who incorporated part of an old Roman basilica into the wall of the strong room. It passed through the hands of several banks – a memorial still stands by the grand main doors of staff who fell in the Great War – before housing the headquarters of NatWest from 1970 until a few years ago. Features include the mosaic floor, a whimsical mural by the imposing staircase, and far too many chandeliers. Shining like a beacon amid the besuited bustle and chatter, the imposing ground-floor island bar serves Chiswick, London Pride and ESB from the Fuller's stable, plus wines ranging from La Capitana merlot from Chile's Rapel Valley (£3.80 a glass) to a bottle of Domaine de Vauroux chablis at £17.95. Early-evening picking platters of Asian, Mediterranean and vegetarian food are a handy option, as are home-made ale-and-meat pies with puff pastry lids (£8), baguettes and sandwiches.
Disabled: toilet. Function room. Games (fruit machine). No-smoking area (lunchtime only). TV (big screen, digital). **Map 6 Q6**.

Crosse Keys

9 Gracechurch Street, EC3V 0DR (7623 4824/www.jdwetherspoon.co.uk). Monument or Bank tube. **Open** 10am-11pm Mon-Fri; 10am-7pm Sat. **Food served** 10am-10pm Mon-Fri; 10am-6pm Sat. **Credit** AmEx, MC, V.
In a setting more suited to the Thatcher Library scene in *Citizen Kane*, this vast, monolithic edifice is one of the more unusual members in the JD Wetherspoon chain. Sure, it has the same improbable beer prices – and, recently, welcome bottled additions from Namibia (Windhoek), Mexico (Negra Modelo) and Poland (Zywiec) – plus the same midweek curry clubs or steak nights you'd find in your local branch. But there's something unsettling about this cavern of a place, with its huge half-globe lamps, vast staircase leading to the downstairs washrooms and echoing voices. Located in a former bank, with imposing green marble pillars and rococo ceiling, the backdrop feels too grandiose for the humble requirement of providing £2 pints of San Miguel to sallow clerks and their suburban squeezes. It's too impersonal, too proper, too proud. Great place for a Rutger Hauer Guinness ad, all the same.
Disabled: toilet. Function rooms. Games (fruit machines, golf machine). No-smoking area. TV (big screen, digital). **Map 6 Q7**.

Hatchet

28 Garlick Hill, EC4V 2BA (7236 0720). Mansion House tube. **Open** 11am-10pm Mon, Tue; 11am-11pm Wed-Fri. **Food served** noon-2.30pm Mon-Fri. **Credit** MC, V.

Squeezed between a Burger King and a Benjy's, on the site of a medieval garlic market, the traditional, Irish-run Hatchet is a reminder of what pubs used to be. Ales on draught include Ruddles Smooth, Greene King IPA and Abbot, plus Scrumpy Jack and a couple of continental lagers (Beck's, Budvar) by the bottle; lunchtime food involves combinations of cod, scampi, chips and salad; pub games are no longer played, but are mounted and framed, just like the old prints of London; and racing takes pride of place on afternoon TV. The wine list is a simplified one of pinot grigio, sauvignon blanc and so on. It's all marvellously unpretentious, and attracts fewer idiots than some of the more laddish establishments nearby.
Games (fruit machine). TV. **Map 6 P7**.

Jamaica Wine House

St Michael's Alley (off Cornhill), EC3V 9DS (7929 6972/www.massivepub.com). Bank or Monument tube. **Open** 11am-11pm Mon-Fri. **Food served** 11am-3pm Mon-Fri. **Credit** AmEx, MC, V.
A Tups pub in the Massive chain, the 'Jampot' (as those rugby types like to call it) isn't your usual oval-ball-dominated sports bar. This one has history. It was built ('at the sign of Pasqua Rosee's Head') by servants of the England's first coffee merchant in 1652 as London's first coffee house, 'a place of commercial gambling, where the *Gazette* and the *Observator* lay generally unturned, where the lottery lists were alone perused'. Razed in the Great Fire, then rebuilt, it later became a meeting place for slave traders and plantation owners. Rebuilt again in 2002 in beautiful dark wood, it's divided into intimate spaces lined with banquettes, with a restaurant upstairs. Wines (rioja £4 a glass, pinot grigio £4.20) compete with draught ale (Bloomsbury, Greene King IPA, Bombardier) for suited custom, along with glasses of Moutard Carte d'Or bubbly (£6.50 a glass). Peculiarities include Somerset cider brandy at £3.60; lunch consists of the usual thick, meaty sandwiches.
Function room. Restaurant. **Map 6 Q6**.

Lamb Tavern

10-12 Leadenhall Market, EC3V 1LR (7626 2454). Monument tube/Bank tube/DLR. **Open** 11am-9pm Mon-Fri. **Food served** noon-2.30pm Mon-Fri. **Credit** AmEx, DC, MC, V.
'Established in 1780', this is the finest and most popular spot in the Leadenhall Market arcade. Although it occupies five floors, lunchtime space is at a premium on the main street-level floor, filled with employees from the nearby Lloyd's of London Building. Below is a wine cellar; immediately above, a modest mezzanine seating area, then a no-smoking floor, then a top-floor restaurant. Trading action takes place on the shop floor, with £5.50 bids quickly put in for roast rib of beef or roast loin of pork sandwiches, the regulars used to a little wait before the big lunchtime chomp. It's a Young's pub, so has their usual bitters and stouts – and it's beautifully photogenic (note the Christopher Wren tiled mural by the side door), so has been used as a backdrop for films starring John Wayne (*Brannigan*) and Robert Mitchum (*The Winds of War*).
Function room. Games (darts, fruit machine). No-smoking room. No piped music or jukebox. Tables outdoors (5, pavement). **Map 6 Q6**.

Leadenhall Wine Bar

27 Leadenhall Market, EC3V 1LR (7623 1818). Monument tube/Bank tube/DLR. **Open** 11.30am-11pm Mon-Fri. **Food served** 11.30am-10pm Mon-Fri. **Credit** AmEx, MC, V.
The colourful Moorish tiling designs (borrowed from Seville) that front the building and line the staircase to this first-floor venue give it away: this is a Spanish-style tapas restaurant, except that here you wait to be seated before perusing the somewhat standard selection of hot and cold dishes. The wine list is similarly (mainly) Spanish, and not especially cheap: a half-decent Castillo Clavijo rioja will cost you £6.50 a glass, or £17.95 a bottle; an equally acceptable Palena sauvignon blanc from Chile costs £5.75 a glass, £15.25 a bottle, while a standard bottle of Cristal cava is £17.95. The service is friendly enough, but tends to get swamped most lunchtimes. Still, the view of Sir Horace Jones' handiwork around the market arcades is always a treat.
Function room. Flamenco (7.30pm 1st Thur of mth; free). Restaurant. **Map 6 Q7**.

Ye Olde Watling

29 Watling Street, EC4M 9BR (7653 9971). Mansion House tube. **Open** 11am-11pm Mon-Fri. **Food served** noon-9pm Mon-Fri. **Credit** AmEx, MC, V.
Legends loom large in this low-ceilinged, wood-beamed boozer on the corner of Watling Street and Bow Lane. Its name and address embedded in Roman lore, its foundations set in a tangle of streets of Saxon origin, Ye Olde Watling was used as Sir Christopher Wren's drawing office when he was rebuilding St Paul's Cathedral. His workers would have enjoyed the ales that are available here today – Adnams, London Pride, Harveys and John Smith's – and the Aberdeen Angus burger (£6.45) and rump steak (£6.95) would have gone down a treat. Modern tastes and occasional female custom see five wines of each colour also available, such as a Chablis Laroche chardonnay (£3.40 a glass) and Rothbury Blue Label shiraz (£3). Meals can also be taken in the first-floor restaurant, where you might find more room than you will at street level amid the stooping white-collar employees on lunch break.
Babies and children admitted (restaurant). Function room. Games (fruit machines). Restaurant. Seating outdoors (courtyard). TVs (digital). **Map 6 P6**.

1 Lombard Street

1 Lombard Street, EC3V 9AA (7929 6611/www.1lombardstreet.com). Bank tube/DLR. **Open** 11am-11pm Mon-Fri. **Food served** 11.30am-10.30pm Mon-Fri.**Credit** AmEx, DC, JCB, MC, V.
Located diagonally opposite the Bank of England, this grand, neo-classical venue is as classy as it gets. Beneath Pietro Agostini's domed skylight, the circular bar dominates the main hall, around which spread brasserie tables, and behind which is the Michelin-starred restaurant of the same name. Lack of back-bar space allows for only a superb cocktail list as opposed to a stupendous one – but that in itself is a feat, as is charging just £6.50 for most of them. Head barman Francesco, previously of Isola and Shumi, pulls out all the stops as he conjures up a Hurricane (Bacardi Oro, Myer's rum, fresh papaya purée, apricot, dashes of angostura) from the mists of time, or a Negroni (gin, red vermouth, Campari) from Florence. House Martinis (£7) are made with Bombay gin and Wyborowa respectively, and prosecco, fresh basil and limoncello inform the 'All Year Round' varieties. The brasserie wine list is encyclopaedic and the tapas (£7-£10) exquisite.
Babies and children admitted (dining only). Disabled: lift; toilet. Function room. Music (pianist & singer, 6.30pm Mon, Fri; free). Restaurant (available for hire; no smoking). **Map 6 Q6**.

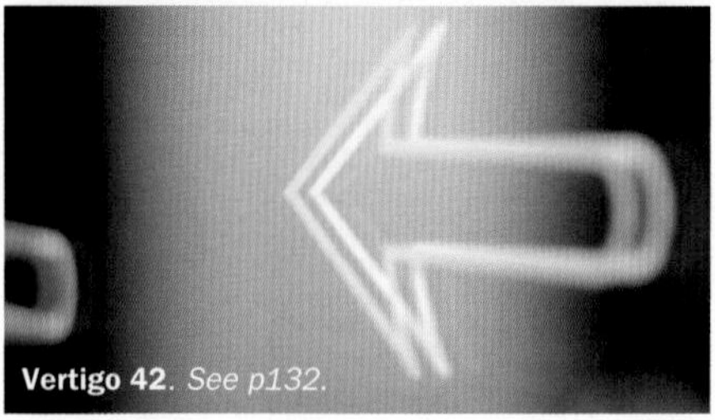

Vertigo 42. *See p132.*

Pacific Oriental

1 Bishopsgate, EC2N 3AQ (7621 9988/www.pacific oriental.co.uk). Monument tube/Bank tube/DLR/ Liverpool Street tube/rail. **Open** 11.30am-11pm Mon-Wed; 11am-1am Thur, Fri. **Food served** 11.45am-3pm, 6-9pm Mon-Fri. **Credit** AmEx, DC, MC, V.

By day, this clubby basement bar is a pan-Asian restaurant; bar snacks like pastry-wrapped king prawns (£7.95) and ginger chicken wings (£5.95) are available of an evening, too. After work, as a bar, it does a roaring trade, despite losing the gimmick of providing home-brewed beer (something went wrong with the brewing process months ago, though the copper vats are still there). Ignoring the Pacific pils and bitter on the drinks menu, nine-to-fivers seek solace in alcopoppy cocktails (£6.50) like a Japanese Slipper of tequila, Midori, lime and syrup, or a Kurrantita of Absolut Kurrant, tequila, Triple Sec and Crème de Cassis. Champagne varieties, like the Pacific Sunset of vodka, Chambord and fruit juices topped with champagne, or Absolut Chambulls of vodka and Red Bull topped with champagne, are £2 extra. If you can't be dealing with Red Bull on a cocktail menu (and who could blame you), the 20-strong wine list is at least affordable, with glasses of sauvignon blanc or cabernet sauvignon in the £3 range.

Babies and children admitted (restaurant). Disabled: toilet. Function rooms. Music (DJ 8.30pm Thur, Fri; free). Restaurant. Specialities (cocktails). TV (digital). **Map 6 Q6**.

Phoenix

26 Throgmorton Street, EC2N 2AN (7588 7289). Bank tube/DLR. **Open** 11am-11pm Mon-Fri. **Food served** noon-9pm Mon-Fri. **Credit** AmEx, MC, V.

A sturdy corner pub converted to suit modern mores, this post-work City trough calls itself 'A Pub with Atmosphere, not Smoke'. We noted the lack of smoke, but the atmosphere was less discernible. 'A Pub without Musical Pap' would be a start. Still, with its Sky Sports and News, rump steak mains (£8), hot roast beef sandwiches (£6) and admittedly decent ales, it suits middle management down to the ground – and it will be interesting to see what happens to trade once other nearby venues (particularly Wetherspoons', already lined up to go smoke-free) follow suit. For the time being, punters fall in two deep at the bar, holding out crisp Ayrtons for pints of Greene King IPA, Spitfire, Adnams or London Pride, or a glass of chablis (£5.45) or Chilean cabernet merlot (£4).

Disabled: toilet. Games (fruit machine). No-smoking. TVs (big screen, satellite).

Prism

147 Leadenhall Street, EC3V 4QT (7256 3888/www.harveynichols.com). Monument tube/Bank tube/DLR. **Open** *Bar* 11am-11pm Mon-Fri. *Lounge bar* 5-11pm Mon-Fri. **Food served** (bar) 11.30am-3pm, 6-10pm Mon-Fri. **Credit** AmEx, DC, JCB, MC, V.

Interesting venue, this one, one of half-a-dozen choice bar-restaurants in the Harvey Nichols chain. Pulling punters in serious numbers to a former Bank of New York building, just beyond the Leadenhall Market lunchtime and post-work magnet, was proving difficult, so Harvey Nick's brought in savvy staff from their booming operation at the Oxo Tower. Hey presto! Half the ground-floor restaurant turns clubby of an evening, with CDs of DJ mixes and a female-friendly atmosphere, and the drinks menu has been souped up considerably. Standard champagne cocktails (£8) are mixed with Ketel One and Seriously, Martinis (£8-£9.50) with Belvedere and other high-end spirits. Wines, ten each by the bottle, six each by the glass, feature rarer finds such as a Gavi La Minaia from Nicola Bergaglio of Piedmont (£6 a bottle) and even the bottled beers include Anchor Steam, Peroni Gran Riserva and Black Sheep. If successful, this clubby upgrade could catch on – quickly.

Disabled: toilet. Function rooms. Restaurant. Specialities (cocktails). **Map 5 R4**.

Swan Tavern

Ship Tavern Passage, 77-80 Gracechurch Street, EC3V 1LY (7283 7712). Monument tube/Bank tube/DLR. **Open** 11am-11pm Mon-Fri. **Food served** noon-2pm Mon-Fri. **Credit** AmEx, MC, V.

Its name writ large over the gateway to a courtyard that's really a cul-de-sac, this Fuller's pub has one star feature: the sleek, black marble-topped Ale Bar, full on our visit with men in suits; half a dozen seemed plenty to fill what claims to be the smallest bar in the City. The first-floor

Swan Bar extends over the gateway without appearing much larger. On our visit, the place was busy with blokes (just one person in a skirt), but our amiable host was well equipped for quiet nights, with a bijou library of dictionaries and fact-books to help him untangle the crossword. The attractive wooden bar puts Chiswick, London Pride and Deuchars alongside your usual draught beers. Some disconcerting display-plates (putting us in mind of narrow boats) and a hearth add character. A small telly shows sport, with the sound charitably turned down. Downstairs can close quite early of an evening, so don't get too settled.
No piped music or jukebox. TV. **Map 6 Q7**.

Throgmorton's

27a Throgmorton Street, EC2N 2AN (7588 5165). Bank tube/DLR/Liverpool Street tube/rail. **Open** noon-11pm Mon-Fri. **Food served** noon-3pm, 6-10pm Mon-Fri. **Credit** AmEx, MC, V.

After the bombastic wrought-iron and gold-lettered name over its entrance, Throgmorton's seems more like a comfortable hotel lobby than a gentlemen's club once you're inside. Starting life in 1900 as J Lyons & Co's flagship restaurant, the building reopened in summer 2004 as a combination deli, restaurant and series of bars, connected by an impressive staircase. It comes complete with caged goods lift, extraordinarily alien globular chandeliers and a fabulous liveried golden mosaic shimmering up the wall. Two floors down, the bar in the Oak Room (pool, table football, tellies mounted among the wooden panels) was closed, so we fetched up in the Mosaic Room Cocktail Bar on a pink sofa beside a portable heater. The spirit selection showed an eye for detail (Pitù, Plymouth gin) without seeming compendious. Of decent draught options, a nice pint of Speckled Hen was the only ale currently on. Peppery cheese straws (£1.50), however, were top-notch.
Babies and children admitted (restaurant). Bar available for hire (weekends). Games (billiards, quiz machine, table football). Restaurant. TVs (satellite). **Map 5 R4**.

Williamson's Tavern

1 Groveland Court, off Bow Lane, EC4M 9EH (7248 5750). Mansion House tube. **Open** 11am-11pm Mon-Fri. **Food served** noon-9pm Mon-Fri. **Credit** AmEx, MC, V.

Occupying most of the Groveland Court alleyway, this historic Nicholson's pub covers three main spaces. At the far end, guarded by wrought iron gates donated by William and Mary, stand two bar spaces: the lower (Martha's Bar) is a comfortable leather-sofa affair, hired out for private dos; the main, beside a row of terrace tables and a set of steps, comprises a wooden interior with stylish leather banquettes, a fireplace with original Roman brickwork, and old lanterns. Ale taps dominate the curved bar counter, of Deuchar's IPA, Harveys, Adnams and London Pride, while the food on offer is suitably manly: filled Yorkshire puddings, Oxford recipe sausages, and meat and chicken platters. Bottled Beck's and Budvar, and draught Addleston's cider provide alternatives for non-ale drinkers. So, amid all this tradition, who was Williamson? Robert, in fact, who bought this property, once the Lord Mayor's, in 1753 and transformed it into a hotel.
Function room. Games (fruit machine, golf machine). TV. **Map 6 P6**.

Also in the area...

All Bar One 103 Cannon Street, EC4N 5AD (7220 9031); 34 Threadneedle Street, EC2R 8AY (7614 9931).
Balls Brothers Bucklersbury House, Budge Row, EC4N 8EL (7248 7557); King's Arms Yard, EC2R 7AD (7796 3049); Minster Court, Mincing Lane, EC3R 7PP (7283 2838); 2 St Mary at Hill, EC3R 8EE (7626 0321).
Bangers Too (Davy's) 1 St Mary at Hill, EC3R 8EE (7283 4443).
City Flogger (Davy's) Fen Court, 120 Fenchurch Street, EC3M 5BA (7623 3251).
City FOB (Davy's) Lower Thames Street, EC3R 6DJ (7621 0619).
City Tup 66 Gresham Street, EC2V 7BB (7606 8176).
Corney & Barrow 16 Royal Exchange, EC3V 3LP (7929 3131); 1 Leadenhall Place, EC3M 7DX (7621 9201); 2B Eastcheap, EC3M 1AB (7929 3220); 12-14 Mason's Avenue, EC2V 5BT (7726 6030).
Fine Line 1 Bow Churchyard, EC4M 9PQ (7248 3262); Equitable House, 1 Monument Street, EC3R 8BG (7623 5446).
Green Man (JD Wetherspoon) 1 Poultry, EC2R 8EJ (7248 3529).
Heeltap & Bumper (Davy's) 2-6 Cannon Street, EC4M 6XX (7248 3371).
Jamaica Wine House (Tup) St Michael's Alley, off Cornhill, EC3V 9DS (7929 6972).
Jamies 54 Gresham Street, EC2V 7BB (7606 1755); 13 Philpot Lane, EC3M 8AA (7621 9577); 107-112 Leadenhall Street, EC3A 4AA (7626 7226); 5 Groveland Court, EC4M 9EH (7248 5551).
Liberty Bounds (JD Wetherspoon) 15 Trinity Square, EC3N 4AA (7481 0513).
Number 25 (Jamies) 25 Birchin Lane, EC3V 9DJ (7623 2505).
O'Neill's 65 Cannon Street, EC4N 5AA (7653 9951).
Pitcher & Piano 28-31 Cornhill, EC3V 3ND (7929 3989).
Pitcher & Piano Calico House, 67-69 Watling Street, EC4M 9DD (7248 0883).
Slug & Lettuce 25 Bucklersbury, EC4N 8DA (7329 6222).

TOWER HILL & ALDGATE

The area betweent the river, Bishopsgate and Whitechapel is currently at the halfway point between the old East End and its new role as southern extremity of the financial district. Bangladeshi restaurateurs and slick corporate pub companies are falling over themselves for their share of the area's leisure cash, while, to the south, St Katharine's Docks show how far you can go to chase the tourist dollar.

Bar 38 Minories

St Clare House, 30-33 The Minories, EC3N 1DY (7702 0470). Aldgate or Tower Hill tube/Tower Gateway DLR. **Open** 11am-11pm Mon-Fri. **Food served** 11am-10pm Mon-Fri. **Happy hour** 3-8pm Mon-Fri. **Credit** AmEx, DC, MC, V.

Bar 38 has had something of a makeover: chrome remains prominent, as does purple paintwork, but the former dark grey has been swapped for a lighter variety and the seating arrangements have been transformed. Chunky black settees

and armchairs around low wooden tables now provide a more intimate setting, and low-level music keeps the mood just so. Backlighting is still de rigueur, and the glass front of the establishment offers the same gawp potential. At the time of our visit, a new menu was being prepared to complement an alcohol range that has seen drastic price reductions, with draught lagers at £1.75 a pint. There are shooters and pitchers, and two-for-a-fiver cocktails available from 3pm to 8pm; wine drinkers are also catered for, an Aussie shiraz or a Fouassier sancerre being just two of the options.
Disabled: lift; toilet. Music (DJ 8pm Fri; free). Venue for hire (Sat only). TVs (big screen, digital). **Map 6 R7**.

Crutched Friar

39-41 Crutched Friars, EC3N 2AE (7264 0041). Tower Hill tube/Tower Gateway DLR. **Open** 11am-11pm Mon-Fri. **Food served** 11am-9pm Mon-Fri. **Credit** AmEx, MC, V.

Wend your way past smokers, exiled from their offices, to the sanctuary of the Crutched Friar. Beneath a copious skylight, besuited gentlemen quaff pints of Kronenbourg, Carling and IPA at the bar; to the left is a dining area where late lunchtime punters graze on the likes of gammon, egg and chips, washed down with an Argentine or Italian red wine; a South African chenin blanc or a NZ sauvignon blanc are among the white wines on offer. The brighter hues of yore have been replaced by subdued grey-greens and cream, although the new red soft seating along the length of wall, leading to a cosily intimate section to the left of the main entrance, adds welcome vibrancy. Across from this, to further compound smokers' persecution complexes, is a recently refurbished no-smoking area.
Disabled: toilet. No-smoking area. Tables outdoors (3 patio; 7 garden). TV. **Map 6 R7**.

Dickens Inn

St Katharine's Way, E1W 1UH (7488 2208). Tower Hill tube/Tower Gateway DLR. **Open** 11am-11pm Mon-Sat; noon-10.30pm Sun. **Food served** noon-4pm Mon-Fri; noon-6pm Sat, Sun. **Credit** AmEx, DC, MC, V.

A three-storey architectural curiosity, the Dickens Inn looks as though it has come all the way from 18th-century Rotterdam rather than the 70m it actually travelled. Confused? In 1976, this former spice warehouse was put on wheels and shifted from the obscure part of the river it had occupied since 1795 to this more tourist-friendly location. The top two floors have been helpfully branded the Grill on the Dock and the Pizza on the Dock to avoid confusion. Inside the bar and restaurant below, it's barrels and maritime paraphernalia and forehead-endangering timbers galore. But the clientele – desk-surfers and tourists in the main – are resolutely unperturbed, content to order from the unchallenging range of on-tap and bottled beers. Draught Coors, and a Belgian Gulpener worth the price-induced wince, are also on offer.
Babies and children admitted: high chairs; nappy-changing facilities. Disabled: toilet. Function room. Games (fruit machine, quiz machine). Tables outdoors (20, garden). TV (widescreen). **Map 6 R7**.

Old Dispensary

19A Leman Street, E1 8EN (7702 1406). Aldgate or Aldgate East tube. **Open** 11am-11pm Mon-Fri. **Food served** 11am-3pm Mon; 11am-3pm, 5.30-9pm Tue-Fri. **Credit** AmEx, DC, MC, V.

High of ceiling, with light wood abounding and dark-green painted metal pillars throughout, this current incarnation of the former charitable dispensary no longer caters for just the sick and poor. At the end of the small bar, where draught Ridley's Rumpus and Tolly Original beckon, with bottles of Duvel and Edett cooling on fridge shelves behind, a sobriety-testing cast-iron staircase spirals up to a raised area. Here, below circular skylights, a handful of tables overlook the Sky Sports-bathed, solid wooden booths of the main bar area below. Standard hearty grub is available at lunchtimes; whites range from £11.45 for a bottle of pinot grigio to just under £25 for a sancerre, with the most expensive red being a £23.95 St Emilion. Intimacy fans and mobile phone junkies have the option of a cosy side room.
Babies and children admitted. Function room. Games (golf machine). No-smoking area. TV (widescreen, digital).

Poet

82 Middlesex Street, E1 7EZ (7422 0000). Liverpool Street tube/rail. **Open** 11am-11pm Mon-Fri. **Food served** 5-9pm Mon; noon-3pm, 5-9pm Tue-Fri. **Credit** AmEx, DC, MC, V.

If the beady glare from the bust of the Bard facing the doorway doesn't grab your attention as you enter the Poet, the blazing red background of the cartoon London-scape on the wall opposite probably will. Elsewhere, dark plum reigns in the paintwork and seating arrangements of this spacious yet cosy establishment, where the staff are as welcoming as the draught 1664 Weiss beer is welcome. Bitburger, Adnams and Ridleys, are also present at the pumps. The wine list is concise but with enough options to accompany tomato and basil soup, lamb's liver and bacon with buttered mash, and mandarin cheesecake from the blackboard menu.
Babies and children admitted (until 5pm). Bar available for hire. Disabled: toilet. TV (satellite). **Map 6 R6**.

White Swan

21 Alie Street, E1 8DA (7702 0448). Aldgate tube/ Tower Gateway DLR. **Open** 11am-11pm Mon-Fri. **Food served** noon-3pm Mon-Fri. **Credit** AmEx, MC, V.

As befits a clean and simple establishment that provides quality beers and nourishing grub, this welcoming side-street Shepherd Neame pub is chock-a-block with office bods of a lunchtime, tucking in to fairly priced bangers 'n' mash or home-made beef and sundried tomato burgers, accompanied by an Early Bird Spring Hop ale or a bottle of Budvar or Asahi. Others sip from glasses of Chilean merlot or Aussie chardonnay, then head for the sprawl-on-me leather settee and armchairs in the larger of the two downstairs sections; an upstairs function room caters for any diner overspill. Kiwi landlady Sally Perkins won the brewery's most recent Manager of the Year award.
Function room. Games (fruit machine). TV (satellite).

Also in the area...

All Bar One 16 Byward Street, EC3R 5BA (7553 0301).
Corney & Barrow 37A Jewry Street, EC3N 2EX (7680 8550).
Fine Line 124-127 The Minories, EC3N 1NT (7481 8195).
Habit & New Waterloo Room Friary Court, 65 Crutched Friars, EC3N 2NP (7481 1131).
Hog's Head 171-176 Aldersgate Street, EC1A 4JA (7600 5852); 1 America Square, EC3N 2LS (7702 2381).
Jamies 2-5 The Minories, EC3N 1BJ (7481 1779); 119-121 The Minories, EC3N 1DR (7709 9900).
Pitcher & Piano The Arches, 9 Crutched Friars, EC3N 2AU (7480 6818).

EAST

EAST

BETHNAL GREEN

Bethnal Green's drinkers are split down the middle. The original residents go for the various no-frills boozers: scary places where England flags are aggressively displayed and the music really does stop when a stranger walks in. But where newer locals once went to less intimidating environs, they no longer have to. The area has hip restaurant Bistrotheque with its hip **Napoleon Bar**, and other new establishments have also opened – the agreeable **Redchurch**, for example. And it would be a mistake to lump a traditional drinking den like the **Sebright Arms** in with other rougher hostelries when it has charm by the bucket load.

Approach Tavern

47 Approach Road, E2 9LY (8980 2321). Bethnal Green tube/rail. **Open** noon-11pm Mon-Sat; noon-10.30pm Sun. **Food served** noon-2.30pm, 6-9.30pm Mon-Fri; noon-9.30pm Sat; noon-4.30pm Sun. **Credit** MC, V.

The Approach is a comfortable, pretty and well-organised pub – it's under the same ownership as the popular Prince George and Royal Inn on the Park (for both, *see p151*), in Hackney. The bar room is heavy with dark wood, handsome with etched glass, and perked up with tea lights on tables and fresh flowers over the fireplace. Our last visit found excellent Fuller's beers on tap – Pride, Chiswick, ESB, Jack Frost – plus Zubr and Litovel lagers, both Czech. The food is great: the £6 Approach brunch appeared in minutes and was delicious; we could also have tried roast rib of beef with parsnips, nachos, or potato wedges with mayonnaise. There was a busy hum as couples, bohos, students, very grown-ups and barely grown-ups with parents did their boozing and eating. The pub is entered through a seasonally tented beer garden, paved but surrounded by plenty of foliage. Jake Miller's highly praised art gallery is on the first floor.

Art gallery (noon-6pm Wed-Sun). Babies and children welcome. Quiz (8.30pm Tue; £1). Specialities (Czech lagers). Tables outdoors (6, garden; 9, heated terrace). TV.

Florist

255 Globe Road, E2 0JD (8981 1100/www.theflorist E2.co.uk). Bethnal Green tube/rail/8 bus. **Open** 2.30-11pm Mon-Sat; 12.30-10pm Sun. **Food served** 2.30-9pm Mon-Sat; 12.30-9pm Sun. **Credit** MC, V.

After a lovely, sensitive conversion a couple of years back, the Florist is happily holding its own at the top end of Bethnal Green's Roman Road. Burgundy walls, battered sofas and an etched-glass mirror add to its pubby, down-at-heel charm. Beers are limited to a few on tap and a few more by the bottle, but the cocktails are top-notch (£5; £6 for champagne varieties) and the Spanish tapas are some of the best going. The crowd is predominantly local, friendly and mixed. On Monday nights, a DJ plays fine blues and soul, and at weekends there are papers to browse, coffees to sip and chilling to be done.

Games (backgammon, chess). Music (DJs 8pm daily; open decks 8pm Tue; free). Tables outdoors (2, pavement).

Napoleon Bar

23-27 Wadeson Street, E2 9DR (8983 7900/ www.bistrotheque.com). Bethnal Green tube/rail. **Open** 5.30pm-midnight Mon-Sat; 5.30-11pm Sun. **Food served** (restaurant) 6-10.30pm Mon-Sat; 1-10.30pm Sun. **Credit** AmEx, MC, V.

Down a deserted-looking cobbled street off Mare Street, Bistrotheque is a classy bar-restaurant that offers a great drinking experience for Hackney folk who can't be bothered to schlep down to Hoxton. It's a handsome place, with bare brick walls, twinkling chandeliers and glass wall sconces; an authentic etched-glass mirror hangs on dark wood panelling behind the bar. Service is friendly and efficient, bar staff serving anything from pints of draught Kronenbourg (£3.30) to bottles of wine (chenin blanc, say, at £13.50). But cocktails are what to order here: a short list includes the ubiquitous Bramble (Dick Bradsell's masterpiece, £6.50) as well as old faves Negroni, Mojito and Sidecar. The restaurant located above the bar has had mixed reviews, but was superb when we visited. The crowd is usually interesting and less self-conscious than you'd find in Hoxton. Beside the bar there's a cabaret venue where we noticed a man fiddling with a wax torso and many blonde bubble wigs.

Babies and children welcome (restaurant). Disabled: toilet. Music (cabaret 9pm Wed-Sat; £3-£7). Restaurant. Specialities (cocktails). Tables outdoors (3, courtyard).

Pleasure Unit

359 Bethnal Green Road, E2 6LG (7729 0167/ www.pleasureunitbar.com). Bethnal Green tube/rail/ 8 bus. **Open/food served** 6pm-midnight Mon-Thur, Sun; 6pm-2am Fri, Sat. **Credit** MC, V.

Formerly the Cock & Comfort, the corner bar Pleasure Unit sounds like somewhere you'd expect find Woody Allen – in *Everything You Always Wanted to Know About Sex* mode. In fact, there's a totally retro feel to this place – purple walls, disco balls, psychedelic lights tripping slowly across the ceiling. Then there's the Vespa that sits beside the DJ box. Live music (of varying quality, but always enthusiastic) is often a feature, and DJs play on several nights. The hottest ticket is the once-monthly Shake (northern soul and underground). Drinks are cheap, the crowd is up for it – and, let that's face it, that's enough to make this bar the best thing along the Bethnal Green Road.

Music (bands 8pm daily; club nights Fri-Sat; £3-£5).

Soma. *See p145.*

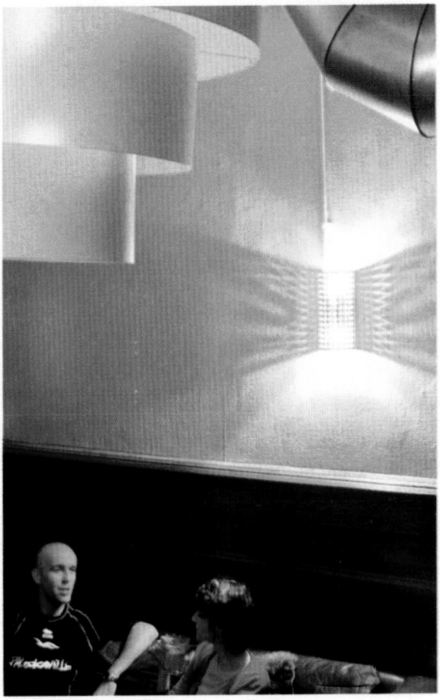

Redchurch

107 Redchurch Street, E2 7DL (7729 8333). Liverpool Street tube/rail then 8 bus. **Open/food served** noon-midnight Mon-Thur, Sun; noon-2am Fri, Sat. **Credit** AmEx, MC, V.

The latest groovy establishment in the area, the Redchurch has wooden floors, 1970s retro plastic swivel chairs and leatherette bar stools. The atmosphere is a little smoky, but the friendly mixed crowd is oblivious to this – they don't even mind sharing a washbasin outside the toilets. The highlights of the Session on Sunday (6pm-midnight) are decent breakfasts and DJs playing Marvin Gaye and Pharcyde; midweek, mellow bluegrass holds sway. Drinks are a treat, including 26 beers and ciders, rums from Cuba, Jamaica, Barbados and Bermuda, Polish vodkas, and gins from Russia and France (all £2.50-£3 a shot). Beers on tap include Maisels' Weisse, German wheat beer and Sierra Nevada pale ale. There's a long list of cocktails (£5.50), plus Choya plum wine, coffees, hot chocolates, builders' tea (£1) and 25 non-alcoholic cold drinks. Food is Spanish-based and uses ingredients from local organic suppliers.

Babies and children welcome. Disabled: toilet. Music (DJs 9pm Fri, Sat; 6pm Sun; free). Specialities (cocktails, continental beers).

Sebright Arms

34 Coate Street, E2 9AG (7729 0937). Bethnal Green tube/rail/Cambridge Heath rail/55 bus. **Open** noon-11pm Mon-Wed, Sun; noon-midnight Thur; noon-2am Fri, Sat. **Food served** noon-4pm Mon-Fri, Sun. **Credit** AmEx, MC, V.

Sebright Passage is a worthy contender for London's most forbidding thoroughfare, but brave this dark alley off Hackney Road and you'll be rewarded with a unique East End experience. The Sebright Arms is a palace of red velvet banquettes, wood panelling, stained glass and framed photos of Frank Sinatra and Dean Martin. You don't come here for what's offered at the bar, which is regular brewery product, but rather for the feel of the place. Cabaret artists perform on a stage framed by gold tasselled curtains, singing along to MP3s played from a laptop, watched by East End characters the likes of which the Queen Vic can only dream of. An added bonus is the outdoor seating area, perfect for old-fashioned Sunday lunchtime slap-ups in the summer. We recommend the fish 'n' chips. Luvverly.

Babies and children admitted (restaurant). Function room. Games (darts, fruit machine, pool table). Music (bands 9.30pm Fri, Sat; 3.30pm Sun). Restaurant. Tables outdoors (5, courtyard).

BOW & MILE END

Bow and Mile End may still be the nether-land between the fashionable East End and the wilder expanses of east London, but drinking options are getting better and better. Not so long ago there wasn't much apart from blokey estate boozers and drink-till-you-snog student faithfuls, but now several pubs here could hold their own in the more competitive zones of central London. That the gastro flag is flown in different styles by the **Crown**, **Morgan Arms** and **L'Oasis** hasn't (yet) sounded the death knell for straightforward fag-and-a-pint pubs; places like the **Palm Tree** and the **Bow Bells** continue to ply their trade in a reassuringly old-fashioned style.

Bow Bells

116 Bow Road, E3 3AA (8981 7317). Bow Road tube/ Docklands DLR. **Open** 11am-11pm Mon-Sat; noon-10.30pm Sun. **Food served** 11.30am-2.45pm Mon-Fri. **No credit cards**.

Were the rest of the pub world not going gastro or late licence, the Bow Bells' L-shaped single room could be the archetype for London boozers. There's a small selection of nicely priced, well-kept real ales (Fuller's Pride, an excellent pint of Brakspear and – off for the evening of our visit – Young's Bitter), a pool table, a CD jukebox, a pull-down screen and corner relay TVs, and blackboards advertising pub food of the sort that doesn't need translation. The unpleasantly vivid orange of the exterior belies some nice interior details (metal poles supporting the bar are twisted like Brighton rock) and some baffling ones (a judge's wig in a case, flanked by a photo of an East End boxer and a Victorian cocoa ad). The theme? Englishness, at a guess. The couple of local coves, lecturers slowly drinking halves and gaggle of boisterous sub-20s here didn't seem to care.

Function room. Games (darts, fruit machines, pool table). Entertainment (DJs/karaoke 8.30pm Fri; Elvis 8.30pm last Sat of mth; free). Quiz (9pm Wed; free). Tables outdoors (3, pavement). TVs (big screen, satellite).

Coborn Arms

8 Coborn Road, E3 2DA (8980 3793). Bow Road or Mile End tube. **Open** 11am-11pm Mon-Sat; noon-10.30pm Sun. **Food served** noon-2pm, 6-9pm Mon-Fri; 1-9pm Sat, Sun. **Credit** MC, V.

The Coborn Arms calls itself 'The pub in Bow with all the charms', before bragging about its plasma TV. More enticing, perhaps, are the two dartboards in a side room and, on a summer's day, the roadside beer garden. The roomy interior is a little too bright, and the spanking-clean pale-green upholstery is not to everyone's taste – but staff are accommodating and the clientele, whether suited or tracksuited, are salt of the earth. Disappointingly for a Young's pub, only the Bitter and Special were on draught, but a vast selection of the brewery's bottled output (Double Chocolate Stout, anyone?) and a wine list on each table should keep everyone happy. While the Morgan Arms (*see p144*), just a minute down the road, will capture aspirational drinkers, the Coborn Arms does an unspectacular job well.

Disabled: toilet. Games (darts, fruit machine, golf machine). Tables outdoors (6, patio). TV (big screen, satellite).

Crown

223 Grove Road, E3 5SN (8981 9998/www.singhboulton.co.uk). Mile End tube/277 bus. **Open** 5-11pm Mon; noon-11pm Tue-Sat; noon-10.30pm Sun. **Food served** 6-10.30pm daily. **Credit** MC, V.

If *Guardian* readers were an endangered species, the Crown would be their protected habitat. Lack of music or TV makes for studious newspaper reading, and the pub soothes the conscience with quality organic food and booze (Pitfield's Shoreditch Stout and SB, Freedom Organic Lager, a blackboard each of reds and whites). You can even buy Natural American Spirit cigs. Blackboards detail the pub's food policy along with the day's fodder; pinboards advertise art expos, yoga and babysitter requirements, giving the place a community feel. After lunch, the hip families melt away with their well-behaved babies, and things can quieten down too much. But this

East

is a handsome place; the gastro norm mix-and-match is enhanced by cut-glass door panes, a mosaic entrance and a wrought-iron 'Saloon Bar' sign over the front door. Bear the upstairs dining room in mind if things get busy: it serves the same menu at the same prices as downstairs, but with table service.
Babies and children welcome; high chairs. Disabled: toilet. Function room. No piped music or jukebox. No-smoking area (restaurant). Restaurant available for hire. Tables outdoors (8, terrace; 5, balcony).

Greenwich Pensioner
2 Bazely Street, E14 0ES (7987 4414/ www.thegreenwichpensioner.com). All Saints DLR. **Open/food served** noon-11pm Mon-Fri; 5-11pm Sat; noon-10.30pm Sun. **Credit** AmEx, MC, V.
Until very recently, this small pub close to the Blackwall Tunnel was probably a downtrodden spot that served the residents of the insalubrious estate that surrounds it – if, indeed, it served anyone at all. But a wildly unlikely renovation has replaced sticky carpet with stripped floorboards, scuzzy barstools with sofas and fluffy white cushions, greasy ashtrays with pink coffee tables, jukebox Sinatra with high-energy house and the dartboard with a huge Roy Lichtenstein. It's all extremely, entertainingly unlikely, though the impact is lessened by a feeble selection of drinks (John Smith's bitter, Guiness, Stella and a few bottled lagers) that can't have changed much since the pub's previous incarnation. The pan-global food menu takes in fish and chips, chicken gnocchi, lamb balti and Thai green curry. A deeply curious place.
Disabled: toilet. Music (karaoke 7-11pm Tue; free). Specialities (cocktails). Tables outdoors (4, pavement).

Half Moon
213-223 Mile End Road, E1 4AA (7790 6810). Stepney Green tube. **Open** 10am-11pm Mon-Sat; 10am-10.30pm Sun. **Food served** 10am-10pm Mon-Sat; 10am-9.30pm Sun. **Credit** AmEx, DC, MC, V.
Being a JD Wetherspoon pub, the Half Moon provides cheap so-so beer (Carling £1.59, Guinness and San Miguel £1.99) and cheap fine beer (Ridleys Rumpus, Marston's Burton Bitter and Pedigree, Harviestoun Bitter & Twisted, Ambree De Koninck, Courage Directors), plus a decent-enough wine list (prices start at £6 a bottle). The food is cheap and cheerful; there's no music. The building, though, sets this Wetherspoon's apart. The usually rather tatty smoking bar was a Welsh Methodist chapel, then a socialist theatre; that theatre's extension is now a big, bright, glass-walled non-smoking bar that looks out on an ample beer garden. The crowd in non-smoking comprises extended families and the kind of single old man who puts on his best suit to have a half of bitter. Students and wizened old fellers, schooling themselves with the *Racing Post*, occupy the smoking half.
Babies and children welcome to eat (until 8.30pm). Disabled: toilet. No piped music or jukebox. No-smoking area. Tables outdoors (8, garden). TV (digital).

Morgan Arms
43 Morgan Street, E3 5AA (8980 6389/ www.geronimo-inns.co.uk). Mile End tube. **Open** noon-11pm Mon-Sat; noon-10.30pm Sun. **Food served** noon-3pm, 7-10pm Mon-Sat. **Credit** MC. V.
We're beginning to tire of rags-to-riches pub conversions, but the transformation of the Morgan into a stylish, spacious gastropub deserves applause. It remains relaxingly pub-like despite Sunday-supplement touches (things made of rushes or dried flowers, a triptych painting of chillies and garlic). The food – gastro-crusted this, with-pancetta that – is good without being exceptional, and the punters are posh enough to suit an unexpectedly handsome portion of Bow. The draught options are adequate (Timothy Taylor Landlord, Adnams Bitter, San Miguel, Bitburger, Kronenbourg 1664, Hoegaarden) and the wine list is broad and nicely organised. Bar snacks are served until closing time: tasty olives and bread were £4.50, but big enough to share. Fairy lights around the windows make the Morgan welcoming from the street, its cosiness enhanced by little lamps on the windowsills with camp diamanté shades. There's a walled beer garden to one side.
Babies and children welcome (dining only). Tables outdoors (11, garden; 4, pavement).

New Globe
359 Mile End Road, E3 4QS (8980 6689). Mile End tube. **Open** noon-midnight Mon-Wed, Sat; noon-2am Thur, Fri; noon-10.30pm Sun. **Food served** noon-3pm Mon-Fri; noon-4pm Sat; noon-2.30pm Sun. **Admission** £2 after 11pm Thur-Sat. **Credit** AmEx, JCB, MC, V.
The New Globe's pricing and plainness of decor point to a rowdy student clientele; pale wood tables and blue café-style chairs leave plenty of breathing space, while bouncers stop things getting out of hand on Thursday and Friday nights. Sensibly doubling as a kind of afternoon café, the place serves solid, keenly priced food (a bacon and avocado salad special with garlic mayo, £4; chips or a bowl of olives, £1), with tea or coffee costing a quid (fancy coffees £1.20). There's nothing remarkable on draught (of three hand pumps for ale, only Pride was available; Stella, Carlsberg and XXXX are the lagers), but exotic shooters and WKD hit the target crowd. A lunchtime visit saw businesslike, middle-aged men in shirtsleeves alongside a table of students embarking on an afternoon bender. Down a metal staircase outside is a series of fixed benches and tables – in pretty poor repair, but right beside the canal.
Games (fruit machine). Music (acoustic night Mon; DJs Thur, Fri). Tables outdoors (3, canalside).

L'Oasis
237 Mile End Road, E1 4AA (7702 7051/ www.loasisstepney.co.uk). Stepney Green tube. **Open** noon-11pm Mon-Sat; noon-10.30pm Sun. **Food served** noon-3pm, 5-9.30pm Mon-Fri; noon-9.30pm Sat, Sun. **Credit** MC, V.
L'Oasis doesn't do anything particularly unusual, but what it does, it does well. The decor is – of course – stripped wood and blackboards, but the clientele is impressively mixed for an area where students, locals and middle-class incomers often sup apart. The draught choices (Timothy Taylor Landlord and Adnams Bitter, Addlestone's Cloudy Cider, Pilsner Urquell and Hoegaarden) are excellent; they're supported by a fine pick of bottled beers (Paulaner, Früli, Nastro Azzurro, Bockstein and Leffe). There's also a decent wine list and, in an alcove behind the long wooden bar, a terrific selection of whisky, whiskey and bourbon. Food, cooked in the open kitchen at the back, includes monkfish wrapped in parma ham, and char-grilled calf's liver with onion mash, along with all-day breakfasts; we reckon the cooking has recently moved up a notch. There are newspapers for the solitary, and an accommodating hubbub for the sociable.
Disabled: toilet.

CRITICS' PICKS

For beers and ales
Birkbeck Tavern (*see p152*), **Black Bull** (*see p157*), **Coborn Arms** (*see p143*), **Crown** (*see p143*), **Dove Freehouse** (*see p150*), **King Edward VII** (*see p156*), **Nag's Head** (*see p156*), **Pride of Spitalfields** (*see p158*), **Prince George** (*see p151*), **Princess of Wales** (*see p146*).

For cocktails
Florist (*see p140*), **Jazz Bar Dalston** (*see p151*), **Napoleon Bar** (*see p140*).

For the strong stuff
L'Oasis (whisky; *see left*), **Redchurch** (gin, rum, vodka; *see p143*).

For wine
Nag's Head (*see p156*), **Via Fossa** (*see p148*).

For sheer style
Lane (*see p158*), **Marie Lloyd Bar** (*see p151*), **Napoleon Bar** (*see p140*), **291** (*see p151*).

For some open sky
Approach Tavern (*see p140*), **Nag's Head** (*see p156*), **Princess of Wales** (*see p146*), **Vibe Bar** (*see p158*).

For a blast from the past
Ferry House (*see p147*), **Flower Pot** (*see p156*), **Grapes** (*see p153*), **Half Moon** (*see left*), **Palm Tree** (*see right*), **Prospect of Whitby** (*see p156*), **Town of Ramsgate** (*see p157*).

For fun and games
Black Lion (pool; *see p154*), **Prince George** (board games, pool, quiz; *see p151*), **Royal Inn on the Park** (board games, quiz; *see p151*).

For real fires
Blind Beggar (*see p157*), **Ferry House** (*see p147*), **Gun** (*see p148*), **Princess of Wales** (*see p146*), **Sir Alfred Hitchcock Hotel** (*see p152*), **Wellington** (*see p152*), **William IV** (*see p152*).

For good food
Approach Tavern (*see p140*), **Gun** (*see p148*), **Cat & Mutton** (*see p150*), **King Edward VII** (*see p156*).

For the sound of music
Big Chill Bar (*see p157*), **Florist** (*see p140*), **Jazz Bar Dalston** (*see p151*), **Pleasure Unit** (*see p140*), **Sebright Arms** (*see p143*), **Vibe Bar** (*see p158*).

Palm Tree
127 Grove Road, E3 5BH (8980 2918). Mile End tube/ 8, 25 bus. **Open** noon-late (last admission 10.45pm) daily. **No credit cards.**

You couldn't make this pub up: everything about the place is a dream. The cash register is a 1950s antique, the gold wallpaper looks even older, and many of the regulars are equally valuable period pieces. There's a drum kit and piano on a small stage in one corner, and in the evenings twinkly eyed would-be Sinatras show their wives they've still got the old magic. The bar serves Boddingtons, guest beers (when we visited it was Dick Turpin's Coach Horse) and Stowford Press cider, plus any spirit you can name and a few you can't. Situated in the middle of Mile End Park and with no surrounding hedge or fence (the postal address is little help; come via Haverfield Road, off Grove Road), the Tree has possibly the largest outdoor seating area in the capital – and one of its warmest welcomes.

Music (jazz, 9.45pm Fri-Sun). Tables outdoors (4, summer only).

Soma
230 Mile End Road, E1 4LJ (7790 3412/ www.somamix.com). Stepney Green tube. **Open/ food served** noon-12.30am Mon, Tue, Sun; noon-1.30am Wed-Sat. **Credit** MC, V.

For just over two years, Soma has made a career out of being the only DJ bar in Stepney. Its secret is pleasing a core crowd: NUS/NHS bargain jugs, for example, or £2 shooters. The draught options are an uninspiring lot (Pilsner Urquell, Grolsch, Carlsberg, Guinness, Scrumpy Jack) and the cocktails more attractive in price (£5 or less) than content, but the alliance of approachable staff and good, loud music keeps the place busy at night. A 2004 refurbishment saw the outside painted blue (it was primer grey before) and the limited interior space rationalised: the decks have migrated from the main floor, and new café-style chairs and tables have appeared. The central U-shaped bar – wooden top, cream surrounds, some elegant carved wood – and an empty hearth survive. Stone-baked pizzas (two for one on Thursday and Sunday) are a boon, but the low brown stools, extra-low brown sofas and even lower tables made of brown lumber remain at the nexus of cool and impractical.

Babies and children welcome (before 8pm). Games (board games). Music (DJs 9pm Tue-Sat; free). Tables outdoors (2, pavement).

Also in the area...
Match Maker (JD Wetherspoon) 580-586 Roman Road, E3 5ES (8709 9760).

CLAPTON

Gentrification might be coming to Hackney in the very near future, but there's little sign of it paying a visit to neighbouring Clapton. Likewise, most of the pubs in the area are forbidding boozers that have seen better days. But the Clapton-based drinker doesn't have to travel – there are three reasons to stay local, and two have a coveted waterside location. And what E5 lacks in elegance, it more than makes up for in hospitality: the warmth of welcome explains why all three pubs we list here have sizeable groups of regulars.

Jazz Bar Dalston. See p151.

Anchor & Hope

15 High Hill Ferry, E5 9HG (8806 1730). Clapton rail/ 253 bus. **Open** noon-11pm Mon-Sat; noon-10.30pm Sun. **No credit cards.**

If you squint really hard you could almost be in the countryside. This curious little pub looks over Walthamstow Marshes Nature Reserve and the River Lea – ignore the railway line and filtration plant – and the water and fields make for a pastoral prospect. The atmosphere has something of the country pub to it, too. This is a tightly knit community and strangers stand out, but a warm welcome is quickly extended. It's almost like being in someone's front room – not least because the pub is extremely compact. The interior is 50 years old and unchanged, the floor is covered in red lino tiles, and the woodwork wears innumerable layers of varnish. The beers are also classics: Fuller's London Pride and ESB enjoy top billing, and are frequently served in Leyton Orient half-pint pots.

Babies and children welcome. Games (darts, fruit machine). Specialities (real ale). TV.

Eclipse

57 Elderfield Road, E5 0LF (8986 1591/ www.the-eclipse.com). Hackney Central or Hackney Downs rail. **Open** 4-11pm Mon-Sat; 1-10.30pm Sun. **Food served** 1-4pm Sun. **Credit** MC, V.

The streets around the Eclipse are gruesome: a vista of cookers and mattresses dumped outside run-down terraces. Residents of this corner of Clapton need a sanctuary to escape to, and the Eclipse is it. The old and the new are skilfully balanced across two bars. One features modern sofas covered in Pucci-style prints, loads of potted plants and muted shades of beige, while the other is wood-panelled with a parquet floor and doesn't look like it's been touched for years. The beer is the same wherever you sit; when we visited Fuller's London Pride, Timothy Taylor Landlord and Harveys Sussex Post were all on tap. A soul night is held on the second and last Wednesday of each month; a knowledgeably stocked jukebox does good service in the meantime.

Babies and children welcome (Sun only). Music (DJs 8pm 2nd & last Wed of mth; free). Games (board games, cards, dominoes). Specialities (cocktails). Tables outdoors (10, pavement).

Princess of Wales

146 Lea Bridge Road, E5 9RB (8533 3463). Clapton rail/48, 55, 56 bus. **Open** 11am-11pm Mon-Sat; noon-10.30pm Sun. **Food served** noon-2.30pm, 6-8.30pm Mon-Sat; noon-3.15pm Sun. **Credit** AmEx, DC, MC, V.

Given the pub's name, you might expect there to be more evidence of the 'people's princess', but thankfully no; there was only one prominent picture of Diana when we visited. This is a huge building split into two main rooms. The public bar has red lino flooring and austere dark-wood panelling and furniture. It's a male environment ideal for games of darts and downing pints of Young's Export, Pilsner, Bitter, Special and Winter Warmer (yes, it's a Young's pub). The lounge bar is larger and more feminine,

with some sofas and an open fire, the effect not dissimilar to a recently renovated country hotel. The pub's waterside location next to the River Lea makes it a popular summer destination, although the buses thundering over the adjacent bridge detract a little from the ambience.
Babies and children welcome (before 9pm). Games (fruit machines). Tables outdoors (15, patio). TV (satellite).

DOCKLANDS

The redevelopment of Docklands may have revitalised the area's economic fortunes, but it has done nothing to improve its nightlife. Of an early evening, its pubs and bars are full of suited ladies and gents (ties loosened), but the lack of imagination – both in the drinks menus and decor – displayed by the entertainment corporations that dominate the Isle of Dogs is depressing. That said, there is some authentic (or, in the case of the **Cat & Canary**, near-authentic) character to be found, as proved by the **Ferry House** and **Gun**.

Cat & Canary

1-24 Fisherman's Walk, Canary Wharf, E14 4DH (7512 9187). Canary Wharf tube/DLR. **Open** 11am-11pm Mon-Sat; 11am-8pm Sun. **Food served** noon-3pm, 6-9pm Mon-Fri; noon-8pm Sat; 11am-6pm Sun. **Credit** AmEx, MC, V.

Looks can be deceiving: this waterside boozer seems ancient, but was in fact built in 1992. The patina of age was transplanted from a Victorian church in Essex in the form of wood panelling and a pulpit (now the telephone kiosk). The pub is situated in the shadow of Canary Wharf (hence the name), so it's no surprise that the clientele is made up of suited City types. They're supplied by a bar that leans heavily towards lager and white wine; you'll also find posh pub grub, a popular 'I can't be bothered to cook' dinner option and a huge TV screen that shows sports on a regular basis. As might be expected for a pub that's geared predominantly to the after-office crowd, the Cat & Canary is busy in the week and dead at weekends.
Disabled: toilet. Games (darts, fruit machines, quiz machine, golf machine). No-smoking area. Tables outdoors (20, terrace). TVs (big screen, plasma, satellite).

City Pride

15 Westferry Road, E14 8JH (7987 3516/ www.glendola.co.uk). Canary Wharf tube/DLR/ South Quays DLR. **Open** noon-11pm Mon-Sat; noon-10.30pm Sun. **Food served** noon-9.30pm daily. **Credit** AmEx, MC, V.

The City Pride first catered for dockers (pre-World War I), but what such folk would think of its modern incarnation is anyone's guess; there isn't an original feature left in the place. So while this is one of the oldest buildings in the area, it has the feel of a travel hub boozer. The pub is painted a dusky pink inside and out; the interior also features much

wood, drive-time music and the type of mid-level lighting that could really do with going up or down a notch. The menu devotes two pages to coffee, which says much about the proprietor's aspirations; San Miguel and Tetley's provide an alternative to the usual nitro-keg lagers. The staff are friendly to a fault, which does much to compensate for blandness in other departments.
Function room. Games (fruit machines, pool tables, quiz machines). Tables outdoors (20, garden).

Ferry House

26 Ferry Street, E14 3DT (7537 9587). Island Gardens DLR. **Open** 2-11pm Mon-Fri; 11am-11pm Sat; noon-10.30pm Sun. **Credit** MC, V.
Could this be the only proper pub on the Isle of Dogs? It's without question one of the oldest buildings on the peninsula – formerly the Greenwich ferry master's house, dating from 1823 – and has an old-world charm that's hard to fake. There's an open fire, loads of beaten-up wood, brass plates and an array of period photographs. The landlady is an East End original, too. While basking in the Merchant Ivory atmosphere, the customers (mostly locals) sup Stella and similar big-brewery products. During the day all eyes are on the TV, invariably tuned to the sport of the moment, and at the weekends there's karaoke, ensuring that the City boys stay away. It's their loss.
Children over 14 welcome. Entertainment (karaoke 9pm Fri; free). Games (darts). Quiz (8.30pm every other Wed; £1). Tables outdoors (3, pavement). TV.

Gun

27 Coldharbour, Isle of Dogs, E14 9NS (7515 5222/ www.thegundocklands.com). Blackwall DLR. **Open** 11am-midnight Mon-Fri; 10.30am-midnight Sat; 10.30am-10.30pm Sun. **Food served** noon-3pm, 6-10.30pm Mon-Fri; 10.30am-4pm, 6-10.30pm Sat; 10.30am-4pm, 6-9.30pm Sun. **Credit** AmEx, MC, V.
The Gun evidently inhabits a very violent neighbourhood: the sign outside sports a cannon-ball hole. The front room is half prim dining room (white tablecloths and all) and half bar, with Martini glasses and a couple of tables with elaborately carved settles. There's also a reassuringly pub-like back room, complete with snugs and wood-burning fires, and a big terrace that affords unsurpassed views of the Dome across the Thames. Real ale fans get only Young's Bitter and a Brakspear, but lager drinkers have San Miguel, Löwenbräu Original and Red Stripe (there's Hoegaarden, too). After a 2001 fire, this 18th-century Grade II listed pub was painstakingly restored: witness the dramatic, dark wood central bar. Run by the people behind the White Swan in EC4, the Gun serves high-class meals and quality bar snacks. Prices suggest the Docklands offices provide most custom, but our Sunday afternoon visit saw several families with children.
Babies and children welcome; high chairs, nappy-changing facilities. Disabled: toilet. Function room. Tables outdoors (12, terrace).

Via Fossa

West India Quay, Canary Wharf, E14 4QT (7515 8549/www.viafossa-canarywharf.co.uk). West India Quay DLR. **Open** 11am-11pm Mon-Wed; 11am-midnight Thur-Sat; noon-10.30pm Sun. **Food served** 11am-10.30pm Mon-Wed; 11am-11.30pm Thur-Sat; noon-10pm Sun. **Credit** AmEx, DC, MC, V.
Although part of a chain (also called Via Fossa), this bar has plenty of character. It's set in one of area's few buildings over 20 years old, a former sugar warehouse from the 1900s. The interior is a rabbit warren and has that 1990s reclaimed church look, with acres of dark ecclesiastical-looking wood partnered with orange rag-rolled walls and leopard-skin sofas. The above-average wine list is less idiosyncratic, reflecting the depth of the suited clientele's wallets, and there's an extensive cocktail menu. The beers are entirely unremarkable: Stella, Fosters and Guinness, among others, on tap; and the likes of Beck's, Budweiser and San Miguel in bottles. The bar food is OK – potato wedges, nachos and burgers – and there's a restaurant upstairs.
Disabled: lift, toilet. Function rooms. Music (DJ 7pm Sat; free). No-smoking area (restaurant). Restaurant. Tables outdoors (45, quayside).

Also in the area...

All Bar One 42 Mackenzie Walk, South Colonnade, E14 5EH (7513 0911).
Bar 38 Unit C, 16 Hertsmere Road, India Quay, E14 4AX (7515 8361).
Corney & Barrow 9 Cabot Square, E14 4EB (7512 0397).
Davy's 31-35 Fisherman's Walk, Cabot Square, E14 4DH (7363 6633).
Fine Line 20-30 Fisherman's Walk, 10 Cabot Square, E14 4DM (7513 0255).
Jamies Unit 1, Westferry Circus, E14 8RR (7536 2861).
Ledger Building (JD Wetherspoon) 4 Hertsmere Road, West India Quay, E14 4AL (7536 7770).
Slug & Lettuce 30 South Colonnade, Canary Wharf, E14 5EZ (7519 1612).

HACKNEY

The East London tube line extension is coming, and preceding it are the young professionals buying up property in anticipation of better transport links and a resulting hike in house prices. While they wait, there are plenty of pubs and bars to keep them occupied, from the upmarket **291** to the recently opened **Marie Lloyd Bar**, next door to and part of the Hackney Empire theatre. As gentrification gathers pace – when visiting one pub in the area we heard Dalston referred to as 'east Islington' – you can be sure these will soon be joined by more.

brb at the Alex

162 Victoria Park Road, E9 7JN (8985 5404). Bethnal Green or Mile End tube/277 bus. **Open** noon-11pm Mon-Sat; noon-10.30pm Sun. *Happy hour* 5-7pm daily. **Food served** noon-10.30pm Mon-Sat; noon-10pm Sun. **Credit** MC, V.
The term 'chav' entered the UK collective consciousness in 2004. It would be unfair to describe this east London outpost of the brb chain thus, but the place exhibits many signs of post-lad culture. So although the interior is airy, sofas are of distressed leather and art exhibitions are a regular feature, there's also a huge TV screen on which football matches are shown. The Alex is popular with local youth as a result, and they often spill on to the road in the summer months to crowd round their cars and smoke funny-smelling cigarettes. Nevertheless, they get along well with the students and off-duty City workers who are drawn here by the competitively priced drinks list – the

RAISE A GLASS: WHEAT BEER

Is Britain's latest beer venture strictly for the birds? In the face of a diminishing and staid lager market sewn up by Stella, Carling, Foster's and Budweiser, one beer variety is punching above its weight: wheat. Wheat beer, known continentally as Weißbier, witbier or bière blanche, now accounts for 20 per cent of all beer sales in the UK. Pioneered by Hoegaarden, followed by Wieckse Witte, wheat beer has a presence in nearly every London local. And the two big brands to break through in 2005, Kronenbourg Blanc and its fruity rival Früli, specifically appeal to the fastest growing section of the drinking public: women.

'The reaction to Früli among women has been extremely pleasing', says Nick Holmes, managing director of the company responsible for introducing it into the UK market, Specialist Brand Development. 'It's a completely different product. The taste is often compared to ice cream or yoghurt.' Served from tall, sexy pumps, generally in half-measures given a hefty price tag on pints, Früli and Blanc are also unusual in that they aren't widespread across the Channel. In fact Blanc, currently being rolled out across the UK by Scottish Courage, isn't on sale in France at all. What started as lucky coincidence, the wheat beer phenomenon is now the industry's most imaginative trump card.

For decades, wheat beer occupied an unhip niche in the markets of its two main producers, Belgium and Germany. More akin to ale than lager, it's concocted with wheat, malt and barley in equal measures by Belgians, who add a litte coriander and orange peel. Germans, particularly Bavarians, brew it with a higher proportion of wheat. A holiday drink in Alpine resorts, wheat beer had an unfashionable cachet in the rest of pils-drinking Germany, its typical drinker considered a cross between ABV-obsessed besweatered beardy and sombrero-wearing, bullfight-poster-brandishing holiday bore. Some even plopped a lemon slice into their glass, something Belgians rarely do. In any case, wheat beer had all but died a death in Belgium until Pierre Celis, a one-time milkman who lived next to a brewery, decided to revive the recipe: Hoegaarden. The cloudy, refreshing result became big in Belgium, so much so that Interbrew bought out Celis in the 1980s. (Celis set up his own brewery in Austin, Texas, but failed to convince cowboys to drop Bud for something feminine and European in a beer glass; he's now back in Belgium.)

London, meanwhile, was riding a wave of Belgiaphilia. With the **Belgo** chain (*see p244*) booming and Eurostar travellers raving about Brussels, Interbrew introduced Hoegaarden in a chunky, hexagonal, logoed glass. Everyone stole one; Interbrew happily provided more. Someone dropped a lemon slice into one – everyone else followed. (Lime and Sol would be a fair analogy.) Bored with blokey lagers, untempted by ale but spoilt for choice in wines and cocktails, discerning Londoners took to the premium-priced (high maintenance, say the distributers) brew like ducks to water. Sexy but not sexually specific, Hoegaarden was a victory of good taste all round. And then along came Früli.

After Früli, Paulaner is next in line to harvest plump profits from the wheat craze. And if you think Früli (strawberry or apple, mmm...) was a fruit too far, somebody may yet launch draught lambic (bacteria-heavy Belgian beer, often flavoured with cherries or raspberries) onto an unsuspecting public. *Peterjon Cresswell*

draught beers and New World wines are all familiar names – and the fantastic pizzas, cooked in a wood-fired oven. Tuesday, two-for-one night, is particularly popular.
Babies and children admitted (before 7pm). Games (fruit machine, quiz machine). TV (big screen, satellite).

Cat & Mutton

76 Broadway Market, E8 4QJ (7254 5599). London Fields rail/Bethnal Green tube then 106, 253 bus/ 26, 48, 55 bus. **Open** 6-11pm Mon; noon-11pm Tue-Sat; noon-10.30pm Sun. **Food served** 6.30-10pm Mon; noon-3pm, 6.30-10pm Tue-Sat; noon-5pm Sun. **Credit** AmEx, MC, V.

'There's a queue for tables,' we were told, with asperity, on a typically frantic Sunday lunchtime. A Saturday return visit was repaid with a quieter pub and a warmer welcome. The familiar but nicely worked gastro refit is enlivened by intriguing original features (a Cat & Mutton mosaic, dull gold pillars flanking the entrance, long-gone ales picked out on the frosted glass), but the stacking school chairs seem blandly functional. Still, the Islington renegades who throng the place seemed comfortable. An open kitchen takes up perhaps a quarter of the floor space; that it's slightly bigger than the bar shows the Cat's priorities. The real ale selection is dismal (just Adnams bitter and a redundant second pump). Still, there are a dozen wines by the glass, plus Pilsner Urquell and San Miguel lagers. The food (orders taken at table) is simple and glorious; the plate of leeks, morcilla and duck eggs (£6.50) was a sensation.
Babies and children admitted; high chairs. Disabled: toilet. Function room. Music (DJs 5.30-10.30pm Sun). Tables outdoors (6, pavement).

Central 1 Lounge Bar & Diner

1-3 Amhurst Road, E8 2AY (8985 2879). Bethnal Green tube/rail/Hackney Central rail. **Open** noon-midnight Tue-Sun. **Food served** noon-10.30pm Tue-Sun. **Credit** MC, V.

There's not much in the way of sophistication in the area around Hackney Central station, but this bar-cum-restaurant is trying. The walls are a muted lilac, the floor is tiled and the bar counter is copper-clad. There are leather sofas in the bar area and designer-like tables and chairs in the restaurant. The bar serves Leffe – both Blonde and Brune – as well as more usual beers, and there's an espresso machine. The menu lists dishes like venison with strawberries and Martini Rosso; DJs play at weekends. If Central 1 sounds like it's trying to be all things to all people, that's because it is. As a consequence, the venue is not quite as classy as it might think. But this is nonetheless a welcome alternative to the neighbouring spit 'n' sawdust pubs.
Babies and children welcome (until 9pm). Bar available for hire. Disabled: toilet. Music (DJs 8pm Fri, Sat; free). Tables outdoors (3, garden; 6, pavement).

Dove Freehouse

24-28 Broadway Market, E8 4QJ (7275 7617/ www.belgianbars.com). Bethnal Green tube then 15min walk or 55 bus. **Open** noon-11pm Mon-Sat; noon-10.30pm Sun. **Food served** noon-3pm, 6-10pm Mon-Thur; noon-3pm, 6-10.30pm Fri; noon-10.30pm Sat; noon-10pm Sun. **Credit** MC, V.

You know you're in capable hands when the guest ale is called Delirium Tremens (at a whopping 9%). Belgian beers are the Dove's speciality, with half a dozen on draught and legions by the bottle. Fuller's Pride, Greene King IPA, Timothy Taylor Landlord and Bass are also on

Boleyn. *See p155.*

tap, there's a healthy wine list and a nice range of spirits – stronger in whiskies (eight single malts and six bourbons) than, say, vodka. The food is hearty: Flemish cod stew, perhaps, or pies and Sunday roasts. The bar room is all classic dark wood, with a hearth and cosy pew seating tucked tight to the tables; plastic chequered tablecloths and candles make the somewhat draughty back room downstairs feel like a continental café. Games (such as Scrabble) help you linger, though we've never needed any assistance. The place gets busy, but a mollifying kind of busy, and staff are friendly beyond the call of duty.
Babies and children welcome (before 6pm). Games (board games). No-smoking area. Restaurant. Specialities (Belgian beers). Tables outdoors (6, pavement).

Jazz Bar Dalston

4 Bradbury Street, N16 8JN (7254 9728). Dalston Kingsland rail. **Open** 5pm-1am Mon-Thur, Sun; 5pm-3am Fri, Sat. **No credit cards**.

It's no good getting the details right if you let yourself down on the basics. There's much to recommend the Jazz Bar: table service, a well-chosen wine list, cocktails that are even better, and a decor that cleverly combines wine bar sophistication, conservatory-sized windows and bohemian tat. But running a bar is all about hospitality. When we visited on a busy Saturday night – packed hardly covers it – the owner had the bouncers oblige a group of people to leave for not relinquishing a chair kept for a member of their party who was buying a round. The reason? The owner wanted to make room for his friends. We'd like to think this was a one-off event – after all, in many respects this is the best bar in the area – but it's still a worrying sign.
Music (DJs 8pm Fri, Sat; jazz 10pm daily). Tables outdoors (7, pavement).

Marie Lloyd Bar

289 Mare Street, E8 1EJ (8510 4500/www.hackney empire.co.uk). Bethnal Green tube then 106 bus/ Hackney Central rail. **Open** 4pm-1am Mon-Fri; 7pm-1am Sat; 7pm-midnight Sun. **Credit** MC, V.

Marie Lloyd was one of the biggest stars of the pre-World War I music hall era. She performed at the Hackney Empire theatre many times, lived around the corner on Graham Road, and helped found the Variety Artists' Association (now part of the actors' union Equity). So it's fitting that the Empire's new wing be named after her. The centrepiece of the extension is this bar, also named after Lloyd, which brings the feel of a swanky hotel to none-too-swish Mare Street. The drinks list is in line with the look: nothing new to the Soho drinker, but a great improvement over the options at the Wetherspoon across the road. Best of all, the bar is open to non-theatregoers, and the management is keen to encourage Hackney residents to show their support for this local institution by popping in for a drink.
Disabled: toilet. Function room. Music (DJs/bands 9pm Thur-Sat; free). No-smoking area.

Prince George

40 Parkholme Road, E8 3AG (7254 6060). Dalston Kingsland rail/30, 38, 56, 242, 277 bus. **Open** 5-11pm Mon-Fri; noon-11pm Sat; noon-10.30pm Sun. **Credit** MC, V.

Every year there's a rumour that the George is going to follow the lead of the Approach Tavern (*see p140*) and the Royal Inn on the Park (*see below*), with whom it shares an owner, and start serving food. Let's hope not: this handsome corner pub, tucked away on a quiet residential street, is a drinkers' pub through and through, and a good one at that. The changes since last year are minimal: a new host for Monday's popular quiz nights (get there by 8.30pm if you want a seat), the replacement of frosted glass with the see-through kind (boo!), better-kept ales (Pride, Abbot, Adnams, Flowers) and higher prices (anyone in doubt that Hackney is gentrifying should see how much the wines cost). Otherwise, it's as you were – which is to say a wide assortment of locals sitting around on haggard wooden furniture, smoking rollies and making boozy conversation to a jukebox-led soundtrack that takes in everything from jazz to post-punk.
Babies and children welcome (until 8.30pm). Games (board games, pool table). Quiz (9pm Mon; £2 per team). Tables outdoors (10, heated forecourt). TV.

Royal Inn on the Park

111 Lauriston Road, E9 7HJ (8985 3321). Bethnal Green or Mile End tube. **Open** noon-11pm Mon-Thur; noon-midnight Fri, Sat; noon-10.30pm Sun. **Food served** noon-3pm, 6-9.30pm Mon-Fri; noon-9.30pm Sat; noon-6pm Sun. **Credit** MC, V.

It's unruly and studenty here, but that doesn't scare off the grown-ups. The decent selection of draught beers includes Fuller's ESB and Pride, Clark's Classic Blonde, Litovel, Zubr and Hoegaarden. There's a reasonable wine list, too, with several by the glass. The half dozen unthreatening but attractive Sunday roasts, a shelf of games (Scrabble, Connect 4 and, rashly, a box of drinking games), plus flyers for the resident psychics, and a quiz night with the Fat Controller, make this a place to settle into for an afternoon – especially in summer when its good-sized beer garden comes into its own. On our visit, a couple of families staked out the little non-smoking annexe, possibly scared away by free jellied eels and prawns on the bar, while the jukebox belted out uni classics (Beatles, Spiritualized, Pulp) at volumes near the pain threshold. No matter: the main room is large enough to provide refuge from the racket.
Babies and children admitted; high chairs; nappy-changing facilities. Disabled: toilet. Function rooms. Games (board games). No-smoking area (restaurant). Quiz (8.30pm Tue; £1). Restaurant. Tables outdoors (30, garden). TV.

291

291 Hackney Road, E2 8NA (7613 5676/ www.291gallery.com). Liverpool Street tube/rail then 26, 48 bus/Bethnal Green tube/rail/55 bus. **Open** 6pm-midnight Tue, Sun; 6pm-2am Wed-Sat. **Credit** MC, V.

Shoreditch's popularity is at an all-time high, and so the fortunes of the abutting neighbourhoods are buoyed. Two years ago, tumbleweed blew across this bar most nights of the week. Not so now, and rightly not so, as it's one of the most visually impressive venues in the whole of London. Black beams vault over the bar, there's an altar-style edifice at the end of the room – the building, which includes an art gallery, used to be a church – and the furnishings are the stuff of interior design magazines. The drinks menu isn't quite as upmarket: the beer is bottled; the wines are decent, not amazing; ditto the cocktails. But this doesn't matter, as 291 is all about decor, even more so since its recent refurbishment. And there really isn't any competition on that score until you get to central London.
Bar available for hire. Digital art event (7.30pm 2nd Wed of mth; free). Disabled: toilet. Gallery space available for hire. Poetry (7.30pm last Mon of mth; £5). Tables outdoors (10, garden).

Wellington

119 Balls Pond Road, N1 4BL (7275 7640). Dalston Kingsland rail/Highbury & Islington tube/30, 38, 56, 277 bus. **Open** 4pm-midnight Mon-Fri; noon-midnight Sat; noon-11.30pm Sun. **Food served** 5-11pm Mon-Fri; noon-midnight Sat; 1-5pm Sun. **Credit** MC, V.

The watchword at the Wellington is cosy. There's an open fire, a white cat napping on a bar stool, and a menu full of comfort food rather than gastropub pretension (highlights include the 'Wellyburger' and syrup pudding and custard). Somehow, decorative curiosities like a china leopard on the bar, exotic bird-of-paradise cut flowers, a toucan and decoy ducks, add to the homey feel, as do the cream walls, large windows, dark wooden floorboards and red ceiling. Greene King IPA and Abbot Ale ennoble the beer selection, and the wine list is streets ahead of local competition. This idiosyncratic boozer attracts a large number of women – it's a very non-threatening establishment – which is a tonic after the plethora of all-male drinking shops in the locality.

Babies and children admitted (separate room). Disabled: toilet. Function room. Tables outdoors (pavement). TV (satellite).

Also in the area...

Baxter's Court (JD Wetherspoon) 282 Mare Street, E8 1HE (8525 9010).

LEYTON & LEYTONSTONE

Located to the east of Hackney Marsh, the twinned Leyton & Leytonstone are something of a haven for the pub connoisseur (compared to neighbouring postcodes, at least). While it has no shortage of old-style, hard-nosed East End boozers in the area, there are also a couple of very good reasons to come here for a drink. The **Birkbeck Tavern** and **William IV** would be a credit to any neighbourhood.

Birkbeck Tavern

45 Langthorne Road, E11 4HL (8539 2584). Leyton tube. **Open** 11am-11pm Mon-Sat; noon-10.30pm Sun. **Food served** noon-6pm Mon, Wed-Sat. **Credit** AmEx, DC, MC, V.

The Birkbeck can be hard to find: it's a five-minute walk from Leyton tube station. Long ago it was a hotel; now, it's a gem of a pub. The saloon bar occupies most of the ground floor, and you can still see where the reception desk and the steep staircase to the rooms upstairs were; on the other side of the mahogany bar, which sits like an island in what was the hotel lobby, there's a smaller public bar. You'll also find an original fireplace and an arch between the door and the bar which must have been quite grand in its day. The proprietors have decorated the walls with period photographs of the area. The drinks list features ales found nowhere else in east London, like Southport Brewery's Carousel and Wharfedale Brewery's Rhylstone Folly.

Function room. Games (darts, fruit machine, pool table). Quiz (8.15pm Sun; £1). Tables outdoors (18, garden). TV (satellite).

North Star

24 Browning Road, E11 3AR (8989 5777). Leytonstone tube. **Open** noon-11.30pm Mon-Sat; noon-10.30pm Sun. **Food served** noon-3pm, 6-9pm Mon-Fri. **No credit cards**.

Lurking on a backstreet at the very northern tip of Leytonstone, the North Star has nearly everything you could want from a pub. The welcome is warm and the atmosphere rowdy – the punters will occasionally stop singing along to the uncommonly loud music to say hello, but more usually will just nod. 'I'm loving angels instead,' crooned the landlady as she winked at us with one hand on a beer pump. The ales are good: Adnams Broadside and Bombardier, as well as Bass. Happily, no one has messed up the interior, which is centred on a fantastic wooden bar, its deep lustre echoed by the orange and brown paintwork. The strong railway theme is all to do with the pub's name, which apparently comes from a steam locomotive – although no one seems to know why.

Games (fruit machine). Tables outdoors (4, garden; 2, pavement). TV (digital, satellite).

Sir Alfred Hitchcock Hotel

147 Whipps Cross Road, E11 1NP (8530 3724). Leytonstone tube/Walthamstow Central tube/rail. **Open** 11am-11pm Mon-Sat; noon-10.30pm Sun. **Food served** noon-3pm, 7-10pm Mon-Sat; 1-5pm Sun. **Credit** MC, V.

The Hitchcock recalls a time when roadside hotels were strung along the country's highways like pearls, and its magnificent Gothic and ivy-clad front elevation looks out on to the southern tip of Epping Forest. The hotel was surely popular with outward-bound London motorists in times past, but its grandeur is now faded and its popularity continues to wane, too. Inaccessibility has to be a major factor, but the beaten-up dark-wood interior and dated semi-timbered ceiling don't help, nor do the sad leather sofas. Perhaps it's the fantastic open fire that keeps customers coming. It's certainly not the selection of drinks, which is standard. For some reason there are old railway signs everywhere; the adjoining restaurant has regular spit roast nights. Hitch would be baffled.

Babies and children welcome (restaurant). Games (fruit machine). Quiz (9pm Tue; £1). Restaurant (available for hire). TV.

William IV

816 Leyton High Road, E10 6AE (8556 2460). Leyton tube/Walthamstow Central tube/rail. **Open** 11am-11pm Mon-Sat; noon-10.30pm Sun. **Food served** noon-10pm Mon-Sat; 12.30-10pm Sun. **Credit** MC, V.

A striking inn dating from 1897, the William IV is all red and white brickwork. It looks more like an asylum than a boozer, although the ivy that covers the building to the first floor does much to soften the imposing edifice. Inside, there are lofty ceilings, vintage mirrors, a deer's head, a fire and an unusual S-shaped bar that snakes through the two main rooms. There used to be a microbrewery here called Sweet William, but sadly it closed down two years ago, which means, alas, that the pub's Just William Bitter is just a memory. Nevertheless, the drinks menu is still better than average for Leyton, and this remains a great pub. With all the foliage obscuring the view outside, you can imagine yourself miles away from E10.

Babies and children admitted (until 7pm). Games (board games, fruit machines). Music (blues 8.30pm Sun; jazz 8.30pm last Thur of mth; free). Tables outdoors (7, patio). TV (big screen, satellite).

Also in the area...

Drum (JD Wetherspoon) 557-559 Lea Bridge Road, E10 7EQ (8539 9845).

George (JD Wetherspoon) 159 High Street, E11 2RL (8989 2921).
O'Neill's 726 Leytonstone High Road, E11 3AW (8532 2411).
Walnut Tree (JD Wetherspoon) 857-861 High Road, E11 1HH (8539 2526).

LIMEHOUSE

This mean-looking patch by the side of the murky river was London's original Chinatown, a place of opium dens and gambling joints. From Victorian times until the decline of the dockyards, Limehouse was a place into which respectable people thought twice about stepping. No change there, then. But the revamping of Docklands, the arrival of the DLR and the gentrification of the area mean there are unambiguous signs of change.

Booty's Riverside Bar

92A Narrow Street, E14 8BP (7987 8343). Westferry DLR. **Open** 11am-11pm Mon-Thur; 11am-midnight Fri, Sat; noon-10.30pm Sun. **Food served** 11am-9.30pm Mon-Fri; noon-6.30pm Sat; noon-9.30pm Sun. **Credit** AmEx, DC, MC, V.

Is it just us, or does the name conjures up some an image of a ghastly hip-hip-hooray chain wine bar in the provinces? No? Never mind. Thankfully, this cosy little spot is nothing of the sort: founded by boxer and businessman Dennis Booty in 1979, it's really just a smart, pokey and slightly eccentric local pub, just far enough from the riverside tourist trail to retain its dignity. The building used to be an engineering stop for barges back in the 19th century; these days, the window tables offer a sweet little view of a not especially scenic corner of the river. The decoration is olde world; the exception is a few maps of French wine regions that have been pinned to the ceiling, presumably to give drunks something to read when they can no longer stand up straight. The beers on tap include Grolsch, Caffrey's and Staropramen, as well as real ales Bass and Tetley's.

Babies and children admitted. Games (fruit machine, quiz machine). Specialities (wines). Tables outdoors (2, pavement). TVs (digital, satellite).

Grapes

76 Narrow Street, E14 8BP (7987 4396). Westferry DLR. **Open** noon-3pm, 5.30-11pm Mon-Fri; noon-11pm Sat; noon-10.30pm Sun. **Food served** noon-2pm, 7-9pm Mon-Sat; noon-3.30pm Sun. **Credit** AmEx, MC, V.

Many pubs claim the honour, but we think it was this pub that Charles Dickens had in mind when wrote in *Our Mutual Friend*, reimagining it as the Six Jolly Fellowship Porters. Either way, it certainly has history: there's been a pub here since 1583, while the current building dates back to 1720. It looks old, too: it's a cramped place, the floorboards slightly off-kilter and the staircase to the toilets and the first-floor restaurant a precariously creaking affair. All of which, of course, only adds to the appeal of a pub that belies its historic appeal by serving, essentially, as a hideout for the largely well-off denizens of this riverside neighbourhood. The beer offering runs from the standards (Carlsberg, Stella) to a clutch of decent real ales (Adnams bitter, Bass, Marston's Pedigree, Tetley's). If it was your local, you'd never leave Limehouse.

No piped music or jukebox. No smoking. Restaurant. Specialities (real ales).

DRINKING ALOUD
TONY CONIGLIARO

Who are you? I'm Bar Operations Manager for Shochu Lounge (*see p45*) and Zuma (*see p56*).
Drinking in London: what's good about it? There's lots of new stuff, ideas, quality – bartenders know what they're talking about, and there's a great sense of community. You can go to a lot of bars and get very good drinks – compared to other cities, London has a much bigger scene.
What's caught your eye in the last year? From personal experience, the interest in shochu – a relatively little-known drink in this country, but the biggest-selling spirit in the world. I suppose London drinkers are becoming more aware of new things, they're willing to try them out, willing to try new drinks.
What's in your crystal ball? I think there are going to be a lot more home-made things – bartenders are making their own syrups, getting more craft-oriented. At Shochu Lounge we make a liquorice syrup, because there isn't one available. And we're working on bottled cocktails, drinks that we make at the beginning of the evening and serve in a bottle with our own label, so people can pour them for themselves. It's not a new idea – there was a guy called Professor Jerry Thomas in 1862 who bottled cocktails for San Francisco miners – but it's a fun idea, and there's more authenticity in a nicely made cocktail in a bottle than in an alcopop.
What could be improved? Service. We are a service industry. Unfriendly service – that's something I really abhor. Things have got a lot better, but when you go to, say, New York, bar staff are inordinately friendly. There needs to be a more of that.
New licensing law: good or bad? Great!

East

Mariners

514 Commercial Road, E1 0HY (7702 7082). Limehouse DLR. **Open** 11am-11pm Mon-Fri; 5-11pm Sat; noon-10.30pm Sun. **Food served** noon-10pm Mon-Fri; 5-10pm Sat; noon-9.30pm Sun. **Credit** MC, V.

We can't say we remember it, but it's easy to imagine what the Mariners must have been like four or five years ago: ragged, dog-eared, home only to the kind of dissolute pub folk who couldn't face going back to their real homes. The renovation it enjoyed a few years back could scarcely be more predictable: huge wooden tables and sofas, and a blackboard on which is detailed an immense menu (everything from fish 'n' chips to nachos). Still, the draught beer selection isn't bad: as well as big-name lagers, you get Adnams bitter and Broadside, Leffe Blonde and Hoegaarden. And while these cheap-as-chips gastropub conversions are ten a penny across London these days, this one is still welcome in an area where eating options generally start with fried chicken or a kebab and end with heartburn or indigestion.

Disabled: toilet.

Narrow Street Pub & Dining Room

44 Narrow Street, E14 8DQ (7265 8931). Limehouse DLR. **Open** noon-11pm Mon-Sat; noon-10.30pm Sun. **Food served** noon-10pm Mon-Sun. **Credit** MC, V.

Formerly the Limehouse Basin Dockmaster's house and then a rather self-conscious 'old' pub called the Barley Mow, this riverside property in a plum location has had a makeover in the last few years, and a dramatic one at that. As well as Going Gastro, it's been kitted out in slightly austere, loft living style; more Habitat than Heal's, but effective enough in its way. The room on the left as you walk in is where most of the diners sit, leaving the smaller space by the bar to the drinkers, who try to keep up a conversation over the cranked-up music and the din of the noisiest extractor fan in the country. The aforementioned drinkers' choices include Affligem, Paulaner and Greene King IPA on draught, and the likes of Budweiser and Beck's in bottles. There's outside seating – and space for a barbecue – in summer.

Babies and children welcome. Disabled: toilet. Restaurant. Tables outdoors (36, riverside terrace).

Queen's Head

8 Flamborough Street, E14 7LS (7791 2504). Limehouse DLR. **Open** 11am-11pm Mon-Sat; noon-10.30pm Sun. **Food served** noon-3.3pm Mon-Fri. **No credit cards**.

As more than a few photographs on its walls will remind you, this is the pub into which the Queen Mother popped in 1987 and pulled a pint of Young's Special for the cameras. She was on a tour of East London at the time, and the organisers could scarcely have picked a more typical – or, indeed, more stereotypical – spot for her to visit. The two-bar Queen's Head, tucked away in a residential street, is the archetype of a cheery East End local: everyone seems to know everyone else, and the atmosphere dial is usually turned to 'knees-up'. It's still a Young's pub, so the beer is good ('ordinary', Special and Ram Rod on tap, Light Ale in bottles), the lighting is way too bright and the seating is less than comfortable – but it's unlikely many of the regulars mind. In days gone by, beer came here by barge; now it's delivered from Wandsworth by lorry.

Babies and children admitted (during the day). Games (darts, fruit machine, quiz machine). Jukebox (free play). TV (satellite).

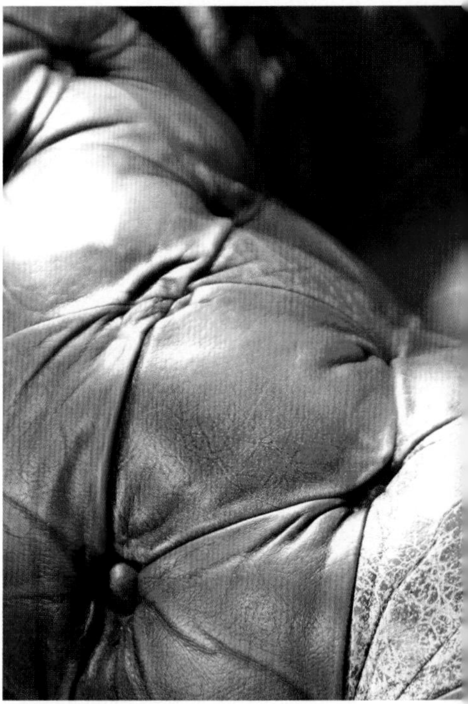

PLAISTOW

Before the 19th century, Plaistow was part of the marshes to the east of London. With industrialisation and the expansion of the capital, dockyards came to dominate the area, but nowadays they are long gone. Not much has replaced them, and the area has a somewhat desolate feel: suburbia at its bleakest. If that doesn't sound promising for drinkers, the reality is even more desolate: there are just two pubs in the area worth mentioning.

Black Lion

59-61 High Street, E13 0AD (8472 2351). Plaistow tube. **Open** 11am-3pm, 5-11pm Mon, Tue; 11am-11pm Wed-Sat; noon-10.30pm Sun. **Food served** noon-2.30pm, 5-7.30pm Mon-Fri. **Credit** MC, V.

People who participate in role-playing games ('gamers', they call themselves) are dubbed geeks by, well, nearly everyone else. So it stands to reason that any place in which they choose to hang out must have a 'live and let live' atmosphere. Every Thursday, the Phoenix Games Club meets at the Black Lion, which is indeed a friendly place. The front bar is stark, with bare floorboards and low beams; the back bar is a little more cosy. There's a beer garden to enjoy on a summer's day (ignore the looming tower block) and a selection of real ales on tap. Apparently, this former coaching inn has connections to highwayman Dick Turpin, but is there a pub in the area that doesn't make such claims? The Black Lion is also home to the West

Vibe Bar. *See p158.*

Ham Boys' Boxing Club (whose members fortunately don't give the Phoenix Gamers any trouble).
Babies and children admitted (until 7pm). Function room. Games (fruit machine, quiz machine). Specialities (guest ales). Tables outdoors (10, garden). TVs (satellite).

Boleyn

1 Barking Road, E6 1PW (8472 2182). Upton Park tube. **Open** 11am-11pm Mon-Sat; noon-10.30pm Sun. **No credit cards**.
This Victorian tipple mansion is right next to West Ham United's Boleyn Ground, and its cavalier anachronisms (Tudor portrait reproductions alongside turn-of-the-20th-century prints) suggest Hammers fans are more regular visitors than Simon Schama. Indeed, we understand that on match days tattooed men in states of undress drench each other with beer and terrace scatology. Midweek, the place is quiet. The red-brick and white frontage is palatial, some of the interior delicious: intricately carved alcoves hold etched mirrors, wooden pillars support deco-style glass over the bar, bay windows have cut-glass panes running beneath. The draught options are less appealing: Calders, Tetley, Stella, Carlsberg and Carlsberg Export. The pub is really two rooms: a not-quite-snug saloon bar with a TV and assorted old chaps; and a large hall, partially divided, with a huge screen and middle-aged men in one part, and lads and lasses playing pool at three tables in the other.
Babies and children welcome (before 7pm). Games (pool tables). No-smoking area. Tables outdoors (3, yard). TVs (big screen, plasma, satellite).

STRATFORD

When it comes to transport, Stratford can compete with any district in London: the tube, rail, DLR and numerous bus routes all come here. Perhaps because it's so easy to travel out of E15, there are so few pubs of note in the district. Most are nondescript, a few are downright rough, and only the two below are worth a visit. Should London get the 2012 Olympics the world will marvel at how well connected east London is – but wonder what its inhabitants do in the evening.

Golden Grove

146-148 The Grove, E15 1NS (8519 0750). Stratford tube/DLR/rail. **Open** 10am-11pm Mon-Sat; 10am-10.30pm Sun. **Food served** 10am-10pm Mon-Sat; 10am-9.30pm Sun. **Credit** AmEx, MC, V.
In other areas of London, the acquisition of a pub by JD Wetherspoon is considered a bad thing, but Stratford isn't a snobbish place and, truth be told, the chain has done a lot of good at the Golden Grove. Most pubs in the district compete on price of beer alone, but though the beer here is cheap, there are plenty of other reasons to recommend the place over its rivals. For a start, there are regular guest ales to accompany the usual fizzy lager; there's a no-smoking area; you'll find reasonably priced and decent wine; the food is cheerful; and the interior, while lacking charisma, is clean. In short, you'd be happy to bring your family here, whereas even a hard-bitten merchant seaman would be worried for his safety at some nearby establishments.

Babies and children admitted (before 9pm if dining). Disabled: toilet. Games (fruit machines). No piped music or jukebox. No-smoking area. Specialities (guest ales). Tables outdoors (15, garden).

King Edward VII

47 Broadway, E15 4BQ (8534 2313/www.kingeddie.co.uk). Stratford tube/DLR/rail. **Open** noon-11pm Mon-Sat; noon-10.30pm Sun. **Food served** noon-10pm Mon-Sat; noon-8pm Sun. **Credit** MC, V.

The Eddie was built in the early 19th century and originally called the King of Prussia, before World War I forced a patriotic name change. It's a squat building compared to its neighbours, but inside the pub is comfortable and has plenty of period features, including an original window etched with an outline of Edward VII. The upstairs bar was recently converted to a restaurant. The landlord's claim to serve the best food in east London seems a trifle boastful, especially if you don't like sausages, but the dishes are certainly pretty good. Similar claims for the beer menu are more honest: Adnams Broadside, Timothy Taylor Dark Mild and Greene King IPA and Abbot Ale were all on draught when we last visited. There's a yard at the back, too.

Babies and children welcome (restaurant). Function room. Games (board games, dominoes, fruit machines, quiz machine). Quiz (8pm Sun; free). Music (acoustic/open mic night 8pm Thur; free). No-smoking area (restaurant). Restaurant. Tables outdoors (7, yard). TV.

WALTHAMSTOW

Walthamstow is something of a mixed bag when it comes to pubs. It has venues where the thought of wine from a bottle instead of a tap, or even the thought of wine full stop, is anathema; but there are some decent places to drink, too. For atmosphere, the **Flower Pot** is especially enticing. It's like a living museum, not just for the interior, apparently untouched since the war (possibly even the first one).

Flower Pot

128 Wood Street, E17 3HX (8520 3600). Walthamstow Central tube/rail. **Open** noon-11pm Mon-Sat; noon-10.30pm Sun. **Food served** 5.30-9.30pm Wed. **Credit** MC, V.

This is a racing pub. Two TVs show horse racing whenever it's on, and Walthamstow men gather during the day to study form, cheer a fancied nag, celebrate a win and commiserate a loss. The ceiling is high, the colour scheme horticultural (olive green, yellow and brown) and pictures of horses adorn the walls. There are loads of original features, from the ancient mirrors advertising Bass and Wenlock to wood panelling and the home-made rolls wrapped in cellophane on a tray behind the bar. As the blackboard puts it, there's an 'ever changing selection of guest beers' – when we visited it was Caledonian Deuchars IPA – but this is not the kind of place in which to order wine. In fact, the guest beer is about the only thing that does change here. Hurrah, say we.

Babies and children welcome. Games (board games, cribbage, retro gaming machine). Music (bands 8.30pm Fri; free). Quiz (8.30pm Sun; £1). Tables outdoors (10, garden). TV (big screen, plasma, satellite).

Nag's Head

9 Orford Road, E17 9LP (8520 9709). Walthamstow Central tube/rail. **Open** 4-11pm Mon-Fri; 2-11pm Sat; 2-10.30pm Sun. **Food served** 2-6pm Sat, Sun. **Credit** MC, V.

The name suggests traditional East End values, but nothing could be further from the truth. Orford Road is a well-to-do street and its residents drink here – hence the large selection of Belgian beers, as well as Old Speckled Hen, Adnams Broadside, Cornish Knocker, Fuller's London Pride, Thwaites Dark Mild and Belle Vue Kriek on draught. The wine list is just as varied and extensive, extending to mulled wine in winter. There's an open fire and tasteful beige walls decorated with pictures of vintage film stars, but the crushed velvet tablecloths are a little tacky (especially the imitation leopard skin). A jazz band plays on Sundays from mid-afternoon. Come summer, an outdoor seating area makes the Nag's Head just the place in Walthamstow at which to enjoy a jug of Pimm's.

Babies and children welcome (garden only). Entertainment (belly dancing 8.30pm Tue; £7). Specialities (real ale, wine). Tables outdoors (8, heated patio; 20, heated garden).

Village

31 Orford Road, E17 9NL (8521 9982). Walthamstow Central tube/rail. **Open** noon-11pm Mon-Sat; noon-10.30pm Sun. **Food served** noon-3pm Mon-Fri; noon-4pm Sat, Sun. **Credit** MC, V.

It's almost as though the Village has been plucked from a provincial town and plonked down in the Borough of Waltham Forest, such is its slightly dishevelled charm. The decor is an appealing symphony of greens and browns, and there's an assortment of bric-a-brac: dusty bottles and a cherishable 1786 sign barring 'skulking loafers and flea-bitten tramps'. The beers are similarly cheering, and include Marston's Pedigree, Courage Directors, Adnams Broadside and Greene King IPA; the wine list is reasonable and contains no hidden horrors. There's a fair number of rock kids (all over 18, of course) among the customers, which might explain why the standard of the piped music is well above average.

Babies and children admitted (snug and garden). Games (fruit machine, quiz machine). Tables outdoors (14, garden). TV.

WAPPING

Wapping's a funny old place. There's the glowering presence of Murdoch's News International and all those warehouses converted into luxury flats; and then there are riverside pubs that date back centuries. The link is the Port of London. Seafarers ensured the place was a riot of boozy skulduggery by the mid 18th century (there were then 36 drinking dens along the High Street), but the terminal decline of the docks has meant that sniffing at house prices in estate agent windows is now as mischievous as things get. Still, a whiff of unsavoury history lingers in the **Prospect of Whitby** and the **Town of Ramsgate**.

Prospect of Whitby

57 Wapping Wall, E1W 3SH (7481 1095). Wapping tube. **Open** 11.30am-11pm Mon-Sat; noon-10.30pm Sun. **Food served** 11.30am-9.30pm Mon-Sat; noon-8.30pm Sun. **Credit** AmEx, DC, MC, V.

Built in 1520, the Prospect of Whitby lays reasonable claim to being the oldest riverside pub in London. The whole place was painstakingly restored in 1955, and the pewter-topped bar, which dates from the 16th century, is still impressive, not least for the pockmarks and bits of patching visible on its surface. Burning stoves and weathered wood keep things cosy. The Thameside beer garden is a boon most of the year (outdoor heaters see to that), especially at high tide, when the hangman's noose outside the pub can seem genuinely chilling; Captain Kidd was one of the desperados whose heels were dangled in this stretch of river. Sadly, the pub never quite seems to muster an independent life, perhaps due to the gangs of tourists periodically shipped in for half pints of English beer (either Young's Bitter, Bombardier or London Pride; Kronenbourg 1664 is the most exciting lager). A 2004 change of management seems to have improved the food. Staff are young and cheerful.
Babies and children welcome. Function room. No-smoking area. Specialities (real ale). Tables outdoors (7, garden).

Town of Ramsgate

62 Wapping High Street, E1W 2PN (7481 8000). Wapping tube/100 bus. **Open** noon-11pm Mon-Sat; noon-10.30pm Sun. **Food served** noon-9pm Mon-Sat; noon-8pm Sun. **Credit** AmEx, MC, V.
This is the lesser of Wapping's two historic pubs and, as a boozer, is all the better for it. Our evening visit saw the roadside bay window touchingly lit with two candles, and the landlady and landlord fussing about, clearly on first-name terms with many locals. The pub comprises a long thin bar room, leading to a nice bit of decking over the Thames. Oxblood planking runs along the side wall, as if the pub were clinker-built, which might be apt given its nautical heritage. Here George 'Hanging Judge' Jeffreys was apprehended in 1688, and a century later Lieutenant Bligh and Fletcher Christian shared a noggin before so impressively falling out aboard HMS *Bounty*. The present Grade II listed building dates from 1758, but isn't hugely impressive. Representatives from Young's, Fuller's and Adnams breweries are on tap, plus the usual run from Strongbow to Kronenbourg. There's a wine rack behind the bar, with several options available by the glass.
Babies and children welcome. Quiz (8.30pm Mon; £2 per team). Tables outdoors (12, riverside garden). TV.

Also in the area...

Vineyard (Davy's) International House, 1 St Katherine's Way, E1 9UN (7480 5088).

WHITECHAPEL

The phrase 'cultural melting pot' is frequently applied to Whitechapel, not without justification. There are substantial communities that hail from the Indian subcontinent and eastern Europe, as well as indigenous Cockney sparrows who haven't yet migrated. Yet, with a few exceptions, such diversity is not reflected in the area's drinking establishments. This could change in the near future; Whitechapel is attracting students and recent London arrivals, but the presence of music venue the Rhythm Factory is also drawing what ad men like to call 'taste makers' to the area. It can't be long before E1's publicans up their game.

Big Chill Bar

Dray Walk (Old Truman Brewery), off Brick Lane, E1 6QL (7680 2850/www.bigchill.net). Aldgate East tube/Liverpool Street tube/rail. **Open** noon-midnight Mon-Sat; noon-11.30pm Sun. **Food served** noon-11pm Mon-Sat; noon-10.30pm Sun. **Credit** DC, MC, V.
At last, Brick Lane's Vibe Bar (*see p158*) has serious competition. The Big Chill is a long, low multipurpose bar, DJ venue and diner, with a car park aesthetic of concrete floors, columns and beams scarcely softened by cinema-style drapes, a lone chandelier and an equally incongruous bison head. A solid and lambently lit bar counter runs the length of one wall with low slung leather seating and tables on the other side of the room. It's almost totally functional, but wholly inviting. Music's a big part of the operation, with DJs playing anything from Afro funk to cheesy lounge every night; if you like the sounds you can get a Big Chill CD with your quality lager (Budvar, König Ludwig or bottled Duval, Moretti or Sagres), draught cider (Westons), wine by the glass and bottle or cocktails (from a list of eight, at around £6). Food is a mix of global tapas, platters and superior sandwiches and burgers.
Babies and children welcome. Disabled: toilet. Film screening (7.30pm 1st Mon of mth). Games (board games). Music (DJs 7pm daily). Quiz (phone for details). Tables outdoors (4, patio).

Black Bull

199 Whitechapel Road, E1 1DE (7247 6707). Whitechapel tube. **Open** 11am-11pm Mon-Sat; noon-10.30pm Sun. **Food served** noon-3pm Mon-Fri. **No credit cards**.
This is a boozers' boozer. Ignore the cod Tudor exterior and interior decoration that runs to a big silhouette of a black bull and a square of flowery red carpet, and glance instead along the pumps. You're in real ale heaven, for this is one of London's very few pubs to serve the great works of Suffolk's Nethergate brewery: India Pale Ale, a porter (Old Growler) and Augustinian, plus a wonderful Adnams Oyster stout as guest. Punters are alike only in their relaxed demeanour, with real ale chaps slightly in the ascendant over students and old geezers. A huge screen shows early 1980s pop vids at a neighbourly volume; small screens relay the action to the green booths to one side.
Games (fruit machine, quiz machine). TV (big screen, satellite).

Blind Beggar

337 Whitechapel Road, E1 1BU (7247 6195). Whitechapel tube. **Open** 11am-1am Mon; 11am-11pm Tue-Sat; noon-10.30pm Sun. **Food served** noon-2.30pm Mon-Sat; noon-3pm Sun. **Credit** MC, V.
This is where gangster Ronnie Kray murdered George Cornell in 1966, but far from regarding the event as a dark chapter in the pub's history, the present management sees it as a unique selling point. Pictures of the Kray twins together with Babs Windsor and assorted East End hard men adorn the walls, lent a sinister edge by the deep red (some might say blood-red) lighting. Despite this ghoulishness, the Beggar is actually quite cosy. There are two open fires – each with cat – and a large number of distressed red leather armchairs and sofas. Beers of note include Brakspear, Courage Directors and Old Speckled Hen; and whatever you do, don't order wine.
Babies and children welcome (dining only). Games (fruit machines, pool table). Music (The Burns Brothers band 9pm Mon). Tables outdoors (10, garden). TV (big screen, satellite).

Indo

133 Whitechapel Road, E1 1DT (7247 4926). Whitechapel or Aldgate East tube. **Open** 11am-11pm Mon-Sat; 11am-10.30pm Sun. **Food served** noon-8pm daily. **Credit** MC, V.

More of a corridor than a bar, Indo is the kind of place that gives corridors a good name. It's particularly welcome given its location on a desolate stretch of the Whitechapel Road (opposite the East London mosque). One side has wooden tables, bench seating and a big chesterfield sofa; the other is an original old bar where anything from beer to a frothy cappuccino can be served by the friendly owners, Richard and Neil. Food includes fresh 'stone-based oven' pizzas (around £5), and all-day breakfasts (with a good veggie option) at weekends. The bar showcases local artists and photographers, and, at weekends, DJs play anything from country to mellow jazz. Draught beers include Heineken, Stella, Guinness and Hoegaarden, while banana beer and strawberry Früli are among the bottled stock.

Games (chess, dominoes). Music (DJs 8pm Sat; open mic bi-monthly; free). Specialities (continental beers). Tables outdoors (2, pavement). TV.

Lane

12 Osborn Street, E1 6TE (7377 1797/www.thelanebar.co.uk). Aldgate East tube. **Open** noon-midnight Mon-Wed; noon-1am Thur, Fri; 6pm-1am Sat. **Food served** noon-3pm, 6-10pm Mon-Fri; 6-10pm Sat. **Credit** AmEx, DC, MC, V.

This is Brick Lane's answer to central London's swanky Sanderson Hotel. The white tiled floor, blocky dark-fabric stools and designer leather sofas scream sophistication; the bar staff angle bottles of wine (from a decent list) for the customer's inspection before pouring; and there's an impressive range of cocktail-making equipment and a spectrum of mixed drinks to match. Yet somehow all this feels out of place: just a few yards away, Osborn Street turns into Brick Lane, curry capital of the East End, where kormas and jalfrezis are washed down with fizzy beer. The Lane's aspirational lifestyle-magazine chic jars with the prevailing 'down at heel but honest fun' atmosphere. So, for the most part, the bar's DJs have only hotel-guest businessmen for company.

Disabled: toilet. Music (DJs 8pm Wed-Sat; free). TVs (plasma screens).

Poet

9-11 Folgate Street, E2 6EH (7426 0495). Liverpool Street tube/rail. **Open** noon-11pm Mon-Fri. **Food served** noon-3pm Mon-Fri. **Credit** AmEx, MC, V.

Given the concentration of financial institutions in the area, it's something of a surprise that this pub, just around the corner from Liverpool Street, doesn't have more competition. It's aimed squarely at the after-work crowd, and suits and imitation Crombie jackets are much in evidence. The punters keep coming because even though there's no one to give the place a run for its money, the Poet is a cut above your average stocks 'n' futures boozer. Bitburger lager and Kronenbourg 1664 Blanc make rare appearances, the bar menu doesn't restrict itself to the usual nachos-and-dips, and the interior decoration concentrates on bold colours and modern art, not faux period frippery. There's also a huge bar round the back that's easy to miss.

Babies and children welcome (until 9pm). Bar available for hire (weekends). Games (fruit machines, pool tables, table football). Music (DJ 8pm Tue, Fri, occasional Sun; free). Poetry (8pm Mon; free). Tables outdoors (15, terrace). TV (big screen, satellite).

Pride of Spitalfields

3 Heneage Street, E1 5LJ (7247 8933). Aldgate East tube. **Open** 11am-11pm Mon-Sat; noon-10.30pm Sun. **Food served** noon-2.30pm Mon-Fri; 1-5pm Sun. **No credit cards.**

Outside, the Pride of Spitalfields looks like somebody's house – a pot plant sits beside the blue-gloss, suburban front door – but within is a friendly, smoky and unpretentious old boozer. Fuller's Pride and ESB are on draught, plus Brewers Gold and Pop Weasel. The impressive range of guest beers over the years is recorded by beer mats on the front of the handsome wooden bar. A brick fireplace with a small, heavy-duty stove does sterling work on a winter's night. Customers include young and old, Shoreditch renegades of the no-hair-product type, and chic Japanese youth. The soundtrack segued from Irish pub rock into Tears for Fears; the red carpet reminded us of the days when pub food meant a pickled egg.

Babies and children welcome. Specialities (real ale). Tables outdoors (4, pavement). TV (big screen).

Urban Bar (LHT)

176 Whitechapel Road, E1 1BJ (7247 8978). Whitechapel or Aldgate East tube/25 bus. **Open/food served** noon-midnight Mon-Wed, Sun; noon-1am Thur-Sat. **Credit** MC, V.

You can't please all the people all the time, but the owners of the Urban Bar have a good go. Most of their customers are nurses (wa-hey!) from the neighbouring hospital and students: hence the garish orange, purple and green paint job (the exterior is painted in tiger stripes). Just in case a passing businessman wanders in, there's a cigar as well as a cigarette machine. Popcorn is sold, too. Salsa classes are run on Tuesdays (beginners welcome), and, bizarrely, there's a coat rack at ceiling level. You can buy pints of Spitfire and London Pride here, but this is more of an Aftershock kind of place. Fun with a capital F.

Function room. Internet access. Jukebox. Music (bands 9pm Wed, Sun; free).

Vibe Bar

The Old Truman Brewery, 91-95 Brick Lane, E1 6QL (7377 2899/www.vibe-bar.co.uk). Aldgate East tube/ Liverpool Street tube/rail. **Open** 11am-11.30pm Mon-Thur, Sun; 11am-1am Fri, Sat. **Food served** 3-8pm Wed-Sun. **Credit** AmEx, DC, MC, V.

The Vibe Bar has been going since before trendy types with asymmetric haircuts even thought of living east of Old Street, and it's still one of the better bars in the area. The venue's enduring popularity is nothing to do with the walls covered in graffiti, the leather sofas and the array of DJs – pretty much the norm for the area now – but is down to the vast outdoor seating area, which proves a huge attraction in the summer. Along with your pint of Pilsner Urquell or glass of white (the wine list is well above average), you can get Thai food and watch the world go by. But avoid the torturous jazz bands that appear on Sundays.

Function room. Music (bands 7.30pm Tue, Sun; DJs 7pm Mon, Wed-Sat). Tables outdoors (70, heated courtyard, marquee).

Also in the area...

Goodman's Field (JD Wetherspoon) Mansell Street, E1 8AN (7680 2850).

Grapeshots (Davy's) 2-3 Artillery Passage, E1 7LJ (7247 8215).

Mint 12 East Smithfield, E1W 1AP (7702 0370).

NORTH

NORTH

BELSIZE PARK

This steep foothill of Hampstead has its fair share of dogwalkers' locals and arriviste gastropubs (particularly in Belsize Village) – the venues listed are a representative selection. The standard of food is excellent in all, a sign of the priorities around here, and decent draught bitter and wine by the glass are guaranteed. On its southern fringe, the more streetwise Primrose Hill area features the **Washington Hotel & Bar**, a place that would stand out in any company.

Belsize

29 Belsize Lane, NW3 5AS (7794 4910). Belsize Park tube. **Open/food served** noon-11pm Mon-Sat; noon-10.30pm Sun. **Credit** AmEx, MC, V.

In the heart of Belsize Village, amid chic Greek restaurants and Mediterranean delis, the makeover of this old favourite was inevitable. The grand, glass-framed entrance has been kept and 'Belsize Tavern' is still etched into the back-bar mirrors, but around them are rescued furniture, retro ad signs and chandeliers. Confit rabbit salad (£6.50) wouldn't have been available in the old days, nor would sandwiches (£6-£7) of smoked salmon and mozzarella, Spanish omelette and cherry tomatoes; a hearty ploughman's costs £7.95. Ales on tap include Adnams, Boddington's and London Pride, and there's a wine list of 20 bottles (ten by the glass). There are cocktails (around £7), too, with Grey Goose and Absolut used in the Martini and Cosmopolitan, and unlikely house varieties like Raspberry Caipirinha (Cachaça 51, Framboise and fresh lime) or a Ginger Mojito (Havana 3 and 7, fresh mint, lime and ginger beer).

Babies and children admitted. Restaurant (available for hire). Tables outdoors (2, pavement). TV (big screen).

Hill

94 Haverstock Hill, NW3 2BD (7267 0033/www.geronimo-inns.co.uk). Belsize Park or Chalk Farm tube. **Open** 4-11pm Mon-Thur; noon-11pm Fri, Sat; noon-10.30pm Sun. **Food served** 7-10pm Mon-Thur; noon-3pm, 7-10pm Fri, Sat; noon-7pm Sun. **Credit** MC, V.

A stylish retreat from the A502 connecting Camden and Hampstead, the Hill is a gastrobar that takes its food and drink seriously. In spacious, dainty surroundings of frilly-covered banquettes, much beige and maroon, a sturdy bar counter stands with imperious taps of König Ludwig wheat beer, Aspall Suffolk cider, Fuller's Honey Dew, Budvar and, of course, flowers. As the back area is for dining, the wine list is categorised to accompany food: reds are 'Mediterranean-style spicy' or 'Fruit-driven', whites are 'Aromatic'. To up the ante, there are bottles of Louis Latour chablis and Les Tuileries sancerre in the £23 range. Mains include seared calf's liver and braised New Zealand lamb shank. A garden area is promised for the summer.

Babies and children admitted. Tables outdoors (20, garden).

Washington Hotel & Bar

50 England's Lane, NW3 4UE (7722 8842). Belsize Park or Chalk Farm tube. **Open** noon-11pm Mon-Sat; noon-10.30pm Sun. **Food served** noon-10pm daily. **Credit** AmEx, MC, V.

The best bar in Belsize Park, the Washington proves how good a pub makeover can be. Its superbly stocked, carved-mahogany counter is staffed by jovial young locals – on our visit a regular with a Zimmer frame was being cleaned up after spilling his bitter. Most other regulars come from Primrose Hill. The weekly Hampstead Comedy Club helps, as does a thought-about soundtrack on other nights. By day, dogwalkers, playwrights and dodderers fill the wooden tables and squishy sofas in the loungey side areas. Draught Bateman's Spring Breeze, Everards Original, Brakspear, Bath Gem and Timothy Taylor Landlord, with bottled Chimay, Erdinger Dunkel and Liefmans Frambozenbier are the highlights of a magnificent range of ales, while the 20-strong wine selection includes a Palena sauvignon blanc (£3.50 a glass) and 1881 Siglo rioja (£3.40). Superior sandwiches (crayfish £5.60, Moroccan chicken breast £5.10) and mains (spicy bean cassoulet £6.50) complete the thoroughly accomplished picture.

Comedy (9pm Thur, Sun; £5-£8). Function room. TV.

CAMDEN TOWN & CHALK FARM

Along with the West End, Camden is set to be transformed as the licensing laws change. Small venues like the Falcon and the Laurel Tree have already been ousted by the increase of chain pubs in the area, and there's concern that later opening hours will eventually stamp out independent ventures altogether.

Abbey

124 Kentish Town Road, NW1 9QB (7267 9449). Kentish Town tube. **Open** 11am-midnight Mon-Wed, Sun; 11am-1am Thur-Sat. **Food served** 11am-10pm daily. **Credit** MC, V.

The Abbey opened in June 2004 with the notion of bringing some refinement to the 'wrong' end of Kentish Town. Airy and chic, it explores the route an All Bar One might take if unchained from head office. Low-watt globes hang above sturdy tables and a long, comfortable leatherette couch, the fridges burst with exotic beers and silty organic ales, and there's Kronenbourg Blanc beside the usual beers on tap. Most drinkers seemed happy to enjoy the light food and light jazz in the bar, but there's a separate dining area should snacks not sate you. The staircase is lined with a blown-up print of a forest, leading to giant roses in the ladies and fireworks in the gents – and each cubicle has its own hand dryer and basin. Wonderfully genteel.

Babies and children admitted. Disabled: toilet. Music (bands 8pm Thur-Sat; free). Restaurant. Tables outdoors (10, garden). TVs (big screen). **Map 8 J25**.

Bar Solo

20 Inverness Street, NW1 7HJ (7482 4611/ www.barsolo.co.uk). Camden Town tube. **Open** 9am-1am daily. **Food served** 9am-11.30pm daily. **Happy hour** 5-7pm daily. **Credit** MC, V.

Music *must* be the food of love. Or latin beats must be, at any rate. They certainly seem to encourage the couples present to intertwine their hands and gaze lovingly over their shared meze plates. Maybe it's the mussels, maybe it's the gold plaster buttocks on the wall, but Bar Solo definitely has a one-track mind. Although there's nothing so vulgar as draught beer on offer, you'll find bottles of Peroni, Corona and Hoegaarden, an eclectic wine list, cocktails and a fine selection of spirits, including 12-year-old Van Winkle and Woodford Reserve bourbons, along with Appleton Estate rum, aged for 21 years. The pumping disco bar downstairs is popular with local after-show parties.

Babies and children admitted. Function room. Tables outdoors (2, terrace). **Map 8 H1**.

Bartok

78-79 Chalk Farm Road, NW1 8AR (7916 0595/ www.meanfiddler.com). Chalk Farm tube. **Open** 5pm-1am Mon-Thur; 5pm-2am Fri; noon-2am Sat; noon-midnight Sun. **Food served** 6-9pm Mon-Fri; noon-9pm Sat, Sun. **Admission** £2 after 11pm, £3 after midnight Fri; £4 after 11pm Sat. **Credit** MC, V.

Although named after a Hungarian composer, Bartok is more about 'classics' and 'classy' than classical. Resident DJs spin anything from loops to electronica, old-school blues and 1960s soul in a room fashioned like an intimate boudoir. The chandeliers, long red curtains, gilt mirrors and pink lilies in vases give the bar a pleasingly decadent feel, and there's an exotic wine list. For those who don't stand on ceremony, there's the usual draught options of Stella, Hoegaarden and Foster's, and a manly selection of sandwiches and fries, as well as more delicate Thai bites.

Babies and children admitted (weekend only). Music (DJs 8.30pm Tue, Fri, Sat; bands 6pm Wed, Thur, Sun). Tables outdoors (3, pavement). **Map 8 G26**.

Bullet

147 Kentish Town Road, NW1 8PB (7485 6040/ www.bulletbar.co.uk). Camden Town or Kentish Town tube. **Open/food served** 5.30pm-midnight Mon-Wed, Sun; 5.30pm-1am Thur; 5.30pm-2am Fri, Sat. **Admission** £5 non-members, £3 members after 10pm. **Membership** £5 6 mths. **No credit cards**.

A revamp has transformed a grungy rockin' dive into Bullet, a swanky cocktail hang-out – and there aren't many of those between Camden and Kentish Town. Many of the stylistic details are familiar: retro leather sofas, wine-red walls, bare bricks, table football – but taken together they create an easy-going, warm and comfortable vibe; there are fine cocktails and tapas bar snacks, too. Owner Adam Marshall clearly wants a creative space, not another joint to get wasted in: there's artwork on the walls, the Sunday's acoustic sessions are open to all, and singer-songwriter Susan McDonald's quartet plays on Wednesdays. It bills itself as 'a cocktail bar and live music venue', but it's DJs that drive the party action from Thursday to Saturday.

Disabled: toilet. Entertainment (cabaret 7.30pm Mon). Music (DJs 7pm Thur-Sat; bands 7pm Tue, Wed, Sun). Tables outdoors (garden). **Map 8 J26**.

Camden Arms

1 Randolph Street, NW1 0SS (7267 9829). Camden Town tube. **Open** noon-11pm Mon-Sat; noon-10.30pm Sun. **Food served** noon-3pm, 6-9pm Mon-Fri; noon-5pm Sat, Sun. **Credit** AmEx, DC, MC, V.

Given that this cosy bar has aimed for the cocktail crowd of late, with just Flowers, San Miguel and Hoegaarden to quench a beer drinker's thirst, the name has been changed from Camden Brewing Co to the far more boring Camden Arms. It's a sparkling jewel, though, dressed rather coquettishly with colourful pouffes, fairy lights, dainty lamps, vases of flowers, two original fireplaces and spiral stairs leading to, on our visit, a Pat Pope rock 'n' roll exhibition. The menu includes snacks like green chicken tikka skewers and a main course of slow-roast belly pork with puy lentils, though food isn't the bar's strongest point. This venue seems to be forever changing hands, but on our latest visit it was thriving, and twenty- and thirtysomethings flood in for the DJ sets on Friday and Saturday nights. Perhaps the hard work is finally paying off.

Disabled: toilet. Function room. Music (DJs 8pm Fri, Sat; free). Restaurant. Tables outdoors (20, garden; 6, pavement). **Map 8 J26**.

Crown & Goose

100 Arlington Road, NW1 7HP (7485 8008). Camden Town tube. **Open** 11am-11pm Mon-Sat; noon-10.30pm Sun. **Food served** noon-3pm, 6-10pm Mon-Sat; noon-9pm Sun. **Credit** AmEx, DC, MC, V.

This regal-looking gastropub tucked away off the main Camden drag also has a restaurant upstairs to cater for the inevitable overspill – for its secret is now well and truly out. We can't help feeling the Crown & Goose would be more at home in Primrose Hill, if not a country estate; the banqueting hall lighting, ornate mirrors and cherubs are all a touch surreal given the pokey square layout, and the cluttered tables and chairs can seem less than relaxing. Nevertheless, the food more than compensates, as the Camden socialites who hunker down for the long haul can confirm. We tucked into wild boar and apple sausages, accompanied by organic wine (the Leffe on tap was just as welcome). Once the fire was lit (at our request), we were in grave danger of getting too comfortable.

Babies and children admitted (before 9pm, dining only). Disabled: toilet. Function room. Tables outdoors (4, pavement). **Map 8 J1**.

Cuban

Stables Market, Chalk Farm Road, NW1 8AH (7424 0692/www.thecuban.co.uk). Camden Town or Chalk Farm Road tube. **Open/food served** 10am-1am Mon-Sat; 10am-midnight Sun. **Credit** MC, V.

Located deep in the heart of the funky Stables market, this bar and restaurant was formerly a trading hall. Of course, there's nothing subtle about the loud Che posters or the Cuban flags festooned across the rough brick interior, but then the place is not aiming for subtle. The diner-style seating is very sociable; the stools lining the long bar encourage you to ogle the staff pounding away at your crushed ice and berries. Once you get into 'customising' a chicken with various latin rubs, or sharing tapas at around a fiver, you'll start to see how this bar puts the emphasis on good times. There are 30 or so strong cocktails, and if you ask for a rum and Coke, you'll invariably get the response: 'Double?'

Babies and children admitted. Disabled: toilet. Music (bands 7pm Fri, Sun, DJ 8.30pm Sat; both free). Tables outdoors (11, pavement). TVs. **Map 8 H26**.

Enterprise

2 Haverstock Hill, NW3 2BL (7485 2659). Chalk Farm tube. **Open** 11am-11pm Mon-Sat; noon-10.30pm Sun. **Food served** noon-8pm daily. **Credit** MC, V.

If you like speciality beers and a good sturdy table, soak up some culture and some thick, raspberry-flavoured Früli at the Enterprise. Framed pictures of noted thespians line the walls, which are also covered with higgledy-piggledy violins, lanterns, tribal drums and assorted junk; the bar is well stocked with Greene King IPA and Worthington's on tap, plus bottled beers from all over Europe. There's an open fire and creaking shelves of books, and the locals always seem ready to chat at the bar. The Barfly Acoustic Club is held upstairs, as well as comedy nights and spoken-word events, which add a young, studenty crowd to the mix.

Babies and children admitted (before 7pm). Comedy (8pm Mon, Sun; £4-£5). Function room. Tables outdoors (4, pavement). TV. **Map 8 G26**.

Hawley Arms

2 Castlehaven Road, NW1 8QU (7428 5979). Camden Town tube. **Open** noon-11pm Mon-Sat; noon-10.30pm Sun. **Food served** noon-8pm Mon-Sat; noon-6pm Sun. **Credit** MC, V.

Finally: the Hawley Arms has found owners who really love it. Their previous experience at Islington's Elbow Room (*see p174*) and the Trafalgar Tavern in Greenwich (*see p212*) has inspired them to create this pastiche of a teenager's bedroom: free nibbles, an awesome jukebox (with slots for unsigned bands) and a matey atmosphere. They have ambitious plans to shift the kitchen upstairs and open the ground floor to make room for a piano; they also aim to use the roof terrace, which regulars probably don't even know exists. Joining the usual on draught are imported Budvar, Hoegaarden, Abbot Ale and a guest ale. Food consists of dollops of comfort food like home-made pies, boiled egg and soldiers, and fresh fish dishes. There's even a tuck shop.

Babies and children admitted (before 7pm). Tables outdoors (4, garden patio). **Map 8 H26**.

Lock Tavern

35 Chalk Farm Road, NW1 8AJ (7482 7163). Camden Town or Chalk Farm tube. **Open** noon-11pm Mon-Sat; noon-10.30pm Sun. **Food served** noon-3pm, 5-10pm Mon-Fri; noon-5pm, 6-9pm Sat; noon-5.30pm, 7-9.30pm Sun. **Credit** MC, V.

The fact that the Lock Tavern calls itself 'a tarted-up boozer on Chalk Farm Road' gives you an idea of its geezerness. In fact, what this pub does best is care for your hangover, which means comfy armchairs and chilled music, along with pies from the Square Pie Company (in addition to a surprisingly refined menu). Owned by DJ Jon Carter, the venue is spread over two floors, with a roof terrace that's fully insulated in winter. This is the most popular spot, with its fairy lights and no-nonsense wooden benches and tables strongly hinting you should get communal. There's a no-frills draught choice of Staropramen, Grolsch, Carling, London Pride, Greene King IPA and Strongbow.

Babies and children admitted. Music (DJs 7pm Thur-Sat, 3pm Sun; free). Tables outdoors (8, roof terrace; 10, garden). TV (projector). **Map 8 H26**.

Lockside Lounge

75-89 West Yard, Camden Lock, NW1 8AF (7284 0007/www.locksidelounge.com). Camden Town tube. **Open** noon-11pm Mon-Thur; 11am-11pm Fri, Sat; 11am-10.30pm Sun. **Food served** noon-10pm daily. **Credit** AmEx, MC, V.

One of countless local bars going for the retro/rustic feel, the Lockside Lounge offers arcade game tables, canned pistachio nuts and exposed beams. Its premises have been given a serious facelift since they housed the dingy HQ club. What the place lacks in originality, it makes up for in consumables – we were pleased to discover imported bottles from Russia, Mexico, Australia, Belgium and the Czech Republic behind the bar, not to mention Magners cider, Adnams Broadside, Old Speckled Hen and Summer Lightning on tap. The cocktail list scores points for thoroughness, with seasonal offers like a Manuka Honey Toddy. The food is warming, with butternut squash spiced soup and goose pâté on toast among the reasonable starters; mains include smoked haddock pie and meat skewers. You can even take a seat on the balcony, if you're not offended by the patchouli wafting up from below.

Babies and children admitted (before 7pm). Disabled: ramp, toilet. Music (DJs 7pm Fri-Sun; free). Tables outdoors (10, terrace). **Map 8 H26**.

Lord Stanley

51 Camden Park Road, NW1 9BH (7428 9488). Camden Town tube/Camden Road rail then 29, 253 bus. **Open** 6-11pm Mon; noon-11pm Tue-Sat; noon-10.30pm Sun. **Food served** 7-10pm Mon; 12.30-3pm, 7-10pm Tue-Sat; 12.30-4pm, 7-9.30pm Sun. **Credit** AmEx, DC, MC, V.

Now this is how a local boozer should be: unpretentious without skimping on character. Take the battered old sofas bearing a billion bum-imprints and the knackered piano for anyone who fancies a tuneless tinkle. Candles flutter welcomingly in the windows, alongside big bunches of wild daisies; inside, toothless old men rub shoulders with poetic types. As well as the usual lager representatives, hand-pumped ales like Adnams Broadside and Exmoor Gold go down a storm. The wine list and food – a superior menu of hearty mains like char-grilled sea bass and home-made sausages – are chalked up on boards; the grub is sizzled before your eyes in the central kitchen.

Babies and children admitted. Function room. Tables outdoors (10, garden; 5 pavement).

Lush

31 Jamestown Road, NW1 7DB (7424 9054). Camden Town tube. **Open** 11am-11pm Mon-Sat; 11am-10.30pm Sun. **Food served** 11am-10pm daily. **Credit** MC, V.

Now the dust has had time to settle after a couple of uninspired takeovers, we returned to Lush to discover that although there haven't been any major changes since the days the premises housed Blakes, things seem to be ticking along nicely. Despite an ongoing battle against local residents to extend the licence (Lush doesn't enjoy the same leniency as other Camden pubs, being off the main drag), the L-shaped bar is usually buzzing with enthusiastic urbanites. Paintings of indie stars adorn the walls, although the decor in general leans towards the medieval, with heavy wooden door and oversized tables. There's a restaurant upstairs, but brunch, wraps and melts are served in the bar, along with an extensive list of cocktails, and Guinness, Heineken and Hoegaarden on tap.

Function room. Specialities (cocktails). Tables outdoors (10, pavement).

Mac Bar

102-104 Camden Road, NW1 9EA (7485 4530/www.macbar.co.uk). Camden Town tube/Camden Road rail. **Open** noon-11pm Mon-Sat; noon-10.30pm Sun. **Food served** noon-3.30pm, 6-9.30pm Mon-Fri; noon-9pm Sat, Sun. **Credit** JCB, MC, V.

The Triangle
1 Ferme Park Road, N4
Tel. 020 8292 0516
Nearest tube: Finsbury Park
Opening hours: Tues - Fri 6pm –midnightSat– Sun 11am-midnight Closed Mondays

This popular little hideaway is an absolute gem of a restaurant that nestles snugly between Crouch End and Finsbury Park. The decor is warm, inviting, a seamless blend of art from all over the world, lush plants and in the summer a simply exquisite garden.

A seasonally changing and highly original menu offers up such delights as pork fillet with apple and potato gratin, seared tuna steak with a crunchy noodle basket, and for the veggies a typical dish might be gratin of stuffed aubergine with vegetable ratatouille, cheese sauce and sunflower seeds.
And of course there are the favourites that just couldn't go away Mediterranean fishcakes - 100% fish, bought locally and always fresh served with homemade chips.

The Triangle draws an eclectic and predominantly creative crowd, On Saturday nights the most exceptionally talented and beautiful belly dancers entwine themselves around the restaurant.

This is the sort of place everbody should have on their doorstep, but if you don't, you seriously need to make a trip to the Triangle.

Written by Clare Cameron

The Mac Bar takes drinking culture very seriously: this is the sort of place where the barman flicks his shaker into the air and catches it with cool nonchalance, all the while pulping your lychee. In addition to quality bar food like hot roast beef, watercress and horseradish mayonnaise on freshly baked bread (£5.95), there's a new, rather makeshift-looking restaurant that's so small it seems like an afterthought. Backlit installations from hip local photographers and artists illuminate the walls, while the low-slung back room plays host to DJs, music and comedy.
Babies and children welcome; high chair. Bar available for hire. Games (board games). Music (DJs 8.30pm Fri, Sat; jazz 3pm Sun; both free). Specialities (cocktails). Tables outdoors (4, pavement). **Map 8 J26**.

Monkey Chews

2 Queen's Crescent, NW5 4EP (7267 6406/ www.monkeychews.com). Chalk Farm tube. **Open** 5-11pm Mon-Thur; 5pm-midnight Fri; noon-midnight Sat; noon-10.30pm Sun. **Food served** 5-11pm Mon-Sat; noon-10.30pm Sun. **Credit** MC, V.

Taking the uninitiated to the hidden grotto that is Monkey Chews usually elicits a wail of 'Why did nobody tell me this was here?' Nestled in a Chalk Farm estate, the bar models itself on LA's drinking dens, the kind Tom Waits sings about. You'll find rotisserie chicken, plates of rock oysters and a Beggar's Banquet feasts for ten or more diners. There's also Hoegaarden, Tetley's, Red Stripe and San Miguel on tap. The decor has a hint of Shanghai, although little touches from the pub's Victorian past, like the magnificent skylight and ornate fireplace, remain. We were entertained by a ska duo on Tuesday's open mic night, but we could have brought our own records on Wednesdays or heard soul on one of the 'Roastin' Sundays'.
Babies and children welcome (before 9pm). Function room. Music (DJs 9pm Thur-Sun; free). Games (quiz machine). Tables outdoors (5, pavement). TV (satellite, widescreen). **Map 8 G25**.

Quinn's

65 Kentish Town Road, NW1 8NY (7267 8240). Camden Town tube. **Open/food served** 11am-midnight Mon-Wed; 11am-2am Thur-Sat; noon-midnight Sun. **Credit** AmEx, MC, V.

If you prefer your Irish bars to conform to some outmoded Emerald Isle fantasy, Quinn's is not the place for you. For a start, the huge range of Belgian beers dwarfs the stouts – Leffe is a better choice than the Guinness (though there's also the likes of Abbot Ale, Greene King IPA, Ruddles County, San Miguel and Budvar on tap). No wonder couples hang on to each other for support. The open fire failed to make the pub (blandly decorated in an Irish style) any more cosy, but Quinn's is no less popular with North London's Irish contingent, and surely a healthy number of Irish punters is a better qualification for declaring a pub Irish than any other.
Babies and children admitted. Music (DJs Fri-Sun; free). Tables outdoors (20, garden). TV. **Map 8 J26**.

Singapore Sling

16 Inverness Street, NW1 7HJ (7424 9527). Camden Town tube. **Open** noon-midnight Mon-Thur, Sun; noon-1am Fri, Sat. **Food served** noon-11pm Mon-Thur; noon-11.30pm Sat; noon-10.30pm Sun. **Credit** MC, V.

Unlike the other bars down Inverness Street, Singapore Sling benefits from space. There's a lobby area with leather couches so comfortable some people progress no further, a friendly upstairs bar with an outside water feature, and a

Queen's Hotel. *See p166.*

main ground-floor dining area (serving pan-Asian cuisine) – all in sumptuous red, with plenty of plants and mirrors. Most importantly, the Sling is nirvana for drink connoisseurs, with almost any cocktail you could conceivably order; there's also saké to lure you off the beaten track. If you're off the sauce, there's a variety of coffees, Malaysian and herbal teas, energy drinks, coconut juice and non-alcoholic cocktails to drink with your spicy oriental bar snacks. Come on a Monday and you can drink twofers all night.
Babies and children admitted (restaurant). Music (DJ 10pm Fri, Sat; free). Restaurant. Tables outdoors (2, pavement).

Also in the area...

Belgo Noord 72 Chalk Farm Road, NW1 8AN (7267 0718).
Camden Tup 2-3 Greenland Place, NW1 0AP (7482 0399).
Hog's Head 55 Parkway, NW1 7PN (7284 1675).

CROUCH END

The giant three-wheel buggies, minor celebs and latte-and-gym bunnies all testify to a 'villagey' (read: poorly connected) enclave rather too conscious of its own charms. Nowhere is this more evident than in the locals' endless speculation about the existence of a decent boozer hearabouts (probable answer: the **Harringay Arms**). Still, the rise of Hornsey High Street, driven by trendy housing and a new outpost of the Burlington Academy, is a welcome evolution in the social scene.

Harringay Arms

153 Crouch Hill, N8 9QH (8340 4243). Finsbury Park tube/rail then W3, W7 bus/Crouch Hill rail. **Open** noon-11pm Mon-Sat; noon-10.30pm Sun. **No credit cards**.
This is a proper old boozer with great atmosphere, populated by a friendly, blokeish crowd who all seem to know each other. Likely as not, they'll count you as one of their chums before the night is out. The Harringay is the sort of place where you'll find yourself joining in an impromptu sweepstake, or bantering as you try to crib answers from the annoyingly well-informed team next to you at the wicked Tuesday night pub quiz. The feel is resolutely old-school: wooden panelling, football on the telly in the background, faded prints of Irish writers, and a well-kept pint of Guinness. There's a tiny 'garden' area at the back, and as this is Crouch End, you might see a famous face or two; Dave Stewart reportedly used to be a regular, and you might spot the odd actor from *EastEnders* as well.
Games (fruit machine). No piped music or jukebox. Quiz (9pm Tue; £1). Tables outdoors (4, garden). TV (satellite).

King's Head

2 Crouch End Hill, N8 8AA (8340 1028). Finsbury Park tube/rail/Crouch Hill rail. **Open** noon-11pm Mon-Sat; noon-10.30pm Sun. **Food served** noon-10pm daily. **Credit** AmEx, MC, V.
The King's Head is best known for its comedy nights in the basement, advertised on a regularly published programme in painfully tiny print. There are try-out nights, magic acts and musicians, too – blues, jazz and salsa; well-known stand-ups come here to test new material. Upstairs is a recently refitted space with a distinctly 1960s, sub-Hoxton

feel: candles, mirrors, George and Mildred wallpaper, a drape partition – and a deeply confused attitude to lighting, with wood-grain patterned lampshades fighting it out with plastic puffballs, chandeliers and an industrial spotlight. Staropramen, Old Empire, Leffe, Hoegaarden and Adnams Broadside are all on draught at the well-stocked bar; food is mostly plates of hot snacks to share. The atmosphere is lively, the acoustics poor, and the clientele look like they all mean well.
Comedy (8pm Thur, Sat, Sun; £6-£8). Disabled: toilet. Function room. Music (jazz 1-5pm Sun; £3). Salsa club (7.30pm-midnight Mon; £5).

Queen's Hotel

26 Broadway Parade, N8 9DE (8340 2031). Finsbury Park tube/rail then W3, W7 bus. **Open** noon-11pm Mon-Wed, Fri; noon-midnight Thur, Sat; noon-10.30pm. **Food served** noon-8pm daily. **Credit** AmEx, MC, V.
Its central location in Crouch End makes the Queen's Hotel an obvious meeting point. Accordingly, the pub does its best to be a good, solid boozer for all. Walk around the huge island bar and you'll get an overview of the constituent parts: the intense pool table section, the quieter areas where couples sit, and the big space where football is screened, above a little stage where musicians play on Thursdays. A fine restoration has left the pub with carved fittings, etched glass and an elaborate ceiling; the surroundings are matched by a few decent real ales (Adnams, London Pride). The hotel is supposedly a local historic landmark, but doesn't really feel like one. Its famous frontage featured in little-remembered Britflick *Final Cut*. The Queen's does its job nicely enough, but a night here is unlikely to change your life.
Games (fruit machines, pool). Music (band 9pm Thur; free). Tables outdoors (7, garden). TVs (big screen, satellite).

Viva Viva

18 High Street, Hornsey, N8 7PB (8341 0999/ www.viva-viva.co.uk). Turnpike Lane tube then 144 bus. **Open** 9am-midnight daily. **Food served** 10am-11pm daily. **Credit** MC, V.
Along with neighbouring eateries Pradera and Le Bistro, Viva Viva is helping to rejuvenate Hornsey High Street, bringing café culture to an area that has long languished in the shadow of Crouch End. No one could fault this self-styled 'West End oasis, here in N8' for effort. Bar, restaurant, world music venue, dance school, children's groups, organic ingredients, fair trade coffee, board games, a special business meeting lunch deal… there's a determination to offer something for everyone. To the uncharitable, this might appear a touch desperate; nonetheless, kicking cocktails and tasty tapas are served with a winning smile. The decor is big on primary colours and makes the most of a narrow layout, with fairy lights, red lamps, leather banquettes and bits of art. A noticeboard loaded with local messages underlines the community feel; programmes of events are published monthly and on the website.
Babies and children welcome (before 9pm; children's menu, high chairs, toys). Disabled: toilet. Games (board games). Music (bands 8.30pm daily; free). Specialities (cocktails). Tables outdoors (2, pavement).

Also in the area…

All Bar One 2-4 The Broadway, N8 9SN (8342 7871).
Tollgate (JD Wetherspoon) 26-30 Turnpike Lane, N8 0PS (8889 9085).

FINSBURY PARK & STROUD GREEN

This is not an area celebrated for its bars, but the **Salisbury Hotel** is an undisputed marvel. Recent refits in the district have tended to bring in hard seats and bare floorboards, though the decor at **Chapter One** and the extraordinarily overblown **Triangle** at least show some imagination.

Chapter One

143 Stroud Green Road, N4 3PZ (7281 9630/ www.chapteronebar.com). Finsbury Park tube/rail/ 210, W3, W7 bus. **Open/food served** 3pm-midnight Mon-Thur; 3pm-12.30am Fri; noon-12.30am Sat; noon-midnight Sun. **Credit** AmEx, MC, V.
Molletes, chilaquiles, quesadillas, Mojitos… there's a distinctly latin quality to this sassy little bar. Chapter One is easily one of the classier drinking venues on patchy Stroud Green Road. Mellow hacienda chic is created by blood-red walls, glass surfaces, strings of discreet fairy lights, dimly lit wooden tables, the odd palm, and leatherette sofas (including an enormous one that wraps around three walls at the back). This is an ideal place for a discreet midweek date, or for a knees-up at the weekend. It is also one of those rare bars that can screen the footie without being taken over by it. Cocktails are advertised on a big blackboard; every weekend they're gulped down by a lively local crowd, to the sound of live music.
Disabled: toilet. Games (quiz machine). Music (DJs 9.30pm Fri, Sat; band 9.30pm Thur). Specialities (cocktails). TVs (digital, satellite, widescreen).

Salisbury Hotel

1 Grand Parade, Green Lanes, N4 1JX (8800 9617). Manor House tube then 29 bus. **Open** 2pm-1am Mon-Wed; noon-2am Thur-Sat; noon-midnight Sun. **Food served** 6-10pm Mon-Thur; noon-3pm, 6-10pm Fri, Sat; noon-6pm Sun. **Credit** MC, V.
You can tell at once from the Salisbury's imposing, bulging Victorian exterior and the decorative ironwork and intricate mosaics of the main entrance that you're on to something special. And the interior exceeds expectations. There are long, tall marble bars, pillars, alcoves, and carved woodwork. The scale and attention to detail are exquisite, the fixtures and fittings vary from one area to the next like the different rooms of a stately home. What's more, there's a strong range of real ales (Fuller's ESB, Chiswick, London Pride and London Porter) and foreign lagers (including Litovel and Zbur from the Czech Republic, plus Leffe and Hoegaarden), a lively quiz night, live jazz and great roasts by a lovely fireside – all in the middle of Green Lanes.
Babies and children admitted (restaurant only). Disabled: toilet. Function room. Music (jazz 8.30pm Sun; free). No-smoking area. Restaurant.

Triangle

1 Ferme Park Road, N4 4DS (8292 0516). Finsbury Park tube/rail then W3 bus/Crouch Hill rail. **Open/ food served** 6pm-midnight Tue-Fri; 11am-midnight Sat, Sun. **Credit** MC, V.
The pungent whiff of incense, the beaten silver doors and, above all, the canvas Moorish marquee appendages stuck on the front of this Moroccan palace: could there be a theme here? Inside, the hard work continues with a full-size raffia motorbike, a bust, gowns and slippers, pouffes, and a

complete restaurant table with menu, glass, ashtray and fork… all stuck to the ceiling. Your first visit will be spent trying to work out what else is up there. Did we mention the mirror tiles, candles, mosaics and through fireplace? There's nothing on draught, but the international collection of bottled beers includes Kirin, Casablanca and, from Estonia, A Le Coq. The menu is surprisingly small but very tasty, and the service is attentive.
Babies and children welcome; high chairs; nappy-changing facilities. Disabled: toilet. Function room. Games (board games). Tables outdoors (5, garden; 7, pavement).

Also in the area...

White Lion of Mortimer (JD Wetherspoon) 125-127 Stroud Green Road, N4 3PX (7561 8880).

HAMPSTEAD

An impossibly pretty tangle of winding backstreets and leafy lanes, Hampstead is undoubtedly one of the loveliest parts of London. It's also an ale drinker's paradise, defiantly resisting the spread of chain bars, and peppered with beautiful and historic pubs.

Flask

14 Flask Walk, NW3 1HE (7435 4580). Hampstead tube. **Open** 11am-11pm Mon-Sat; noon-10.30pm Sun. **Food served** noon-3pm Mon; noon-3pm, 6-8.30pm Tue-Sat; noon-4pm Sun. **Credit** MC, V.
This rather strait-laced old boozer is frequented by a brooding, almost curmudgeonly bunch of hardy old fellows (who keep themselves mostly confined to the small, semi-detached saloon bar), and a more varied mixture of ages and dispositions (who inhabit the relatively spacious seating areas at the front and out back). The Irish barman chatted to us happily, while pulling pints of Young's Special, Bitter and Waggledance. To the rear is an attractive conservatory, overrun with a colourful (but fake) hop plant, and decorated with a raffish collection of old photos and fin-de-siècle poster art. Don't confuse this place with the more illustrious Flask in Highgate (*see p169*).
Babies and children admitted (until 7pm). Disabled: toilet. Function room (conservatory). Games (board games, fruit machine, quiz machine). No piped music or jukebox. Restaurant. Tables outdoors (7, pavement, terrace). TV.

Freemasons Arms

32 Downshire Hill, NW3 1NT (7433 6811). Belsize Park or Hampstead tube/Hampstead Heath rail. **Open** 11am-11pm Mon-Sat; noon-10.30pm Sun. **Food served** noon-2.30pm, 7-10pm Mon-Sat; noon-7pm Sun. **Credit** AmEx, MC, V.
A pub for people who don't like pubs. From the outside, it doesn't look so different from the other buildings lining the exclusive road on which it sits. Manicured hedges border the modest front courtyard, and a plunging stream works its way through the lush and sizeable beer garden. Inside, things are bright and open-plan, with seating arranged, restaurant-style, around polished wooden tables. The coolly efficient bar staff dispense pints of Leffe, London Pride and Staropramen. Food is all of the gastropub variety, with an emphasis on hearty char-grills and spit roasts – a popular choice for the swathes of weary Heath walkers who form the backbone of the pub's clientele.
Babies and children admitted (dining area & garden). Disabled: toilet. Games (skittles). Restaurant (no-smoking). Tables outdoors (40, garden).

Garden Gate

14 South End Road, NW3 2QE (7433 6891). Belsize Park tube/Hampstead rail. **Open** noon-11pm Mon-Sat; noon-10.30pm Sun. **Food served** noon-3pm, 5.30-9.30pm Mon-Fri; noon-9.30pm Sat; noon-9pm Sun. **Credit** MC, V.
Despite the Garden Gate's proximity to the Heath, its bucolic moniker has a somewhat optimistic ring to it: this pretty old boozer sits atop one of the noisiest junctions in Hampstead. No matter, for this is an excellent little spot. The decor walks a nice line between rustic charm and voguish flair; the oversized brick hearth that loosely separates the rear seating area has been retained, for instance, but instead of containing a blazing fire, it's been decorated with artfully hung oil lamps. There's a solid selection of mainly Belgian beers on tap, together with a handful of real ales, including Timothy Taylor Landlord. You'll also find a decent wine list and a surprisingly good selection of champagne available by the glass.
Babies and children admitted (until 7pm). Disabled: toilet. Music (jazz 4pm 2nd Sun of mth; free). Tables outdoors (25, garden). TVs.

Magdala

2A South Hill Park, NW3 2SB (7435 2503). Hampstead Heath rail/C11, 24, 46, 168 bus. **Open** 11am-11pm Mon-Sat; noon-10.30pm Sun. **Food served** noon-2.30pm, 6-10pm Mon-Fri; noon-10pm Sat; noon-9.30pm Sun. **Credit** MC, V.
The sad history of this interesting café-bar is all but hidden away now, save for a few framed press cuttings and two weather-worn bullet holes on the front wall outside. This is where Ruth Ellis shot David Blakely, on Easter Day 1955: a crime for which she later became the last woman in Britain to be hanged. Today, the Magdala is a sedate spot; light pours in through the oversized, partly stained-glass windows, and the pink and terracotta decor is reminiscent of an old seaside café. The overall vibe is one of rarefied hippiness. Chirpy young bar staff pull pints of London Pride, Abbot Ale and Greene King IPA; the Magdala is also known for its nice pints of Guinness.
Babies and children admitted. Function room. Games (board games, cards). Restaurant. Tables outdoors (4, patio).

Spaniards Inn

Spaniards Road, NW3 7JJ (8731 6571). Hampstead tube/210 bus. **Open** 11am-11pm Mon-Sat; noon-10.30pm Sun. **Food served** 11am-10pm daily. **Happy hour** 5-8pm daily. **Credit** AmEx, MC, V.
It would be an injustice if a creaky old place like this were not haunted and, sure enough, the Spaniards drips with tall tales of ghostly goings-on. This is an immensely welcoming pub, as popular today as it was with its illustrious former regulars, including Charles Dickens, Bram Stoker and Mary Shelley. Low-beamed ceilings undulate above timeworn stone floors, and the air is infused with evocawood smoke. The pub can be almost unbearably crowded at Sunday lunchtime, understandably so, as the food is excellent (although expect to pay Hampstead prices – £10 for Icelandic cod and chips, for example). At other times, finding a secluded corner isn't too challenging, and in

THE HARRINGAY ARMS

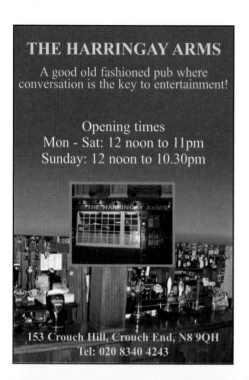

summer an agreeable beer garden comes into its own. The pleasing range of draught ales includes Pedigree, Spitfire, Bombardier and Adnams Bitter.
Babies and children admitted. Entertainment (poetry club 8pm Tue; free). Function room. Games (board games, fruit machine). Music (Irish folk 8pm Tue & 3rd Fri of mth; free). No piped music or jukebox. No-smoking area. Tables outdoors (90, garden).

Wells

30 Well Walk, NW3 1BX (7794 3785/www.thewells hampstead.co.uk). Hampstead tube. Bar **Open** noon-11pm Mon-Sat; noon-10.30pm Sun. **Food served** noon-10.30pm Mon-Sat; noon-10pm Sun. **Credit** MC, V.
Originally built to cash in on the steady stream of passing trade from Hampstead Spa (which some enterprising soul turned into public baths in 1701), this handsome old pub is a far more respectable place today than in past centuries. The plaque out front describes, in wonderfully euphemistic terms, how the Well was once renowned for offering 'facilities for the celebration of unpremeditated and clandestine marriages'. Such lascivious chicanery having long since dried up, the pub is now home to a much more refined crowd. Deep-green walls and black leather sofas set an appropriately modern tone, although this is not just your average gastropub. The food is extremely good – both in the ground-floor bar and the more elegant, upstairs restaurant – and the wine list is long and perfectly judged. There's also a small but satisfying range of ales on tap, including Wadworth 6X and Fuller's London Pride.
Babies and children admitted. Disabled: toilet. Function room. Games (board games, chess). Music (musicians 8.30pm Mon; free). Quiz (8.30pm Tue; £2). Restaurant (no-smoking). Tables outdoors (15, patio).

HIGHGATE

Distant Highgate is one of the few places in London that fully deserves its 'village' title. There's a real community feel here, so dozy old boozers filled with gossipy locals are the predominant strain of pub life. Which is why the **Boogaloo** is such a welcome option.

Angel Inn

37 Highgate High Street, N6 5JT (8347 2921). Archway or Highgate tube. **Open** noon-11pm Mon-Fri; 11am-11pm Sat; noon-10.30pm Sun. **Food served** noon-10pm Mon-Fri, Sun; 11am-10pm Sat. **Credit** MC, V.
Squeezed between estate agents, ringed by people on mobiles, the Angel has the right sort of punter – and it probably got a few tips from its property market neighbours. Angel is makeover heaven, with an open kitchen, burgundy walls, and spindly silver twig arrangements in a corner. It's a conversion of a 1930s conversion, split into two, with light wood, benches by the large, square-paned windows at the front and squishy brown sofas with dark wood panels and low tables in a loungey area to the back. The blue-lit fish tank is quite distracting while you're ordering a drink – a problem also because the beer selection is so extensive. Belgian-themed, it has draught Fruli, as well as De Konnick and Leffe Blonde; in bottles, you'll find malty Mexican beer Dos Equis, along with Duvel. Wines are a brand bonanza – Deakin, Douglas Green and Rothbury. An impressive menu includes bread with oil to dip in (£2.50) and steak and ale pie (£8.90).
Comedy (8.30pm last Thur of mth; £4). Disabled: toilet. Music (jazz 8pm Sun; free). Quiz (9pm Wed; £1). Tables outdoors (3, pavement). TV.

Boogaloo

312 Archway Road, N6 5AT (8340 2928). Highgate tube. **Open** 5.30-11pm Mon-Wed; 5.30pm-midnight Thur; 5.30pm-1.30am Fri; noon-1.30am Sat; noon-10.30pm Sun. **Food served** 5.30-9pm Mon-Fri; noon-7pm Sat, Sun. **Credit** MC, V.
This corner pub is run by Gerry O'Boyle, former boss of Filthy MacNasty's (*see p174*), and the connection shows: this is a similarly raffish, lively drinking hole. While Filthy's took an Irish theme, the Boogaloo is a music pub through and through. The jukebox is impeccable, music-related paintings line the walls, and on Tuesdays, teams with names like Willie Nelson's Column and Nazi Sinatra battle for supremacy at the popular music quiz. DJs play everything from punk to classic soul most Fridays and Saturdays, and there are regular gigs: Pete Doherty and Shane MacGowan (a regular fixture at the bar when he's in London) somehow kept it together for long enough to play on St Patrick's Night. It's all very convivial, and not as blokey as you might expect. Our big complaint, save for the cringeworthy name, is the highly erratic Guinness. Poor form for a pub with no ales, a landlord with an Irish heritage and beer with a £2.90 price tag.
Babies and children admitted. Disabled: toilet. Music (band 5.30-8.30pm Sun; free). Quiz (8.30pm Tue; £1). Tables outdoors (15, garden).

Flask

77 Highgate West Hill, N6 6BU (8348 7346). Archway or Highgate tube/143, 210, 214, 271 bus. **Open** noon-11pm Mon-Sat; noon-10.30pm Sun. **Food served** noon-3pm, 6-10pm Mon-Fri; noon-10pm Sat; noon-4pm, 6-9.30pm Sun. **Credit** MC, V.
This classic 18th-century pub, with low ceilings, timber-beams and rooms big enough for pixies, has been given an unusual style bar twist. The owners of the nearby Angel Inn (*see above*) have brought in the same burgundy paint and lined a few walls with trendy beige banquettes. They've kept the original layout, with dark old wood splitting up five rooms, but the bar has moved to the top one. Now the original bar, a large wooden semi-circular structure is something of irrelevance, filled with punters rather than staff – all a bit disconcerting. Flask gives a taste of the city without having to venture beyond the semi-rural trappings of Highgate. Couples straight out of a car advert loll in the corner, wealthy fiftyish men in suits discuss brake horse power and posh blonde girls wait for their boyfriends to arrive. It's rammed on Sundays, with the offer of four doggy snacks for 20p drawing in hounds and their owners. The selection of ales has more from Belgium than the Angel's line-up, including the thick, dark syrup of Old Growler on draught, and a good selection of malts, albeit from large drink company Diageo's 'Classic' stable, includes Dalwhinnie 15 year old and Talisker 10.
Babies and children admitted. Music (jazz 8pm Mon; free). No-smoking areas. Tables outdoors (15, garden).

Wrestlers

98 North Road, N6 4AA (8340 4297). Highgate tube. **Open** 4.30-11pm Mon-Fri; noon-11pm Sat; noon-10.30pm Sun. **Food served** noon-4pm Sun. **Credit** MC, V.
Lovers of history will have a field day at the Wrestlers. Part of a parade of Georgian houses, at one of which Charles Dickens stayed in 1832, and smack opposite

Flask. *See p169.*

Lubetkin's classic High Point flats, this pub dates from 1921 (a pub has stood on the site since 1547). There's a huge blazing fire inside, panelled walls, stained glass windows and communion candles that give a Home Counties manor feel. Pictures of the Eton wall game, Cheltenham Festival winners in 2000 and copies of the *Daily Telegraph* suggest it's well-matched to its crowd – two girls to every twelve blokes, and lots of rugby shirts and suits at the bar. This is a really cosy winter pub, but the beer garden would make a good spot in the summer, and is surprisingly modern – a plant-fringed, blue-painted wall rises behind wood decking. Beers on draught include Young's Bitter, Greene King IPA, London Pride, Abbot Ale and Staropramen. Wines number 21, with nine by the glass. Dom Pérignon 1995 is well-priced for a special occasion, at £90.
Bar available for hire. Games (board games). Tables outdoors (15, garden, 6, pavement).

Also in the area...

Gatehouse (JD Wetherspoon) 1 North Road, N6 6BD (8340 8054).

HOLLOWAY

Although it's still rather a rough and ready neighbourhood, pub-wise, Holloway hasn't been spared the inexorable spread of the chain bar and gastropub. Rising house prices indicate that this trend is likely to continue, even if pickings remain slim for the moment. The finest venues are to be found away from the main thoroughfare – two gems being the **Swimmer** and the **Landseer**.

Coronet

338-346 Holloway Road, N7 0RN (7609 5014/ www.jdwetherspoon.co.uk). Holloway Road tube. **Open** 10am-11pm Mon-Sat; noon-10.30pm Sun. **Food served** 10am-10pm Mon-Sat; 10am-9.30pm Sun. **Credit** AmEx, DC, MC, V.

From the outside, it's not hard to hazard a guess at the history of this enormous structure. To this day, a small percentage of customers who pass through its vast double doors probably expect to catch a movie, for the grand art deco exterior of this former cinema has been faithfully preserved. The last film was shown here back in 1983, but Wetherspoon's has converted the building into a boozer. Many original features have been restored – including a splendid 1930s chandelier, suspended above a creaky old film projector. Yet we almost wish something more imaginative had been done with the huge, cavernous interior. A lively mix of hardy old sorts and dour-looking regulars sit alongside waves of impoverished students (attracted, no doubt, by the bargain basement prices). The overall vibe, while hardly intimate, is appealingly unaffected. The fine range of ales on tap includes Shepherd Neame Spitfire.
Babies and children admitted (before 7pm, dining only). Disabled: lift, toilet. Games (fruit machines). No piped music or jukebox. No-smoking area. Specialities (real ales). Tables outdoors (3, patio).

Landseer

37 Landseer Road, N19 4JU (7263 4658/www.thelandseer.com). Archway or Holloway Road tube/17, 43, 217 bus. **Open** noon-midnight Mon-Fri; 10am-midnight Sat; noon-11.30pm Sun. **Food served** noon-5pm, 6-10pm Mon-Fri; 10am-5pm, 6-10.30pm Sat; 11am-9.30pm Sun. **Credit** AmEx, MC, V.

In creating such a stylish, comfortable little watering hole, the Landseer's proprietors have pulled off a feat in an area that isn't usually celebrated for its gastropubs. Minimalist decor, neutral tones and pine furniture don't win many points for originality, but the atmosphere here is congenial and the crowd relaxed. Seating is arranged around a mixture of wooden tables (some of them communal), including the prerequisite comfy sofas. The most attractive corners, though, are to be found in the conservatory, with its decorative tiles and unusual, vaulted glass roof. Greene King IPA, Marston's Pedigree and Flowers Original were the draught ales on our last visit, but the selection on tap seems to change with pleasing regularity. There's a decent wine list, too. The fairly standard gastropub food offers few surprises, but it's all good, honest stuff.
Babies and children welcome. Games (board games). Restaurant (no-smoking). Tables outdoors (15, pavement).

Nambucca

596 Holloway Road, N7 5LB (7263 6939/ www.hollowayroad.co.uk). Archway or Holloway Road tube. **Open** 6pm-minight daily. **Food served** 6-9pm daily. **Credit** (over £10) MC, V.

The Holloway Road is not London's most salubrious thoroughfare, but this new establishment, located pretty much midway between Archway and Holloway tubes, is doing its best to liven things up. It's a big corner space, with an airy L-shaped front bar and a large, spacious raised area at the back. Nambucca calls itself 'the best pub in north London', which might be pushing it, but this operation deserves credit for attempting to be more than just a drinking place: there are art exhibitions, music nights with DJs and bands, and film screenings; the owners are keen to run as many different events as possible. Beer and cocktails are the standard batch, but there's a reasonable Thai menu, plus £5 roasts on Sunday. Lively without being trendy, and smart without being snooty, Nambucca is an endeavour that should be supported.
Art exhibitions. Film screenings (check website). Games (arcade machines, board games, fruit machines). Music (country 6pm Fri; bands 6pm Sat; open mic 6pm Sun; all free-£1). Tables outdoors (2, pavement). TVs (projector, satellite).

Swimmer at the Grafton Arms

13 Eburne Road, N7 6AR (7281 4632). Archway or Holloway Road tube/Finsbury Park tube/rail. **Open** noon-2.30pm, 5-11pm Mon-Thur; noon-11pm Fri, Sat; noon-10.30pm Sun. **Food served** noon-2pm, 6-9.30pm Tue-Fri; noon-9.30pm Sat; noon-4pm Sun. **Credit** MC, V.

Hidden away down an unassuming sidestreet, this enjoyable little pub is considered a well-kept secret by much of its regular clientele. They may well have a point; certainly the Swimmer feels like an oasis amid an otherwise lacklustre selection of boozers in this neck of the woods. The modern decor is fetching and well judged. Wooden benches and endearingly shabby sofas flank the cream-coloured walls, while an open recess gives a goldfish-bowl view of the adjoining kitchen, from which a spot-on range of upper-class bar food is dispensed to appreciative punters. The owners take pride in their booze, too; the recent switch from Ruddles to Fuller's has brought with it a suitably fine medley of real ales, including Pride, ESB and Honey Dew, while the range of Czech lagers on tap is little short of revelatory – there's precious few places serving draught Zubr in this town, for instance.

Babies and children welcome (garden). Games (board games, chess). Jukebox. Restaurant (no-smoking). Tables outdoors (15 garden). TV.

ISLINGTON

Islington straddles a demographic fault line. In street after street, gentrified Georgian civility slaps up against down-to-earth estates, and bright white townhouses give way to industrial units and murky canal-scape. This duality is reflected in the district's pubs and bars. The environs of Upper Street, the main drag, offer the full spectrum, from characterful theatre pubs and understated gastro-bars to working men's locals, middlebrow chain boozers and loud, late-licence cattle markets.

Anam

3 Chapel Market, N1 9EZ (7278 1001). Angel tube. **Open** 5pm-2am Tue-Fri; 5pm-3am; 1-11.30pm Sun. **Food served** 6-11pm Tue-Sun. **Admission** £3 after 10pm Fri, Sat. **Credit** MC, V.

London's first Irish cocktail bar is a retro-stylish two-floor space about the size of a static caravan. It reminds us of Soho's Lab bar (*see p84*) – lots of curved lines and rounded corners, plus funky club graphics – and of Bayswater's Harlem (*see p18*) – the glass window in the floor providing up-skirt thrills for those below. The drinks list is terrific, with cocktails created by Tony Conigliaro (*see p153*) utilising premium brand spirits (Belvedere and Grey Goose vodkas, for instance) and rare Irish whiskeys (Kilbeggan, Tyrconnell and Middleton Very Rare). Size is a problem. Upstairs has seating for only about a dozen, supplemented by stools at the bar ('watch your backs, coming through!'), while downstairs, which has a second bar area and the obligatory DJ booth, is hardly any bigger. We struggled to squeeze in on a recent midweek visit, and hate to think how rammed it must get towards the weekend, especially given the lure of that late, late licence.

Disabled: toilet. Function room. Music (DJs 9pm Wed-Sun). TV (big screen, satellite). **Map 9 N2**.

Angelic

57 Liverpool Road, N1 0RJ (7278 8433). Angel tube. **Open** noon-11pm Mon-Sat; noon-10.30pm Sun. **Food served** noon-10pm Mon-Sat; noon-9.30pm Sun. **Credit** MC, V.

Like many of the area's upmarket gastropubs, the Angelic is as much in its element by day as by night. Café culture comes naturally to this beautifully refitted space, with its high ceiling, huge, open-plan layout, period tiling and fireplace, and exceptional service. Indeed, the term 'pub' seems wholly inadequate for an establishment that offers flavoured coffees, a fresh juice bar and a menu featuring solid, rustic fare (pork and rabbit terrine, baked potato with red leicester, ox tongue, poached skate). Draught beers include San Miguel and Charles Wells Bombardier, and there's an extensive wine and champagne list. Politely boisterous by night, the Angelic is also a great place in which to while away a lazy afternoon browsing your *Guardian* and sipping your cappuccino.

Babies and children admitted (before 6pm). Bar available for hire. Disabled: toilet. Games (board games). TV (big screen, satellite). **Map 9 N2**.

Barnsbury

209-211 Liverpool Road, N1 1LX (7607 5519/ www.thebarnsbury.co.uk). Angel tube/Highbury & Islington tube/rail. **Open** noon-11pm Mon-Sat; noon-10.30pm Sun. **Food served** noon-3pm, 6.30-10pm Mon-Fri; noon-4pm, 6.30-10pm Sat; noon-4pm, 6.30-9.30pm Sun. **Credit** AmEx, MC, V.

Barnsbury is one of London's duller precincts, but this gastropub is not at all bad. Beneath chandeliers fashioned out of upturned wine glasses, heavy-smoking locals are kept happy with London Pride, Timothy Taylor Landlord and guest ales. Tucked at the back, excellent global cuisine is brought over by unassuming bar staff: from Thai, through Italian and Welsh (rarebit), to a Barnsbury chicken pie (presumably made from local chickens). At the pumps, Amstel, Grolsch, San Miguel and Bavarian wheat beer all add to the global flavour, while an excellent, mostly organic wine list (including ten wines by the glass) helpfully recommends matches with various dishes on the menu. Standard lamps, duck-egg coloured walls, a photography exhibition and a display-case of toy cars add to the unusual, but generally endearing drinking experience.

Babies and children welcome; high chairs. No-smoking area. Restaurant available for hire. Tables outdoors (4, pavement; 6, garden). **Map 9 N1**.

Camden Head

2 Camden Walk, N1 8DY (7359 0851). Angel tube. **Open** 11am-11pm Mon-Sat; noon-10.30pm Sun. **Food served** noon-9.30pm daily. **Credit** MC, V.

Set back from the nocturnal chaos of Upper Street beside the stone flags of Dickensian little Camden Passage, the Head is a perfectly preserved (all right, restored) shrine to the ghosts of drinkers past. Imagine acid-etched glass, antique optics and taps, gas light fittings, cosy booths and (non-working) bells to press for service. Take away the admirably indie-heavy juke box, dim the lights, throw in a few frock coats, and on a frosty December night you could almost make out Bob Cratchit sneaking a snifter. As well as the usual lagers, there's Bombardier on tap plus two guests (Greene King IPA and Adnams Broadside recently). In summer, an acrobat performs for the crowd swelling to fill the large pub 'garden'. Musos, estate agents, crusties, media types, locals from the nearby estate, and the odd famous face (Timothy Spall, John Hegley) make for a happy mingling space.

Babies and children admitted (heated garden). Comedy club (8.30pm Wed-Sun, every other Mon; £3-£5). Function room. Games (fruit machines, quiz machines). Tables outdoors (12, heated terrace). TVs. **Map 9 O2**.

Centuria

100 St Paul's Road, N1 2QP (7704 2345). Highbury & Islington tube/rail/30, 277 bus. **Open** 5-11pm Mon-Fri; noon-11pm Sat; noon-10.30pm Sun. **Food served** 6-11pm Mon-Fri; 12.30-11pm Sat; 12.30-10.30pm Sun. **Credit** MC, V.

A good ten-minute trot from Highbury Corner, down St Paul's Road, this cool venue is well worth the walk. Resolutely a thirtysomethings' hangout, Centuria comes with a palatable Café del Mar soundtrack that helps create the perfect atmosphere for a relaxed few drinks with friends. It's a good call for a first date, too. The building itself is impressive, with huge windows all around and high ceilings that make the smallish bar seem airy and spacious. The standard range of beers and wines is available, in addition to a selection of reasonably priced cocktail jugs for the party-minded. You can eat in both rooms, but the

larger of the two, with its open kitchen, is a roomy restaurant (slightly lacking in atmosphere) in which to enjoy the usual choice of gastropub tuck. There's nothing try-hard about this place, which in some ways makes for a refreshing change round these parts.
Children admitted; high chairs. Restaurant available for hire. Tables outdoors (6, pavement). **Map 9 P25**.

Chapel

29A Penton Street, N1 9PX (7833 4090/www.thechapelbar.co.uk). Angel tube. **Open** 5-11pm Mon-Wed; 5pm-midnight Thur; noon-2am Fri, Sat; noon-11pm Sun. **Food served** 2-6pm Sun. **Happy hour** 5-9pm Mon-Wed; 5-7pm Thur-Sat. **Credit** AmEx, DC, MC, V.
There's a sign on the encaged balcony above the Chapel that says something like 'This party could be your party', giving a phone number. Calling up might be no bad idea, as this is a good-times sort of pub, with its cod-Gothic monastery decor; a bar serving everything from Flatliners and Slippery Nipples to draught Hoegaarden, Tetley's and bottled speciality wheat beers; a lively dancefloor; and the slouchiest sofas in Christendom. There's also a restaurant called the Moroccan Chamber (delicious tagines), salsa classes on Wednesday night, and 'deep dirty funky house' until 3am on a Saturday. OK, so the Chapel has no idea what it wants to be, but that's all part of the fun. Great for an after-works knees-up, the place is even more energetic at the weekend when a gay-friendly crowd enjoys choons over two floors and a 'sun terrace'. Nicely naughty.
Babies and children admitted (before 6pm). Function room with heated roof terrace. Music (DJs 8pm Fri, Sat; free-£5). Tables outdoors (6, terrace). Specialities (cocktails). TV (big screen, satellite). **Map 9 N2**.

Compton Arms

4 Compton Avenue, N1 2XD (7359 6883). Highbury & Islington tube/rail. **Open** noon-11pm Mon-Sat; noon-10.30pm Sun. **Food served** noon-2.30pm, 6-8.30pm Mon-Fri; noon-4pm Sat, Sun. **Credit** MC, V.
Seated incongruously among the gentrified villas of Canonbury, this squat yellow block-plus-beer-garden feels like a real local, and a country local at that. The kindly landlady appears to know everyone by name, as does everyone else. A blokeish crowd chats loudly over the sport on the telly. The decor is formulaic local pub, down to the pew-like benches and old black-and-white brewery photos. Honest pub grub of the 'ham and eggs' school is served. So, this is indeed a friendly and, yes, real place where the art of conversation is still thriving – and not a champagne cocktail or game of giant Jenga or scuffed leather pouffe in sight. Instead you'll find Greene King ales (IPA, Abbot, Old Speckled Hen) and a regularly changing guest beer.
Babies and children admitted (before 8.30pm, separate area). No piped music or jukebox. Tables outdoors (10, garden). TV (satellite). **Map 9 O26**.

Duchess of Kent

441 Liverpool Road, N7 8PR (7609 7104/www.geronimo-inns.co.uk). Highbury & Islington tube/rail. **Open** noon-11pm Mon-Sat; noon-10.30pm Sun. **Food served** noon-3pm, 7-10pm Mon-Fri; noon-4pm, 7-10pm Sat, Sun. **Credit** MC, V.
Down at the 'wrong' (non-Angel) end of Liverpool Street, here's a fetching, friendly lady who's managed to solve that eternal gastro conundrum: how do we serve great, restaurant-style food, but still feel like a pub? The lovingly refitted Duchess is a pub of two very different yet happily

DRINKING ALOUD
STEVE WILLIAMS

Who are you? I'm the CAMRA (Campaign for Real Ale) regional director for Greater London.
Drinking in London: what's good about it? We have some very good pubs, good beer, and food's becoming more and more sophisticated – and though we don't have many free houses (where the pub is free of ties and can take beer from whichever brewery it chooses) – there are a handful, and those free houses that lead on real ale are really fantastic places.
What could be improved? A large proportion of our pubs in this country are owned by two companies, Enterprise and Punch – and their licensees have to take beers from their owners' lists. It would be great if the government started a guest beer policy to allow licensees from any pubco to take one beer from whichever brewery they choose: then the local pubs could take the local beer.
What's caught your eye in the last year? The main trend is a negative one – we're finding more and more pubs are closing for redevelopment into housing. That's happening across the country, but mainly in London, because housing is so rare and so expensive.
What's in your crystal ball? The national breweries are not interested in real ale, so breweries like Greene King, Young's and Fuller's will continue to focus on it. And more very small breweries will open up: concerns like the new Twickenham brewery called Twickenham Fine Ales – 20-odd pubs are taking its beers, and its beers are good.
New licensing law: good or bad? Good. It needn't mean 24-hour drinking, but pubs can be more flexible and satisfy different people.

North

overlapping halves, with a real fire in each: yellow walls and shiny stripped wood by the bar; and a maroon-walled, den-like, L-shaped back half where most of the dining takes place. Between the two there's a bookshelf bearing reference works and board games – all arranged so untidily that you know they get used. Real fires, big tables, comfy chairs, idiosyncratic ornaments and corny paintings create an atmosphere of friendly jumble that's very welcoming. The menu is akin to that of a superior wine-bar; it's supported by an extensive wine list and a well-stocked bar boasting draught Adnams bitter and Timothy Taylor Landlord, as well as Bitburger and Amstel lagers.
Babies and children admitted (before 6pm). Disabled: toilet. Games (board games). No-smoking area. Tables outdoors (10, pavement). **Map 9 N1**.

Duke of Cambridge

30 St Peter's Street, N1 8JT (7359 3066/www.singhboulton.co.uk). Angel tube. **Open** noon-11pm Mon-Sat; noon-10.30pm Sun. **Food served** 12.30-3pm, 6.30-10.30pm Mon-Fri; 12.30-3.30pm, 6.30-10.30pm Sat; 12.30-3.30pm, 6.30-10pm Sun. **Credit** MC, V.
It's hard to find anything to dislike about this organic gastropub. In fact, there's a lot to recommend it. Inside you'll find the bare-wood floors, sturdy wooden tables and mix-and-match chairs and benches of your standard 1990s renovation. The bar sells organic bitters, a great selection of wines, and even organic juices (the apple is exceptional). The open kitchen, tucked away in the corner of the room, produces excellent organic food that's high on imagination and relatively light on the stomach. The crowd is predominantly local – that is, media types in their early thirties. The only problem is a slight lack of atmosphere. In fact, on wet and windy nights, the Duke can seem a little sombre. Still, a few pints of Eco Warrior (the best of the beers, produced by local microbrewery Pitfield) seemed to dissipate the aura of austerity about the place. Funny, that.
Babies and children welcome; high chairs. Restaurant available for hire (no-smoking). No piped music or jukebox. Specialities (organic food, wines, beers). Tables outdoors (5, courtyard; 5, pavement). **Map 9 O2**.

Elbow Room

89-91 Chapel Market, N1 9EX (7278 3244/www.theelbowroom.co.uk). Angel tube. **Open** 5pm-2am Mon; noon-2am Tue-Thur; noon-3am Fri, Sat; noon-midnight Sun. **Food served** noon-11pm daily. **Admission** £2 9-10pm, £5 after 10pm Fri, Sat. **Credit** MC, V.
This enormous Chapel Market institution is one of a chain of temples to American-style pool, with swish oblongs of baize stretching into the distance. If you come expecting little red and yellows balls on a compact six by three, you'll be disappointed; this is a bigger, brasher version of the British pub game. The Elbow Room is a great place to shoot some frames by day, though in the evenings you can wait an age for a table. Things get livelier (and it takes longer to get served) as the evenings and the week wear on. The bar's curved leather booths, impromptu dance area and loud DJ-led urban music create an animated pulling zone. There are regular student nights (Wednesday), and cult-movie screenings (Monday) complete with popcorn and bean bags. Coors lager from the States is the most interesting choice on tap, though the two for one cocktail deal (5-8pm) has its fans.
Disabled: toilet. Games (11 pool tables). Music (DJs 9pm Tue-Sat; bands 9pm Sun). **Map 9 N2**.

Embassy Bar

119 Essex Road, N1 2SN (7226 7901/www.embassybar.com). Angel tube/38, 56, 73 bus. **Open** 4pm-midnight Mon-Thur, Sun; 4pm-2am Fri, Sat. **Admission** £3-£4 after 9pm Fri, Sat. **Credit** AmEx, MC, V.
For our money, the Embassy has a strong claim to the title of coolest bar in Islington. Not that it would ever be so gauche as to boast about such a thing. Indeed, the whole proposition – from the leather swivel high chairs to the softly glowing red wall-lights, the miniature palms, the art deco mirrors, the unapologetic flock wallpaper and the impeccable soundtrack – speaks of an effortlessly low-temperature sensibility that's louche, loungey and lovable all at once. Downstairs, well-chosen DJs do their thing for a tightly packed but ample dancefloor. You can never quite remember what was playing, but it always feels right at the time. There's Carlsberg, Carling, Guinness and Export on tap, plus a handful of red and white wines to supplement the modest cocktail and shooter menu. Even if you're not feeling very cool yourself, the Embassy will never hold it against you.
Bar available for hire. Music (DJs 8pm Thur, Sun; 9pm Fri, Sat). TV (satellite). **Map 9 O1**.

Filthy McNasty's

68 Amwell Street, EC1R 1UU (7837 6067). Angel tube. **Open** noon-11pm Mon-Sat; noon-10.30pm Sun. **Food served** noon-3pm Mon-Fri; 3-8pm Sun. **Credit** MC, V.
An interesting oddity, just off the beaten track, Filthy's is great for a no-frills booze-up. Somehow, despite hosting publishers' book readings in the roomy back bar, this is the most unpretentious of pubs. The beer choice on tap could be more varied, but there's Red Stripe among the lagers, and a single guest ale (Adnams Broadside on our visit). Staff are a cheery bunch of scruffniks, and customers are a mix of young hipsters, old soaks and the odd waif or stray. The music tends to crank up as the small front bar gets busy, so come here for a few lively drinks and a laugh rather than a quiet, intimate chat. The decor is a bit tatty, but the atmosphere is magic. The Thai food at lunchtimes isn't the main attraction, though it's wholesome and fairly priced. If you sometimes confuse the phrases 'intellectual debate' and 'drunken rant', welcome to your spiritual home.
Babies and children admitted (before 6pm). Disabled: toilet. Literary readings (8.30pm weekly, call for times; free). Music (bands, call for dates; free). Tables outdoors (7, pavement). TV (big screen). **Map 9 N3**.

House

63-69 Canonbury Road, N1 2DG (7704 7410/www.inthehouse.biz). Highbury & Islington tube/rail. **Open** 5-11pm Mon; noon-11pm Tue-Sat; noon-10.30pm Sun. **Food served** 6-10.30pm Mon; noon-2.30pm, 6.30-10.30pm Tue-Sat; noon-3.30pm, 6-10pm Sun. **Credit** MC, V.
Even by the standards of the area, this is a very upmarket establishment indeed. It feels much more like a restaurant that's giving House room to a bar. The clean-cut decor is elegantly understated, without having any great distinction: a hexagonal island bar, a neat modern brick fireplace, designer stools and sofas, posh flora, a plasma screen and an enormous silver Taittinger champagne bucket. Choose from champagne cocktails, regulation beers (including San Miguel on tap), an extensive wine list, and a delicious first-class menu: game terrine with spiced pear chutney, char-grilled yellow-fin tuna, and steamed

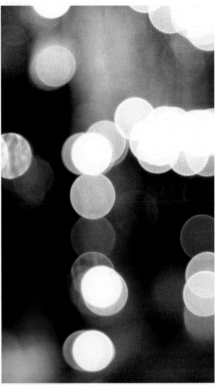

Medicine Bar. *See p177.*

sea bass mouginoise (with buttered baby spinach and onions, and sauternes velouté, £16.95). You'll feel more at home here sporting a camel coat and a cocker spaniel than with a donkey jacket and pitbull terrier.
Babies and children admitted. Disabled: toilet. Music (8pm Sun; free). Tables outdoors (6, garden). Restaurant (no-smoking). **Map 9 O26**.

Island Queen

87 Noel Road, N1 8HD (7704 7631). Angel tube. **Open** noon-11pm Mon-Fri, Sun; 11am-11pm Sat. **Food served** noon-3pm, 6-10.30pm Mon-Thur; noon-10.30pm Fri, Sun; 11am-11pm Sat. **Credit** MC, V.
The Island Queen is tucked away in a network of gentrified streets. As pubs go, it is about as well-brought up and presentable as they come. The high Victorian interior is spectacular, a beautifully proportioned composition of expansive etched-glass frontage, art-deco light fittings, dark woods and velvet drapes. A vast island bar dominates the main room (there's a lounge area upstairs) and a battered wooden figurehead points to an understated nautical theme. The menu is pure gastropub: all Sicilian casseroles and rustic platters. 'If you think your head is too large on your beer, we will gladly top it up,' says a sign. Classy, inoffensive and never knowingly kicking, this is the sort of typical 'London, England' pub that Hollywood would set a film in. There's a good range of beers on tap, including London Pride and two guest ales, Addlestone's cider, plus Früli, Staropramen, and De Koninck.
Function room. No-smoking area. Quiz (8pm Tue; £1). Tables outdoors (8, pavement). TV. **Map 9 O2**.

Keston Lodge

131 Upper Street, N1 1QP (7354 9535). Angel tube. **Open** noon-11.30pm Mon-Thur, Sun; noon-2am Fri, Sat. **Food served** noon-3pm, 5-10pm Mon-Fri; noon-5pm, 6pm-1am Sat; noon-5pm, 6-10pm Sun. **Admission** £3-£4 after 10.30pm Fri, Sat. **Credit** MC, V.
The pegboard walls, metal piping handrails and plethora of crosshead screws at Keston Lodge provide a welcome change in decor for those City types who slope up the Northern Line for their fix of Berry Martinis and Peach Bellinis. But while these folk recline at obtuse angles on the capacious furniture, there's an older contingent nearby, attracted by the muted sounds and the unusually inexpensive food. In a part of London where it's almost compulsory to charge around £12 for a main course, most dishes here cost under £8. What's more, the daily changing menu uses produce fresh from Borough Market. The plonk is more pricy – £11 for house wine – but it's the cocktails that give the staff a chance to shine; chilled glasses and painstakingly poured champagne lift the drinks way above the local competition. Saturday nights are packed, but the Lodge makes for an exceptional weekday treat.
Babies and children admitted (until 6pm). Disabled: toilet. Music (DJs 7.30pm Mon; 9.30pm Fri, Sat; 8.30pm Sun; free). Tables outdoors (2, garden).

King's Head

115 Upper Street, N1 1QN (7226 0364/ www.kingsheadtheatre.org). Angel tube/Highbury & Islington tube/rail. **Open** 11am-1am Mon-Thur; 11am-2am Fri, Sat; noon-1am Sun. **Food served** (pre-booked theatre dinner only) 7-8pm Tue-Sat. **No credit cards**.
The famous in-house theatre has made the King's Head what it is; the framed pictures of thesps adorning the walls deserve inspection by any 'Before They Were Famous' enthusiast. A high-spirited pre-show crowd in jeans and jumpers prepares for the imminent performance with pints of bitter: real ales come from Adnams and Young's; rows of lager taps are conspicuous by their absence. As for wine, there's only a house red and white to choose from, so non-beer-lovers should head down the spirit and mixer route. Perched above the bar are spotlights turned on the assembled drinkers, but these are fortunately for decoration only and not used to force people out of the building at closing time. Post-performance drinking is still a tradition, as is the old-fashioned till and quaint custom of hanging up a small sign with details of 'tonight's pianist'.
Babies and children admitted (until 9pm). Disabled: toilet. Music (bands 10pm daily; £3 after 10pm Fri, Sat). Tables outdoors (2, pavement). Theatre (box office 7226 1916). **Map 9 O1**.

Matt & Matt Bar

112 Upper Street, N1 1QN (7226 6035/ www.mattandmatt.co.uk). Angel tube. **Open** 5pm-1am Tue-Thur; 5pm-2am Fri, Sat. **Happy hour** 5-8pm Tue-Fri. **Admission** £4 after 10pm Fri, Sat. **Credit** MC, V.
Lacking the gastronomic pretensions found at nearby pubs, Matt – along with his friend, Matt – sticks to serving up vodka shots, bottled beers and Sex On The Beach cocktails into the early hours. There's a slight package-holiday sensation to the place; you never seem to be more than six feet away from someone drinking Malibu and pineapple. But the on-tap lager selection is perfectly fair (Amstel, Staropramen, Heineken Export) and the wines (three reds and three whites by the glass) are palatable. Retro video games, pinball and table football keep the lads happy, while girlfriends sip on amaretto sours, swaying gently to the persistently upbeat sounds. Until now, Matt & Matt's unique selling point has been its late opening hours; with changes in the licensing laws it remains to be seen whether the good-time music policy and stack of tequilas can retain the crowd. We hope so: staff here are easily the most welcoming on Upper Street.
Bar available for hire (weekdays only). Games (pinball, table football, video games). Music (open decks 8pm Tue-Thur; DJs 9pm Thur-Sat). **Map 9 O1**.

Medicine Bar

181 Upper Street, N1 1RQ (7704 9536/ www.medicinebar.net). Angel tube/Highbury & Islington tube/rail. **Open** 5pm-midnight Mon-Thur; 5pm-2am Fri; 2pm-2am Sat; 2pm-midnight Sun. **Admission** £4 after 9.30pm Fri, Sat. **Credit** MC, V.
The sheer number of punters engulfing this small bar at the weekend is inexplicable. The decor is tatty, reminiscent of a decaying fairground ride, and the air is filled with the word 'What?' bellowed at high volume above the fizz-thump of the DJ's speaker cabinets. Anyone here who isn't under the age of 25 certainly wishes to be. But there are saving graces: Beck's and San Miguel are on tap; the Guinness is passable; and the wine list, which looks as if it has been Letraset on to the wall, does the job (although it's a little unadventurous. The large fronds of greenery make a soothing antidote to the sensory overload. Acupuncture charts, fixed to the wall, provide a handy reference tool should you or a drinking partner begin to suffer from stress.
Function room. Music (DJs 8.30pm Thur-Sun). Tables outdoors (10, pavement). **Map 9 O1**.

Mucky Pup

39 Queen's Head Street, N1 8NQ (7226 2572/ www.muckypup-london.com). Angel tube. **Open** 5-11pm Mon-Thur; noon-11pm Fri, Sat; noon-10.30pm Sun. **Food served** 6-9pm Tue-Thur; noon-9pm Fri, Sat, Sun. **Credit** AmEx, MC, V.

This new and welcome addition to the Islington boozescape probably wrenched many of its punters out of their comfort zone to enter a Brave New World down little Queens Head Street towards the canal. Once the home of an embattled gay bar, it's now the happy kingdom of an enthusiastic young couple who have created an atmosphere of genuine friendliness within a matter of months. You get great food (Sunday lunches are popular), there's an animated quiz night, a small outer courtyard, and a separate area for sociable games of pool and darts. Throw in the low-slung sofas and the mucky pup himself – a tiger-striped gentle giant of cartoon proportions – and yes, they've actually done it, creating that elusive 'front room with a bar in it' feel. Greene King IPA is the one cask beer, and Hoegaarden is also on tap, along with the usual lagers (Foster's, Stella, Kronenbourg) and various bottled beers.

Bar available for hire. Games (board games, darts, pool). Jukebox. Quiz (8.30pm Wed; £1.50). Tables outdoors (3, garden). TV (digital). **Map 9 O2**.

Narrow Boat

119 St Peter Street, N1 8PZ (7288 0572). Angel tube. **Open** 11am-11pm Mon-Sat; noon-10.30pm Sun. **Food served** noon-3pm, 6-9.30pm Mon-Fri; noon-9.30pm Sat; noon-5.30pm Sun. **Credit** MC, V.

There has been a revamp here, but the faithful old customers still hang out, looking with bemusement at the stripped floorboards, pine tables and the computer monitor displaying the pub's website behind the bar. They're also unmoved by the various medallions and parcels on the gastropub menu, but the food is reliable and reasonably priced (mains around £6). Plasma screens at either end of the long, narrow room beam out Sky Sports relentlessly. Even the toilets have the audio. Having said all this, we love the wonderful views of the Regent's Canal, now enhanced with full-length windows. Another plus is the reasonably diverse drinks selection: guest ales including Adnams and London Pride; 'amusingly' named shooters (has anyone ever ordered a Slippery Nipple?); and a laminated wine list that, as it's encased in plastic, presumably doesn't change often. One for a long, Sunday afternoon in the summer – if you like sport.

Babies and children admitted. Games (board games, fruit machines). Music (DJs 7pm Fri; Irish band, 8.30pm Thur; free). Quiz (8.30pm Sun; £1). Restaurant. TVs (big screen, satellite). **Map 9 P2**.

Northgate

113 Southgate Road, N1 3JS (7359 7392). Angel tube/Essex Road rail/38, 73 bus. **Open** 5-11pm Mon-Thur; 5pm-midnight Fri; noon-midnight Sat; noon-10.30pm Sun. **Food served** 6.30-10.30pm Mon-Fri; 12.30-4pm, 6.30-10.30pm Sat; 12.30-4pm, 6.30-9.30pm Sun. **Credit** MC, V.

There's been quite a turnaround at this pub. It used to belong to the people who own the Junction Tavern (*see p187*), but now, the small stage that families now sit on to work their way through three-course meals was once used for displays of amateur boxing. The crowd presumably roared on the action from what is now the open-plan kitchen. The food is ambitious (spiced lentil and coriander soup with yoghurt, followed by confit of duck leg, say), pushing the Northgate into the upper echelons of pub grubbery – but the drinkers haven't been forgotten. There are regularly changing guest ales, and a summer beer festival. The extensive wine list of chenins, Chablis and syrahs doesn't come cheap. A mixed crowd, from exquisitely manicured young women to local builders, spreads itself around the spacious interior. Everyone feels perfectly at home: not least because of the incredibly sunny disposition of the staff.

Babies and children admitted (garden, restaurant). Disabled: toilet. Function room. Restaurant. Specialities (real ales). Tables outdoors (10, patio).

Old Red Lion

418 St John Street, EC1V 4NJ (7837 7816/ www.oldredliontheatre.co.uk). Angel tube. **Open** noon-11pm Mon-Sat; noon-10.30pm Sun. **Food served** noon-3pm Mon-Fri. **Credit** MC, V.

With an old joanna stuck in the corner, and a small blackboard containing a nondescript menu of sandwiches and 'bangers', this minuscule theatre bar is undrizzled with olive oil or balsamic. It's one of the few remaining ungentrified pubs in the area. There's been a boozer on this site since the 13th century, so the Red Lion should know a thing or two about longevity. It continues to play to its strengths, providing an excellent pint of London Pride, a decent house white and businesslike service. The place is divided into two by etched-glass panels, which presumably once kept the saloon riff-raff away from the more polite customers in the lounge; these days it's a free-for-all. Secure a banquette and nurse a quiet pint along with the grizzled regulars, while you steel yourself for the more physically demanding hostelries on the other side of Angel tube station.

Babies and children admitted (until 6pm). Games (board games, fruit machine). Tables outdoors (3, patio). Theatre (comedy Mon, plays Tue-Sun; £8-£12). TV (satellite). **Map 9 N3**.

Rosemary Branch

2 Shepperton Road, N1 3DT (7704 2730/ www.rosemarybranch.co.uk). Angel tube/Old Street tube/rail. **Open** noon-11.30pm Mon-Thur; noon-midnight Fri, Sat; noon-10.30pm Sun. **Food served** noon-3pm, 6-9.30pm Mon-Sat; noon-6pm Sun. **Credit** MC, V.

This place is quite a trek from the nearest tube, but most definitely worth it. The Rosemary Branch has the kind of sophisticated jukebox that provokes good-natured arguments among its muso customers. It also offers the chance on Mondays for these musos to do battle in a pop quiz. In short – a highbrow pub with a down-to-earth welcome. Affligem and Litovel on tap provide rare treats for lager lovers, and together with Adnams, Fuller's ESB, London Pride and guest ales, make for a beer-drinking oasis. An inexplicable Battle of Britain theme, with large model aeroplanes suspended from the ceiling, contrasts starkly with the pot plants strewn around the scruffy tables. This isn't a place where you'll be persuaded to leave at closing time by someone spraying noxious chemicals and wielding a duster. If there's a decent play on at the theatre upstairs, that's all the more reason to pay a visit. Something to treasure.

Babies and children admitted (before 7pm). Function room. Games (board games). No-smoking area. Quiz (8.30pm Mon, Thur; £1). Theatre (7.30pm Tue-Sat; £8-£10). Tables outdoors (12, patio). TV. **Map 9 P1**.

Social

33 Linton Street, Arlington Square, N1 7DU (7354 5809/www.thesocial.com). Angel tube. **Open** 5-11pm Mon-Fri; noon-11pm Sat; noon-10.30pm Sun. **Food served** 5-10.30pm Mon-Fri; 12.30-10.30pm Sat; 12.30-9.30pm Sun. **Credit** AmEx, MC, V.

This wood-panelled boozer has been painstakingly polished up by Heavenly Records to become a laid-back, sensible cousin to the West End bar of the same name. The Social is tucked away behind a rather grim backstreet housing estate, an odd location for one the hipper jukeboxes in town. But although the slick sounds are an undeniable draw, they're far from obtrusive; you'll be as keen to come back for the high-quality food prepared in the open-plan kitchen as for those obscure James Brown outtakes. Equal care has been taken over the selection of beers, wines and spirits: Kirin, Red Stripe and Erdinger edge out the standard trio (Foster's, Stella, Kronenbourg), and you can sample an unusually large range of whiskies at one of the candlelit tables. Service was attentive and friendly, making for a thoroughly pleasant evening.

Babies and children admitted (until 6pm, weekends). Function room. Games (pool). Music (DJs 4.30pm Sun; free). Quiz (8pm, 3rd Wed of mth; £2). Restaurant. Tables outdoors (2, pavement). **Map 9 P2**.

25 Canonbury Lane

25 Canonbury Lane, N1 2AS (7226 0955). Highbury & Islington tube/rail. **Open** 5-11pm Mon-Fri; noon-11pm Sat, Sun. **Food served** 6-10pm Mon-Thur; noon-3.30pm; 1-4.30pm Sun. **Credit** MC, V.

Here's yet another Islington bar with a deep-red colour scheme (did a job-lot of crimson paint fall off the back of a lorry on Upper Street recently?). But there's more attention to detail at this venue: chandeliers, low tables, pouffes, and a fairy grotto of a room situated at the back where only the most beautiful people hang out. Coats are placed firmly on coat hooks; sitting around in a Parka will almost certainly raise a few perfectly plucked eyebrows. Snacks are served tapas-style (so, in small portions), while the cocktails read like a mouth-watering pudding menu: Strawberry Daiquiris, Blackberry Caprioskas, and the curiously named Toblerone. The owners claim to have 'redefined bar culture', which is probably not true; but the 'luscious selection of fine wines and cocktails' is certainly close to the mark. If you're wearing a smart shirt and you've just got paid, give No.25 a whirl.

Babies and children admitted (before 6pm). Tables outdoors (5, conservatory). **Map 9 O26**.

Also in the area...

All Bar One 1 Liverpool Road, N1 0RP (7843 0021).
Angel (JD Wetherspoon) 3-5 Islington Street, N1 9LQ (7837 2218).
Babushka 125 Caledonian Road, N1 9RG (7837 1924).
Bierodrome 173-174 Upper Street, N1 1XS (7226 5835).
Elk in the Woods 37 Camden Passage, N1 8EA (7226 3535).
Glass Works (JD Wetherspoon) N1 Centre, 21 Parkfield Street, N1 0PS (7354 6100).
Pitcher & Piano 68 Upper Street, N1 0NY (7704 9974).
Slug & Lettuce 1A Islington Green, N1 2XH (7226 3864).
Walkabout 56 Upper Street, N1 0NY (7359 2097).
White Swan (JD Wetherspoon) 255-256 Upper Street, N1 1RY (7288 9050).

KENTISH TOWN & GOSPEL OAK

Leading from the grotty underworld along Kentish Town Road to the leafier slopes of Gospel Oak at the base of Parliament Hill, this area contains clutches of urban Irish pubs and haughty gastrobars. Rarely do the twain mix, although the rebirth of the previously low-grade gastro Jorene Celeste as the foodie **Oxford** is an interesting case in point. For a genuinely good bar, you can't go much wrong with the **Pineapple**.

Oxford

256 Kentish Town Road, NW5 2AA (7485 3521/ www.realpubs.co.uk). Kentish Town tube/Kentish Town West rail. **Open** noon-11pm Mon-Sat; noon-10.30pm Sun. **Food served** noon-3.30pm, 6-10pm Mon-Fri; noon-10pm Sat; noon-9pm Sun. **Credit** MC, V.

A recent addition to the Real Pubs chain ('real beers and European cuisine' – and a more choosy clientele), the former low-grade Jorene Celeste is now an all-seared, all-panfried eaterie with bar attached. At the back, an imposing blackboard boasts of skate and Barnsley chop dinners (£9-£13). Around the drinking area of institutional wooden tables, leather-topped bar stools along a busy counter and inevitable corner of squishy sofas, more casual lunch menus include organic suckling pig sausages and mash (£6). To complement these delights are two dozen wines, eight by the glass. London Pride, Deuchar's IPA, Flower's, Red Stripe and Hoegaarden are on draught; Pilsner Urquell and Nastro Azzurro are in bottles.

Disabled: toilet. Function room. Music (DJs 5pm Sun; free). Restaurant. Tables outdoors (6, pavement).

Pineapple

51 Leverton Street, NW5 2NX (7284 4631/www.the pineapplelondon.com). Kentish Town tube. **Open** noon-11pm Mon-Sat; noon-10.30pm Sun. **Food served** noon-2.30pm, 7-10pm Tue-Sat; 1-4pm Sun. **Credit** MC, V.

Appealing to both the streetwise and young salaried, the subtly themed Pineapple is pleasingly bar-sized, yet sussed enough to offer a good gastro selection. Soul, Trojan and indie sounds vibrate from the speakers above the tiny bar, around which are comfortable old corner banquettes, untouched by any revamp. Behind hides a small back room of leather armchairs and paved back garden; framed retro pineapple ads lead to a conservatory and upstairs dining room, both available for hire. Adnams, Boddington's and Marston's Pedigree stand out beside the standard lagers – wine is available but not selectively listed. Bar food includes prawn and smoked haddock fish cakes (£7.50), organic sausage and mash (£7.50). A welcome lack of affectation is the keynote of the regulars of the shirttail-over-jeans, last-shaved-Tuesday type.

Babies and children admitted (before 7.30pm). Function room. Games (cards, chess, darts). Quiz (8.30pm Mon; £1). Restaurant (no-smoking tables). Tables outdoors (9, garden; 16, pavement).

Vine

86 Highgate Road, NW5 1PB (7209 0038/ www.thevinelondon.co.uk). Tufnell Park tube/Kentish Town tube/rail. **Open** 11am-11pm Mon-Sat; noon-

10.30pm Sun. **Food served** 12.30-3.30pm, 6.30-10.30pm Mon-Fri; 12.30-10.30pm Sat-Sun. **Credit** AmEx, DC, MC, V.
This gastropub makes the most of its impressive grounds and Edwardian building. With a front terrace and leafy, roofed, paved back garden, Vine still has plenty of room for a front dining area with big bay windows, a side bar with ethno arty touches, and prop-uppable zinc bar counter along which the bar stools spilling out stuffing are a touch too authentic. Wines are plentiful, with standard merlots, riojas and pinot grigios by the glass (£3.50-£4.25), plus more choice labels such as Tindall Marlborough, Vega del Rayo and Domaine Champeau pouilly fumé (£22-£26) by the bottle. Draught Spitfire, London Pride, Hoegaarden and San Miguel keep a regular clientele of mithering freelance journos ('When *is* that cheque going to come?') at least temporarily satisfied, as do budget-pleasing bar snacks (£3.95) such as lamb merguez or whitebait. Upscale mains such as linguini dressed with fresh blue swimmer crab, and oven-roast barramundi, tip over the tenner barrier – set lunch (£6.50) and early-evening dinner (£7.95) options prove popular.
Babies and children welcome; children's menu Sat; high chairs. Function rooms. Tables outdoors (22, garden).

KILBURN

Kilburn High Road, main artery of London's Irish community, is no longer the scruffy stout 'n' shamrock thoroughfare it once was. Gentrification is slowly seeping in from neighbouring Maida Vale, and much of the Guinness paraphernalia has been swept away in the new tide of gastropubs.

Black Lion
274 Kilburn High Road, NW6 2BY (7624 1424/ www.blackliongueshouse.com). Kilburn tube/ Brondesbury rail. **Open** noon-midnight Mon-Fri; 11am-midnight Sat; noon-11.30pm Sun. **Food served** noon-3pm, 6-10pm Mon-Fri; 11am-10pm Sat; noon-9.30pm Sun. **Credit** MC, V.
Kilburn's original gastropub has become a benchmark for the High Road's watering holes. The vast, late-Victorian interior has been cleverly updated to create a cosy pub and dining room, with most of the original features left in place – open fireplace, eccentric, gold-embossed ceiling, and wood panelling. Faux antique touches such as silk lampshades and battered leather sofas complete the faded look. The main room is moodily lit with flickering candles and brass chandeliers, which suits the handful of old soaks hanging around the bar, although it's mostly Kilburn's young and Diesel-clad who come for the good selection of beers (including Adnams and Hoegaarden) and excellent food. The menu is a big draw, although it's pricey and a touch pompous: Toulouse sausages with rosemary jus translate as bangers and mash (ringing in at £9.95), and the cod comes with truffle potatoes, not chips.
Babies and children admitted (before 6pm). Restaurant (no-smoking). Tables outdoors (6, garden).

North London Tavern
375 Kilburn High Road, NW6 7QB (7625 6634). Kilburn tube. **Open** noon-11pm Mon-Sat; noon-10.30pm Sun. **Food served** noon-3.30pm, 6.30-10.30pm Mon-Fri; 12.30-4.30pm, 6.30-10.30pm Sat; 12.30-9.30pm Sun. **Credit** MC, V.

CRITICS' PICKS

For beers and ales
Angel Inn (*see p169*), **Enterprise** (*see p162*), **Lockside Lounge** (*see p162*), **Quinn's** (*see p164*), **Salisbury Hotel** (*see p166*), **Swimmer at the Grafton Arms** (*see p171*), **Washington Hotel & Bar** (*see p160*),

For cocktails
Anam (*see p172*), **Cuban** (*see p161*), **Keston Lodge** (*see p177*), **Singapore Sling** (*see p164*), **25 Canonbury Lane** (*see p179*).

For the strong stuff
Bar Solo (*see p161*), **Flask** (*see p169*), **Matt & Matt Bar** (*see p177*),

For wine
Angelic (*see p172*), **Barnsbury** (organic; *see p172*), **Duke of Cambridge** (organic; *see p174*), **House** (*see p174*), **No.77 Wine Bar** (*see p188*).

For a blast from the past
Camden Head (*see p172*), **Salisbury Hotel** (*see p166*), **Spaniards Inn** (*see p167*).

For real fires
Crown & Goose (*see p161*), **Duchess of Kent** (*see p173*), **Garden Gate** (*see p167*).

For surroundings with a theme
Cuban (Cuba; *see p161*) **Triangle** (Morocco; *see p166*).

For good food
Bridge House (*see right*), **House** (*see p174*), **Queens** (*see p184*), **Wells** (*see p169*).

For the sound of music
Boogaloo (*see p169*), **Bullet** (*see p161*), **Hawley Arms** (*see p162*).

A recent refurb has replaced mumbling pensioners with moneyed Kilburnites in this old Victorian pub, although the tip-happy staff don't seem to be mourning the loss. Old regulars may have shifted, but hip bits of Victoriana still abound – acid-etched glass, a dark-wood bar and gilded mirrors – complemented by an eclectic bunch of chandeliers and predictable teal-and-crimson walls. Well-groomed couples lounge along the walls and on banks of sofas, nodding to trip hop. There's a good selection of wines by the glass, and beers include Marston's Pedigree, London Pride and Leffe, as well as the usual Stella-style suspects. The function room at the back has been converted into a bright dining room (fishcakes, risotto and steaks are the norm), and pistachios and olives are dished up from glass jars behind the bar, as are pickled eggs. Irony, we presume.
Babies and children welcome. Disabled: toilet. Function room. Restaurant. Specialities (real ales). Tables outdoors (5, pavement). TV.

Also in the area...

Beaten Docket (JD Wetherspoon) 50-56 Cricklewood Broadway, NW2 3DT (8450 2972).

MAIDA VALE

Who'da thunk it? Maida Vale, in particular its canal area of Little Venice, contains some absolute gems. Right by the canal, **Bridge House** mixes cool bar credibility with a solid cultural agenda, while across the water the **Prince Alfred** is a treat to behold, architecturally and gastronomically. And the legendarily louche **Warrington Hotel** is bar in a million.

Bridge House

13 Westbourne Terrace Road, W2 6NG (7432 1361). Warwick Avenue tube/Paddington tube/rail. **Open** noon-11pm Mon-Sat; noon-10.30pm Sun. **Food served** noon-10pm Mon-Sat; noon-9.30pm Sun. **Credit** (over £5) AmEx, DC, MC, V.

Fabulous bar, this, its small square of paved terrace just within earshot of the putt-putting of canal boats across the street, and its long-established NewsRevue satirical theatre upstairs attracting an inquisitive, cosmopolitan clientele. The foxy, vampish decor involves chintzy red lights over the bar, a pink mural at the back and a thought-about mishmash of seating both squishy and kitsch. Food and drink both do justice to the setting. Beers include draught Küppers Kölsch, Black Sheep, Abbot, Leffe, Hoegaarden and Früli, and bottled Asahi, Beck's and Dos Equis; the two dozen wines range from a simple Bottega Vinai pinot grigio (£3.60 a glass) to bottles of Boisset pinot noir (£17). Light bites (spinach, cheese and tomato quesadilla, chicken yakitori) and sandwiches (grilled halloumi, pork-and-leek sausage) are about a fiver; mains (lamb rump steak, 8oz Angus cheeseburger) in the £8 range.

Babies and children welcome (before 6pm). Disabled: toilet. Entertainment (theatre 7.30pm, 9.30pm Mon-Sat; 7pm, 9pm Sun; £7-£9). Games (board games, cards). Tables outdoors (8, terrace).

Graze

215 Sutherland Avenue, W9 1RU (7266 3131/ www.graze.co.uk). Maida Vale tube. **Open** 6pm-1am Tue-Sun. **Food served** 6pm-12.30am Tue-Sun. **Credit** AmEx, DC, MC, V.

Softening hard-ass minimalism with rust-coloured net curtains, antique chandeliers and a lick of red paint, new owners have remade Otto as bar-restaurant Graze. The result is like a school gym tarted up for the Christmas dance, yet punters seem to be flocking in – J-Lo booties, Jude Law lookalikes and all. The huge bar room is where the action is, with drinks dispensed from a full-length bar counter staffed by black-shirted men. The range of quality spirits and fresh juices is impressive – our cocktail of persimmon, Southern Comfort, apple juice and chilli was a treat. The menu lists a big selection of French-style and north European 'tapas' – if you like trying imaginative dishes (Herdwick mutton kebab, pig's trotter on toast with pan-fried foie gras), it's all brilliant fun. But cocktails cost £7-£8 and each small plate £4-£5, so you could spend less on an evening's hedonism in a fashionable West End restaurant.

Babies and children admitted (restaurant). Bar available for hire. Restaurant (no-smoking). Specialities (cocktails).

Prince Alfred & Formosa Dining Rooms

5A Formosa Street, W9 1EE (7286 3287). Warwick Avenue tube. **Open** 11am-11pm Mon-Sat; noon-10.30pm Sun. **Food served** noon-3pm, 6-10.30pm Mon-Sat; noon-4pm, 6-10pm Sun. **Credit** AmEx, MC, V.

The beautiful old tiling and exquisitely curved frosted glass frontage barely prepare you for the architectural delight within: a complex series of snugs (free to hire!) with a fabulously ornate half-moon dark-wood bar as centrepiece and the swish, modern Formosa Dining Rooms behind. Locals are treated to an excellent range of beers, cocktails, wines and foodstuffs: Paulaner wheat and Affligem on draught, Cruzcampo and Michelob by the bottle, and £6 cocktails (Brandy Alexander hot or cold, Cosmopolitans with Absolut Citron) are only the tip of the iceberg. Two dozen wines by the glass, and 30 by the bottle, run up to a Petaluma cabernet merlot (£49.50) from Coonawarra. A swift kitchen turns out pea, mint and parmesan risotto (£9) or Cumberland sausage and mash (£8.50), the latter part of a £10 two-course lunch deal.

Babies and children welcome; high chairs. Disabled: toilet. Restaurant available for hire (no-smoking). Tables outdoors (3, pavement).

Warrington Hotel

93 Warrington Crescent, W9 1EH (7286 2929). Maida Vale tube. **Open** 11am-11pm Mon-Sat; noon-10.30pm Sun. **Food served** noon-2.30pm, 6-10pm daily. **Credit** MC, V.

The trek was eulogised in the Yobs' Christmas punk classic 'The Ballad of the Warrington': even the walk to this tatty palace of opulence is part of pop legend. An imposing entrance is marked by an apron of mosaic tiles and a rash of old phone boxes. Once inside... wow! OTT, semi-erotic art nouveau nymphs grace the elaborately carved back bar and concave wing; if this wasn't a brothel, it should have been. Amid coloured glaze and marble, pop has-beens bide their time before disappearing to do panto or pier shows; a more fitting care home you could not imagine. Once they're back, and the bottles of El Jinador and Jim Beam are caned, they make do with Young's, Fuller's ESB, London Pride, Spitfire, Everards Perfick and Spitfire. Bottles of wine are set up over the bar as at a fairground gallery, bearing £2.50 and £12 price tags. Upstairs, Ben's Thai restaurant offers quality curries and grills.

Babies and children admitted (restaurant). Games (darts, fruit machine, quiz machine). No piped music or jukebox (main bar). Restaurant (no-smoking). Tables outdoors (12 courtyard). TV (big screen, satellite).

Waterway

54 Formosa Street, W9 2JU (7266 3557/www.the waterway.co.uk). Warwick Avenue tube. **Open** noon-11pm Mon-Sat; noon-10.30pm Sun. **Food served** 12.30-3.30pm, 6.30-10.30pm daily. **Credit** AmEx, MC, V.

A classy operation, with an open-plan bar and outdoor decking overlooking the canal. Couples and young professionals with laptops peruse the leather-bound menus while attentive waitresses buzz around the smart brown furniture. Cocktails are a speciality, well priced and well made. Among the Martinis (£5.50), the Norsk (muddled blackberries, gomme, fresh lemon juice and Smirnoff Norsk) and Benedictine (Benedictine and Biscuit cognac, shaken with Martini Dry) stand out; the Vodka Collins (£5.50) is made with Seriously, the Mojito (£5.50) with Havana 3. Five wines of each colour come by the glass; the 20 bottles (£12.50-£30) are categorised as 'Rhône Spice', 'Bordeaux

Style', 'Fragrant Italian' and so on. Budvar, Flower's and Hoegaarden are all on draught, Mort Subite in two flavours by the bottle, and bar food includes steamed mussels (£8) and bavette steak (£12.50).
Babies and children admitted (before 7pm). Restaurant. Tables outdoors (20, garden).

Also in the area…

Slug & Lettuce 47 Hereford Road, W2 5AH (7229 1503).

MUSWELL HILL & ALEXANDRA PALACE

Following a brief flurry of openings, Muswell Hill's bar scene has languished in recent years. The best pubs also involve the steepest treks – either uphill to Alexandra Palace, or down from the Broadway to the area's leafier corners.

Over the Hill

96 Alexandra Park Road, N10 2AE (8444 2524). Bounds Green tube. **Open** 5-11pm Mon; 10am-11pm Tue-Sun. **Food served** 6-10.30pm Mon; noon-10.30pm Tue-Sun. **Credit** MC, V.
More of a local hangout than a bar, OTH feels like you've stumbled into someone's private party. Everyone knows everyone else (on our last visit we overheard people ordering 'the usual'). It has a Paris brasserie feel, with woven wicker furniture, flickering tea lights and daffodils poking from tiny vases. The staff are happy to chat about the wine list, which is long and heavy on New World wines; there's an organic wine of the month, too, although the groups of locals propping up the bar seem to prefer the draught Bitburger. Live funk and soul music ups the beat at weekends, while downstairs in the basement there are salsa classes. Given the continental feel of the place, the food is a bit of a surprise – heavy on comfort dishes like lamb casserole or shepherd's pie.
Babies and children admitted (until 7pm). Entertainment (salsa classes 7.30pm Tue, Fri). Function room. Music (band 7.30pm Sun). Tables outdoors (14, garden terrace).

Phoenix

Alexandra Palace Way, N22 7AY (8365 4356). Wood Green tube/Alexandra Palace rail/W3 bus. **Open** *Winter* 10.30am-8pm Mon-Thur; 10.30am-11pm Fri, Sat; 10.30am-10.30pm Sun. *Summer* 10am-11pm daily. **Food served** 11.30am-4pm daily. **Credit** MC, V.
The merits (or drawbacks) of a trip to the Phoenix depend entirely on what's on at Ally Pally. Tucked into a corner of the main bulk of the palace, it might be filled with suited businessmen from a conference one day, or with chavs sucking down pre-gig alcopops on another. You can't count on the clientele, but the view remains the same: a stunning panorama of the city, best enjoyed from the tables set outside in summertime. Inside, the high ceilings, mirrored pillars, potted palms and oversized globe lights give it a touch of turn-of-the-century Brighton, a seaside-jaunt feel helped along by the ice cream, Mars Bars and Vimto being served alongside run-of-the-mill draught beers. Cheap portions of fish and chips complete the picture, dished out from a heated trolley by jovial dinner ladies.
Babies and children admitted (garden only); nappy-changing facilities. Disabled: toilet. Function rooms. Game (fruit machine). Tables outdoors (50, garden terrace). TV (satellite).

Victoria Stakes

1 Muswell Hill, N10 3TH (8815 1793/www.victoriastakes.co.uk). Finsbury Park tube/rail then W3, W7 bus. **Open** 5-11pm Mon-Thur; noon-midnight Fri, Sat; noon-10.30pm Sun. **Food served** 6-10.30pm Mon-Thur; noon-4pm, 6-10.30pm Fri, Sat; noon-9pm Sun. **Credit** AmEx, DC, MC, V.
Set a stiff downhill walk from the centre of Muswell Hill, Victoria Stakes made a big impact when it morphed into a gastropub a couple of years ago. Its blood-red walls, low leather sofas and rough wood floors were a welcome injection of sophistication, although it's looking a little faded these days. The fraying feel gives it an appealing Sunday-afternoon atmosphere, though, even on Friday nights when boho-chic north Londoners cram round the tables to quaff bottles of red wine or pints of Abbot. The moodily lit restaurant upstairs (and the balmy beer garden in summer) offer new slants on bistro classics, such as roast poussin with chorizo. Punters downstairs can graze on bar snacks (moules frites, or sweet potato wedges), chalked up alongside cocktail specials (£5 a pop). Beer buffs should check out the bottled beers, which include Russian Baltica and Mort Subite in cherry or raspberry flavours.
Babies and children welcome; high chairs. Games (board games). Music (acoustic 8pm 1st Mon of mth; free). No-smoking area. Restaurant. Tables outdoors (20, garden).

Also in the area…

Wetherspoons Unit 5, Spouter's Corner, High Road, N22 6EJ (8881 3891).

PRIMROSE HILL

Surprisingly, Primrose Hill doesn't have one bar for class-A posing. It's more the sort of place for low-key drinking spots, with the classy **Landsdowne** pub laureate among them. Although celebs certainly do reside in these parts, you'll wait a long time trying to spot Jude, Kate and the like in the local boozers.

Albert

11 Princess Road, NW1 8JR (7722 1886). Chalk Farm tube. **Open** 11am-11pm Mon-Sat; noon-10.30pm Sun. **Food served** noon-2.30pm, 6.30-10pm Mon-Fri; noon-10pm Sat; noon-9.30pm Sun. **No credit cards**.
Unpretentious and laid-back, the Albert is one of the most family-friendly pubs in the area: on a Sunday you're as likely to bump into roaming toddlers with mums in anxious pursuit as couples, groups of friends or dog walkers. The pub conveys the happy atmosphere of a country establishment, eschewing the more self-conscious trend-setting of its neighbours. Its best-kept secret is (whisper it) a very pretty sun-trap of a garden, which is a godsend for long summer afternoons. Tables, unsurprisingly, get snapped up quickly. London Pride and Bombardier are reliable draught options, even if the wine list by the glass is disappointing. Staff are possibly the most efficient in the vicinity, and – even when the sun comes out – the pub never, ever feels overcrowded.

RAISE A GLASS: BOOZERS ON FILM

According to the London Film Commission, there are film crews shooting on the streets of London every single day – which means there may, at some time or other, have been clapperboard action at your local.

Not that a London boozer has to mean London once the cameras start to roll. Take **Madame Jo Jo's** (*see p255*), which crosses the Atlantic in Stanley Kubrick's last film, *Eyes Wide Shut*, to become Club Sonata, the New York jazz club where Tom Cruise learns a password to take him into an orgy. Then there's Harringay's **Salisbury Hotel** (*see p166*), whose elaborate Victorian interior makes it a highly desirable location for film-makers. In John Mackenzie's *The Long Good Friday* (1990), it stands in for a Northern Ireland pub ('Fagan's') where Bob Hoskins' right-hand man Paul Freeman gets involved in some shady wheeler-dealing. Then it appears (back in London, but sporting another postcode) as the Covent Garden pub in Richard Attenborough's *Chaplin* (1992): it's here that Robert Downey's Charlie gets a dressing-down from a drunk. Then it turns up in David Cronenberg's *Spider* as a big, bustling pub of no precise location, in which Miranda Richardson looks for Gabriel Byrne.

Richardson was rather more agitated when, as Ruth Ellis in *Dance with a Stranger* (1985), she made an appearance at Clerkenwell's **Three Kings** (*see p119*). The pub was a stand-in for the real **Magdala** (*see p167*), the Hampstead pub where the real Ruth Ellis shot her upper-class boyfriend. Death also comes to the boozer in Michael Powell's psycho-thriller *Peeping Tom* (1959), in which quintessentially English drinking establishment the **Newman Arms** (*see p44*) doubles as the bordello where prostitute Brenda Bruce meets her end at the hands of photographer Karl Böhm. To up the film's frisson factor, Powell threw in a suggestion that the arched Newman passage next to the pub was previously known as Jekyll & Hyde Alley.

A name change is part of the long history of the **Lamb and Flag** (*see p35*), said to have worn the grisly moniker 'Bucket of Blood'. It was one of Charles Dickens's favourite taverns, and in more recent times did duty as the site of a money pick-up (bloodless, admittedly) in George Cukor's comic drama *Travels with my Aunt* (1972). Another historic pub is the **George Inn** (*see p199*), that was doing business during the reign of Henry VIII. It's the last galleried inn in London, and plays the coaching tavern that Tom's coach leaves from in *Tom Brown's Schooldays* (1951).

London's film pubs have seen cowboys as well as schoolboys. In *Brannigan* (1975), John Wayne chases bad guy Del Henney all the way to the British capital, and stops for an all-out brawl in Leadenhall Market's **Lamb** (*see p135*). Physical contact of a different kind is the nub of Patrice Chéreau's *Intimacy*; in it, leading man Mark Rylance is seen working behind the bar at **AKA** (*see p24*). Taking a lighter look at affairs of the heart, *Sliding Doors* (1998) also offers a glimpse of the **Blue Anchor** (*see p235*), while in *About A Boy* (2002), Hugh Grant choses to reveal his complicated life to Rachel Weisz in upmarket **Hakkasan** (*see p41*).

Far less swanky is Southwark's **Anchor** (34 Park Street, SE1, 7407 1577), which pops up in Brian de Palma's *Mission: Impossible* (1996) and, in the same year, Meera Syal's urban fairytale *Beautiful Thing*. Meanwhile, further west, swish **Mother Black Cap** (41 Tavistock Crescent, W11, 7727 9250) was the screen double for a scruffy Camden boozer in Bruce Robinson's cult comedy *Withnail & I* (1987). It's here that Withnail (Richard E Grant) orders 'Two large gins; two pints of cider; ice in the cider'. The boozer, formerly known as Babushka, recently adopted its celluloid name; **Shaw's Booksellers** (*see p121*) has also done something similar. Movie magic – there's clearly something in it. *Janice Fuscoe*

Babies and children welcome. Games (board games). Tables outdoors (16, garden). TV. **Map 8 G1**.

Lansdowne

90 Gloucester Avenue, NW1 8HX (7483 0409). Chalk Farm tube/31, 168 bus. **Open** 6-11pm Mon; noon-11pm Tue-Sat; noon-10.30pm Sun. **Food served** 7-10pm Mon; 12.30-3pm, 7-10pm Tue-Sat; 12.30-4pm, 7-9.30pm Sun. **Credit** MC, V.

The Lansdowne has kept hold of its vintage cream-tiled frontage (now chipped and cracked), and so beckons in customers with the unfulfillable promise of Charrington's Ales. Yet this is no boozer living off its faded glory: a common room for the upper bourgeoisie would be more accurate. The lovely black lacquer ceiling is matched by wall skirting and charcoal-hued fireplace; near the fire is a squishy sofa (a Sunday paper hotspot). The rest of the room is dressed in tastefully scuffed wood. There's Everards Tiger, Deuchars IPS, Caffrey's and Staropramen on tap, and the likes of Breton cider and organic ginger beer in bottles. The pub is favoured by Primrose Hill gals out for a gossip and men who resemble famous Russian violinists, plus a fair few sprogs at the weekend. The gastropub menu includes good, comforting dishes such as smoked haddock risotto with poached egg (£9.50).

Babies and children welcome (restaurant; before 7pm in bar). Disabled: toilet. Games (board games). Restaurant. Tables outdoors (8, pavement).

Pembroke Castle

150 Gloucester Avenue, NW1 8JA (7483 2927). Chalk Farm tube. **Open** 11am-11pm Mon-Sat; noon-10.30pm Sun. **Food served** noon-3pm, 6.30-9.45pm Mon-Fri; noon-6pm Sat, Sun. **Credit** AmEx, MC, V.

This diminutive corner pub, with its curvaceous zinc bar and chandeliered restaurant, is an attractive place in which to hang out with the well-groomed, high-earning Primrose Hill set. It's treated like a local – almost everyone piles a coat on top of the others behind the door – but looks rather smarter, what with the pine floors, gilt mirrors and bunches of lilies (not to mention a few designer dresses). The open kitchen hatch and the television screen (active on match days) make the pub seem less self-conscious, and bar staff are friendly. Drinks include Timothy Taylor Landlord, along with the more familiar London Pride, Grolsch, Carling and Guinness. At the back is a large and lovely walled beer garden, with plenty of picnic-bench seating, dangling ivy and warm yellow lamps in the evening.

Babies and children admitted (before 7pm). Function room. Games (fruit machine, quiz machine, pool). Tables outdoors (25, terrace). TVs (big screen, satellite).

Princess of Wales

22 Chalcot Road, NW1 8LL (7722 0354). Chalk Farm tube. **Open** 11am-11pm Mon-Sat; noon-10.30pm Sun. **Food served** noon-4pm, 7-9.30pm Mon-Sat; noon-5.30pm Sun. **No credit cards**.

No 'destination' venue, the Princess of Wales is all the better for being one for locals. Not quite an old-fashioned boozer, the place's clientele are, on the whole, not in the first flush of youth – and we like that. It means there's jazz on a Sunday lunchtime (we've even learnt to applaud at the end of solos); there's Timothy Taylor Landlord, as well as Bombardier and Adnams on tap; and, best of all, there's the best by-the-glass wine selection in the area, offered at best-value prices (the Navajas crianza rioja is sumptuous). Walls are crammed with pictures of all shapes and sizes, and shelves are piled high with well-thumbed, dusty books, but the pub remains bright in creams and greens and staff are friendly and good at what they do. Another bonus: the huge Sunday roasts are fine value at £6.75.

Babies and children welcome. Function room. Music (jazz 8.30pm Thur, noon Sun). Quiz (9pm Tue). Tables outdoors (10, patio garden; 5, pavement). TV. **Map 8 G1**.

Queens

49 Regent's Park Road, NW1 8XD (7586 0408/ www.geronimo-inns.co.uk). Chalk Farm tube/31, 168, 274 bus. **Open** 11am-11pm Mon-Sat; noon-10.30pm Sun. **Food served** noon-3pm, 7-10pm Mon-Sat; 12.30-4pm, 7-9pm Sun. **Credit** MC, V.

At the bottom of lovely Primrose Hill, Queens is two parts faded country pub to one part London gastropub. It's not a pulse-quickening mix, though there's some very good food to be had, either from a long menu or a short but sweet list of bar snacks (salt and pepper squid with coriander, £3.50; crumbled brandade balls, £2.50). The bar stretches down a long corridor-like space, with rather dilapidated banquettes at one end and a curved window seat at the other. Assorted knick-knacks (a wooden crocodile, a wire bird cage) are dotted about, along with a few pieces of glaringly average modern art. The whole place could use a facelift, but could never be called pretentious. Young's ales are on draught, plus Red Stripe and Hoegaarden. In summer, the pavement tables are much in demand.

Babies and children admitted (restaurant). Restaurant. Tables outdoors (3, balcony; 3, pavement). TV (digital, satellite).

ST JOHN'S WOOD

At first sight, the exclusive, grand housefronts of St John's Wood would not appear to yield any drinking utopias, yet scattered around these stern residential streets are a few gems whose idiosyncracy would grace more acclaimed swaths of north London. Their battiness – and anonymity – mean that they attract the occasional B-list face equally attracted by the area's musical legacy.

Abbey Road Pub & Dining Room

63 Abbey Road, NW8 0AE (7328 6626). St John's Wood or Kilburn Park tube. **Open** 5-11pm Mon; noon-11pm Tue-Fri; 11am-11pm Sat; 11am-10.30pm Sun. **Food served** 7-10.30pm Mon; 12.30-3.30pm, 7-10.30pm Tue-Fri; noon-3.30pm, 7-10.30pm Sat; noon-4pm, 7-10pm Sun. **Credit** AmEx, MC, V.

Although a fair walk from the iconic zebra crossing and recording studios, the Abbey Road name is one most recently settled on by this imposing corner pub-restaurant. In a previous incarnation as the Salt House, it gained a good gastropub reputation, one that the new management (also responsible for the Salusbury in NW6 and Bollo in W4) are keen to maintain. With a starter of panfried king scallops (£8), watercress and ricotta ravioli as a starter or main (£7.50/£10), and panfried red bream (£13.50) as a serious main – plus a sparkling roast cod lunch special at £5 – all is fine in the food department. Wines come two dozen to

the bottle, with eight by the glass, draught beers include Abbot, Greene King and Budvar. All can be enjoyed in a comfortable boho space upon Ottomans and church pews, surrounded by stripped wood, in the terrace beer garden or sunken restaurant.
Babies and children welcome (before 7pm); high chairs. Function room. Restaurant. Specialities (cocktails). Tables outdoors (12, terrace).

Duke of York

2A St Anne's Terrace, NW8 6PJ (7722 1933). St John's Wood tube. **Open** 11am-11pm Mon-Sat; noon-10.30pm Sun. **Food served** noon-11pm Mon-Sat; noon-10pm Sun. **Credit** MC, V.
The wicker chairs covering the corner of pavement where St Anne's and St John's Wood Terraces meet prepare you for a continental-style bar-brasserie with arty touches – which is exactly what awaits behind the lattice shutters. A well-to-do clientele sip a pint of Old Speckled Hen or a glass of red bergerac (£15.95 a bottle) in the front bar area while diners at the back tuck into peppered tuna with pak choi (£12.95) or blackened rib-eye steak (£11.95). Equally upmarket but snackier foodstuffs are available, too – say, frittata of crayfish with shaved parmesan and wild rocket (£5.50) or pan-fried lemon crumbed goat's cheese (£4.95). Beer choices include John Smith's and Hoegaarden on tap, plus bottled San Miguel, Tiger, Cobra and Beck's.
Babies and children admitted (before 8pm). No-smoking area. Restaurant. Tables outdoors (8, pavement). TV.

Star

38 St John's Wood Terrace, NW8 6LS (7722 1051). St John's Wood tube. **Open** 11am-11pm Mon-Sat; noon-10.30pm Sun. **Credit** MC, V.
If someone suggests St John's Wood is only upmarket gastro joints and upholstered pubs for toffs, send them here. This delightfully quirky, communal corner pub would be anyone's local. The decor makes the first impression, the cabin-like wooden interior, comfortably carpeted, done out with glass stars hanging from the lattice work and 1940s film stars framed around the fireplace. A small back room for sports on TV is covered with caricatures of jockeys and photos of Best and Ali; complete sets of Typhoo cards and coin collections are mounted elsewhere. At the square bar counter, Bass, Worthington and Caffrey's indicate an older clientele (who enjoy a drop of evening sun out on the front terrace), although there are standard cocktails (£4 a glass, £11 a jug), too. There's not much by way of food, but with bonhomie this warm, who could wish for more?
Games (fruit machine). Jukebox. Tables outdoors (5, patio). TV (big screen).

Also in the area...

All Bar One 60 St John's Wood, NW8 7SH (7483 9931).

STOKE NEWINGTON

Granted, there are a couple of decent watering holes on the High Street, and a couple more tucked away in the heart of residential areas (seek out the Shakespeare if you can), but it's still all about Church Street, a skinny stretch of road lined with bookshops, pubs, restaurants and London's loveliest cemetery.

Auld Shillelagh

105 Stoke Newington Church Street, N16 0UD (7249 5951). Manor House or Seven Sisters tube/ 73, 476 bus. **Open** 11am-11pm Mon-Sat; noon-10.30pm Sun. **Credit** AmEx, DC, MC, V.
While other pubs in the neighbourhood let people stare proudly in through plate glass, the Auld Shillelagh has stuck with the frosted glass, shutting out those who aren't already au fait with the place and keeping the world from those who've come in to escape it. Still, it's hardly a threatening pub: step through the beat-up door and you'll find the warmest welcome in N16. This is an Irish pub, not an Oirish pub. The air is dense with the fog of Marlboro Lights, the atmosphere is never oppressive, and the Guinness – if you're drinking anything else, you should be drinking somewhere else – will be poured in its own time and brought to your table unprompted by staff never slow to smile. Musically themed evenings add a little colour, but really, this is just a place in which get mashed in convivial company. On good nights, it's the best pub in Stokey.
Babies and children admitted (before 7pm). Games (fruit machine). TV (big screen, satellite).

Daniel Defoe

102 Stoke Newington Church Street, N16 0LA (7254 2906). Stoke Newington rail/73, 393, 476 bus. **Open** 1-11pm Mon-Fri; noon-11pm Sat; noon-10.30pm Sun. **Food served** 1-10pm Mon-Fri; noon-6pm Sat, Sun. **Credit** MC, V.
Defoe's statue has been vandalised and removed from the nearby Stoke Newington library, but this grand 19th-century building is very much alive and well. The decor is non-PC dark brown walls and a tobacco-stained yellow ceiling, with curtains tied up by enormous gold tassels; big blackboards scream out 'cream of mushroom soup' and 'Sunday roast – chicken, beef, pork', in multicoloured chalk. The look is old northern railway pub, with men playing on a pool table in the back room. Shepherd Neame own the place, and their Bombadier is on tap, along with Marston's Pedigree and St Austell, as well as an ale made specially for the pub in nearby Stratford – the delicious, malty, aptly named Defoe.
Games (fruit machine, pool table). Tables outdoors (10, garden). Specialities (real ales). TV.

Fox Reformed

176 Stoke Newington Church Street, N16 0JL (7254 5975/www.fox-reformed.co.uk). Stoke Newington rail/ 73, 393, 476 bus. **Open** 5-11pm Mon-Fri; noon-11pm Sat, Sun. **Food served** 6.30-10.30pm Mon-Fri; noon-3pm, 6.30-10.30pm Sat, Sun. **Credit** AmEx, DC, MC, V.
An attempt to bring the French bistro to north London – 'Apéritifs de Marque' is etched on the front window – this well-known Stokey bar is more like Café Rouge meets *Antiques Roadshow.* There's an impressive array of liqueurs from Dijon, and wines number 30, with nine by the glass (try the Myall Road shiraz from Australia, £4.40). The outside is classically British, painted telephone box red, and the front room is Taunton B&B, with toby jugs and a ticking grandfather clock. When we visited, the owner was taking turns doing the crossword with a chap in half glasses and a couple of refugees from Woodstock were sitting on the church pew seating. Board games – Scrabble, backgammon and chess – are popular, but after 7.30pm you'll have to move if people want to eat.
Games (board games). Entertainment (backgammon club 7.30pm Mon). No-smoking tables. Tables outdoors (5, heated garden).

Prince

59 Kynaston Road, N16 0EB (7923 4766). Stoke Newington rail/73, 106 bus. **Open** noon-11pm Mon-Sat; noon-10.30pm Sun. **Food served** noon-2.30pm, 5-10pm Mon-Fri; noon-4pm, 5.30-10pm Sat; noon-4pm, 5.30-9pm Sun. **Credit** MC, V.

The Prince is now owned by the people who once operated the Red Lion on Church Street, and while they haven't brought all their customers along with them for the ride, there's still a reasonable buzz about this place. It's another reworking of an old corner boozer, which is to say that the lighting is careful, the paints come from Farrow & Ball (or look like they do), the drinkers are relatively affluent and the wines are decent. A feeble vegetarian pasta dish raised suspicions that reopening the kitchen may not have been such a good idea, but we're assured that the meatier portions of the menu, from prosaic burgers to more exotic belly pork, is better. A major plus is the location, far enough away from Church Street to deter those who don't already know about it. There's a music quiz on Tuesdays.

Babies and children admitted (before 5pm); children's menu, high chairs. Disabled: toilet. Function room. Music quiz (8.30pm Tue; £1). Tables outdoors (8, garden). TV (satellite).

Rose & Crown

199 Stoke Newington Church Street, N16 9ES (7254 7497). Stoke Newington rail/73, 393, 476 bus. **Open** 11.30am-11pm Mon-Sat; noon-10.30pm Sun. **Food served** noon-2.30pm Mon-Fri; noon-3.30pm Sat, Sun. **Credit** MC, V.

When, in their song 'Seven Days', perennial local underachievers Animals That Swim chose a pub to illustrate the boozy vortex into which life in Stoke Newington can carelessly descend for long-term, dole-happy residents, they chose this one. Good call. While other pubs have been reworked into gastroboozers or Wetherspoonian pits, the Rose & Crown remains just what it's always been: a matey room in which to slowly take the edge off the day with people willingly stuck in the same small circle of activity as you. Progress in the last decade has been largely limited to a gradual, infinitessimally stepped but undeniable turning-up of the dimmer switch; the fruit machine still blinks, but less noisily than before. The menu boasts of a Sunday roast seven days a week, which seems curiously appropriate; wash it down with Marston's Pedigree. As for Animals That Swim, *I Was the King, I Really Was the King* can be found in all scruffy second-hand record shops for about three quid. It's a terrific record.

Babies and children welcome (before 7pm). Games (fruit machine, quiz machine). Quiz (8.30pm Tue; £1). Tables outdoors (2, pavement). TV (satellite).

Shakespeare

57 Allen Road, N16 8RY (7254 4190). 73, 476 bus. **Open** 5-11pm Mon-Fri; noon-11pm Sat; noon-10.30pm Sun. **Credit** MC, V.

The Shakespeare is owned by the same group who run – among others – the Approach Tavern (*see p140*), the Prince George (*see p151*) and the Royal Inn on the Park (*see p151*), and drinkers who've stopped in any of those pubs will clock the resemblance in a heartbeat. The wallpaper appears artfully stained by nicotine, the jukebox throws out anything from vintage punk to jazz, and the wines are more expensive than they should be. However, while it looks like its siblings, the Shakespeare carries an ambience that's pure Stokey: raffish, leftist, vaguely bohemian and keen on getting another round in when last call is announced. And then another. The ales include London Pride, Adnams and, most appetisingly, something or other from the Ridley's brewery in Essex – all the better to wash down your disappointment when you come third from last in the fiendishly tough Monday-night quiz.

Babies and children admitted. Games (board games, cards, cribbage, dominoes). Quiz (8.45pm Mon; £1). Tables outdoors (12, covered garden). TV (satellite).

Also in the area...

Lion (Tup) 132 Stoke Newington Church Street, N16 0JX (7249 1318).
Rochester Castle (JD Wetherspoon) 145 High Street, N16 0NY (7249 6016).

SWISS COTTAGE

The name conjures up images of pastoral calm, which only makes the grim reality harder to take. Swiss Cottage is an urban nightmare entwined around a cute Tyrolean-style chalet, the tavern which gave the tube station and immediate area its name. Little else cottagey remains; it's all northbound traffic roar, tacky commerce and mall rats. When ready, chic new apartment blocks around the tube stop may sprout a bar or two.

Ye Olde Swiss Cottage

98 Finchley Road, NW3 5EL (7722 3487). Swiss Cottage tube. **Open** 11am-11pm Mon-Sat; noon-10.30pm Sun. **Food served** noon-8pm Mon-Sat; noon-5pm Sun. **Credit** MC, V.

When this chintzy chalet was erected as a tavern in 1840, it was at a tollgate set up for the newly laid Finchley Road. Swiss was hip. Adolphe Adam had a hit with the opera *Chalet*, and Prince Albert built an Alpine hut on the Isle of Wight. Run by a famous boxer who handed out free beer on fight days, this inn became a landmark, giving its name to the tube station and surrounding area, now an ugly traffic fly-past. Tacking 'Ye Olde' on the name doesn't begin to address the anomaly. It's a large Samuel Smith's pub of Hovis vintage and flat-cap characters where you can hear a crisp packet rustle. Outside, on the terrace, it's like drinking lager on the launch pad of Cape Canaveral. Along with Ayingerbrau, Sovereign and Sam Smith's staples, there's food of the gammon-egg-and-chips (£6.95) variety.

Babies and children admitted (dining only). Function room. Games (chess, darts, fruit machines, pool). No piped music or jukebox. Tables outdoors (30, pavement).

Also in the area...

brb at Hampstead 48 Rosslyn Hill, NW3 1NH (7431 8802).
Wetherspoons Level 2, 02 Centre, 255 Finchley Road, NW3 6LU (7433 0920).
Walkabout 02 Centre, 255 Finchley Road, NW3 6LU (7433 6570).

TUFNELL PARK & ARCHWAY

A changing demographic seems to be bringing some much-needed life to the local beer economy. The area around Tufnell Park tube contains some old locals revived with young

No.77 Wine Bar. See p188.

money. The **Lord Palmerston** has long made a feature of good food and wine, while former fleapits – like the **Junction Tavern** and **St John's** – are being turned into gastropubs.

Dartmouth Arms

35 York Rise, NW5 1SP (7485 3267). Tufnell Park tube. **Open** 11am-11pm Mon-Fri; 10am-11pm Sat; 10am-10.30pm Sun. **Food served** 11am-3pm, 6-10pm Mon-Fri; 10am-10pm Sat, Sun. **Credit** MC, V.

'Beer, wine, gravy, cake and mussels' is painted in big letters on the outside of this pub; but what it doesn't say is 'blokes'. When we visited, the place was packed with tattooed lads in Ted Baker T-shirts, bald-headed guys in Tacchini zip-tops, and chaps in patent leather shoes and V-necks. It's a lively, welcoming place, though, and bar staff are prompt – even though there's a saloon bar at the back with further demanding drinkers to deal with. The saloon has a New England hunting-lodge look – varnished dark wood, antlers, plenty of brass fittings – and attracts older fellers and women students making roll-ups – but nary a lumberjack. The excellent ciders stand out, notably Dunkertons Organic (£2.95 for 33cl) from Herefordshire, but there's also a must-try 40-year-old Krohn Colheita port (£5 for 50ml). Good food, too: an 8oz ribeye steak comes with a glass of wine (£11) or there are oysters (£5 for six).

Babies and children admitted (before 8pm). Games (board games). Knitting club (all day, last Sat of mth; free). Quiz (8pm every other Tue; £1). Restaurant available for hire. TV (big screen, satellite).

Junction Tavern

101 Fortess Road, NW5 1AG (7485 9400). Tufnell Park tube/Kentish Town tube/rail. **Open** noon-11pm Mon-Sat; noon-10.30pm Sun. **Food served** noon-3pm, 6.30-10.30pm Mon-Fri; noon-4pm, 6.30-10.30pm Sat; noon-4pm, 6.30-9.30pm Sun. **Credit** MC, V.

The popular Junction has a sub-baronial look, with wood-panelled walls, highly decorative ceiling plaster and chandeliers. The dining room at the front feels like a Harrogate tea room – families and older couples sitting up straight and not making too much noise – but a smattering of wood tables, some sofas and a scuffed wood floor make the back room more relaxed. Here, students, retirees, engineers and journalists sup real ales (Deuchars IPA, great works from the Itchen Valley brewery) or make the best of a disappointing wine selection. A bright and airy, plastic-framed conservatory tacked on at the back provides more seating for those tucking into well made, well priced food, with two courses for £13.50 on a Sunday. There are also picnic benches for summer drinking outside.

Babies and children welcome. Restaurant. Tables outdoors (15, garden).

Lord Palmerston

33 Dartmouth Park Hill, NW5 1HU (7485 1578). Tufnell Park tube. **Open** noon-11pm Mon-Sat; noon-10.30pm Sun. **Food served** 12.30-3pm, 7-10pm Mon-Sat; 1-4pm, 7-9pm Sun. **Credit** MC, V.

This sparse gastropub is full of Hampstead ladies and wealthy, former dance music entrepreneurs, rather than Gooner replica shirt-wearers with pint in hand. It's a riot of minimalism, with blue-grey walls – the shade they use in mental hospitals to calm patients – and without pictures or decoration. A back dining room is delightful in summer, although the fully glass-paned ceiling makes it rather chilly at night. Staff can be a bit cold, too, but they're always helpful and will explain an impressive range of drinks that includes 28 wines. There's also great Guillet Frères cider from Brittany, rather than the more usual Normandy, and Young's Light Ale in bottles. The food has a couple of vegetarian options, including roast butternut squash, with spices, broad beans and goat's cheese (£8.95).

Babies and children admitted. Function room. Tables outdoors (5, garden; 13, pavement).

Settle Inn

17-19 Archway Road, N19 3TX (7272 7872). Archway tube. **Open** 11am-11pm Mon-Sat; noon-10.30pm Sun. **Food served** noon-3pm, 6-10pm Mon-Fri; noon-9.30pm Sat, Sun. **Credit** MC, V.

You know where you are with the Settle Inn: a road sign right outside says 'M1 5 miles, Watford 15 miles', next to which a blackboard proudly tells of 'VK Blue, VK Ice and VK Ice Cranberry'. Within the drinks selection is better than one might expect, with Flowers IPA, Bass and Staropramen on tap, as well as Budvar and Leffe by the bottle. Of nine wines (four by the glass), only the 2003 Berri Estates colombard (£10.50 a bottle) impresses. The place is gastropub-standard (open kitchen, pine benches, diners in groups of four), with a couple of comedy chairs adding 'character' – made from double-height planks of wood, they look like they were reclaimed from a water mill. But plastic lamp lighting is still in place from when this was the Dog, along with bumpy wallpaper and blokes that resemble music festival bouncers. The food, inevitably, is Thai, though there are some decent Sunday roasts (£6.50), too.

Babies and children admitted (dining only). Games (board games, quiz machine). Quiz (8.30pm Tue; free). TV (satellite).

St John's

91 Junction Road, N19 5QU (7272 1587). Archway tube. **Open** 5-11pm Mon; noon-11pm Tue-Sat; noon-10.30pm Sun. **Food served** 6.30-11pm Mon; noon-3.30pm, 6.30-11pm Tue-Fri; noon-4pm, 6.30-11pm Sat; noon-4pm, 6.30-10.30pm Sun. **Credit** AmEx, MC, V.

This popular gastropub has built up a loyal following with wealthier locals who'll embrace anything rather than the grotty boozers on Holloway Road. From the outside the cream tiles and brown brick trim suggest a public toilet, but the St John's interior is a jewel of Victorian detailing: Corinthian pillars, picked out in gold at the tip, rise to the patterned plaster ceiling; there's a sweeping wooden bar; and oak tables and chairs stand beneath large-paned windows. There's a decent selection of real ales (Deuchars IPA, Wadworth 6X, Old Speckled Hen) and 18 wines by the glass, featuring the lovely, rose-scented Viña Esmeralda from Miguel Torres (£4 a glass) and an English wine from the fast-improving Gloucestershire winery, Three Choirs (£3.75 for a glass). The adjoining restaurant offers classy food, including roast pheasant, confit leg of pheasant, rösti, kale and redcurrant jus for £11.50.

Babies and children admitted; booster seats. Games (backgammon, chess). Restaurant. Tables outdoors (7, patio).

WEST HAMPSTEAD

The hilly village of West Hampstead keeps its eateries and few bars beside the cycle surgeries and charity shops of West End Lane, the main drag. At its northern tip, the verdant junction with Fortune Green is abundant with ethnic restaurants and terraces – but not one bar.

Gallery

190 Broadhurst Gardens, NW6 3AY (7625 9184/ www.gallerybarhampstead.co.uk). West Hampstead tube/rail. **Open** 4-11pm Mon; 4-11.30pm Tue-Thur; noon-midnight Fri, Sat; noon-11pm Sun. **Food served** 5-9pm Mon-Fri; 12.30-4.30pm, 6-9pm Sat, Sun. **Happy hour** 5-7pm daily. **Credit** DC, MC, V.

Round the corner from West Hampstead tube station, the stylish Gallery appeals to a more discerning clientele than that which gathers at nearby post-work troughs. It's a bar and restaurant, the latter a candlelit affair tucked away down a staircase. Although set on three levels, the bar space is intimate, with the prime comfy spots in the titular gallery, overlooking a modest mezzanine of squishy seating and old Hitchcock posters, and a main area around the counter spotted with small, polished tables; street-facing windows open in summer. On the counter, a huge Erdinger tap towers over others for Bitburger, Red Stripe and Leffe, and there are standard cocktails (£5.50-£6), too. Wine, listed a dozen of each colour on huge blackboards either side of the bar, comes three of each by the glass.

Babies and children welcome (until 6pm). Games (board games). Restaurant (no-smoking area). Specialities (cocktails). Tables outdoors (2, pavement).

No.77 Wine Bar

77 Mill Lane, NW6 1NB (7435 7787). West Hampstead tube/rail. **Open** noon-11pm Mon, Tue; noon-midnight Wed-Sat; noon-10.30pm Sun. **Food served** noon-3pm Mon-Fri; noon-midnight Sat; noon-10pm Sun. **Credit** MC, V.

More party bar than wine bar, No.77 is a popular hangout for rugger types of both sexes and hemispheres, whose regular events (such as morris dancing on St George's Day) has punters spilling out on to the pavement. It takes its wine seriously enough to enjoy, with ten each of red and white available by the glass. A Château Senailhac is a nice find at £3.95 a glass, as is a Rooiberg Winery sauvignon blanc (£3.30). A solitary Budvar beer tap is backed up by bottles of Hahn, plus Steinlager and Tooheys from New Zealand, while 'the sexiest food in West Hampstead' features panfried scallops (£5.75), vegetarian haggis (£7.95) and £2.50 'bits on the side' – focaccia and olive oil, and so on. Framed rugby shirts are given as much presence as the ethno art in the labyrinthine network of little spaces.

Babies and children welcome. Function room. Games (board games). Restaurant. Specialities (wine). Tables outdoors (8, pavement).

SOUTH

SOUTH

BALHAM

It'll be a long time before Balham completes any process of gentrification, and this is undoubtedly a good thing; you get the best of both worlds, with Young's bitters and quality cocktails served side by side in many pubs, all with reasonably priced, reliably good grub. Perfect examples are the Grove or **Duke Of Devonshire**; or, if you'd rather pretend you're drinking on Old Compton Street, the **Kitchen & Bar** is a good place to act out your fantasy.

Balham Kitchen & Bar

15-19 Bedford Hill, SW12 9EX (8675 6900/www.balhamkitchen.com). Balham tube/rail. **Open** 8am-11pm Mon-Sat; 8am-10.30pm Sun. **Food served** 8am-10.30pm Mon-Sat; 8am-10pm Sun. **Credit** AmEx, MC, V.

The smooth curves and sleek, highly polished surfaces in this split-level bar and restaurant immediately make you wish you'd ironed your shirt before you came out – though you'd be hard pushed to match the crisp whiteness of the uniforms on the staff who serve up the impressive range of wines and cocktails. The cocktails come in 'new school' and 'old school' varieties, all at a reasonable £6. The wine list includes five whites, five reds and a couple of rosés; many choices are available by the glass for about a fiver. Catering perfectly for the Clapham overspill, the BK&B is extremely busy upstairs. If perching on a bar stool gives you cramp in your toes, you can always descend to the Playroom: no, not a haven for partner-swappers, but a quieter lounge area, where slightly dubious animal-skin rugs and leather sofas revive 1970s decadence.

Babies and children welcome (before 6pm). Disabled: toilet. Function rooms. No-smoking area. Tables outdoors (4, pavement). TVs (big screen, satellite).

Bedford

77 Bedford Hill, SW12 9HD (8682 8940). Balham tube/rail. **Open** 11am-11pm Mon-Wed; 11am-midnight Thur; 11am-2am Fri, Sat; noon-10.30pm Sun. **Food served** noon-2.45pm, 7-10pm Mon-Fri; noon-4pm, 7-10pm Sat; noon-5pm, 7-9.45pm Sun. **Credit** AmEx, MC, V.

Many Londoners will be familiar with this endearingly shabby place, remembering picking their way through the haphazardly laid-out tables and chairs to attend the top-notch comedy nights or low-key acoustic performances that take place in the back rooms. But the main bar is not without entertainment; jazz duos work their way through soul classics on a small stage in the corner, while chefs noisily sling together 'Balhamburgers' and 'Bedford Salads' in the open-plan kitchen. An open fire provides a great backdrop for a relaxing quaff of wine or two. The bottles aren't cheap (£11 and up), but the selection is reasonably left-field, and there's a varied choice by the glass. Men in posh shirts and jumpers prefer supping their pints of London Pride, Wadworth 6X, Young's or one of a host of strong lagers while watching football on TV.

Babies and children admitted (until 6pm). Comedy (9pm Tue, £3; 7.30pm Fri, £8-£12; 6.30pm Sat, £12-£15). Dance (line dancing 7.30pm Mon; £5; swing classes 8pm Tue, £8-£10; salsa classes 7.45pm Wed, £5). Disabled: toilet. Function rooms. Games (board games, fruit machines). Music (jazz 8pm Sun, £5; acoustic 9pm Wed, free; bands 9pm Thur, free). Nightclub (11.15pm-2am Fri, Sat; £5). Quiz (8.30pm Wed; £1). TV (big screen, satellite).

Duke of Devonshire

39 Balham High Road, SW12 9AN (8673 1363). Balham tube/rail. **Open** noon-midnight Mon-Thur, Sun; noon-2am Fri, Sat. **Food served** noon-11pm Mon-Fri; noon-1am Sat, Sun. **Credit** MC, V.

It's almost two distinct pubs rolled into one. At the front, the quiz machine and TV are stared at without interest by older local customers working their way through pints of Young's bitter, Special or (when appropriate) Winter Warmer. In the spacious back room, there's a hipper crowd indulging in the trusty triumvirate of Foster's, Carlsberg and Stella. During weekday evenings, the Duke is hard to beat as a meeting place. The standard pub fare of pastas, roasts, pies and burgers is impressive in both quality and quantity. Fairy lights and table lamps tend to obscure any small facial blemishes that might otherwise ruin a first date, and on late-opening weekend nights, the music is ramped up at regular intervals throughout the evening, so that by last admissions at 11pm, conversation is relegated to second place. By which time most of the crowd are too merry to care.

Disabled: toilet. Games (darts, fruit machines, table football). Music (DJ 9.30pm-2am, last entry 11pm Fri, Sat; free). Tables outdoors (12, garden). TV.

Exhibit

12 Balham Station Road, SW12 9SG (8772 6556/www.theexhibitbarandrestaurant.com). Balham tube/rail. **Open** 11.30am-11pm Mon-Thur; 11.30am-midnight Fri, Sat; 11.30am-10.30pm Sun. **Food served** noon-3pm, 7-11.30pm Mon-Sat; noon-4pm Sun. **Credit** MC, V.

Almost certainly the best bar in London to adjoin a supermarket carpark. The grimness of the location belies the swankiness of the joint, which has recently expanded to include a cocktail bar and a screening room showing sport and classic films. The wine list is divided into categories such as 'supple', 'elegant', 'smooth' and 'aromatic', and you could divide the clientele similarly; the flashing smiles and tanned midriffs give you the impression that you've stumbled into a modelling convention, and even the fish in the bar-side aquarium seem distracted by all the healthy, glowing complexions. Amstel, Kirin and Red Stripe are on tap; the only bitter – Bombardier and Banana Bread – is

in bottles. The cocktails have slight twists on traditional themes, with the Chilli Mary (using chilli vodka) being the pick of the bunch. If you're peckish, try the restaurant upstairs, which has recently received plaudits from chef and *Masterchef* presenter John Torode.
Babies and children admitted (until 7pm). Disabled: toilet. Function room. Restaurant. Tables outdoors (8 garden; 6 pavement).

Lounge

76 Bedford Hill, SW12 9HR (8673 8787/www.the balhamlounge.co.uk). Balham tube/rail. **Open** 5pm-midnight Tue-Fri; 10.30am-midnight Sat; 11.30am-10pm Sun. **Food served** 5-10.30pm Tue-Fri; 10.30am-10pm Sat; 11.30am-9pm Sun. **Credit** MC, V.
Snug under a railway bridge, Lounge has a dingy location that's offset nicely by its haphazard, bright interior. The place comes across as more of a diner than a lounge; almost a transport café with upmarket ambitions. Salt and pepper pots sit on pine tables, a ceiling fan whispers and the slightly disorganised service contributes to an unusual but not unpleasant atmosphere. The dishes on the tapas menu are excellent value at around £4, and the draught Greene King IPA shows that the owners are making an effort to accommodate more than the Beck's/chardonnay brigade. Bottles of white are brought out in natty orange ice buckets to thirtysomethings who are trying to forget about their grim day in the office; pints of Guinness are slurped by other thirtysomethings who have already forgotten.
Babies and children admitted. Disabled: toilet. Function room. TV (digital, satellite).

Also in the area...

Balham Tup 21 Chestnut Grove, SW12 8JB (8772 0546).
Moon Under Water (JD Wetherspoon) 194 Balham High Street, SW12 9BP (8673 0535).

BATTERSEA

Battersea was once the mousey little sister of cheerleader Clapham, though there are signs it may be blossoming. Regeneration is everywhere – the area's bars included. The slick **Dovedale** and urbane **Dusk** are all signs of a coming of age – but the quiet and reliable charm of Battersea's earlier self is not forgotten at the 'Sunday roast' boozers of the **Masons Arms**, the **Latchmere** and the **Fox & Hounds**. All this, and one of the finest parks in London.

Artesian Well

693 Wandsworth Road, SW8 3JF (7627 3353/ www.artesianwell.co.uk). Clapham Common tube/ Wandsworth Town rail. **Open** 5pm-1am Thur; 5pm-3am Fri, Sat. **Food served** 6-11pm Thur-Sat. **Admission** (club only) £3-£5 Fri, Sat. **Credit** AmEx, MC, V.
Long-established late-night bar for the revellers of Battersea and Clapham, the insanely decorative Artesian Well overflows with faux-baroque furnishings, gargoyles and more. Once inside you'll find mood and music evolve by floor (there are three): the higher you go, the more manic things get, especially at weekends when DJs spin. House aficionados will probably wince at the commercial musings of the DJ, but the dancefloor heaves nonetheless. The management changed just as we were going to press, but the new incumbents seem likely to foster the same boisterous hedonism as before. Weekend queues are not unusual, and there's an additional entrance fee to the upper rooms of £3 and £5 on Friday and Saturday night respectively.
Babies and children admitted (before 9pm). Function rooms. Music (open mic 7pm Thur, free; DJs 9.30pm Fri-Sun, £3-£5). Tables outdoors (3, terrace).

Royal Oak. *See p200.*

Le Bouchon Bordelais

5-9 Battersea Rise, SW11 1HG (7738 0307/www.lebouchon.co.uk). Clapham Junction rail/35, 37 bus. **Open** 10am-11pm Mon-Sat; 10am-10.30pm Sun. **Food served** 10am-10pm daily. **Credit** AmEx, MC, V.

Le Bouchon isn't new, but it has had a new injection of culinary expertise, by Michel Roux of Le Gavroche, in the bistro side of its operation. The food (filet de boeuf with flaxen frites, for instance, or a starter of pan-fried foie gras on savoy cabbage drizzled with port sauce) is certainly pretty good, but you're not obliged to eat: Le Bouchon has plenty of liquid inducements to visit, wines in particular. There are 20-odd bottles (an excellent 2001 Gigondas, for instance, at £28), of which four reds and four whites are available by the glass. The staff are French, the nibbles are French, there's even Ricard, and Canal+ plays on the TV to keep you informed of goings-on across the Channel. Come the Six Nations rugby tournament, this place is the scene of much shouting and downing of claret.

Babies and children welcome: children's menu; crèche (Sat-Sun); high chairs. Function room. No-smoking tables. Restaurant. Tables outdoors (8, terrace). TV (big screen, satellite).

Corum

30-32 Queenstown Road, SW8 3RX (7720 5445). Battersea Park, Queenstown Road or Clapham Junction rail/77, 137, 156, 345 bus. **Open** noon-3pm, 5pm-1am Mon-Wed; noon-3pm, 5pm-2am Thur; noon-3pm, 5pm-3am Fri; noon-3am Sat; noon-1am Sun. **Food served** 6pm-11pm daily. **Credit** AmEx, MC, V.

Much has been made of Corum's head chef John Simeoni (he worked at River Café and the Ivy), which means the adjoining bar here is often overlooked. This, combined with the overly bright lighting and draughty condensation-covered glass façade, does not encourage the pre- or post-dinner crowd to linger too long by the linen-covered tables, or to teeter upon the low leather pouffes. Which is a shame, given the absence of any other late-licence bars in this neck of Battersea, as the cocktails are reasonably cheap (though not overly creative) and the wine list is extensive. Beers are an uninspired collection: same-old-same-old lagers and a small bottled range that includes Tiger and Hoegaarden.

Babies and children admitted (restaurant). Disabled: toilet. Music (DJs 10pm Fri, sat; free). No-smoking area. Tables outdoors (2, pavement). TV (big screen).

Dovedale House

441 Battersea Park Road, SW11 4LR (7223 7721). Battersea Park rail/44, 49, 344, 345 bus. **Open** noon-11pm Mon-Sat; noon-10.30pm Sun. **Food served** noon-3pm, 6-10pm Mon-Fri; noon-10pm Sat, Sun. **Credit** MC, V.

Opened in 2003 by the imaginative Spirit Group, the Dovedale was a welcome addition to this slightly sleepy corner of Battersea. The curvaceous bar is tolerably well stocked: as well as the usual big-name lagers and stout, there's Adnams Bitter and Paulaner in lager and wheat varieties. There are several tables around a gas fire and some slightly raised diner-style seating: useful when ordering from the open kitchen. An eclectic mix of paintings and prints hangs from the walls, while curious teacup-inspired chandeliers bathe the thirtysomething crowd in a warm amber glow. There's a fine breakfast menu, too.

Babies and children welcome. Disabled: toilet. Music (live jazz 8pm Sun). Tables outdoors (15, garden).

Drawing Room & Sofa Bar

103 Lavender Hill, SW11 5QL (7350 2564). Clapham Junction rail/77, 77A, 345 bus. **Open/food served** noon-11pm Mon-Sat; noon-10.30pm Sun. **Credit** AmEx, MC, V.

The designer of the Sofa Bar had the Midas touch – or a mate with a vanload of 1950s gold clocks. The walls of this quirky bar are lined with battered star-shaped timepieces and fish-eye mirrors; the rest of the decor is a dusty and faux opulent combo of peach walls, turquoise ceiling emblazoned with gold stars, Persian carpets and squidgy sofas with brocaded throws. The atmosphere is relaxed, with a boho crowd enjoying either a glass of red wine or flicking through the handwritten cocktail menu – Sex on the Sofa, anyone? Although there are no beers on tap, there's a great selection of aperitifs, from limoncello and a good choice of single malts, including 16-year-old Glenfiddich. On weeknights, the majority of customers retire to crash in the sofas after dinner in the adjoining drawing room, where you can enjoy a simple menu Mediterranean dishes.

Babies and children admitted. Bar available for hire. Function rooms. Tables outdoors (4, pavement).

Dusk

339 Battersea Park Road, SW11 4LF (7622 2112/www.duskbar.co.uk). Battersea Park rail. **Open** 6pm-12.30am Mon-Wed; 6pm-1.30am Thur-Sat. **Food served** 6-10.30pm Mon-Sat. **Credit** AmEx, MC, V.

The much-lauded Dusk (it was a runner-up in Time Out's 2004 Eating & Drinking awards) continues to impress and pull in the crowds from Battersea and beyond. A luscious red ceiling canopies three distinct areas: the lounge, bordered by hand-stitched leather cube chairs and low tables; the members' section, a diminutive space which, despite being roped off, is more crowded than anywhere else; and the glowing space towards the back, which has a little more room in which to move to the sounds of the DJ. Outside is a patio (there are plans to incorporate a grill/barbecue). Cocktails are the thing here, of course, and all are made with premium spirits. The attention to detail can, however, make for long waits on busy nights.

Function room. Music (DJs 9pm Wed-Sat). Tables outdoors (10, terrace). TV (big screen).

Fox & Hounds

66-68 Latchmere Road, SW11 2JU (7924 5483). Clapham Junction rail. **Open** 5-11pm Mon; noon-2.30pm, 5-11pm Tue-Thur; noon-11pm Fri, Sat; noon-10.30pm Sun. **Food served** 7-10.30pm Mon; 12.30-2.30pm, 7-10.30pm Tue-Thur; 12.30-3pm, 7-10.30pm Fri, Sat; 12.30-3pm, 7-10pm Sun. **Credit** MC, V.

Occupying the ground floor of an impressive Victorian building, this oasis of gastropubbery on an otherwise bleak stretch of road has decent ales – Bass, London Pride and Greene King IPA are all on tap – and a decent wine list. Nicely renovated a few years back, it has pale yellow walls, a red ceiling and vintage mirrors, with ornate pillars twisting up from the rough wood floor. The blackboard menu lists the dishes of the day – creations such as citrus-braised lamb shanks with rice salad and rocket (£13.50) or braised cod fillet with savoy cabbage and sweet onions (£11). The gentle clatter from the open kitchen provides a pleasant echo of the trains rattling over the nearby rail bridge.

Babies and children admitted (before 7pm). Disabled: toilet. Tables outdoors (10, garden). TV.

Holy Drinker

59 Northcote Road, SW11 1NP (7801 0544). Clapham Junction rail/35, 37 bus. **Open** 4.30-11pm Mon-Fri; noon-11pm Sat; 1-10.30pm Sun. **Credit** MC, V.

The Holy has certainly stood the test of time. One of the first style bars in Battersea, it staked its claim a good seven years BC (Before Chains). Comfy yet sleek, it's a happy hybrid of wine bar and style bar, and attracts a much more discerning, trendier crowd than your average Battersea hooray hangout; and, just as important, it has a very well stocked beer fridge. Towards the back, low-slung couches illuminated with numerous penny candles provide escape from the corridor of people that lend something of a house-party atmosphere to proceedings. The bar boasts 16 world ales and lagers, including EB, Bitburger, Schneider wheat beer and Everard's Tiger. Wines, too, are well chosen and there's a decent music policy.

Babies and children admitted (until 7pm). Music (DJs 6pm occasional Sat, Sun). Tables outdoors (4, pavement). TV.

Latchmere

503 Battersea Park Road, SW11 3BW (7223 3549). Battersea Park or Clapham Junction rail/44, 49, 344, 345 bus. **Open** noon-11pm Mon-Sat; noon-10.30pm Sun. **Food served** noon-3pm, 5-10pm Mon-Fri; noon-9pm Sat, Sun. **Credit** MC, V.

An welcome escape from the traffic blasting up to the bridge, this vast old corner pub oozes character. It's a vintage space, with dark polished wood panels lit by a mix of beautiful antique lights and candles; battered and studded leather sofas cluster around the fireplace at one side of the bar. Upstairs, the Latchmere theatre provides dramatic icing on the cake as one of London's best fringe venues. There's nothing better after a spot of theatre than a debate over a pint, and the draught selection includes Young's and Adnams Bitters, John Smith's and Kronenbourg; in bottles, there's Stella, Budvar, Michelob and others, alongside alcopops. The big football games are shown, but the screen is promptly dispatched on final whistle.

Babies and children admitted (until 6pm). Games (fruit machines, golf machine). Quiz (9pm Thur; £1). Tables outdoors (10, garden). Theatre (nightly; box office 7978 7040). TVs (big screen, satellite).

Masons Arms

169 Battersea Park Road, SW8 4BT (7622 2007). Battersea Park rail/137, 417 bus. **Open** noon-11pm Mon-Sat; noon-10.30pm Sun. **Food served** noon-3pm, 6-10pm Mon-Fri; noon-4pm, 6-10pm Sat; noon-4pm, 6-9pm Sun. **Credit** AmEx, MC, V.

Needing no introduction to the regulars of the Pilot and the Stonemason's Arms in West London, with which it shares owners, the Masons is an exemplary gastropub. Black and white prints hang on the pale yellow walls, while rag-tag wooden furniture is spaced around a large, rough-floored interior. To eat, there's the likes of goat's cheese tart with sesame pastry (£5), baked Portobello mushroom with couscous (£9) or springbuck steak with curried butternut squash purée (£12.50). The wide selection of draught beers includes Marston's Pedigree, Adnams Best, Amstel, Leffe, Staropramen and Hoegaarden. Warm and cosy in winter, bright and airy in summer, the Masons is a pub for all seasons. Style bars are opening all the time in this part of town, so it's nice to have an old-fashioned alternative.

Babies and children welcome. Disabled: toilet. Music (DJs 6.30pm last Fri of mth; free). Tables outdoors (6, pavement).

Matilda

74-76 Battersea Bridge Road, SW11 3AG (7228 6482). Clapham Junction rail then 319 bus/South Kensington tube then 45 or 345 bus. **Open/food served** noon-11pm daily. **Credit** MC, V.

Just a few hundred yards from Battersea Bridge, a turquoise fluorescent sign announces this pleasant bar-cum-restaurant. The interior is a subtle mix of mint green and vanilla, with interesting tapestries hung around the compact but extensively stocked bar. The food served in the back-room restaurant (booking essential) is good, but there's also a more casual bar menu that offers picks from the chef's specials board, along with a fine choice of Italian hams and bread. The wine list is well thought-out, too, and there's a small number of beers on tap: Pilsner Urquell, Amstel and Adnams Bitter. Well worth a visit.

Babies and children welcome. Disabled: toilet. Function rooms. Restaurant. Tables outdoors (10, garden & pavement).

Microbar

14 Lavender Hill, SW11 5RW (7228 5300/www.microbar.org). Clapham Common tube/Clapham Junction or Wandsworth Road rail/77, 77A, 137 159 bus. **Open** 6-11pm daily. **Credit** MC, V.

Tired of the same old lagers? Try this smashing little bar. It stocks an outlandishly varied choice of beer – beers like Alaskan Smoked Porter that the list says is 'like black forest ham', the ruby-red Brooklyn and the Belgian Trappist ale Westvleteren Blonde. And that's just for starters: get through those, and there's still a huge range of American, Czech, Belgian, German, Dutch and Scottish versions to sample – mostly in bottles, though there are also a couple on tap. Staff are friendly and clued up (they know who invented Hoegaarden, for instance), and there's an apt note on the wall: 'Not only was beer proof that there was a God, but it proved that he loves us.' Amen.

Games (backgammon, cards). Specialities (beers).

S Bar

37 Battersea Bridge Road, SW11 (7223 3322). Sloane square tube then 19, 49, 319 bus. **Open** noon-11pm Mon-Thur; noon-midnight Fri, Sat; noon-10.30pm Sun. **Food served** noon-3pm, 6-10pm Mon-Sat; 1-6pm Sun. **Credit** MC, V.

This is a lovely place, with potted plants and generous space between candlelit wooden tables. The result is a welcome sense of intimacy, whether you hide behind one of the pillars or slouch on the sofa beneath the window. There's a good wine list and some fine cocktails, with a choice of over 16 Bloody Marys, including the exotic Sumo Mary made with soy sauce and wasabi. Perhaps the most striking thing about S Bar, though, is the free booze. Yes, you read right. Every Tuesday night, the bar hosts a tasting evening to push the merits of new wines, spirits and cocktails. We were bitterly disappointed to have missed the absinthe night by 24 hours; the same mistake wasn't made for the armagnac night.

Babies and children admitted (until 6pm). Disabled: toilet. Function rooms. Music (DJs 8pm Fri, Sat; free). TVs (satellite, widescreen).

Tea Rooms des Artistes

697 Wandsworth Road, SW8 3JF (7652 6526/www.tearoomsdesartistes.com). Wandsworth Road rail/77, 77A bus. **Open** 6.30pm-1am Fri, Sat. **Food served** 6.30-11.30pm Fri, Sat. **Credit** MC, V.

The Tea Rooms des Artistes opened in 1982, and in the bar world that sort of longevity isn't a bad sign. Housed in a 16th-century barn with a later butcher's frontage, it has for the last 20-odd years been a Clapham drinking institution. Most famously, it was home to Rob da Bank and his band of Sunday Best revellers, and when Rob left, the chilled-out quality sounds and relaxed vibe stayed. This is a more discerning Clapham local than many of the new kids on the block, although it's only open on Friday and Saturday (a good spot for a private hire during the rest of the week). It has a pretty patio, but a limited selection of drinks: just four beers (bottled), 14 wines and standard cocktails.
Function room. Games (backgammon, chess, table football). Music (DJs 9pm Fri, Sat; free). Tables outdoors (7, garden).

Tim Bobbins

1-3 Lilleshall Road, SW4 0LN (7738 8953). Clapham South tube. **Open** 11.30am-11pm Mon-Sat; noon-10.30pm Sun. **Food served** 11.30am-3pm, 7-10pm Mon-Sat; noon-4pm, 7-9pm Sun. **Credit** AmEx, MC, V.
A cracking little local, this, and one that has added good food to its repertoire without losing its old-boozer charm. The one room of creaking floorboards and black and fawn walls plays host to an eclectic crowd: older drinkers who remember the time when pubs offered two kinds of grub (crisps and scratchings) and a younger, professional bunch. A big bar (London Pride, Wadworth 6X and Young's bitter are the ales on tap) dominates the room, which is book-ended by two fireplaces. The only entertainment is piped Motown that mingles with the murmurs of conversation, and the occasional thud on the dartboard.
Babies and children welcome. Function room. Games (darts). Restaurant. Tables outdoors (5, pavement). TVs (satellite).

Woodman

60 Battersea High Street, SW11 3HX (7228 2968). Clapham Junction rail then 319 bus. **Open** 11am-11pm Mon-Sat; noon-10.30pm Sun. **Food served** noon-3pm, 7-10pm Mon-Sat; 12.30-4pm Sun. **Credit** MC, V.
The Woodman seems to fare well, despite its quiet location. A Hall & Woodhouse establishment, it has the standard (and fine) H&W line-up of beers on tap, including Badger Best, Tanglefoot and Hofbrau lager. Appropriately enough, there are wood-panelled walls, a wooden floor and wooden bar, together fostering a cosy atmosphere. At the back of the long bar is a great beer garden that opens in the summer; during the winter, sturdy cooking is available from the kitchen: fish pies, home-made burgers and decent steaks. Satellite TV is available, but doesn't dominate. Well worth the extra few yards' stroll off Latchmere Road.
Babies and children welcome. Games (board games). Tables outdoors (10, garden). TV (satellite).

Also in the area...

All Bar One 32-38 Northcote Road, SW11 1NZ (7801 9951).
Asparagus (JD Wetherspoon) 1-13 Falcon Road, SW11 2PD (7801 0046).
Fine Line 33-37 Northcote Road, SW11 1NJ (7924 7387).
O'Neill's 66A-C Battersea Rise, SW11 1EQ (7350 0349).
Pitcher & Piano 94 Northcote Road, SW11 6QW (7738 9781).
Slug & Lettuce 4 St John's Hill, SW11 1RU (7924 1322).

BERMONDSEY & ROTHERHITHE

The formerly bleak area just south of the Thames now has drinking establishments reflecting the recent social divide: gastrobars such as the **Garrison** and **Hartley** for the newly arrived loft-dwelling professionals, and timeless community boozers like the superb **Blacksmith's Arms**. By the river, the **Mayflower** picks up decent trade from tourists through its historic connections.

Blacksmith's Arms

257 Rotherhithe Street, SE16 5EJ (7237 1349). Canada Water or Rotherhithe tube/225 bus. **Open** noon-11pm Mon-Sat; noon-10.30pm Sun. **Food served** noon-3pm, 6.30-10pm daily. **Credit** MC, V.
A great little community pub this, miles from anywhere in a bend of winding Rotherhithe Street – right by the No.225 bus stop. All around are tower communal housing and high-security riverview yuppie developments; within are warmth, cheer and good beers. On a horseshoe bar counter, you'll find pumps of London Pride, Fuller's ESB and a guest ale (perhaps Greene King's IPA), with dining tables at either side. Solid, home-made fare is accompanied by more creative daily specials, perhaps a Mediterranean hotpot at £6.95. The walls tell of riverside life of yore and of the Queen Mum manning the beer taps here. Kids are accommodated – nay, celebrated – and on special occasions locals gather around the Joanna (yes, it really does happen). At the back is a games room with comfy sofas. It's the kind of place that gives the area a good name.
Babies and children welcome. Games (darts, fruit machines, pool table). Tables outdoors (3, garden). TV.

South

Garrison

99-101 Bermondsey Street, SE1 3XB (7089 9355/ www.thegarrison.co.uk). London Bridge tube/rail. **Open** noon-11pm Mon-Sat; noon-10.30pm Sun. **Food served** 12.30-3.30pm, 6.30-10pm Mon-Sat; 12.30-4pm, 6.30-9.30pm Sun. **Credit** AmEx, MC, V.
This industrial-style gastrobar attracts loft-dwelling professionals, delighted to find a fine wine, a rare beer and a superior bar snack or two. Grabbing a perch at one of the tall tables with wooden dividers can be paramount, as there's no room for standing. A basement for overspill is also used for private parties and occasional films, for which a separate entrance is signposted. The bar dispenses Czech Zatec by the 33cl bottle (£2), Adnams Bitter in imperial measures, and bottles of Pilsner Urquell, Paulaner, St Peter's Golden Ale and Celis Wheat beer. The wine list is large: 15 bottles of each colour, a fine selection priced from £33 to £76; by the glass you can get a Trinity Hall sauvignon blanc from Hawkes Bay, New Zealand (£6.30), or an Espiga Tinto Quinta de Boavista from Portugal (£4). Bar snacks include salt-and-pepper squid (£4.50) and – colloquial, this – £3.30 fish finger sarnies.
Disabled: toilet. Function room. No-smoking area. Theatre.

Hartley

64 Tower Bridge Road, SE1 4TR (7394 7023/ www.thehartley.com). Borough tube/Elephant & Castle tube/rail then 1 or 188 bus. **Open** noon-11.30pm Mon-Fri; 11am-11pm Sat; noon-10.30pm Sun. **Food served** noon-4pm, 6-10pm Mon-Fri; 11am-4pm, 6-10pm Sat; 11am-6pm Sun. **Credit** AmEx, MC, V.

Wine Wharf. See p200.

A cool gastropub, its name derived from the old jam factory seen through the picture windows, ideally from the raised lounge seating at the front. Before you stretches a long, zinc bar counter, backed with rows of wine bottles. The main area is lined with rows of wooden tables, the back ones wafted with heat from the kitchen hatch. Here, an expert hand prepares honey-roast pork, seared sea bass and, recently, brunches. Decorative primary colours set the tone for the steady chatter and clink of glasses. There's a good choice of wines: Chilean Neblina merlot (£4.25), Marqués de Cáceres rioja blanca (£5.50) and Château d'Or costières de nîmes (£5.50) are among the 16 sold by the glass. Draught Boddingtons, Staropramen and Guinness are complemented by bottles of Früli, Leffe, Tiger, Paulaner and Pilsner Urquell – there are even standard cocktails at £6.
Babies and children admitted (before 6pm). Music (DJ 7.30pm Sun; live jazz 8pm Tue; Free). No-smoking area. Specialities (cocktails).

Mayflower

117 Rotherhithe Street, SE16 4NF (7237 4088). Rotherhithe tube. **Open** noon-11pm Mon-Sat; noon-10.30pm Sun. **Food served** noon-3pm, 6.30-9pm Mon-Sat; noon-4pm Sun. **Credit** MC, V.
The legend, detailed on the menus in a main dining area of rebuilt 17th-century pew seating, lives on lucratively in this low-ceilinged, wooden-beamed, traditional boozer. Right here, 'from a pub called the Shippe, the Pilgrim Fathers set sail in 1620, returning to Rotherhithe in 1621'. They and the pub were gradually forgotten about, until the latter was rebuilt as the Spread Eagle & Crown in the 1700s. Bombed in the war, it was later rebuilt in historic style, renamed the Mayflower and, as if tourists needed anything else to encourage them, licensed to sell British and American postage stamps, bizarrely. Today it's just T-shirts, plates and mugs – plus Morland Old Speckled Hen and Greene King's IPA and Abbot. Flip over the history, and you'll find 'Traditional fayre' of pan-fried lamb's liver (£9.95) and old English sausages with crispy beetroot (£8.95).
Babies and children admitted (restaurant). Quiz (8.30pm Tue; £1). Restaurant. Tables outdoors (25, riverside terrace).

Spice Island

163 Rotherhithe Street, SE16 5QU (7394 7108). Rotherhithe tube. **Open** 11am-11pm Mon-Thur; 11am-midnight Fri, Sat; noon-10.30pm Sun. **Food served** noon-9.30pm Mon-Sat; noon-8.30pm Sun. **Credit** AmEx, MC, V.
This one is a landmark venue – not for its history, nor its beers (although there's little wrong with Greene King IPA, Hoegaarden and Staropramen). No, Spice Island, a two-floor pub-restaurant just across the walkway from Surrey Water, stands out because local families fill its expansive space with satisfied chatter, their kids making nuisances of themselves on the pool table. Housed in an old wharf warehouse, its centrepiece is a large, octagonal bar counter slap in the centre of the ground floor; ascend by lift or stairs and you can see the names of spices on the beams of the first floor, where you'll also find balcony tables with river views. Pastas and salads are the main constituents of the family-oriented menu, with 8oz steaks (rump, sirloin, fillet, £10-£13) and roast racks of New Zealand lamb with port and redcurrant jus (£12) there for the ravenous.
Babies and children admitted (until 7pm): children's menu; high chairs. Disabled: lift; toilet. Games (fruit machine, pool, quiz machine). Music (jazz band 8pm Thur; free). No-smoking area (restaurant). Restaurant. Tables outdoors (20, riverside terrace). TV.

Wibbley Wobbley

Greenland Dock, Rope Street, SE16 7SZ (7232 2320). Canada Water or Surrey Quays tube. **Open** noon-11pm Mon-Sat; noon-10.30pm Sun. **Food served** 6.30-10pm Thur-Sat; noon-5pm Sun. **Credit** (restaurant only) AmEx, MC, V.
Herein lies a tale – a recent tragedy, in fact. Early in 2005, alternative comedian Malcolm Hardee slipped and drowned in the Thames after a few too many at this boat

bar he co-owned. An original, abrasive character (a plaque inside lists the friends who gave him credit – and those who refused – to open this operation in 2001), Hardee was one of the founding fathers of the stand-up scene. ('But I can't bloody stand up', would have been a typical Hardee riposte.) But what of his bar? Well, it's surprisingly low key and tranquil. Retro tack and nautical knick-knacks fill the low-ceilinged space, crowned by a ship's compass and Wurlitzer jukebox (jazz, blues, ska) by the bar. There, taps of Greene King IPA, Ruddles Best and Hoegaarden are accompanied by bottles of Beck's and Nastro Azzurro. If sandwiches don't suffice, you can dine at French Fred's upper-deck restaurant (7740 1411). Both establishments have tables on deck.
Babies and children welcome (before 8pm). Games (quiz machine). No-smoking (restaurant). Restaurant. Tables outdoors (12, pontoon).

Also in the area...

Surrey Docks (JD Wetherspoon) 185 Lower Road, SE16 2LW (7394 2832).

BLACKHEATH

Blackheath's bar action takes place in the small cluster of streets sloping towards the station, known to all as 'the Village'. Quaint, historic and steeped in rugby tradition, its preservation is the cause of the influential Blackheath Society, who frown on any loud, late-opening overspill from a new breed of bars like the **Cave Austin** or **Railway**.

Cave Austin

7-9 Montpelier Vale, SE3 0TA (8852 0492/www.caveaustin.co.uk). Blackheath rail. **Open** 10am-11.30pm Mon, Tue; 10am-1am Wed-Sat; 10am-10.30pm Sun. **Food served** 6-10pm Mon-Thur; 10am-10pm Fri, Sat; 10am-3.30pm, 6-10pm Sun. **Credit** MC, V.
A recent change of management at this wine bar and restaurant should do the place a lot of good. Its biggest trade was for the basement club at weekends, and still is; but in the summer a back garden beer tent, complete with San Miguel on, will come into its own. There's also a swishy, red chill-out bar upstairs. The new team plans to increase the wine choice and to downgrade the main meals to snacks and tapas. For the moment, you can get eight or so wines of each colour by the bottle (Curée St Vincent chablis, £20; Marqués de Riscal rioja reserva, £18), and only a couple by the glass (£2.95 for a standard muscadet or Sangre de Toro Miguel Torres). There's a good selection of standard cocktails (£5) and a few choice malts (Talisker, Glenlivet). Beck's and Kronenbourg in bottles.
Babies and children welcome (before 6.30pm). Music (DJs basement bar, 9pm Wed-Sat, £7; musicians 8.30pm occasional Sun). Restaurant (no-smoking). Specialities (separate cocktail bar). Tables outdoors (15, garden). TV (big screen, satellite).

Hare & Billet

1A Elliot Cottages, Hare & Billet Road, SE3 0QJ (8852 2352). Blackheath rail. **Open** 11am-11pm Mon-Sat; noon-10.30pm Sun. **Food served** noon-3.30pm, 5.30-9pm daily. **Credit** MC, V.
Shining a welcoming light across Blackheath for the best part of four centuries, this former coaching inn on the main London-to-Dover road today attracts discerning drinkers, darts players and teams coming in from games on the heath. It's won awards for doing so, in fact: a team hospitality award for rugby, cricket and football, posted on one of the pillars that support a friendly, spacious, wooden interior. Adnams Bitter, Greene King IPA, London Pride, Hoegaarden and Staropramen line the well-run bar counter, behind which bottles of Beck's, Budvar and Leffe stand to chill. Dalwood Côtes du Rhône is the house tipple (£2.70 a glass), accompanied by a handful of other affordable and quaffable varieties; rather decent pub grub of the steak-and-ale-pie type is served through the day.
Babies and children admitted (lunch only). Games (quiz machine). No-smoking area. TV.

Princess of Wales

1A Montpelier Row, SE3 0RL (8297 5911). Blackheath rail. **Open** noon-11pm Mon-Sat; noon-10.30pm Sun. **Food served** noon-3pm, 5-9pm Mon-Fri; noon-9pm Sat; noon-8pm Sun. **Credit** MC, V.
Well, well, what have we here? Named after Caroline of Brunswick and steeped in rugby tradition (England players gathered here before the world's first international in Edinburgh in 1871), this imposing, three-lounge Georgian edifice used to be filled with estate agents and Tory-voting outdoor types with their labradors. Walk in now and what do you find? A face-studded Aussie in an apron serving pints of Früli and Leffe to hip young punters from a low-slung bar counter against an aural backdrop of heavy dub – that's what. The palace revolution came in September 2004, and brought a loungey refit to the long back room, the addition of an armchair area and 'deckchair wine of the month' promotions. Who was responsible for this outrage? And when can we buy him a drink?
Babies and children welcome (before 5pm). Disabled: toilet. Quiz (8.30pm Tue: £1). Games (fruit machine, golf machine). Tables outdoors (30, garden, patio).

Railway

16 Blackheath Village, SE3 9LE (8852 2390). Blackheath rail. **Open** noon-11pm Mon-Wed; noon-midnight Thur-Sat; noon-10.30pm Sun. **Food served** noon-3pm, 5-9pm Mon-Fri; noon-8pm Sat, Sun. **Credit** AmEx, MC, V.
This spacious, loungey bar/pub was once the haunt of beer lovers. They still fill it by day, but by night the Railway becomes party central, a rather loud and brash pick-up joint. The beers have barely changed – draught Spitfire, Hoegaarden, Früli, Staropramen, De Koninck, Black Sheep and Young's Special (plus bottled Bellevue Kriek, Duvel, Chimay Bleu and Erdinger) – but after dark the people who want to drink them prefer to be at the tables by the front window. Everyone else, average age 19, gathers and flirts around the back lounge, now bereft of its Pop Art posters of Paul Weller, Ray Davies et al. Who needs history when you can get hammered and horny? Bin-end wines dissolve the inhibitions of lads' quarry – a shoo-in considering the proximity of bus stops and Blackheath station.
Disabled: toilet. Games (fruit machine). Music (DJ 8pm Sat; jazz 8pm Wed, free). Tables outdoors (5, garden). TV (Sat only).

Zero Degrees

29-31 Montpelier Vale, SE3 0TJ (8852 5619/www.zerodegrees-microbrewery.co.uk). Blackheath rail. **Open** noon-midnight Mon-Sat; noon-11.30pm Sun. **Food served** noon-11pm Mon-Sat; noon-10.30pm Sun. **Credit** AmEx, MC, V.

A sleek operation, this one, combining microbrewery and pizza restaurant – and it's popular with Blackheath's young professionals. 'Zero' is something to do with the nearby meridian and the brewing process; the menus are a cumbersome 0 shape, but full of adventurous house specialities. The 'hand-crafted beers on tap', all at £2.40 a pint (£1.75 6-7pm weekdays), comprise Pilsner, Pale Ale, Black (a real treat) and Wheat; they're also sold in five-litre party kegs from the shop next door. Wines are not forgotten: there's the house Condeza de Leganza Vinra (£2.95 a glass), La Mancha and Distinto Sangiovese merlot, Calatrasi from Sicily, as well as decent pinot grigios and Riojas by the bottle (£15-£17). Leave room for the good wood-roasted pizzas (salmon and mascarpone, carne asada, grilled steak) at under £10; starters include seared beef carpaccio (£5.95) and baba ganoush (£3.95). The open-plan design stretches over two floors, and there's a vast screen for TV sports.
Babies and children welcome: high chairs. Restaurant (available for hire). Specialities (own-brewed beers). TV (big screen, satellite).

Also in the area...

O'Neill's 52 Tranquil Vale, SE3 0BH (8297 5901).

BOROUGH & SOUTHWARK

London's most atmospherically filmic street, Stoney Street runs beside the cast-iron framework of Borough Market and under the high brick arches of the railway as it curves in to London Bridge. It's a fine place for a pub crawl, with four splendid venues (**Market Porter**, **Wine Wharf**) within a very short walk of each other. After these, you're within strolling distance of what we consider to be one of the very best pubs in town, the **Royal Oak**.

Bridge House

218 Tower Bridge Road, SE1 2UP (7407 5818). Tower Hill tube or London Bridge tube/rail. **Open** 11.30am-11pm Mon-Sat; noon-10.30pm Sun. **Food served** 11.30am-10pm Mon-Sat; noon-9.30pm Sun. **Credit** AmEx, MC, V.
Drinking options in the vicinity of Tower Bridge are limited, but this place is a winner. A rock's lob from the high-campery of the bridge, it's a smart little bar-cum-pub, all blonde wood and sienna-coloured walls. Yes, the Bridge House is a bit high street, but there are some nice details – the original cast-iron I-beam columns, for instance. Then there's the view: large picture windows offer a panorama of the testicular new City Hall, the river and the City towers beyond. Lit up at night it's almost Manhattan (well, maybe Poughskeepsie). The Adnams brewery owns the place, so expect a decent line up of ales (Bitter, Broadside and maybe Oyster Stout); there's an interesting range of wines, too, and a menu of baguettes to complement the usual roster of sausages and fish 'n' chips.
Babies and children admitted (restaurant). Disabled: toilet. Function room. Restaurant. TV.

Founder's Arms

52 Hopton Street, SE1 9JH (7928 1899). Blackfriars tube/rail. **Open** 9am-11pm Mon-Sat; 9am-10.30pm Sun. **Food served** 9-11am, noon-8.30pm Mon-Sat; 9-11am, noon-7pm Sun. **Credit** AmEx, MC, V.
From the outside, the Founder's is a squat, modern brick bunker; inside, it resembles the kind of bar you might find at a provincial airport. However, where it scores big time is with sublime panoramas along the Thames, taking in the neighbouring Millennium Bridge and the dome of St Paul's. The place is at its best in the summer, when you can take your beer out to the riverside terrace (it's a Young's house, so the beer's reliably good). There's a decent wine list, let down by hefty mark-ups, and a routine food menu (panini, sandwiches, burgers, fish, sausage and a soup of the day), although, again, prices are over the odds. Still, with such a prime location, beside Tate Modern and just down from the Globe Theatre, the Founder's has no shortage of punters.
Babies and children admitted. Disabled: toilet. Games (fruit machines). No-smoking area. Tables outdoors (30, riverside patio).

George Inn

77 Borough High Street, SE1 1NH (7407 2056). London Bridge tube/rail. **Open** 11am-11pm Mon-Sat; noon-10.30pm Sun. **Food served** noon-3pm, 5-10pm Mon-Fri; noon-4pm, 5-10pm Sat; noon-4pm Sun. **Credit** MC, V.
Rebuilt over medieval foundations following fire damage in 1676, this capacious, multi-roomed spot is London's last remaining galleried coaching inn. Indeed, it's now owned by the National Trust. Pretty to look at from the outside, it's a horror within. Modern additions like the 'Elizabethan' kiosk that serves as an open kitchen, the 'rustic' light fittings bought as a job lot from B&Q, and wall decor that mixes corporate pub ephemera with olde worlde knick-knacks, make the George seem like a cut-price, ham-fisted theme park stab at heritage. It doesn't help that it's also a magnet for coach parties and office groups. We could tell you about the beers (Adnams ales), wine and food but, honestly, we don't think it's worth it. The George shares a large seated courtyard with a branch of the atrocious Heeltap & Bumper bar-café-bar™ chain, and that says it all.
Babies and children admitted. Function rooms. Games (darts, fruit machine). No-smoking area (lunch). Tables outdoors (35, courtyard).

Lord Clyde

27 Clennam Street, SE1 1ER (7407 3397). Borough tube. **Open/food served** 11am-11pm Mon-Fri; noon-11pm Sat; noon-7pm Sun. **Credit** AmEx, DC, MC, V.
The Clyde is an authentic neighbourhood pub with a landlady who greeted us with a cheery 'Allo luv', though she didn't know us from Adam. An inn has stood here for three centuries, although the name and current pile date from 1863: a memento of the Scottish soldier and scourge of the sepoys, Sir Colin Campbell. The elaborate green and cream glazed earthenware tiles date from 1913, when landlord EJ Bayling took over and ensured his name appeared prominently beside that of the brewers, Truman's. Thick red velvet curtains around the two street doors lend an air of theatricality to the place; deep red carpets and red upholstery add a cocoon-like warmth. Ales are a fine line up of London Pride, Shepherd Neame Spitfire, Greene King IPA, Young's 'ordinary' and Adnams Bitter. The grub is pubby.
Babies and children admitted (before 9pm). Games (darts, fruit machines). TV (satellite).

Market Porter

9 Stoney Street, SE1 9AA (7407 2495). London Bridge tube/rail. **Open** 6-8.30am, 11am-11pm Mon-Fri; noon-11pm Sat; noon-10.30pm Sun. **Food served** noon-3pm daily. **Credit** AmEx, MC, V.

South

Apparently the Porter has been used as a location in the filming of the next Harry Potter movie (it appears as the wizards' pub, the Leaky Cauldron), so we suggest you visit now before the crowds descend. Actually, it's too late, as the crowds have been descending for decades now, with standing room only on most nights. This is an attractive place with an appealing location beneath the railway arches on the edge of Borough Market, but most customers are here because the Porter is recognised as one of London's finest real ale pubs. Up to eight different, strangely named brews are on tap most nights. Funnily enough, this doesn't translate into a bar full of elderly, bearded and tedious gents – there are usually as many women present as men, and the age range is pleasingly wide. Some customers even manage to keep a straight face while ordering pints of Loddon Hoppit and Slater's Top Totty.
Babies and children welcome (lunch). Disabled: toilet. Function room. Games (fruit machines). Restaurant. Specialities (real ale).

Royal Oak

44 Tabard Street, SE1 4JU (7357 7173). Borough tube/London Bridge tube/rail. **Open** 11.30am-11pm Mon-Fri; noon-6pm Sat, Sun. **Food served** noon-3pm, **Credit** AmEx, DC, MC, V.

The handsome and wonderfully maintained Royal Oak is the only pub in the capital tied to excellent Lewes brewer Harveys. The beer is fantastic: the typical line up is Best, IPA, a seasonal and, wonder of wonders, Mild (which, we reckon, makes the Oak one of only three pubs in central London to have mild as a standard). There might be a lager, but sadly the sign that read 'Lager drinkers will be served only if accompanied by a responsible adult' is gone. The pub food is of a high standard and fairly priced, there's no music, and service is sharp and witty whenever co-landlord Frank is around the bar. Very much a locals' pub, the Oak also exerts a pull across town to draw a committed crowd of maverick music promoters, small-press publishers, procrastinating crime novelists and sometime pornographers – not to mention demanding beer aficionados.
Disabled: toilet. Function room. No piped music or jukebox. No-smoking tables.

Wine Wharf

Stoney Street, Borough Market, SE1 9AD (7940 8335/www.winewharf.com). London Bridge tube/ rail. **Open** 11.30am-11pm Mon-Fri; 11am-11pm Sat. **Food served** noon-9.30pm Mon-Sat. **Credit** AmEx, DC, MC, V.

This has to be one of the best places in London for oenophiles. Wine Wharf is the bar attached to Vinopolis (the wine museum) and, as such, it offers a suitably extensive and global selection of interesting wines. Come here to experiment: you can roam from a Château Musar from Lebanon's Bekaa Valley to a £65 pinot noir from New Zealand. Options by the glass are strewn all over the menu, meaning choice is exceptional. The young, friendly staff are wine-savvy and always let you try before you buy. For those with the balls to ask for them, the bar also stocks a few brands of imported bottled beers like Heineken and Budweiser. Bar food includes cheese platters, naturally, as well as snacks such as bowls of chips and squid rings. This is a good-looking place: a modish wharf-style interior of bare bricks, beams and metal, softened by sofas and low lighting.
Babies and children welcome (until 8pm). Bar available for hire. Disabled: toilet. Specialities (wine).

Also in the area…

All Bar One 28-30 London Bridge Street, SE1 9SG (7940 9981).
Balls Brothers Hay's Galleria, Tooley Street, SE1 2HD (7407 4301).
Bermondsey (Davy's) 63 Bermondsey Street, SE1 3XF (7407 1096).
Cooperage (Davy's) 48-50 Tooley Street, SE1 2SZ (7403 5775).
Heeltap & Bumper (Davy's) Chaucer House, White Hart Yard, Borough High Street, SE1 1NX (7407 2829).
Pommeler's Rest (JD Wetherspoon) 196-198 Tower Bridge Road, SE1 2UN (7378 1399).
Skinkers (Davy's) 42 Tooley Street, SE1 2SZ (7407 9189).
Slug & Lettuce 32 Borough High Street, SE1 1UX (7378 9999).
Wetherspoon's Metro Central Heights, Newington Causeway, SE1 6EJ (7940 0890).

BRIXTON & STREATHAM

Traditionalists can still stand their ground at such old-school drinking holes as the **Effra** and **Trinity Arms**, but it's as a pre-clubbing destination, with places like **Dogstar** – and, indeed, as a clutch of hot clubs – that Brixton really shines. For the latter, see our Clubs section, starting on p247.

Brixton Bar & Grill

15 Atlantic Road, SW9 8HX (7737 6777/www.bbag. me.uk). Brixton tube/rail. **Open** 4.30pm-midnight Tue, Wed; 4.30pm-1am Thur; 4.30pm-2am Fri, Sat; 3.30-11pm Sun. **Food served** 6-midnight Tue-Sat; 4-10.30pm Sun. **Credit** MC, V.

When this venue first opened in place of a popular pizza joint, its primary function was as a tapas bar. In the past year, though, the drinks list has become more important. The concise cocktail menu features the appealing Mango Mumm, as well as some non-alcoholic alternatives like Virgin Mary. On the bottled beer front, the range takes in Czech Zatec lager and Liefman's cherry beer, and the rare St Peter's Best Bitter from Suffolk. If you aren't happy to pay up to £5 a bottle for these, you could always sample one of the standard-issue beers on draught, including Stella and Guinness. The tapas here are well above average; a few dishes from the snacks selection make the perfect accompaniment to a shared bottle of wine. Opt for antipasti for two and a generous portion of bread, oil and tapenade.
Disabled: toilet. Music (live bands 8pm Tue, 6pm Sun; DJs 9pm Fri, Sat; both free). Tables outdoors (4, pavement).

Brixtonian Havana Club

11 Beehive Place, SW9 7QR (7924 9262/www.brixton ian.co.uk). Brixton tube/rail. **Open** 5.30pm-midnight Mon-Wed; 5.30pm-2am Thur-Sat; noon-midnight Sun. **Food served** 6-11pm Mon-Wed; 6pm-midnight Thur-Sat; noon-4pm Sun. **No credit cards**.

This backstreet Havana-style club was in the middle of a revamp when we visited, promising a new cocktail list – boosting its collection of over 300 global rum varieties that line the bar – as soon as the paint had dried. We see no reason why, in its new clothes, it won't be as busy as ever, with mixed crowds shuffling to soundtracks of Cuban

beats or 1960s pop or DJs playing until the early hours. In addition to the handful of bottled beers (Coors, Stella, both £2.50), there's a superb range of cocktail classics alongside the bar's own inventions (try the Brixton Riot, £5.50), priced between £5 and £7. As well as new drinks, 2005 will bring tastings, Cuban cigars and a renovated terrace that could prove to be a summer hotspot. A daily menu featuring hot Caribbean dishes is also available.
Music (jazz 9pm Wed; DJs 9.30pm Thur-Sat; live gospel 3pm Sun; opera recital monthly, call for details). Restaurant. Tables outdoors (25, terrace).

Dogstar

389 Coldharbour Lane, SW9 8LQ (7733 7515/www.thedogstar.com). Brixton tube/rail. **Open** noon-2am Mon-Thur, Sun; noon-4am Fri, Sat. **Food served** 6-midnight Tue-Sat; noon-7pm Sun. **Admission** £3 10-11pm, £5 after 11pm Fri, Sat. **Credit** MC, V.
Nothing much has changed here over the years, but there's life in the old dog yet. In fact, this Brixton pioneer is still very popular, and still manages to pull in a loyal crowd of Brixtonites for nightly doses of retro pop, hip hop and drum 'n' bass. Weekends, naturally, are when it's at its most manic; but however packed it becomes, the punters are generally a friendly throng who foster an upbeat, happy vibe. There's nothing extraordinary to be found behind the bar (unless you're impressed by alcopops and self-important bar staff), but with its wooden tables and large sink-into sofas the place doubles as a comfortable daytime haven – more so now a modern Caribbean restaurant has opened upstairs promising 'the best lunch in Brixton'.
Babies and children admitted (until 6pm). Disabled: toilet. Function room. Games (video games). Music (DJs 9pm Mon-Sat, 3pm Sun). Tables outdoors (5, garden). TV (big screen).

Duke of Edinburgh

204 Ferndale Road, SW9 8AG (7924 0509). Clapham North tube/Brixton tube/rail. **Open/food served** noon-11pm Mon-Sat; noon-10.30pm Sun. **Credit** MC, V.
A short walk from Brixton station, the Duke is a desirable destination during the summer, thanks to its expansive garden. When the weather forbids outdoor drinking, the wood-panelled bar area has a cosy, contemporary feel, with flowers in metal containers resting against an antique mirrored fireplace. Trendy drinkers sit around the large wooden tables and watch sport on the large TV screen, while an older set stays further back, relaxing on leather sofas. A pool table just inside the entrance is host to knockout challenges (with a free buffet) on Tuesdays; DJs take over at the weekends. A small hand-written cocktail list sits on the bar, and there are displays of various bottled mixers, along with Kronenbourg, Foster's and Stella on tap – all served by pleasant, unassuming staff.
Games (fruit machine, pool, table football). Music (DJs, 8pm Thur-Sat; free). Tables outdoors (60, garden, heated marquee). TVs (big screen, satellite).

Effra

38A Kellet Road, SW2 1EB (7274 4180). Brixton tube/rail. **Open** 3-11pm daily. **Food served** 3-10pm daily. **No credit cards**.
The Effra is probably the least pretentious and most relaxed drinking hole in Brixton, its patrons kept sweet with a constant ska/reggae soundtrack, stylised Victorian decor and proper Jamaican grub. The two sides of this 19th-century pub feel quite divided: one half draws a bohemian crowd (especially when Latin/jazz bands play in the back); the other, with its busy pool table, tends to attract older regulars. Standard-issue bottled drinks and spirits are reasonably priced, and there's a long-running 'two Carlings for £4' deal. The menu often features a daily special, with such delights as goat's foot soup; the standard list includes the likes of extra-hot jerk chicken and filled baguettes.
Games (dominoes). Music (live jazz 8.30pm Tue-Thur, Sat, Sun; free). Tables outdoors (3, garden). TV.

Far Side

144 Stockwell Rd, SW9 9TQ (7095 1401/www.thefarsidebar.co.uk). Stockwell tube/Brixton tube/rail. **Open** noon-11pm Mon-Thur; noon-midnight Fri, Sat; noon-10.30pm Sun. **Food served** noon-3pm, 6-9.30pm Mon-Fri; noon-9.30pm Sat, Sun. **Credit** MC, V.
Next door to a Portuguese café and just a step away from the Brixton Academy, this smallish gastropub offers a cosy retreat as well as some pretty decent food. Sports fans arrange themselves on the pews to watch the big TV, while those looking for a cosier space can ease into leather couches and feel the warm glow of the fire nearer the back. Chatty bar staff officiate behind taps of Hoegaarden, Leffe Blonde and Brune, Staropramen and everyday Stella and Guinness; at the time of our visit they were planning to add an ale to the line-up in the near future, as well as Belgian and German beers in bottles. There are basic wines and spirits, too. Diners ordering from the good-value menu during the evening are treated to a warming choice of gastro fare, such as wild boar sausage 'n' mash in thick gravy (£7.90) or organic burgers with generous piles of chips (£6.95). During the summer, a back garden adds to the appeal of this fairly formulaic yet pleasant establishment.
Babies and children welcome (before 7pm). Music (DJs/bands 9.30pm Fri, Sat; free). Tables outdoors (garden). TV (big screen, satellite).

SW9

11 Dorrell Place, SW9 8EG (7738 3116). Brixton tube/rail. **Open** 10am-11pm Mon-Thur; 10am-1am Fri, Sat; 10am-11pm Sun. **Food served** 10am-10pm daily. **Happy hour** 4.30-7pm Mon-Fri. **Credit** AmEx, MC, V.
This compact, purple-hued space is probably the closest Brixton gets to café-bar culture: there's a petite bar, tables packed together, tobacco smoke, newspapers and an amiably dishevelled vibe. Post-clubbing strays come here for breakfasts at weekend, and pounding music is supplied to keep them in the mood: not the sort of soundtrack most people would chose for the first meal of the day. Still, there's a good menu of hangover cures in the shape of home-made burgers and full English breakfasts, as well as a handsome array of snacks. As well as a fair range of wines and spirits, there's Guinness, Foster's and – less predictably – Kirin on tap. The outside area by the entrance is covered and heated during winter, but in summer SW9 spills out into the street.
Babies and children admitted. Music (jazz 9pm Fri, Sat). Tables outdoors (heated patio).

Tongue & Groove

50 Atlantic Road, SW9 8JN (7274 8600). Brixton tube/rail. **Open** 9pm-3am Thur; 9pm-5am Fri, Sat. **Admission** £5 after 11pm Thur-Sat. **Credit** AmEx, MC, V.
T&G opens just three nights a week – late, and it stays open late. Its lustrous decor and wall-hugging sofas foster a slick, classy aura, and the red façade conceal it from passers-by, which probably accounts for its relaxed vibe.

Early evenings see a good-looking cool-list clientele slowly filtering in to spend a few hours sipping excellent cocktails and lounging. Then, around midnight, DJs up the tempo and drown out the conversation with a pleasing mix of global music (anything from Afro to house to kitsch); most of the seating is whisked away, producing a small but serviceable dancefloor. Cocktails start at £6, and bottled Beck's and Peroni's (there are no beers on tap) cost £3.
Bar available for hire. Disabled: toilet. Music (DJs 9.30pm Thur-Sat). Specialities (cocktails).

Trinity Arms

45 Trinity Gardens, SW9 8DR (7274 4544). Brixton tube/rail. **Open** 11am-11pm Mon-Sat; noon-10.30pm Sun. **Food served** noon-3pm Mon-Fri. **Credit** MC, V.
We wonder whether much will ever change at this quaint, traditional Young's pub, built in 1840 on what's still a small, quiet square. Every time we come here, we see the same flat-capped man smoking his pipe and enjoying a peaceful pint, and feel like we've stepped into a sepia photograph. The smartly attired barman seems to have been imported from another era, too – though the prices are disappointingly contemporary. The selection of Young's ales encompasses seasonal specials (Winter Warmer in winter, Waggledance in summer); there's also Stella and Carling on tap, an extensive wine list, plus various malts including vintage Glenlivet. A bar menu is available most days, and in the warm months there's a small garden area.
Babies and children welcome (garden only). Games (fruit machine). No piped music or jukebox. Tables outdoors (6, garden, 6 pavement). TV.

White Horse

94 Brixton Hill, SW2 1QN (8678 6666/www.whitehorsebrixton.com). Brixton tube/rail then 59, 118, 133, 159, 250 bus. **Open** 5pm-1am Mon-Thur; 2pm-3am Fri; noon-3am Sat; noon-1am Sun. **Food served** 6-10pm Mon-Thur; 6-9pm Fri; noon-8pm Sat; noon-6pm Sun. **Credit** MC, V.
With its clash of unfinished brick walls and smart-retro wooden furniture, the White Horse, a short bus ride from Brixton's centre, strikes a comfortable, unstuffy balance between boozer and trendy bar. Blackboards adorn the walls, advertising well-priced tapas and a few main dishes, with some unusual variations for vegetarians. There's a decent wine list for the thirtysomething couples and hip young things who lounge on the sofas taking phonecam pics; for beer-drinkers, the range includes Kronenbourg and Kronenbourg Blanc, San Miguel, John Smith's and Old Speckled Hen. Music slides almost unnoticed from the sound system, and when there's a big match on TV it gets screened on the wall next to the bar; DJs entertain at weekends, with hip hop, soul and 1980s-inspired beats. There's also a pool area at the back that's usually pretty busy.
Disabled: toilet. Games (pool). Music (DJs 9pm Fri, Sat; live jazz/funk 5pm Sun; £5 after 9pm Fri, Sat). Tables outdoors (6, courtyard). TV (projector).

Windmill

22 Blenheim Gardens, SW2 5BZ (8671 0700/www.windmillbrixton.co.uk). Brixton tube then 49, 59, 118, 133, 159, 250 bus. **Open** 11am-midnight daily. **Admission** £3 after 8pm daily. **No credit cards.**
Entirely different from any other pub you'll find at this end of Brixton, the Windmill feels like a proper, old-fashioned indie rock joint. Bands play here pretty much every night (with the admission fee rarely exceeding £3 for the pleasure). Weekday evenings are generally quiet, but when Friday night comes round, the place fills with a bohemian multitude and the regular old rocker barflies are, for once, outnumbered. There's not much in the way of seating, which is generally fine as people are happy standing up to watch the bands. The small, predictably stocked bar is reasonably cheap, although you can expect a painful wait when things are busy. If you love live music, but can't fork out for gig tickets very often, the Windmill could become your favourite hangout this side of town.
Babies and children welcome (until 7pm). Comedy/poetry (9pm alternate Thur; £3). Games (fruit machine). Music (8pm nightly; £3). Tables outdoors (4, garden, 4 pavement). TV (big screen).

Also in the area...

Beehive (JD Wetherspoon) 407-409 Brixton Road, SW9 7DG (7738 3643).
Crown & Sceptre (JD Wetherspoon) 2A Streatham Hill, SW2 4AH (8671 0843).
Holland Tringham (JD Wetherspoon) 107-109 Streatham High Road, SW16 1HJ (8769 3062).

CAMBERWELL

Party-hearty art students, long-term residents and, increasingly, young professionals in search of vaguely affordable but central housing, are the most common subscribers to Camberwell's drinking scene. While the latter group is slowly driving things upmarket, the change is gradual, and there's still enough variety to keep everyone happy.

Castle

65 Camberwell Church Street, SE5 8TR (7277 2601). Oval tube/Denmark Hill rail/12, 35, 68, 176, 185, 345 bus. **Open** noon-midnight Mon-Thur; noon-2am Fri, Sat; noon-10.30pm Sun. **Food served** noon-10pm daily. **Credit** AmEx, DC, JCB, MC, V.
The 'over-21s only' sign on the door indicates that the Castle is not quite the comfy student hangout it was in its previous life as the Snug. Accordingly, there's not a cocktail in sight, though the mostly thirtysomething customers have little cause for complaint about the choice of premium spirits, boutique European beers and draught Adnams Broadside. Seafood and red meat dominate a mod European menu that aims high enough for us to forgive its pretensions (sandwiches listed as 'between bread'). The setting for all this is appropriately gastro-modish; white walls and dark pews create a stark, ecclesiastical space against which the art displays sometimes seem incongruous. Nevertheless, the ironic retro touches – velvet-topped bar stools, old-fashioned drinks price list, cut-glass light fittings, the stuffed fox crouching over the door – look tastefully antique. A snoozing Weimaraner dog at the end of the bar and a cosy open fire at the back soften the effect.
Babies and children welcome. Games (board games). Function room. Music (DJs 9pm Thur-Sun; free). TVs (big screen, satellite).

Funky Munky

25 Camberwell Church Street, SE5 8TR (7277 1806). Denmark Hill rail/12, 36, 171, 176, 185, 436 bus. **Open** noon-midnight Mon-Wed, Sun; noon-2am Thur-Sat. **Food served** noon-6pm Tue; noon-9pm Wed-Fri; noon-6pm Sat, Sun. **Happy hour** 5-7pm daily. **Credit** MC, V.

To the relief of most, last year's remodelling has changed neither the vibe nor the look of the Funky Munky. There's now a more practical layout, avoiding the crush around the bar, but this is still an inviting, twinkling grotto of warm-orange walls, house plants, multicoloured fairy lights and other cheap but cheerful mood lighting. Not all the seating is comfortable, but no one seems to mind; happy hour specials and DJs draw in the art college crowd, and the convivial atmosphere makes them stay. At weekends, the joint is jumping, the party continuing into the night with the club upstairs (often free of charge, but rarely costing more than £2). Bison-grass vodka is popular and the choice of cocktails has expanded, but the emphasis is still on Sea Breezes, Cosmopolitans and other girlie stalwarts. Beer options are limited. Rump steak, breaded chicken and pancakes feature on the menu of student-friendly 'classics'.
Babies and children welcome (before 5pm). Dance classes (tango 7.30pm Mon). Function room. Music (DJs 9pm Thur-Sun; free). Tables outdoors (6, pavement).

Hermit's Cave

28 Camberwell Church Street, SE5 8QU (7703 3188). Denmark Hill rail/12, 36, 171 bus. **Open** 11am-11pm Mon-Sat; noon-10.30pm Sun. **Food served** 11am-4pm Mon-Sat; noon-5pm Sun. **No credit cards.**
Around since 1908 (according to the old gent on constant glass-collection), the Hermit's Cave is now something of a relic among Camberwell's funky new bars. Yet it's this fact that makes the pub stand out from the crowd. The Cave's many loyal regulars don't want a makeover for this Victorian-style boozer of etched glass, dark wood and smoke-dulled flock wallpaper. Local competition's hardly fierce, but the place is busy day and night. Its claim to serve the 'best beer around here' is justified, with Old Speckled Hen, Shrimpers AVS (brewed in Harrogate) and Shepherd Neame Spitfire among the draught options. In amused defiance of Camberwell's cocktail revolution, the pub has a long list of the likes of Bombay Sapphire and tonic, or Famous Grouse and Coke advertised on one blackboard. Another lists liqueur coffees and hearty grub such as stroganoff and paprika pork for under a fiver per dish.
Babies and children welcome (lunchtime only). Specialities (whisky). Tables outdoors (3, pavement). TV (big screen, satellite).

Old Dispensary

325 Camberwell New Road, SE5 0TF (7708 8831). Elephant & Castle tube/rail then 12 or 176 bus/36, 185, 436 bus. **Open/food served** noon-midnight Mon-Sat; noon-10.30pm Sun. **Credit** AmEx, DC, MC, V.
Finally making use of this long-empty space, the Old Dispensary is a bold new arrival. Its philosophy of grown-up decadence was embraced wholeheartedly on our last visit by a man surely old enough to know better than to drink a bottle of champagne through a straw. From the vast vase of fresh flowers adorning the small bar, to the colossal chandelier hanging in the octagonal skylight and the sleek tabletops of mirror and marble, subtle glamour is the clear aim. In fact, if it weren't for the goofy snapshots stuck in the gilt frame behind the bar, this place would be almost too slick. The choice of draught beers is reasonable (highlights are Leffe Blonde and Leffe wheat, alongside cherry and strawberry beers), but takes a back seat to wines and to cocktails that are resolutely adult in price, strength and concoction. Food ranges from half-pints of prawns to all-day brunches and more substantial main courses.
Disabled: toilet. Specialities (cocktails).

Sun & Doves

61 Coldharbour Lane, SE5 9NS (7733 1525/www.sunanddoves.co.uk). Brixton tube/rail then 35, 45, 345 bus/Loughborough Junction rail. **Open** noon-11pm Mon-Thur; noon-midnight Fri, Sat; noon-10.30pm Sun. **Food served** noon-10.30pm Mon-Sat; noon-6pm Sun. **Credit** MC, V.
'Food, bar and art' are promised in large letters in the window, and that's just what this bright, airy boozer delivers. The art college contingent is colourfully represented through the changing exhibits on the walls, but this is a place more beloved of relaxed locals and off-duty medics from nearby King's. The pub is considerably removed from the main drag, and has a big garden perfect for Sunday roasts among the oddball sculptures. It's a shame that the once-great execution of the simple menu has gone so drastically downhill, but the friendliness of the staff is such that few seem able to complain. Old Speckled Hen and Ruddles are welcome choices among the usual suspects on the beer pumps. The cocktail list shows some care and attention, being divided into velvets, warmers, classics, moderns, shooters and 'seasonal'. The winter selection nostalgically includes the likes of Snowballs and hot buttered rum.
Babies and children welcome: children's menu; high chairs. Gallery. Music (open mic 8.30pm, alternate Sun). No-smoking area. Restaurant. Specialities (cocktails). Tables outdoors (20, garden; 6, pavement).

Also in the area...

Fox on the Hill (JD Wetherspoon) 149 Denmark Hill, SE5 8EH (7738 4756).
O'Neill's Windsor Walk, SE5 8BB (7701 8282).

South

CATFORD

To say Catford suffers from an image problem is an understatement. It's more Lewisham than Lewisham, given over to bland commerce and blokey pubs clustered around the station and nearby main intersection. It's also impenetrable. Two of the venues we list (the **Ram** is right in Catford) require a bus journey from the station, on a dark stretch of the South Circular or parallel Perry Hill. Dare anyone open a decent new bar here?

Blythe Hill Tavern

319 Stanstead Road, SE23 1JB (8690 5176). Catford or Catford Bridge rail. **Open** 11am-11pm Mon-Sat; noon-10.30pm Sun. **No credit cards.**
Large, landmark boozer, this one, slap on the South Circular; an Irish pub that takes its sport seriously. The cosy front bar is decked out in rare old golf paraphernalia, including unusual advertising carved in wood, while the back bar is a shrine to the sport of kings. Framed jockey shirts are mounted alongside snooker and horse-racing souvenirs, with the constant colourful blur of a sports channel from the TV screen above. London Pride provides an ale alternative to the standard lagers, Guinness and bottles of Magners cider. The food is suitably hearty. An unexpected back garden features a kiddies' play area, while the grown-ups can indulge in darts indoors. There's live Irish music once a week and a lovely roaring fire in winter.
Babies and children welcome (before 7pm). Games (darts, fruit machine). Quiz (9pm Mon; free). Music (Irish traditional, 9pm Thur). Tables outdoors (20, garden). TV (big screen, satellite).

Catford Ram

9 Winslade Way, SE6 4JU (8690 6206). Catford Bridge rail. **Open** 11am-11pm Mon-Sat; noon-10.30pm Sun. **Food served** 11am-3pm, 5-9pm Mon-Fri; noon-4pm Sun. **No credit cards**.

Penned in under the Catford shopping centre walkway by a cavernous branch of Iceland, with a dark, estate-pub frontage, the Ram promises little but trouble and cheap house doubles. The truth is otherwise. The Ram is a community pub for sure, but a well-run Young's one – vast, carpeted, with tables suitable for private conversation set around the edges, offset by a pictorial wall of local history. At the long bar, blokes talk over the Beefheart back catalogue and old scaffolding jobs over the standard but welcome Young's range of ales (draught Export, Pilsner and Special, bottled Ramrod and Waggledance). To say the food is cheap would be an injustice. Who needs Wetherspoon's when mains start at £3.50 and don't rise much higher? Steak and onions and a few decent pints with yer old muckers – cancel that villa in Fuengirola!

Disabled: toilet. Games (darts, fruit machine, quiz machine, pinball machine). TV (big screen, satellite).

Rutland Arms

55 Perry Hill, SE6 4LF (8291 9426). Catford Bridge rail/54, 185 bus. **Open** 11am-11pm Mon-Sat; noon-10.30pm Sun. **Food served** noon-10pm Mon-Sat; noon-2.30pm Sun. **No credit cards**.

What a lovely place this is. A jazz bar, yes, but so much more – and we're not just referring to the R&B Thursday 'alternative' that is slotted between the quality regular live stuff of a Tuesday, Saturday night and Sunday lunchtime. No, the Rutland, adrift on a backwater of the 54 bus route, attracts a busy, chatty crowd to its spacious, L-shaped interior. Why? Because it's a free house (Fuller's ESB, London Pride, Toby, Bass, Caffreys and Grolsch) and damn friendly at that. Amiable chaps nod and keep time to the tonking sounds of the Stan Robinson Quartet, breaking out in applause at any nifty sax solo, while the less well initiated relax on comfy green banquettes or drift to the other side of the bar and catch the game on TV. Swift and accommodating bar staff keep things ticking over nicely.

Function room. Games (darts, fruit machines). Music (trad jazz 8.30pm Sat; modern jazz 8.30pm Tue, 1pm Sun; R&B 9pm Thur; all free). Quiz (1st Sun of month; £1). Tables outdoors (2, pavement). TV (satellite).

Also in the area...

London & Rye (JD Wetherspoon) 109 Rushey Green, SE6 4AF (8697 5028).
Tiger's Head (JD Wetherspoon) 350 Bromley Road, SE6 2RZ (8698 8645).

CLAPHAM

Clapham probably has the widest variety of watering holes in south London. There are noisy DJ bars, cocktail-focused style bars, trad real ale boozers, gay cruise joints, you name it.

Arch 635

15-16 Lendal Terrace, SW4 7UX (7720 7343/www.arch635.co.uk). Clapham North tube/Clapham High Street rail. **Open** 5pm-midnight Mon-Thur; 5pm-1am Fri; 4pm-2am Sat; 4pm-midnight Sun. **Credit** (over £10) MC, V.

Before hitting some of the less enticing venues on Clapham High Street, it seems that many of Clapham's young PR crowd, in a rare show of good taste, head to the less than salubrious railway arch that houses 635. A fine choice, too, and though the leather sofas, bare bricks, exposed piping and terminally dull beer selection are as familiar to Londoners as a backpacker on a night bus, there's an enjoyable conviviality among the bar staff and rag-tag south London geezers who circulate among the handbag lovers. It gets rammed on weekends, so is best appreciated, in our opinion, on a Sunday afternoon. Refreshment comes in the form of a fine cocktail list and great choice of bottled beer.

Disabled: toilet. Games (table football, pool). Music (DJs 9pm Fri, Sat; 8pm Sun; free). TV (satellite). **Map 11 L16**.

Bar Local

4 Clapham Common Southside, SW4 7AA (7622 9406/www.barlocal.co.uk). Clapham Common tube. **Open** 5pm-midnight Mon-Fri; noon-midnight Sat; noon-11.30pm Sun. **Food served** 5-10pm Mon-Fri; noon-10pm Sat, Sun. **Credit** MC, V.

This Lilliputian bar next to Clapham Common tube compensates in style for what it lacks in size. Fine-looking cocktails are dealt out by fine-looking staff, the beers on tap include Leffe, Staropramen, Stella and Cobra, and to soak up the alcohol there are some heart-stopping offerings from the Clapham Burger Company: behold the half-pound Bar Local Bad Boy Burger, enough to reduce any nearby vegetarian to tears. DJs turn up the heat from Thursdays to Sundays, when – true to the bar's witty sauna-style design – the temperature soars. Getting here early will allow you to grab one of the window seats; otherwise, you're left with a drink in your hand and the very remote possibility of snaffling one of the sofas at the back.

Music (DJs 8pm Thur-Sun). **Map 11 L17**.

Bread & Roses

68 Clapham Manor Street, SW4 6DZ (7498 1779/www.breadandrosespub.com). Clapham Common or Clapham North tube. **Open** noon-11pm Mon-Sat; noon-10.30pm Sun. **Food served** noon-3pm, 6-9.30pm Mon-Fri; noon-4pm, 6-9.30pm Sat; 1-7pm Sun. **Credit** MC, V.

When James Oppenheim wrote socialist anthem 'Bread and Roses' in 1912, it's doubtful whether he had this pub, with its lush interior of curved, blonde woods and warm leather couches, in mind. Still, B&R does have leftist foundations: it's owned by trade union fundraiser the Workers Beer Company. Gone are the days where debates on the socialist state would be aired here, but the pub's metamorphosis has meant survival. Good food, a fine outdoor area, and a good set of beers (including Timothy Taylor Landlord, Spitfire, Leffe, San Miguel and Workers Ale) help, too.

Babies and children welcome (before 9pm): high chairs; nappy-changing facilities. Comedy (8.30pm alternate Wed; £5 with free drink). Disabled: toilet. Function room. Games (board games). Music (live band 1st & last Sun of mth; £3). No-smoking area (conservatory). Quiz (8.30pm 3rd Mon of mth; £2). Tables outdoors (8, conservatory; 15, heated garden; 8, patio). **Map 11 L16**.

Coach & Horses

173-175 Clapham Park Road, SW4 7EX (7622 3815/www.barbeerian-inns.com). Clapham Common tube. **Open** 11am-11pm Mon-Sat; noon-10.30pm Sun. **Food served** noon-2.30pm, 6-9.30pm Mon-Fri; noon-3pm, 6.30-9pm Sat; 12.30-5pm, 7-9pm Sun. **Happy hour** 6-7pm Fri, Sat. **Credit** MC, V.

Blythe Hill Tavern. *See p203.*

This book-lined, green-walled pub serves a local rugby-loving crowd. The well-appointed rectangular bar is topped and tailed by two big screens. Beers on draught include London Pride, Adnams Bitter, Shepherd Neame Spitfire and Old Speckled Hen, and there's a good range of single malts. Come spring and the Six Nations, the Coach creates an atmosphere on which Twickenham would be proud. Outside match days, this bar could never be described as a wallflower – but it does offer the chance for a quieter drink than perhaps you'd get on nearby Clapham High Street.
Babies and children admitted (lunchtime only). Disabled: toilet. Function room. Games (board games). Tables outdoors (8, enclosed terrace). TVs (big screen, satellite). **Map 11 L17**.

Exhibit B

13 Old Town, SW4 0JT (7498 5559). Clapham Common tube. **Open** 11.30am-11pm Mon-Sat; 11.30am-10.30pm Sun. **Food served** noon-10pm Mon-Sat; 12.30-9pm Sun. **Credit** MC, V.
This is an industrial-style, modernist space that lies somewhere between funky student bar and Bauhaus. The electric sliding doors part to reveal a concrete floor equipped with canteen seating and low, leather-cushioned, tubular-steel chairs. The sunken area in front of the well-stocked bar provides cover from the vast plate-glass windowed façade. Snacks are served until 10pm, but the restaurant is the real draw for those seeking more than a few nibbles to consume alongside the spectacular cocktails. An illuminated marbled mural glows warmly and points the way to the 50-seat dining area, and an enormous, semi-transparent, blood-red screen separates the bar from the restaurant.
Babies and children welcome (until 6pm). Disabled: toilet. Music (DJs 5pm Sun). No-smoking (restaurant). Restaurant. Specialities (cocktails). **Map 11 K6**.

Landor

70 Landor Road, SW9 9PH (7274 4386/www.landortheatre.com). Clapham North tube/Clapham High Street rail. **Open** noon-11pm Mon-Sat; noon-10.30pm Sun. **Food served** noon-2.30pm, 6-9.30pm Mon-Fri; 1-9.30pm Sat; 1.15-5pm Sun. **Credit** MC, V.
An uncommon venue midway down the road from which it takes its name. The jet-black ceiling accentuates the intimacy of the various nooks and crannies within; the walls groan with sporting memorabilia chosen with seemingly no rhyme or reason. Real ales are a highlight; the choice regularly changes, but London Pride and Greene King IPA are regulars, and microbreweries feature among the guest ales: Smuggler from Buckinghamshire's Rebellion Beer Company, for instance. Originally famous for its upstairs theatre, the bar now attracts a crowd that's happy to play pool on one of the three tables or watch the footie on TV.
Babies and children admitted (garden until 7pm). Games (fruit machine, pool, quiz machine). Tables outdoors (12, garden). Theatre (7.30pm Tue-Sat; £7-£10). TV (big screen, satellite). **Map 11 M16**.

Royal Oak

8-10 Clapham High Street, SW4 7UT (7720 5678). Clapham North tube. **Open** noon-11pm Mon-Sat; noon-10.30pm Sun. **Food served** noon-10.30pm Mon-Sat; noon-10.00pm Sun. **Credit** AmEx, MC, V.
Another boozer that has recently benefited from a little spit 'n' polish. Goodbye scraggy carpet, so long bad lighting, begone blinking games machine; hello steak pies and sausage mash, well-kept taps and shiny pumps (including Scrumpy Jack cider and Adnams Broadside), bottled beers and decent wines, low-level lights and hardwood floors. Sounds like an identikit gastropub? Happily, it isn't. The Victorian glass conical lampshades that hang from the circling sepia fans, the wallpapered ceiling, the wood-panelled walls, and the brass footrail fencing the bar all are reminders that the Oak has been oiling Clapham North for decades.
Babies and children welcome (before 6pm). Function room. Tables outdoors (4, pavement). TV (big screen, satellite). **Map 11 K16**.

Sand

156 Clapham Park Road, SW4 7DE (7622 3022). Clapham Common tube/Brixton tube/rail, 35, 37 bus. **Open/food served** 6pm-2am Mon-Sat; 6pm-1am Sun. **Admission** £5 after 9.30pm Fri; £5 after 9.30pm, £8 after 11pm Sat. **Credit** MC, V.

Now well established on this grimy stretch of Clapham Park Road, this desert-themed place caused quite a storm when it opened a few years back with its shrewd attempt to bring a bit of panache to the Clapham bar scene. Not that there's anything outrageous about Sand. Rather, the emphasis is on providing just the right mixture of great cocktails and shorts, above-par food and a vibe as seductive as it is accessible. The ambiguous desert theme is nicely understated (not a stuffed camel to be seen) and – neat touch – there are a few tiny TV sets (the sort you find in airline seats) set into the walls.
Disabled: toilet. Function room. Games (board games). Music (DJs 10.30pm Wed-Sat). Tables outdoors (7, roof terrace). TVs (big screen, miniature). **Map 11 L17**.

SO.UK

165 Clapham High Street, SW4 7SS (7622 4004/ www.soukclapham.co.uk). Clapham Common tube. **Open** 5pm-midnight Mon, Sun; 5pm-2am Tue-Sat. **Food served** 6-10pm daily. **Credit** MC, V.
Combining Bedouin bohemia and Soho style, SO.UK has become a near-compulsory stop for anyone taking in the High Street's high points. The wonderful zinc bar and the low brass tables that partner luxuriant red sofas form a walkway of sorts to the lounge, with its billowing taffeta curtains. Pacific Rim cuisine is served throughout, along with a vast selection of cocktails, boosted by one of the best champagne lists in south London. A hotch-potch of styles it may be, but the overriding atmosphere is one of surprising warmth and friendliness, given the often intimidating tendencies of other inferior venues nearby.
Bar available for hire. Disabled: toilet. Music (DJs 8pm Tue-Sun; free). Specialities (cocktails). Tables outdoors (2, pavement). **Map 11 L17**.

Windmill on the Common

Windmill Drive, Clapham Common Southside, SW4 7AA (8673 4578). Clapham Common or Clapham South tube. **Open** 11am-11pm Mon-Sat; noon-10.30pm Sun. **Food served** noon-3pm, 6-10pm Mon-Fri; noon-10pm Sat; noon-9pm Sun. **Credit** AmEx, DC, MC, V.
This Young's hotel has been serving the walkers and Sunday-leaguers of the Common for decades. From afar, it appears to be an old pub, but due to a Holiday Inn-style refit the Windmill is clean, comfortable and somewhat anodyne. Still, the Young's stock is good, with the seasonal Winter Warmer most welcome after a chilly stroll; at other times, expect St George's or Waggledance. The venue is made up of four distinct areas, with the pick of the bunch being the non-smoking restaurant towards the back. There are better bars in the area, but few enjoy such a location: the vastness of the Common becomes a de facto beer garden in summer.
Babies and children welcome: high chairs. Disabled: toilet. Function room. Restaurant (no smoking). Tables outdoors (8, garden). TV (big screen, satellite). **Map 11 K18**.

Also in the area...

Bierodrome 44-48 Clapham High Street, SW4 7UR (7720 1118).
Fine Line 182-184 Clapham High Street, SW4 7UG (7622 4436).

DEPTFORD

By rights, the main bar action in Deptford should be along its historic High Street, Christopher Marlowe's old drinking haunt; today it musters only a couple of seedy boozers. Many locals (and Goldsmiths' and Laban students) frequent adjoining New Cross just as much as Deptford.

Dog & Bell

116 Prince Street, SE8 3JD (8692 5664). New Cross tube/rail/Deptford rail. **Open** noon-11pm Mon-Sat; noon-10.30pm Sun. **Food served** noon-2.30pm, 6-9pm Mon-Fri; 2-4pm Sun. **No credit cards**.
Easily the best pub Deptford has to offer, albeit tucked away down a dark side street beyond the creek end of the High Street, the classic Dog & Bell offers superb ales at cut-rates, communal warmth and local character, all within a cheery, intimate two-lounge space. Starting with the real ales (note the CAMRA London Pub of the Year 2004 sticker), Fuller's ESB and London Pride, Admiral's Battersea and Boggart's Sun Dial are the current incumbents, at prices ranging from £1.85 to £2.70 per pint; the the beermats pinned above the bar counter also tell of Old Stroker and Scutcher's Autumn Ale – casks are regularly changed. The best lager on offer is bottled and Belgian, starting with Kriek, and there's decent pub grub available in two daily servings. Equally attractive is the offbeat decor – matching the local boho clientele – of arty photos and chefs' heads on plates. The bar billiards table could be a pub game or an art statement, ideally both.
Disabled: toilet. Games (bar billiards, shove hapenny). Specialities (real ales). Tables outdoors (6, garden). TV.

Live Bar

41-42 Deptford Broadway, SE8 0PL (8469 2121). Deptford Bridge DLR/53, 177 bus. **Open** 5-11pm Mon, Tue; 5pm-2am Wed-Sun. **Admission** £5 after 10pm Thur-Sat; £3 after 9pm Sun. **Credit** AmEx, MC, V.
A real Deptford success story, the vibrant Live Bar offers entertainment and late drinking every night of the week. Set in a high-ceilinged old bank, the Live Bar has created a little hub of activity along a once moribund stretch of road by Deptford Bridge DLR station. Just up the road, the Polar Bar (*see p211*) is the latest newcomer, and there are bound to be more. Meanwhile, the Live Bar goes from strength to strength, and a main bar area with DJ decks and plenty of dance space fills from mid-evening. Draught San Miguel, Kronenbourg and Kronenbourg Blanc – and bottled Budvar or Corona – are the drinks of choice. A pool area and chill-out room (hired out as the VIP Room) help with overspill. Live music (and open mic) on Sundays, with a 2am bar, is the latest addition to the weekly programme.
Games (pool). Music (DJs 9pm Wed-Sun; musicians 8pm Sun).

DULWICH

No, it's not the new Clapham – but walk down Lordship Lane of a Friday night and you can certainly spot a resemblance. **Franklins** is typical of the easygoing gastrobars, but there are several other exponents, as well as taverns of a more historic cast, such as the **Crown & Greyhound**.

Clock House

196A Peckham Rye, SE22 9QA (8693 2901). East Dulwich or Peckham Rye rail/12, 63, 312 bus. **Open** 11am-11pm Mon-Sat; noon-10.30pm Sun. **Food served** noon-2.30pm, 6-8.30pm Mon-Fri; noon-8.30pm Sat, Sun. **Credit** AmEx, MC, V.

At its best in summer – when the terrace's blooming flowers and its prime position opposite Peckham Rye Common prove irresistible to weekend walkers and picnickers – the Clock House is the boozer of choice in this, the posh part of Peckham. Inside, the walls are green, the fish are stuffed and mounted in cases and the tankards are of the vintage variety. In your pint glass, you can choose from a very respectable range of ales, including Young's ('ordinary', Special, St George's and Ram Rod) and guest appearances by Waggledance and (in summer) Golden Zest. Lager drinkers will have to make do with Stella, Carlsberg and more Young's (Export and Pilsner). If you get hungry, you're looking at jacket spuds, ploughman's and the like.
Babies & children welcome (patio only). Disabled: toilet. Quiz (9pm Tue). Tables outdoors (patio).

Crown & Greyhound

73 Dulwich Village, SE21 7BJ (8299 4976). West Dulwich rail. **Open** 11am-11pm Mon-Sat; noon-10.30pm Sun. **Food served** noon-10pm Mon-Sat; noon-3pm, 4.30-9pm Sun. **Credit** AmEx, MC, V.
Whenever a Englishman abroad starts to long for the simple, familiar pleasures of a well-pulled pint and a quiet snug to drink it in, you can be sure it's an establishment exactly like this one that shimmers so enticingly in his mind's eye. The drone of bees and the twitter of birdsong in the beer garden, the creaking of armchairs and the flicker of firelight on dark winter days – these are what make the C&G one of London's best-loved pubs. Its four saloon areas cling to the wide arc of its polished-wood and stained-glass bar, where smart Dulwich Villagers choose between four weekly ales – Badger Best Bitter, perhaps, or Everards Beacon – and a dozen wines by the glass. There are also blackboard menus advertising a spread of decent grub, and a pleasant little dining room to eat it in.
Babies and children welcome: high chairs; nappy-changing facilities. Disabled: toilet. Function room. Restaurant (no-smoking area). Tables outdoors (15, garden).

East Dulwich Tavern

1 Lordship Lane, SE22 8EW (8693 1316/1817). East Dulwich rail/12, 40, 176, 185 bus. **Open** 11am-11pm Mon-Wed; 11am-midnight Thur-Sat; noon-10.30pm Sun. **Food served** noon-4pm Sat. **Credit** MC, V.
Despite increasing competition, the EDT continues to be the busiest and, in many ways, the best boozer on the strip. There's no fancy interior design here; this is bog-standard contemporary pub decor, from the tiled floors, large storefront windows and splashes of modern art to the big screen (for professional football matches) and the Babyfoot table (for amateur ones). Partly owing to this accessible, open-plan format, and partly because of its prime location at the very start of Lordship Lane, the place is always full (and, on the weekends, just the right side of raucous). To drink, Young's ('ordinary' and Special), Staropramen, Stella, Grolsch and Guinness are on tap; there are also a few wines by the glass. Should you become hungry at any point, there's a perfectly decent restaurant upstairs.
Babies and children welcome (before 6pm). Games (quiz machine, table football). Restaurant. Tables outdoors (5, pavement). TVs (big screen, digital).

Franklins

157 Lordship Lane, SE22 8HX (8299 9598). East Dulwich rail. **Open** noon-11pm Mon-Wed; noon-midnight Thur-Sat; noon-10.30pm Sun. **Food served** noon-4pm, 6-10.30pm Mon-Sat; 1-10pm Sun. **Credit** AmEx, MC, V.
Stripped and sanded walls give this cosy bar a warm, convivial vibe, helped along by some good-natured banter between locals and bar staff – not *Cheers*, perhaps, but as close as you'd ever want to get to it. There's a more formal restaurant area at the back (where starched tablecloths and a busy open kitchen set the scene for some ambitious modern British cooking), but imaginative, tasty snacks are also available to those seated on the leather sofas or at the café-style tables in the bar. Draught beers are Guinness and Young's 'ordinary', lagers are the usual Beck's, Foster's and Kronenbourg line-up, while on the nicely varied wine list you'll also find four reds and as many whites by the glass. In a word: civilised.
Babies and children welcome: high chairs. Disabled: toilet. Function room. Tables outdoors (3, pavement).

Liquorish

123 Lordship Lane, SE22 8HU (8693 7744). East Dulwich rail/P13 bus. **Open/food served** 5pm-midnight Mon-Fri; 11am-midnight Sat; 11am-11.30pm Sun. **Credit** MC, V.
From the moment Liquorish wriggled into its tunnel-like premises on Lordship Lane, the place has been regularly packed to the rafters. The formula is simple: one part sleek cocktail bar, one part simple diner, with some decks discreetly positioned towards the back for after-dark vibe control. But this is no ordinary DJ bar, nor is it exactly a gastropub (you'll find no farmhouse tables or Sunday papers here); no, this is something altogether more sophisticated. Take, for example, English Summer, one of the cocktails we selected from a long and impressively diverse list. Its combination of gin, Campari, grapefruit juice, coriander and cucumber had the pleasantly dreamy effect of evoking sunlit lawns and the sound of leather on willow, as if the whole PG Wodehouse canon had been distilled in a single drink. The wine list also has an excellent selection by the glass.
Babies and children welcome (lunch only). Games (board games). Music (DJs 9pm Fri, Sat; free). Restaurant. Specialities (cocktails). Tables outdoors (3, terrace).

FOREST HILL

Bar activity is confined to the confluence of traffic-swamped streets leading to the station, each lined with late-night shops and takeaway joints, while Blokey pubs can be spotted at various points along the South Circular.

Bar Equal

68-70 Honor Oak Park, SE23 1DY (8699 6674/www.barequal.com). Honor Oak Park rail/P4, P12, 122, 171, 172 bus. **Open** 6pm-midnight Mon-Wed, Sun; 6pm-2am Thur-Sat. **Food served** 6.30pm-10pm Mon-Thur, Sun; 6.30-10.30pm Fri, Sat. **Credit** AmEx, MC, V.
More Honor Oak Park than Forest Hill – in fact, it's right by the station – but with a bar this good, who's quibbling? Experienced, partly French bar staff mix up a whole mess of decent cocktails in the cool confines of a two-space, modern bar design, while an equally adept kitchen keeps regulars in Mediterranean risotto, steamed wild sea bass (£8-£9) and the like. The attractive prices – you're in Forest Hill, not Fulham, remember – hold true for the cocktails as well, an across-the-board £5.25 from Sunday to Thursday, and £6 on Friday and Saturday. Along with the classic varieties, there's a regularly changing range of lesser known, lethal concoctions: a d.o.a. of absinthe, Archer's,

cranberry juice and fraise fuzzed the edges of the blue squares lining the walls. Good backing track, too – though not at weekends, when handy DJing comes to the fore.
Disabled: toilet. Music (DJs 9pm Thur-Sat; free). Restaurant. Specialities (cocktails).

Casa Tequila

66-68 Brockley Rise, SE23 1LN (8690 7323). Honor Oak Park rail. **Open** 5.30-11pm Mon-Fri; noon-11pm Sat; noon-10.30pm Sun. **Food served** 6-10.30pm Mon-Fri; noon-4pm, 6-10.30pm Sat; noon-4pm, 6-10pm Sun. **Credit** MC, V.

This beacon of Latino drinking opened at the end of 2004; it's an unexpected find amid an otherwise nondescript parade of shops. Behind the big glass frontage, a tiny grey and red bar provides an unadorned backdrop for the enjoyment of (surprise!) tequila, which is cheerily dispensed by the knowledgeable owner. The 20 or so varieties range from slugs of cheaper stuff for the salt 'n' lime brigade to generous measures of fine sippin' Reposados. Tequila- and chilli-flavoured bottled beers, and a worm-filled Mexican vodka, complement the main specialism. Latin musicians bring in punters during the week, while weekenders can enjoy a brunch menu featuring the likes of vegetarian burrito, alongside more usual brunch dishes. A small dining room at the back continues the Mexican theme with main courses like steak marinated in (surprise!) tequila.
Babies and children welcome: children's menu; high chair. Disabled: ramps, toilet. Function room. Music (musician 8.30pm Thur; free). Restaurant (no-smoking). Specialities (cocktails). Tables outdoors (5, terrace).

Dartmouth Arms

7 Dartmouth Road, SE23 3HN (8488 3117). Forest Hill rail. **Open** 11am-11pm Mon-Sat; 11am-10.30pm Sun. **Food served** noon-2.30pm, 6.30-10pm Mon-Fri; noon-4pm, 6.30-10pm Sat; noon-9pm Sun. **Credit** AmEx, MC, V.

Once a fag-end of a place where old geezers muttered into their pints, the Dartmouth Arms has been reborn as a fine gastropub. Rather than ripping out its guts, the proprietors have given the place a judicious makeover: polishing the old wood for sepia-toned warmth, adding a couple of slouchable leather sofas here, red '60s-style perspex lights there. A mural of coffee cups reflects the daytime offer of caffeine alongside the alcohol; there's London Pride and Bombardier on draught, and an eight-strong list of keenly priced classic cocktails. But it's the food in the rear dining room that stands out; an open-plan kitchen knocks out a weekly changing menu of beautifully cooked, robust Modern European dishes. In summer, the beer garden is the venue for alfresco barbecues beneath a pear tree. The Dartmouth provides genuine rivalry to East Dulwich stars such as Franklins (*see p207*).
Babies and children welcome: high chairs. Disabled: toilet. Restaurant. Tables outdoors (10, garden).

Hobgoblin

7 Devonshire Road, SE23 3HE (8291 2225). Forest Hill rail/176, 185 bus. **Open** 2-11pm Mon-Thur; 2pm-2am Fri, Sat; 2-10.30pm Sun. **Credit** MC, V.

This Forest Hill landmark opposite the station means different things to different people. Late on Friday nights, T-shirted yoof piles in to neck lager while local bands blast through raucous sets until the small hours. More cerebral punters grab one of the bottled Wychwood ales (including Hobgoblin, naturally), or maybe one of half a dozen cocktails before going upstairs for comedy (Saturdays) or theatre (Fridays). During the week, though, the Hob chills. Fish drift through a tank behind the bar, snowboarders flip across the giant plasma screen by the pool table, and decent music plays at a decent level. It's a nice space, painted in pale yellows and reds, with tiny blue lights hanging through netting above battered sofas and old wooden tables. Board games, internet PCs and an old pinball machine add to the laid-back community feel of the place.
Comedy (8pm Sat; £6-£9). Games (board games, fruit machines, pinball, pool, quiz machine). Music (bands 9pm Fri; £2-£5). Tables outdoors (4, courtyard). TV (big screen, satellite).

Railway Telegraph

112 Stanstead Road, SE23 1BS (8699 6644). Forest Hill rail/122, 185 bus. **Open** 11am-11pm Mon-Sat; noon-10.30pm Sun. **Food served** noon-2.30pm Mon-Fri. **Credit** MC, V.

This large, landmark Shepherd Neame pub, set back from a Monte Carlo-style chicane on the South Circular, is favoured by discerning ale drinkers, pool players and families. Spitfire and Master Brew are joined by Oranjeboom Hürlimann, Holsten Export and Bishops Finger along the bar counter, around which all kinds of pub entertainment has been laid out. A man-sized pool table (with associated rules strictly illustrated on a blackboard) has commandeered one side area; another of conservatory appearance allows parents to watch over their kids in the garden. Board games seem to be popular here, and there's more than enough room for a dartboard elsewhere. Sky TV is another crowd-puller, but mostly you'll find locals sitting around whispering along to the lyrics of the AOR playlist.
Babies and children admitted (until 7pm). Games (board games, darts, fruit machines, pool). Tables outdoors (11, garden). TV (big screen, satellite).

GREENWICH

Easily the most happening place in south-east London, riverside Greenwich comes into its own at weekends. A busy market, historic attractions and an attractive park all feature complementary pubs of similar ilk (**Coach**, **Trafalgar Tavern**) alongside – but family pub lunches are not the only attractions these days. Night owls now revel in cute style bars, **Inc Bar** and the **Polar Bar** being the classic after-dark examples; the **North Pole** and **Oliver's** are equally fêted as party venues, and more are bound to follow before long.

Ashburnham Arms

25 Ashburnham Grove, SE10 8UH (8692 2007). Greenwich rail/DLR. **Open** noon-11pm Mon-Sat; noon-10.30pm Sun. **Food served** noon-2.30pm, 6-10pm Tue-Sat; noon-8pm Sun. **Credit** MC, V.

The classic, community-oriented Ashburnham is the paradigm of what a local pub should be. First off, it's a friendly focus of the neighbourhood, with folks chatting in the intimate front bar, gathered around the fire or perched in the bar billiards area surrounded by pictures of the pub cricket team. Secondly, it serves excellent ales, namely Porter, Shepherd Neame Best, Spitfire and Master Brew, plus quality draught lagers in Oranjeboom and Holsten Pils; Kriek, Leffe and other Belgian offerings come by the bottle. Thirdly, the food is first-rate: thick steaks, tuna ones of

equal succulence, and always a non-meat option. A conservatory, through the loungey corridor away from the grown ups, accommodates children, with special menus and high chairs provided before you even ask. A garden and patio complete the accomplished picture.
Babies and children welcome (conservatory): children's menu; high chairs. Games (bar billiards, board games). No-smoking area. Quiz (9pm Tue; free). Spanish classes 7pm Mon; £7). Tables outdoors (6, garden; 12, patio).

Bar du Musée

17 Nelson Road, SE10 9JB (8858 4710/www.bardumusee.com). Cutty Sark DLR. **Open** 11am-midnight Mon-Fri; 11am-1am Sat. **Food served** (restaurant) noon-4pm, 6-10pm Mon-Fri; 11am-4pm, 6-10pm Sat, Sun. **Credit** MC, V.

Opinions vary wildly about this landmark wine bar backing on to Greenwich Market. Locals enthuse over the BDM of yesteryear, a carefree gem of a bar, run by Old Dave. Since Dave's passing, and the subsequent change of ownership, three large conservatories have been tacked on the end, and a full restaurant menu is offered. Locals now gripe. The food, average at best, is expensive and served by unmotivated staff – far too few to manage 250 diners. So, treat the bar as before; intimate, late-opening and foxy to a fault, and you won't go wrong. Breeze past the bouncer any time before 1am, grab a slice of counter in the narrow bar area done out with art nouveau pretensions, order up a glass of Guerrieri Rizzardi pinot grigio, and get involved. If already *à deux*, order one of the 25 wines by the bottle, a San Biagio barolo, perhaps, or a Daniel Dampf chablis. See? Social drinking at its best.
Babies and children welcome: high chairs. Function room. Restaurant. Tables outdoors (22, garden).

Coach

13 Greenwich Market, SE10 9HZ (8293 0880). Cutty Sark or Greenwich rail/DLR. **Open** 11am-11pm Mon-Sat; 11am-10.30pm Sun. **Food served** noon-10pm Mon-Sun. **Credit** AmEx, MC, V.

At once a bar, pub and market meeting place (with outside tables jutting onto the trestled morass of junk and jewellery), the Coach covers all bases. With its 'Coach & Horses' pub sign still proudly atop its intimate right-angle of a bar, it offers hearty ales and fine wines, a fireplace and Med cuisine. Abbot, Bombardier, London Pride and Morland Old Speckled Hen comprise the ales on tap, Amstel, Affligem and Wieckse Witte the beers. Trapiche malbec (£4.10 a glass) is one of a dozen wines by the glass, complementing dishes (£6-£7) such as leek, mushroom and lemon risotto, or linguine with clams, chili, olive oil and pancetta. The modern gastrobar touch is accentuated by a side area of low-level loungey furniture and the day's papers. Stake your claim early at weekends.
Babies and children admitted (until 9pm). Tables outdoors (12, patio).

Cutty Sark Tavern

4-6 Ballast Quay, SE10 9PD (8858 3146). Greenwich rail/DLR/Maze Hill rail. **Open** 11am-11pm Mon-Sat; noon-10.30pm Sun. **Food served** noon-9pm Mon-Fri, Sun; noon-10pm Sat. **Credit** MC, V.

It doesn't get more traditional than this listed (and listing) building, anachronistically set as it is beside the new waterfront Anchor Iron Wharf housing development. Its dateline of 1695 stamped on the outside and, etched into the coloured glass of the front door, the words 'Cutty Sark Tavern', it may have been built a century later – but who's counting? In summer, ten terrace tables overlooking the Thames justify the long trek through this obscure stretch of North Greenwich, although the attraction of a roaring fire and a pint of Spitfire, London Pride or Adnams Broadside in a cosy, upholstered snug is just as strong in winter. Wines, at around £4 a glass and £12 a bottle, include Domaine de Pajot sauvignon, Argentine chardonnay and Chilean merlot. Duck breast, lamb shank, and broccoli and three cheese bake figure among the hearty mains (£8-£10), while nautical knick-knacks and beer barrel tables give the two-storey space a rustic feel.
Babies and children welcome (children's menu). Games (fruit machine). Tables outdoors (10, riverside terrace).

Greenwich Union

56 Royal Hill, SE10 8RT (8692 6258). Greenwich rail/DLR. **Open** 11am-11pm Mon-Fri; 10am-11pm Sat; 10am-10.30pm Sun. **Food served** noon-9.30pm Mon-Fri; 10am-9pm Sat, Sun. **Credit** MC, V.

Not much change at this much-lauded bar, and why should there be? Flagship outlet of Alistair Hook's equally lauded Meantime Brewing Company, the Union flaunts the fruits of a labour which began with Hook's beer apprenticeship in Munich, where techniques are age-old and authenticity is sacrosanct. Thus the house Blonde is cask-preserved in the traditional way; signature Union, Chocolate, Golden, Pilsner, Raspberry, Stout, White and a rather excellent Kölsch, all by the barrel, can be tasted in miniature in a handy try-before-you-buy exercise. The staff are friendly and knowledgeable, swiftly manning a bar which divides the beerhall-like front area from the loungey back, all done out in orange and brown, with a solid flagstone floor. A back patio opens in summer. The classy mains includes daily specials (roast quail and baby spinach, £7.95), served until 10pm, by which time there's live music (jazz, blues, R&B) twice a week.
Babies and children welcome (before 9pm). Games (board games). Music (live bands weekly, call to chk). Specialities (continental beers). Tables outdoors (12, garden).

Inc Bar & Restaurant

7 College Approach, SE10 9HY (8858 6721/www.incbar.com). Cutty Sark DLR/177, 180, 286 bus. **Open** 5pm-midnight Mon-Thur, Sun; 5pm-1am Fri, Sat. **Food served** 6-10pm daily. **Credit** MC, V.

Sliding doors – *zzzhhhhh* – open to reveal a doorman and a desk, neither of which require any cash, only the optional and nominal choice of a coat check. Up a flight of stairs, and ahead stretches a spacious main bar with DJ decks at the far end, and a busy, well-manned bar counter at the near one. Signature spots of detail reveal the collaborative hand of Laurence Llewelyn-Bowen in the design: colourful gems, Nelson in various poses, clocks of all sorts. Above the DJ is a balcony mezzanine covered with tables, ideal for tucking into the bar food (£3.50) of stuffed chicken or prawn pâté with herb crostini while observing the local, party-oriented clientele. Behind the balcony bar extends a mini warren of secretive rooms; exploring them compares favourably with finding the coolest room at a house party. One intimate room has low lights, a fire and erotic wallpaper, while another bar lurks across a narrow corridor. Drinks here are as cheap and well made as downstairs: £6 cocktails (Cosmopolitans with Ketel One Citron, French Martinis with Stoli Raspberi), long and short varieties at £6.75, such as the house recommendation of tequila slammers

with Pannier Rosé. Eight wines by the glass, Leffe and Hoegaarden by the half-pint, plenty of malts. Is there a better bar south of the river right now?
Babies and children admitted. Music (DJs 8pm Fri, Sat; free). Restaurant. Specialities (cocktails).

North Pole

131 Greenwich High Road, SE10 8JA (8853 3020/ www.northpolegreenwich.com). Greenwich rail/DLR. **Open** noon-11pm Mon-Sat; noon-10.30pm Sun. **Food served** noon-3pm Mon-Sat; noon-4pm, 6.30-10pm Sun. **Happy hour** 4.30-7pm daily. **Credit** AmEx, DC, MC, V.

Premier party venue since 1999, this stylish three-floor club-bar-restaurant has been surpassed by recent arrivals ten minutes away in downtown Greenwich – but the North Pole can still get some action. In the main street-level bar, the zebra-patterned bar stools have given way to plain brown ones, but the three-area space doesn't lack for tack. There's some kind of necklace over the bar counter, and an aquarium effect separating it from the loungey front of house. Bar and lipstick-coloured comfy side room both sport TV screens. Potent cocktails (£6 a glass, £13.50 a jug), include a Killer Zombie with Appleton's, Myer's, Morgan's Spice and Woods 100 rums, and a Sex At The Pole of Finlandia, peach schnapps and juices. Spitfire, Staropramen and Hoegaarden are available on draught, and wine (as in the continental restaurant upstairs) comes eight of each colour by the bottle, four by the glass, starting with a standard pinot grigio and merlot at £3. DJs hit the decks at the South Pole downstairs at weekends. Breakfast and live jazz bookend Sundays.
Babies and children welcome: children's menu; high chairs. Function room. Music (DJs 7.30pm Thur-Sat; live jazz 6-8pm Sun). No-smoking area. Restaurant. Tables outdoors (8, pavement). TV (big screen, digital).

Oliver's

9 Nevada Street, SE10 9JL (8858 5855). Greenwich rail/DLR. **Open** noon-11pm daily. **Food served** 7-11pm daily. **No credit cards.**

Flavour of the month in these parts, this cosy jazz cellar is both a landmark live venue and an intimate destination for a drink à deux. A cover charge (£3/£4) is levied most nights of the week, but the live music on offer is generally of a decent standard – with more offbeat offerings at Tuesday's Twist – and most are happy to pay it for the ambience in any case. Set in the cobbled alley behind and below the Spreadeagle restaurant, Oliver's feels medieval – no surprise, as it was a staging-post hostelry in the late 1600s. A scattering of tables and an area of half-moon seating is squeezed into a dimly lit space bookended by a low stage, accessed through a tiny bar area. There you'll find a rare tap of Italian Moretti, but most stick with wine. Standard chardonnay, pinot grigio and shiraz come by the glass (£3-£4), and there's decent Chilean merlot or New Zealand sauvignon blanc at £17 a bottle. This being a favoured birthday spot, Jean Milan house champagne comes at £6.50 a glass, £31 a bottle.
Music (musicians 8pm Tue-Sun; £3-£5). Specialities (cocktails). Tables outdoors (6, pavement).

Polar Bar

13 Blackheath Road, SE10 8PE (8691 1555). Deptford bridge DLR. **Open** noon-1am Mon-Thur; noon-2am Fri, Sat; noon-10.30pm Sun. **Food served** noon-10pm daily. **Credit** MC, V.

DRINKING ALOUD
CHARLOTTE VOISEY

Who are you? I'm the general manager of Apartment 195 [*see p29*] and a hands-on mixologist – I won *Class* magazine's Best Bartender award in 2004.
Drinking in London: what's good about it? The creativity and attention to detail that you find in cocktail bars. London's the best place for drink cocktails in the world – it's certainly overtaken New York in the last four years.
What's not so good? Prices. And the pretentious attitude you get in a lot of 'quality' venues. They have wonderful cocktails, very passionate bartenders, the music's great – but people might not get that far because they've had an unpleasant experience at the door.
What's caught your eye in the last year? The sheer range of ingredients available. I recently discovered some Colombian fruits that most people in London won't know. There's the lulo, a green fruit unlike anything I've ever seen, with a spiky exterior and taste similar to a gooseberry; and the mora, which is an Andean blackberry. It's exciting to get such products and present them via cocktails.
What's in your crystal ball? More focus on the base spirit of a cocktail, as opposed to throwing lots of things in a blender and coming up with something pink and fruity. Everyone knows about Cuban rum, but the working classes in Cuba drink something called aguardiente, a white spirit similar to rum, but made in a different way. Things like that will make their way into the limelight over here.
New licensing law: good or bad? I think there are going to be teething problems. But we'll never be ready for it if we don't give it a try.

Inc Bar & Restaurant. *See p210.*

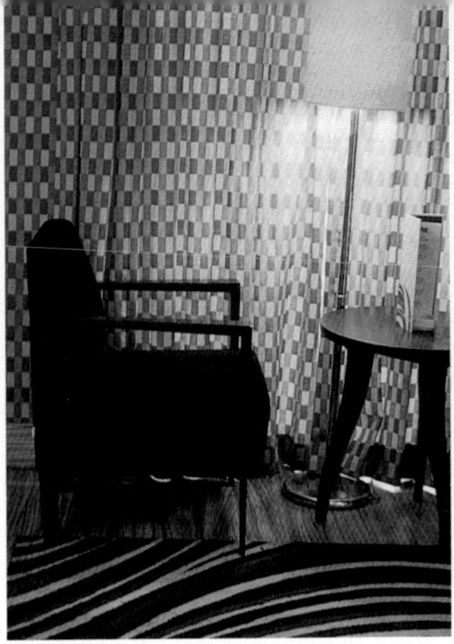

The party-oriented Polar Bar – the latest late-opening DJ bar on the burgeoning scene where Deptford and Greenwich meet – takes cool seriously. The air conditioning is switched to 'chill', the beer (Grolsch) comes in frozen glasses and blue is the colour of choice. Cocktails (£5.50 a glass, £12 a jug) are similarly themed, although made of unspecified base spirit: Arctic Breeze (rums and orange juice), Arctic Summer (gin, apricot brandy and bitter lemon), Polar Bar Cooler (dark rum, port and orange juice), and so on. The food and music are suitably hot, piri piri chicken (£8) and spicy tapas available on a daily basis, with occasional salsa on Sundays, R&B on Thursday and funky house and live percussion on Saturdays. Club nights incur a door charge (£3-£8) and mild dress code (no caps or tracksuits), but the salsa is free. Greenwich Magistrates' Court is next door, so don't go overboard on the large shooters (£5).
Babies and children welcome (before 8pm). Music (DJs 9pm Wed-Sat; £5 after 9pm Fri, Sat only). Specialities (cocktails). Tables outdoors (15, garden). TV (satellite).

Richard I

52-54 Royal Hill, SE10 8RT (8692 2996). Greenwich rail/DLR. **Open** 11am-11pm Mon-Sat; noon-10.30pm Sun. **Food served** noon-9pm daily. **Credit** MC, V.
The success of the Greenwich Union (*see p210*) next door has not dented the popularity or quality of this exemplary Young's pub. Fronted by attractive bay windows, this comfortable boozer is divided into two bar areas, one full of diners chomping into pies and slabs of fish, the other a little quieter and lined with pictures of cheery postwar pub outings. The full range of Young's beers (Pilsner, Special and bitter on draught, Ramrod, Waggledance, Oatmeal Stout and Champion by the bottle) and wines (decent sauvignon blanc and merlot in the £14 a bottle range) are served from a busy, sturdy bar counter exuding winter bonhomie. In summer, an extensive back garden comes into its own, where children can be let loose – grown ups can enjoy a quieter, alfresco pint at the tables outside the front door.
Babies and children admitted (garden only). No piped music. Tables outdoors (15, garden; 2, pavement).

Trafalgar Tavern

Park Row, SE10 9NW (8858 2437/www.trafalgartavern.co.uk). Cutty Sark Gardens DLR/Maze Hill rail. **Open** noon-11pm Mon-Thur; noon-midnight Fri, Sat; noon-10.30pm Sun. **Food served** noon-3pm, 6-9pm Mon-Sat; noon-4pm Sun. **Credit** MC, V.
Stately in appearance, the landmark Trafalgar is no authentic naval institution from the time of Nelson – although the grand portraits of heroic admirals in the main bar would suggest otherwise. It open in 1837, but within a century or so fell into disuse and disrepair – strange, really, considering its superb location by the lapping Thames. Restored in regal style in 1965, it accommodates tourists and discerning drinkers with considerable aplomb. The four ground-floor rooms increase in grandeur, from high-ceilinged bar rooms to the old-fashioned, upholstered wine lounge and fully fledged restaurant at the back; upstairs is the chandeliered Nelson Room, used for special occasions. Most crowd into the middle bar, where draught Boddington's, Flowers, Slater's and Nelson's Blood are served by rushed but polite staff. Outdoor riverside tables are the best spots for tucking into superior pub lunches, such as the house burger of ground veal and organic beef.
Babies and children welcome: children's menu; high chairs. Function rooms. Music (jazz 9pm Sat; free). Restaurant. Tables outdoors (20, riverwalk).

Also in the area...

Davy's Wine Vaults 161 Greenwich High Road, SE10 8JA (8853 0585).
Gate Clock (JD Wetherspoon) Cutty Sark Station, Creek Road, SE10 9RB (8269 2000).

HERNE HILL

At the edge of Dulwich's all-encompassing sprawl, Herne Hill is a green and pleasant place where everybody's made quite a bit of money lately in the housing market. Gentrification has brought many changes to the district, including polished

wooden floors, Belgian beers and loft conversions. If it's a drink you're after, head towards the busy train station; all the worthwhile establishments are within stumbling distance of here.

Commercial

210-212 Railton Road, SE24 0JT (7501 9051). Brixton tube/rail then 3, 196 bus/Herne Hill rail. **Open** noon-11pm Mon-Sat; noon-10.30pm Sun. **Food served** noon-3pm, 5-10pm Mon-Fri; noon-10pm Sat; noon-9pm Sun. **Credit** AmEx, MC, V.

An extensive renovation has transformed what was an old railway boozer into the trendiest pub in Herne Hill. With lots of polished wood, brass details, big windows, comfortable couches and real fires blazing on cool nights, the Commercial has been a huge success since it reopened in November 2004. The crowd is lured by an extensive list of beers on tap, including Hoegaarden, De Konink, Leffe and Früli, as well as the usual suspects – Grolsch, Staropramen, London Pride, Guinness – and three regularly changing guest ales. Prices are high for the suburbs; the cheapest draught is £2.50 a pint, and a pint of Hoegaarden will set you back £3.60. But what the heck – the place looks good, it's buzzing, and there's a menu of thick hamburgers, potato wedges and the like.

Babies and children welcome. Disabled: toilet. Games (board games). No-smoking area. Tables outdoors (5, garden).

Half Moon

10 Half Moon Lane, SE24 9HU (7274 2733). Herne Hill rail/68 bus. **Open** noon-11pm Mon-Thur; noon-1.30am Fri, Sat; noon-10.30pm Sun. **Credit** AmEx, DC, MC, V.

We're happy to report that Herne Hill's gentrification has not yet consumed this place: indeed, there are no signs that the stubbornly blokey Half Moon will fly the gastropub flag any time soon. The boxing gym upstairs keeps the clientele mostly male and sometimes muscular, and there's a music venue at the rear where bands occasionally bring in startlingly big crowds. The interior is mercifully unreconstructed: high of ceiling, dark of wood panelling and softened by etched glass; unsurprisingly, what with the gym above, there's a sporty theme to the decor. The drinkers, mostly locals, have Courage beers (Directors, Best), Beck's, Kronenbourg, John Smith's and Foster's; bottled options all start with B (Budweiser, Budvar, Beck's).

Games (darts, pool). Music (live bands 8pm Fri, Sat; £3-£5). Tables outdoors (12, pavement). TV (satellite).

Number 22

22 Half Moon Lane, SE24 9HU (7095 9922/www.number-22.com). Herne Hill rail/3, 37, 68 bus. **Open/food served** 10am-11pm Mon-Sat; noon-10.30pm Sun. **Credit** MC, V.

Herne Hill's newest arrival is small, well-rounded and classy. A subtle Spanish theme runs through bar and restaurant, from the draught Cruzcampo and immaculate sherry list to the stylish contemporary tapas menu. Unsurprisingly, given that there's ex-Match Group expertise at work here, the selection of spirits behind the generously proportioned bar is flawless; the cocktails are impressive, too. Among the bespoke creations, the 22 Martini is a miniature work of art in a coupette, and one served, refreshingly, with Latin friendliness rather than shaker-twizzling flair. The seasonally updated wine list boasts an admirable number of organic choices and even a biodynamically produced cava. For such a modest space, 22's ambitions seem boundless, but the enthusiasm of those involved is infectious – with talk of regular mix-your-own Bloody Mary brunches, we can't wait to return.

Babies and children welcome: high chairs. No-smoking. Restaurant. Specialities (cocktails, wine tasting). Tables outdoors (4, patio; 2, pavement).

Pullens

293-295 Railton Road, SE24 0JP (7274 9163). Herne Hill rail/3, 196 bus. **Open/food served** 11am-11pm Mon-Sat; 11am-10.30pm Sun. **Happy hour** 5-7pm Mon-Fri. **Credit** MC, V.

The cosiest and friendliest venue of all the Herne Hill options, Pullens is an all-purpose restaurant, bar, breakfast spot, gathering place, coffee shop – you name it. It's not too big and not too small, with plenty of wood and brick. Staff are so adorable, you scarcely mind that there are hardly any chairs in the bar. The wine list features a dozen or so bottles of red and white, and while there's no beer on draught, bottles include St Peter's Ale, Everards Tiger and Bishops Finger. The bar is at its busiest during happy hour (5-7pm Mon-Fri), when most beers and wines are half price. This is one place where you can stay for dinner (and many do): specials in the small adjacent restaurant change regularly, but usually feature grilled fish, steak and hamburgers at reasonable prices.

Babies and children welcome. Restaurant (no-smoking area). Tables outdoors (10, pavement).

KENNINGTON, LAMBETH & OVAL

Although this heading covers a fair sweep of south-east London – part of it gentrifying, much of it not – there isn't a great deal around here except estate pubs and more estate pubs. Camberwell is next door but a million miles away. Kennington has the most bar action, but the area belongs to Ireland, really; the two Irish venues we list here are the **Greyhound** and **Three Stags**.

Beehive

60 Carter Street, SE17 3EW (7703 4992). Kennington tube/12, 68, 68A, 171, 176, P5 bus. **Open** 11am-11pm Mon-Sat; noon-10.30pm Sun. **Food served** noon-3pm, 5.30-10pm Mon-Fri; noon-10pm Sat, Sun. **Credit** MC, V.
A lovely community pub this, appealing to white collar employee and workman alike. Many come here for the ales alone. Old Speckled Hen, Courage Directors, London Pride and John Smith's line up on the counter of the cosy, two-space interior, warmed by a fire in winter and giving on to a modest terrace that's kept for summer use. There's Beck's on tap; a back bar of whiskies from either side of the Irish Sea (Ballygeary, Ragganmore, Balvenie, Glenmorangie, Oban); and a blackboard of wines, four each by the glass, eight each by the bottle, starting with a chenin blanc from South Africa and a Morin merlot/grenache (both £2.60 a glass) and moving on to a bottle of Oyster Bay sauvignon blanc (£14.95 a bottle) and Louis Latour pinot noir (£12.95). Diners in the back lounge are thus equipped to enjoy braised lamb steak (£6.50) or tagliatelle with chicken (£5.50). Political figures on the walls hint at a radical past.
Babies and children welcome (until 7pm): children's menu. Specialities (real ales). Tables outdoors (30, patio). TV.

Dog House

293 Kennington Road, SE11 6BY (7820 9310). Kennington or Oval tube. **Open** noon-11pm Mon-Sat; noon-10.30pm Sun. **Food served** noon-3.30pm, 5.30-9.30pm Mon-Fri; noon-9pm Sat, Sun. **Credit** MC, V.
A cool, boho bar, this, on a busy intersection opposite the landmark, but tediously themed Finca. Divided into cosy front bar and lovely back space around a fireplace, the Dog House offers Abbot Ale, Bombardier, Grolsch and Red Stripe on draught, plus five red and five white wines starting with a standard Australian moondarra at £2.75 a glass. Although most come here to hang out among the arty photographs, there's a serious kitchen at work, too. Offerings, chalked up on the huge board in a front bar festooned with uncontrollable house plants, begin with freshly baked baguettes and focaccias at £4.50. For keen diners, pan-fried salmon fillets, roast sea bass, cod supreme and prawn seafood chowder, plus braised lamb shank and Thai green chicken curry, come at £7.95 each. The music rarely falls a notch below acceptable, and is often pretty good.
Babies and children welcome (upstairs only). Comedy (8pm 1st Mon of mth; free). Function room. Games (board games). Music (musicians 6pm, alternate Sun; jazz/Latin 8.30pm, alternate Tue; free). Tables outdoors (3, pavement). TV.

Greyhound

336 Kennington Park Road, SE11 4PP (7735 2594). Oval tube. **Open** 11am-11pm Mon-Sat; noon-10.30pm Sun. **Food served** noon-3pm Mon-Fri; noon-4pm Sun. **Credit** AmEx, MC, V.
This friendly corner community pub, shamrock-shaped and proud of it, is not limited to serving the needs of the local Irish diaspora – although hurling, Gaelic football and live Irish music on a Sunday night are regular features. Thesps from local drama schools and the Oval House Theatre drift in after rehearsals; in summer, cricket fans head across to the Oval, recently bereft of its main pub; and when we visited, a gaggle of Chilean poets sat plotting on the green banquettes of this long, low-ceilinged, three-space venue. Bombardier, Courage Best, London Pride and bottled Beck's provide refreshment for all, and rows of rarely seen Irish whiskeys (Midleton, Powers, Locker's, Hewitt's, Connemara, Green Spot) give the regulars a taste of home. The place serves hearty, well-priced pub lunches through the week, and roasts on Sundays.
Babies and children welcome (Sun lunch only). Games (fruit machine, golf machine). Music (Irish music, 9pm Sun). TV (big screen, satellite).

Prince of Wales

48 Cleaver Square, SE11 4EA (7735 9916). Kennington tube. **Open** noon-11pm Mon-Sat; noon-10.30pm Sun. **Food served** noon-2.30pm, 6-9pm; Mon-Thur; noon-2.30pm Fri, Sat; noon-3pm Sun. **Credit** MC, V.
A world away from the screeching brakes the other side of Kennington Park Road, this homely pub is set on the corner of a tranquil landscaped square. Built in 1901, its very discretion made it a notorious hangout for gangsters and politicians playing away – but since its takeover by Faversham's Shepherd Neame brewery, it's become a safe haven for satisfied two-income couples to read broadsheets and swap school-run stories. Holsten and Oranjeboom provide strong-lager draught alternatives to standards from the Shepherd Neame stable (Best, Spitfire), while the 16-bottle wine list, chalked over the bar, includes an El Coto rioja for £14.95 and a Clos des Bouffants sancerre at £17.50. Food is of the pan-fried variety, and the mounted prints of famous old cricketers hint at the relative proximity of the Oval.
Tables outdoors (2, pavement).

Three Stags

67-69 Kennington Road, SE1 7PZ (7928 5974). Lambeth North tube/159 bus. **Open** 11am-11pm Mon-Sat; noon-10.30pm Sun. **Food served** noon-8pm Mon-Fri; noon-6pm Sat, Sun. **Credit** MC, V.
Rather smart these days with glitzy chandeliers, bare light bulbs and live jazz on Mondays, this sturdy corner boozer diagonally opposite the Imperial War Museum wasn't always thus. This was the pub where the Charlie Chaplin's father drank himself to death while his young son was sent to a nearby poorhouse – a story alluded to (but not explained, as the details were removed in the recent revamp) by calling the sassy corner snug the Chaplin Corner. These days the Stags has a decent range of wines, draught ales such as Greene King IPA, Abbot Ale, Ruddles Best and Old Speckled Hen, plus sandwiches and ciabattas such as open poached salmon or prawn (£5.95) and chargrilled steak and caramelised onions (£7.95). Steak also features in the hefty mains, pleasing many a tourist hungry after a morning's stroll around tanks and soldiers.
Disabled: toilet. Games (fruit machine). Music (jazz 8pm Mon; open mic 8.30pm Tue; free). No-smoking area. Tables outdoors (5, pavement).

LEE

This somewhat nondescript extension of Lewisham, bounded from Blackheath by the Eltham Road, has its principal pub hub right on the border with its snobby, upmarket neighbour. Up the slope of Burnt Ash Hill, past Lee station, the **Crown** has a certain bucolic appeal.

Crown

117 Burnt Ash Hill, SE12 0AJ (8857 6607). Lee rail. **Open** 11am-11pm Mon-Sat; noon-10.30pm Sun. **Food served** noon-3pm, 6-9.30pm Mon-Sat; noon-6pm Sun. **Credit** MC, V.

Nothing much wrong with this large, well-run Young's pub, where the food is as big a draw as the full range of Young's beers on tap and by the bottle. Set back from the hill by its spacious car park and terrace, the Crown provides comfy seats for diners by the front windows, and big screen TV for sports fans in the extensive interior. On Sundays, the Crown comes into its own when it offers humungous three-course roasts (£10.95) along with the usual dishes of smoked haddock or Cumberland sausage (both £5.50), plus Premiership football or rugby. Glasses of El Coto rioja, red and white, keep wine drinkers cheaply happy at £3, and in summer everyone steps out into the garden for a pint or two in the sunshine.
Entertainment (karaoke 9pm Fri; free). Function room. Games (fruit machine, quiz machine). Quiz (8.30pm Sun; £1). Tables outdoors (12, garden). TV (big screen, digital).

Also in the area...

Edmund Halley (JD Wetherspoon) 25-27 Lee Gate Centre, Burnt Ash Road, SE12 8RG (8318 7475).

LEWISHAM

The two venues listed here are away from central Lewisham – and, in the case of the **Dacre Arms**, very far away – and there's a reason for that. Central Lewisham is horrible. You'd be hard pushed to find a quiet pint, much less a decent one. At weekends, the vast Yates' Wine Lodge and other venues around the market and shopping centre take on the atmosphere of Wild West saloons. Avoid.

Dacre Arms

11 Kingswood Place, SE13 5BU (8852 6779). Lewisham DLR/rail then 321 bus/Blackheath rail. **Open** 11am-11pm Mon-Sat; noon-10.30pm Sun. **Credit** MC, V.
Tricky to find, this homely pub is worth the effort once you get here. In the no man's land on the borders of Lee, Lewisham and Blackheath, far from the train stations of all three, you walk up from Dacre Park from the bus stop on Lee High Road. Past a boarded-up pub and grim housing blocks, third on the left and there you are: instant bonhomie. In a dark wood decor with plush, well-kept carpets gather old couples and blokes who know their beer. Courage Best, Bombardier, Greene King IPA and Deuchar's IPA, with a couple of Continental lagers by the bottle (Nastro Azzurro, *per essempio*), keep the punters cheery. Cigarette card collections, pictures of trams in Deptford High Street, Arsenal paraphernalia and an ex-serviceman's knick-knacks deck the bar and walls. Alongside hang framed pictures of guide dogs funded here.
Games (fruit machine). No piped music or jukebox. Tables outdoors (16, garden). TV.

Jordan

354 Lewisham High Street, SE13 6LE (8690 2054). Ladywell rail. **Open** 11am-11pm Mon-Sat; noon-10.30pm Sun. **Food served** noon-2pm Mon-Fri. **Credit** AmEx, DC, MC, V.
Once the local Hogshead, this cabin-like real ale boozer by Lewisham University Hospital has hardly changed since its current owner bought the lease three years ago. Its old, wooden, beamed interior, dotted with beer barrels, ceramics and brewing accoutrements and set out with small glazed-window dividers, has a long, narrow bar counter between square-shaped front and back areas for boozers and diners. Cask ales, their ABVs faithfully recorded on a board behind the bar, include Cambridge, Stonehenge Green and Orkney Raven among the better known choices of Young's and Greene King IPA. Non-ale drinkers are not forgotten – there's Hoegaarden on draught and several Belgian choices by the bottle. Prices are reasonable – cheap, even – and the standard lunchtime meals fly out of the kitchen at under a fiver a throw.
Babies and children welcome (beer garden, summer only). Games (fruit machine, giant Jenga, quiz machine). Tables outdoors (6, garden). TV (satellite).

Also in the area...

Watch House (JD Wetherspoon) 198-204 High Street, SE13 6JP (8318 3136).

NEW CROSS

The drinking action in New Cross takes place in a small Bermuda Triangle a short distance from Goldsmiths College and New Cross station – although the clientele is not limited to students. Dingy, late-night dives have been replaced by lively, modern-style drinkeries still open just as late (if not later). Typified by the **Goldsmiths Tavern** and the **New Cross Inn** opposite, they attract a more diverse crowd than the crusty mob of yore, and the music is more clubby than the previous retro thrash. It's still edgy enough to be interesting, and mercifully bereft of trendy chains.

Goldsmiths Tavern

316 New Cross Road, SE14 6AF (8692 7381/www.goldsmithstavern.co.uk). New Cross or New Cross Gate tube. **Open** noon-2am Mon-Sat; noon-midnight Sun. **Food served** noon-10pm daily. **Credit** MC, V.
'A cappuccino, a merlot and some oven-baked sea bass, please...' If this seems run-of-the-mill to readers in Belsize Park or Clapham, here it's revolutionary. By Goldsmiths College, in a hub of late-night outlets and takeaways, the Tavern was a cabaret venue in the 1980s (Vic Reeves a regular performer) and a grunge/DJ venue in the 1990s. Seriously grunge. Vomit and needles on the floor, and the men's toilet connecting the two bars. Redone in 2003, it's now an all-in-one pool lounge with squishy sofas and a floor that isn't fuzzy, selling wine (Tinto Monte Clavijo rioja at £3.35 a glass, La Serre sauvignon blanc at £3.20 a glass) and food (decent pastas and salads) from the restaurant, Aldo's, upstairs. Beers include Beck's and Red Stripe on tap and Budvar, Grolsch and Grimbergen by the bottle, served till 2am to a good bunch of young regulars by laconic Aussie Wayne and his sidekick Krystyna. The back room is still used for DJs six nights a week.
Babies and children welcome (restaurant only). Disabled: toilet. Function room. Games (fruit machines, pool). Music (DJs 10pm Mon-Sat; £2-£4 Fri, Sat; occasional live bands). Restaurant. Tables outdoors (12, patio). TV (big screen, digital, widescreen).

Hobgoblin

272 New Cross Road, SE14 6AA (8692 3193). New Cross Gate tube/rail/36, 89, 136, 171, 177 bus. **Open** 11am-11pm Mon-Sat; noon-10.30pm Sun. **Food served** noon-8.30pm Mon-Thur; noon-4pm Fri-Sun. **Happy hour** (students with ID only) 2-8pm Mon-Fri. **No credit cards**.

This Wychwood Brewery pub opposite New Cross Gate station need not sell quality draught ales such as its namesake Hobgoblin, Greene King IPA or Bombardier. Its clientele, perched and slowly slumped on the scuffed wooden tables in the all-in-one main bar, drink standard lagers by the bucketload and feed the jukebox for blasts of the Pixies, White Stripes and Manics. Blokey types do use the place – not least for TV sports, when pitchers of beer are sold at £8 – but this is a pre-party venue for Goldsmiths' students and the eternal adolescents of the neighbourhood. Retro advertising posters, a welcome enclosed back beer garden and Thai food make vague attempts at appealing to the homeowners up on nearby Telegraph Hill, but it's all drowned out in the noise of Nirvana and a sea of lager served by a spiky type in a 'Yoga Kills' T-shirt.

Babies and children welcome (before 7pm; conservatory, garden only). Disabled: toilet. Games (fruit machines, quiz machines). Tables outdoors (8, conservatory; 12, garden). TV (satellite).

Montague Arms

289 Queens Road, SE15 2PA (7639 4923). New Cross or New Cross Gate tube. **Open** 7.30-11.30pm Mon, Tue, Thur-Sat; noon-4pm, 8-10.30pm Sun. **Food served** noon-4pm Sun. **No credit cards**.

Jutting out on a corner of the one-way system by the Old Kent Road estuary, the marvellously kitsch Montague serves coachloads of continental punters on their way down to Dover. That's the theory, anyway, somewhat surpassed by budget air travel and the fact that the locals who fill the place revere it more than any Dutchman could. A live music venue (it was used as a warm-up for the Gang of Four in 2005), it's the regular haunt of keyboard maestro Peter 'Two Moogs' London, one of the first synthesiser players to have graced the capital. The dark, cavernous interior is decked out with zebra heads, old carriages and knick-knacks from landlord Stan's crazy stint in the services. Black Sheep, Deuchar's IPA, London Pride and Ayingerbräu are served , along with mountainous Sunday lunches of whole pheasant (£7.50), fresh trout (£5.50) and roast English gammon in large or jumbo sizes (£5/£6).

Games (fruit machine). Music (musician 9pm Sat; 1.30pm Sun).

PECKHAM

Central Peckham, at the bus-clogged confluence of Peckham Road, Hill Street and High Street, is still best avoided, despite considerable efforts (like the award-winning library) to raise its profile. Up Rye Lane towards Dulwich, however, the area is changing dramatically. The streets are sprouting sculptures and funky lamp-posts, and the pubs are disappearing or turning into bars.

Rye Hotel

31 Peckham Rye, SE15 3NX (7639 5397). Peckham Rye rail/12, 37, 63 bus. **Open** noon-11pm Mon-Thur, Sun; noon-midnight Fri, Sat. **Food served** noon-4pm, 6-10pm Mon-Fri; noon-10pm Sat, Sun. **Credit** MC, V.

The most successful conversion job in these parts, the buzzing Rye Hotel makes its good-natured, young clientele feel appreciated. Fresh flowers, original art (by the chef's husband), newspapers for lazy afternoons and a relaxed attitude at the closing bell augment the bonhomie generated by the energetic and personable bar service. On tap are Fox's Nob, Young's, Hoegaarden and Guinness, while a decent wine list runs up to Craigow pinot noir at £29. The menu is English/Thai, ranging from healthy to exceedingly hearty. Thai fish cakes, green chicken curry with jasmine rice, and spicy lamb 'n' mint sausages all fall in the £8 range, with puddings (including the divine chocolate and coffee variety) at £4. The music is clubby, but not intrusive; squidgy leather sofas and the candlelit, dark-panelled interior complete the classy picture.

Babies and children welcome (before 6pm). Function room. No-smoking area. Specialities (cocktails). Tables outdoors (30, garden).

Wishing Well Inn

79 Choumert Road, SE15 4AR (7639 6444). Peckham Rye rail. **Open** 11am-11pm Mon-Sat; 11am-10.30pm Sun. **Food served** noon-3pm, 6.30-11pm Mon-Fri; noon-5pm Sat, Sun. **No credit cards**.

Close to Peckham Rye station, this remains a good local boozer whose clientele covers a broad spectrum of age and income. Although the titular wishing well was taken out to make room for more outside tables, the dark wood and etched glass interior was restored with the pub drinker in mind. It's not only the Marston's Pedigree on draught, the Hoegaarden, nor even the stellar bangers and mash – it's the fact that the multitude of monitors and big screens are blank except from kick-off time to final whistle, so the quiet pint is still sacrosanct. The atmospheric vault boasts a jukebox and a couple of pool tables; upstairs, as old masters gaze down from the walls, the smart and chatty staff help generate a genial ambience.

Babies and children welcome. Games (pool tables). Jukebox. Quiz (9pm Thur; free). Tables outdoors (5, pavement). TVs (big screen, satellite).

Also in the area...

Kentish Drovers (JD Wetherspoon) 71-79 Peckham High Street, SE15 5RS (7277 4283).

PUTNEY

There are some fine old boozers down by the river at Putney: highly civilised places, steeped in history, at which to chew the fat and enjoy the view. The modern world has a foot in the door, though, especially on the High Street, which until recently was bereft of decent drinking venues.

Bar M

The Star & Garter, 4 Lower Richmond Road, SW15 1JN (8788 0345/www.barm.co.uk). Putney Bridge tube/Putney rail. **Open** 11am-11pm Mon-Sat; noon-10.30pm Sun. **Food served** 11am-10pm Mon-Thur; 11am-9pm Fri, Sat; noon-9pm Sun. **Credit** MC, V.

Loosen the tie, stuff the coat in the corner and get on with the serious matter of post-work drinking: such seems to be the mantra of almost everyone in the rectangular ground-floor room of this no-frills bar. The backdrop for the boozing is prime, though – a splendid sweep of the river by Putney Pier. Bar M's decor (from a page that fell out of the All Bar One design catalogue) and drinks selection (nitrokeg lagers, John Smith's) are less inspiring – but that didn't seem to be a problem for the crowd of off-duty

RAISE A GLASS: WINING OUT

On a recent walk through the West End, I stopped off at a dozen or so wine bars and pubs to check out their wine service by the glass. It was by no means a scientific survey, but it gave me a snapshot of what's happening at the coalface: the meeting point between wine producers and the punters who buy their products in ordinary, non-glam outlets. And it brought some good news and some bad news.

First, the good news. Wines are treated better, on the whole, than they would have been ten years ago in comparable joints. In most of the bars where I asked about wine storage overnight, for instance, they said they took special measures to conserve the freshness of open bottles. The most popular measure is the immensely successful Vacu-Vin, a rubber stopper with a slit cut into its top. You shove the stopper in the bottle, clamp a pump over it and pump till you suck all the air out. Air is the great enemy of wine, and Vacu-Vin is a cheap, easy way of keeping the two apart. It's not perfect – some of the aromatic qualities are pumped out with the air – but it's the best the catering trade can do without investing in more expensive technology. It was in evidence at **Cork & Bottle** (*see p56*), **Grape Street Wine Bar** (*see p26*), **Vats Wine Bar** (*see p49*), and even at All Bar One. **Truckles of Pied Bull Yard** (*see p28*) goes one better by using a machine to pump in inert gas, thus protecting the wine from air even more efficiently.

Now for the bad news. First of all, some of the wines I saw on display were kept at temperatures that do not serve them well in the glass. This applied especially to reds, which were often held on high shelves in quantities that clearly indicated they would be there for awhile. When the term 'room temperature' was devised for serving red wine, rooms were cooler than they are now – and bars can be very warm indeed. Keeping a light, fruity red at warm temperatures will eventually rob it of its freshness, and you'd notice the difference if you tasted it alongside a properly kept bottle. (This is a good reason, by the way, to avoid shops where they keep the wine by a window.) Temperatures for white wine are less crucial, although there's a tendency to keep some of them too cold: in the warmth of the room, they'll soon get up to a better drinking temperature.

Turnover, too, is crucial. If a wine bar keeps its stock in the bar for just a few days, you won't notice any drop-off in quality. More than a week and you should start worrying. Problem

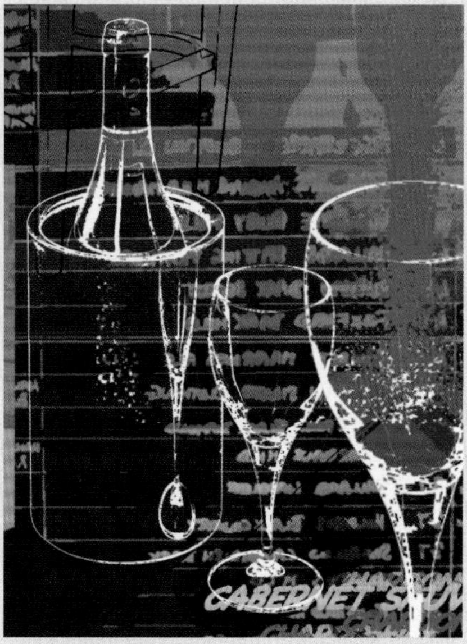

is, it can be hard to get a straight answer when you ask how long various establishments keep their reds at these temperatures, but it's worth asking anyway. Alternatively, use a trick I learned from a source now forgotten, and when you order your glass, ask for it to be poured from the bottle they opened most recently.

The other bad news: the quality of glassware leaves a lot to be desired, especially in pubs. It's a well established fact that the aromas and flavours of different wines are best revealed by glasses of different shapes, yet most of the places I visited had just two types of glass: one type for still wines and a flute version for champagne. And proper glasses – with an elegantly slim stem and bowl curving decisively inward at the rim – were used in only three or four places.

Still, poor glassware isn't the end of the world. Truth be told, if you're in a wine bar for a drink and a snack, you won't be savouring every sip as you would in an expensive restaurant. But that's no reason to accept low standards. If a wine is too warm, explain why you're dissatisfied and ask for another glass. If the glass itself is inferior, find a different place to drink. And remember that last-bottle-opened rule. It may be the best way of all to ensure that the vino is at its best when it makes the journey from bottle to mouth. *Richard Ehrlich*

CID officers cavorting around the tables on our visit. There's also a small basement bar that, although it doesn't stay open past midnight, plays host to DJ nights. *Babies and children admitted (before 7pm): high chairs. Function rooms (2). No-smoking area. Games (fruit machine, quiz machine). TV (big screen, digital).*

Duke's Head

8 Lower Richmond Road, SW15 1JN (8788 2552). Putney Bridge tube/22, 265 bus. **Open** 11am-11pm Mon-Sat; noon-10.30pm Sun. **Food served** noon-2.30pm, 6-10pm Mon-Fri; 11am-10pm Sat; noon-9pm Sun. **Credit** AmEx, MC, V.

This beautiful Victorian pile on the bank of the Thames is partitioned into three areas. The public bar, with its fine circular counter planted in the centre, is a rough and ready place where grizzled regulars tap their feet on the mosaic floor and chat to the affable barmaid, while supping on well-kept Young's ales. The saloon is a larger, more genteel affair, its roaring fire, high ceilings and framed pencil drawings of Thames scenic spots reminiscent of a country manor's drawing room. The third area is the dining room, from where you can gaze through big picture windows at the river, while tucking into roasts, bangers 'n' mash and such like. There are also a few tables outside (ringside seats for the Varsity boat race).

Games (table football). No piped music or jukebox. Tables outdoors (9, riverside patio). TV (satellite).

Green Man

Wildcroft Road, Putney Heath, SW15 3NG (8788 8096). East Putney tube/Putney rail/14, 39, 85, 93, 170 bus. **Open** 11am-11pm Mon-Sat; noon-10.30pm Sun. **Food served** noon-3pm, 6-9.30pm Mon-Fri; noon-9pm Sat; noon-5pm Sun. **Credit** AmEx, MC, V.

The clock set in the whitewashed wall above the front door of this lovely old boozer was running about 20 minutes slow when we came, which seems about right. Refurbished in 2004, the Green Man has lost none of its charm. A warren of small rooms opens off the bar, offering intimacy, if not privacy, on busy Saturday nights. On winter nights an open fire gives the place a country pub feel, and there's a pretty courtyard garden to enjoy in the summer. Warming and generous servings of good pub grub staples are available alongside a short but decent wine list. The wood-panelled walls are decorated with an array of old prints that hint at the history of this area – the Heath was a popular duelling spot in the 1700s – and the ales are from Young's.

Games (fruit machine). Music (live music 9pm Thur; free). Quiz (9pm Tue; £1). Tables outdoors (25, garden). TV.

Half Moon

93 Lower Richmond Road, SW15 1EU (8780 9383/ www.halfmoon.co.uk). Putney Bridge tube/Putney rail. **Open** noon-11pm Mon-Sat; noon-10.30pm Sun. **Credit** MC, V.

A blackboard outside this barn-like Young's boozer highlights the musicians (mostly folk and country, plus tribute bands and DJs) that have appeared here over the years. The tiny writing suggests a certain diligent pride, a feeling that's kept going by the interior's framed pictures of the great, good and bearded musicians that have graced the back room. Nights *sans* music can be slightly dispiriting, though, as lonesome men straddle stools, scruffy locals chat in dark corners, and the vibe seems redolent of a party that's never going to heat up. It's a nice place in which to hide with a paper and a pint of Young's Special, but the Half Moon is undeniably at its best when there's a band in.

Games (board games, pool, quiz machine). Music (bands 8.30pm most nights; from £2.50; Jazz 2-5pm Sun; free). Tables outdoors (8, garden).

Putney Station

94-98 Upper Richmond Road, SW15 2SP (8780 0242/ www.brinkleys.com). East Putney tube. **Open/food served** noon-11pm Mon-Sat; noon-10.30pm Sun. **Happy hour** 5-7pm daily. **Credit** MC, V.

Most of the weary commuters pouring out of East Putney station in the early evening seem to be giving this new wine bar a miss. Pity, really, as the wine list is both adventurous and accessible, starting with a pinot grigio at £9 and including some more obscure South African wines such as a Stellenbosch Rust en Vrede merlot at £15.50. The other shame is that Putney Station, despite its groovy signage, exudes the air of a would-be sophisticated wine bar circa 1982: strip lighting, metal blinds and distressingly Sadé-like soundtrack makes you worry that the next group to walk through the door will be dressed like Bananarama.

Babies and children welcome: high chairs. Disabled: toilet. Music (bands 8pm Wed; free). No-smoking tables. Restaurant. Tables outdoors (4, pavement).

Whistle & Flute

46-8 Putney High Street, SW15 1SQ (8780 5437/ www.fullers.co.uk). Putney Bridge tube/Putney rail. **Open** noon-11pm Mon; 11am-11pm Tue-Sat; noon-10.30pm Sun. **Food served** noon-10pm daily. **Credit** AmEx, MC, V.

Putney High Street has long suffered from a paucity of original drinking venues. In another part of town the Whistle & Flute would be fairly anonymous; compared to much of the competition on this thoroughfare, though, it's a pretty tempting offer. The interior is not especially cosy despite the heavy use of candles and dark-red paint; but it is a great place in which to sample Fuller's ales (including Jack Frost, on our visit), and catch up on gossip with a group of mates – the big tables would make more small-scale get-togethers seem awkward. Two TVs were on during our visit, but everyone was ignoring them in favour of various discussions, most of which seemed to revolve around football.

Disabled: toilet. Babies and children welcome (before 6pm). Games (fruit machine, quiz machine). No-smoking area. TV (satellite).

Also in the area...

Railway (JD Wetherspoon) 202 Upper Richmond Road, SW15 6TD (8788 8190).
Slug & Lettuce 14-16 Putney High Street, SW15 1SL (8785 3081).

SOUTH NORWOOD

Football fans heading towards Selhurst Park for a Crystal Palace game will struggle to find a decent local hostelry for a pre-match pint. The pubs around South Norwood provide little in the way of style: sadly, most of the handsome old venues in the area have had their interiors ripped out and modified beyond recognition. Thank goodness, then, for **Oceans Apart** – a striking break from the norm in an area ripe for some innovation.

Alliance
91 High Street, SE25 6EA (8653 3604). Norwood Junction rail. **Open** 10am-11pm Mon-Sat; noon-10.30pm Sun. **No credit cards**.
Walking through the door that leads into this cosy little corner pub by Norwood Junction station is like entering the *EastEnders* Queen Vic, circa 1985: is that Arfur Fowler scrutinising the *Racing Post*? All the hallmarks of the traditional English pub are in place: decent real ales (from Archers of Swindon), brass saucepans hanging from the ceiling, curmudgeonly old gents grumbling about the tube network, and so on. All well and good, but these old-school values also mean there are no female customers, there's a very smoky atmosphere and there's a cacophony of hacking coughs from the old gents. Still, what's another packet of pork scratchings and a fag between friends? Every pub in London used to be like this, you know.
Babies and children welcome (before 4pm). Games (fruit machines). No-smoking area. TV.

Oceans Apart
152 Portland Road, SE25 4PT (8663 8881/ www.oceansapart-bars.com). Norwood Junction rail/ 30, 197, 312 bus. **Open** noon-11pm Mon-Sat; noon-10.30pm Sun. **Food served** noon-10pm daily. **Credit** AmEx, DC, MC, V.
It's a long trek down the Portland Road to this newcomer. But keep going past the abandoned boozer and the launderette that still advertises its rates in shillings and pence, and you'll find a stylish new pub conversion that, if not oceans, is at least a good few estuaries apart from anything else trading around here. First impressions are of a typical blond wood and blond lager makeover, but there are enough quirky touches to ensure Oceans' definition as a style bar. We're talking about the cute little illuminated pod tables, the cool transparent plastic chairs, and the toffee-coloured sofas that don't look like they've seen too many sprawling drunks. The Motown and soul DJ nights at the weekends are proving a draw as well. Boy, does South Norwood need more places like this.
Babies and children welcome. Disabled: toilet. Games (board games, fruit machines). Music (DJs 7pm Fri-Sat, 1-6pm Sun; free). Tables outdoors (20, garden). TVs (satellite, widescreen).

Also in the area...
William Stanley (JD Wetherspoon) 7-8 High Street, SE25 6EP (8653 0678).

STOCKWELL

SW8 is not the best area for bar hopping, but it still has one or two spots worth seeking out. The north of the South Lambeth Road has a cluster of convivial Portuguese establishments, of which **Bar Estrela** is the star; the whole street came to a standstill for the Euro 2004 final – and the party may still have been going on had Portugal won.

Bar Estrela
111-115 South Lambeth Road, SW8 1UZ (7793 1051). Stockwell tube/Vauxhall tube/rail. **Food served** 8am-midnight daily. **Credit** AmEx, DC, MC, V.
The Estrela (Star) is the brightest and most popular of the Portuguese bars along this stretch of Stockwell's main thoroughfare. In the summer, diners and boozers can log the progress of Mayor Ken's bus proliferation policy from the recently facelifted triangle of pavement outside. The emphasis inside is on function and simplicity, with two TV screens dominated by football and Portuguese broadcasting. The besuited staff stay on the case efficiently enough to keep business ticking along without too much ceremony. Ceres and Sagres are the draught beer options; there's also a decent selection of reasonably priced Spanish and Portuguese wine, and plenty of food options – from small snacks to traditional favourites such as garlic chicken, and *bacalhau* (salt cod), along with sweet treats such as the sublime egg custard and pastry combination *pastel de nata*.
Babies and children welcome: high chairs. Booking advisable. Tables outdoors (10, pavement).

Canton Arms
177 South Lambeth Road, SW8 1XP (7587 3819/www.barbeerian-inns.com). Stockwell tube/Vauxhall tube/rail. **Open** 11am-11pm Mon-Sat; noon-10.30pm Sun. **Food served** noon-2.30pm, 6-9.30pm Mon-Fri; 12.30-3pm, 6.30-9pm Sat; 12.30-4pm, 7-9pm Sun. **Happy hour** 6-7pm Fri, Sat. **Credit** MC, V.
A comfortable and warm neighbourhood local that's large enough to accommodate several micro-cultures of drinkers simultaneously. At one end, big-screen football viewers can enjoy the game from large leather sofas while tucking into pub grub (veal osso bucco, £9.50; mushroom fettuccine, £7.50; twofer burgers in happy hour; and, for some reason, Australian specials). The more bookish crowd gets a corner next to the shelves (and the toilets). On the other side of the octagonal central bar, pub quizzers can test their knowledge as table football players flick their wrists. Only here for the beer? Choose from cask ales such as Old Speckled Hen, Bombardier and Greene King IPA. A predictable range of dodgily named 'Shooters' is offered for those who are after a speedier route to oblivion. The all-Sunday two-for-one Bloody Mary offer is a nice touch.
Babies and children welcome (before 8pm). Games (quiz machine, table football). Quiz (Mon). Tables outdoors (8, patio). TV (big screen, satellite).

Priory Arms
83 Lansdowne Way, SW8 2PB (7622 1884). Stockwell tube. **Open** 11am-11pm Mon-Sat; noon-10.30pm Sun. **Food served** noon-3pm Mon; noon-3pm, 5.30-9.30pm Tue-Sat; 12.30-3.30pm Sun. **Credit** MC, V.
Ghosts of beers past line the walls of this small neighbourhood free house, the best option in Stockwell for quality ale. The Priory mainly attracts older locals, who should be delighted to have such a pub on their doorsteps. There are usually six cask ales to choose from, as well as bottled Belgian and German beers. If you fancy testing your palate further, try the fruit wines, birch, perhaps, or dandelion and apricot. There's seating outside, next to a road full of buses from the nearby depot. New owners have introduced a 'fish at the Priory' evening menu, featuring £3.95 starters (prawns, salmon) and mains such as cod in Adnams ale batter with chips (£6.95). Sunday roasts are served, too. There are chessboards embedded in a couple of the tables, plus a small selection of board games, and a fruit machine. Keen backgammon players abound on Sundays.
Children admitted (Sun lunch only; no pushchairs or under 5s). Function room. Games (fruit machine; backgammon club, Sun afternoon; chess club, Wed afternoon). Quiz (9pm Sun; free). Tables outdoors (8, patio). TV (2, satellite).

Surprise

16 Southville, SW8 2PP (7622 4623). Stockwell tube/Vauxhall tube/rail. **Open** 11am-11pm Mon-Sat; noon-10.30pm Sun. **Food served** noon-3pm daily. **Credit** MC, V.

One to remember when the sun is shining, or when you have kids to entertain or a dog to walk (and fancy a pint at the same time). This small Young's pub is on the edge of Larkhill Park and has its own terrace area; there are barbecues and boules nights held here in the summer. The beer is the usual Young's range – plus Pilsener, Export, Triple A and bottled Ramrod. Food options are pretty basic, but run to jacket potatoes and sandwiches. The front bar is very small, yet there are two large back rooms with fires, one of which is full of caricatures of regulars. The pub dog, Toffee, always gets a lot of attention.

Babies and children welcome. Games (board games, boules pitch, fruit machine). Tables outdoors (12, patio). TV (satellite).

Swan

215 Clapham Road, SW9 9BE (7978 9778/www.theswanstockwell.co.uk). Stockwell tube. **Open** 6pm-2am Thur; 6pm-3am Fri; 7pm-3am Sat; 7pm-2am Sun. **Food served** 9pm-2am daily (bar snacks). **Admission** (prices may vary) free Thur; £3 after 8pm, £5/£6 after 10pm Fri; £3 before 9pm, £6 after 9pm Sat; £3 after 10pm Sun. **Credit** AmEx, DC, MC, V.

A real meat market for the over-refreshed, the Swan is popular with London's Antipodean residents. The pub stands right opposite the tube, and only opens four nights a week, but it often draws large crowds who queue round the block. They come for the heady combination of sketchy tribute acts (bring on the ersatz Red Hot Chili Peppers, Robbie Williams, U2), a disco and, most importantly, the chance to pull a Slovakian nurse or rugby player (depending on persuasions and how many lagers have been sunk). The bouncers have a bit of a reputation – particularly for obscure entrance questions – but they don't bite if handled gently. Bar food (chicken and chips) is included in the admission price and can help stave off total inebriation.

Babies and children welcome (before 7pm weekdays only). Dress code (smart casual, weekends). Music (DJs 8.30pm nightly; bands 9.30pm nightly). TVs.

SYDENHAM

Down-at-heel Sydenham. Its glory days ended with the burning down of the Crystal Palace in the 1930s. The whole area needs a lick of paint, frankly, and most of the local pubs are slightly seedy depressing places where staff grudgingly serve you the bare minimum of nitrokeg lagers and alcopops. The happy exception is below.

Dulwich Wood House

39 Sydenham Hill, SE26 6RS (8693 5666). Sydenham Hill rail/63, 202 bus. **Open** 11am-11pm Mon-Sat; noon-10.30pm Sun. **Food served** noon-3pm, 6-9pm Mon-Sat; noon-4pm Sun. **Credit** MC, V.

Remember John Major's misty-eyed speech about England: cycling spinsters drinking warm beer and all that? Something as quintessentially English is evoked at this gorgeous retreat from the modern world. Built by Joseph Paxton (the man responsible for the mammoth Crystal Palace, which stood down the road until the devastating fire of 1936), the Dulwich Wood House is a solid gem of a boozer with a clutch of wood-panelled rooms. To eat, there's bar food (bangers 'n' mash) and a more substantial restaurant menu (salmon supreme); to drink, there are Young's ales (bitter, Special, Waggledance and a seasonal addition), Young's Pilsner, plus Stella and Guinness.

Babies and children admitted (outside only). Games (fruit machines, quiz machine). No-smoking area. Quiz (7.30pm last Tue of mnth). Tables outdoors (50, garden). TV.

TOOTING

It's a shame, with Tooting supposedly the singles capital of the UK, that so few boozers here have created an environment where they might actually want to meet up. The **Trafalgar** is undoubtedly the pick of the bunch, with the **King's Head** coasting on its reputation a little, and the newer crop of bars still firmly in the shadow of far better alternatives five minutes up the Northern Line.

King's Head

84 Upper Tooting Road, SW17 7PB (8767 6708). Tooting Bec tube. **Open** 11am-11pm Mon-Sat; noon-10.30pm Sun. **Food served** noon-10pm daily. **Credit** MC, V.

More a multiscreen football experience than a pub, the King's Head has goal-mouths visible in every direction, distracting your attention from what has been a remarkable restoration job. Elegant wooden panelling, etched-glass partitions and fronds of greenery give an authentic Victorian feel. There are no such allusions behind the bar, though, with that ubiquitous fridge full of Aftershock and an underwhelming lager selection. Empty glasses slung on real ale pumps to indicate they're 'off' is a regular and predictable sight, and the bar staff seem rather jaded with their 'young and lively' (or is it 'pissed and rowdy'?) clientele. Yet there are saving graces: an extensive menu featuring salads, sandwiches, main courses and desserts is chalked up in friendly lower-case letters; and the place is so huge that if you arrive early you're certain of a table and a seat. How long you'll want to stay is another matter.

Disabled: toilet. Games (pool, quiz machine). Quiz (8pm Sun; £1). Tables outdoors (14, garden). TV (big screen, satellite).

smoke bar diner

14 Trinity Road, SW17 7RE (8767 3902/www.smokebardiner.com). Tooting Bec tube. **Open** 5pm-midnight Mon-Fri; noon-midnight Sat; noon-10.30pm Sun. **Food served** 5-10pm Mon-Fri; noon-10pm Sat, Sun. **Credit** MC, V.

Appearing deceptively small from the front – almost like a scaled-down All Bar One – this increasingly well-patronised bar has a more unusual and spacious back room. Enter here and you'll find the kind of office furniture that ten years ago would have passed for junk, but now is most definitely vintage. It's certainly comfortable, and a chic crowd nestles gently amid the leather and the steel tubing, while examples from the range of particularly sugary cocktails perch on glass-topped coffee tables. A combination of passion-fruit vodka and chambord is the pick of the bunch at £5.50. Customers with not quite as

Half Moon.
See p213.

sweet a tooth go for pints of Staropramen or Boddingtons, poured by attentive and amiable staff. The grim landscapes and glass bricks add to the corporate 1980s feel, but the sounds are up-to-date (matching the taste of the alterno crowd) and range from driving drum 'n' bass to pounding indie guitar.
Disabled: toilet. Function room. Music (DJs 7pm Fri; free). TV (big screen, satellite).

Spirit Bar Café
94 Tooting High Street, SW17 0RR (8767 3311). Tooting Broadway tube. **Open** 11am-midnight Mon-Sat; 11am-10.30pm Sun. **Food served** noon-3pm, 6-10pm Mon-Fri; 11am-10pm Sat; 11am-6pm Sun. **Credit** AmEx, MC, V.
Taking the place of a grim wine bar, Spirit has been persistently popular ever since it opened in the late 1990s. The owners try to attract a glamorous crowd – difficult in SW17 – and they almost manage it; football fans make up the rest of the clientele, sitting in the rear room in front of a large plasma screen. Food-wise, mains are cheap at around £7, but the menu sometimes writes cheques the kitchen can't cash: peach salsa, anyone? On similar lines, it's probably a bad idea to hold a cocktail promotion when your bar staff think that a Mojito consists of half a glass of soda water with a couple of mint leaves floating in it. But the gentle lounge sounds are pleasant and unobtrusive, while the wine list (featuring zinfandel, grenache and chenin blanc) is a cut above the usual pub selection.
Babies and children admitted. Function room. No-smoking area. Tables outdoors (pavement). TV (2, satellite).

South

Trafalgar Arms
148 Tooting High Street, SW17 0RT (8767 6059). Tooting Broadway tube. **Open** noon-11pm Mon-Sat; noon-10.30pm Sun. **Food served** noon-9pm daily. **Credit** MC, V.
This glorious pub seems to be earning more pink pounds than ever, with ear-splitting nights of transvestite bingo and camp karaoke held regularly; meanwhile, the local straight crowd is still perfectly happy with its combo of burgers, beers and board games. Discounts for those working at the nearby St George's Hospital ensure that the Trafalgar is always busy (spot the inebriated doctor). The food is plentiful, cheap and high on carbs, and the beer selection rotates regularly (on our visit the pumps ran from nitrokeg lagers to Shepherd Neame Spitfire and Greene King IPA). In summer months, customers spill out on to benches arrayed on the black tarmac forecourt; it's hardly a beer garden, with the A23 within spitting distance, but it's a highly popular spot all the same. Efficient, friendly service, plus a blazing fire and candlelit tables, add to the laid-back atmosphere. Highly recommended.
Babies and children admitted (until 9pm). Drag bingo (Thur). Games (board games, fruit machines). No-smoking area. Tables outdoors (20, pavement).

VAUXHALL

Though long a centre of the capital's gay scene, with clubs blaring away into the small hours for massed ranks of hedonistic boyz, Vauxhall's boozing scene is slight. The recent makeover of the **Fentiman Arms** is certainly progress, though.

Fentiman Arms
64 Fentiman Road, SW8 1LA (7793 9796/www.geronimo-inns.co.uk). Vauxhall or Oval rail/tube. **Open** 11am-11pm Mon-Sat; noon-10.30pm Sun. **Food served** 11am-3.30pm, 7-9.30pm Mon-Fri; 11am-4pm, 7-9.30pm Sat; noon-4pm, 7-9.30pm Sun. **Credit** MC, V.
Once renowned for having the slowest and rudest staff of any pub south of the Thames, the Fentiman (a branch of the usually reliable Geronimo Inns group) has recently had its brusque customer service replaced with, if not outright smiles, then at least something approaching conviviality. The pub itself is a welcoming spot, occupying a cosy corner site hidden snugly between the elegant townhouses of this more moneyed niche of Oval. Its pebbled beer garden is an attractive proposition come the summer, and the beer, although pricey, is an admirable selection that includes San Miguel, Wadworth 6X, Greene King IPA and Bombardier on draught. With all this to brag about, you'd have thought the staff would have cheered up long ago.
Babies and children admitted. Comedy (8pm Tue). Function room. Music (jazz, Sun, free). No-smoking area. Tables outdoors (15, garden). TV (satellite).

WANDSWORTH

Popular with well-heeled young familes, this area has some array of smart and sensible boozers. The **Hope** continues to flourish as one of the best pubs south of any river, let alone the Thames, with wonderful views of the common; and there's a quota of quirkiness on offer in places like the lovingly preserved and restored **Ship**. The pubs we list are spread over a wide area, so wear decent shoes if you're planning a crawl.

Alma
499 Old York Road, SW18 1TF (8870 2537/www.thealma.co.uk). Wandsworth Town rail. **Open** 11am-11pm Mon-Sat; noon-10.30pm Sun. **Credit** AmEx, MC, V.
Walk out of Wandsworth Town station and you have little choice but to step straight in through the front door of this ever-lively gem. The large circular bar in the middle is frantic with staff tending to the needs of a smart after-work crowd, serving Young's ales made at the brewery less than half a mile away. When the fire is aflame and the restaurant room at the back is full (good gastropub food is served), there are few more welcoming places south of the river. The Alma is popular for the big rugby games, and there's a wide variety of champagne, which should come in handy next time England win the Six Nations.
Babies and children admitted; high chairs. Booking advisable. Disabled: toilet. Function room. TVs.

ditto
55-57 East Hill, SW18 2QE (8877 0110/www.doditto.co.uk). Wandsworth Town/Clapham Junction rail. **Open** noon-11pm Mon-Fri; 9.30am-11pm Sat, Sun. **Food served** noon-2.30pm, 6.30-11pm Mon-Fri; 9.30am-11pm Sat, Sun. **Credit** MC, V.
Given a long sliver of space with a paucity of natural light, you might feel that the options are bound to be limited. But the owners here have done much to overcome feelings of dinginess, with candles, pale walls, and lovely saggy sofas. There are classic cocktails at £5.25 or £6.25, draught beers

include Stella and Staropramen, and the menu includes Mod-Euro dishes and comfort food. Wine is something of a specialism here: the globe-trotting list has 20 or so reds and the same number of whites, roughly half are available by the glass, and there are regular 'Wine Dinners', where a guest speaker from a wine estate comes to explain the merits of the wine you're eating with your meal. Oh, and the silk-shirted barmen are exceptionally polite.
Babies and children admitted. Function room. Games (backgammon). No-smoking area. Restaurant. TV (big screen, satellite).

East Hill

21 Alma Road, SW18 1AA (8874 1833). Wandsworth Town rail. **Open** 11am-11pm Mon-Sat; noon-10.30pm Sun. **Food served** noon-3pm, 6-10pm Mon-Fri; noon-9pm Sat, Sun. **Credit** MC, V.
Tucked away on a backstreet corner off East Hill, this pleasant little place has a laid-back decor of yellow paint and scuffed wood. Open bookcases help break up the space around a semi-circular bar offering London Pride bitter, guest ales like Adnams Broadside and Marston's Pedigree, as well as big-brand lagers, and Aspall cider from Suffolk. Patrons are encouraged to take out and peruse the books on the shelves, though it's a mongrel library, for sure: *Just William* or *How to Keep Ponies*, for example. The menu lists gastro staples (when will the craze for fish cakes end?) and there's a pile of board games.
Babies and children admitted. Games (board games). Quiz (8pm Sun; £1). Tables outdoors (4, paved area). TVs (satellite).

Freemasons

2 Wandsworth Common Northside, SW18 2SS (7326 8580). Clapham Junction rail. **Open** noon-11pm Mon-Sat; noon-10.30pm Sun. **Food served** noon-3pm, 6.30-10pm Mon-Fri; 12.30-3.30pm, 6.30-10pm Sat; 12.30-4pm, 6.30-9.30pm Sun. **Credit** AmEx, MC, V.
The people squeezed into this new, stylish little bar on the north side of Wandsworth Common are young, good-looking and very well-bred. Their good taste shows in their choice of venue as much as their choice of clothing, for the Freemasons' food menu is terrific: pan-fried venison, on our visit, made in an open kitchen that sent out a succession of wonderfully moreish aromas. The ales (Everards Tiger and Timothy Taylor Landlord) are well kept, and the other draught options include Früli, Staropramen, Leffe Blonde and Hoegaarden. The place was bursting at the seams on our midweek evening visit: a good sign.
Babies and children welcome: high chairs. Disabled: toilet. No-smoking area. Restaurant. Tables outdoors (8, patio). TV (widescreen).

Hope

1 Bellevue Road, SW17 7EG (8672 8717). Wandsworth Common rail. **Open** noon-11pm Mon-Sat; noon-10.30pm Sun. **Food served** noon-10pm Mon-Sat; noon-9pm Sun. **Credit** AmEx, MC, V.
The Hope has some fine qualities, but puns aren't among them: 'Don't wine with our fine selection of wines', warns the blackboard outside. Things improve from here on in: the array of fairy lights inside creates a festive feel, and the good cheer continues with deluxe comfort food like a fish-finger sandwich with lime and mayo. There's a good choice of beers on draught, including Staropramen, Grolsch, and regularly changing ales (recently Deuchars IPA, London Pride and Black Sheep). A Tuesday night ale club and an acoustic night on Fridays are further attractions. There's a nice mix of mismatched tables and seats (we like the red 1950s diner seats by the window), all of which were full of young, laid-back locals on our visit.
Disabled: toilet. Music (bands 7.30pm Fri; free). Quiz (8.30pm Mon; £3). Tables outdoors (15, patio).

Nightingale

97 Nightingale Lane, SW12 8NX (8673 1637). Clapham South tube/Wandsworth Common rail.
Open 11am-11pm Mon-Sat; noon-10.30pm Sun.
Food served noon-2.30pm, 6pm-9.30pm Mon-Fri; noon-3pm Sat; 1pm-4pm Sun. **Credit** MC, V.
This no-nonsense boozer from the Young's stable has been around for over 150 years. Middle-aged couples looked perfectly happy eating at the bar, though that's not to say the Nightingale has undergone a gastro revolution: steak and kidney pudding, and smoked haddock and spinach fish cakes are two of the choices. There's a lovely walled beer garden (reached through a tiny side room), but the pub is just as popular in winter, when a diverse crowd of lads, gents and couples come to enjoy the lively and homely atmosphere. The beers include Young's lagers (Pilsner and Export) and ales ('ordinary', Special and one seasonal extra), as well as less ambitious choices like Stella.
Babies and children admitted (no-smoking area). Games (board games, darts, fruit machine). No-smoking area. Quiz (7.30pm first Tue of mth). Tables outdoors (12, garden). TV.

Ship

41 Jew's Row, SW18 1TB (8870 9667). Wandsworth Town rail. **Open** 11am-11pm Mon-Sat; noon-10.30pm Sun. **Food served** noon-10.30pm Mon-Sat; noon-10pm Sun. **Credit** AmEx, DC, MC, V.
A lovely pub in unlovely surroundings – right by an urban wasteland near the river – but the Ship shines like a beacon, part of a quartet of pubs (including the nearby Alma, *see p222*, and the Grove) owned by farming couple Charles and Linda Gotto. The interior was revamped a few years ago, and the unpolished, stripped-down tables and floors, fine vintage jukebox (unplugged on our visit), huge industrial boiler fire (clamped to the middle of the conservatory floor) and general rough-round-the-edges feel means the Ship's legacy as a working-class dockers' pub has been remembered – even if customers these days are a far more monied bunch. Young's ales are the beers of choice, though there's also Young's Pilsner, Hoegaarden, Stella, Foster's, Kronenbourg and Guinness on draught. The back garden is a popular draw in summer for its barbecues. A split-level riverside beer garden is the scene of some serious barbecues in summer.
Babies and children admitted (before 7pm). Function room. Restaurant. Specialities (real ales). Tables outdoors (30, riverside garden). TV.

Also in the area…

Pitcher & Piano 11 Bellevue Road, SW17 7EG (8767 6982).
Tonsley Tup 1 Ballantine Street, SW18 1AL (8877 3766).

WIMBLEDON & EARLSFIELD

Wimbledon's drinking scene is much as it's always been: the livelier joints tend to be on the Broadway; classier and daytime venues

CRITICS' PICKS

For beers and ales
Blacksmith's Arms (*see p195*), **Dog & Bell** (*see p206*), **Greenwich Union** (*see p210*), **Jordan** (*see p215*), **Market Porter** (*see p199*), **Microbar** (*see p194*), **Royal Oak** (*see p200*), **Zero Degrees** (*see p197*).

For cocktails
Crown (*see p214*), **Exhibit** (*see p190*) **Inc Bar & Restaurant** (*see p210*), **Sand** (*see p205*), **Tongue & Groove** (*see p201*).

For the strong stuff
Brixtonian Havana Club (rum; *see p200*), **Coach & Horses** (whisky; *see p204*), **Inc Bar & Restaurant** (whisky; *see p210*), **Number 22** (*see p213*).

For wine
Corum (*see p193*), **Garrison** (*see p195*), **Matilda** (*see p194*), **S Bar** (*see p194*), **SO.UK** (*see p206*), **Wine Wharf** (*see p200*).

For sheer style
Dusk (*see p193*), **Inc Bar & Restaurant** (*see p210*), **SO.UK** (*see p206*).

For some open sky
Richard I (*see p212*), **Surprise** (*see p220*), **Trafalgar Tavern** (*see p212*), **Wibbley Wobbley** (*see p196*), **Woodman** (*see p195*).

For fine views
Bridge House (*see p199*), **Cutty Sark Tavern** (*see p210*), **Founder's Arms** (*see p199*).

For a blast from the past
Cutty Sark Tavern (*see p210*), **Lord Clyde** (*see p199*), **Trinity Arms** (*see p202*).

For fun and games
Hobgoblin (pool; *see p209*), **Tea Room des Artistes** (chess, table football; *see p194*).

For real fires
Bedford (*see p190*), **Beehive** (*see p214*), **Blythe Hill Tavern** (*see p203*), **Commercial** (*see p213*), **Far Side** (*see p201*).

For good food
Le Bouchon Bordelais (*see p193*), **Corum** (*see p193*), **Dartmouth Arms** (*see p209*), **Greenwich Union** (*see p210*), **Hartley** (*see p195*), **Matilda** (*see p194*).

For the sound of music
Bedford (*see p190*), **Oliver's** (*see p211*), **Rutland Arms** (*see p204*), **Swan** (*see p220*), **Windmill** (*see p202*).

are closer to the famous tennis courts and the Common in Wimbledon Village, atop Wimbledon Hill Road. This year's newcomer is the **Suburban Bar & Lounge**, which stands on the site of the popular Hartfield's Wine Bar.

Alexandra
33 Wimbledon Hill Road, SW19 7NE (8947 7691). Wimbledon tube/rail. **Open** *Pub* 11am-11pm Mon-Sat; noon-10.30pm Sun. *Wine bar* noon-11pm Mon-Thur; noon-1am Fri, Sat; noon-10.30pm Sun. **Food served** noon-3pm, 6-9.30pm Mon-Sat; noon-6pm Sun. **Admission** £5 after 9.30pm Fri, Sat. **Credit** AmEx, DC, MC, V.

This Young's establishment, a stone's throw from Wimbledon station, was built in 1874. The main pub is flanked by a sports bar and saloon, but you're best off heading to the large and buzzy wine bar ('the Smart Alex') that adjoins it. This does a busy lunchtime trade in old-school pub grub (pie 'n' mash, fish 'n' chips, pasta, sarnies, steaks) and is full of cheerful young professionals come evening. The wine bar also has a late licence and hosts occasional live music. In summer, the small roof garden is a pleasant spot that comes with its own bar (though the view is of the busy main road below – look at the hanging baskets instead). The boozer, meanwhile, is for older, crossword-loving locals, and has some good Young's ales on tap: St George's, Special and Waggledance on our visit.

Disabled: toilet (wine bar). Games (fruit machine, quiz machine, golf machine). Music (band 9.30pm Fri, Sat; £5 after 9.30pm). No-smoking area. Quiz (7.30pm alternate Tue; £1). Tables outdoors (15, roof garden; 6, pavement). TVs (big screen, satellite).

Bar Café
153-161 The Broadway, SW19 1NE (8543 5083). South Wimbledon tube/Wimbledon tube/rail. **Open/food served** 11am-11.30pm daily. **Credit** AmEx, MC, V.

On a stretch of road that has long been a little drab compared to the rest of Wimbledon, the Bar Café has done a fair bit to liven things up. On Fridays and Saturdays, this large space (with a capacity of up to 550) sees DJ John Garcia playing soul and house from the past three decades, plus R&B and other grooves. There are also salsa classes every Wednesday evening (the space in front of the bar easily adapts to dancefloor duties). Outside there's pavement seating and room for drinking at the front. Simple bar food and snacks are on the menu, along with a varied choice of bottled beers from £2.50; the limited draught selection includes Kronenbourg Blanc and John Smith's. Take heed, though – prices increase at peak times; the price list in the porch helps predict the night's expenditure.

Disabled: toilet. Dress: weekend evenings, smart. Function room. Music (DJs 8pm Fri, Sat). Salsa classes (7.30pm beginner, 8.30pm intermediate, Wed; £4). Tables outdoors (6-18, patio). TV (satellite).

Bar Sia
105-109 The Broadway, SW19 1QG (8540 8339/www.barsia.com). South Wimbledon tube/Wimbledon tube/rail. **Open/food served** 4pm-midnight Mon-Thur; 4pm-2am Fri; noon-2am Sat; noon-11.30pm Sun. **Credit** AmEx, DC, MC, V.

The stylish Bar Sia, apparently named after the owner's grandmother, is now a bouncing three-year-old. It's housed in one of Wimbledon's most interesting buildings: the

downstairs bar/function room used to be Turkish baths that were once frequented by actors from the Wimbledon Theatre, which still stands next door. Inside, the main drinking den has adopted a wood, metal and concrete look, with brown leather sofas occupied by a crowd up for some fun. The usual Foster's, Kronenbourg, John Smith's and Guinness are on tap, and cocktails run from £5.70 to £6.90. Thursdays (dedicated to jazz) and Fridays (house and funk) see DJs liven up the atmosphere further. Table service means that there's little inducement to move on.
Bar available for hire. Dress: smart casual. Music (jazz 8pm alternate Thur; DJs 8pm Fri, Sat). TV (satellite).

Common Room

18 High Street, SW19 5DX (8944 1909/www.jamies bars.co.uk). Wimbledon tube/rail. **Open and Food served** 11am-11pm Mon-Thur; 11am-midnight Sat; 11am-10.30pm Sun. **Credit** AmEx, MC, V.
This spacious place is all about joviality and living-room comfort. There are pastel shades, brown leather sofas, a big telly, children, inoffensive music and a sweet back yard that's nice in summer. You can get satisfying snacks for around a fiver (tapas and the like), while mains range from modish (spinach filo parcels with salmon) to comforting (burgers), with kids' versions of meals also provided. On the drinks list are nearly 30 wines (this is a branch of the Jamies wine bar chain, after all), and if the beers on tap are uninspiring, there are bottles of more unusual beers like Warsteiner, Steinlager and König. A list of 17 cocktails completes the picture; the Wimbledon Shake (Bailey's, Cointreau, strawberries and cream, £7) reminds you that the All England Lawn Tennis Club is just down the hill.
Babies and children welcome: children's menu; high chairs. Disabled toilet. Games (board games). No-smoking area (until 6pm). Tables outdoors (12, patio). TV (satellite).

Earl Spencer

260-262 Merton Road, SW18 5JL (8870 9244/www.theearlspencer.co.uk). Southfields tube. **Open** 11am-11pm Mon-Sat; noon-10.30pm Sun. **Food served** 12.30-2.30pm, 7-10pm Mon-Sat; 12.30-3pm, 7-9.30pm Sun. **Credit** AmEx, MC, V.
This large, spacious pub and dining room has no music, but remains lively enough with the chat and bustle of young professionals. There's plenty to drink on draught; as well as the regulars (Beck's, Foster's, Guinness, London Pride, Spitfire), there's Hook Norton bitter from the Oxfordshire village of the same name. Vinophiles have a 38-strong wine list (£10-£30), with 11 available by the glass, plus rosés, sparkling and dessert options. Served in the separate dining area is a varied menu of global cuisine. Lunch could be pan-fried skate wings (£11.50) or chicken liver and foie gras parfait toast and plum chutney (£6.50); dinner might include New England smoked haddock, clam chowder, peas and cornbread (£11.50). There are some nice veggie dishes, too. A winner.
Babies and children admitted; high chairs. Function room. Live music (1st Wed of mth). No piped music or jukebox. Tables outdoors (10, patio).

Eclipse

57 High Street, SW19 5EE (8944 7722/www.eclipse-ventures.com). Wimbledon tube/rail/93 bus. **Open/food served** 5pm-midnight Tue-Thur; 4pm-midnight Fri; 1-10.30pm Sat, Sun. **Admission** £5 (after 11pm Thur; 10.30pm Fri, Sat). **Credit** AmEx, MC, V.
The choice of bars in Wimbledon has changed little over the past couple of years – so the small Eclipse remains one of the district's best evenings-only establishments. As the venue is located in Wimbledon Village, it comes into its own during the tennis fortnight (the All England Lawn Tennis Club is down the hill, along nearby Church Road). Inside, there's just one room of leather brown chairs and banquettes that can stuff in about 70 or so people (well-dressed, of course); the remainder spill outside in summer. Punters spend around £5 to £7 a throw on the bar's cocktails; there's a smattering of deli-style snacks on the menu, too. No beers on tap, but the bottled selection includes Nastro Azzurro and Finland's Lapin Kulta. Pitch up on Friday and Saturday nights for the live bongo player.
Tables outdoors (10, pavement). TV (big screen, tennis only).

Fire Stables

27-29 Church Road, SW19 5DQ (8946 3197). Wimbledon tube/rail, then 93, 200, 493 bus. **Open** 11am-11pm Mon-Sat; 11.30am-10.30pm Sun. **Food served** noon-3pm, 6-10.30pm Mon-Fri; noon-4pm, 6-10.30pm Sat; noon-4pm, 6-10pm Sun. **Credit** MC, V.
The Fire Stables is Wimbledon Village's last port of call before Church Road slopes down to the lawn tennis clubs. It's also one of Wimbledon's classiest haunts. The stylish contemporary look includes the requisite brown leather sofas, two open fires and a garden area at the back that makes for a pretty view (though it's too small to hold any seats). Lunchtime sees happy lone diners and groups of pals treating themselves from the admirable wine and food list. There are 20 red and 20 white wines on the blackboard; the menu, which changes daily, includes the likes of beef tagine (£11.50), sea bass with saffron risotto (£14) and old faithfuls like lamb burgers with chips (£8.50). Eavesdropping on staff, we learned that the place was fully booked for food that evening – not bad for a Monday.
Babies and children admitted (high chairs). Disabled: toilet. No-smoking area. Restaurant. TV (digital, widescreen).

Fox & Grapes

9 Camp Road, SW19 4UN (8946 5599). Wimbledon tube/rail. **Open** 11am-11pm Mon-Sat; noon-10.30pm Sun. **Food served** noon-9.45pm Mon-Sat; noon-9.30pm Sun. **Credit** MC, V.
This one-time riding stable (and sometime changing room for Wimbledon football club) occupies a small spot on the edge of Wimbledon Common. By and large, walkers and their dogs make up the lunchtime habitués, the latter ending up asleep on the floor. While they doze, their owners listen to piped music and decide which ale to drink; there's Courage Best, Directors and Bombardier on draught. Children are welcome, and at lunchtime add to the noisy-cosy atmosphere. The F&G also ensures its diners are well fed; the separate dining area has a makeshift deli counter, where pork pies and pâtés are among the provisions on offer. Sit-down lunches include lamb chops, lasagnes, smoked haddock and sausages, and cost around £7.50. There's an in-house cash machine, too.
Babies and children welcome (before 8pm). Function room. No-smoking bar. TV (big screen, satellite).

Garage

20 Replingham Road, SW18 5LS (8874 9370). Southfields tube. **Open** noon-11pm Mon-Sat; noon-10.30pm Sun. **Food served** noon-8pm daily. **Credit** MC, V.

This reasonably sized, single-room bar just a short walk from Southfields station has ditched its 'Old' prefix and now attracts an upbeat, young crowd. The owners nobly dedicate themselves to showing football and rugby on a regular basis: the bar's fashionably bare-brick walls are dotted with small screens. As for drinks, the Garage is the proverbial Foster's-on-tap kind of place. Its beer pumps are encased in ice to produce an extra-cool pint (ace in summer), and though the cocktail list is small, this is one of the cheapest places in Wimbledon in which to mix your drinks; cocktail prices start at £4, which explains why alcopops, pitchers and shooters remain the order of the day.
Disabled: toilet. Games (fruit machines). TV (satellite).

Hand in Hand

6 Crooked Billet, SW19 4RQ (8946 5720). Wimbledon tube/rail. **Open** 11am-11pm Mon-Sat; noon-10.30pm Sun. **Food served** 12.30-3pm, 7-9.30pm Mon-Sat; noon-4pm, 7-9pm Sun. **Credit** AmEx, MC, V.
A quaint Young's pub, the Hand in Hand is deceptively small on the outside, though it's large and spacious within. It's the sort of place where local Kiwis sit and chat to the staff behind the bar, with no music to interrupt proceedings. Young's ales are on draught, but we recommend opting instead for the wines; there are 12 or so each of whites and reds, but also a couple of interesting fruit wines, including peach, redcurrant and blackcurrant flavours at £2.50 a glass. In summer, punters who spill out into the twee front yard get an eyeful of part of the Common and the prestigious King's College School. Yes, it's posh in these parts.
Babies and children admitted (separate area): children's menu. Games (darts, quiz machine). Tables outdoors (3, courtyard).

Leather Bottle

538 Garratt Lane, SW17 0NY (8946 2309). Earlsfield rail. **Open** 11am-11pm Mon-Sat; noon-10.30pm Sun. **Food served** noon-3pm, 6-10pm Mon-Fri; noon-10pm Sat, Sun. **Credit** MC, V.
This handsome 18th-century Young's pub is yet another place that the comfortably-off and professionals of Wimbledon and Earlsfield use for skiving purposes. The Leather Bottle merrily caters for all seasons. A large front patio (overlooking busy Garratt Lane and the school opposite), and a covered yard at the back, are appealing summer assets, while the back yard also contains a barbecue. In winter, drinkers warm themselves next to an open fire. Those who stick indoors are treated to dark wood furnishings, and decorations including stuffed animals and (yes) a leather bottle. A narrow main bar area dispenses the beers (on our visit, 'ordinary', St George's, Special and Waggledance); there's some basic pub grub on offer, too.
Babies and children admitted. Disabled: toilet. Restaurant. Tables outdoors (85, garden). TV.

Rose & Crown

55 High Street, SW19 5BA (8947 4713). Wimbledon tube/rail/93 bus. **Open** 11am-11pm Mon-Sat; noon-10.30pm Sun. **Food served** noon-3pm, 6-10pm Mon-Thur; noon-10pm Sat; noon-9pm Sun. **Credit** AmEx, DC, MC, V.
There's been a pub on this site since the 17th century, and it was something of a literary haunt during Victoria's reign; the poet Swinburne used to drink here. Today, the Rose & Crown is still a cosy spot, the sort of pub where moneyed middle-aged locals read the *FT* and compare ski resorts; the lack of music means the pub hums with chatter. The drinks list encompasses the usual keg beers (Foster's, Stella, Guinness and so on), but, this being a Young's pub, Young's Bitter, Special and the brewery's seasonal ales are also available on draught. A very decent wine list includes 14 options by the glass (and several bottles costing around £12). Main meals (fish, sausages, pies, chips, smoked haddock, pastas, salads and risottos) hover around the £8 mark. There's an open fire in winter and a beer garden for the summer.
Babies and children admitted (conservatory). Disabled: toilet. Games (fruit machine). No-smoking area. Tables outdoors (14, patio). TV (satellite).

Suburban Bar & Lounge

27 Hartfield Road, SW19 3SG (8543 9788/www.suburbanbar.com). Wimbledon tube/rail. **Open** 5-11pm Mon-Sat; 5-10.30pm Sun. **Credit** AmEx, MC, V.
Hartfield's Wine Bar has gone, and the Suburban has taken its place. It's a smart affair, with rich, brown furnishings, chocolate-coloured walls and terracotta tiles decorating the face of the bar. It's primarily a cocktail bar for the young and lively (and the well-turned-out – the sign on the door says that if you're wearing work wear, you ain't coming in). The cocktail list includes non-alcoholic varieties and ingredients such as ice-cream; most of them are well priced at around a fiver. We can't tell whether the Suburban will be as popular as Hartfield's, but given its style, value and site (within staggering distance of Wimbledon station) we reckon it stands a good chance.
Disabled: toilet. Specialities (cocktails). Tables outdoors (garden).

Sultan

78 Norman Road, SW19 1BT (8542 4532). Colliers Wood tube. **Open** noon-11pm Mon-Sat; noon-10.30pm Sun. **Credit** MC, V.
It might be a grand name for a modest backstreet location, but this king among boozers is named after a great racehorse of the 1830s. Inside, the Sultan is a magnet for ale lovers: this is the only London pub owned by Salisbury's Hopback Brewery, and it serves that establishment's wonderful GFB, Summer Lightning and Entire Stout. You can even take a polypin or minipin of draught ale home with you. Beer lovers will also appreciate the beer club every Wednesday evening, when real ale is just £1.70 a pint; they'll be reassured, too, by the many CAMRA award certificates around one of the pub's three open fires. New pine tables and bar stools furnish the interior, with unobtrusive piped radio providing the backing track. Outside, there's an appealing beer garden, which comes complete with barbecue for the summer months. A worthy winner of the Best Pub category in Time Out's 2004 Eating & Drinking awards.
Disabled: toilet. Quiz (9pm Tue; £1). Specialities (real ales). Tables outdoors (11, patio).

Also in the area...

All Bar One 37-39 Wimbledon Hill Road, SW19 7NA (8971 9871).
Slug & Lettuce 21 Worple Road, SW19 4DH (8971 6790).
Walkabout 74-78 The Broadway, SW19 1RQ (8543 8624).
Wibbas Down Inn (JD Wetherspoon) 6-12 Gladstone Road, SW19 1QT (8540 6788).

WEST

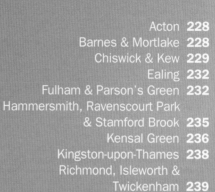

Kwak glass & Beer from Belgo

WEST

ACTON

Acton's contribution to the West London pub scene is, at best, modest – though the **Grand Junction Arms** is an unexpected find in an unpromising neighbourhood. Otherwise, the best pickings are to be found near Uxbridge Road, the Steyne Road and the High Street, which offers a slew of chain bars.

Grand Junction Arms

Acton Lane, NW10 7AD (8965 5670). Harlesden tube. **Open** *Front bar* 11am-11pm Mon-Sat; noon-10.30pm Sun. *Back bar* noon-11pm Mon-Thur; noon-midnight Fri, Sat; noon-10.30pm Sun. **Food served** noon-3pm, 6-9pm Mon-Sat; noon-4pm Sun. **Credit** AmEx, MC, V.

It's hard to imagine a less appealing location for a pub, amid the industrial hinterland of call centres and courier depots that comprise much of this rather grotty corner of West London; but, to be fair, the Grand Junction Arms is rather a likeable old joint. In addition to the relatively small front bar, which fills up with the local office crowd at lunchtime, there are a couple of more spacious side rooms, and a large beer garden overlooking the Grand Union Canal (this place was originally built as a stable to serve the nearby moorings). On tap are Young's Export plus a couple of seasonal ales.

Babies and children admitted (before 7pm, weekends only); play area. Disabled: toilet. Games (football machine, fruit machine, pool). Music (band or karaoke 9pm Fri; free-£7). Tables outdoors (20, garden). TVs (digital, satellite, widescreen).

Also in the area...

Red Lion & Pineapple (JD Wetherspoon) 281 High Street, W3 9PJ (8896 2248).

BARNES & MORTLAKE

Often overlooked in favour of Richmond and Hammersmith, their more imposing neighbours, these attractive little pockets of West London were once entirely separate villages. That still shows today, though they can now be reached by more than just marsh or river. The **Sun Inn** on Barnes village green is perhaps the most idyllically positioned boozer of this bunch, although all but two directly overlook the Thames.

Bull's Head

373 Lonsdale Road, SW13 9PY (8876 5241). Hammersmith tube, then 209 or 283 bus/ Barnes Bridge rail. **Open** 11am-11pm Mon-Sat; noon-10.30pm Sun. **Food served** noon-2.30pm, 6-10.30pm daily. **Credit** AmEx, MC, V.

An unlikely marriage of jazz and Thai food is consummated nightly in this appealing old riverside pub, and while it is not quite the world-famous music mecca it promotes itself as, the Bull's Head has hit upon a successful formula that has been pulling in the crowds for years now. During the day, it's a sedate kind of place; a refuge for walkers and flat-capped locals, who give way to a smarter, more eclectic crowd come the evening. Although they're drawn here as much by the excellent food as the nightly programme of live jazz, it is, indeed excellent. There's a handful of real ales on offer, but more of a revelation is the superb wine list; there's a selection of 80 malt whiskies, too.

Babies and children admitted (family area). Function room. Games (board games). Music (live jazz 8.30pm Mon-Sat; 2-4.30pm, 8-10.30pm Sun; £5-£10). No-smoking tables. Specialities (malt whisky). Tables outdoors (3, terrace). TVs (big screen, satellite).

Coach & Horses

27 Barnes High Street, SW13 9LW (8876 2695). Hammersmith tube, then 209 or 283 bus/Barnes Bridge rail. **Open** 11am-11pm Mon-Sat; noon-10.30pm Sun. **Food served** noon-3pm, 6-9pm Mon-Sat; noon-4pm Sun. **Credit** MC, V.

A few years ago, West London was full of places such as this musty little boozer, frequented by locals who appreciate its resolute character and unfussy, take-it-or-leave-it charm. Now the Coach & Horses seems like something of a rarity, a venerable old place without even the merest hint of a leather sofa or distressed pine banquette. This is the certainly the cosiest in the string of Young's pubs in this area, and the most unaffected, too; hardy old regulars prop up the bar, eschewing the wine list for pints of Young's Special or bitter, while the ebullient bar staff help foster a homely air. The large, attractive beer garden is popular with families, although nippers are kept appropriately far from the inner sanctum of the bar. Barbecues are occasionally held here in the summer months.

Babies and children admitted (garden only); children's play area. Function room. Games (bowls). Tables outdoors (40, garden). TV.

Ship

10 Thames Bank, SW14 7QR (8876 1439). Mortlake rail. **Open** 11am-11pm Mon-Sat; noon-10.30pm Sun. **Food served** noon-3pm, 6.30-9.30pm daily. **Credit** AmEx, DC, MC, V.

The scent of hops and malt hangs heavy in the air around this pretty riverside boozer. The Ship was here long before the Budweiser factory on to which it backs, and although the mass-produced fruits of the fragrant behemoth's labour are offered here on tap, this is, otherwise, an unaffected little place. The small range of draught ales

includes Pride, Bombadier and two guests per month (on a recent visit, the relentlessly chipper barman was extolling the virtues of Wychwood's alarmingly named – but delicious – Dirty Tackle). The atmosphere is sedate, if hardly electric, and while neither the pub-by-numbers decor nor the piped dad-rock provide much inspiration, we've always found this to be a perfectly pleasant spot in which to while away a summer afternoon. Its site by the finishing line of the Varsity boat race means the place packs out at least once a year.
Babies and children admitted (until 8pm). Function room. Games (bar billiards, board games, fruit machines, quiz machine). Quiz (9pm Tue; free). Music (musicians 9pm Sat; free). Tables outdoors (25, garden). TV (satellite).

Sun Inn

7 Church Road, SW13 9HE (8876 5256). Hammersmith tube then 209 or 283 bus/Barnes Bridge rail. **Open** noon-11pm Mon-Sat; noon-10.30pm Sun. **Food served** noon-3pm, 6-9.30pm Mon-Thur; noon-9.30pm Fri-Sun. **Credit** AmEx, MC, V.
'Friday is Fish, Chips and Champagne Night!' declared the specials board on our last visit to this funky little pub overlooking Barnes village green. It's a combination that sums up the place pretty well, and certainly one that meets approval from the boho crowd that inhabits its designer nooks and upholstered crannies. Hip young bar staff dispense Broadside, Bombardier and Spitfire alongside an above-average wine list, while ambient jazz and techno set an art-school-ish tone to the proceedings. In fairness, the Sun is perhaps one of the more successful reinventions of this type around these parts (and the environs of Richmond are full of them); the atmosphere is relaxed, and the whole place has a faintly self-aware feel that becomes it well.
Babies and children admitted (until 7pm). Games (video game). Music (musicians 9pm Thur; free). No-smoking tables. Quiz (9pm Tue: £1). Tables outdoors (15, terrace).

Ye White Hart

The Terrace, Riverside, SW13 0NR (8876 5177). Barnes Bridge rail/209, 419 bus. **Open** 11am-11pm Mon-Sat; noon-10.30pm Sun. **Food served** noon-2.30pm, 6.30-9.30pm Mon-Sat; noon-4pm Sun. **Credit** MC, V.
There is an undeniable air of grandeur to this deceptively small old pub; the high-beamed ceiling soars above tall windows, while a huge, oval-shaped bar dominates the centre of the room. Unfortunately, the management has long since cottoned on to its commercial appeal; before we even walked through the door, we had been made all-too-aware of the various facilities available for hire. A pity, as the appeal of this place more than speaks for itself, especially on sunny days, when it simply glows with warmth and congeniality. The selection of real ales is adequate, but the wine list is outstanding; this place has won the Young's wine pub of the year award twice in the last five years. The exterior terraces get predictably jam-packed on the afternoon of the Varsity boat race, but with the possible exception of the Dove in Hammersmith (*see p235*), one can scarcely imagine a better pub vantage point from which to observe the action.
Function room. Games (fruit machine). Music (musician 8pm Sun in winter; free). Tables outdoors (6, balcony, riverside terrace; 8 garden; 8, tow path). TV (big screen, satellite).

CHISWICK & KEW

With its village feel and resolutely child-centric orientation, Chiswick is more a place for the older, more settled pub-goer rather than the young, trendy drinker. The river is an obvious draw in the summer for families. Just off the High Road is the area's most distinguished hostelry, **Devonshire House**.

Bell & Crown

11-13 Thames Road, Strand-on-the-Green, W4 3PL (8994 4164). Gunnersbury tube/rail. **Open** 11am-11pm Mon-Sat; noon-10.30pm Sun. **Food served** noon-3pm, 6-9pm Mon-Sat; noon-7pm Sun. **Credit** AmEx, DC, MC, V.
One of a cluster of pubs lining the towpath by Kew Bridge, the Bell & Crown is a top spot for riverside summer supping or winter warmers by the open fire. Fuller's – near ubiquitous in these parts – provides the liquid interest, and the kitchen turns out good grub that has never failed to satisfy us. At weekend lunchtimes there's a family crowd; not the best time to visit, if children set your teeth on edge. The decor is a tad on the chintzy side, but the river views make for better contemplation than the wallpaper. There's no sign of the smugglers who, according to the signage, used to frequent the place – just plenty of young locals entertaining their nearest and dearest.
Babies and children admitted (until 7pm). Function room. No-smoking tables. Tables outdoors (10, riverside patio). TV (satellite).

Bollo

13-15 Bollo Lane, W4 5LR (8994 6037). Chiswick Park tube. **Open** noon-11pm Mon-Sat; noon-10.30pm Sun. **Food served** noon-3pm, 7-10.15pm Mon-Fri; 12.30-3.30pm, 7-10.15pm Sat; 12.30-4pm, 7-10pm Sun. **Credit** AmEx, MC, V.

Dove. *See p235.*

The Blue Anchor

Traditional 18th Century Riverside Alehouse
Unique Pewter Bar
Real Ales and Fresh Home Cooked Fayre
Featured in Many Films and Television Documentaries
Open 11 til 11

13 Lower Mall
Hammersmith Bridge North Side
London
W6 9DJ
Tel: 020 8748 5774

WILLIAM · IV

BAR · RESTAURANT · GARDEN

786 HARROW RD LONDON NW10 5JX
TEL: 020 ~ 8969 5944 FAX: 020 ~ 8964 9218
www.william-iv.co.uk

baroque

the kiwi kitchen @ baroque
94 Uxbridge Road
West Ealing
London W13 8RA
Tel: 020 8567 7346

A little slice of clubby NYC cool on the Uxbridge Road, it provides a sophisticated haunt for local companies by day, and chilled 70s lounge bar by night.
Relaxed brasserie food by day, with a more extensive restaurant menu till 10pm.

What really draws in the crowds is the extensive and imaginative cocktail menu.

The bartenders are the stars behind the bar and can make everything from the perfect Martini to the freshest Mojito.

Live jazz every Sunday.

Every second Saturday the bar takes on a funky house mantle with resident House Foundation DJ.
Baroque has a clubby upstairs bar/chillout lounge available for private parties of up to 50.

Open seven days a week;
Sunday 12:00 - 10:30pm
Monday - Thursday 12:00 - 11:00pm
Friday & Saturday 12:00 - 2am

Castilla

Best kept secret after MI5

Tel: 020-7738 9597

To anyone caught between Acton and Chiswick and looking for an excellent pub in which to refuel, we'd recommend the Bollo unreservedly. It's set on a cut-through road between a railway bridge and a level crossing, but the outside area, with ample seating, is a lovely spot on a Saturday night – or Sunday afternoon – in the summer. Inside is a spacious L-shaped room with a cavernous eating area and a table with banquette in one corner (perfect for a big group celebration). There's a good wine list and a menu sporting imaginative dishes with plenty of choice at reasonable prices. And it doesn't get too busy on week nights.
Babies and children welcome (until 7pm); high chairs. Tables outdoors (12, pavement). TV (big screen, digital, plasma).

City Barge

27 Strand-on-the-Green, W4 3PH (8994 2148). Gunnersbury tube/rail/Kew Bridge rail. **Open** 11am-11pm Mon-Sat; noon-10.30pm Sun. **Food served** noon-9.30pm daily. **Credit** AmEx, DC, MC, V.
The Barge was already in operation when Agincourt was a recent memory. One of a handful of good riverside pit stops that make up the Strand-on-the-Green pub-hub, it's a cracker in its own right. Fuller's supplies the ales, and there's a wholesome, if old-school menu of generously served pies and burgers to choose from. Outside, the half-dozen tables on the water's edge, in the lee of Oliver's Island – comrade Cromwell's Civil War bolthole – make a fine spot at which to spend a summer evening or relax over a pint on a Sunday lunchtime. Naturally, the place buzzes when the sun's out, so get here early for an seat.
Babies and children admitted (until 9pm). Music (live jazz 8.30 Thur; free). No-smoking tables. Tables outdoors (6, riverside terrace).

Coach & Horses

8 Kew Green, TW9 3BH (8940 1208). Kew Gardens tube/rail. **Open** 11am-11pm Mon-Sat; noon-10.30pm Sun. **Food served** noon-2.30pm, 7-9.30pm Mon-Sat; noon-9pm Sun. **Credit** AmEx, MC, V.
The thought of retiring afterwards to this large, airy and congenial pub will make a visit to nearby Kew Gardens seem like an even better idea. It's a Young's pub, and the draught ales (bitter, Special, Waggledance and a couple of seasonal options – St George's on our visit) are well kept and served by jolly bar staff. There's a much more extensive sampler of Young's output in 500ml bottles, too, including Lord's, Old Nick and Kew Brew, and the Coach operates a takeaway service: four bottles for a fiver. There's Sky Sports on the box at the weekends, and plenty of room to sit down and enjoy the good pub grub; there are also rooms in which to crash out in the hotel upstairs. The Coach's full English is famous around these parts.
Babies and children admitted (dining area). Disabled: toilet. Function room. Games (board games, fruit machines, quiz machine). No-smoking area. Tables outdoors (6, patio; 8, garden). TV (big screen, satellite).

Devonshire House

126 Devonshire Road, W4 2JJ (8987 2626/www.thedevonshirehouse.co.uk). Turnham Green tube. **Open** noon-11pm Tue-Sat; noon-10.30pm Sun. **Food served** noon-2.30pm, 7-10.30pm Tue-Fri; noon-3pm, 7-10.30pm Sat; noon-3pm, 7-10pm Sun. **Credit** AmEx, MC, V.
Surrounded by Chiswick's less salubrious elements, slap bang in the middle of its estates, the Dev is the jewel in its crown of pubs. Indeed, it's not so much a pub that serves excellent food as a gourmet restaurant that happens to be situated in an old boozer (now done up), the former Manor Tavern. The beautifully understated interior has plenty of tables and banquettes down one wall of the long, thin main room, and the food is imaginative; even the bar menu impresses, with dishes like croque monsieur with Bayonne ham (£6.95) or risotto cakes with buffalo mozzarella and wild mushrooms (£2.75). The wine list is a corker, with plenty of choices of each colour by the glass, bottles priced from £12.50 to £55, and a small but tasty array of champagne and dessert wine.
Babies and children welcome. Bar available for hire. Tables outdoors (10, garden; 4, pavement).

Mawson Arms

110 Chiswick Lane South, W4 2QA (8994 2936). Turnham Green tube. **Open** 11am-8pm Mon-Fri. **Food served** noon-3pm Mon-Fri. **Credit** MC, V.
Why would you go to a pub that's stuck right on one of West London's busiest roundabouts, especially one that closes at 8pm every night? For the beer, that's why. This is a pub that simply concentrates on serving excellently kept bitters – and as such it's become a magnet for lovers of real British ale. The stars in the bar are supplied by London's oldest surviving brewery, Fuller's, whose premises are right next door. Standards are unsurprisingly high: a better drop of London Pride you won't find anywhere, and the refreshing, light, fragrant Honey Dew is a delight. After you've supped here, keep the evening going by heading east along the towpath to the delightful Old Ship (*see p234*).
Function room. No-smoking area. TV.

Old Pack Horse

434 Chiswick High Road, W4 5TF (8994 2872). Chiswick Park tube. **Open** 11am-11pm Mon-Sat; noon-10.30pm Sun. **Food served** noon-10pm Mon-Sat; noon-9pm Sun. **Credit** AmEx, MC, V.
In the winter, assuming you arrive early enough, you'd do well to grab a seat by one of the two open fires in this rather spacious red-brick boozer. It's a Fuller's establishment, and has a good spread of that brewery's beers: on tap, there's London Pride, ESP and Chiswick, plus regular guests (IPA and Hock, for example); in bottles, the Fuller's options run from London Porter and 1845 to Honey Dew and Golden Pride, as well as outsiders like Tiger, Singer and Bitburger. Leather sofas dotted through the bar give this old fave a slightly more contemporary feel; at the rear there's a rather standard-issue Thai restaurant. The Pack Horse fills up at the weekends with a mixed, if not out-and-out trendy, crowd, and we're told the lead singer of Iron Maiden is a regular. One of the better pubs on this stretch.
Babies and children admitted (restaurant only). Games (fruit machine, golf machine). Restaurant. Tables outdoors (6, pavement; 5, garden).

Swan

Evershed Walk, 119 Acton Lane, W4 5HH (8994 8262). Chiswick Park tube/94 bus. **Open** 5-11pm Mon-Fri; noon-11pm Sat; noon-10.30pm Sun. **Food served** 7-10.30pm Mon-Fri; 12.30-3pm, 7-10.30pm Sat; 12.30-3pm, 7-10pm Sun. **Credit** MC, V.
There's a distinct Dickensian feel to the decor of this little gem. In the main bar, huge Victorian windows take up one side of the large-ish room; oak panels and ancient leather sofas set the scene in the rear salon. The hearty gastropub grub served here (Italian sausage with polenta, perhaps, or chicken breast with pancetta, rosemary and sage), all in the £9 to £12 range, help make this a great winter pub; a pretty and (for London) spacious patio garden make it a

cracking summer spot, too. The beer taps include London Pride, Spitfire, Deuchars and John Smith's, as well as everyday lagers; there are also 14 wines of each colour, with seven of each available by the glass.
Babies and children welcome (before 7pm). Tables outdoors (30, garden).

Also in the area...

All Bar One 197-199 Chiswick High Road, W4 2DR (8987 8211).
Pitcher & Piano 18-20 Chiswick High Road, W4 1TE (8742 7731).

EALING

While the area's oldest and most attractive pubs still tend to be found in the vicinity of St Mary's Road, where the original Ealing village developed – take the **Red Lion**, a stone's throw from Ealing Film Studios – Ealing has produced a crop of new bars and gastropubs over the last couple of years, from the traditional **Ealing Park Tavern** to the sassy **Baroque**.

Baroque

94 Uxbridge Road, W13 8RA (8567 7346/www.baroque-ealing.co.uk). West Ealing rail. **Open** noon-11pm Mon-Thur; noon-2am Fri, Sat; noon-10.30pm Sun. **Food served** noon-3pm, 5-10pm daily. **Credit** MC, V.
It's hard to dislike this sassy, good-humoured little joint. True, one could so easily get the wrong idea from the arty, black and white photos of the Manhattan skyline that adorn the raspberry-coloured walls, or from the decidedly hip-looking crowd that pack the place out every Friday and Saturday night. But it doesn't take long to realise that Baroque is not, in fact, taking itself seriously (thank goodness). The thoroughly friendly staff do their best to keep things upbeat, while in less frenetic hours a battered selection of board games sits at one end of the highly polished bar, adding to the prevailing atmosphere of fun. The range of beers on tap may not be much to sing about, but there's a huge selection of bottles, and the cocktail menu is solid.
Function room. Games (board games). Music (live jazz 7pm Thur, 2-5pm Sun; free). Tables outdoors (5, garden).

Drayton Court

2 The Avenue, W13 8PH (8997 1019). West Ealing rail. **Open** 11am-11pm Mon-Sat; noon-10.30pm Sun. **Food served** noon-3pm, 5-9pm Mon-Fri; noon-9pm Sat, Sun. **Credit** AmEx, MC, V.
It's been over a year now since the grand old Drayton Court had a drastic refit, and the results have been successful. It's certainly as popular as it ever was, although the sheer size of the place usually means that finding a seat isn't a challenge – especially when it's warm enough for punters to decamp, en masse, to the huge, landscaped beer garden. Adjoining the pleasant main bar (where Chiswick, Pride and ESB are served on tap), there's now an entirely separate lounge room, lined with comfy sofas and chairs, where a quieter atmosphere generally prevails. And what a wise decision it was to place it at the opposite end of the building to the additional sports bar (to which the TVs are confined) – a commendable attempt to please everyone.
Babies and children admitted (until 9pm); play area. Disabled: toilet. Function room. Games (board games, fruit machine, pool table, quiz machine). Music (jazz, 8pm last Wed of mth; free). Tables outdoors (40, garden). TVs (big screen, projector, satellite).

Ealing Park Tavern

222 South Ealing Road, W5 4RL (8758 1879). South Ealing tube. **Open** 5-11pm Mon; 11am-11pm Tue-Sat; noon-10.30pm Sun. **Food served** 5-10.30pm Mon-Sat; 5-9pm Sun. **Credit** AmEx, MC, V.
Phenomenally popular with locals, this beautiful old pub was completely transformed a couple of years ago from a rather dingy watering hole into the elegant and atmospheric gastropub it is today. Light pours in through the windows, oak-panelled walls enclose the spacious bar-cum-dining area, and a faint aroma of wood lends the place an almost serene feel, especially during quieter hours. Not that punters are in short supply: people flock here for the food (both the restaurant and tapas-style bar menus are good) and the congenial, slightly old-fashioned atmosphere. The range of beers is what really sets this place apart, though; on draught, in addition to Hoegaarden, Leffe and IPA, there's 6X, Ruddles County, Grand Union Special, and Wychwood's Hobgoblin. During the summer months, a pretty, walled beer garden comes into play.
Babies and children welcome; high chairs; toys. Restaurant (no smoking). Tables outdoors (25, garden).

Red Lion

13 St Mary's Road, W5 5RA (8567 2541). South Ealing tube. **Open** 11am-11pm Mon-Sat; noon-10.30pm Sun. **Food served** noon-3pm, 7-9.30pm Mon-Sat; noon-5pm Sun. **Credit** AmEx, MC, V.
A modest brass plaque by the entrance gives the unofficial name of this cosy little pub – Stage Six, known as such to generations of actors and technicians from nearby Ealing Film Studios; today's incumbents still come here after a hard day's work on the real stages one to five. The decor tastefully acknowledges Ealing's stalwart contribution to British cinema, with photos of various cinematic luminaries hanging alongside vintage posters for *The Ladykillers* and the like. The crowd is a lively mixture: mostly regulars in the day, but on a busy Saturday night you might just as easily watch a group of bright young things jostle for position at the bar with some venerable old gent in tweeds and a flat cap. Ales on tap include Jack Frost, Chiswick, and Honey Dew, although people come here as much for the excellent bar food as anything else.
Disabled: toilet. Tables outdoors (15, garden).

Also in the area...

All Bar One 64-65 The Mall, W5 5LS (8280 9611).
Hog's Head 46-47 The Mall, Ealing Broadway, W5 3TJ (8579 3006).
O'Neill's 23-25 High Street, W5 5DB (8579 4107).

FULHAM & PARSONS GREEN

Our Fulham boundary stretches far and wide, taking in everything from the riverside to the busy lower stretches of the King's and Fulham Roads. Pastoral pleasures are to be found in Parsons Green – the **White Horse** is one of London's finest boozers – but generally this is a lively playground for SW6's young carousers and football supporters along to watch Fulham and Chelsea at the nearby grounds.

Aragon House

247 New King's Road, SW6 4XG (7731 7313/www.aragonhouse.net). Parsons Green or Putney Bridge tube/22 bus. **Open** 11am-11pm Mon-Sat; 11am-10.30pm Sun. **Food served** noon-3pm, 6-10pm Mon-Fri; noon-8pm Sat; noon-4pm Sun. **Credit** AmEx, DC, MC, V.

Standing in the luxuriant environs of Parsons Green, this neo-Georgian boozer announces itself with the utmost discretion by means of a diminutive plaque on its ivy-covered façade. The interior is bolder, though, with medieval-style murals, tapestries, ornate tables and gold-coloured chairs. There's a good wine list, a decent selection of whiskies, hell, even pricey cigars; and draught beers include San Miguel and Kronenbourg Blanc, with Hog's Back Tea and Bombardier as the two real ales. In summer, cocktails are served in the vast beer garden at the back (a rare asset in this neck of the woods), and there's also some fine seating overlooking the green on the patio at the front.

Function rooms. Music (musicians 8pm Mon in winter). Tables outdoors (5, garden; 12, patio).

Finch's

190 Fulham Road, SW10 9PN (7351 5043). Earl's Court, Fulham Broadway or South Kensington tube/14 bus. **Open** 11am-11pm Mon-Sat; noon-10.30pm Sun. **Food served** noon-2.15pm, 6-8pm Mon-Sat; noon-3pm Sun. **Credit** MC, V.

Finch's is something of an institution. Granted, there have been some half-hearted attempts to gloss up the place, but its stained-glass skylight and superb Victorian tiled walls still provide evidence of former grandeur. In the 1950s and '60s, Chelsea's boho set – Augustus John, Brendan Behan, Elisabeth Frink and Robert Graves, among others – imbibed here. We hope the management will be mindful of history and not make further alterations along the lines of the carpeted area at the back. Young's provides the ales, but, sadly, the customers these days – comfortable, monied Chelsea types – don't measure up to their illustrious and eccentric predecessors. Finch's is still the best pub on this busy stretch of Fulham Road.

Games (fruit machines). TV (big screen, plasma, satellite).

Fox & Pheasant

1 Billing Road, SW10 9UJ (7352 2943). Fulham Broadway tube. **Open** 11am-11pm Mon-Sat; noon-10.30pm Sun. **Food served** noon-2.30pm Mon-Fri. **Credit** MC, V.

The creaking floorboards of this two-room boozer has seen many a drinker's foot since it opened in the mid 19th century. All brass and wood and rough-and-ready tables, the F&Ph seems like little bit of the West Country; while the bars of the surrounding area compete with the size of their cocktail lists, this unassuming establishment simply gets on with the business of serving good beer (Greene King IPA and Hobbit are the real ales here, alongside a couple of everyday lagers), a decent plate of food and the odd bottle of wine. Not refurbished, not remixed, not reinvented – just one of the nicest little pubs in west London.

Babies and children welcome (garden). Games (darts). Tables outdoors (8, heated garden). TV (satellite).

Mitre

81 Dawes Road, SW6 7DU (7386 8877). Fulham Broadway tube. **Open** noon-11pm Mon-Sat; noon-10.30pm Sun. **Food served** noon-4pm, 6-9.30pm Mon-Sat; 1-8pm Sun. **Credit** AmEx, MC, V.

DRINKING ALOUD
ALEX KAMMERLING

Who are you? I'm an ex-bartender. I've worked all over the world, though my last London job was at Detroit (*see p35*). Since then I've been writing for *Class* magazine, *Time Out*, *Square Meal* – and I've just published a book, *Blend Me, Shake Me*. A cocktail book, obviously...

Drinking in London: what's good about it? Great energy, bartenders are friendly, it's a very sociable industry. It's got so big, there are so many good bartenders, and so many new bars, that it's hard to keep track. There's a new bar opening every week, it seems.

What could be improved? Service. It's getting better, but still only at the top end of the market.

What's caught your eye in the last year? There's the whole cocktail culture – the M-word, mixology – and we're seeing more brand-calling: customers asking for Grey Goose in Martinis, rather than just 'a vodka Martini'. And drinking more premium spirits. There's more training for bartenders, too – I'm currently involved with that – showing them how spirits are made, differences between brands, which means they're equipped to sell the products to the consumers, to educate customers. But it's a long process.

What's in your crystal ball? I think the whole responsible drinking thing is going to kick in, and we're going to see more responsible bartending to help counteract binge drinking.

New licensing law: good or bad? I don't know what's going to happen. I think it's good, but it's going to get much worse before it gets better. The British have a sort of mad obsession to get absolutely paralytic, and it goes back a long way – don't ask me why.

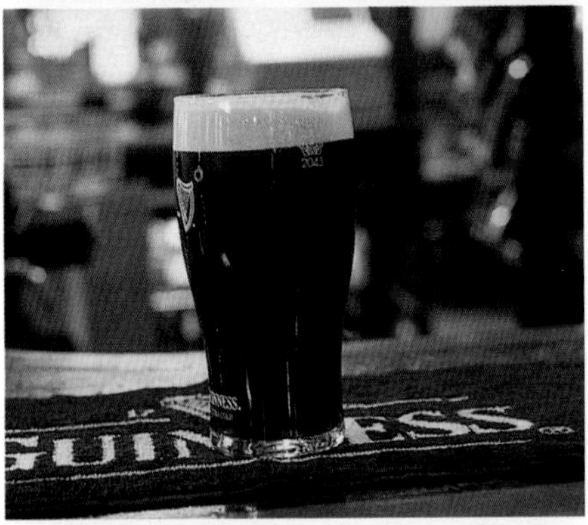

Hope & Anchor

The mock Tudor exterior hides a recent refurbishment that has done away with the previously underwhelming decor, in favour of a contemporary look. Spotlights dot the ceiling, and sauna-style wooden slats hug the walls. The bar holds an unexciting array of lagers, but there's a choice of three real ales (Adnams bitter, London Pride and Greene King IPA). Regulars, a relaxed local crowd, seem to appreciate the pub, and there's certainly not much competition at this end of winding Dawes Road.

Babies and children welcome (before 6pm). Disabled: toilet. No-smoking area. Tables outdoors (30, garden). TV (plasma, satellite).

La Perla

803 Fulham Road, SW6 5HE (7471 4895). Parsons Green tube. **Open** 5-11pm Mon-Fri; noon-11pm Sat; noon-10.30pm Sun. **Food served** 5-10.15pm Mon-Fri; noon-10.30pm Sat; noon-9.45pm Sun. **Happy hour** 5-7pm daily. **Credit** AmEx, MC, V.

What you won't get at this newish outcrop of the Café Pacifico/La Perla chain is an overabundance of Tex-Mex kitsch; what you will get is a measure of Central American panache. Thankfully the ceiling is devoid of hanging sombreros; instead, there's a polished wooden bar and photos and murals depicting Mexican beach life. The drinks list is wide in scope, ranging from a monumental list of tequilas to over a dozen rums and more Mexican beers than you can shake a fajita at. Bar snacks and Tex-Mex mains are served from the open kitchen at the back. On weekend afternoons, this a family joint; during the week, the local after-work crowd heads here for a spot of spirit slamming.

Babies and children admitted (restaurant only). Restaurant.

Vamos de Tapas

575 King's Road, SW6 2EB (7371 9044). Fulham Broadway tube/22 bus. **Open/food served** 7-11pm Mon-Wed; noon-midnight Thur-Sat; noon-3pm Sun. **Credit** AmEx, MC, V.

A bar with an excellent wine list, well-kept beers and a tapas menu to rival many in Madrid would be welcome in most areas, but given the lack of gastrobars on this stretch of the King's Road, Vamos de Tapas is especially so. Occupying the premises of the former Lunasa, this is a bold affair: big windows shed light on its large, foliage-rich ground floor, and there's a dedicated dining area up the winding staircase. The bar can be drawn on for its liquid offerings alone (its draught beers run to Staropramen and Boddington's, plus Stella and Guinness), but it would be a shame to miss out on the tapas.

Babies and children welcome (before 9pm). Bar available for hire. Disabled: toilet. Tables outdoors (3, pavement).

White Horse

1-3 Parsons Green, SW6 4UL (7736 2115). Parsons Green tube. **Open** 11am-11pm Mon-Sat; 11am-10.30pm Sun. **Food served** noon-10pm Mon-Fri; 11am-10pm Sat, Sun. **Credit** AmEx, MC, V.

At the apex of the Green, this lovely old Victorian pub, the boozer of choice for posh locals, has earned the nickname Sloaney Pony. Don't be put off. Down one side of the horseshoe bar, black polished flags extend past a huge fireplace into a small, formal dining room looking on to a tiny courtyard. Pink walls on one side add a merry note, and elsewhere tightly bound Chesterfields sit beside long wooden tables. An fine gastro menu suggests both wine and beer to accompany each dish, and it's a joy to find beer treated with such respect. The taps

dispense the likes of Harveys, Adnams Broadside and Firefly, as well as Chimay and De Koninck, and there's a good pick of bottled beers.
Babies and children welcome. Disabled: toilet. No piped music or jukebox. Restaurant. Specialities (organic wines). Tables outdoors (30, garden).

Also in the area...

Slug & Lettuce 474-476 Fulham Road, SW6 1BY (7385 3209).
Fulham Tup 1 Harwood Terrace, SW6 2AF (7610 6131).
O'Neill's 90-90A High Street, SW6 3LF (7384 3573).
Oyster Rooms (JD Wetherspoon) Fulham Broadway, SW6 1AA (7471 0310).

HAMMERSMITH, RAVENSCOURT PARK & STAMFORD BROOK

Hammersmith has a raw edge to it, and an interesting mix of pubs on its High Street and by the river. There are plenty to choose from in a relatively compact area, but the pick of the bunch – a happy marriage of river views, outside space and lively crowd – has to be the **Old Ship** on Upper Mall.

Blue Anchor

13 Lower Mall, W6 9DJ (8748 5774). Hammersmith tube. **Open** 11am-11pm Mon-Sat; noon-10.30pm Sun. **Food served** noon-3pm, 6-9pm Mon-Fri; noon-4pm, 6-9pm Sat, Sun. **Credit** MC, V.
One of a handful of decent riverside pubs within a five-minute stroll of Hammersmith Bridge, the Blue Anchor is an 18th-century building that has retained much of its olde world charm. It's small inside, with half a dozen tables offering rest for the weary in an almost soporific atmosphere; outside, on a summer night, there's a similar number of picnic bench tables tucked against the riverside wall. If you manage to snag one, settle in and watch the lights come on along the bridge and an ever-changing menagerie of walkers, cyclists, rollerbladers and rowers in wellies. At the pumps, there's Budweiser, Guinness, Kronenbourg, London Pride and Brakspear bitter.
Babies and children admitted. Function room. Tables outdoors (10, riverside). TV.

Brook Green Hotel

170 Shepherd's Bush Road, W6 7PB (7603 2516). Hammersmith tube. **Open** *Ground floor bar* 8-11pm Wed; 8pm-midnight Thur, Fri; 6pm-1am Sat; 7pm-midnight Sun. *1st floor bar* 7am-11pm Mon-Thur; 8am-11pm Fri, Sat; 8am-10.30pm Sun. **Food served** (1st floor only) 7am-9.30am, noon-3pm, 6-10pm Mon-Thur; 8am-10am, noon-3pm, 6-10pm Fri, Sat; noon-4pm, 6-10pm Sun. **Credit** AmEx, DC, MC, V.
Prominently sited on the main Hammersmith–Shepherd's Bush Road is this amply proportioned Victorian pub. The decor in its main bar is all scarlet and gold, with a set of odd, pendulous orb lights dangling over the bar, a yellow ceiling and chequered upholstery. Young's is responsible for the draught beers (bitter, Special and St George's on our visit), and it has a basement bar with a separate entrance that's used for stand-up comedy nights, jazz and blues. It's a hotel in more than name, too: the Brook Green also provides accommodation, with 14 bedrooms for those too plastered to get home.
Comedy (8pm Thur; £5). Disabled: toilet. Function room. Music (DJ and swing dancing 7pm Sun; live blues 8pm Fri; live jazz 8pm Wed; £5-£7). No-smoking area. Tables outdoors (12, garden). TVs (big screen, satellite).

Dove

19 Upper Mall, W6 9TA (8748 5405). Hammersmith or Ravenscourt Park tube. **Open** 11am-11pm Mon-Sat; noon-10.30pm Sun. **Food served** noon-2.30pm, 5-9pm Mon-Sat; noon-4pm Sun. **Credit** AmEx, MC, V.
If you're looking to take a visitor from out of town to a landmark London boozer, you couldn't pick a better one than this 400-year-old beauty. It ticks all the boxes: dangerously low-beamed ceiling, dark panelled walls, rickety furniture, terrace overlooking Father Thames and history oozing from every pore. It even has a record-breaking bar room, the smallest, measuring four feet by seven (though there is another, much larger room as well). This is a Fuller's pub, and dispenses London Pride, ESP and, on our visit, Jack Frost, as well as the usual nitrokeg lagers. It does get very busy in the evenings – so much so that an early arrival is no guarantee of a seat. AP Herbert put the Dove into his *Water Gypsies*, as the Pigeon.
No piped music or jukebox. Tables outdoors (15, riverside terrace).

Hope & Anchor

20 Macbeth Street, W6 9JJ (8748 1873). Hammersmith tube/266 bus. **Open** 11am-11pm Mon-Sat; noon-10.30pm Sun. **No credit cards.**
One of Hammersmith's many no-frills locals, this corker has managed to escape the makeover merchants who have ruined most of the pubs in the area. It remains true to its 1930s roots in looks and has a pleasant, locals' local atmosphere – although it can get a tad quiet side on week nights. Old-school entertainment abounds here, with big-screen sports action, darts and a pool table. It's an unremarkable place, which makes it stand out as a proper pub still run with local patrons in mind; the beers are unremarkable as well (Guinness, Foster's, Kronenbourg and John Smith's on tap, with Beck's and Budweiser in bottles alongside the breezers). It'll never win any awards but, you suspect, the locals want it to stay exactly as it is.
Babies and children welcome. Games (darts, fruit machines, pool). Jukebox. Music (musicians 8.30pm Sat; free). Tables outdoors (8, garden). TVs (big screen, satellite).

Old Ship

25 Upper Mall, W6 9TD (8748 2593/www.oldshipw6.co.uk). Hammersmith, Ravenscourt Park or Stamford Brook tube. **Open** 9am-11pm Mon-Sat; 9am-10.30pm Sun. **Food served** 9am-10.30pm daily. **Credit** AmEx, MC, V.
During the summer, this splendid, ivy-clad riverside hangout is mobbed by a boisterous crowd of young hipsters, chisel-jawed yahoos and faintly bewildered tourists. Loud music booms inside, but it makes the atmosphere rather than kills it; if you can, try to snaffle a table on the expansive balcony, from where you'll have the best seat in London from which to watch rowers in training on the river. (For the same reason, the Ship is a popular venue come the Varsity boat race.) There's a stupefying array of flavoured vodkas behind the bar, and a decent array of Fuller's ales, with London Pride a fixture and seasonal options including India Pale Ale, London Porter and Hock.
Babies and children admitted; children's menu; high chairs, nappy-changing facilities. Disabled: toilet.

Function rooms. Games (fruit machine). Restaurant (no smoking). Tables outdoors (17, riverside terrace; 7, balcony). TV (big screen, satellite).

Salutation

154 King Street, W6 0QU (8748 3668). Hammersmith tube. **Open** 11am-11pm Mon-Sat; noon-10.30pm Sun. **Food served** noon-2.30pm, 5.30-9.30pm daily. **Credit** MC, V.

They don't make 'em like they used to – beautifully ornate Victorian pub fronts, that is. Slap bang in the heart of busy Hammersmith, this remarkable building is, from the outside, stunning to look at. Inside, it's a half-decent, no-frills place with the buzz of the streets about it. The garden at the back of the pub is a wonderful refuge from the fumes and noise of King Street, while the bar in front is a great spot in which to watch the football on a well-placed big screen. This is a Fuller's establishment, so the beer line-up includes London Pride, Chiswick and ESB, a couple of the brewery's seasonal ales, and lagers like Grolsch and Stella.

Babies and children welcome (before 6pm). Games (arcade machine). Tables outdoors (24, garden). TV (big screen, satellite).

Also in the area...

Bar 38 1 Blacks Road, W6 9DT (8748 3951).
Plough & Harrow (JD Wetherspoon) 120-124 King Street, W6 0QU (8735 6020).
William Morris (JD Wetherspoon) 2-4 Swan Island, King Street, W6 0QA (8741 7175).

KENSAL GREEN

Inauspiciously bordered by Wormwood Scrubs prison and the Grand Union canal, Kensal Green has had a Notting Hill-esque revamp in the last couple of years; and while there has yet to be a full-scale yuppy invasion, there are enough bohos around to give this otherwise run-down area an intriguing feeling of diversity. This is reflected in local pubs, from the stylish **William IV** to the weird and wonderful **Paradise by Way of Kesnal Green**.

Greyhound

64-66 Chamberlayne Road, NW10 3JJ (8969 8080). Kensal Green tube/Kensal Rise rail. **Open** 6.30-11pm Mon; noon-11pm Tue-Thur; noon-midnight Fri, Sat; noon-10.30pm Sun. **Food served** 6.30-10pm Mon; 12.30-3.30pm, 6.30-10.30pm Tue-Sat; 12.30-7pm Sun **Credit** MC, V.

Don't be fooled by the artfully aged decor: this place was created from two separate premises just a few years back. The result is a strange and rather charming little gastropub. The interior is split into separate bar and dining areas. Table seating makes good use of the deceptively limited space, but at busy times it's standing room only. And while we see the idea behind the pictures of Tommy Cooper beside the front door, the subdued light, atmospheric red lamps and unusual decorative flourishes are really more 19th-century magic show than 1970s cabaret. The bar menu is smart but unpretentious (beef burger with tomato and chilli relish, for instance), while the restaurant serves an expanded menu including, on our last visit, such appropriately old-fashioned dishes as stuffed rabbit and venison steak. Adnams Best is on tap, plus a bi-weekly guest ale; San Miguel and Bitburger are among the lagers.

Babies and children welcome. Disabled: toilet. Games night (7.30pm 4th Sun of mth; free). Music (DJ 7.30pm 1st, 3rd Sun of mth; free). Quiz (7.30pm 2nd Sun of mth; £5). Restaurant. Tables outdoors (7, pavement; 15, garden).

North Pole

13-15 North Pole Road, W10 6QH (8964 9384/ www.massivepub.com). Latimer Road or White City tube. **Open** noon-11pm Mon-Sat; noon-10.30pm Sun. **Food served** noon-3pm, 6-9.30pm Mon-Thur, Sat; noon-4pm, 6-9.30pm Fri, Sun. **Credit** AmEx, DC, MC, V.

Given that the proximity of Television Centre makes this a favourite hangout for BBC employees, North Pole manages remarkably well to resist the sort of pretentious trappings you might expect from a media-friendly gastropub on the fringes of Notting Hill. This is really just an unfussy, take-it-or-leave-it sort of place, and despite its attempts to cultivate a funky vibe, a very appealing one at that. Solid, hearty food is served, both in the main bar and the separate dining area; Bombardier and Bloomsbury are the real ales on draught, along with a reasonable selection of lagers (including Kronenbourg Blanc and San Miguel); and the wine list is above average, too. Some of the seating is a little cramped when the bar gets busy (which it regularly does, especially on Saturday nights), so try to secure one of the sought-after leather sofas.

Babies and children admitted (restaurant). No-smoking area. Restaurant available for hire. Tables outdoors (6, pavement).

Paradise by Way of Kensal Green

19 Kilburn Lane, W10 4AE (8969 0098). Kensal Green tube/Kensal Rise rail/52, 302 bus. **Open** 12.30-11pm Mon-Sat; noon-10.30pm Sun. **Food served** 12.30-4pm, 7.30-11pm Mon-Sat; noon-9pm Sun. **Credit** MC, V.

Named after GK Chesterton's bittersweet eulogy to the English drunkard, the endearingly weird Paradise is certainly unique among the disparate clutch of gastropubs that inhabit this small corner of Kensal Green. A sense of artful entropy pervades the battered-looking walls (with ivy spreading out of every nook and corner), and the huge, Gothic angel keeping watch from one end of the room. The furniture is similarly chaotic; you're just as likely to sit on a gilded chaise longue or a battered old church pew as on anything resembling a bar stool. There are two more intimate side rooms, crammed with board games and dusty old books. On tap are Red Stripe, Spitfire and Old Speckled Hen; the popular little restaurant to the rear offers a fine, Asian-European menu. The crowd is eclectic: families on Sunday lunchtimes, more bohemian types of an evening.

Babies and children admitted; children's menus; high chairs; nappy-changing facilities. Function room. Games (board games). Tables outdoors (10, garden). TV (digital, widescreen).

William IV

786 Harrow Road, NW18 1TF (8969 5944/www. william-iv.co.uk). Kensal Green tube. **Open** noon-11pm Mon-Wed; noon-midnight Thur-Sat; noon-10.30pm Sun. **Food served** noon-3pm, 6-10.30pm Mon-Wed; noon-3pm, 6-11pm Thur, Fri; 12.30-4pm, 7-11pm Sat; noon-4.30pm, 6.30-9.30pm Sun. **Credit** AmEx, DC, MC, V.

Although there's a slightly musty, 1930s feel to this place – with its wood panelling and earthy green and brown colour scheme – the William IV is, in fact, a far sassier proposition than it might at first appear. Thoughtful design touches are scattered about the spacious bar area,

RAISE A GLASS: GOOD SPORTS

So intrinsic is sport – particularly football and international rugby – to the leisure boom that come match day every third pub instantly transforms itself into a makeshift cinema-cum-Crusade. Battle is done with a fleet of St George's flags and a sea of nitrokeg lager. Was it like this in '66? No, people watched the game at home then, *en famille*. The Sky TV revolution, which marketed football's Premiership so successfully through the '90s, has ensured that match day means pub day. And big match day can mean mayhem – consider the horrendous scenes in Croydon during Euro 2004. It's not as if most sports-themed bars – bland, corporate or both – show and more class. The American-style **Sports Café** (*see p58*) caters well for children but treats adults like burger-chain brats; JD Young's Sports Bar (2 Lidlington Place, NW1, 7387 2988), by the tower blocks of Camden Town, has little to recommend it. Extra Time (1 Long Lane, EC1, 7726 8292) is a notch above, but it is for City types.

The new antipodean Camel chain (www.thecamel.co.uk), with branches in Fulham, Mayfair, Tower Bridge, Victoria and Waterloo, makes an effort with food (teriyaki, slow roasted lamb shoulder) and slices real limes into the standard cocktails. They show NASN, the new North American sports network for Europe. The Mayfair branch (actually Marylebone, it's the old Liquid Blue bar on Duke Street) actually also shows promise – but it also has Playboy Bunny nights. What is it about sports bars that brings out the beast or the bonehead in everyone?

The well-bred watch their sport in the rugger pubs of West London, and those holding down responsible jobs gather in shouty bars in the City. Catering for both are two chains, the **Tups** (*see p246*) and Page pubs. Tups, for 'twenty-thirtysomethings who like to work and play hard' are smart – even the one in Camden. As for Page, *Time Out* described the **Sporting Page** (*see p31*) in Chelsea as 'some rich bloke's kitchen'.

Where, then, is the happy medium (let alone a hip one) where decent, intelligent folk of either sex can enjoy sport over a few drinks without having to cane it with the chavs or tart up their act to do tiffin with the toffs?

For individuality, look no further than the ivy-clad **Faltering Fullback** (19 Perth Road, N4, 7272 5834), tucked away in football-swamped Finsbury Park. From its *Beano*-style pub sign to its bizarre knick-knacks (PSV

Eindhoven scarf, Wolves shirt, furry Goofy in a cage), this marvellous boozer exudes scruffy irreverence and loves its sport with passionate irony. Good Thai food, too. For character, the Irish-tinted **Greyhound** (*see p214*), near the Oval, caters to the hurling fraternity and cricket lovers. For convenience, the **George** (55 Great Portland Street, W1, 7636 0863) is an old-style Greene King pub round the corner from the BBC, whose mix of media types and proper workers puts it on an egalitarian footing. For tradition, venues such as boxing's **Ring** (*see p106*), cricket's **Australian** (*see p54*) and rugby's **White Swan** (*see p240*) and **Princess of Wales** (*see p197*) have footnotes in sporting history. For Latin verve, the Bar Italia (22 Frith Street, W1, 7437 4520) now sells alcohol and the **Bar Estrela** (*see p219*) offers Portuguese footie and fare.

The **Famous 3 Kings** (171 North End Road, W14, 7603 6071) by West Ken Tube stop, once the leaner, far meaner F3K, has greatly improved, introducing neat primary-coloured seats, pesto sauce with its pasta and a continuation of the commentary of the main game in the pool-table area as you nip to the loos. But still the best best, for cosmopolitan atmosphere, cool decor, good beers and excellent food, is the table-football themed Kick duo (**Café Kick**, *see p111*; **Bar Kick**, *see p124*). Fun and sexy, the Kicks offer the perfect pitch of sport and leisure, without insulting your intelligence. The game needs more flair players like these. *Peterjon Cresswell*

revealing a certain style-conscious sensibility. Modish art canvases hang from the walls, fairy lights cascade from the windows, and the two small fireplaces are bejewelled with fragments of broken mirror. This is a favourite hangout of staff from nearby Virgin Records; more of a mixed bunch comes here at the weekend, though, when the fine restaurant menu attracts families during the day, and the varied and imaginative live music programme makes for a packed house in the evening. On tap are Hoegaarden, Staropramen and Leffe, and there's a limited wine and cocktail choice.
Babies and children welcome; high chairs. Function room. Music (DJ 9pm Fri, Sat; free). Restaurant. Tables outdoors (30, garden).

KINGSTON-UPON-THAMES

Though the borough's renaissance has continued over the past year with gusto, it's the club, theatre and restaurant industries that have seen the most change. Still, the area's boozers continue to satisfy local and visiting imbibers. The best pubs can be found in two main districts: the residential quarter between Kingston station and the very southern tip of Richmond Park; and, of course, on the banks of the Thames.

Boaters Inn

Canbury Gardens, Lower Ham Road, Kingston-upon-Thames, KT2 5AU (8541 4672). Kingston rail.
Open 11am-11pm Mon-Sat; noon-10.30pm Sun.
Food served noon-9.30pm Mon-Sat; noon-9pm Sun.
Credit AmEx, MC, V.
Folk at the Boaters like to believe this is a pub for people who really appreciate the river. Getting here requires a pleasant walk along the Thames towpath beside Canbury Gardens; once inside, rowers are rewarded with a 10% discount. In summer you'll spot fishermen casting their nets outside, and all year long, Friday is 'fish day' – when the popular 'haddock and chips, bangers and mash' brasserie menu is boosted by plates of sea bass, skate, oysters and platters for £8 a pop. There are two other things of importance to the Boaters' chatty and comfortably-off punters: the drink, which includes Greene King IPA, Adnams Broadside, Brakspear and Spitfire on draught (along with the requisite wines and spirits); and Sunday's long-running jazz night. There's a large space outside, complete with bench seating, that's unsurprisingly popular in summer.
Babies and children admitted; children's menu; nappy-changing facilities. Games (board games, fruit machines). Music (live jazz 8.30pm Sun; free). No-smoking area. Restaurant. Tables outdoors (30, riverside patio). TV.

Canbury Arms

49 Canbury Park Road, Kingston-upon-Thames, KT2 6LQ (8288 1882). Kingston rail. **Open/food served** 11am-11pm Mon-Sat; noon-10.30pm Sun. **Credit** MC, V.
The looming top-floor sign and blacked-out windows make the Canbury an imposing sight – yet inside you'll find a locals' local, with bantering barmen, bare-brick bar, eclectic decor, reddish-brown carpet, open fire and a sleeping dog. Customers requiring further entertainment can look to the big screen (we doubt it has ever shown anything other than sport), the pool table, the fruit machine or the dartboard; those content with liquid pleasures can drink London Pride, Shepherd Neame Spitfire or any of the weekly changing guest ales on draught. Other plus points include some pavement seating at the front and a cash machine inside. Don't be fooled by the pub's address, though; the Boaters Inn (*see above*) is far, far closer to the business end of Canbury Gardens.
Babies and children admitted (separate room). Games (board games). Tables outdoors (8, forecourt; 10, garden). TV (big screen).

Gazebo

King's Passage, Thames Street, Kingston-upon-Thames, KT1 1PG (8546 4495). Kingston rail.
Open 11am-11pm Mon-Sat; noon-10.30pm Sun.
Food served noon-2.30pm, 6-9pm Mon-Thur; noon-2.30pm Fri, Sat; noon-4pm Sun. **Credit** MC, V.
If you can't be bothered to walk from Kingston town centre to the Boaters Inn to be beside the river, then the cheerful Gazebo (also on the river) is your next best bet. It's a Samuel Smith's 'café by day, bar by night' affair, with outdoor seating and a first-floor terrace bar that, come summer, gets absolutely rammed with moneyed drinkers. Inside, the ground floor is decked out with stripped-pine

CRITICS' PICKS

For beers and ales
Coach & Horses (*see p231*), **Ealing Park Tavern** (*see p232*), **Eel Pie** (*see right*), **Mawson Arms** (*see p231*), **Red Lion** (*see p240*).

For cocktails
Bush Bar & Grill (*see p241*), **Defectors Weld** (*see p242*), **Seven Stars Bar & Dining Room** (*see p242*).

For the strong stuff
La Perla (tequila; *see p234*).

For wine
Albertine (*see p241*), **Ye White Hart** (*see p229*).

For fine views
Boaters Inn (*see left*), **Cricketers** (*see right*), **Ship** (*see p228*).

For a blast from the past
City Barge (*see p231*), **Red Lion** (*see p232*), **Finch's** (*see p233*), **Dove** (*see p235*).

For fun and games
Hope & Anchor (*see p235*).

For real fires
Bell & Crown (*see p229*), **Canbury Arms** (*see left*), **Old Pack Horse** (*see p231*).

For good food
Devonshire House (*see p231*).

For the sound of music
Boaters Inn (*see left*), **Bull's Head** (*see p228*).

walls and furniture, and there are large windows through which to view the river when it's nippy outside. Drinks include Old Brewery Bitter, Prinz and Ayingerbrau; note that Gazebo has a strict over-21s policy.
Function room. Games (fruit machine, quiz machine, pool table). No piped music or jukebox. Tables outdoors (10, pavement).

Wych Elm
93 Elm Road, Kingston-upon-Thames, KT2 6HT (8546 3271). Kingston rail. **Open** 11am-3pm, 5-11pm Mon-Fri; 11am-11pm Sat; noon-10.30pm Sun. **Food served** noon-2.30pm Mon-Sat. **No credit cards.**
Just down the road from the Canbury Arms (*see left*), on the other side of the primary school, is this more friendly, CAMRA award-winning hostelry with public and saloon bars. The Wych Elm is a smart Fuller's outfit; the dark-wood furniture, open fireplace and green and cream decor are all in good nick. There are ornate floral displays and containers at the front and in the garden at the back; neither your granny, nor her great-grandchildren would look out of place here. Yet there are also solid pub trappings: the TV (showing sport), the dartboard (with plenty of room to play) and the beer (a selection of Fuller's best, including London Porter, ESB and Chiswick on draught).
Babies and children admitted (dining area only). Games (darts, fruit machine). Tables outdoors (8, garden). TV.

Also in the area...
Kingston Tup 88 London Road, KT2 6PX (8546 6471).
O'Neill's 3 Eden Street, KT1 1BQ (8481 0131).
Slug & Lettuce Turks Boatyard, Thames Side, KT1 1PX (8547 2323).

RICHMOND, ISLEWORTH & TWICKENHAM

Most of the finest pubs in these historic parts follow the path of the river Thames. Twickenham has a bigger town centre, with slightly more to offer the discerning pub goer, although real ale aficionados may want to head straight down to Isleworth and the sample the award-winning delights of the **Red Lion**.

A Bar & Restaurant
93 Colne Road, Twickenham, TW2 6QL (8898 8000). Twickenham or Strawberry Hill rail. **Open/food served** 6pm-12.30am Mon-Thur; 11am-11pm Fri, Sat; 9.30am-5pm Sun. **Credit** AmEx, DC, MC, V.
The atmosphere was so lively when this place opened in the summer of 2004 that Richmond Council promptly slapped a noise abatement order on it. Things seem to have calmed down, but A Bar (also known as Austin's) remains buzzy. The venue is certainly a drastic improvement on the rather seedy Duke's Head pub that preceded it. Pop art now hangs on the cream-coloured walls in the main bar, and leather sofas and high-backed chairs are arranged down heavy wooden tables. There's a fair selection of draught beers, but far better is the long and carefully put together wine list. We opted for a bottle of the house white, a Georges Duboeuf burgundy at a reasonable £11. If you're feeling flush, venture to the adjoining restaurant to sample the alluring, Mediterranean-influenced menu; alternatively, try the good, tapas-style bar snacks.
Babies and children welcome. Bar available for hire. Restaurant. Tables outdoors (8, garden). TV (plasma, satellite).

Coach & Horses
183 London Road, Isleworth, TW7 5BQ (8560 1447). Syon Lane rail. **Open** 11am-11pm Mon, Wed, Thur; 11am-midnight Tue, Fri, Sat; noon-10.30pm Sun. **Food served** noon-3pm, 6-10pm Mon-Fri; noon-10pm Sat; noon-6pm Sun. **Credit** AmEx, MC, V.
The pretty, ivy-covered exterior of this former coaching inn is somewhat spoilt by the cacophonous roar of the busy road on which it stands. A pity, because the Coach & Horses is a jovial sort of place, popular with locals and passing trade from nearby Syon Park. Few risks have been taken with the decor: it's all nice and traditional, with the merest hint of a chain pub about the place. The selection of Young's ales includes Special, Pilsner and seasonal guests. The bar menu, with its emphasis on Thai fare, is surprisingly good; presumably this is why the pub can get almost as crowded at lunchtime as it does in the evening. There's also an extensive programme of music here, with bands playing most nights of the week.
Babies and children admitted (until 8pm). Games (fruit machines). Music (bands 9.30pm Mon, Tue, Fri, Sat; 2.30pm Sun; free). Quiz (Wed 9pm; £1). Tables outdoors (12, courtyard). TV (big screen, satellite).

Cricketers
The Green, Richmond, TW9 1LX (8940 4372). Richmond tube/rail. **Open** noon-11pm Mon-Sat; noon-10.30pm Sun. **Food served** noon-2.30pm Mon-Fri; noon-3pm Sat, Sun. **Credit** AmEx, MC, V.
It's hard to imagine a better location for this diminutive pub, overlooking the cricket on Richmond Green. The picturesque view doesn't seem to have changed much in a century or more, and indeed, the pub still fields a cricket team during the summer months. But we've always found the Cricketers to be an unremarkable boozer; predictable items of sports memorabilia adorn the walls, and the cramped seating can be almost unbearable once the crowds arrive. And arrive they do – for reasons we've never quite been able to fathom, this place is vastly more popular than any other pub on Richmond Green, especially on hot summer afternoons. Come to watch a match, by all means, but join the plastic glass brigade and watch from the Green. On tap are Old Speckled Hen and Greene King IPA, plus Budvar and other lagers.
Babies and children admitted (restaurant). Function room. Games (fruit machine, golf machine, quiz machine). Quiz (8.30pm Wed; £1). Restaurant. Tables outdoors (3, pavement). TV (big screen).

Eel Pie
9-11 Church Street, Twickenham, TW1 3NJ (8891 1717). Twickenham rail. **Open** 11am-11pm Mon-Sat; noon-10.30pm Sun. **Food served** noon-4.15pm daily. **Credit** MC, V.
The rather beguiling sign to this grand old pub describes a scene from local folklore. The men of Twickenham, so the legend goes, would regularly spirit their mistresses off to Eel Pie Island for a spot of medieval loving; until one day, their aggrieved spouses decided to follow them. In order to prove infidelity, however, the women had to hire the only boat in the vicinity, but their rakish husbands had withheld payment from the owner until he had returned

them (the men) safely to dry land. Hence the expression, 'He who pays the Ferryman…' No doubt the story is apocryphal, but the Eel Pie pub remains a dependable old watering hole. Plentiful seating is arranged under low-beamed ceilings, and there's an excellent selection of draught ales including Adnams Mild, Badger Best, Tanglefoot and Wadworth 6X. Although the pub shares the rugby obsession that is a virtual prerequisite for boozers in these parts, the regular crowd seems perfectly good-natured.
Babies and children admitted (until 7pm). Games (fruit machine). Quiz (9pm Thur; £1). TVs (big screen, satellite).

London Apprentice

62 Church Street, Isleworth, TW7 6BG (8560 1915). Isleworth rail. **Open** 11am-11pm Mon-Sat; noon-10.30pm Sun. **Food served** 11am-2.30pm, 6-9.30pm Mon-Thur; 11am-9.30pm Fri, Sat; noon-9pm Sun. **Credit** AmEx, DC, MC, V.
History drips from the beams of this pretty riverside pub, originally built to cash in on passing trade from the London livery apprentices. Henry VIII held secret liaisons here, and it's thought that Dick Turpin made nefarious use of the secret passageway that connects the building with the nearby church. But just as the picturesque skyline of old Isleworth is slowly being ruined by building sites, the Apprentice seems a little the worse for years of careless redecoration. From the Georgian façade that obscures the original Tudor frontage to the noisy video games that flank the interior today, the whole place feels, if not unloved, then certainly somewhat maltreated. Nevertheless, this is still a fine location for a pint or two, preferably on the terrace overlooking the river. On tap are Adnams, London Pride and Bombardier, and there's a passable food menu, too.
Babies and children admitted (until 9.30pm, dining area only); children's menus. Function room. Games (fruit machine, video games). No-smoking area. Tables outdoors (10, riverside terrace). TV (digital, widescreen).

Prince's Head

28 The Green, Richmond, Surrey, TW9 1LX (8940 1572). Richmond tube/rail/St Margarets rail. **Open** 11am-11pm Mon-Sat; noon-10.30pm Sun. **Food served** noon-9pm Mon-Sat; noon-6pm Sun. **Credit** MC, V.
Regulars held their breath when, in the closing months of 2004, the Prince's Head reopened after a long refurbishment. Not too much seems to have changed – and thank goodness, for this is probably the finest among the gaggle of pubs overlooking this stretch of Richmond Green. The original oak panelling has been retained, and a new wooden floor added, as well as some much-needed comfy seating in the expanded back room. The Prince's Head has also joined the wave of pubs in Richmond that have moved towards a ban on smoking: only partially, in this case, but for how long remains to be seen. The pub has also maintained its well deserved reputation for excellent bar food: all hearty, traditional stuff, which is quite refreshing in these parts. It's a Fuller's pub, so expect London Pride, ESB and the like on tap.
Games (fruit machine). No-smoking area. Tables outdoors (6, pavement). TVs (satellite, widescreen).

Red Lion

92 Linkfield Road, Isleworth, TW7 6QJ (8560 1457). Isleworth rail. **Open/food served** 11am-11pm Mon-Sat; noon-10.30pm Sun. **No credit cards**.
Situated in the middle of an otherwise nondescript residential street, this humble boozer seems, at first glance, to be an unlikely recipient for the multifarious accolades with which it has been showered over the years. Its owners deserve all the praise they can get for sheer dedication to the cause of real ale. This establishment has been the local CAMRA pub of the year twice since 2003, and was one of the 50 best pubs in London in a *Time Out* survey in 2004. There are up to nine beers from specialist breweries on tap here, including a rotating beer of the month and a couple of Young's ales, plus draught lagers, ciders and stouts. Appropriately, a beer festival is held twice a year, and there are regular music and comedy nights, too.
Beer festivals (live music and family events, call for dates). Games (backgammon, board games, cards, chess, darts, pool). Music (live bands 8.30pm Sat, Sun; free). Quiz (9pm Thur; £1). Specialities (real ale). Tables outdoors (20, garden). TVs (digital, satellite).

White Cross

Riverside, Richmond, TW9 1TJ (8940 6844). Richmond tube/rail. **Open** 11am-11pm Mon-Sat; noon-10.30pm Sun. **Food served** noon-3.30pm Mon-Sat; noon-4pm Sun. **Credit** MC, V.
You could be forgiven for thinking that the whole of west London has spent a summer afternoon at the White Cross at one time or another – and possibly all at once. The grande dame of Richmond pubs has been packing in the crowds like nobody's business for generations, and it's easy to see what makes this such a fine location for a spot of alfresco drinking. The building is perched on a quiet, dead-end street down by the Thames, and punters are free to spread out far along the riverbank or take in the fine view from the pub's own summer terrace. Come winter, the White Cross goes into a state of semi-hibernation, but at least it's then possible to get a seat. The pub is owned by Young's, so expect bitter and Special alongside one seasonal ale – St George's, perhaps, or Waggledance.
Babies and children welcome (garden only). Function room (Mon-Fri). No piped music or jukebox. Tables outdoors (15, garden).

White Swan

Riverside, Twickenham, TW1 3DN (8892 2166). Twickenham rail. **Open/food served** noon-2.30pm, 6-9.30pm Mon-Fri; noon-2.30pm Sat, Sun. **Credit** MC, V.
Nestling on the north bank of the Thames, the White Swan can be found down a maze of narrow old streets that seem impossibly idyllic – when they're not crawling with people. The pub also overlooks that final refuge for keepers of the countercultural flame, Eel Pie Island, but while this cosy little spot still plays host to the occasional free spirit, the vibe is generally more sporty than hippy. This being Twickenham, the disparate memorabilia lining the walls is mostly rugby-related. Yet there's also a curious form of guestbook above the bar. For decades, passing punters have slipped their business cards into a long plastic case; there are now thousands of them, some brand new, others too yellowed to read. On tap is a fine selection of ales and bitters, including Courage Directors, Greene King IPA and Shepherd Neame Spitfire. The bar menu contains a hearty choice of pub grub.
Babies and children admitted (before 7.30pm). Quiz (8.30pm, alternate Mon, winter only; £1.50). Tables outdoors (3, balcony; 15, riverside garden). TV (big screen, satellite).

Also in the area…

All Bar One 11 Hill Street, TW9 1SY (8332 7141).
O'Neill's 28 The Quadrant, TW9 1DN (8334 0111).
Pitcher & Piano 11 Bridge Street, TW9 1TQ (8332 2524).

Slug & Lettuce Riverside House, Water Lane, TW9 1TJ (8948 7733).
Twickenham Tup 13 Richmond Road, TW1 3AB (8891 1863).

SHEPHERD'S BUSH

Once notable for very little other than the BBC and a half-decent music venue, Shepherd's Bush is slowly liberating itself from the chain pubs and grotty boozers that once held sway here. There's still some way to go, but at least the local drinker need not venture into Notting Hill to find some class-act bars; with luck, newcomers such as **Defector's Weld** are a sign of things to come.

Albertine

1 Wood Lane, W12 7DP (8743 9593). Shepherd's Bush tube. **Open** 11am-11pm Mon-Fri; 6.30-11pm Sat. **Food served** noon-10.30pm Mon-Fri; 6.30-10.30pm Sat. **Credit** MC, V.

More suited to the backstreets of Montmartre than the debatable charms of Wood Lane, Albertine is a gorgeous, unaffected little wine bar. When we entered the tiny and ever so slightly scruffy bar-cum-dining room, an elegantly dishevelled older gentleman was perched behind the bar, patiently going over the vast wine list with a couple of punters, while the gentle strains of Marvin Gaye played on the stereo. The place is furnished with an appealingly mismatched selection of furniture, and enormous blackboards stretch down half the length of the walls, detailing the outstanding selection on offer. Food here is bistro-style fare, simple but delicious; alternatively, opt for a selection of nibbles, such as the excellent cheeseboard – a perfect accompaniment for a fine glass of red. They just don't make places like this any more.

Function room. Games (board games). Specialities (wine).

Anglesea Arms

35 Wingate Road, W6 0UR (8749 1291). Goldhawk Road or Ravenscourt Park tube. **Open/food served** 11am-11pm Mon-Sat; noon-10.30pm Sun. **Credit** MC, V.

Situated on the corner of a surprisingly idyllic suburban street, given that the traffic hell of Goldhawk Road is a mere petrol fume's waft away, the Anglesea Arms is a chilled and appealing little spot. Specials boards cover almost every available patch of the wood-panelled bar, detailing the various culinary delights of the day, in addition to a smaller range of upper-class snacks ('prawns and a pint' for £6.25) and an excellent wine list. The bar staff are charming and friendly, while the crowd is a pleasantly ramshackle array of locals, media types and, we couldn't help noticing, young trustafarians (and, yup, the hits of Bob Marley were blaring from the speakers). The ales you'll find on tap include London Pride, Old Speckled Hen and IPA.

Babies and children welcome; high chairs. Tables outdoors (5, pavement). No piped music or jukebox. Restaurant.

Bush Bar & Grill

45A Goldhawk Road, W12 8QP (8746 2111/www.bushbar.co.uk). Goldhawk Road tube. **Open/food served** noon-11pm Mon-Sat; noon-4pm Sun. **Credit** AmEx, MC, V.

Launched a few years ago by the folk behind such enclaves of exclusivity as the Groucho Club and Woody's Bar, this place has carved out something of a niche as a beacon of metropolitan cool in a rather drab neighbourhood. You enter via a short passageway – spotless white walls, red strip lights – off the main road. Inside, the place faintly resembles an industrial greenhouse: soaring ceilings, huge windows and row upon row of long, bench-like tables. The staff are well groomed and approachable, and take a genuine interest in the imaginative cocktails they serve; a Berry Fever (peaches and berry cordial with pear cognac and tequila) was spicy and excellent, while the Bellini was sweet and perfectly mixed. The range of bottled beers is rather limited, but commendable in its choices, which include rare treats like Duvel and Sleemans Honey Brown.

Babies and children welcome; children's menu (Sat, Sun); high chairs. Disabled: toilet. Restaurant. Specialities (cocktails). Tables outdoors (9, courtyard).

Crown & Sceptre

57 Melina Road, W12 9HY (8746 0060). Goldhawk Road or Shepherd's Bush tube. **Open** noon-11pm Mon-Sat; noon-10.30pm Sun. **Food served** noon-3pm, 6-10pm Mon-Fri; noon-10pm Sat; 12.30-4pm, 6-9.30pm Sun. **Credit** AmEx, MC, V.

Defectors Weld. *See p242.*

You could almost hear a collective sigh of relief among the committed drinkers of West London when this wonderful old place was taken over by Fuller's in 2004. Admittedly, things have been spruced up a little – but just a little; so the Crown & Sceptre still has the air of a place that hasn't changed much since the 1950s. Frosted glass doors swing into a bright, open seating area, into which light pours through tall windows, and diminutive wooden tables are pushed into almost every available space – which makes legroom something of a luxury at busy times. Good, honest pub grub is served from the old-fashioned but ugly stainless steel serving hatch that rather spoils one end of the room, and the fine selection of Fuller's favourites on tap includes Chiswick, ESB and Honeydew.
Babies and children admitted (high chairs). Disabled: toilet. Quiz (9pm Mon; £1). No-smoking area. Tables outdoors (10, garden; 3, pavement). TV.

Defector's Weld

170 Uxbridge Road, W12 8AA (8749 0008). Shepherd's Bush tube. **Open** noon-11pm Mon-Thur; noon-midnight Fri, Sat; noon-10.30pm Sun. **Food served** noon-3pm, 5-11pm Mon-Thur; noon-3pm, 5-midnight Fri; noon-midnight Sat; noon-10.30pm Sun. **Credit** MC, V.
The vibe at this excellent new venue reminds us of how Cherry Jam (*see p18*) felt in its early days, but with a more inclusive, down-to-earth atmosphere. Downstairs is a stylish and modern pub, where talkative bar staff dispense pints of Staropramen and London Pride, and the small but hearty food menu includes such pleasing, almost-local touches as Borough Market sausages. The most intimate seating is to be found to the rear, either in a few alarmingly soft armchairs, or a series of small wooden booths lit by low-hanging fabric lamps that almost give the impression of a dozen simultaneous seances when the place is full. Upstairs is the 'snug bar', a smaller, smarter cocktail lounge with table service and slightly more elaborate food. The music policy is effortlessly cool, but with a classy and well-judged caveat – piped music is kept to a sociable volume, and the frequent live sets include 'DJs not generally playing house music after 9pm'.
Disabled: toilet. Function room. Music (DJs 9pm Fri-Sun; free). No-smoking area.

Havelock Tavern

57 Masbro Road, W14 0LS (7603 5374/www.thehavelocktavern.co.uk). Shepherd's Bush tube/Kensington (Olympia) tube/rail. **Open** 11am-11pm Mon-Sat; noon-10.30pm Sun. **Food served** 12.30-2.30pm, 7-10pm Mon-Sat; 12.30-3pm, 7-9.30pm Sun. **No credit cards.**
Often imitated and rarely matched, this hardy old gem of a place is the daddy among the plethora of gastropubs scattered around the increasingly chi-chi borderland between Shepherd's Bush, Hammersmith and Notting Hill. The atmosphere is convivial and homely, like a proper local; lone drinkers chat with affable bar staff, while larger groups and families pack the place out at mealtimes, even mid-week. It's not hard to see why: the food is excellent – varied and truly eclectic – with full lunch and evening menus daily. The decor is infused with a slightly arty, bohemian air; seating is arranged down large, communal pine tables in the main bar, while at the back, a more snug retreat acts as a sanctuary in which to nurse a solitary pint. On tap is are Marston's Pedigree, Brakspear Bitter and London Pride.
Babies and children welcome; high chairs. Disabled: ramp. Tables outdoors (6, garden; 2, pavement).

Seven Stars Bar & Dining Room

243 Goldhawk Road., W12 8EU (8748 0229/www.sevenstarsdining.co.uk). Goldhawk Road tube. **Open** noon-11pm Mon-Wed; noon-midnight Thur-Sat; noon-10.30pm Sun. **Food served** noon-3pm; 6-10.30pm Mon-Sat; noon-10pm Sun. **Credit** MC, V.
The self-appointed mission of this rather hip little place – to become the best restaurant in West London – seems a little ambitious, but it's precisely the kind of tenacity and pluck that made us warm to it in the first place. We've not tried the formal restaurant (the 'lunch for a fiver' option in the bar is more than satisfying), so we can't vouch for that aspect of the master plan; but in other respects this is turning into a smooth and pleasant operation. A suitably well-groomed crowd occupies leather sofas in the elegantly underlit main bar, while efficient bar staff potter around to the strains of cool Latin beats on the stereo. The cocktail list is small but perfectly formed, and the selection of beers on tap is perhaps the only off note – just Pilsner Urquell and Hoegaarden to choose from, in addition to a handful of predictable lagers.
Disabled: toilet. Music (jazz 7pm Sun; free). No-smoking area. Restaurant. Tables outdoors (3 long tables, garden).

Also in the area...

Central Bar (JD Wetherspoon) West 12 Shopping Centre, Shepherds Bush Green, W12 8PH (8746 4290).
O'Neill's 2 Goldhawk Road, W12 8QD (8746 1288).
Slug & Lettuce 96-98 Uxbridge Road, W12 8LR (8749 1987).
Walkabout 56 Shepherds Bush Green, W12 8QE (8740 4339).

SOUTHALL

The contribution that this rather far-flung corner of West London has made to the capital's bar scene has hitherto been rather sparse. The message is tread carefully: Southall is one of the most crime-ridden parts of the city – a reputation that nearly cost the inclusion of the boozer below.

Glassy Junction

97 South Road, Southall, UB1 1SQ (8574 1626). Southall rail. **Open** 11am-11.30pm Mon-Wed; 11am-1am Thur; 11am-2am Fri, Sat; noon-11pm Sun. **Food served** noon-10.30pm Mon-Wed; noon-midnight Thur-Sat; 12.30-10pm Sun. **No credit cards.**
Entire sociology papers have been written about this place, which depending upon your point of view, is either a bold outpost of the Punjab diaspora, or just a joyous explosion of bad taste. From the outside, the only hint of anything unusual is the sign that declares it to be the first pub in the UK to accept rupees, but to walk inside is like entering a treasure trove of tat. Pictures of Bollywood stars adorn the lavishly decorated walls, and there's even a faux-jewel-encrusted panel on the back of the front door. However, our enthusiasm for this place was tempered when, in the summer of 2003, three men were shot here during a fight – a shocking event, and even more given the friendly and tolerant atmosphere for which the place is usually known. The wide range of Indian lagers on tap includes Lal Toofan.
Babies and children admitted. Function room. Games (pool tables). TV (satellite).

THE CHAIN GANG

Champagne from Veuve Clicquot

THE CHAIN GANG

For Dog & Duck and Red Lion read All Bar One and O'Neill's. London pub life has changed in many ways since we published the first edition of this guide in 1998, but the most significant development has been the proliferation of chain bars: identikit pubs dreamed up in boardrooms.

Discerning drinkers have become immune to these places; indeed, most natives couldn't tell you what differentiates one brand from another. Generally speaking, each attempts to take the same classic formula of meeting, eating and drinking and make it as characterless, undemanding and dependable as possible for its clientele (as identified and profiled by focus groups, surveys and berks from marketing). The good news is that the public has shown signs of tiring of such places. Of all the chains surveyed for this edition, only two have increased their total number of branches in the last couple of years; all the rest have cut back.

You'll find few reviews of individual chain branches in this guide. We give a brief write-up here and list branches in the **Also in the area...** postscript to each district. Branches are also listed on each chain's website, supplied below.

All Bar One

www.mbplc.com/allbarone

All Bar One (owned by the massive Six Continents pubco) is about as predictable as drinking-holes can get. Huge wall-to-ceiling windows let plentiful light into pine-saturated Ikea-inspired interiors (rarely have so many trees died for so little), giving passers-by the opportunity to gaze upon dozens of identical young commutobots feverishly texting their identical friends on identical mobile phones. The attractions are as obvious as the deficiencies: plenty of space, lots of seating and enormous bar counters with a very average selection of beers and a slightly better array of wines. They do provide an unintimidating atmosphere for women – but that in turn attracts lots of wolfish males. There's a curious over-21s door policy at most branches, though one wonders why anybody under the age of 30 would want to drink here.

Balls Brothers

www.ballsbrothers.co.uk

Balls Brothers is the king of fake olde worldness. It was one of the first in the chain wine bar game and is holding its own against the younger breed of competitors. Its cellar bars, kitted out with wood-panelled walls and drawing room prints, originally catered exclusively for gangs of smartly dressed City slickers, but more recently forays have been made to the west with sites in places like Victoria. Newer venues have a much more contemporary feel aimed at introducing BB to a younger, more mixed crowd. In keeping with the essentially classical image and clientele, house wine lists tend to be traditional and strong on Old World favourites, particularly bordeaux and burgundy.

Bar 38

www.scottish-newcastle.com

This is Scottish & Newcastle's brash bar concept, aimed at those who think they're too hip for All Bar One but aren't confident enough for Hoxton-style bars. In fact, the first 38s (in Covent Garden and Hammersmith) started off not dissimilar in look to the ABOs, but later additions (Canary Wharf, the Minories) have been individually styled and come across as the kind of thing you might find attached to a cinema multiplex: lots of bright colours and cheap finishes. Shooters, long drinks and cocktail pitchers are pushed over beers, plus there's food and a Starbuck's worth of coffees to draw in the lunchtime crowd.

Belgo & Bierodrome

www.belgo-restaurants.com

Created in 1992 by a French-Canadian and an Anglo-Belgian, Belgo began with a quirky restopub in Camden (Belgo Noord). A more cutting-edge version, Belgo Centraal,

Jamies

opened three years later in Covent Garden, followed by Belgo Zuid in Notting Hill (which, sadly, closed in 2002). Three Bierodromes (Clapham, Holborn and Islington) also share the same basic 'Belge est bien' philosophy with house menus of a wide spread of Belgian beers – amber, blond, dark and fruity – backed by huge platters of mussels and chips, or sausage in beer sauces. However, they've never quite got the acoustics right and the venues tend to be loud and shouty, as well as a touch too corporate and tanked up for the kind of connoisseur who might truly appreciate a choice of several dozen fine ales.

Pitcher & Piano. *See p246.*

Corney & Barrow

www.corneyandbarrow.com

Corney & Barrow chooses some prominent sites for its glam City wine bars – Broadgate Circle and Cabot Square being two perfect examples. Decor in all the bars is sleek and sexy – as is the clientele, which tends to get younger as the evening goes on. Bar offerings include a substantial mix of designer beers, but the real draw is the well-thought-out and frequently changing wine list, with more than 60 wines by the glass. Food is a creative take on modern eclectic brasserie fare, with slight variations to suit each bar. Prices aren't the cheapest in town.

Davy's

www.davy.co.uk

More of a bar chain with a wine list than a genuine wine specialist, making it less of a destination for oenophiles than, say, branches of Corney & Barrow and Balls Brothers. That said, there's a compact and very approachable wine selection. There are also plenty of Davy's own label options, making choosing even easier as you don't have to negotiate extra hurdles such as names of producers and regions. In addition, the list hasn't changed in the past couple of years, so if you find something you like, chances are it'll still be there next time. There's no particular house style and interiors can vary from spit and sawdust to polished, gleaming and spotlit.

Fine Line

www.fullers.co.uk

Fuller's take on the style bar follows a familiar formula of big display windows, pale wood, light paintwork, and lots of chairs and tables. There's a definite brasserie feel, with a prominence placed on lunchtime food. Menus are sensibly unambitious and tend towards fish cakes, steak baguettes, fancy sausages and the like, priced around £5-£8. Evenings are more boozy (light snacks are available) but the company's excellent draught beers are largely sidelined in favour of a decent wine list and house cocktails. Fine Lines are very female-friendly, welcoming of office crowds and, like the shopfronts at Gap, perfect for mannequins in suits.

Hog's Head

www.laurelpubco.com

It was only to be expected that the concept of the Hogsheads (note the rebranded title) would fade once its begetters, Whitbread, sold it on. It was originally conceived as a chain serving a cornucopia of real ales, Belgian beers and other boozy delights, but these days the accent is on lager, alcopops and cheap food. The only cask-conditioned ale available at many branches now is London Pride. A real shame because take away the beers and there's nothing left. Fatuous PR makes claims for 'an entirely new experience which challenges pub orthodoxy', but what this boils down to is table service. More pig's ear than hog's head.

Jamies

www.jamiesbars.co.uk

Jamies branches vary dramatically in stature and setting, from the huge, glam Thameside affair in Docklands at Westferry Circus to the much more intimate and uniquely located bar in the pavilion of an EC2 lawn bowling club. But overall the decor is smart and modish. The undaunting wine list is split into Old and New World, so you can dive straight into your preferred section; each country is represented by a snapshot selection of its best-known wines. Lesser-known producers are also given opportunities to shine, which is great for the more adventurous drinkers. Food is better than average, ranging from nibbles to mains, and served in some bars until 10pm.

JD Wetherspoon

www.jdwetherspoon.co.uk

A formula of cheap booze, no smoking, no music and quick-serve canteen cuisine at bargain prices has seen the chain (owned by golden boy of beer Tim Martin) expand to around 600 pubs nationwide. We like them for their devotion to real ale and for the out-of-the-ordinary premises some of the pubs occupy, including a cinema (Holloway), a ballroom (Liverpool Street station) and a chapel (Whitechapel). On the other hand, decor can be cheap and cheesy and the atmosphere more redolent of Batley Labour Club than hip, style-wise London – but where else inside the M25 are you going to get a pint and a curry for £3.99? JDW's 'bright, brash and fun' new sub-division Lloyds No.1 provides a more youth-oriented package, with cheap coffee and unusual bottled beers from places like New Zealand, Poland and South Africa.

JD Wetherspoon. See p245.

O'Neill's

www.mbplc.com/oneills

This ghastly cod-Irish chain must be doing something right – it has outlasted its marginally more sophisticated rival Scruffy Murphy's, for starters, and continues to expand (more's the pity). Each branch is cast in the same mould – a multi-boothed emporium of manufactured craic and bogus blarney, littered with Emerald Isle trinkets: this is Donald Duck's idea of Ireland. Guinness, Murphy's and Caffrey's are all on tap, though most drinkers seem to stick to lagers; food is of the Irish stew variety. The branch on lower Wardour Street is hugely popular for its late licence, and the final-stretch atmosphere is easily imagined. Funnily enough, O'Neill's are not often frequented by the Irish.

Pitcher & Piano

www.pitcherandpiano.com

All Bar One's lairier cousin, P&Ps – again with the pine! – tend to attract lager-swilling young suits on the lash and keen up-for-anything secretaries. Add some head-thumping music and a cavernous interior and you've got quite an atmosphere: hectic, smoky, exceptionally noisy and clearly a whole lot of fun for those in the mood. It certainly isn't the place for quiet contemplation, but fortunately the drinks selection doesn't require much scrutiny: choice is limited to the usual lagers, Pedigree, Scrumpy Jack and the now ubiquitous Hoegaarden, none of which come particularly cheap. The odd sofa is provided for those who can't stand up/it.

Slug & Lettuce

www.slugandlettuce.co.uk

The godfather of all chains, Slug & Lettuce was started back in the early 1980s by Hugh Corbett (who subsequently went on to do the Tups and Larricks). Back then it was a breath of fresh air, introducing some revolutionary concepts into the London bar scene such as windows that people could see through, non-sticky carpets and edible food. But that was some 20 years ago. No one could accuse S&L (now owned by the SFI Group) of being revolutionary these days. Suits dominate the current average branch, with an even split between the sexes, and an age range typically older than that of All Bar One. Food remains central to the operation. Bars for sensible folk.

Tup

www.massivepub.com

Also founded by Hugh Corbett (see Slug & Lettuce) but now owned by the Massive pubco, the Tups are smart, airy pubs that blend a sporting interest with a curious fascination with copulating sheep. Although branches share these common associations, they also retain enough individuality to avoid identikit anodynity; some can even attain an almost local-like atmosphere. They're customer-friendly, too, in a way that doesn't smack of marketing strategy handed down from on high. Many branches allow drinkers to order takeaway food from outside, and even keep menus and cutlery behind the bar for patrons, while the Camden Tup provides plastic glasses so slow drinkers can take unfinished pints with them come closing. Beers are standard, though some branch into adventurous territory (Tonsley has Victoria Bitter from Suffolk's Earl Soham Brewery).

Walkabout Inn

www.walkabout.eu.com

Antipodean visitors pack these Australian theme bars, despite travelling halfway across the world to (presumably) escape the very things they celebrate. They're unashamed party joints, where expats, long-term tourists, lost souls and the just plain unadventurous can settle down in a clichéd but familiar environment with like-minded compatriots who don't need every colloquialism or last bit of slang explained to them. Brits who can stand the stench of spilt lager are attracted by the Sheilas and surfer boys and late closing at weekends – notably the branch on the corner of Charing Cross Road and Shaftesbury Avenue in what used to be the Limelight club. Be warned, boasts of sporting supremacy are as legion in conversation as the orange 'Kangaroo Crossing' signs are plentiful on the walls. And no less irritating.

Zone One Bars

www.zoneonebars.com

The company that owned Babushka and sibling Bed was bought by Zone One Bars early in 2005; under the new owners, many of the bars have kept their original names. The concept looks unlikely to change in the near future, though the new owners have added a handful of new venues, including a late-licence Bed on Basingwall Street, and a place called Apartment on Threadneedle Street. The original Notting Hill Babushka, once the ramshackle boozer in which Richard E Grant was called a 'perfumed ponce' in *Withnail and I*, has been renamed Mother Black Cap, the name it wore in the film. Most Babushkas trade on the same qualities, attracting a young urban crowd to medium-sized, darkish, Moorish-influenced and vaguely Gothic grottoes that specialise in DJ nights and numerous varieties of flavoured vodkas – plus bottled beer, the odd keg of stout or lager and a little wine. Music tends towards the ambient in the week, but at weekends things can get very noisy indeed, making Babushkas a favoured venue with those who fancy a night out but really can't be arsed with a club.

CLUBS

CLUBS

Clubbing in London rocks. Right now the city is far more vibrant than any other on the planet: just ask anyone from Berlin, Tokyo, New York or Sydney. These cities do well, but on a much smaller, far more segregated scale ('if this is Berlin, then it must be electro'). There's a reason why so many DJs across the world are falling over themselves to play here, and it's this: once they've made it in London, they've made it full stop. So whatever gets you running for the dancefloor – electro, drum 'n' bass, hard house, screaming guitars, world grooves, old school rave – you'll find it here every night of the week. Unless you're into queercore or silent clubs, of course – but even then, you've got at least a couple of nights a month.

Rumours of clubland's death have proven to be somewhat premature. There are more round-the-block queues at more clubs than ever before, and fresh new sounds, such as grime, straight out of the East End, are tearing up dancefloors across the capital. And another thing: the days when you had to choose between a bar *or* a club are long gone – now the bar and the club are often under the same roof. So when you walk into **Cargo**, you can peel left for the restaurant, walk through the first arch for some loungin' action – or carry on through to the back and jump around to a band. This section of the guide covers venues whose primary function is to cater to clubbers; for DJ bars, consult the index. Now get out there!

Aquarium

256 Old Street, EC1V 9DD (7251 6136/www.clubaquarium.co.uk). Old Street tube/rail. **Open** *Bar* noon-11pm Mon-Fri; 7-11pm Sat; noon-3pm Sun. *Club* 9am-3am Wed, Thur, Sun; 9pm-4am Fri; 10pm-4am Sat. **Food served** *Bar* noon-3pm, 5-7pm Mon-Fri; noon-3pm Sun. **Admission** *Club* £8-£15. **Credit** MC, V.

Apparently the only club in the country with its own swimming pool and jacuzzi, Aquarium lives up to its watery name with a T-shaped Roman pool complete with life guards and fluffy towels; the 500-capacity venue also has two dancefloors and a cosy lounge bar with capacious sofas. Hardly surprising, then, that it's been the location for so many pop videos and films. Despite its setting in achingly cool Old Street, its nights tend to be tongue-in-cheek. Carwash is the unstoppable '70s funkfest that sends clubbers to their dressing-up box every Saturday.

Map 5 Q4.

Barfly

49 Chalk Farm Road, NW1 8AN (7691 4244/www.barflyclub.com). Camden Town or Chalk Farm tube. **Open** 7.30pm-midnight Mon-Thur; 7.30pm-3am Fri, Sat; 7.30-11pm Sun. **Admission** £5-£8. **No credit cards**.

In the dark and dusty minds of a few old rockers, this is the Monarch; to everyone else, it's the Barfly. Without much ado, it's established itself as a Camden institution to eclipse its predecessor. Primarily a small gig venue, it has two rooms with the essential bare brick walls and odd posters. This is still Camden, so expect balding once-were-rockers moshing against girls in designer vintage and perfectly ironed hair. The Queens of Noize still rule the DJ roost every Friday bar one, and you'll find the outrageously fun Filthy Dukes here every couple of weeks, with the rock 'n' roll circus they call Kill 'Em All Let God Sort It Out.

Map 8 H26.

Bar Rumba

36 Shaftesbury Avenue, W1V 7DD (7287 6933/www.barrumba.co.uk). Piccadilly Circus tube. **Open** 9pm-3.30am Mon, Sat; 6pm-3am Tue; 9pm-3am Wed; 6pm-3.30am Thur, Fri; 8.30pm-2am Sun. **Admission** £3-£12; free before 9pm Tue, Fri; before 8.30pm Thur. **Credit** AmEx, MC, V.

Open for over a decade, but still going strong, this basement venue is home to some of the most respected sessions in town. Their happy hour goes on for hours, and don't fret if you don't nab one of the booths: this place was made for groovin' on the dancefloor with the lights down low every night of the week. That's How It Is 2 is Monday's jazz-funk party, Tuesdays gets sexy salsa dancers at Barrio Latino, while Movement keeps the junglists jumping with plenty of international drum 'n' bass action every Thursday. Friday's all about hip hop and bashment at Get Down.

Map 7 K7.

Blag

First Floor, 68 Notting Hill Gate, W11 3HT (7243 0123/www.blagclub.com). Notting Hill Gate tube. **Open** 7.30pm-1am Wed-Sat; 8pm-12.30am Sun. **Admission** £5 after 9pm. **Credit** MC, V.

Check at which Blag Club you're meeting your mates: there's another one in the Canalot Studios on Kensal Road. Both microclubs are more bar than club, but plenty of people come to dance even when it gets squishy – and with a capacity of just 100, that happens pretty fast. Tucked away (up a floor in Notting Hill; behind some nondescript doors on Kensal Road), both have Indonesian-minimalist decor, and as many people come as part of a big guest-list group, it often feels like you're walking into a friendly party.

Map 10 A7.

Bug Bar

The Crypt, St Matthew's Church, Brixton Hill, SW2 1JF (7738 3366/www.bugbrixton.co.uk). Brixton tube/rail. **Open** *Lounge Bar* 5-11pm Tue-Sat;

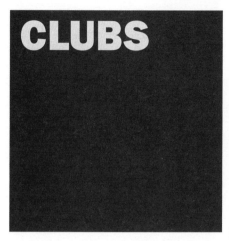

1-9pm Sun. *Bug Bar* 8pm-1am Thur; 8pm-3am Sat; 8pm-2am Sun. **Credit** MC, V.
Deep in the crypt of what was once St Matthew's Church, a postal address it shares with Mass (*see p257*), the Bug Bar has been rocking with underground sounds since 1997. Its vaulted chambers are full of red velvet sofas, wooden tables, old pews (naturally) and flickering candles – but all is not half as gothic as it sounds. The attached restaurant has expanded its once-veggie menu to include organic fish and meat, and the Lounge serves snack food and some fine cocktails. It's for the club that most come, though, where DJs dish up anything from soulful house through to bassquaking breaks. Come summer and you'll want to lounge under one of the ancient yew trees and enjoy frosty beers and food late into the evening.

Canvas

King's Cross Goods Yard, N1 0UZ (7833 8301/ www.canvaslondon.net). King's Cross tube/rail.
Open 10pm-6am Fri, Sat. **Admission** £10-£20.
Credit (bar only) MC, V.
While the nearby Key and Cross are open all weekend, every weekend, Canvas is open as and when promoters fancy biting off a whole lot of space. It easily accommodates 3,000 if all three room and two bars are open, and would need one hell of a refurb to prevent it feeling like a monolithic warehouse. No bad thing, really, as it's currently perfect for the weekly Roller Disco, which sees disco, hip hop, party classics and big house choons thrown down over three rooms every Thursday; then there's free (yup, free!) bi-monthly Hum Allnighters for breaks fans, and the occasional indie guitar mosh pit that is Kill All Hippies.

Cargo

83 Rivington Street, EC2A 3AY (7749 7844/ www.cargo-london.com). Old Street tube/rail/55 bus.
Open/food served 6pm-1am Mon-Thur; 6pm-3am Fri, Sat; 6pm-midnight Sun. **Admission** £4-£10.
Credit MC, V.
Housed in a Victorian railway arch, this is one venue where it's the music that matters. They've been championing the live-bands-at-clubs malarkey since their inception some four years ago, and are nothing if not eclectic when it comes to booking DJs and promoters. Inside, there's a restaurant that serves international tapas-style grub, and the middle bar has an elevated lounge space that's filled with big brown cushions. The main room can get pretty jammed when there's a band on, but the joy of Cargo is that whatever your taste – Gilles Peterson's world music, Bobby Friction's Asian underground, international hip hop – you'll find a night for you. Tuesdays are Demo City (Youth of Britain are one recent young band). The excellent website delivers live recordings if you miss an essential gig.
Map 5 R4.

Crash

Arch 66, Goding Street, SE11 5AW (7793 9262/ www.crashlondon.co.uk). Vauxhall tube/rail. **Open** 10.30pm-6am 2nd & 4th Sat of mth. **Admission** £12-£15. **Credit** MC, V.
This popular gay club is situated in two enormous rooms under a murky railway arch in Vauxhall. It prides itself on monthly residencies that cater for every gay subset, but it's their flagship event Crash Afterhours that really

EGG

attracts the boys. Kicking off at 4.30am on a Sunday, it's definitely not for the faint of heart. Recent improvements have included a new bar and more comfortable areas in which to chill out or get it on. Proof of success comes in the form of dozens of barechested blokes queuing to get in.

Cross

Arches, 27-31 King's Cross Goods Yard, N1 0UZ (7837 0828/www.the-cross.co.uk). King's Cross tube/rail. **Open** 11pm-5am Fri, Sun; 10pm-6am Sat. **Admission** £12-£20. **Credit** MC, V.

What occupied just two railway arches over a decade ago has since expanded to five and a garden: a cavernous venue for house lovers who quite like dressing up, thank you. Its nights aim for the middle of the road and create huge queues: Renaissance, Seb Fontaine's Type and the Italo-house Vertigo are all regulars here. The crowd is good looking, friendly and unafraid to wear sunglasses, and there's a big quotient of Italians and Spanish clubbers. The walls might be bare bricks, but the rest is pure style: enormous leather sofas, red drapes, elevated seating areas and lots of plants. It really does make you think (as it proudly states): who needs Ibiza when you can have the Cross?

Dunes

20 Kensington Church Street, W8 5EP (7795 6656/ www.duneslondon.com). High Street Kensington tube. **Open/food served** 8pm-2am Tue-Sat; 8pm-1am Sun. **Admission** £10-£15. **Credit** AmEx, DC, MC, V.

Chances are, Kensington Church Street isn't going to be your first (or fifth, even) thought when it comes to raving the night away: so if the new Dunes is going to be anything more than swanky watering hole with music, it's got its work cut out. Happily, it's very easy on the eye: the sumptious, red-lit basement venue has more than enough sofas, a long leather bar, plenty of twinkly lights and the bar staff certainly know their way around the cocktail menu. The nights include Arabian Nights, which certainly suits the decor, every Wednesday, and lots of R&B on the weekend.

EGG

200 York Way, N7 9AX (7609 8364/www.egglondon. net). King's Cross tube/rail then free shuttle bus from bus stop G every 15 mins until 1am. **Open** 10pm-5am Fri; 10pm-6am Sat. **Admission** free-£15. **Credit** (bar only) MC, V.

If only all clubs could be as good-looking as EGG. Three floors inside to play on: the loft bar boasting gorgeous red leather banquettes to lounge on; the middle straight out of a warehouse dance studio, with a flashy disco-lit bar if you (ahem) lose your way on the dancefloor; and the basement, half art gallery, half super-swanky apartment. A well designed outdoor terrace and courtyard complete with bar, astroturf and loungers is perfect for sunny weather. While never living up to its Electroclash mothership, it's nonetheless attracting some strong resident nights that take in house, techno and the odd bit of afterhours debauchery.

Electrowerkz

7 Torrens Street, EC1V 1NQ (7837 6419/ www.electrowerkz.com). Angel tube. **Open** 10pm-7.30am Sat; times vary on weekdays. **Admission** £5-£15. **No credit cards**.

Given its location, it's no small surprise that a developer with dollars in his eyes hasn't snapped up Electrowerkz. It's more than a tad skanky: you certainly don't want to fall on the floor, or shod your feet in anything that you can't

london's QUEER
alternative
TRASH PALACE
LATE NITE SOHO SOUNDZ BAR
CHEAP BOOZE - DJS - 2 FLOORS
11 WARDOUR ST - LONDON W1
MON-THU & SUN 5PM-LATE
FRI-SAT 5PM-SUPER LATE
WWW.TRASHPALACE.CO.UK
Ghetto
THE FAG UNDERGROUND
SOHO CLUBBIN
10.30PM-LATE 7 NITES A WEEK
FALCONBERG COURT - LONDON W1
WWW.GHETTO-LONDON.CO.UK
popstarz
THE UK'S BIGGEST QUEER CLUBBING ALTERNATIVE!
EVERY FRIDAY, 10PM-LATE @ THE SCALA KINGS CROSS LONDON N1
WWW.POPSTARZ.ORG
filthy gorgeous
get yer rocks off

wash. Not that you'd be allowed in on Saturday nights if your feet were dressed in anything but black: Electrowerkz is home to Slimelight, the capital's biggest goth night (both modern and traditional variants welcome). You have to be a member to get in, and can only apply by turning up (they like to check you out in person): unless you look like an extra from *Dracula*, expect to be disappointed. Saturdays aside, Soul Jazz also host their popular reggae night, 100% Dynamite, here, and there are also regular one-offs, particularly from electronica labels.
Map 9 N2.

End

18 West Central Street, WC1A 1JJ (7419 9199/ www.endclub.com). Holborn or Tottenham Court Road tube. **Open** 10pm-3am Mon; 10.30pm-3am Wed; 10pm-4am Thur; 10pm-5am Fri; 10pm-7am Sat; phone for details Sun. **Admission** £4-£15. **Credit** MC, V.
Down here, any kind of electronic sound goes, as long as it's not commercial. The reason? It's owned by Mr C and Layo, both of whom have been at the cutting edge of dance music for more than a decade. The main room is either loved or loathed by DJs for its island booth, but the Lounge is universally popular. AKA (*see p24*) gets dragged in to proceedings every Saturday, turning it into a three room affair. On a monthly rotation you'll find the breaks magic of Chew The Fat, leftfield electro/house/techno at Bugged Out!, tech/house at Underwater, and Layo & Bushwacka! All Night Long. However, it's the Monday night Trash that everyone keeps talking about. Run by Erol Alkan (he's also the resident), it's a meeting of indie and dance, with frequent ahead-of-the-curve live acts. The Trash dress code – thrift shop meets haute couture – is as cutting-edge as the music, and evidence of effort made is required for entry.
Map 1 L6.

Fabric

77A Charterhouse Street, EC1M 3HN (7336 8898/ www.fabriclondon.com). Farringdon tube/rail. **Open** 9.30pm-5am Fri; 10pm-7am Sat. **Admission** £12-£15. **Credit** MC, V.
Open only at weekends, it has achingly hip DJ line-ups, with clever bookers getting in live acts and DJs months before most people have even heard of them. Fridays bring leftfield drum 'n' bass, hip hop, grime and breaks, while Saturdays see a healthy dose of house and techno into the mix. Although the two big rooms are hard to get out of once you find a space, do check the small room in the rafters: this is where the real experimental stuff happens. With three subterranean spaces and a capacity of 1,500, it can sometimes feel like you need a map – but getting lost and making new friends on the stairs is half the fun. If you turn up just as the pubs are closing, expect huge queues.
Map 3 O5.

Fridge Bar

1 Town Hall Parade, Brixton Hill, SW2 1RJ (7326 5100). Brixton tube/rail. **Open** *Bar* 6pm-2am Mon-Thur; 6pm-4am Fri; 8pm-4am Sat; 8pm-3am Sun. *Happy hour* 6-10pm daily. *Club* 10pm-6am Fri, Sat. **Admission** *Bar* free before 10.30pm then £5-£10 Fri, Sat; £3 occasional Sun. *Club* £12-£18. **Credit** *Both* (over £10) MC, V.
Fridge is London's hard dance mecca (we'll ignore the brief, ill-advised swerve into R&B not long back), and its recent refurb has made the space cleaner and added lights and lasers, but the atmosphere's still anarchic. It's a veritable home from home for nutters who, depending on the night, range from dreadlocked trancers to glo-stick-carrying, furry-booted ravers. One or two nights lean toward out-and-proud gay parties; but the rest are straight-up, hard dance marathons. Which is just the way they like it.

Ghetto

5-6 Falconberg Court, W1D 3AB (7287 3726/ www.ghetto-london.co.uk). Tottenham Court Road tube. **Open** 10.30pm-3am Mon-Thur, Sun; 10.30pm-4am Fri; 10.30pm-5am Sat. **Admission** £1-£7. **No credit cards**.
Done out in raving red, this fabulously sweaty basement venue is home to two of London's hippest electro synth fests. Nag Nag Nag might not get headlines these days, but there's no doubt it has one of the most forward-thinking music policies around, with the talented JoJo de Freq playing bang-up-to-date (not banging) electronica and techno, and Johnny Slut mixing up old and new electro-disco. Friday's mostly gay (though straight-friendly) Cock is not as cutting-edge but outdoes Nag for sheer energy: it's the night that prompted gay bible *Attitude* to dub Ghetto 'a welcome break from your typical homo hangout'.
Map 7 K6.

Hammersmith Palais

230 Shepherds Bush Road, W6 7NL (7341 5300/ www.hammersmithpalais.com). Hammersmith tube. **Open** 10pm-3am Fri, Sat. **Admission** £5-£10. **Credit** (bar only) MC, V.
Owned by the Barvest group, the Palais shows little evidence of its past as a grungy rock 'n' roll venue, but instead plenty of red drapes, ironwork and Middle Eastern decor. Stand on the balcony overlooking the simply massive main floor, and it's easy to see why it's so popular for corporate events and awards ceremonies. Drive past on a Saturday night and you're likely to look twice or even thrice: queues of adults dressed in school uniforms can mean one thing – the phenomenally successful Schooldisco.com. More of a meat market than our school discos ever were (and that's saying something), it's hugely popular with groups of guys and girls out on the prowl. Fridays are Classics for those who like their retro to come from the quality box.

Heaven

Under the Arches, Villiers Street, WC2N 6NG (7930 2020/www.heaven-london.com). Embankment tube/ Charing Cross tube/rail. **Open** 10am-6am Mon, Wed, Fri, Sat. **Admission** £2-£12. **Credit** (advance bookings only) AmEx, MC, V.
Ask anyone who raved in London's earliest days about Heaven, and they're likely to go misty eyed and talk about hearing the likes of Grooverider and Fabio cutting their DJ teeth. Fast forward a decade, and it's mostly 'the most famous gay club in the world'. The main room is super-club-sized, while towards the back, the Soundshaft is a much smaller affair that has a wrap-around balony to throw shapes on; there's also a diner and a VIP room with fishtanks and red velvet seats. Nights are usually loudly and proudly gay, with Saturday nights heaving with sweating men. Gatecrasher and Wildchild, two of London's most popular hard dance parties, have residencies here.
Map 2 J7.

Herbal

10-14 Kingsland Road, E2 8DA (7613 4462/ www.herbaluk.com). Old Street tube/rail/55 bus. **Open** 9pm-2am Tue-Thur-Sun; 9am-3am Fri, Sat.

5 mins 'til the Weekend
www.carwash.co.uk
Get Funked Harder
0870 246 1966

Admission £3 after 10pm Wed; £3-£5 Thur; £4-£8 Fri, Sat; £6-£8 Sun (women free before 11pm). **Credit** MC, V.

This well designed two-floor club and bar maintains a warm and cosy vibe with a house party feel. It's only a 500-capacity club, yet no expense was spared in rigging up a sound system that makes such nights as Grooverider's weekly Grace into real roof-raisers. The upstairs bar, overlooking down-at-heel Kingsland Road, pleases pre-club drinkers with draught Red Stripe and Hoegaarden, quality whisky, Stolis and Polstars – all in a cosy decor of bare brick and reclaimed timber. The owners have worked hard to avoid attracting the bridge 'n' tunnel brigade, partly by forever exhibiting new underground talents. **Map 5 R3**.

Jamm

261 Brixton Road, SW9 6LH (7274 5537/www.brixton jamm.org). Brixton tube/rail. **Open** 5pm-2am Mon-Thur; noon-6am Fri, Sat; noon-midnight Sun. **Admission** £3-£8. **Credit** AmEx, DC, MC, V.

Despite the name change (and a big neon sign), people are finding it hard to stop calling this club Bar Lorca. A brisk walk from Brixton tube and you come to a hefty bar complete with outdoor terrace and carpark. It's on the right side of rundown; there's a lounge area kitted out with sofas, a few plants, posters and a good-sized bar. The main room was made for small gigs and blistering club nights, with a small stage and a bar running the length of one side. Basement Jaxx lay on their monthly Inside Out parties here (they drape white acid house sheets over the bare walls), and there are plenty of drum 'n' bass parties pulling in impressive talent several nights of the week.

Karma Bar

266 Fulham Road, SW10 9EL (7352 6200/www.kbar chelsea.com). Earls Court or Fulham Broadway tube. **Open** 10pm-2am Tue-Sat. **Admission** £12-£15. **Credit** AmEx, DC, MC, V.

Sure, it's yet another bar-restaurant-club; but let's face it, there's hardly a row of superclubs down Chelsea way. Whatever it is, it's rightly popular. The theme – yes – is karma, so you'll see the Buddha wherever you look; and if we're ever faced by an international cushion shortage, we'll know who to blame. Alcoves and semi-private areas put it a world away from the average sardine-tin bar, and the music is more about swaying nicely than going crazy. As at most places of this ilk, you'd do well to get your name on the 'guest list' to ensure entry: it can get pretty busy and unless you're Kate Moss (not that she would ever go here), you'll struggle to get in on Thursday, Friday and Saturday.

Key

King's Cross Freight Depot, King's Cross, N1 9AA (7837 1027/www.thekeylondon.com). King's Cross tube/rail. **Open** 10.30pm-6am Fri, Sat. **Admission** £7-£20. **Credit** (bar only) MC, V.

Whatever you do, don't rock up to the Key at any time before midnight, or you'll be in for a lonely start to the evening. Things only really get going at around 1am, but it stays open late – sometimes really late. The Key was only added two years ago to the growing complex of clubs behind King's Cross railway station, and perhaps the ten-minute walk along bleak-looking roads encourages the late-arrival-late-departure culture. Either way, the disco-tastic illuminated dancefloor, back-to-basics approach and intimate vibe make the trek more than worthwhile.

KOKO

1A Camden High Street, NW1 9JE (0870 432 5527/ www.koko.uk.com). Mornington Crescent tube. **Open** 10pm-4am Sat; 10pm-3am Fri; phone to check other times. **Admission** £3-£15. **Credit** (bar only) MC, V.

Famous for being the Camden Palace (we wish they'd kept the old name; KOKO is a bit daft), where many music legends did legendary things, it was allowed to run down in quite criminal fashion. The few million pounds for refurbishment last year was money well spent, for the old music hall now looks a treat. Opulent in an old-fashioned way – gloss claret and gold paint, plenty of Greek gods holding up columns – KOKO is all about vertical levels. You'll no doubt get lost in the many stairwells as you try to get from balcony over here to balcony over there. The sound system is beyond awesome and works for both DJs and live shows. The cheesy post-relaunch programming was widely criticised, but now Saturdays are hyper-credible, with house, techno and live acts worthy of the coolest venues. **Map 8 J2**.

Madame Jo Jo's

8-10 Brewer Street, W1S 0SP (7734 3040/www. madamejojos.com). Leicester Square or Piccadilly Circus tube. **Open** 10pm-3am Wed, Fri; 9pm-3am Thur; 7pm-3am Sat. **Admission** £5-£15. **Credit** (bar only) AmEx, MC, V.

The combination of that name and a Soho location (not to mention the garish red decor) suggests drag and cabaret – and with the likes of the Kitsch Cabaret and the occasional Burlesque Bazaar, you get both in bucketloads. The hen

CRITICS' PICKS

For dancing till dawn
Cross (*see p250*), **EGG** (*see p250*), **End** (*see p253*), **Fabric** (*see p253*), **Turnmills** (*see p259*).

For showing off the glad rags
Aquarium (*see p248*), **Cross** (*see p250*), **Hammersmith Palais** (*see p253*), **Pacha** (*see p258*), **Rouge** (*see p259*).

For catching superstar DJs
Cross (*see p250*), **End** (*see p253*), **KOKO** (*see above*), **Ministry of Sound** (*see p257*), **Turnmills** (*see p259*).

For discovering the next big thing
Cargo (*see p249*), **Fabric** (*see p253*), **Key** (*see left*), **Notting Hill Arts Club** (*see p258*), **333** (*see p259*).

For sound system junkies
Fabric (*see p253*), **KOKO** (*see above*), **Ministry of Sound** (*see p257*), **Plastic People** (*see p258*).

For achingly hip hipsters
Fabric (*see p253*), **Herbal** (*see p253*), **Key** (*see left*), **Plastic People** (*see p258*), **333** (*see p259*).

parties that come here are invited to stay on for Groove Sanctuary, the deep house night that takes over at 10pm. Much cooler is Keb Darge's Deep Funk night on Fridays, the last word in rare funk singles and the legacy of the capital's '80s rare groove scene. The dancefloor is invariably packed. We're glad to hear Mark Moore (from S-Express, no less) is back every Thursday with Electrogogo, a mix of '80s synth pop, punk-funk and Euro-techno. **Map 7 K6**.

Mass

St Matthew's Church, Brixton Hill, SW2 1JF (7738 7875). Brixton tube/rail. **Open** 8.30pm-3am Thur; 10pm-6am Fri; noon-7pm, 10pm-6am Sat; phone to check other times. **Admission** £4-£15. **No credit cards**.

New owners and a promotional reshuffle have put Mass back on the clubbing map. Legendary reggae broadcaster David Rodigan has made his Wednesday reggae session an essential one, hitting the spot for a local multicultured crowd with soundclash greats such as Saxon Sound. Fridays are thriving as an underground R&B, soulful alternative to Ministry of Sound's Smoove; it's a lycra-wearing, booty affair which as a sign-of-the-times necessity has put a large metal detector front of house – all a long way from the loved-up, illegal parties of the '80s for which the venue is still fondly remembered. There are regular hard house and old school drum 'n' bass nights, too.

Medicine

89 Great Eastern Street, EC2A 3HX (7739 5173/ www.medicinebar.net). Old Street tube/rail/55 bus. **Open/food served** 5-11pm Mon-Wed; 5pm-2am Thur, Sat; 4pm-2am Fri. *Happy hour* 5-9pm Mon-Fri. **Admission** £4-£6 after 9pm Fri, Sat. **Credit** MC, V.

Thanks to the groundbreaking work of its big brother on Upper Street, the Medicine Bar has muscled in on the DJ bar turf of ruthlessly competitive Shoreditch – and toughed it out to good effect. Quality DJing and a pristine sound system have, above all, drawn the punters in. Large-to-medium names – Norman Jay plays occasionally, as does the Sonar Kollectiv – pull in a respectable, albeit disparate crowd at the weekends, while during the week City types wander up from Liverpool Street to take advantage of frequent drinks promotions and the late licence. As for the bar, it's cool by rote, laid-back and louche downstairs; interestingly lit, subtle and spacious at street level. **Map 5 Q4**.

Ministry of Sound

103 Gaunt Street, SE1 6DP (0870 0600 010/ www.ministryofsound.com). Elephant & Castle tube/ rail. **Open** 10pm-3am Wed; 10.30pm-5am Fri; 11pm-7am Sat. **Admission** £4 Wed; £12 Fri; £15 Sat. **Credit** MC, V.

There's no arguing that MoS is the world's most famous clubbing brand – if only because of prolific compilation albums and near-constant international touring. All in all, it's difficult to get away from the feeling that it isn't a club, it's a corporation. Once inside, it's as far removed from the days of raves as it's possible to get. A recent refurbishment threw even more money at the sound system; say what you will about the Ministry, its sound is gobsmackingly great. The main room (the 'box') could be confused with a warehouse, albeit a very clean one, while the bar with its overlooking balcony is often just as heaving as the main room. This is one place where the VIP room is to be avoided like the plague: they've installed glass cubes for extra-special VIPs – fine only if you like impersonating goldfish.

Madame Jo Jo's. *See p255.*

Neighbourhood

12 Acklam Road, W10 5QZ (7524 7979/www.neighbourhoodclub.net). Ladbroke Grove or Westbourne Park tube. **Open** 8pm-2am Thur-Sat; 5pm-midnight Sun. **Admission** £5-£15. **No credit cards**.

His confidence no doubt galvanised by the success of Cherry Jam, Ben Watt (of Everything But the Girl) has breathed new life into this spot under the Westway, previously occupied by Subterrania. It's not just the decor that's been juiced up; the menu boasts champagne cocktails and sushi, served by friendly bar staff and lapped up by a merry muddle of people dressed a little smarter than the Subterrania crowd. The beloved balcony upstairs is still a great feature, but there are now lots of convivial seating areas if you aren't in a moving-and-grooving kinda mood. This time round the music has a stronger tilt towards quality house music, with nights such as One Starry Night on Fridays, while Mr Watt gives Sundays a kick in the pants with his hugely successful Buzzin' Fly. **Map 10 Az5**.

93 Feet East

150 Brick Lane, E1 6QN (7247 3293/www.93feeteast.co.uk). Aldgate East tube/Liverpool Street tube/rail. **Open** 5-11pm Mon-Thur; 5pm-1am Fri; noon-1am Sat; noon-10.30pm Sun. **Admission** £5-£10; free before 9pm Fri, Sat. **Credit** (advance bookings & bar only) MC, V.

There may be a load of bars rubbing shoulders with the curry houses now, but there used to be just two Brick Lane originals: the Vibe bar and this. During the week, it's predominantly a live venue; at weekends, however, dance music played by DJs still holds sway. The nights are a mix of one-offs and monthlies, and tend to be a pile-up of all that's great, good and downright unusual: house, hip hop, soundclashes, techno, raggae, twisted mentalness. Toast Battles are great fun (the resident hip hop DJs take on anyone silly enough to have a go), while Liverpool's excellent Chibuku Shake Shake rock the tech house crowd. It's a shame it's not open later (noise complaints), but they make the most of what they've got, and it's a destination venue all summer long, thanks to its great courtyard.

Notting Hill Arts Club

21 Notting Hill Gate, W11 3JQ (7460 4459/ www.nottinghillartsclub.com). Notting Hill Gate tube. **Open** 6pm-1am Mon-Wed; 6pm-2am Thur, Fri; 4pm-2am Sat; 4pm-1am Sun. **Admission** £5-£8. **Credit** (bar only) MC, V.

This no-frills subterranean den has been rolling out nights to sate every musical taste for quite a while. DJs and live music are the main order or the day, but some of the more avant-garde promotions have surprises up their sleeves. Alan McGee's Death Disco is still giving shaggy-haired White Stripe wannabes something to rock to; Thursday's YoYo is all about soul, funk and house classics. Other regular nights take in Scando-house, Mediterranean flavours, Berlin electronica, Latino and Asian underground. And fear not, Sloane-loathers: despite its location, Notting Hillbillies rarely join the crowd of musos and boozos. **Map 10 B7**.

Pacha

Terminus Place, SW1E 5NE (7833 3139/www.pacha london.com). Victoria tube/rail. **Open** 10pm-5am Fri; 10pm-6am Sat. **Admission** £15-£25. **Credit** MC, V.

Everyone knows that Pacha in Ibiza is one of the world's very best clubs. Those chasing the double cherries (cherries are the club logo) to Victoria, though, are in for a shock. Sure, once you get in, it's glitzy and sleek; but it's nowhere near as massive as its Balearic counterpart, and the Astroturf terrace overlooks a bus depot. The main room works well, on occasion, with a large raised platform for exhibitionists, and the baby room upstairs is perfectly formed. After a run through different nights that simply didn't work, they've struck a successful chord with glammed-up house nights: Kinki Malinki, Defected, Gate 21. Many a night sees a long queue now, too. It often costs £20 just to get through the door, which says a lot about the clientele: more big spenders than cool clubbers.

Plan B

418 Brixton Road, SW9 7AY (7733 0926/www.planbrixton.co.uk). Brixton tube/rail. **Open** 5pm-2am Tue-Thur, Sun; 5pm-4am Fri, Sat. **Admission** £5 after 10pm Thur; £5 after 9pm, £7 after 11pm Fri, Sat. **Credit** AmEx, MC, V.

This slick, industrial amalgam of concrete, steel and bare brick is the best thing that's happened to Brixton Road. Fresh music promotions have helped shed the area's reputation as a mecca of ragga, riots and resin, and resident DJs book guest spinners from Thursday to Sunday, all free (except for a token entry tax at weekends). Friday's Fidgit is a feel-good hip hop success; Saturdays see B Side welcome up-and-coming house names, plus some heavyweight spinners. The high bar spans the entire back wall and serves the usual bottled beers, some inspired cocktails and generously poured measures of spirits.

Plastic People

147-149 Curtain Road, EC2A 3QE (7739 6471/ www.plasticpeople.co.uk). Liverpool Street or Old Street tube/rail/8, 55, 133, 344 bus. **Open** 10pm-2am Thur; 10pm-3.30am Fri, Sat; 7.30pm-midnight Sun. Times can vary, so check website. **Admission** £5-£10. **No credit cards**.

Plastic People subscribes to the old school line that says all you need for a kicking party is a dark basement and a sound system. But what it lacks in size and decor it makes up for in sound quality (the rig embarrasses those in many larger clubs) and some of London's most progressive club nights. On the last Thursday of the month Forward showcases the latest developments in dub-step, two-step and grime; Friday nights see Rory Phillips (Erol Alkan's righthand man at Trash) go it alone with And Did We Mention

TEN CLUBBING COMMANDMENTS

You shall use
All of the days of the week to rave.

You shall not covet
Your neighbour's handbag or Stella McCartney designed Converse. Together, you are *all* beautiful people on the dancefloor.

You shall hold
Your frothy pint and lit cigarette carefully as you move across the dancefloor.

You shall never share
A toilet cubicle with any other person (unless you fancy a speedy eviction from the club).

You shall never climb into
Illegal minicabs, nor let your friends use them. The risks are just too great.

You shall know
The methods of the nightbuses, for they shall be your saviour.

You shall not attempt
To adjust the EQ for the DJ, nor explain at length why he or she is better than sliced bread. Your presence on the dancefloor is praise enough.

You shall not talk
About things being better 'back in the day'.

You shall visit
The four corners of London, for verily, there is life beyond Hoxton and the West End.

You shall keep
A thoroughly open mind and taste all the fruits of London's clubland.

Our Disco; flagship Saturday night Balance treads a middle ground of Latin, jazz, hip hop, house and techno; and the second and last Sundays of the month see Co Op roll out future jazz and broken beats.
Map 5 R4.

Rouge

144 Charing Cross Road, WC2H 0LB (7240 1900/ www.rougeclublondon.com). Tottenham Court Road tube. **Open** 10pm-4am Wed-Sat; 10pm-3am Sun. **Admission** £8-£15. **Credit** (bar only) MC, V.
Famous for its after parties, this sprawling 600-capacity club is the place for celeb-spotting – or at the very least dancing on a spot which was previously hoofed on by the Darkness or Kevin Spacey. The dark burgundy decor dictates smart-casual wear, cocktail-drinking and fairly high prices – but with four dancefloors and music that spans burlesque, club classics, electro and R&B, a night out at Rouge never gets dull. A new spate of after-hours gigs sees the dancefloor getting a good workout during the day, too.
Map 7 K6.

seOne

41-43 St Thomas Street, SE1 3QX (7407 1617/ www.seonelondon.com). London Bridge tube/rail. **Open** 10pm-6am Fri, Sat. **Admission** £10-£18. **Credit** (advance bookings only) AmEx, MC, V.
It must be disconcerting for drivers who turn into the Weston Street tunnel to see hundreds of ravers wearing funny things in their hair queuing to get into a club. Set in the enormous archways under London Bridge, seOne can get pretty frosty (and pretty steamy). The two main rooms that parallel each other are gargantuan, but when filled with a successful night, they take you back to the early days of warehouse raves. Depending on the night, there are several smaller rooms, usually for chilling out or VIPs. Mostly home to 'relive the day' raves and massive psychedelic trance affairs, this is a basic and grimy venue.

Telegraph

228 Brixton Hill, SW2 1HE (8678 0777/www.the brixtontelegraph.co.uk). Brixton tube/rail then 45, 59, 118, 133, 159, 250 bus. **Open** noon-2am Mon-Thur; noon-4am Fri; noon-6am Sat; noon-midnight Sun. **Food served** 5.30-11.30pm daily. **Credit** AmEx, MC, V.
One of south London's most relaxing hangouts, for which you'll be thankful after the hill-climb to get there. The layout is designed for multi-space enjoyment; the idea, probably, is to fill up on Thai food at the chunky wooden tables before moving on to the bar. Then, in one corner, you can warm up to a DJ before retiring to the air-conned club/ parlour. If it all sounds rather grand, it is – and don't local SW2 dwellers appreciate it. (Be warned that in the cold light of day, the shabby exterior gives a slightly different impression; early drinkers may notice the tatty wallpaper.) Thursdays are Hunk Pappa's Pure Reggae, while 3-D gets proper house bods through the door.

333

333 Old Street, EC1V 9LE (7739 5949/www.333 mother.com). Old Street tube/rail. **Open** *Bar* 8pm-3am Mon-Wed; 8pm-4am Thur, Sun; 8pm-1am Fri, Sat. *Club* 8pm-3am Wed; 10pm-4am Thur, Sun; 10pm-5am Fri, Sat. **Admission** £5-£10. **Credit** (bar only) MC, V.
What a long running success story the 333 is. The queues in rain, hail and shine are testament to the fact that you can rely on this club to get some of the most exciting line-ups in all of London. Three floors (dark basement, big main, Mother bar upstairs, all filled with oh-so-cool party people) lay on everything from Jamaican dancehall to jazz-tinged house, electro-disco to drum 'n' bass – usually all on the same evening. A good thing, because in this area, there's not an enormous amount of late-night choice.
Map 5 R4.

333

Turnmills

63B Clerkenwell Road, EC1M 5PT (7250 3409/ www.turnmills.co.uk). Farringdon tube/rail. **Open** 8pm-1am Wed; 9pm-3am Thur; 10.30pm-7.30am Fri; 10pm-6am Sat. **Admission** £12-£15. **Credit** (bar only) MC, V.
Some great clubs have resided here: Trade, Heavenly Social, Headstart, the Gallery… Despite its Mediterranean decor, the main room still has an acid house feel, helped by its rectangular shape, lasers and the fact that it's usually pitch black. The small room is tucked away under some stairs, and there can be some irritating bottlenecks (who put a bar right by a major thoroughfare?); the top room is part neo-classic, part Ibizan nightspot. A few larger 'small rooms' through the back never have that much going on, but you can be sure that with trance and hard house nights like the Gallery, everyone will be throwing their hands in the air in the main room. And Turnmills attracts the friendliest and most international crowd in town.
Map 3 N4.

WHERE TO GO FOR...

ART

BEER

Belgian beer

Bottled beers

Real ales (good range of)

Central:

City:

East:

North:

South:

West:

CRITICS' PICKS

COMEDY

DANCE CLASSES

DISABLED TOILETS

DRINKING ALOUD

INTERNET ACCESS

IRISH PUBS

KARAOKE

LATE LICENCES

MEMBERS BARS

MUSIC (LIVE)

NO PIPED MUSIC

NO-SMOKING AREAS

OPEN FIRES

ORGANIC FOOD AND/OR DRINK

OUTDOOR DRINKING

(*See also* Riverside & Canalside pubs)

Gardens

Patios, yards & terraces

POETRY/ SPOKEN WORD

QUIZ

RIVERSIDE & CANALSIDE PUBS

SPIRITS

SPORTS

THEATRES

THEMED OR QUIRKY SURROUNDINGS

VIEWS

WINE

A-Z INDEX

ADVERTISERS' INDEX

Please refer to relevant sections for addresses/ telephone numbers

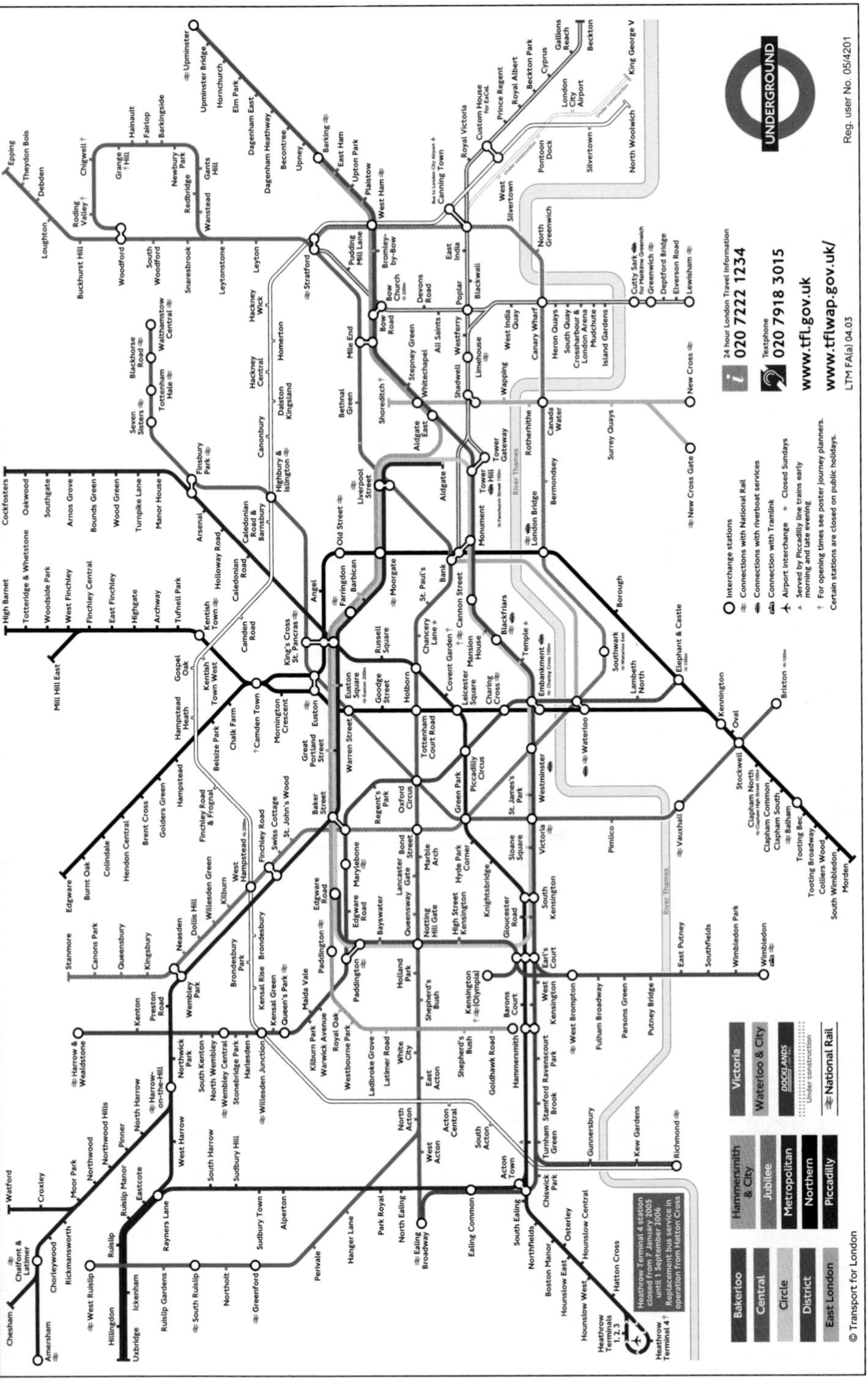
UNDERGROUND
Reg. user No. 05/4201
24 hour London Travel Information
020 7222 1234
Textphone
020 7918 3015
www.tfl.gov.uk
www.tfl.gov.uk/
LTM FA(a) 04.03
Interchange stations
Connections with National Rail
Connections with riverboat services
Connection with Tramlink
Airport interchange
Closed Sundays
Served by Piccadilly line trains early morning and late evening
For opening times see poster journey planners.
Certain stations are closed on public holidays.
Heathrow Terminal 4 station closed from 7 January 2005 until 1 September 2006
Replacement bus service in operation from Hatton Cross
Bakerloo
Central
Circle
District
East London
Hammersmith & City
Jubilee
Metropolitan
Northern
Piccadilly
Victoria
Waterloo & City
DOCKLANDS
Under construction
National Rail
© Transport for London
River Thames
Under construction
Bus to London City Airport
Upminster
Upminster Bridge
Hornchurch
Elm Park
Dagenham East
Dagenham Heathway
Becontree
Upney
Barking
East Ham
Upton Park
Plaistow
West Ham
Epping
Theydon Bois
Debden
Loughton
Buckhurst Hill
Woodford
South Woodford
Snaresbrook
Leytonstone
Leyton
Stratford
Hainault
Fairlop
Barkingside
Chigwell
Grange Hill
Roding Valley
Newbury Park
Gants Hill
Redbridge
Wanstead
Beckton
Gallions Reach
Cyprus
Beckton Park
Royal Albert
Prince Regent
Custom House
Royal Victoria
Canning Town
King George V
London City Airport
Pontoon Dock
Silvertown
North Woolwich
West Silvertown
North Greenwich
East India
Blackwall
Poplar
Pudding Mill Lane
Bromley-by-Bow
Bow Church
Devons Road
Bow Road
Mile End
All Saints
Westferry
Limehouse
West India Quay
Canary Wharf
Heron Quays
South Quay
Crossharbour & London Arena
Mudchute
Island Gardens
Cutty Sark
Greenwich
Deptford Bridge
Elverson Road
Lewisham
Walthamstow Central
Blackhorse Road
Tottenham Hale
Seven Sisters
Hackney Wick
Homerton
Hackney Central
Dalston Kingsland
Canonbury
Highbury & Islington
Finsbury Park
Stepney Green
Whitechapel
Bethnal Green
Shoreditch
Shadwell
Wapping
Rotherhithe
Canada Water
Surrey Quays
New Cross
New Cross Gate
Aldgate East
Aldgate
Tower Gateway
Tower Hill
Liverpool Street
Bermondsey
London Bridge
Monument
Bank
Cockfosters
Oakwood
Southgate
Arnos Grove
Bounds Green
Wood Green
Turnpike Lane
Manor House
Arsenal
Holloway Road
Caledonian Road & Barnsbury
Caledonian Road
Old Street
Moorgate
Barbican
Farringdon
Angel
St. Paul's
Cannon Street
Mansion House
Blackfriars
Temple
Borough
Elephant & Castle
Southwark
Lambeth North
Kennington
Oval
Stockwell
Brixton
High Barnet
Totteridge & Whetstone
Woodside Park
West Finchley
Finchley Central
East Finchley
Highgate
Archway
Tufnell Park
Mill Hill East
Kentish Town
Camden Road
King's Cross St. Pancras
Russell Square
Chancery Lane
Covent Garden
Gospel Oak
Kentish Town West
Camden Town
Euston Square
Goodge Street
Holborn
Leicester Square
Charing Cross
Embankment
Waterloo
Hampstead Heath
Chalk Farm
Mornington Crescent
Euston
Warren Street
Tottenham Court Road
Piccadilly Circus
Westminster
Belsize Park
Great Portland Street
Regent's Park
Oxford Circus
Green Park
St. James's Park
Hampstead
Finchley Road & Frognal
Swiss Cottage
St. John's Wood
Baker Street
Bond Street
Marble Arch
Hyde Park Corner
Victoria
Vauxhall
Pimlico
Clapham North
Clapham Common
Clapham South
Balham
Tooting Bec
Tooting Broadway
Colliers Wood
South Wimbledon
Morden
Edgware
Burnt Oak
Colindale
Hendon Central
Brent Cross
Golders Green
Finchley Road
West Hampstead
Willesden Green
Kilburn
Dollis Hill
Neasden
Marylebone
Lancaster Gate
Sloane Square
Knightsbridge
Edgware Road
Bayswater
Queensway
Notting Hill Gate
High Street Kensington
Gloucester Road
South Kensington
Stanmore
Canons Park
Queensbury
Kingsbury
Wembley Park
Brondesbury Park
Brondesbury
Kensal Rise
Kensal Green
Queen's Park
Maida Vale
Paddington
Holland Park
Shepherd's Bush
Kensington (Olympia)
Earl's Court
West Brompton
Fulham Broadway
Parsons Green
Putney Bridge
East Putney
Southfields
Wimbledon Park
Wimbledon
Harrow & Wealdstone
Kenton
Preston Road
Northwick Park
South Kenton
North Wembley
Wembley Central
Stonebridge Park
Harlesden
Willesden Junction
Kilburn Park
Warwick Avenue
Royal Oak
Westbourne Park
Ladbroke Grove
Latimer Road
White City
East Acton
Goldhawk Road
Hammersmith
Barons Court
West Kensington
Ravenscourt Park
Stamford Brook
Turnham Green
Gunnersbury
Kew Gardens
Richmond
Harrow-on-the-Hill
West Harrow
South Harrow
Sudbury Hill
North Harrow
Pinner
Northwood Hills
Northwood
Moor Park
Watford
Croxley
Rickmansworth
Chorleywood
Chalfont & Latimer
Chesham
Amersham
North Acton
West Acton
Acton Central
South Acton
Acton Town
Chiswick Park
Ealing Common
Ealing Broadway
North Ealing
Park Royal
Hanger Lane
Perivale
Alperton
Sudbury Town
Greenford
Northolt
South Ruislip
Ruislip Gardens
Rayners Lane
Eastcote
Ruislip Manor
Ruislip
Ickenham
Hillingdon
Uxbridge
West Ruislip
South Ealing
Northfields
Boston Manor
Osterley
Hounslow East
Hounslow Central
Hounslow West
Hatton Cross
Heathrow Terminals 1, 2, 3
Heathrow Terminal 4

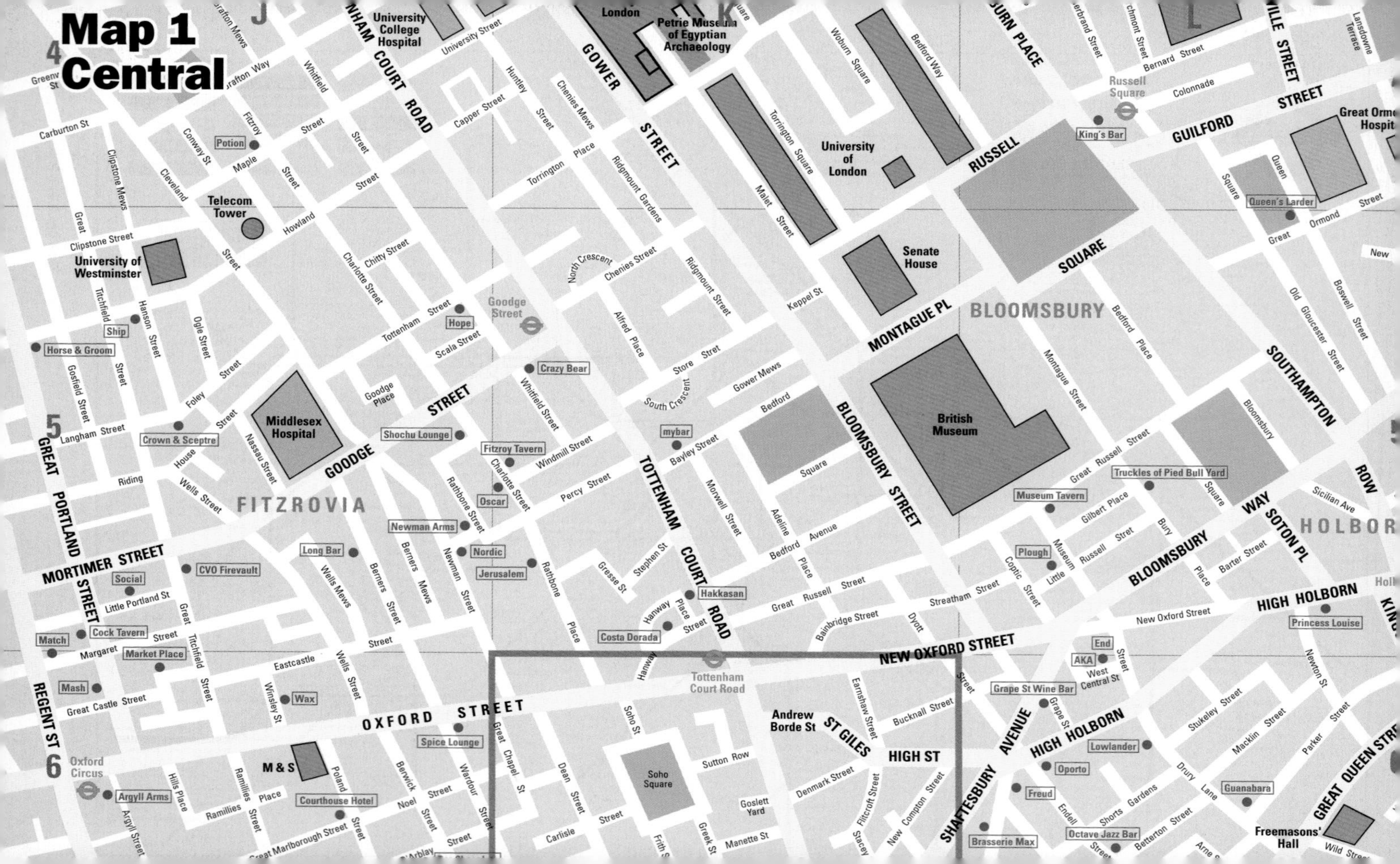

Map 1
Central
4
5
6
J
K
L
FITZROVIA
BLOOMSBURY
HOLBORN
University College Hospital
London
Petrie Museum of Egyptian Archaeology
University of London
Senate House
British Museum
Telecom Tower
University of Westminster
Middlesex Hospital
Soho Square
Great Ormond Hospital
Freemasons' Hall
M & S
Russell Square
Goodge Street
Tottenham Court Road
Oxford Circus
Potion
Ship
Horse & Groom
Crown & Sceptre
Hope
Crazy Bear
Shochu Lounge
Fitzroy Tavern
Oscar
Newman Arms
Long Bar
Nordic
Jerusalem
CVO Firevault
Social
Match
Cock Tavern
Market Place
Mash
Wax
Spice Lounge
Argyll Arms
Courthouse Hotel
mybar
Hakkasan
Costa Dorada
King's Bar
Queen's Larder
Truckles of Pied Bull Yard
Museum Tavern
Plough
Princess Louise
End
AKA
Grape St Wine Bar
Lowlander
Oporto
Freud
Guanabara
Octave Jazz Bar
Brasserie Max
TOTTENHAM COURT ROAD
GOWER STREET
GOODGE STREET
GREAT PORTLAND STREET
MORTIMER STREET
REGENT ST
OXFORD STREET
NEW OXFORD STREET
BLOOMSBURY STREET
MONTAGUE PL
RUSSELL SQUARE
GUILFORD STREET
SOUTHAMPTON ROW
SOTON PL
BLOOMSBURY WAY
HIGH HOLBORN
SHAFTESBURY AVENUE
ST GILES HIGH ST
GREAT QUEEN STREET
Andrew Borde St

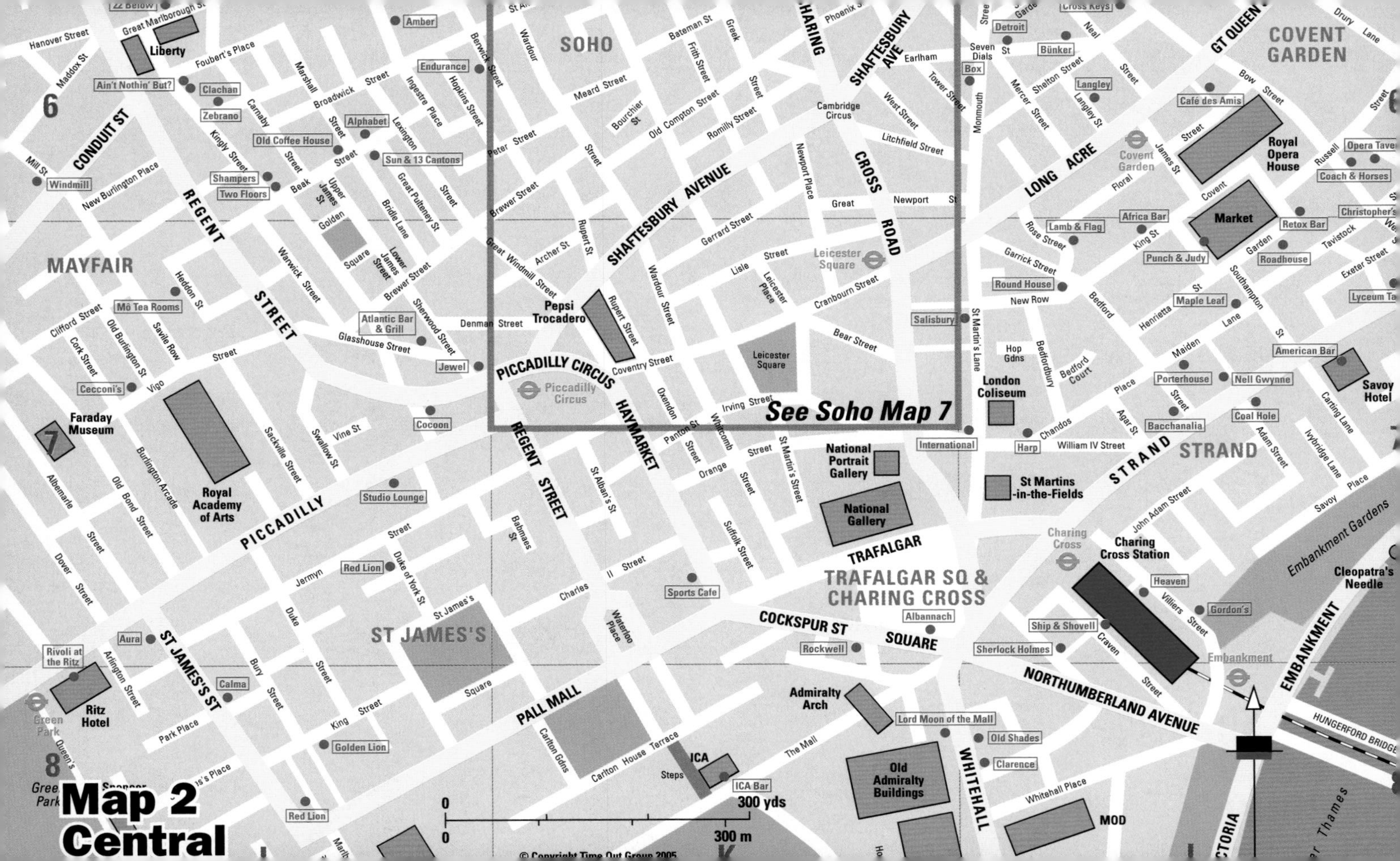
Map 2
Central
See Soho Map 7
COVENT GARDEN
SOHO
MAYFAIR
ST JAMES'S
STRAND
TRAFALGAR SQ & CHARING CROSS
Royal Opera House
Market
Liberty
Faraday Museum
Royal Academy of Arts
Ritz Hotel
Pepsi Trocadero
London Coliseum
St Martins -in-the-Fields
National Portrait Gallery
National Gallery
Charing Cross Station
Savoy Hotel
Cleopatra's Needle
Admiralty Arch
Old Admiralty Buildings
MOD
ICA
Steps
Leicester Square
Piccadilly Circus
Covent Garden
Charing Cross
Embankment
Green Park
Amber
Endurance
Ain't Nothin' But?
Clachan
Zebrano
Alphabet
Old Coffee House
Sun & 13 Cantons
Shampers
Two Floors
Windmill
Mô Tea Rooms
Atlantic Bar & Grill
Jewel
Cecconi's
Cocoon
Studio Lounge
Red Lion
Aura
Rivoli at the Ritz
Calma
Golden Lion
Red Lion
Salisbury
Round House
Lamb & Flag
Africa Bar
Punch & Judy
Maple Leaf
Retox Bar
Roadhouse
Christopher's
Coach & Horses
Café des Amis
Langley
Bünker
Detroit
Box
American Bar
Nell Gwynne
Porterhouse
Coal Hole
Bacchanalia
Harp
International
Heaven
Gordon's
Ship & Shovell
Sherlock Holmes
Albannach
Rockwell
Sports Cafe
Lord Moon of the Mall
Old Shades
Clarence
ICA Bar
REGENT STREET
PICCADILLY
PICCADILLY CIRCUS
HAYMARKET
SHAFTESBURY AVENUE
CHARING CROSS ROAD
LONG ACRE
GT QUEEN
CONDUIT ST
ST JAMES'S ST
PALL MALL
COCKSPUR ST
TRAFALGAR SQUARE
NORTHUMBERLAND AVENUE
WHITEHALL
EMBANKMENT
STRAND
Hungerford Bridge
Embankment Gardens
River Thames
300 yds
300 m
© Copyright Time Out Group 2005

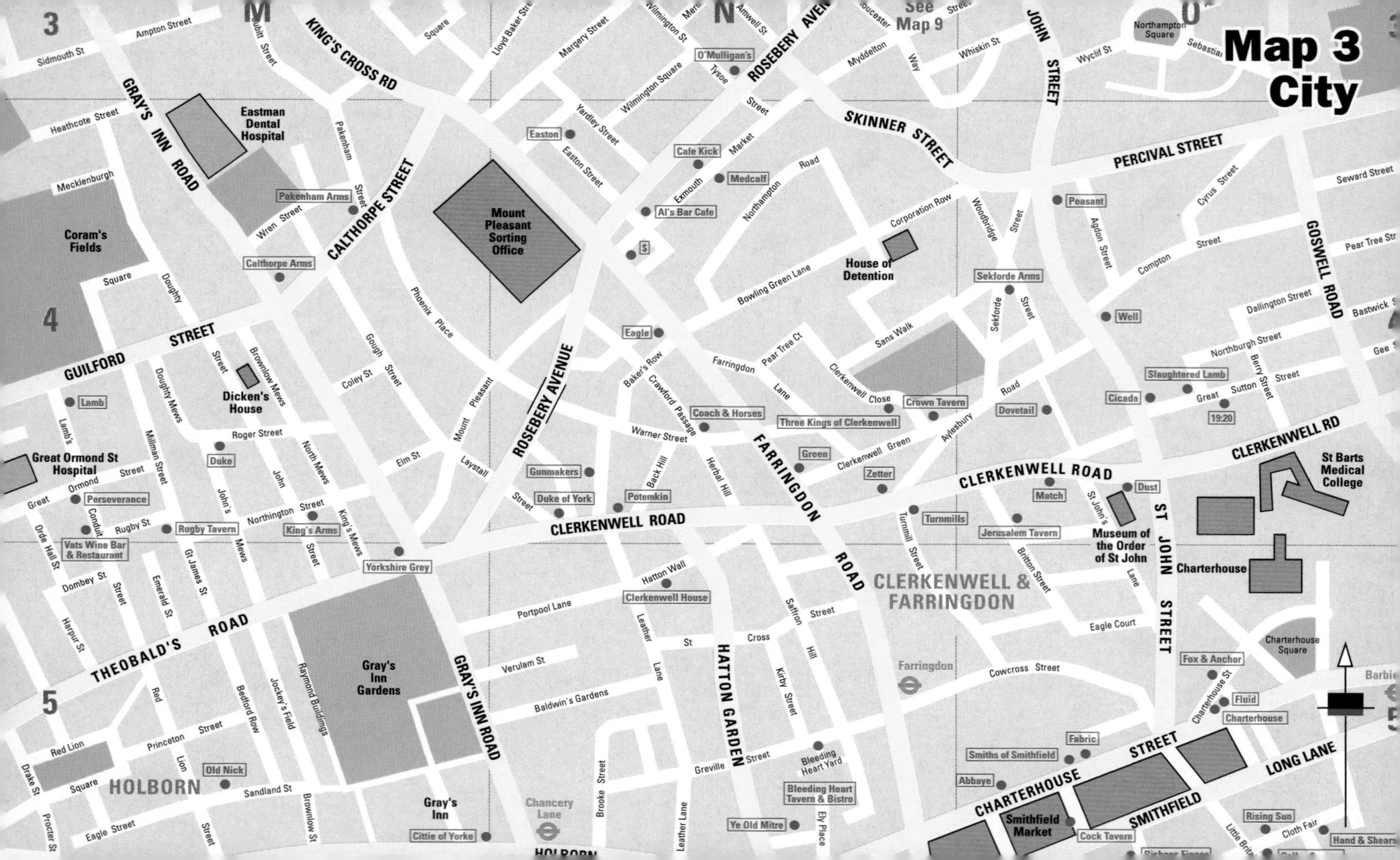
Map 3
City
GRAY'S INN ROAD
KING'S CROSS RD
ROSEBERY AVENUE
SKINNER STREET
PERCIVAL STREET
JOHN STREET
GOSWELL ROAD
CALTHORPE STREET
GUILFORD STREET
CLERKENWELL ROAD
CLERKENWELL RD
FARRINGDON ROAD
ST JOHN STREET
THEOBALD'S ROAD
HATTON GARDEN
CHARTERHOUSE STREET
LONG LANE
SMITHFIELD
CLERKENWELL & FARRINGDON
HOLBORN
See Map 9
Eastman Dental Hospital
Coram's Fields
Mount Pleasant Sorting Office
House of Detention
Dicken's House
Great Ormond St Hospital
Gray's Inn Gardens
Gray's Inn
Museum of the Order of St John
Charterhouse
St Barts Medical College
Charterhouse Square
Northampton Square
Smithfield Market
Farringdon
Chancery Lane
O'Mulligan's
Easton
Cafe Kick
Medcalf
Al's Bar Cafe
Pakenham Arms
Calthorpe Arms
Peasant
Sekforde Arms
Well
Eagle
Coach & Horses
Three Kings of Clerkenwell
Crown Tavern
Slaughtered Lamb
Cicada
19:20
Dovetail
Green
Zetter
Gunmakers
Duke of York
Potemkin
Match
Dust
Turnmills
Jerusalem Tavern
Lamb
Duke
Perseverance
Rugby Tavern
King's Arms
Vats Wine Bar & Restaurant
Yorkshire Grey
Clerkenwell House
Old Nick
Cittie of Yorke
Ye Old Mitre
Bleeding Heart Tavern & Bistro
Bleeding Heart Yard
Fox & Anchor
Fluid
Charterhouse
Fabric
Smiths of Smithfield
Abbaye
Cock Tavern
Rising Sun
Hand & Shears
Sidmouth St
Ampton Street
Heathcote Street
Mecklenburgh Square
Doughty Street
Doughty Mews
Wren Street
Pakenham Street
Cubitt Street
Square
Lloyd Baker Street
Margery Street
Wilmington St
Wilmington Square
Amwell St
Tysoe Street
Myddelton Way
Whiskin St
Wyclif St
Sebastian Street
Yardley Street
Easton Street
Market Street
Exmouth Market
Northampton Road
Corporation Row
Woodbridge Street
Bowling Green Lane
Sans Walk
Sekforde Street
Agdon Street
Compton Street
Cyrus Street
Seward Street
Pear Tree Street
Dallington Street
Bastwick Street
Northburgh Street
Berry Street
Great Sutton Street
Gee St
Aylesbury Road
Clerkenwell Close
Clerkenwell Green
Farringdon Lane
Pear Tree Ct
Baker's Row
Crawford Passage
Warner Street
Herbal Hill
Back Hill
Phoenix Place
Mount Pleasant
Laystall Street
Gough Street
Coley St
Elm St
Roger Street
Brownlow Mews
North Mews
John Street
John's Mews
Northington Street
King's Mews
Millman Street
Lamb's Conduit Street
Great Ormond Street
Rugby St
Orde Hall St
Dombey St
Harpur St
Emerald St
Gt James St
Jockey's Field
Raymond Buildings
Bedford Row
Princeton Street
Lion
Red Lion Square
Drake St
Procter St
Eagle Street
Sandland St
Brownlow St
Hatton Wall
Portpool Lane
Leather Lane
Verulam St
Baldwin's Gardens
Brooke Street
Greville Street
Saffron Hill
Cross St
Kirby Street
Ely Place
Turnmill Street
Britton Street
Eagle Court
Cowcross Street
St John's Lane
Charterhouse St
Cloth Fair
Little Britain
Barbican
M
N
O
3
4
5

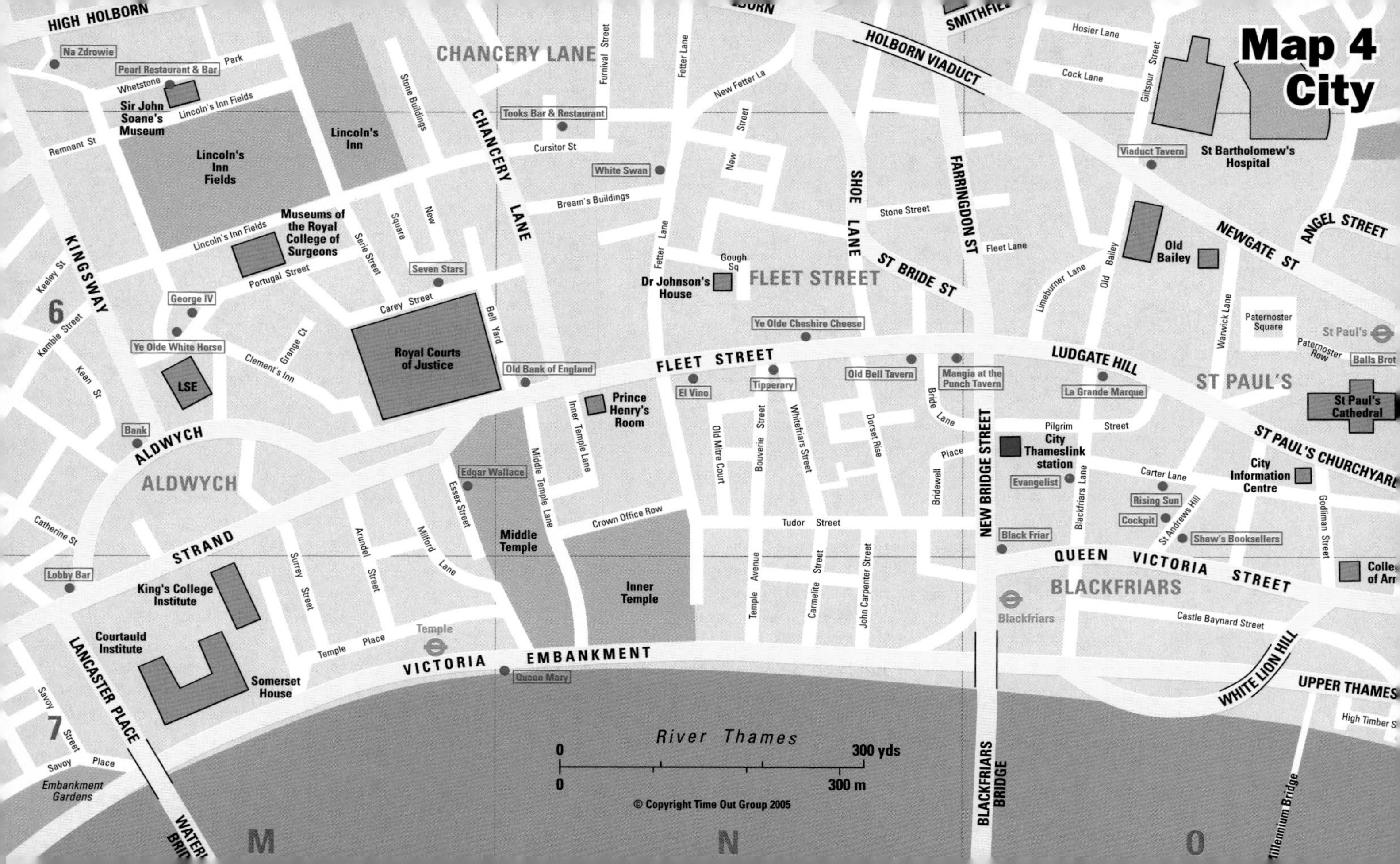
Map 4
City
HIGH HOLBORN
Na Zdrowie
Pearl Restaurant & Bar
Park
Whetstone
Sir John Soane's Museum
Lincoln's Inn Fields
Remnant St
Lincoln's Inn Fields
Lincoln's Inn
Stone Buildings
CHANCERY LANE
Furnival Street
Fetter Lane
New Fetter La
HOLBORN VIADUCT
SMITHFIE
Hosier Lane
Cock Lane
Giltspur Street
St Bartholomew's Hospital
Viaduct Tavern
Tooks Bar & Restaurant
Cursitor St
White Swan
Bream's Buildings
New Street
Stone Street
FARRINGDON ST
SHOE LANE
ST BRIDE ST
Fleet Lane
Limeburner Lane
Old Bailey
NEWGATE ST
ANGEL STREET
KINGSWAY
Keeley St
Kemble Street
Kean St
6
Museums of the Royal College of Surgeons
Portugal Street
Serle Street
Square
New
Seven Stars
George IV
Ye Olde White Horse
Grange Ct
Clement's Inn
Carey Street
Bell Yard
Royal Courts of Justice
LSE
Old Bank of England
Fetter Lane
Gough Sq
Dr Johnson's House
FLEET STREET
Ye Olde Cheshire Cheese
FLEET STREET
El Vino
Tipperary
Old Bell Tavern
Mangia at the Punch Tavern
LUDGATE HILL
La Grande Marque
Warwick Lane
Paternoster Square
St Paul's
Paternoster Row
Balls Brot
ST PAUL'S
St Paul's Cathedral
Bank
ALDWYCH
ALDWYCH
Prince Henry's Room
Inner Temple Lane
Old Mitre Court
Bouverie Street
Whitefriars Street
Dorset Rise
Bride Lane
NEW BRIDGE STREET
Pilgrim Street
City Thameslink station
Evangelist
Blackfriars Lane
Carter Lane
Rising Sun
Cockpit
St Andrews Hill
Shaw's Booksellers
City Information Centre
Godliman Street
ST PAUL'S CHURCHYARD
Catherine St
Edgar Wallace
Essex Street
Middle Temple Lane
Crown Office Row
Tudor Street
Bridewell Place
Black Friar
QUEEN VICTORIA STREET
BLACKFRIARS
Blackfriars
Colle of Arr
STRAND
Lobby Bar
King's College Institute
Surrey Street
Arundel Street
Milford Lane
Middle Temple
Inner Temple
Temple Avenue
Carmelite Street
John Carpenter Street
Castle Baynard Street
WHITE LION HILL
UPPER THAMES
High Timber S
Courtauld Institute
LANCASTER PLACE
Temple Place
Temple
VICTORIA EMBANKMENT
Queen Mary
Somerset House
Savoy Street
7
Savoy Place
Embankment Gardens
River Thames
0
300 yds
0
300 m
© Copyright Time Out Group 2005
BLACKFRIARS BRIDGE
Millennium Bridge
WATER BRI
M
N
O

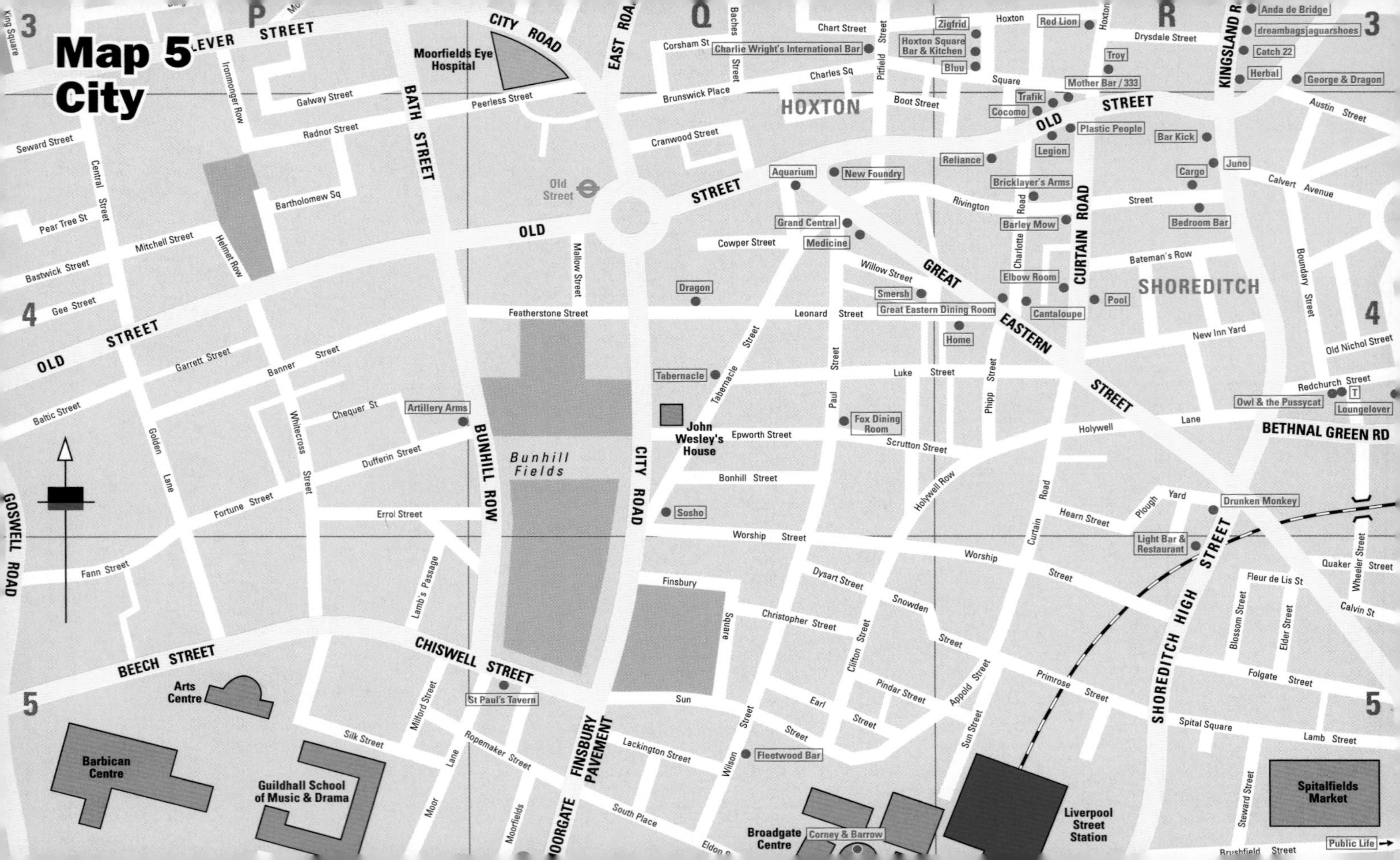

Map 5
City
Moorfields Eye Hospital
HOXTON
SHOREDITCH
Old Street
Bunhill Fields
John Wesley's House
Arts Centre
Barbican Centre
Guildhall School of Music & Drama
Broadgate Centre
Liverpool Street Station
Spitalfields Market
Public Life
Charlie Wright's International Bar
Zigfrid
Hoxton Square Bar & Kitchen
Bluu
Red Lion
Troy
Mother Bar / 333
Trafik
Cocomo
Plastic People
Legion
Anda de Bridge
dreambagsjaguarshoes
Catch 22
Herbal
George & Dragon
Bar Kick
Juno
Cargo
Bedroom Bar
Reliance
Aquarium
New Foundry
Bricklayer's Arms
Barley Mow
Grand Central
Medicine
Elbow Room
Dragon
Smersh
Great Eastern Dining Room
Cantaloupe
Pool
Home
Tabernacle
Fox Dining Room
Artillery Arms
Sosho
Owl & the Pussycat
Loungelover
Drunken Monkey
Light Bar & Restaurant
St Paul's Tavern
Fleetwood Bar
Corney & Barrow
CITY ROAD
OLD STREET
EAST ROAD
BATH STREET
LEVER STREET
BUNHILL ROW
CHISWELL STREET
BEECH STREET
GOSWELL ROAD
FINSBURY PAVEMENT
MOORGATE
GREAT EASTERN STREET
CURTAIN ROAD
SHOREDITCH HIGH STREET
BETHNAL GREEN RD
KINGSLAND R
King Square
Ironmonger Row
Galway Street
Peerless Street
Radnor Street
Seward Street
Central Street
Bartholomew Sq
Pear Tree St
Mitchell Street
Helmet Row
Bastwick Street
Gee Street
Garrett Street
Banner Street
Baltic Street
Golden Lane
Whitecross Street
Chequer St
Dufferin Street
Fortune Street
Errol Street
Fann Street
Lamb's Passage
Milford Street
Silk Street
Moor Lane
Ropemaker Street
Moorfields
South Place
Eldon S
Corsham St
Baches Street
Chart Street
Pitfield Street
Charles Sq
Brunswick Place
Boot Street
Hoxton Square
Hoxton
Drysdale Street
Cranwood Street
Mallow Street
Featherstone Street
Cowper Street
Rivington Street
Charlotte Road
Bateman's Row
Boundary Street
Calvert Avenue
Austin Street
Willow Street
Leonard Street
New Inn Yard
Old Nichol Street
Redchurch Street
Luke Street
Paul Street
Phipp Street
Holywell Lane
Holywell Row
Epworth Street
Scrutton Street
Bonhill Street
Worship Street
Curtain Road
Hearn Street
Plough Yard
Quaker Street
Wheeler Street
Fleur de Lis St
Calvin St
Blossom Street
Elder Street
Folgate Street
Finsbury Square
Dysart Street
Christopher Street
Snowden Street
Clifton Street
Pindar Street
Earl Street
Appold Street
Primrose Street
Sun Street
Wilson Street
Lackington Street
Spital Square
Lamb Street
Steward Street
Brushfield Street
3
4
5
P
Q
R

Map 6
City
Museum of London
ALDERSGATE ST
LONDON WALL
MOORGATE
Jamies at the Pavilion
Circus
Liverpool St
Dirty Dick's
Artillery Lane
Gun
5
BISHOPSGATE
Hamilton Hall
BLOMFIELD ST
LIVERPOOL ST
New Street
George
MIDDLESEX STREET
Bell Lane
LIVERPOOL STREET
Poet
Cobb Street
Wentworth Street
Devonshire Square
Harrow Place
Haberdashers' Hall
Noble Street
Addle St
Aldermanbury Square
Basinghall Avenue
Aldermanbury
Love Lane
Wood Street
Goldsmiths' Hall
Red Herring
Guildhall
Basinghall Street
Coleman Street
Great Swan Alley
Copthall Avenue
Carpenters' Hall
Great Winchester Street
One of Two
Throgmorton Avenue
Austin Friars
OLD BROAD STREET
NatWest Tower
Twentyfour/Vertigo 42
CAMOMILE ST
HOUNDSDITCH
Cutler Street
Stoney Lane
Gravel Lane
6
Foster Lane
Gutter Lane
Gresham Street
Wood Street
Milk Street
Trump Street
King Street
Ironmonger Lane
Old Jewry
Drapers' Hall
Phoenix
Throgmorton's
Throgmorton Street
BISHOPSGATE
St. Helen's Pl
St Mary Axe
BEVIS MARKS
Bury Street
Aldgate
ST. BOTOLPH STREET
CHEAPSIDE
PRINCES ST
Bank of England
Museum
Stock Exchange
THREADNEEDLE STREET
Bonds Bar & Restaurant
Undershaft
Creechurch Lane
DUKE'S PL
ALDGATE
Bank
Watling Street
Bow Wine Vaults
Bowchurchyard
Williamson's Tavern
Bread Street
Pacific Oriental
Prism
CORNHILL
Mansion House
1 Lombard Street
Jamaica Wine House
Counting House
Lloyd's Building
LEADENHALL STREET
Bow Lane
Ye Olde Watling
CANNON STREET
Bar Under the Clock
Walbrook
KING WILLIAM STREET
Birchin Lane
Lamb Tavern
Lime Street
Billiter Street
Jewry Street
MINORIES
Bar 38 Minories
QUEEN VICTORIA STREET
Mansion House
MANSION HOUSE, MONUMENT & BANK
St Swithins Lane
Crosse Keys
Leadenhall Market
Leadenhall Wine Bar
Fenchurch Avenue
Lombard Street
Nicholas Lane
Painters' Hall
Garlick Hill
Hatchet
Bar Bourse
College Hill
Abchurch Lane
Clements Lane
GRACECHURCH STREET
Swan Tavern
Cullum Street
Lloyds Avenue
Haydon Street
Skinners Lane
Queen St
College Street
Cannon St
CANNON STREET
FENCHURCH STREET
Crutched Friar
Portsoken Street
Crosswall
Monument
Philpott Lane
Fenchurch St Station
Crutched Friars
Coopers Row
GOODMAN'S YARD
UPPER THAMES STREET
Skinners' Hall
BUSH LANE
Rood Lane
Mincing Lane
Mark Lane
7
High Timber Street
Vintners' Hall
Bell
Arthur Street
EASTCHEAP
Pepys Street
Tower Gateway
Samuel Pepys
L Pourtney Lane
Monument Street
TOWER HILL & ALDGATE
River Thames
SOUTHWARK BRIDGE
Cannon Street Station
The Monument
Pudding Lane
Seething Lane
Trinity Square
Tower Hill
Shorter St
0
300 yds
0
300 m
P
Fishmongers' Hall
Q
St. Mary at Hill
St. Dunstans Hill
GREAT TOWER STREET
R
TOWER HILL

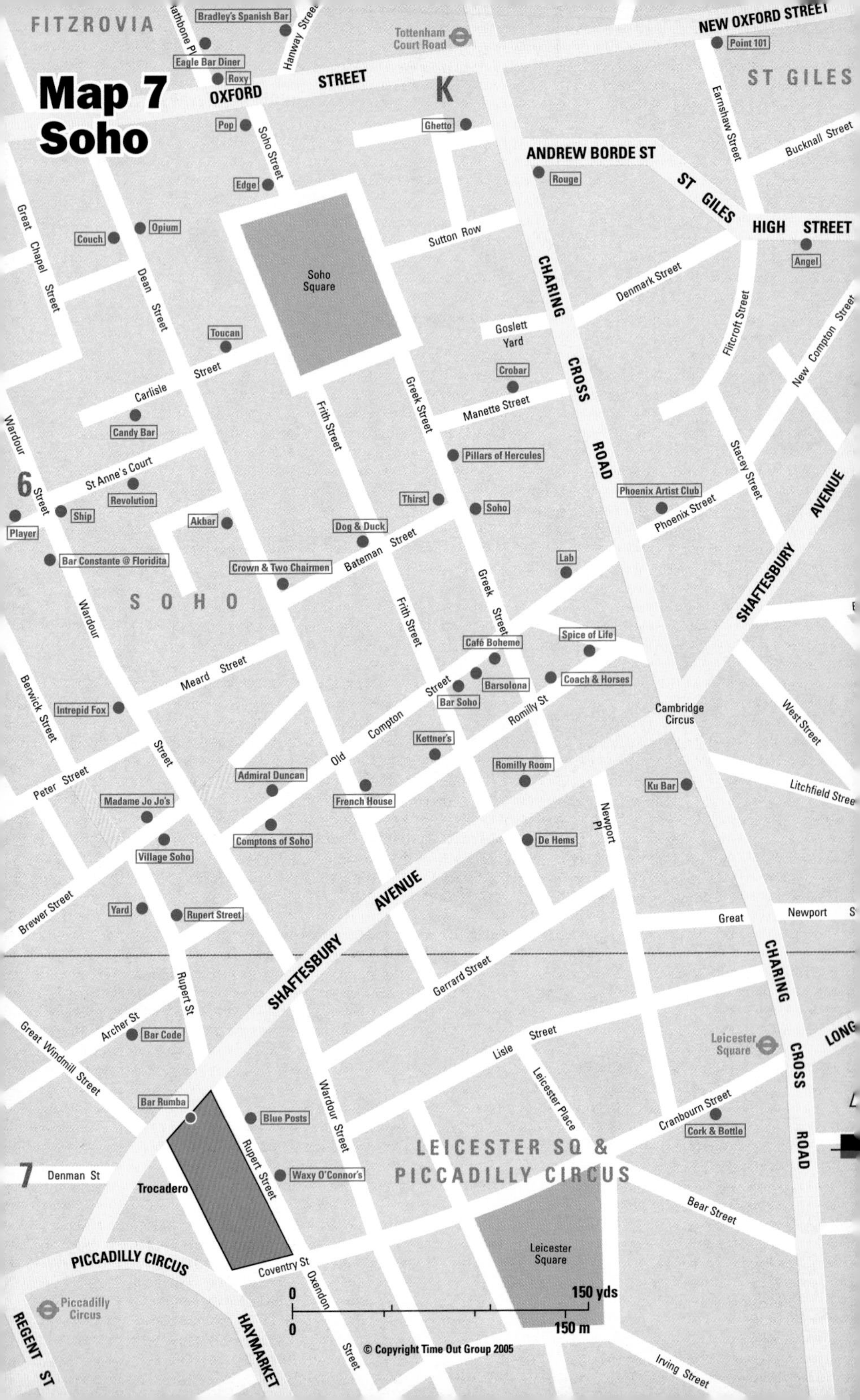
Map 7
Soho
FITZROVIA
ST GILES
SOHO
LEICESTER SQ &
PICCADILLY CIRCUS
K
6
7
NEW OXFORD STREET
OXFORD STREET
Tottenham Court Road
Bradley's Spanish Bar
Hanway Street
Eagle Bar Diner
Roxy
Point 101
Pop
Soho Street
Ghetto
Edge
Earnshaw Street
Bucknall Street
ANDREW BORDE ST
Rouge
ST GILES HIGH STREET
Angel
Great Chapel Street
Couch
Opium
Dean Street
Soho Square
Sutton Row
CHARING CROSS ROAD
Denmark Street
Flitcroft Street
New Compton Street
Goslett Yard
Toucan
Carlisle Street
Crobar
Manette Street
Greek Street
Frith Street
Candy Bar
Wardour Street
St Anne's Court
Revolution
Pillars of Hercules
Stacey Street
Phoenix Artist Club
Phoenix Street
SHAFTESBURY AVENUE
Thirst
Soho
Ship
Player
Akbar
Dog & Duck
Bateman Street
Bar Constante @ Floridita
Crown & Two Chairmen
Lab
Café Boheme
Spice of Life
Meard Street
Berwick Street
Intrepid Fox
Barsolona
Coach & Horses
Bar Soho
Old Compton Street
Romilly St
Cambridge Circus
West Street
Kettner's
Romilly Room
Admiral Duncan
Ku Bar
Litchfield Street
Peter Street
Madame Jo Jo's
French House
Newport Pl
Comptons of Soho
De Hems
Village Soho
Brewer Street
Yard
Rupert Street
Great Newport St
Gerrard Street
Rupert St
Archer St
Bar Code
Great Windmill Street
Lisle Street
Leicester Square
LONG
Leicester Place
Cranbourn Street
Bar Rumba
Blue Posts
Cork & Bottle
Denman St
Waxy O'Connor's
Trocadero
Bear Street
PICCADILLY CIRCUS
Coventry St
Oxendon Street
Piccadilly Circus
REGENT ST
HAYMARKET
0
150 yds
150 m
Irving Street
© Copyright Time Out Group 2005

Map 8 Camden

G
H
J
24
25
26
1
Kentish Town
Kentish Town West
Camden Road
Chalk Farm
Camden Town
Mornington Crescent
KENTISH TOWN
CHALK FARM
CAMDEN TOWN
PRIMROSE HILL
Primrose Hill
REGENT'S PARK
London Zoo
Regent's Park Barracks
Pineapple
Bull & Gate
Jorene Celeste
Barfly
Monkey Chews
The Hill
Abbey
Bullet
Enterprise
Bartok
Barfly
Quinn's
Lock Tavern
Hawley Arms
Cuban
Camden Arms
Pembroke Castle
Lockside Lounge
Lansdowne
Mac Bar
Engineer
Queen's
Princess of Wales
Blakes
Singapore Sling
Bar Vinyl
Bar Solo
Albert
Dublin Castle
Spread Eagle
Crown & Goose
KOKO
Leverton St
Leighton Road
Regis Road
Holmes Road
Islip Street
Hammond St
Caversham Road
Gaisford Street
Patshull Road
Lawford Road
Bartholomew Road
Bartholomew Villas
Wolsey Mews
Raglan Street
Alma St
Angler's Lane
Willes Road
Grafton Road
Ryland Road
Spring Lane
Warden Rd
Athlone Street
Wilkin Street
Weedington Road
Grafton Road
Queen's Crescent
Allcroft Road
Bassett Street
Grafton Terrace
Herbert St
Maitland Park Villas
Queen's Crescent
MALDEN ROAD
Marsden St
Talacre Road
Prince of Wales Road
HAVERSTOCK HILL
MALDEN CRES
FERDINAND ST
Ferdinand Place
Harmood Street
Hadley Street
Grafton Cres
Kelly Street
Castle Road
Castlehaven Road
Lewis Street
Clarence Way
Hartland Road
Hawley Road
HAWLEY ROAD
KENTISH TOWN ROAD
KENTISH TOWN RD
Rochester Road
Rochester Terrace
Rochester Place
Wilmot Place
ST PANCRAS WAY
Jeffreys St
Prowse Place
Bonny St
Randolph St
Baynes
ROYAL COLLEGE ST
Eton College Road
Provost Rd
Crogsland Road
ADELAIDE ROAD
CHALK FARM ROAD
Regents Park Road
Gloucester Avenue
Chalcot Road
Fitzroy Road
Princess Road
Regents Park Road
Gilbeys Yard
Hawley Crescent
Buck St
CAMDEN ROAD
CAMDEN ST
Lyme Street
Jamestown Road
Inverness Street
Arlington Road
Greenland Road
Georgiana St
Gloucester Crescent
Oval Road
St Marks Crescent
Gloucester Avenue
HIGH STREET
PARKWAY
Albert St
Bayham Street
Pratt Street
Mandela St
ALBERT ROAD
DELANCEY STREET
Plender Street
Bayham Pl
CROWNDALE
Outer Circle
Gloucester Gate
Park Village West
Park Village East
Mornington Terrace
Mornington Street
Albert Street
Mornington Place
Mornington Crescent
EVERSHOLT
Oakley
Lidlington Place
Harrington Sq
Granby Terr
Augustus St
ALBANY STREET
Cumberland Terrace
Outer Circle
0
300 yds
0
300 m
© Copyright Time Out Group 2005

Map 9 Islington

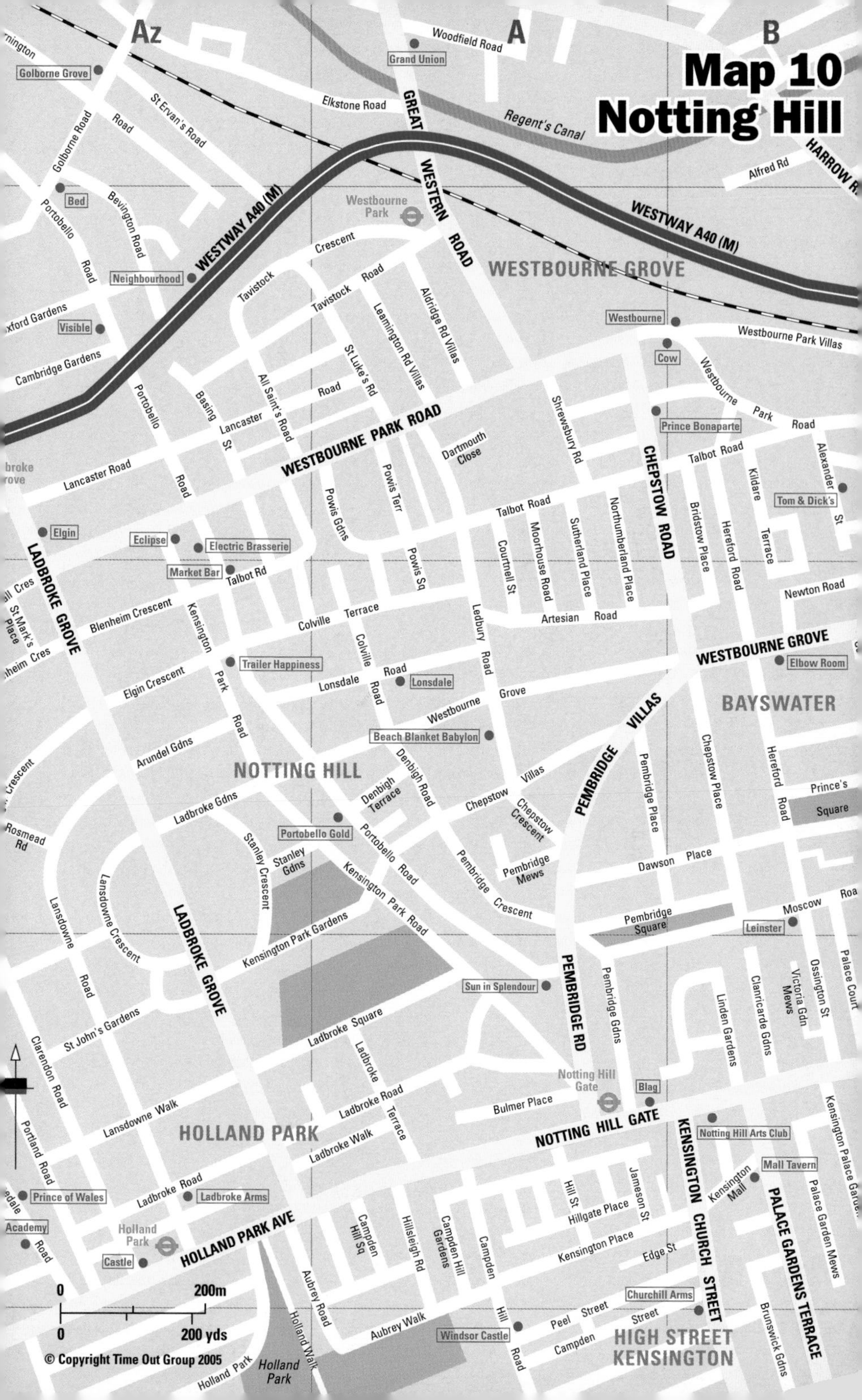
Map 10
Notting Hill
Az
A
B
Woodfield Road
Grand Union
Golborne Grove
Elkstone Road
St Ervan's Road
Regent's Canal
Golborne Road
Road
GREAT WESTERN ROAD
HARROW R
Alfred Rd
Bed
Portobello Road
Bevington Road
Westbourne Park
WESTWAY A40 (M)
Crescent
WESTBOURNE GROVE
Neighbourhood
Tavistock
Tavistock Road
Aldridge Rd Villas
Leamington Rd Villas
xford Gardens
Visible
Westbourne
Westbourne Park Villas
Cow
St Luke's Rd
All Saint's Road
Road
Cambridge Gardens
Westbourne Park Road
Portobello
Basing St
Lancaster
Prince Bonaparte
Shrewsbury Rd
Dartmouth Close
WESTBOURNE PARK ROAD
CHEPSTOW ROAD
Talbot Road
Alexander St
broke
rove
Lancaster Road
Powis Gdns
Powis Terr
Kildare Terrace
Road
Talbot Road
Tom & Dick's
Elgin
Moorhouse Road
Sutherland Place
Northumberland Place
Bridstow Place
Hereford Road
Eclipse
Electric Brasserie
Courtnell St
LADBROKE GROVE
Market Bar
Talbot Rd
Powis Sq
ll Cres
Newton Road
St Mark's Place
Kensington
Blenheim Crescent
Colville Terrace
Ledbury Road
Artesian Road
heim Cres
Colville Road
WESTBOURNE GROVE
Trailer Happiness
Elbow Room
Elgin Crescent
Park
Lonsdale Road
Lonsdale
Road
Westbourne Grove
BAYSWATER
Road
Beach Blanket Babylon
Arundel Gdns
Denbigh Road
PEMBRIDGE VILLAS
Crescent
NOTTING HILL
Denbigh Terrace
Chepstow Villas
Pembridge Place
Chepstow Place
Hereford Road
Prince's Square
Ladbroke Gdns
Chepstow Crescent
Rosmead Rd
Portobello Gold
Stanley Crescent
Stanley Gdns
Portobello Road
Pembridge Mews
Dawson Place
Lansdowne Crescent
Kensington Park Road
Pembridge Crescent
Moscow Road
Roa
Lansdowne Road
LADBROKE GROVE
Kensington Park Gardens
Pembridge Square
Leinster
Palace Court
PEMBRIDGE RD
Pembridge Gdns
Clanricarde Gdns
Victoria Gdn Mews
Ossington St
Sun in Splendour
Linden Gardens
St John's Gardens
Ladbroke Square
Clarendon Road
Ladbroke
Notting Hill Gate
Blag
Kensington Palace Gardens
Lansdowne Walk
Ladbroke Road
Terrace
Bulmer Place
Portland Road
HOLLAND PARK
NOTTING HILL GATE
KENSINGTON CHURCH STREET
Notting Hill Arts Club
Ladbroke Walk
Mall Tavern
Hill St
Jameson St
Kensington Mall
Ladbroke Road
Prince of Wales
Ladbroke Arms
Hillgate Place
PALACE GARDENS TERRACE
Palace Garden Mews
Academy
Road
Holland Park
Campden Hill Sq
Hillsleigh Rd
Campden Hill Gardens
Campden
Kensington Place
HOLLAND PARK AVE
Castle
Edge St
0
200m
200 yds
Aubrey Road
Churchill Arms
Holland Walk
Hill Road
Peel Street
Brunswick Gdns
Aubrey Walk
Windsor Castle
Campden Street
HIGH STREET KENSINGTON
© Copyright Time Out Group 2005
Holland Park
Holland Park

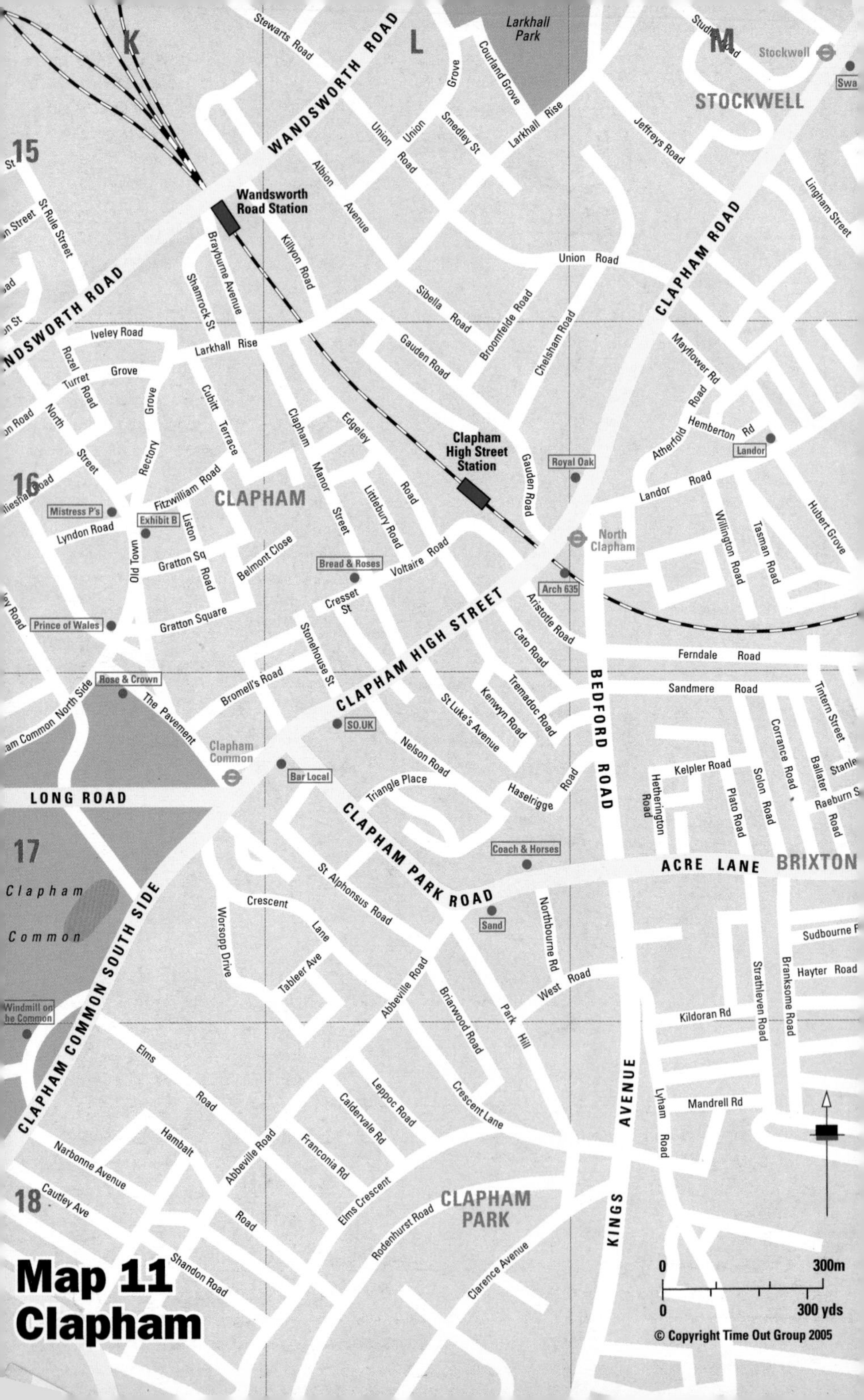

Map 11 Clapham